SOUTH-WESTERN
EDUCATIONAL PUBLISHING

Business Principles and Management

TENTH EDITION

BY

KENNETH E. EVERARD
Professor of Management, Trenton State College
Trenton, New Jersey

JAMES L. BURROW
Associate Professor, North Carolina State University
Raleigh, North Carolina

Editor in Chief: Dennis M. Kokoruda
Developmental Editor: Willis S. Vincent
Marketing Manager: Larry Qualls
Production Manager: Carol Sturzenberger
Senior Production Editor: Jane Congdon
Art Director: John Robb
Staff Designer: Ann Small
Photo Editor: Linda Ellis
Cover and Book Design by Lamson Design, Cincinnati

Library of Congress Cataloging-in-Publication Data

Everard, Kenneth E.
    Business principles & management / Kenneth E. Everard, Jim Burrow.
  —10th ed.
     p. cm.
   ISBN 0-538-62466-3
    1. Business.   2. Management.   I. Burrow, Jim.   II. Title.
  III. Title: Business principles and management.
  HF5351.E89   1996
658—dc20   94-47501
                                        CIP

I(T)P

International Thomson Publishing
South-Western Educational Publishing is an ITP Company. The ITP trademark is used under license.

ISBN: 0-538-62466-3

7 8 9 10 D2 02 01 00

Printed in the United States of America

Professional Profiles (pages 2, 106, 180, 240, 366, 508, and 592) were reprinted with permission from *Pathways to Success,* by Michael D. Ames, Berrett-Koehler Publishers, San Francisco, California.

Preface

Welcome to the dynamic and changing world of business and your opportunity to learn more about it. For years, the United States was a country admired for creating valuable new products that provided jobs and an increased standard of living for its people. Later, however, other countries not only copied our business practices but became competitive rivals. Today, global competition is the driving force for survival in world markets.

Change requires that companies adapt to endure. In recent years, global competition has required firms to modify their organizational structures, to learn different ways to satisfy customer needs, and to invent new ways to compete nationally and internationally. The dramatic changes have caused some firms to downsize, be bought by other firms, or file for bankruptcy. Other firms, however, have seen competitive challenges as opportunities. A former top executive recently stated, "Get better or get beaten." You will soon discover how the rebirth of challenged firms as well as the development of new businesses provide consumers around the world with higher-quality products in greater varieties and at lower prices than in the past.

The Tenth Edition of *Business Principles and Management* provides you with knowledge about the recent and rapid evolutionary changes, which includes the role of multinational corporations that operate in many countries. Several other themes are provided, one of which is starting and managing your own business. Business ethics, an issue of rising importance, is another theme that is woven throughout most chapters.

The central focus of the text, however, is to build a solid foundation of established business principles and practices that form the groundwork for all business operations. Business fundamentals such as economic, legal, and social foundations are presented along with a close look at organizing businesses, marketing products and services, financing operations, managing and developing employees, and making difficult business decisions in a dynamic competitive atmosphere.

CAREERS AND GOALS

A basic understanding of business principles and management is needed by everyone who plans a career in business. For this reason, this book is written especially for you if you plan to:

- Explore the possibility of a career in business.
- Enter business as a beginning employee.
- Return to the classroom after having gained some business experience.
- Eventually have an opportunity to manage a business for others.
- Ultimately own and operate your own business.

The information presented in this completely updated edition is designed to facilitate the accomplishment of basic goals for all readers. Learners will achieve the following goals:

- Acquire a working vocabulary of common business terms.
- Obtain an awareness of the many activities, problems, and decisions involved in successfully operating a business.
- Gain an appreciation of the importance of business in our economy.
- Develop insights for deciding on specific career objectives from among the great number of employment opportunities in the business world.
- Understand facts, procedures, principles, and concepts needed to become effective members of profit-making and not-for-profit making organizations.
- Appreciate the dynamic elements of business that are represented by such things as organizational change, diversity in the workforce, ethics, world competition, and the link between business and society.

ORGANIZATION OF CONTENTS

Business Principles and Management contains 27 chapters that are divided into seven units. Most of the content found in the earlier edition has been retained, modified, or expanded. Two new chapters have been added, some chapters have been repositioned, and one unit has been moved forward.

Business and Its Environment, Unit 1, describes the characteristics of business and the economic and social elements that affect organizations. Recent critical changes that affect American firms are described, including total quality management, reengineering, worker empowerment, work teams, and privatization of government functions. The ethical principles presented set the stage for treatment in other units. A new chapter that closes the unit is devoted entirely to international business.

Forms of Business Ownership and the Law, Unit 2, describes the nature and formation of sole proprietorships, partnerships, and corporations. Newer forms of organizations that have been added include the subchapter S corporation, joint ventures, and nonprofit organizations. The legal environment of business chapter that draws this unit to a close incorporates topics such as laws that regulate and control competition, bankruptcy, regulatory agencies, and taxes related to business.

Although *Information and Communication Systems*, Unit 3, is the shortest unit, it is a critical unit. The two chapters on technology and information management and organizational communications have been updated and placed closer to the beginning of the text. Because the role of computers now penetrates deeply into all organizational activities, its coverage has been updated and expanded.

Production and Marketing Management, Unit 4, is composed of five critical chapters that deal with operations related to producing and marketing goods and services. The focus is on satisfying customers creatively as well as efficiently and effectively. Chapters have been reorganized in this unit in order to add greater understanding of important production and marketing concepts.

Financial Management, Unit 5, consists of six chapters and covers the types and sources of capital needed for running firms, budgeting, recordkeeping and accounting, banking and other financial services, handling credit, and dealing with risk through insurance and other risk management activities. Most of the content from the former edition has been retained and updated.

Human Resources Management, Unit 6, deals with the most important asset of a business—employees—and covers how to hire, pay, train, appraise, promote, and retain workers while organizations undergo mild and major changes. The growing importance of this unit resulted in the inclusion of creative new methods of human resource management that are used in leading firms.

Management Responsibilities, Unit 7, examines the basic functions of managers, including planning, organizing, implementing, and controlling. These vital activities are discussed in a new and unique way emphasizing the changing role and work of managers. Making and implementing decisions are included as is the psychology that enables managers to lead empowered workers effectively in a growing world of work teams.

TEXT FEATURES FOR STUDENTS

Valuable new features have been added to the Tenth Edition and special features from the past edition have been preserved. Here are highlights of particular interest to students:

- Newly added are objectives that provide an overview of what will be learned in each unit. Unit objectives are followed by a quotation from a noted business personality. The quotation is followed by a career story about a successful business leader who serves as a role model for the topic covered in the unit.
- Each unit ends with a review of the unit objectives highlighted by a summary of the key points found in the unit.
- A new feature is the glossary at the end of the text containing definitions of all terms that appear in bold print throughout the text.
- Each chapter starts with objectives that are usually followed by a realistic story tailored to the chapter's contents. The vignette sets the stage for motivating students to read the chapter.
- Each chapter also includes a one-page high-interest feature story that extends learning by integrating topics of interest into the chapter. The special features used throughout the text—Global Perspectives, Ethical Issues, and Manage-

ment Close-Ups—are followed by thought-provoking questions written to
encourage critical thinking.

- Each chapter ends with carefully designed exercises that begin with easy
review questions and gradually proceed to realistic application problems and
cases that generate critical thinking and lively discussions.

PROGRAM COMPONENTS FOR TEACHERS

All the major components from the prior edition have been retained. Several
significant new features are included that will greatly benefit teachers:

- An entirely new Teacher's Annotated Edition of the student text is provided
that contains chapter lesson plans and notes in the margins for enhancing
instruction. These notes contain reinforcement and extension/enrichment
activities along with subject matter notes and references to transparency
masters for reteaching.
- Also included in the new Teacher's Annotated Edition are suggested motiva-
tional activities for launching each unit, discussion questions related to the
business quotation in the student's edition, and specific questions that can be
raised to generate spirited discussions about a business leader profiled. Each
unit concludes with at least three or four portfolio assignments and a testing
suggestion for assessing student performance.
- An enriched Teacher's Resource Manual contains answers to end-of-chapter
activities, tests, and workbook exercises. At least four transparency masters
are provided for each chapter. A chapter outline and an abundance of teaching notes and strategies are included in addition to those provided in the
Teacher's Annotated Edition.
- An activity-packed workbook is available that contains a wide range of exercises for each chapter that will capture the attention of students. For each
chapter, teachers can select assignments that include study guide questions
to aid content review, controversial issues to analyze, numerous problems to
solve, and a special continuing project for a business that includes enriching
chapter-by-chapter activities.
- New in this edition are chapter tests, unit tests, and a final examination. A
computer test bank is available in addition to printed tests.

The Tenth Edition of *Business Principles and Management* is the result of
input from many individuals. We are deeply indebted to the dedicated classroom
teachers, college professors, and business people whose ideas, comments, and
helpful suggestions have contributed so much to the development of this text.
We only wish that space would permit recognizing each by name. All have contributed greatly to the creation of a publication milestone in this Tenth Edition.

Kenneth E. Everard
Jim Burrow

Contents in Brief

Contents

International

Ethics

Business and Its Environment

"... in big business or small, we observe that there are only two ways to create and sustain superior performance over the long haul. First, take exceptional care of your customers ... via superior service and superior quality. Second, constantly innovate. That's it. There are no alternatives in achieving long-term superior performance, or sustaining strategic competitive advantage ..."

Tom Peters
Nancy Austin
A PASSION FOR
EXCELLENCE, 1985

OBJECTIVES

1-1 Describe the general nature and extent of business and how global competition affects business operations.

1-2 Summarize key features of entrepreneurship, causes of failure, and the risks and opportunities that exist.

1-3 Discuss how society's economic, social, and environmental problems influence business policies and practices.

1-4 Explain basic social responsibilities and ethical issues as well as how ethics relates to business situations.

1-5 Identify basic economic concepts and problems, fundamental principles of capitalism, and other economic-political systems.

1-6 Outline the importance, dimensions, and theories of international business, especially on how it impacts on the balance of trade and on importing and exporting operations.

Professional Profile

A LEADER IN BUSINESS DEVELOPMENT

Jacqueline Phillips wanted to become a nurse because it was a way to help people in need. After spending four years as a nurse in general surgery for a large hospital, she decided that the hospital bureaucracy was too focused on the bottom line (profitability) rather than the patients. She believed that a business committed to improving the product and providing quality care could be a successful and profitable business. So she left the hospital and, with the help of a partner, formed Advanced Nursing Services of St. Louis.

Advanced Nursing Services of St. Louis and a second company, Advanced Home Health Services, provide a complete range of private duty nursing services for people in their own homes or in hospitals and nursing homes. Some patients require intensive care for long periods of time while others need only a sitter service for as little as one day. Ms. Phillips' companies employ a large number of nurses and carefully identify the needs of each patient and select the nurse most capable of providing the services needed. The company is even careful to avoid personality conflicts when assigning a nurse.

Begun with a vision—the patient is the primary focus—and one patient, the two companies owned by Ms. Phillips now have revenues of over $2 million. The partners now manage a full-time staff of eight and provide their services through 250 nurses. Jacqueline Phillips states, "We care about our nurses, so they care about our patients. As managers, we are vitally concerned about the care each of our clients receives."

INSPIRATIONAL IDEAS

Jacqueline B. Phillips, R.N., B.S.N., President, Advanced Nursing Services of St. Louis

"Success in business does not come naturally. The only way to be a success in business is to try. First and foremost you must be honest. Second, be willing to take risks. Finally, do right in business and give back to the community. By giving back you foster a strong, united community which, in turn, helps your business."

Photo courtesy of Event Medical Care.

CHARACTERISTICS OF BUSINESS

CHAPTER 1

After studying this chapter you will be able to:

1-1 Explain the general types and changing nature of businesses.

1-2 Describe how global competition has affected how American businesses operate.

1-3 Show how businesses have grown and improved the economic well-being of people.

1-4 Discuss the role and nature of entrepreneurship and the opportunities, problems, and obligations of small businesses.

1-5 Summarize the value of plans that allow employees to become or feel like entrepreneurs inside businesses.

1-6 Explain the importance of studying business principles and management.

Leslie Hanes waited at the roadside curb for the school bus with her son, Mark. He was growing so fast. It seemed she had to buy something new for him every week—clothes, shoes, school supplies, baseballs, and now a bicycle. Her younger daughter, Marla, would soon have similar demands. In fact, she already had. Last week it was a teddy bear; this week, her first visit to the dentist; and next week, a tricycle.

"When will all these expenses stop," she thought. "What did you say, Mom?" asked Mark. "I'm just thinking out loud, Mark. Here comes your bus. Don't forget your Little League game later this afternoon." Mark promptly retorted, "How could I forget this important game? Don't forget the new catcher's mitt we have to buy before the game starts."

Leslie had forgotten, but she could always rely on Mark and Marla to remind her of things to buy. Of course, her husband Tim was good at sending out "don't forget" signals as well. Fortunately, with his good job at the manufacturing plant and her half-time computer job at the department store, the family's income was adequate to meet most expenses if they budgeted carefully. While waving goodbye to Mark as the bus pulled away, she recalled reminding Tim to schedule his vacation time for late June when the family could drive to the mountains and camp out under the stars. "That should keep costs down," she mused, "but I'd better start putting money aside for a new tent, sleeping bags, and gas for the long trip. Maybe the money we make on Saturday's garage sale will pay for some of it."

American businesses work for Leslie Hanes and her family. As the family's financial manager, she pays the bills. Leslie and Tim, along with Mark and Marla, are consumers. They buy goods such as clothes, shoes, tricycles, and tents. Likewise, they buy services such as trips to the dentist and to movies. Businesses work very hard to provide the goods and services needed by the Hanes family and everyone else.

Illus. 1-1

Whether they are individuals, families, or other businesses, customers are the reason businesses exist. Can you think of a business that could survive without customers? Does a government have customers?

Jeff Greenberg, Photographer

About 19 million businesses currently exist in the United States. They vary in size from one employee to more than 700,000 employees and in assets from a few dollars to over $200 billion. Some of these businesses have only a few customers, while others have millions of customers located throughout the world.

These vast differences make the story of American business fascinating. Products found in most homes come from countless producers. The flowering plant in the Hanes' front window could have been purchased from a greenhouse operated by a single person. The light bulbs the Hanes family uses could have been made by a business with 100,000 employees, their carpet from a business with 500 employees, and the cake for Marla's birthday from a bakery with only 10 workers. These and scores of other items found in homes, offices, stores, and factories are produced by every kind of business.

NATURE OF BUSINESS

An organization that produces or distributes a good or service for profit is called a **business.** *Profit* is the difference between earned income and costs. Every business engages in at least three major activities. The first activity, **production,** involves making a product or providing a service. **Manufacturing firms** produce goods whereas **service firms** provide assistance to satisfy specialized needs through skilled workers such as doctors, travel agents, entertainers, and taxi drivers. Today the number of service firms far exceeds the number of manufacturing firms. For this reason, it is sometimes said that we live in a service society.

The second activity that businesses are involved in is marketing. *Marketing* deals with how goods or services are exchanged between producers and consumers. The third activity, **finance,** deals with all money matters related to running a business. Whether a business has one worker or thousands of workers, it is involved with production, marketing, and finance. The price that Leslie Hanes pays for Mark's catcher's mitt will be based in large part upon supply and demand for the glove. *Supply* of a product refers to the number of similar products that will be offered for sale at a particular time and at a particular price. *Demand,* on the other hand, refers to the number of similar products that will be bought at a given time at a given price. This book will focus on the various activities involved in managing a business successfully. But before examining those activities in detail, let's take a look at the general nature of business.

TYPES OF BUSINESSES

Generally speaking, there are two major kinds of businesses—industrial and commercial. **Industrial businesses** produce goods that are often used by other businesses or organizations to make things. Mining ore for making metal products, manufacturing catchers' mitts and tricycles, and constructing buildings are types of industrial businesses. Highly industrialized nations that produce thousands of products, such as the United States, Japan, and Germany, can be distinguished from **third world nations** that are underdeveloped, have few manufacturing firms, and have large numbers of poor people who possess few goods. Some of the third world nations have made progress by becoming developing nations.

Unlike industrial businesses, **commercial businesses** are engaged in marketing (wholesalers and retailers), in finance (banks and investment companies), and in furnishing services (dental services, sports centers, motels, and video rental shops). *Services* are intangible products that result from a high degree of labor input and that satisfy consumer needs.

An indication of the importance of the major types of businesses is shown in Fig. 1-1. The graph shows the number of persons employed in selected types of production and service industries. **Industry** is a word often used to refer to all businesses within a category. For example, the publishing industry includes any business that deals with producing and selling books, magazines, newspapers, and other printed documents prepared by authors. Even a government can be considered an industry because it produces services such as fire and police protection. This industry would include all services provided by local, state, and federal governments.

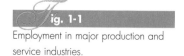

Employment in major production and service industries.

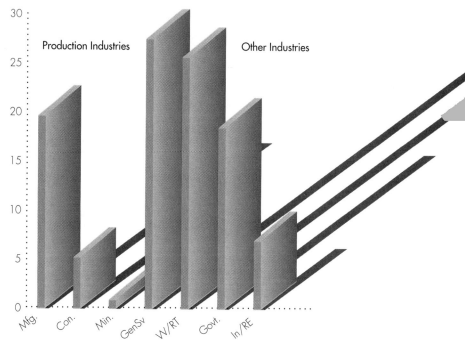

No. of Employees (in Millions)

Source: *Statistical Abstract of the United States, 1992.*

CHANGING NATURE OF BUSINESS

An important characteristic of business is that it is dynamic, or constantly changing. Most businesses react quickly to the changing nature of society. For instance, travel by horse was the principal means of transportation until the invention of steam power. Then, with the emergence of the first cross-country railroad in 1869, goods and services traveled mainly by rail for about 50 years. When the gasoline engine arrived, travel patterns shifted from train to car, bus, and truck. Shortly thereafter, airplanes gliding along at 100 miles an hour were soon replaced by jets criss-crossing countries and oceans, carrying people and goods to their destinations in a matter of hours.

Similar changes are visible in other industries. For many centuries, only natural fibers such as wool and cotton were used for making clothing and assorted products. As a result of chemical research, synthetic fibers—rayon, nylon, acetate, and polyester—were developed and are now used to make clothing, carpets, and many other products.

Not only have changes occurred in the products made and the services offered, but changes

Tony Stone Images

have also taken place in the way businesses operate. Marketing methods that involve buying, selling, advertising, and shipping goods, for example, have changed in recent decades and will continue to change.

The dynamic nature of business is also indicated by major changes in selected categories of businesses over the years. As shown in Fig. 1-2, the number of businesses increased in all categories since 1975. However, several categories of businesses increased at faster rates than others. In particular, service businesses multiplied so swiftly that they far outnumber manufacturing businesses.

Fig. 1-2

Growth in number of selected types of businesses.

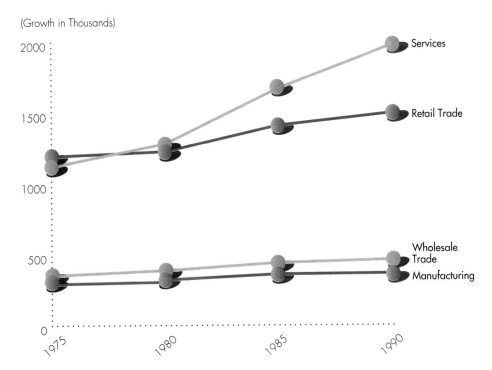

Source: Statistical Abstract of the United States, 1992.

IMPACT OF GLOBAL COMPETITION ON BUSINESS

For hundreds of years, American businesses led the way in producing new goods and services that were bought around the world. Consumers worldwide eagerly purchased exciting new products that were invented and made in the United States. Factories hummed with activity, workers from other countries arrived by the thousands to find jobs, and people spent their wages buying the goods that the firms produced. Many leaders from foreign countries also arrived to find out how American businesses were managed.

Over the last 25 years, however, the situation slowly changed. Other countries became industrialized after learning how to invent and produce new products for their consumers. Americans gradually began to purchase these foreign products. Foreign firms also learned how to use efficient methods for making goods. To satisfy the growing number of American buyers, foreign manufacturers concentrated on satisfying the American demand for higher-quality products with greater varieties and at lower prices.

American business leaders soon realized that other countries were producing goods and services at breakneck speed. It was time for change, a time to challenge foreign competitors, and a time to rely on America's abundant human talent to meet the challenge of global competition. **Global competition** is the ability of profit-making organizations to compete with other businesses in other countries. Let's look at what is happening to help America compete in a global economy.

FOCUSING ON THE RIGHT THINGS

Businesses often study themselves in terms of whether they are doing the right things and whether they are doing the right things well. Two terms are used to describe the two points. First, **effectiveness** occurs when an organization makes the right decisions in deciding what products or services to offer customers or other users. Also included is making the right decisions in how to produce the products and deliver them to consumers. Second, **efficiency** occurs when an organization produces needed goods or services quickly at low cost. Firms that provide products at the lowest cost while maintaining desired quality will succeed. Some firms are extremely efficient but very ineffective while others are effective but inefficient. Good managers focus on both effectiveness and efficiency at all times.

ACHIEVING EFFECTIVENESS

Making the right decisions requires both common sense and skill. Knowing what customers want is critical to business success and to achieving effectiveness. What kind of tent, for example, will best satisfy the needs of the Hanes family when they take their summer vacation in the mountains? In the past, customers bought whatever was available because there were few brands, colors, and styles from which to select. Today, the choices for most goods have increased because of competition among domestic and foreign firms.

Domestic goods (products made by firms in the United States) must compete with **foreign goods** (products made by firms in other countries).

Unlike the past, firms today focus more on gathering information from customers, studying their buying habits, testing new products with customers, and adding new features to existing products. New designs, different shapes, bright colors, readable instructions, and simplicity of product use are features customers like. Major corporations spend millions of dollars examining customers' preferences. Equally important is that successful firms also invest heavily in keeping customers satisfied after products are sold. Product guarantees and conversations with customers about the product help keep customers loyal.

Customers not only want products that best meet their needs but they also want quality products. A major new emphasis of American producers is to make products of high quality. Japanese car makers are excellent examples of how foreign producers captured a large portion of the market worldwide by providing customers with reliable cars. In the past, American car producers were not meeting the needs of many buyers. Too many cars had too many defects that required numerous trips to car dealers to correct. On the other hand, Japanese cars had fewer flaws.

American producers learned important lessons about quality from the Japanese. Today, American car producers are building products that equal or exceed Japanese and European standards. To accomplish this, American car manufacturers and producers of many other products vigorously campaigned to stress the importance of quality. The concept is called **total quality management (TQM),** which is a commitment to excellence that is accomplished by teamwork and continual improvement. Where TQM is practiced, managers and employees receive a great deal of training on the topic of quality from experts. The result is a return to what customers want—well-made products.

A further encouragement for quality comes from the Malcolm Baldrige National Quality Award program. The program is managed by an agency of the federal government. Each year, hundreds of firms apply for this distinctive national honor. Eight awards may be given yearly. Organizations that win this award usually notice an upturn in demand for their products. Quality awards are also offered in Europe. The Japanese offer the Deming Award, which is named after an American who was an expert on quality. Competition based on quality has grown in importance worldwide.

Jeff Greenberg, Photographer

Illus. 1-3

American car producers have learned to equal or exceed foreign car makers in the quality of their products. Is quality an important factor when you buy a car or other expensive product?

ACHIEVING EFFICIENCY

Not only must firms do the right things, such as offering high-quality products, but they must produce their products efficiently. While many older methods for achieving efficiency have been discarded, some still work well. Newer methods, however, are replacing older methods. The extent to which businesses are efficient is measured by **output**—the quantity, or amount, produced within a given time. **Productivity,** on the other hand, refers to producing the largest quantity in the least amount of time by using efficient methods and modern equipment. Workers are more productive when they are well equipped, well trained, and well managed. Productivity for employees has grown over the years in manufacturing firms, as shown in Fig. 1-3, but the growth has not been as rapid as in a few other industrialized nations.

Efficiency—including improved productivity—can be achieved in three ways. Specialization of effort is one approach; another is through better technology and innovation; and the most challenging way to achieve efficiency is through reorganization.

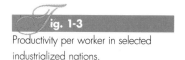
Fig. 1-3

Productivity per worker in selected industrialized nations.

Output-Per-Hour Index for Manufacturing Employees (Index: 1982 = 100)

COUNTRY	1970	1980	1985	1990
United States	77.2	96.6	114.8	136.6
Canada	76.9	99.9	119.8	121.8
France	58.5	90.6	108.8	127.7
Germany	67.0	98.4	112.9	126.2
Japan	52.0	92.1	112.0	138.0
England	70.8	89.9	117.8	145.0

Source: Statistical Abstract of the United States, 1992.

Specialization

In any business with more than a few employees, it is desirable to have workers become specialists. In a large automobile repair shop, for example, not all workers are general mechanics. Rather, some workers specialize in body repair work while others specialize in repairing transmissions or engines. When workers specialize, they become expert at what they do. As a result, specialization improves quality while the amount produced increases. Because specialization improves efficiency, it is no wonder that businesses hire or train employees for many specialized jobs.

Effectiveness can also be improved through **mass production,** the use of up-to-date equipment and assembly line methods to produce large quantities of identical goods. Through mass production, the cost of goods manufactured decreases because it is possible to produce more items in less time. Today, electronically driven equipment, including computers and robots, makes it possible to mass-produce large numbers of items with fewer workers.

Technology and Innovation

Effectiveness can also be improved through advanced technology. Technology includes equipment, manufacturing processes, and materials from which products are made. Because of new discoveries and inventions, better-quality goods and services are built at a faster pace and often at a lower cost. Improved materials, for example, may weigh less, last longer, and permit faster product assembly. Examples of new technology are found in everyday items such as cars, clothing, computers, and electronic appliances. With advanced technology, a business can enjoy a powerful advantage over competitors. And because technology has a significant impact on productivity, businesses spend billions of dollars annually on buying and using new technology.

Innovation requires creative workers who create or use new methods, ideas, and devices to make goods and services available to customers. One of the strengths of American business is its ability to produce new ideas, products, and processes. The United States has always been one of the world's leading contributors of new inventions. Inventiveness is a hallmark of success. But creating new ideas is one thing. Business success also depends upon whether firms can convert inventions to high-quality products at reasonable prices that will satisfy customers. To boost efficiency, firms are focusing on the process of reorganizing how work gets done.

Reorganization

The third and most difficult way to obtain increased efficiency is through reorganization, which usually produces the greatest results. During the late 1970s, early 1980s, and early 1990s, companies experienced slow growth for reasons explained in a later chapter. However, one key reason for the slow growth arose from the competition of other industrialized nations. The typical reaction to slow growth caused by global competition was to cut back production costs by laying off workers. A business would **downsize** by cutting back on the goods and services provided and thereby shrink the size of a firm and the number of employees. By laying off workers, dropping unprofitable products or selling them to other firms, or by increasing the use of technology, firms were able to downsize; but the problem of producing excellent products inexpensively still existed. Better ways were needed to compete with foreign firms, many of which had lower labor costs. Some firms boldly decided to move in a direction that was similar to tearing down the business and rebuilding it.

Major firms arrived at the conclusion that employees are the most important resource of an organization. Further, managers learned that by empowering workers, firms became more productive. **Empowerment** is letting workers decide how to perform their work tasks and offer ideas on how to improve the work process. This dramatic change viewed the role of the worker far differently than in the past, when workers performed narrow tasks on assembly lines and had no decision-making rights.

After empowering workers, firms found that the quality of work often improved as did the efficiency of production. Although better-trained and highly skilled workers were required, fewer managers were needed. Companies were able to reduce the number of levels of management by pushing down the day-to-day decisions directly to workers rather than to managers. Workers were taught to use computers, to work in teams, and to be responsible for quality.

While practicing empowerment, some managers were also redesigning the work flow throughout their organizations. Instead of typical assembly lines found in factories and offices, steps were eliminated, abbreviated, or placed entirely into the hands of employees. Customer complaints dropped. Fewer well-trained workers with computers could better satisfy customers than outdated methods from the past. Most major firms—and many smaller ones—adopted these newer practices and are finding that customer satisfaction has risen along with productivity. The concept of redesigned work and work flow will appear in more detail in a later chapter.

American firms are again becoming strong players in world business as a result of restructuring efforts and a more intensive focus on quality and customers' needs. Empowering workers has contributed a great deal to the rebuilding of firms. Those firms are now doing the right things well. Furthermore, no large or small business in an industrialized society should think only about customers in their own countries. Their customers are located around the corner and around the world. American factories exist in other countries, and businesses in other countries make and sell products in this country.

American firms also form joint agreements with domestic and foreign firms. For example, Ford Motor Company and Mazda Motors work with each other to either make car parts or entire cars for each other. Similar arrangements exist with European firms. Toshiba, a large electronics manufacturer in Japan, formed alliances with over eighteen firms, many of which are American. You will learn more about international business in Chapter 4.

B USINESS GROWTH AND PROSPERITY

Overall, the United States is a prosperous nation. Much of its prosperity is due to business growth. Around the world, people admire and envy this country's economic strength. Let us look at two ways in which a nation measures its economic wealth and its benefits to citizens.

GROSS DOMESTIC PRODUCT

The first measure of a nation's economic wealth is the gross domestic product. The **gross domestic product (GDP)** is the total market value of all goods produced and services provided in a country in a year. Whenever a product or service is purchased, the dollar amount is recorded by the federal government. The GDP of the United States is compared from year to year and is compared with the GDP of other countries. In this way it provides a measure of economic success.

Illus. 1-4

Garage sales are part of the underground economy. Are babysitting, house sitting, or bake sales also part of the underground economy?

Certain types of transactions, however, are never included in the GDP. These transactions are not recorded because they are unlawful or do not occur as part of normal business operations. For example, when a youngster is hired to mow lawns, formal business records are not normally prepared and the income is usually unrecorded. When drugs are sold illegally, such transactions are not recorded. Income that escapes being recorded in the GDP is referred to as the **underground economy.** Business transactions that occur in the underground economy have increased in recent years in relation to the total GDP. Some economists believe that estimates range between 5 percent during a brisk economy to 20 percent of the GDP during a lagging economy. The size of the underground economy concerns government officials.

In a recent year, the total known and recorded GDP for the United States reached the staggering $6.2 trillion mark, as can be seen in Fig. 1-4 on page 14. The one trillion dollar mark was reached by 1970. And in a recent year, the GDP nearly equaled the total GDP of four major countries combined—Japan, Germany, England, and Brazil. The rate of growth and the current size of the GDP indicate, in a rather striking way, the economic strength of the country.

Growth in GDP since 1960.

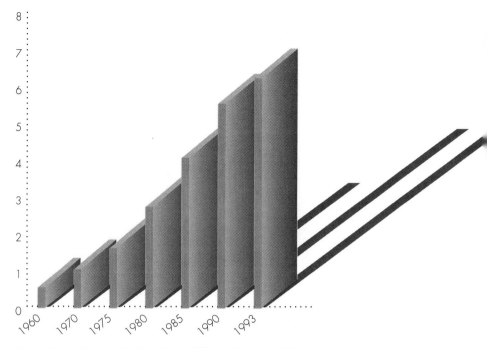

United States GDP (in Trillions of Dollars)

Source: Statistical Abstract of the United States, 1992, and Department of Commerce.

INDIVIDUAL WELL-BEING

A second measure of a nation's wealth is the individual well-being of its citizens. While GDP figures are helpful in judging the overall growth of a nation, such figures by themselves tell little about the economic worth of individuals. However, the U.S. Department of Commerce gathered information that reveals the financial well-being of U.S. citizens.

Family income has increased steadily, with the average yearly family income currently nearing $40,000—much more than it was a decade ago. In a recent year, the average individual yearly income for a male without a high school diploma was $19,000 but after earning a high school diploma, it jumped to $27,000. College graduates earned over $43,000. Generally, females earn somewhat less than males. You will find an interesting discussion on this topic in Chapter 2.

With increased income, an average family improves its level of living. In a recent government study, the worth of a typical American household exceeded $42,000. Over half of all families live in homes they own. As shown in Fig. 1-5 on page 15, items once considered luxuries are now owned by many families. For example, refrigerators, televisions, VCRs, ranges, microwave ovens, and cars are found in a majority of households. Four out of five households have cars. In addition, Americans still invest large sums of money in education, with many adults receiving some education beyond high school. Further, individuals invest in life-enrichment activities by traveling in this country and abroad. Despite these large expenditures on material goods and services, Americans saved nearly $715 billion in a recent year.

Percentage of Households Owning Selected Items

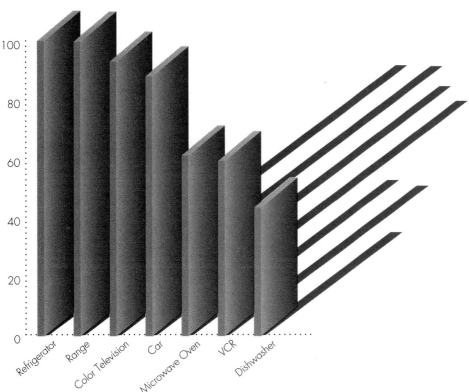

Fig. 1-5
Families buy cars and appliances with their incomes.

Source: Statistical Abstract of the United States, 1992.

Even though the typical American has done well when compared to people in other countries, some problems still exist. For example, slow economic periods may create job shortages, layoffs, and reduced incomes. People are finding fewer jobs in higher-paying manufacturing industries and, therefore, are taking lower-paying service jobs. Some people cannot find employment because of inadequate skills. When incomes drop, it becomes more difficult to buy homes and to send children to college. Lower incomes could also lead to poverty. Moreover, financial hardships exist for larger numbers of older people who have limited incomes and greater health care needs. You will learn more about these and similar problems in later chapters.

E NTREPRENEURSHIP

The successful growth of business in the United States happened as a result of many factors. The strong desire by individuals to own their own businesses and the ease with which a business can be started are two reasons for business growth. One who starts, manages, and owns a business is called an **entrepreneur.**

POPULARITY OF SMALL BUSINESS

It is the tradition of this country to encourage individuals to become entrepreneurs. Few government controls, for example, prevent a person from launching a new business. Almost anyone who wishes to do so may start a business. As a result, many new businesses spring up yearly in shopping malls and along highways and byways.

Small business is the term applied to any business that is operated by one or a few individuals. Because it is normally costly to start a manufacturing business, few small firms produce goods. Most small businesses are commonly found in service and retail trade fields that usually employ fewer than 100 people. Nearly 98 percent of all businesses in the country are classified as small. However, over half the total number of workers in this country are employed by businesses with fewer than 500 employees. In addition, the revenue generated from all small businesses accounts for about half of the GDP.

In recent years, when many large firms were laying off thousands of workers, small businesses with less than 20 employees were hiring in large numbers. Often, the new entrepreneurs were highly skilled managers who were displaced by large firms that were downsizing. Small firms, on the other hand, were reported to be hiring twice as many applicants as the number of employees laid off by large firms. In addition, many of these small firms were adding more high-paying jobs than low-paying jobs.

Many small businesses are one-person or family operations with only a few employees. Examples include restaurants, gift shops, real estate services, and bakeries. Many businesses also operate on a part-time or seasonal basis. Some examples include outdoor foodstands and souvenir shops found at popular lake and ocean resorts. According to the U.S. Department of Commerce, many businesses earn less than $250,000 in yearly revenue, with many of the very small shops earning far less.

GROWTH OF SMALL BUSINESS

Most large businesses today began as very small businesses. Because they supplied products and services desired by the public and because they were well managed, they became larger and larger. An example includes Tandy, which started as a leather shop in 1923 and grew to over 7,000 Radio Shack outlets. Likewise, Procter and Gamble started as a partnership that grew to 58 manufacturing plants in 23 countries. In a similar manner, Sears, Roebuck and Co. got its start by selling watches and later becoming one of the nation's largest retail businesses.

GROWTH OF FRANCHISE BUSINESS

For the person with an entrepreneurial spirit, a popular way to launch a small business is through a franchise. A **franchise** is a legal agreement between a company and a distributor to sell a product or service under special conditions. Many Docktor Pet Centers, Pizza Huts, and Roy Rogers Restaurants are operated by small business owners under such agreements. The two parties to a franchise agreement are the **franchisor,** the parent company of a franchise agreement that provides the product or service, and the **franchisee,** the distributor of a franchised product or service.

In a typical franchise agreement, the franchisee pays an initial fee to the franchisor and a percentage—usually 3 to 9 percent—of weekly sales. In return, the franchisee gets help in selecting a store site and gets exclusive rights to sell the franchised product or service in a specified geographic area. These services are particularly valuable to inexperienced entrepreneurs.

The franchisor also provides special training and advice in how to operate the franchise efficiently. Therefore, a franchise business has a far greater chance of success than a firm starting on its own. While 5 to 10 percent of franchised businesses fail, the failure rate is far lower than the failure rate of non-franchised businesses.

For anyone planning to become a franchisee, great care should be taken to check out the franchisor. Fraudulent dealers have deceived many innocent people. Franchise agreements may require franchisees to buy all items from the franchisor, often at a price substantially higher than available

Illus. 1-5

Franchise businesses have grown in popularity. How many franchise businesses operate in your community?

elsewhere. In recent years, some franchisors have been charged with allowing other franchises to open businesses too close to each other. Some states have passed laws to protect franchisees. Potential franchisees should seek the help of lawyers and accountants before signing franchising agreements.

In spite of possible dangers, the number of franchises has grown steadily over the years, especially in the retail area. About twelve percent of all retail sales are made by franchise businesses, such as those listed in Fig. 1-6 on page 18. The two areas with the greatest number of franchises are auto and truck dealerships and gasoline service stations. However, fast food restaurants and convenience shops such as Seven Eleven food stores are also quite popular. In recent years, the number of franchises for service-type businesses that do not require large sums of money to get started have steadily increased.

Franchises From A to Z

Athlete's Foot	**Nathan's Famous, Inc.**
Budget Rent-A-Car	**Orange Julius of America**
Century 21	**Pizza Hut**
Deck the Walls	**Quik Print, Inc.**
Eureka Log Homes, Inc.	**Roy Rogers**
Flowerama	**Sbarro, Inc.**
Greetings, Inc.	**The Medicine Shoppes**
Hickory Farms	**U.S.A. Treats**
International Tours, Inc.	**Video Biz, Inc.**
Jiffy Lube	**Western Auto Supply**
Kwik Copy	**Yogi Bear's Jellystone Park**
Lawn Doctor, Inc.	**Zarex Business Centre**
Mini Maid Services, Inc.	

Fig. 1-6
Many business firms are franchise operations.

RISKS OF OWNERSHIP

The success of a business depends greatly on managerial effectiveness. If a business is well managed, an adequate income will likely be earned. From an adequate income, it is possible to pay all expenses and to earn a profit as well. If a business does not earn a profit, it cannot continue for long. An entrepreneur assumes the risk of success or failure.

Risk—the possibility of failure—is one of the characteristics of business that all entrepreneurs must face. Risk—which will also be discussed in Chapter 20—involves competition from other businesses, changes in prices, changes in style, competition from new products, and changes that arise from economic conditions. Whenever risks are high, the risk of failure is also high.

Businesses close for a number of reasons. Thousands fail yearly for financial reasons, as shown in Fig. 1-7. According to popular statistics, one out of every four to five businesses fails within three years, and about half cease operations within six to seven years. However, those figures include firms that voluntarily go out of business, such as by selling to someone else or by adding more owners. The results of a recent study shown in Fig. 1-8 clearly indicate that only 18 percent should fall into the failure category. The reported causes of failures are shown in Fig. 1-9 on page 20. Most often, economic and financial factors cause businesses to fail.

Business Failures: 1984-1992

Reported Failures (in Thousands)

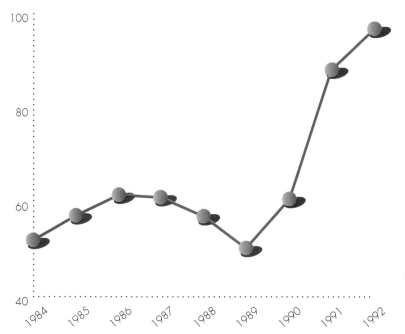

Source: Adapted from Business Failure Record. The Dun & Bradstreet Corporation, 1992.

Fig. 1-7
Yearly financial failures of business firms.

The Results of 814,000 Firms 8 Years After Starting (in Percent)

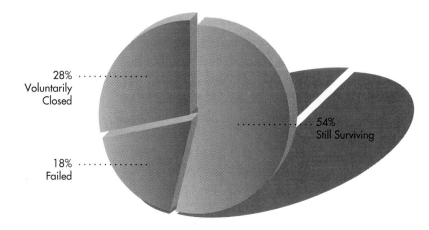

28%
Voluntarily
Closed

54%
Still Surviving

18%
Failed

Fig. 1-8
Many of the businesses reported as failures are not failures.

Fig. 1-9

Causes of business failures.

PRIMARY REASONS FOR FAILURES	PERCENT OF FAILURES
ECONOMIC CAUSES	64.1
Industry weakness, low profits, and low sales	
FINANCE CAUSES	23.9
Heavy expenses and burdensome debts	
DISASTER AND FRAUD	6.7
Hurricanes, floods, and theft	
NEGLECT CAUSES	3.7
Business conflicts, family problems, and poor work habits	
STRATEGY CAUSES	0.9
Overexpansion and difficulty collecting from customers	
EXPERIENCE CAUSES	0.8
Inadequate planning and inexperience	

Source: Adapted from *Business Failure Record. The Dun & Bradstreet Corporation, 1992.*

Obligations of Ownership

Anyone who starts a business has a responsibility to the entire community in which the business operates. Customers, employees, suppliers, and even competitors are affected by a single business. Therefore, a business that fails creates an economic loss that is shared by others in society. For example, an unsuccessful business probably owes money to other firms that will also suffer a loss because they cannot collect. In fact, a business that cannot collect from several other businesses may be placed in a weakened financial condition and it, too, may fail.

An executive of a major business association pointed out the following obligations of business owners:

1. TO CUSTOMERS: That they may have the best at the lowest cost, consistent with fairness to all those engaged in production and distribution.
2. TO WORKERS: That their welfare will not be sacrificed for the benefit of others, and in their employment relations, their rights will be respected.
3. TO MANAGEMENT: That it may be recognized in proportion to its demonstrated ability, considering always the interest of others.
4. TO COMPETITORS: That there will be avoidance of every form of unfair competition.
5. TO INVESTORS: That their rights will be safeguarded and they will be kept so informed that they can exercise their own judgment respecting their interests.
6. TO THE PUBLIC: That the business will strive in all its operations and relations to promote the general welfare and to observe faithfully the laws of the land.

Just as every business has an obligation to the community, the community has an obligation to each business. Society should be aware that owners face many risks while trying to earn a fair profit on the investment made in the business. Consumers should realize that the prices of goods and services are affected by expenses that arise from operating a business. Employees should also realize that a business cannot operate successfully, and thereby provide jobs, unless each worker is properly trained and eager to work. The economic health of a community is improved when groups in the community are aware of each other's obligations. Some of the social and ethical dilemmas faced by businesses are examined in Chapter 2.

I NTRAPRENEURSHIP

Rather than lose creative employees who may quit to start their own businesses, employers now encourage creativity through intrapreneurships. An **intrapreneur** is an employee who is given funds and freedom to create a special unit or department within a company in order to develop a new product, process, or service. Although the new venture is financed by the main company, intrapreneurs enjoy the freedom of running their operations with little or no interference from upper-level managers.

Some of the largest corporations in the United States provide intrapreneurship opportunities. By so doing, valuable employees provide the company with innovative products and services. International Business Machines (IBM), for example, entered late into the personal computer market. When IBM decided to make a small computer, it needed a good product in a hurry. An intrapreneurship unit was created. Within a brief period, the employees who voluntarily joined the unit made a personal computer that soon outsold other brands.

IBM and other major corporations such as 3M and General Electric have also captured the innovative abilities of employees with entrepreneurial characteristics. Employees benefit because they risk neither their salaries nor their savings to launch a new business. Employers also benefit by keeping creative employees who might have started successful competing businesses. Furthermore, employers and consumers benefit because new and better products, processes, and services are introduced at a quickened pace through intrapreneurships.

In recent years, businesses that struggled for survival in a global economy offered an ownership opportunity to employees. That opportunity became known as an **employee stock ownership plan (ESOP),** which permits employees to directly own the company in which they work by allowing them to buy shares in it. Companies benefit by obtaining funds from employees who buy shares and thereby become highly motivated to make their company a success. ESOPs have been shown to increase productivity. For instance, Avis, the car rental firm, has an ESOP that created employee participation groups that focused on solving problems. Avis became a more profitable company because employees worked harder and better when they knew they would share in the profits as owners.

SATURN REINVENTS HOW CARS SHOULD BE MADE

Questions:

1 Why did Roger Smith feel it was necessary to create the Saturn division of General Motors?

2 What new strategies did Saturn use that most contributed to the car's success?

3 Can you offer reasons why transferring Saturn vice presidents to other car divisions had little effect in getting Saturn innovations accepted there?

4 Why has it been difficult for GM to change the way it operates?

In 1985 General Motors (GM)—the company that makes Chevrolets, Buicks, and other popular models—took a bold move. It created a separate company that used an entirely different approach to make a new car. The old mass production methods where workers performed narrow, specialized tasks were tossed aside.

Roger B. Smith, the top manager at GM, decided to experiment by creating a division that would include empowering employees to work with managers to produce a new car. Five years later the Saturn Corporation, a subdivision of GM, proudly presented its first batch of cars. Suspicious buyers were hesitant, but after kicking tires and test driving three new models, some bought. The good news spread quickly. The small cars had few flaws, were inexpensive, attractive, and ran well. By the end of the second year, buyers had to be turned away. Demand exceeded supply.

How did Saturn accomplish this miracle? Critics were skeptical of Roger Smith's bold idea. But those union members and managers who volunteered to move to Spring Hill, Tennessee, to make new lives and three new car models smiled at the skeptics for different reasons. They had ideas of succeeding. They set high goals for themselves and for Saturn that included teamwork, a commitment to excellence, trust and respect for one another, and—perhaps most important—an emphasis on customer satisfaction. They also created new methods that were used when working with companies that sold supplies and parts to Saturn. These "partner" suppliers had to support the same goals that Saturn employees set for themselves—stand behind their products and incorporate teamwork in a decision-making environment while aiming for maximum customer satisfaction.

Saturn workers and managers became equals. They discussed problems and worked out solutions together. They offered ideas, implemented changes, and talked with suppliers. Work teams hired their own workers and trained them. These decision-making workers created a car that placed Saturn ahead of Toyota, Mercedes-Benz, and Acura in a recent customer-satisfaction poll.

Serious problems exist in spite of the many innovations introduced by Saturn. Millions of dollars were invested in Saturn and GM has been concerned about when it will make a reasonable profit. The introduction of Saturn's innovations into other General Motors' car divisions will not be easy. Several vice presidents were transferred to other plants but could not successfully transport Saturn's innovations. Changing the giant corporation to operate like Saturn may take many years. Only time will tell whether GM can reinvent itself in a timely manner.

IMPORTANCE OF STUDYING BUSINESS PRINCIPLES AND MANAGEMENT

Whether you plan to operate a business of your own or become an employee who expects to rise to a top-level position, you must be well informed about the production, marketing, and financial activities of a business. As an owner, you must have a complete understanding of all phases of business operations, including employee relations and government regulations. In a similar manner, such understandings are also necessary to become a competent employee in a specialized job or department. Moreover, if you expect to become a supervisor or an executive of a company, you must fully understand how the activities of all departments are coordinated in a smoothly operating business. Finally, if you plan to work in organizations other than in business, such as in government, you will also benefit by knowing more about how successful businesses operate.

CHAPTER REVIEW

BUILDING VOCABULARY POWER

Define the following terms and concepts.

1. business
2. production
3. manufacturing firms ✓
4. service firms
5. finance ✓
6. supply ✓
7. demand ✓
8. industrial businesses
9. third world nations ✓
10. commercial businesses
11. industry
12. services
13. global competition ✓
14. effectiveness
15. efficiency ✓
16. domestic goods
17. foreign goods ✓
18. total quality management (TQM) ✓
19. output ✓
20. productivity
21. mass production ✓
22. downsize ✓
23. empowerment ✓
24. gross domestic product (GDP) ✓
25. underground economy ✓
26. entrepreneur ✓
27. small business
28. franchise ✓
29. franchisor ✓
30. franchisee ✓
31. intrapreneur ✗
32. employee stock ownership plan ✓ (ESOP)

REVIEWING FACTS

1. About how many businesses of all kinds are there in the United States?
2. What three activities do all businesses perform?
3. Which two types of businesses, shown in Fig. 1-1, employ the most workers?
4. Which type of business has grown so rapidly that it now outnumbers manufacturing, wholesaling, and retailing businesses?
5. Name three techniques that American businesses can use to improve efficiency and productivity.
6. When workers are empowered, what happens in an organization?
7. Why is the gross domestic product (GDP) important?
8. What proof is there that the average American family is financially well off?
9. Is the typical person prevented from starting a small firm?
10. How much do small businesses contribute to the GDP yearly, and how much of the total workforce is employed by small businesses?
11. In a typical franchise arrangement, what are the advantages to the franchisee?
12. Are there any dangers to consider when seeking a franchisor?
13. What are the two main causes for business failure?
14. Why would a large business encourage intrapreneurship?
15. How does a company benefit if it has an Employee Stock Ownership Plan?

DISCUSSING IDEAS

1. How does an industrial firm differ from a manufacturing firm?
2. Study Fig. 1-2, which shows changes in the growth of businesses by selected categories. (a) Discuss what is happening to manufacturing when compared to the other categories, (b) offer reasons for the cause of the condition, and (c) indicate what might be done to improve it.
3. Discuss which is more important, effectiveness or efficiency.
4. Discuss a plan of worker specialization and mass production for a company that makes motorcycles.
5. Many new products and methods have been created in this country, but does the number of new inventions always lead to business success over competitors? Explain your answer.
6. Discuss what types of people might prefer to be specialists on an assembly line doing the same tasks continuously, and who would most prefer to be empowered employees.
7. How might it be possible for the GDP to be larger than the reported amount in a given year? What can be done to prevent inaccurate GDP amounts that are reported?

REVIEW

8. Why might a person who wishes to go into business not want to consider a franchise arrangement?

9. Give examples of risks that the owner of a gasoline service station might have.

10. Not only does the owner of a business have an obligation to employees, but each employee has an obligation to the employer. Mention some specific obligations that each has.

11. Discuss why it is important for employees, consumers, or citizens to understand how American business operates.

A NALYZING INFORMATION

1. Compare the total of industrial types of businesses in Fig. 1-1 with the total of the service industries shown.
   a. Approximately what is the total employment for the production industries and for the other industries?
   b. By what percentage is the one group larger than the other?

2. Use the actual GDP figures (shown below) between 1960 and 1990: (a) what is the actual number of dollars for 1960 showing all the necessary digits; (b) show the percent of increase for each decade; (c) calculate the total percent of increase from 1960 to 1990, and (d) determine the average yearly increase in the GDP for the period shown.

1960	$ .513 trillion
1970	1.011
1980	2.708
1990	5.514

3. From his regular job, Drew earned $25,000 last year, on which he paid his federal taxes. He also paid taxes on a week-long job held before getting his full-time job, from which he earned $600. In addition, Drew earned $12,500 painting homes for relatives, neighbors, and friends. Early in the year, he bought an antique car in poor condition for $3,500. After spending $6,000 on special parts and many hours remodeling the car, he sold it for $31,000 and received cash for the full amount. Neither the money made when the antique car was sold nor the money earned for painting homes was reported on his income tax return. (a) How much of Drew's earnings were taxed last year? (b) How much income earned was a part of the underground economy on which no taxes were paid? (c) What percent of his total income for the year was from his underground economy earnings? (d) Does Drew have a moral obligation to report his underground economy earnings? Explain your answer.

4. Talk to the owner of a franchise about the advantages and disadvantages of managing a franchise. Also discuss the general advantages and disadvantages of entrepreneurship. Report your findings to the class.

5. With the help of a librarian, find a recent article on productivity or on problems a U.S. company or industry may have when competing with

foreign countries. Read the article and make a report following the instructions of your teacher.

S OLVING BUSINESS PROBLEMS

CASE 1-1

The Trimm family came to this country early in the 20th Century and made a bicycle that soon became known for its quality. Through much of the century, Trimm was the "Cadillac" of American bicycles. A former U.S. president was featured in a Trimm advertisement and the company sponsored its own TV show. In the 1960s, it ran circles around numerous competitors; one in four bikes was a Trimm. Throughout this time, the Trimm family managed the company.

The success of Trimm's line of bicycles gave the company great confidence, perhaps too much confidence. During the last three years sales dropped, slipping from one million bikes sold yearly to 500,000 the next year and 250,000 last year. Three major competitors with nifty lower-priced bikes who sold to K-Mart, Sears, and other large stores were stealing customers. When mountain bikes became popular, Trimm management ridiculed this new fad.

In the meantime, the quality of Trimm bikes faded. To cut costs, employees were let go and lower-quality parts were bought from foreign firms and installed. Trimm managers made no attempt to talk to biking customers. Neither did the managers listen to the hundreds of dealers who sold Trimm bicycles in specialty shops. Loyal dealers started adding competitors' products to survive. Bike deliveries were running late. The changes made to cut costs did not correct the situation. For the last three years, Trimm operated at a loss. Something drastic had to occur.

Recently, Trimm was purchased by another company. Headquarters for the company was set up in Colorado where biking is popular. Trimm's new managers talked to customers and dealers. As a result, new products rolled off the assembly line that were satisfying loyal dealers and older bikers who recalled the excellent quality of the Trimm two-wheelers. But can the new Trimm adequately rebuild itself to compete in a tough market? Quality Trimm bikes sold only at specialty shops cost $250 to $2,500, which is far more than most bikes purchased at discount stores. Plenty of persuading will be needed to convert the price-conscious casual bikers or the more serious riders who put on 25 to 100 miles a week.

Signs of success appear on the horizon. A small profit is expected this year for the struggling firm. Whether the new managers can reestablish Trimm's earlier lead in the marketplace is yet to be determined.

Required:

1. What was the main reason why the old Trimm company failed? Explain your answer.

REVIEW

2. What should the new managers do to help improve Trimm's effectiveness?
3. What might the company do to help improve its efficiency?
4. Create a title for this case that provides the theme to the story.

CASE 1-2

Four weeks ago, two close friends lost their jobs as a result of a slow period with the company. They expect to be called back, but they are not certain about that. Meanwhile, they often spend their afternoons together jogging, playing tennis, or going to the nearby YMCA to play basketball. Often, they just chat about different things, including how difficult it is to be without work and without a steady income. One afternoon, the following conversation took place.

Jim: I have payments to make on my house and car. Fortunately, I paid cash for my new console TV. I hope the company calls us back to work soon.

Bill: I know what you mean, but just think. While we are out of work, we still have a pretty good deal. You have your own home and car. Lots of people in other countries have almost nothing.

Jim: If we made a list of things that most of the workers at the factory own, how long would it be? Two cars each, maybe? Two TVs, a lawn mower, . . .

Bill: Throw in radios, stereos, electric razors, and hair dryers. Everyone has furniture, clothes, telephones, washers . . . . We could go on forever.

Jim: Don't forget the items in closets and drawers. Most people have at least one camera, a watch, a ring . . . .

Bill: You gave me an idea, Jim. If we are not called back to work by next weekend, let's have a garage sale so we can get rid of some of the extra things we have lying around in our attics and basements. We can each raise enough money to buy new tennis racquets. We sure need them.

Jim: Better yet, we could buy tickets to see the pros play in the big tournament coming up next month. That would be a great weekend for both of us.

Required:
1. Should Jim and Bill be looking for other jobs rather than wait to be called back by the companies that laid them off?
2. Are the benefits of the U.S. business system revealed in this conversation? Explain.
3. Do you believe that most U.S. families would have the items mentioned in the conversation? Explain.
4. What items that Americans often buy were not mentioned by Jim and Bill that show the economic well-being of Americans?
5. If a garage sale is held, is it likely that the money earned would be included in the GDP? Explain.

SOCIAL AND ETHICAL ENVIRONMENT OF BUSINESS

CHAPTER 2

After studying this chapter you will be able to:

2-1 Describe the changing nature of the population, the labor force, and some of the major social issues that face businesses today.

2-2 Discuss how the values of Americans have changed and how business has adapted to those changed values.

2-3 Debate the dilemma of the growth of business in relation to protecting the environment.

2-4 Explain the basic principles of ethics and how ethics applies to business situations.

2-5 Suggest ways in which businesses can be socially responsible.

2-6 Predict how changes in society and business will impact on employment in the future.

S hawn picked up the file folder and walked to his supervisor's office. He had finally saved enough money for the down payment and other costs for a small stone house on the lake that his wife had long wanted. He now needed his supervisor's signature on several documents that the bank required to approve the home loan. Shawn was excited; he had a skip in his walk.

The Marathon Company where Shawn worked was the main employer in this small town in Michigan. The company had been around for a long time. Because the firm paid high wages, the town had nice stores, good restaurants, and colorful festivals. Taxes paid by the company supported the police and fire departments, the public school system, and the recreation center.

In recent years, however, Marathon was struggling to keep up. Sales fell while unsold goods began to pile up. Some employees were let go. To survive, Marathon had to cut costs and update its buildings and machinery. Rather than continue operations in Michigan, Marathon decided to relocate in Georgia where taxes and wages were lower, as well as utility and raw material costs. Of course, employees were not aware of Marathon's serious problem.

Only yesterday Shawn's supervisor, Mr. Woodward, had been informed that the town's factory would shut down over the next twelve months. He was being promoted but would move to the new Georgia plant. Some of the workers would be given the option to move to Georgia but many others, like Shawn, would lose their jobs.

Therefore, when Shawn excitedly asked Mr. Woodward to sign the bank papers for his lakeside home, Mr. Woodward was disturbed. Should he sign the loan papers when he knew Shawn's job would barely last a year? If he did not sign, everyone would soon find out why. Morale among employees would drop. Then production would slump as people looked for jobs elsewhere. It was important to keep the plant closure decision a secret for as long as possible. The town would be devastated when it learned that its main employer would soon be relocating. Mr. Woodward pondered the decision as he thought about how much the community and country had changed in his short lifetime.

Since its establishment more than 200 years ago, the United States has attained remarkable goals, especially technically and economically. The country has the world's largest economy and relies on highly sophisticated and modern means of production, transportation, and communication. Most Americans enjoy a high standard of living. All these achievements can be attributed to the enormous resources that the country possesses, the ingenuity of its people, a democratic form of government, a social system that rewards individualism, and policies that encourage business.

Despite enormous successes, difficult issues continue to exist with regard to solving serious problems such as employment, poverty, discrimination, environmental damage, ethical conduct, and social responsibility. As a result, the business system must be seen as part of the total society in which it operates. As a major element of society, businesses affect people in material ways, as Shawn will soon discover. Society, in turn, influences the conduct of business. Thus, one cannot study business principles and management without also having an understanding of the social forces that shape business.

HUMAN RESOURCE ISSUES

People are a firm's most important resource. A business cannot isolate itself from the people who help achieve organizational goals. The challenges faced by business are closely interwoven with those experienced by the workforce. In particular, such issues as those caused by changes in population and life styles have a direct bearing on business operations and also on the well-being of the nation.

POPULATION

The gross domestic product (GDP) of a country cannot increase unless there are enough people to provide the labor and to purchase the goods and services that are produced. Population statistics help businesses plan how much and what kinds of goods and services to offer. However, the GDP of a country must grow at a faster rate than its population in order to improve its living standard. Not only the size but also the nature of the population are important elements in business planning.

Growing Population

The population of the United States has grown slowly but steadily over the years, as can be seen in Fig. 2-1. The growth rate is controlled mostly by the birth rate. The birth rate fluctuates modestly over time but in recent years has stayed close to the level of **zero population growth (ZPG),** the point at which births and deaths balance.

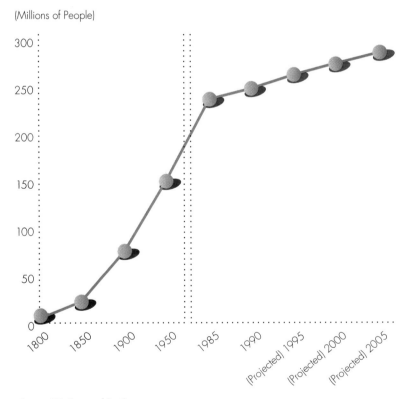

(Millions of People)

Fig. 2-1

The population of the United States continues to grow, but at a slower pace.

Source: U.S. Bureau of the Census.

In spite of ZPG, the population increases in two other ways. First, because of improved health care, people are living to rather advanced ages. Second, the population also increases in legal and illegal ways through immigration. The United States annually accepts more legal immigrants than any other country in the world, with large numbers coming from Asian and Latin American nations. However, many immigrants enter the country illegally to seek a better life.

Changing Population

The nature of the population has been undergoing a change as well. Currently, more than eighty percent of Americans are racially classified as white. However, because of higher birth rates among nonwhite Hispanic and African Americans and recent immigrants, their proportions in the population have been growing.

Changes in the birth rate have also caused shifts in the number of people in different age groups. For example, because of the high birth rate between 1945-1965, there are more Americans in the 30-50 age group than any other group. The 1945-1965 high birth rate period is referred to as the **baby boom** period. The number of people 55 years of age and older will increase substantially in number by the year 2000. The low birth rate period that followed the boomer period is called the **baby bust** period. The baby bust period has created a shortage of young workers called busters. This shortage will continue to create serious problems, especially when the boomers retire in large numbers.

Businesses must be prepared to offer the kinds of goods and services needed by people of different age and racial groups. For instance, with increasing numbers of Spanish-speaking people, some newspapers publish a Spanish-language edition. As people live longer, food companies continue to develop special foods and products for the elderly.

Illus. 2-1

Young "baby bust" workers are in short supply for filling full-time and part-time jobs. What types of jobs are advertised most by retail or other types of businesses that seek young workers?

Jeff Greenberg, Photographer

Moving Population

A feature of the American population is that people move frequently. Every year, on average, one out of five Americans will change his or her address. People move short distances, often from cities to suburbs; and long distances, such as from the **Frost Belt**—the colder northern half of the country, to the **Sun Belt**—the warmer southern half of the nation. As businesses relocate to where customers and workers are located, they affect where other people move in order to find jobs. For example, factories have relocated to the southeastern states where wage rates are lower than in the **Rust Belt**—the north central and northeastern states where the major manufacturing centers once dominated. As revealed in the opening story, the Marathon Company decided to move from Michigan to Georgia to lower its labor and other costs.

The continuing movement of people from the city to the suburbs, and from the north to the south, have led to many unintended consequences. When families and businesses left cities in large numbers, the cities lost the financial ability to provide high-quality services. As a result, crime and poverty rates are high in some large cities. Many southern states such as Georgia and Florida have experienced enormous economic and industrial growth. When businesses moved from the Rust Belt, they left behind unemployed workers, closed factories, decaying towns, and homeless people.

LABOR FORCE

As the population grows, so does the labor force. The **labor force** includes most people aged 16 or over who are available for work, whether employed or unemployed. Of course, many of the people in the labor force may be available for work but are not actively seeking employment, such as students and full-time homemakers. The growth rate in the labor force is shown in Fig. 2-2.

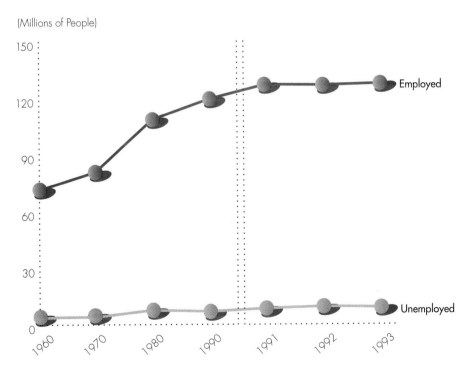

(Millions of People)

Fig. 2-2
Trends in the labor force.

Source: U.S. Bureau of Labor Statistics.

The relationship between the population and the labor force is shown by the **labor participation rate**—the percentage of the labor force that is either employed or actively seeking employment. In the last three decades, the labor participation rate increased primarily because many more women became employed outside the home. In 1970, around 58 percent of women worked outside the home; but by 1990, the figure had risen to nearly 72 percent. Women were also not marrying, delaying marriage, or marrying but pursuing careers before raising children. Fig. 2-3 shows the trend in labor participation rates for males and females.

Fig. 2-3

The labor participation rate for men and women aged 20–24 years of age.

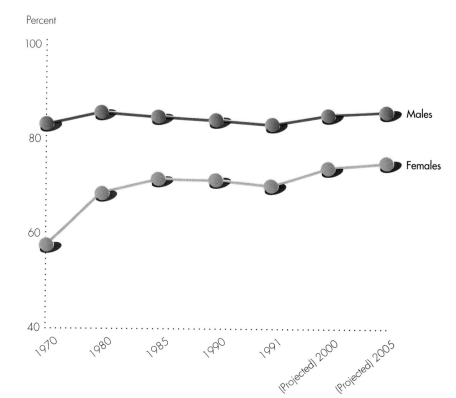

Source: U.S. Bureau of Labor Statistics.

As a result of economic growth, the shifting population, and technological advances, many new jobs have emerged. One of the great strengths of the American economy has been the ability to create new jobs. A large number of new jobs are in small businesses and in service industries such as banking, insurance, computer, travel, food, and entertainment. Many of the new jobs require more skills, which means workers must be educated. As a result, more people are going to college or acquiring training in new areas. As new technology increases and old jobs disappear, it becomes necessary to retrain workers. At the same time, jobs such as short-order cooks and clerks have been simplified, require little training, and pay low wages. A large number of workers are in dead-end jobs and are not earning an adequate income to maintain a reasonable standard of living.

For various reasons, including lack of financial resources, public schools in many urban areas are failing to provide the quality and level of education historically expected of high school graduates. A recent major study revealed that half the adults lacked basic skills as revealed by their inability to write a brief letter explaining an error on a credit card statement or by their inability to use a calculator to determine the difference between a sale price and a regular price. Particularly deficient are math, computer, social, and communication skills (reading and writing). Businesses are being forced to provide remedial education in basic skills when hiring workers.

POVERTY

The prosperity of Americans is not equally distributed among the population. According to the United States Bureau of the Census, between 12 and 15 percent of the population—nearly one in seven people—live in poverty. These people are usually poorly housed, poorly clothed, and poorly fed. Many of them live in inner-city slums as well as in rural areas of some states. Statistics suggest that the richest 20 percent of American families have continued to earn more over the past twenty years while the income of the lowest fifth has remained the same. Thus, the gap between the rich and poor widens. This gap is not just economic, but also ethnic—many of the poor are black or Hispanic.

Both governments and businesses have programs that reduce poverty. By setting minimum wage rates and by providing unemployment benefits, food aid, and medical care, poverty-stricken people are somewhat protected. Businesses increasingly offer training programs to provide skills that enable people to get jobs.

EQUAL EMPLOYMENT

Equality for all is one of the basic principles on which the United States was formed. Yet, many groups of Americans have found it difficult to obtain jobs or get promoted on an equal basis. Several laws have been passed to outlaw discrimination on the basis of race, gender, national origin, religion, age, handicap, and other characteristics.

In many occupations, the numbers of women and racial minorities are few. Even when jobs are found, these groups encounter difficulties in being promoted above a certain level. This situation is known as the **glass ceiling**—an invisible barrier to job advancement. The barriers are often difficult to detect, for example a white male's discomfort with having a female or black supervisor. Employers are now legally obligated to provide equal employment opportunities for all.

COMPARABLE WORTH

On average, females are paid only 75 percent of what males are paid for most jobs. The difference in pay is more nearly equal for young workers but the gap widens with age. For example, a newly employed female college graduate earns 92 percent of what similar males earn; but as the female nears retirement, she earns only 54 percent of what males earn.

Most people would agree that men and women who are hired to do the same job should earn the same pay. But what happens when the jobs are similar

Ilus. 2-2
Women and minorities may hit the "glass ceiling" as they attempt to move to higher level jobs. Have any of your friends or family members found it impossible to rise in their jobs because of racial or gender-based discrimination?

Jeff Greenberg, Photographer

but not the same? **Comparable worth** means paying workers equally for jobs with similar but not identical job requirements. The concept is also called "equal pay for comparable work." Jobs being compared may be distinctly different as between legal secretaries and carpenters. However, if it can be determined that comparable factors are needed to perform both jobs, the pay scale for the two jobs should be the same, or legal secretaries should be paid more than what they currently earn. To determine whether work is of equal value, factors such as special skills, physical strength, job dangers, job responsibilities, and education are compared.

Major problems arise, however, in determining specific factors that measure the worth of jobs. Should physical strength, for instance, be used to compare the worth of a legal secretary to a carpenter? And if few applicants are available for the carpenter's position and many are available for legal secretaries, is it fair to pay legal secretaries more than carpenters? And what about the social status of carpenters or their having to work in cold, rain, and snow?

These and other factors make it difficult for employers to design and implement comparable worth plans. But businesses are trying. More than one-third of the states have passed laws that promote using comparable worth for determining wages in government jobs. However, businesses fear comparable worth will raise labor costs. Thus far, courts have not favored comparable worth. Equal pay for comparable work will evolve slowly. With more and more women entering traditionally male dominated jobs, gaps in pay between women and men should eventually disappear.

SOCIETAL VALUES

The United States is a country where people readily accept change. New products, new ideas, new ways of doing things, and new attitudes regularly emerge in American society before they are adopted in other countries. In recent decades, societal values have been undergoing change at a fast pace.

An especially striking development has been the transformation of adult life, especially in relation to families and child-rearing practices throughout the past few decades. These changes have not only affected the nature of the American family but of Americans' work lives as well.

The number of children living with both parents continues to fall because of rising divorce rates and children born out of wedlock. The birth rate too has declined as people delay marriage and pursue fulfilling professional careers outside the home. The traditional ideal of a working husband, a homemaker wife, two children, and a dog is now an exception; less than one-fourth of America's families fit this picture.

With affluence has come the desire to enjoy work and time away from work. For instance, more vacation time is demanded, as are flexible work hours. Job absenteeism is on the rise, especially among women. Romance has blossomed in the workplace, but so have charges of sexual harassment. People are placing more emphasis on recreational opportunities, as reflected in the growth of the travel industry. With increasing numbers of adult singles and working couples, dining at home is being replaced by dining out. More money is spent by American consumers on restaurant meals than on grocery purchases.

An aspect of contemporary American society is the use of illegal drugs. Another concern deals with the dreaded and costly AIDS disease, a disease that destroys the body's ability to resist infection. The law protects people suffering from AIDS, tuberculosis, and other harmful diseases from being fired by employers. Similarly, alcoholism remains a stubborn problem. Evidence now reveals that many Americans are also addicted to gambling. All these factors gravely affect both business and society.

EMPLOYER PRACTICES

A changing society impacts on individuals as well as on organizations. Many of the social issues transfer to work settings. Employees leave home each work day thinking about personal problems. Responsibilities may be enormous for workers with preschool children, aging parents, family illnesses, and financial burdens. Concerns such as these follow employees to their work sites and affect their job performance.

Retaining capable and loyal employees is as important a concern as is attracting qualified job applicants. To attract and retain competent workers, employers have been conscious of the changes in individual life styles, pressures on families, and needs of workers at all age levels. Managers have responded to these social changes by taking action to improve the way work is done, to assure healthier and safer working conditions, and to help workers deal with some personal problems.

Redesigning Jobs

As you will learn in other chapters, when jobs consist of mainly dull repetitive tasks, workers get bored, productivity drops, and morale is low. Many workers leave to find jobs with other employers offering more interesting jobs. Thus, to retain workers, employers are redesigning jobs to make them varied and interesting. In some cases, employees learn each others' jobs and regularly switch jobs with others. For instance, if one employee has always done Task A, another Task B, and still another Task C, they can shift from one task to another on a scheduled basis. Jobs take on added interest, morale jumps, and coworkers fill in for absentees or pinch hit when needed for other tasks.

Workers may also be given a chance to participate more in making job decisions, providing suggestions, or serving on committees that look for ways to improve work quality. When work teams are formed, not only does the quality of work improve but so does the quantity produced. The emphasis in modern firms is on improving job satisfaction through empowering workers and thereby improving the quality of work life. Employees and employers both benefit.

Improving Health and Safety

In response to concerns over health, businesses operate wellness and fitness programs. A physically unfit employee is absent more and is less productive than a fit employee. As a result, many corporations encourage physical fitness by providing financial incentives to smokers to quit, health clubs for employees to exercise, counseling services where workers can receive support for stress or emotional problems, drug tests to discourage drug abuse, and rehabilitation programs for drug addicts and alcoholics. Employers thereby reduce medical costs. Corporations report that with active physical fitness programs in place, their life and health insurance costs on employees are reduced.

Two changes directly relate to the health of workers. One change safeguards the work environment by outlawing smoking; the second warns employees who are exposed to work conditions that could affect their health. The second change has caused firms to adapt equipment to a safe and comfortable work environment.

Adapting to Worker Needs

Given the changes in the family structure, employers are making efforts to respond to the personal side of a worker's life. Government agencies and alert businesses have responded by helping entire families, not just individual employees. Major corporations such as Aetna Life & Casualty, Johnson & Johnson, and Continental Corporation are learning that it pays to help today's family cope better when linking jobs to family responsibilities. Firms are also learning that some problems are so severe that policies are needed that some workers may not like.

For example, with each passing year more firms provide day-care facilities for employees. A recent law also provides family leave for new parents, which allows employees three months of unpaid leave time to adopt, give birth, and to care for newborn children. Another important benefit that permits employees to start work early and leave early as well as to start late and leave late is a flexible work schedule. Flexible schedules help employees avoid rush-hour traffic jams and also allow parents to adjust schedules that meet family needs and life styles. Yet another way that employers are responding to the changing life styles of workers is to permit telecommuting. **Telecommuting** allows employees to work at home using computers rather than at the business. Working mothers and handicapped employees especially appreciate telecommuting.

Many employers have instituted policies concerning drug use. Drug testing before employment is a growing requirement for large firms. However, many of these same firms provide medical treatment to help employees overcome dependencies on drugs and alcohol. When drugs interfere with work performance and employees do not attempt to solve their problems, employees are fired. Why? Drug abuse leads to poor job performance and causes accidents.

Because of the changing makeup of the population and a predicted future shortage of workers, employers are making efforts to hire women and minorities who have been overlooked in the past. Progress is being made in breaking the glass ceiling that restricts job advancement. At the same time, businesses are adopting work environments that allow disabled and older workers to function in an effective manner. Managing a diverse workforce is a new challenge for America's employers.

NATURAL RESOURCE ISSUES

As society grows, people purchase more things. More purchases mean more paper wrappings, boxes, and worn out products to throw away. When worn out plastic, chemical, and metal products grow in number, disposing of them becomes harder to accomplish. Moreover, some products may be harmful if not disposed of properly. On the other hand, to produce the goods that consumers want places great pressure on natural resources such as land, water, minerals, and air. America must address these resource issues.

MANAGING THE ENVIRONMENT

Better management of our limited natural resources and improved disposal methods of waste products are critical concerns of society and business. Fortunately, increasing attention is being given to preserving our resources, intelligently discarding our trash, and recovering discarded materials that may be transformed into new products. As landfills become stuffed, focus has shifted to reduce the growth of waste and to **recycle**—the reuse of products or product packaging whenever possible. Attention is especially focused on conserving resources that are nonrenewable, such as natural gas, oil, and iron ore. At the same time, more ways to use renewable resources continue to unfold, such as generating electricity from the sun (solar power).

Solar power is used to expand more traditional power sources. Do you know a person or business using solar cells to heat water or to heat a building?

Bob Wallace/Stock, Boston

At times, pollution control goals, such as improvement of air quality, may be at odds with energy conservation goals. For example, the use of coal, which is currently in great supply, generally pollutes air more than natural gas, which is in short supply. A business changing from coal to natural gas meets environmental goals but violates conservation goals. On the other hand, a business changing from natural gas to coal conserves natural gas but creates additional pollution. In time, scientists may discover ways to use coal without creating a great deal of pollution. Until then, Americans must decide how best to conserve natural resources and protect the environment as well.

Pollution dangers have become more and more apparent. Large cities are often covered by smog that contains pollutants generated by large numbers of motor vehicles. As a result, many residents suffer from breathing problems. In numerous rivers and lakes, pollutants have killed fish and other marine life. In addition, chemical products used to destroy insects and plant life have especially endangered waterways and land areas.

GOVERNING OUR ACTIONS

Many groups have pressured governments and employers to tighten pollution standards and to conserve natural resources. The federal government created the Environmental Protection Agency (EPA) in 1970 to help control and reduce pollution in the basic areas of air, water, waste, pesticides, noise, and radiation. The EPA enforces such laws as the Clean Air Act, Clean Water Act, Resource Recovery Act, Federal Water Pollution Control Act, Federal Environmental Pesticide Control Act, Noise Control Act, and Resource Conservation and Recovery Act. For instance, regulations have been developed that require engines in cars to be both fuel-efficient and to reduce air pollution.

New waste disposal rules, especially for hazardous materials like medical and nuclear waste, are strictly enforced and often costly to carry out. These high costs sometimes lead to illegal dumping in bodies of water or on remote land areas. To conserve resources and to protect the environment, more and more companies are using recycled materials in their production processes.

In the aftermath of the Exxon Valdez accident, which spilled oil along coastal Alaska in 1989 and killed large numbers of fish and waterfowl, environmentalists and socially minded groups formed the Coalition for Environmentally

Responsible Economies to encourage companies to behave responsibly. The Coalition developed a list of ten environmental guidelines named the Valdez Principles. Organizations are voluntarily asked to follow the principles although they are not legally required to do so. Sun Oil Company (Sunoco) was the first major company that promised to follow the Valdez Principles listed in Fig. 2-4.

1. **Protect the environment from the release of pollutants, especially hazardous substances that may damage the environment.**
2. **Conserve nonrenewable natural resources through efficient use and careful planning.**
3. **Minimize the creation of waste, especially hazardous waste, and dispose of such materials in a safe, responsible manner.**
4. **Make every effort to use environmentally safe and sustainable energy sources to meet organizational needs.**
5. **Reduce environmental, health, and safety risks to employees and surrounding communities.**
6. **Sell products that cause as little damage to the environment as possible and are safe to use.**
7. **Accept responsibility for any harm the company causes to the environment; correct damages made to the environment, and compensate injured parties.**
8. **Keep the public informed of incidents relating to operations that harm the environment or pose health or safety hazards.**
9. **Appoint one person to represent environmental interests to serve on the highest-level decision-making committee that represents owner interests.**
10. **Produce and publicize a yearly self-evaluation of progress toward implementing these principles and meeting all applicable laws worldwide.**

Fig. 2-4

Organizations that voluntarily follow the Valdez Principles safeguard the environment.

Source: Adapted from Rajib N. Sanyal and Joao S. Neves, The Valdez Principles: Implications for Corporate Social Responsibility in The Journal of Business Ethics, Vol. 10, #12, December 1991, pp. 888–889. Original source: CERES: 1990, The 1990 CERES Guide to the Valdez Principles, The Social Investment Forum, Boston, MA. Reprinted by permission of KLUWER Academic Publishers.

Laws against polluting as well as demands for conserving natural resources are costly to businesses. An issue arises when foreign countries have weaker laws, law enforcement is lax, or public concern over pollution and conservation is not as carefully observed as in the United States. As a result, companies in these foreign countries can make goods more cheaply than products made in America. One of the objections to increasing trade with Mexico, for example, is that pollution laws in Mexico are much weaker than in the United States. To help reduce manufacturing costs, therefore, some American companies have moved factories to Mexico.

E THICAL ISSUES

Laws provide a minimum standard of behavior for people and businesses to follow. However, there are many behaviors that are neither allowed nor disallowed by law. The guide that then comes into play is ethics. **Ethics** refers to a code of moral conduct that sets standards for what is valued as right or wrong behavior for a person or group. Ethical behavior relates to practices that are considered acceptable or unacceptable.

Ethical behavior is closely linked to personal values—underlying beliefs and attitudes that individuals or groups possess. To decide whether a particular action is ethical or not, we have to ask questions such as: Is the action right or is it wrong regardless of what the laws state? Therefore, ethical conduct goes beyond state and federal laws.

BUSINESS ETHICS

A collection of principles and rules of conduct based on what is right and what is wrong for an organization is called **business ethics.** Any action that conforms to these moral principles is ethical behavior. Not all firms have the same rules of conduct, however. What is right and wrong can vary from manager to manager, business to business, and country to country. Generally, however, moral conduct that is favorable to the largest number of people is considered ethically desirable. Many organizations have established codes of ethics in the belief that ethical behavior is in the best long-term interest of the business. A **code of ethics** is a formal, published collection of values and rules that are used to guide the behavior of an organization toward its various stakeholders. An established code removes or reduces opportunities for unethical conduct. These codes deal with

Illus. 2-4

Good business ethics is good business. Can you identify the unethical practice taking place here?

Jeff Greenberg, Photographer

such issues as accepting business gifts, bribing government officials, and using company property for personal use.

Ethical codes must be communicated to employees in memos, newsletters, posters, and employee manuals. Procedures must also be devised to handle situations that arise when codes are violated. To carry weight, codes of ethics must have the full support of the organization's top-level managers. Lack of top-level support is a primary reason why codes of ethics often fail.

ETHICAL DILEMMAS

The issue of ethics often arises because it is not clear whether a particular action is legal or illegal. While it is illegal to pay men and women differently in the United States for doing the same job, should a business pay men and women differently in its office located in a foreign country where no such law exists? Many philosophers have debated the issue of right and wrong for centuries. One well-known approach is to ask this question: What is the value or worth of a specific behavior for society as a whole? The best behavior is that which does the most good for the most people. For example, assume a company employed 200 people and it eliminated 50 people so that it could continue to operate. While 50 people were left jobless, 150 benefitted by retaining their jobs.

Businesses are constantly faced with ethical dilemmas of various kinds. Should a lumber company cut a forest of trees although a rare species of bird nests there? Should oil drilling be permitted off a coast, thus destroying its natural beauty? Should a manager accept a request from a foreign official to arrange for his daughter's admission to an American university if the company wants to land a contract? How businesses handle these issues determines whether they are acting in an ethical manner. Notions of what is right or wrong can change over time. Clear-cut answers are not always available. Similarly, morals and values differ from culture to culture.

Because values differ among nations, problems sometimes arise for firms involved in international business. The dilemma firms face is whether to choose the ethical practices of the foreign country or of their home country. For instance, it is an accepted business practice in Japan for employees to give expensive gifts to their bosses. Such behavior in the United States is generally discouraged. Should an American company behave in Japan as it does in the United States or should it follow the Japanese practice? Ethical managers search for answers among employees and the general public.

SOCIAL RESPONSIBILITY OF BUSINESS

In the process of trying to solve the country's various social issues, new issues arise. For example, experts have raised questions regarding the responsibilities of business toward solving the nation's ills. At the same, time employers and employees are constantly faced with situations to which there are no easy solutions, such as when the profit motive and the good of society conflict with one another. Should profit, for instance, be reduced in order to reduce possible harm to others? In such cases, decisions have to be made on what is right and what is wrong.

The primary goal of business is to make a profit for the owners. Businesses cannot survive for long if owners are not rewarded for their efforts. Although profit plays a key role in our business system, businesses today also place a great deal of attention on another business goal—social responsibility. **Social responsibility** refers to the duty of a business to contribute to the well-being of society. Because a community provides a business with certain resources and rights, the business has an obligation to aid the community in which it operates.

Many groups and individuals have a stake in a business. These **stakeholders** —the owners, customers, suppliers, employees, creditors, government, the public, and other groups who are affected by a firm's action—expect a business to be responsible and responsive to their interests. Such responsibility may mean a variety of things. Examples include donating money to flood victims, sponsoring an exhibition on Hindu art at local museums, providing scholarships to colleges for needy students, training gang members in job-related skills, and setting up day-care centers for employees' children.

Thus, social responsibility on the part of business means an acceptance of a duty to contribute to the well-being of its stakeholders. It is often believed that a business has the resources to contribute to a community's well-being, and good deeds also translate into favorable publicity for the business, which translates into more sales and profits. A large donation, for example, to support the construction of a new public swimming pool receives much attention on radio and television as well as in the newspapers.

Illus. 2-5

Large and small businesses often sponsor community activities such as softball leagues. Can you name a local business that sponsors a softball or bowling team or other event?

Joseph Nettis/Stock, Boston

Milton Friedman, a famous economist, once said that "the business of business is business." His view reflects those who believe that if a business becomes involved in being socially responsible, it will get distracted from its main goal. If that happens, the company will not remain very profitable and, thus, workers will get lower wages, customers will pay higher prices, and the owners will make less profit. Questions are also raised about the ability of a business to solve social problems. Does a manager know how to solve drug abuse? Should a business be responsible for promoting sporting events in the company or in the community? Is this not a role for government to perform?

Despite these serious concerns, it is now widely recognized that business has an important responsibility to its stakeholders. Business has also realized that by getting involved socially it advances its own interests. When goodwill in the community is enhanced, the desire of government to regulate business is often discouraged. To that end, some businesses review their social programs at regular intervals. The reviews show what the business is doing to fulfill its social responsibilities, its success in accomplishing its goals, and its involvement in pursuing future activities.

THE FUTURE

Given the fast pace of change in the world today, the issues that will face society in the future will change. While some of the current problems will persist into the foreseeable future, unexpected concerns and demands will rise and reshape society. Trends occurring today permit a brief glimpse into the future.

The U.S. Department of Labor reported its economic and employment projections for the year 2005. It predicts that jobs will continue to be created at a faster rate in service rather than in manufacturing industries. Occupations demanding higher levels of education will grow faster than average. The percentage of whites in the labor force will decline. Jobs with the greatest growth potential throughout the 1990s will continue to be for salespeople, authors, computer experts, insurance adjusters, financial managers, economists, lawyers, and company presidents. On the other hand, jobs with the least potential for employment will be jobs that require low-level skills.

Businesses are apt to become more and more involved in providing social services to the community that, in the past, likely had been provided by families, funded by government, or purchased by individuals. Employers will have to learn to work with a multicultural workforce in a fiercely competitive world economy. Concern over the environment and respectful treatment of workers on the job will take on added importance. As values change, each business will continue to shape and be shaped by the society in which it functions.

Ethical Issues

I Don't Eat Whale Meat; Neither Should You

Questions:

1 Suggest a strategy for how Big Fish might deal with the boycott.

2 Explain the behavior in foreign countries of the environmentalists and their supporters.

3 Are Norway and Big Fish reacting in a socially responsible way? Why or why not?

4 Should one society force its ethical standards on another? Why or why not?

After a recent conference of countries interested in conserving whales, the biggest creatures on earth, Norway announced it was going to resume whale hunting. Norway is a seafaring nation with a long and rich history of hunting whales, and whale meat is a delicacy.

A Norwegian fishing company, Big Fish Inc., operates a fleet of ships to harpoon whales. Over the years, the firm refined its whale-catching techniques, thereby reducing the suffering endured by the few hundred whales caught yearly. In addition to processing whale meat, Big Fish catches and cans other marine products such as cod and sardines. Whale meat is only a small portion of Big Fish's overall business. While nearly all whale meat is consumed in Norway, its other products are sold abroad. The United States is its largest market.

Following the Norwegian government's decision to allow whale hunting, outrage was expressed by conservation organizations like Greenpeace and Save the Whales. Their volunteers got into small but fast boats, trailed Big Fish's ships to whaling grounds, harassed and encircled the ships, and effectively prevented the harpooning of whales. Serious collisions between the small boats and the hunting ships were only narrowly avoided. At the same time, "Boycott Big Fish" campaigns appeared in the United States.

Supermarkets were asked to stop carrying Big Fish's cod and other marine products until whale hunting was called off. School children around the world submitted petitions to Norwegian embassies. In front of the United Nations in New York, demonstrators carried imitation spears to dramatize the state of harpooned whales. The campaign soon escalated from a protest against Big Fish to a protest against Norway. Tourists were asked to cancel vacation plans. Threats were made to disrupt the forthcoming Winter Olympics in that country. All in all, the coordinated campaign was turning into a financial and public relations disaster for Big Fish and Norway.

The Norwegian government tried to explain its position. Only a few hundred whales would be hunted; the particular species was not an endangered one; whale hunting and whale meat were part of Norway's tradition; and Norway's record on protecting the environment was second to none. The government also stated that it was unfair for foreign countries and for environmentalists to criticize Norway.

CHAPTER
REVIEW
2

Building Vocabulary Power

Define the following terms and concepts.

1. zero population growth (ZPG)
2. baby boom
3. baby bust
4. Frost Belt
5. Sun Belt
6. Rust Belt
7. labor force
8. labor participation rate
9. glass ceiling
10. comparable worth
11. telecommuting
12. recycle
13. ethics
14. business ethics
15. code of ethics
16. social responsibility
17. stakeholders

Reviewing Facts

1. Despite zero population growth, why is the population of the United States growing?
2. What caused the decline in the number of young workers in recent years?
3. Why is the age and racial makeup of the population important to business?
4. How has the movement of people from the cities to the suburbs affected the cities?
5. What major factor caused the rise in the labor participation rate in recent decades?
6. Why is it difficult for employers to design and implement comparable worth plans?
7. Give two examples of how values have changed in the United States in the past twenty years.
8. Why have wellness and fitness programs been adopted by forward-looking businesses?
9. What action has the federal government taken to protect the environment?
10. What situation occurred that caused the development of the Valdez Principles?
11. Why don't all firms have the same rules of conduct?
12. Which does ethics do? (a) Corrects bad laws. (b) Replaces existing laws. (c) Goes beyond existing laws.
13. Give two reasons why someone might feel that business should not get involved in socially responsible projects.
14. Give two reasons why businesses should be socially responsible.

15. During the decade of the 1990s, (a) what types of occupations will have the greatest growth potential and (b) what types of occupations will have the least potential for growth?

D ISCUSSING IDEAS

1. Why should one who studies American business principles and management also study the social problems of the United States?
2. What types of businesses will be most affected by the makeup of the population that will exist around the year 2005?
3. Because of slow growth and rapid business changes, employers cannot always find people to fill some of the new jobs that have been created. Discuss what future employers, the education system, and business organizations can do to correct this problem.
4. List and discuss those factors that most contribute to poverty.
5. Most city bus drivers are males but nearly all dental hygienists are female. Bus drivers earn more money than dental hygienists. (a) Does the idea of comparable worth apply to both jobs? (b) How might you argue that the dental hygienists should be paid the same, more, or less than bus drivers?
6. Develop a list of new employer practices that have contributed to the quality of work life for employees.
7. Why have Americans become conscious of the need to reduce pollution and conserve resources?
8. Give two examples of how environmental goals can be at odds with energy conservation goals.
9. How can a code of ethics help employees act ethically?
10. Give three reasons why employees behave unethically.
11. On prom night at your school, your town's Taxicab Association announced that it would provide free drop-off and pick-up services to all students participating in the event. Give three reasons why the Taxicab Association is likely providing this service.
12. How does social responsibility differ from business ethics?

A NALYZING INFORMATION

1. Use the library to obtain information on a list of American cities. Using data from the Bureau of the Census, look at the population of these cities in 1970 and 1990. Explain why and how they have changed.
2. Refer to Fig. 2-2, which provides information about the labor force, and answer these questions.
   a. In what year did unemployment reach its highest point?
   b. In what year was unemployment the lowest?
   c. When the employment rate rises, will the unemployment rate also rise? Give reasons for your answer.

REVIEW 2

d. Do you believe there is a relationship between unemployment and poverty? Explain your answer.

3. Assume the total population of the United States is 270 million, of which 200 million are 16 years of age and above. Of this 200 million, 35 million are full-time homemakers, 45 million are students, and 20 million are retirees. Eight million are unemployed but looking for work. The rest are employed. With this information, answer the following questions.
   a. What is the size of the labor force?
   b. Calculate the labor participation rate.
   c. Which groups are not considered part of the labor force?

4. Consider any business with which you are familiar. It might be a gas station, a fast food restaurant, a supermarket, or a bank. Assume that the business has agreed to follow the Valdez Principles. Develop a list of specific activities the business must perform if it is to live up to the Principles.

5. In a recent study on ethics of over two thousand employees who work in offices, an attempt was made to determine whether those who attend religious services weekly are more ethical than those who attend rarely. The following results were reported in percents. Answer the questions that follow the reported results.

	Attend Religious Services	
Do You . . .	*Weekly*	*Rarely*
Twist rules when dealing with others	22	33
Bend the truth a bit in what you tell others	21	31
Use office equipment for personal projects	22	37
Take time off from work when you should not have	8	19
Feel somewhat less than completely honest when filing tax returns	8	6

   a. Do those who attend religious services weekly or rarely act in unethical ways?
   b. For which question is there the greatest percentage difference between those who attend religious services weekly and rarely?
   c. Why might the people who attend religious services weekly be more unethical than those who attend rarely in regard to filing tax returns?
   d. In one sentence, what conclusion can you make from this study?

S OLVING BUSINESS PROBLEMS

CASE 2-1

Greengrocers is a major food company in the United States. In its factories it processes fruits, vegetables, and grains into a wide variety of packaged food products. The quality of the food in the packages declines over time. Therefore, an expiration date is stamped on the containers, after which the product cannot be sold. Supermarkets offer discounts on slow-moving items to hasten their sale as expiration dates near. Even then, significant numbers of packages with expired dates are returned to Greengrocers' warehouses, although the food has not spoiled and is still edible. Were it not for strict rules laid down by a governmental agency, the expiration date could easily be pushed to the future and the food would still be fit for human consumption. But in the United States, it is illegal to sell products beyond expiration dates marked on products.

The returned packages became a problem and an expense because Greengrocers had to destroy the expired products. Recently an opportunity appeared that made Greengrocers' managers high-five their good luck. With reports and coverage of famine in the small African country of Somalia dominating the news, the company decided to make a generous donation of free packaged food to the starving Somalis. With great fanfare, the company announced that $500,000 worth of food would be donated. The U.S. military transported the food on one of its relief flights. Donations were reported in the national media and Greengrocers received favorable publicity as a socially responsible firm stepping in to lessen human misery in the highest tradition of American generosity.

The donated packages, of course, had expired dates. Somalia had no law against selling products with expired dates and Greengrocers' managers assumed that starving people would rather have food with expired dates than no food. In any case, the food was still edible. In addition, Greengrocers could claim a charitable contribution tax deduction in the United States.

Once the military plane arrived in Somalia, the donated food was turned over to a relief organization, Save the Children Fund, for distribution to the hungry. While several young American volunteers unpacked the boxes, they noticed that the packages had expired dates. A huge group of starving Somalis was waiting for the packages while the correspondent of a television network waited to broadcast the event in the United States. What was broadcast, instead, was information about the expired dates on the donated food.

Required:
1. Since Somalia has no law on food dates and the food was still edible, do you think Greengrocers acted in a socially responsible manner? Explain.
2. If you were the president of Greengrocers, how would you explain your conduct now that the details of the donation were revealed?
3. Suggest some ways by which Greengrocers can discourage unethical conduct by its employees in the future.

CASE 2-2

Waste Processors Inc. has contracted to remove garbage from the city of Philadelphia and dispose of it in accordance with regulations set up by the federal and state governments. Because of environmental concerns and the "not in my back yard" philosophy of the public, disposing of garbage has become a difficult and expensive ordeal. This is especially true for hazardous

waste like medical products. Landfills (approved places where garbage could be dumped) have been exhausted and disputes arise when new landfill sites are suggested. Incineration, or burning of waste, has become nearly impossible to handle because of concerns over air quality. Therefore, more and more communities are ready to transport their trash elsewhere but not accept anyone else's.

It was becoming increasingly difficult for Waste Processors to handle Philadelphia's garbage. The company did not have enough money to buy the sophisticated machinery needed to get rid of waste, especially hazardous waste. When truckloads of medical waste were turned away from landfill areas and incinerators located around the country, or when Waste Processors were asked to pay high disposal costs, the managers started to look for cheaper disposal methods.

Waste Processors' president took a plane to the capital of Haiti, the poorest country in the western hemisphere. The president met the military ruler of the nation and offered $1 million annually for the right to own and operate a landfill in Haiti. It was pointed out that the landfill facility would create 25 jobs for Haitians who would be paid good wages. Haiti has no law on waste disposal and even if laws existed, Haiti lacks the technical capability to either dispose of garbage or enforce disposal laws. Haiti accepted the offer because Waste Processors' president pointed out that if rejected, waste smuggling into Haiti would occur and it would be unregulated. Further, dumping would provide the military chief with a handsome income.

Soon after signing the agreement, a ship loaded with medical waste products from the United States arrived off the coast of Haiti. Several Haitians were hired to dig huge holes near a deserted beach, dump the waste into them, cover the holes, and send the boat back for other shipments.

Required:
1. Is the behavior of Waste Processors socially responsible? Explain.
2. Is there a good reason why poor countries should not accept another country's waste even if they are paid well?
3. Should the American government ban such trade in garbage? Why or why not?
4. Suggest ways to handle the dilemma posed by the growing quantities of garbage and inadequate disposal methods.

ECONOMIC ENVIRONMENT OF BUSINESS

CHAPTER **3**

After studying this chapter you will be able to:

3-1 Describe economic concepts that apply to satisfying economic wants.

3-2 Discuss three economic systems and three economic-political systems.

3-3 Summarize five fundamental elements of capitalism.

3-4 Explain how economic growth can be promoted and measured.

3-5 List basic economic problems that exist and state what government can do to correct the problems.

Boris Popovich came to the United States from Russia where he had lived until after the communist form of government was dissolved. While in a training program to become an electrician, he met Christine Doby at a party. As the two were becoming friendly, Boris learned of Christine's interest in starting a business. "I have considered many types of firms," she said, "but most types have many competitors, which means my chance of success is not good. I want a retail shop selling something for which demand would be steady." Boris thought for a moment and then suggested: "Have you considered a lighting store? You know, one that sells all types of lamps, ceiling lights, outdoor lights—a complete lighting shop."

Christine muttered, "What do I know about lamps?" Boris answered, "You can learn quickly; and when I finish my training in two months, we can open side-by-side businesses—you sell them and I install and repair them." Somewhat slowly Christine grew to like the idea. "There is no business like that around here.

Demand would be stable. We could add overhead lights with paddle fans, work with new home builders, and make contacts with home remodeling decorators and contractors."

The plan came together within days, but Boris was hesitant. "I know a great deal about electrical repairs, Christine, but I know nearly nothing about your free enterprise system and very little about economics or American business." "Leave that part to me," she responded. "As an economics major in school, I learned about supply and demand, about setting prices, and about raising capital. And you have been learning how our economic system works. You're a consumer. Together we'll become producers, and if we do well we can call ourselves capitalists." With that comment came laughter and an agreement to join forces. "We'll light up this town—inside and out," Boris added.

All societies face the problem of trying to satisfy the wants of their citizens for goods and services. Although all societies share this problem, many different systems have been developed for producing and using goods and services. The body of knowledge that relates to producing and using goods and services that satisfy human wants is called **economics**.

Concepts that are essential to the understanding of any economic system are discussed first in this chapter. The world's economic systems, along with economic-political systems, are then described. Finally, fundamentals of capitalism are presented as well as factors related to economic growth.

SATISFYING OUR ECONOMIC WANTS

Businesses help to make the economic system work by producing and distributing the particular goods and services that people want. A good place to begin the study of economics is with the two types of wants found throughout an economic system.

Illus. 3-1

Everyone has wants for scarce goods and services, and not all wants can be satisfied. What do you want most that you cannot afford? And what are the greatest wants of your closest friend or your parents?

Jeff Greenberg, Photographer

People have many kinds of wants. The economic system, however, is concerned only with **economic wants**—the desire for scarce material goods and services. People want material goods, such as food, clothing, housing, and automobiles. They also want services, such as hair care, medical attention, and public transportation. Items such as these are scarce because the economic system cannot satisfy all the wants of all people for all material goods and services.

People have another kind of want known as a noneconomic want.

Noneconomic wants are those desired wants that are not scarce. Another characteristic of noneconomic wants is that they are nonmaterial. Some examples of noneconomic wants include air, sunshine, friendship, and happiness.

The goods and services that people want have to be produced. Clothes must be made. Homes must be built. Personal services must be supplied. And as we learned in the opening scenario, Christine expects her customers to want home lighting products, and Boris expects them to want his electrical light installation and repair services.

UTILITY

Utility is the ability of a good or a service to satisfy a want. In other words, a good or a service that has utility is a useful good or service. Something is not useful, however, unless it is available for use in the right form and place and at the right time. As a result, four common types of utility exist: form, place, time, and possession. Definitions of the four types of utility, with examples, appear in Fig. 3-1.

Anyone who aids in creating a utility is a **producer**. A producer is entitled to a reward for the usefulness that is added to a good or service. Hair stylists are entitled to a reward for the usefulness of their services. The price you pay for a pen includes a reward for the manufacturer who made the pen, the shipping company that delivered it to the merchant, and the retailer who made it possible for you to buy the pen at the time you wanted it.

Types of Economic Utility

Fig. 3-1

Satisfying wants involves four common types of utility.

FORM UTILITY

Created by changes in the form or shape of a product to make it useful. (Form utility usually applies only to goods and not to services.) Example: Is the swimsuit you desire to buy available in a particular fabric and style?

PLACE UTILITY

Created by having a good or service at the place where it is needed or wanted. Example: Is the swimsuit you desire available in a nearby store where it can be purchased?

TIME UTILITY

Created when a product or service is available when it is needed or wanted. Example: Is the store open when you are ready to buy and use your swimsuit?

POSSESSION UTILITY

Created when ownership of a good or service is transferred from one person to another, but may also occur through renting and borrowing. Example: Is the swimsuit available at a price you can afford and are willing to pay?

FACTORS OF PRODUCTION

In creating useful goods and services, a producer uses four basic resources. These resources, called **factors of production**, are natural resources or land, labor, capital goods, and management.

Natural Resources

The extent to which a country is able to produce goods and services is, in part, determined by its natural resources. **Natural resources** relate to anything provided by nature that affects the productive ability of a country. The productive ability of the United States, for example, is related to its fertile soil, minerals, water and timber resources, and its mild climate.

Labor

Labor is the human effort, either physical or mental, that goes into the production of goods and services. Goods and services would be in short supply without labor. A part of labor is **human capital**, the accumulated knowledge and skills of human beings—the total value of each person's education and acquired skills. In a highly technological world, the need for human capital has increased significantly. Christine's knowledge of economics and Boris's knowledge of electricity are examples of labor and human capital.

Capital Goods

Before producing goods that people want, it is necessary to have capital goods. **Capital goods** are buildings, tools, machines, and other equipment used to produce other goods but do not directly satisfy human wants. A robot on a car assembly line is an example of a capital good. Capital goods do not directly satisfy human wants. However, capital goods make it possible to produce goods such as cars that consumers want. Capital goods allow the production of goods in large quantities which, in turn, should decrease production costs and increase the productivity of labor and management.

Management

For the production of goods, more is needed than the mere availability of natural resources, labor, and capital goods. Someone, or some group, must bring these factors together to plan and organize the production of the final product. Management is the fourth factor of production that brings together the other three factors—natural resources, labor, and capital. The many aspects of management are treated in Unit 7.

Because government provides many services that are essential to the operation of a business, it is often listed as a fifth factor of production by economists. Some of the essential services provided by government are streets and highways, police and fire protection, and courts that settle disputes.

CAPITAL FORMATION

The production of capital goods is called **capital formation**. Capital goods, such as buildings and equipment, are needed to produce consumer goods and services. Unlike capital goods, **consumer goods and services** are those goods and services that directly satisfy people's economic wants.

A country is capable of producing a fixed quantity of goods and services at any one time. As a result, total production is divided between capital goods and consumer goods and services. When the production of consumer goods increases, the production of capital goods and services decreases. On the other hand, when the production of consumer goods decreases, the production of capital goods increases. New capital goods must be made—capital formation— in order to add to the total supply and to replace worn-out capital goods. Capital formation takes place, for example, when steel is used to produce the tools and machinery (capital goods) that make automobiles rather than to produce the automobiles themselves (consumer goods).

When productive resources are used for capital formation, it becomes possible to produce more consumer goods. For example, when robots and other tools and machinery are produced for making automobiles, it is then possible to increase the production of automobiles.

However, using steel, labor, and management to produce tools and machinery (capital goods) means that these same resources cannot also be used for automobiles (consumer goods). The immediate result is that consumers have fewer automobiles to buy. But, because the tools and machinery were made, consumers will have more automobiles to buy in the future. China is a current example of a country that uses a large portion of its productive resources in capital formation rather than in the production of consumer goods and services.

Economic Systems

Remember that no country has enough resources to satisfy all the wants of all people for material goods and services. Because productive resources are scarce, difficult decisions must be made about how to use these limited resources. For example, what is needed is a way to decide whether to produce more capital goods and fewer consumer goods or more consumer goods and fewer capital goods.

An **economic system** is an organized way for a country to decide how to use its productive resources; that is, to decide what, how, and for whom goods and services will be produced. What goods and services to produce must be determined. How these goods and services will be made and provided to others must also be determined. Equally important, the economic system must decide who will be entitled to obtain the goods and services. While there are many countries in the world, only three types of economic systems exist. Even the number of political systems is rather limited. Next you will learn about these basic economic and political systems.

TYPES OF ECONOMIC SYSTEMS

The primary types of economic systems are a market economy, a command economy, and a mixed economy. Each of these systems can be found in one form or another in various countries of the world.

A **market economy** is an economic system that determines what, how, and for whom goods and services are produced by coordinating individual choices through arrangements that aid buying and selling goods and services. In a market economy, consumers and producers act independently to determine what, how, and for whom goods and services are produced. The free enterprise system found in the United States is the best example of a market economy.

A **command economy** is an economic system in which the method for determining what, how, and for whom goods and services are produced is decided by a central planning authority. Countries that adopt a command economy are often dictatorships. Decisions are not made by consumers but by the ruling government. A number of command economies may be found in Asia—China, North Korea, Cambodia, and Vietnam—and in other small countries such as Cuba.

A **mixed economy** is an economic system in which a combination of a market and a command economy are blended together to make decisions about what, how, and for whom goods and services are produced. In a mixed economy, the national government makes production decisions for certain goods and services. For example, the post office, telephone system, schools, health care facilities, and public utilities are often owned and operated by governments.

No one country has a truly pure market economy or command economy. Most countries have mixed economies, although some tend to stress the market economy elements more than others. The United States and Canada, for example, stress the market economy more than Cuba and Sweden. Even countries of the former Soviet Union allowed limited forms of a market economy, as do China and Iraq.

Today the tendency is for the majority of countries to become more like the United States by placing greater stress on market economy characteristics. For example, England, France, Sweden, Mexico, and Eastern European countries have restricted the number of goods and services owned and controlled by national governments.

When a country or state transfers its authority to provide a good or service to individuals or businesses, it is called **privatization**. Former communist countries often sold telephone and transportation services to private firms. Some states and cities in this country have privatized by paying businesses to operate jails, collect trash, run cafeterias in government buildings, and perform data processing activities. The incentive is to reduce costs for the taxpayers and to increase efficiency.

UNIPHOTO

Illus. 3-2

Each nation decides whether to have a market, command, or mixed economic system. These same nations may change economic systems from time to time. Can you name any countries that have changed their economic systems in recent years?

TYPES OF ECONOMIC-POLITICAL SYSTEMS

Each country has an economic system and a political system as well. The political system influences the economic system. The economic system is nearly always determined by the political system. Because the two systems cannot be separated, we refer to them as an economic-political system.

The importance of the individual citizen has always been emphasized in the United States. Therefore, a political and an economic system was designed that permits a great deal of individual freedom. History tells us that there is a relationship between political and economic freedom; that is, political freedom usually is found in countries where individuals have economic freedom. And political freedom is quite limited in countries that do not give people and organizations much economic freedom.

Three economic-political systems exist. They are capitalism, socialism, and communism. An understanding of other political-economic systems allows us to gain a better understanding of our own system. As you read about these three economic-political systems, compare their features as shown in Fig. 3-2, page 61.

Capitalism

The economic-political system found in the United States is called capitalism, or the free enterprise system, which operates in a democracy. **Capitalism** is an economic-political system in which private citizens are free to go into business for themselves, to produce whatever they choose to produce, and to distribute what they produce. Also included is the right to own one's own property. Some state and federal regulations exist to assure an orderly marketplace that does not harm the public.

This strict definition of capitalism would have accurately described our economic system during much of the nineteenth century and the early part of the twentieth century. In recent decades, however, government has assumed an important economic role in the United States. As the economy developed without controls by government, certain abuses took place. For example, some people began to interfere with the economic freedom of others. Some large businesses began to exploit small businesses. In addition, manufacturing firms did not take into account the cost of pollution. In essence, these costs were passed on to the public. For example, assume a firm produced a new type of pesticide and sold it to farmers and gardeners. Several years after some had washed into streams and lakes, the pesticide was found to kill fish and harm swimmers. Neither the producer nor the buyers of the pesticide were required to pay for damages. The public ultimately pays in the form of poor health and medical costs as well as in the form of banning swimming in lakes. To protect the public and to correct such abuses, Congress passed laws, many of which require producers to help prevent or reduce costs to the public.

Further attention to the regulation of business by government is given in Chapter 7. However, detailed features of capitalism are provided later in this chapter.

Socialism

Socialism is an economic-political system in which the government controls and regulates the means of production. How scarce resources are used to satisfy the many wants of people is decided, in part, by the government.

Socialists do not agree as to how much of the productive resources government should own. The most extreme socialists want government to own all natural resources and capital goods. Middle-of-the-road socialists believe that planning production for the whole economy can be achieved if government owns certain key industries, but they also believe that other productive resources should be owned by individuals and businesses. As a result, socialism is often associated with mixed economies.

Socialism is generally disliked in the United States because it limits the right of the individual to own property for productive purposes. The right to own property, however, exists in socialistic economies in different degrees, depending upon the amount of government ownership and control. Socialism in its different forms exists in many countries, particularly in the Western European countries of Sweden, Italy, and Great Britain.

Communism

Communism is forced socialism where all or almost all the productive resources of a nation are owned by the government. Decisions regarding what is to be produced, how much is to be produced, and how the results of production are to be divided among the citizens are made by government agencies on the basis of a government plan. Government measures how well producers perform on the basis of volume of goods and services produced without much regard for the quality of or demand for the goods or services. A command economy is practiced by communist countries.

Consumer goods are often in short supply in communist countries, such as Cuba and China, because heavy emphasis is placed on capital formation. Even Chinese leaders have recognized the shortcomings of the system when it comes to meeting the needs of consumers. As a result, some adjustments are being made that introduce market economy principles. Two such adjustments include judging the performance of producers by the demand for their products and permitting control of production in terms of consumer demand.

Workers in a communist system cannot move easily from one job to another. And managers of businesses do not decide what is to be produced. A communist country's central planning agency makes most such decisions. Capitalism relies, instead, on consumers and managers to make these decisions. People in a communist society do not own property. All economic decisions are made by government leaders. These leaders decide how scarce resources will be used. The members of a communist country have few of the economic freedoms that Americans believe are important.

Comparison of Economic-Political Systems

Fig. 3-2

Three main economic-political systems exist throughout the world.

	CAPITALISM	SOCIALISM	COMMUNISM
	Market/ Mixed Economy	Mixed Economy	Command/ Mixed Economy
Who may own natural resources and capital goods?	Businesses and individuals	Government for some, but not all	Government for most
How are resources allocated?	By customers based on competition	By government for some and customers for others	By government only
To what extent does government attempt to control business decisions?	Limited	Extensive over the allocation of some resources, but little over distribution	Extensive
How are marketing decisions made?	By market conditions	By market conditions	By government
What one country is a good example of this economic system?	United States	Sweden	China

Kentucky Fried Chicken (KFC) Corporation, Louisville, Ky.

FUNDAMENTALS OF CAPITALISM

As you learned earlier, some economic-political systems either do not permit ownership of property (communism) or may impose limitations to ownership (socialism). One of the basic features of capitalism is the right to private property. Others include the right of each business to make a profit, to set its own prices, to compete, and to determine the wages paid to workers.

PRIVATE PROPERTY

The principle of private property is essential to our capitalistic system. **Private property** consists of items of value that individuals have the right to own, use, and sell. Thus, individuals can control productive resources. They can own land, hire labor, and own capital goods. They can use these resources to produce goods and services. Also, individuals own the products made from their use of land, labor, and capital goods. Thus, the company that produces furniture owns the furniture it makes. The furniture company may sell its furniture, and it owns the money received from the buyer.

PROFIT

In a capitalistic system, the incentive as well as the reward for producing goods and services is **profit**, which is computed by subtracting total costs from total earned receipts. The company making furniture, for example, has costs for land, labor, capital goods, and materials. Profit is what the furniture company has left after subtracting these costs from the amount received from selling its furniture.

The profit earned by a business is often overestimated by society. The average profit is about 5 percent of total receipts while the remainder, 95 percent, represents costs. Consider a motel with yearly receipts of $300,000. If the profit amounts to 5 percent, then the owner earns $15,000; that is, $300,000 times .05. Costs for the year are .95 times $300,000, or $285,000. Some types of businesses have higher average profit percentages, but many have lower ones or even losses. Owners, of course, try to earn a profit percentage that is better than average.

Being in business does not guarantee that a company will make a profit. Among other things, to be successful, a company must produce goods or services that people want at a price they are willing to pay. Other fundamental features of capitalism covered next deal with competition and the distribution of income.

PRICE DETERMINATION

Demand for a product refers to the number of products that will be bought at a given time at a given price. Thus, demand is not the same as want. Wanting an expensive luxury car without having the money to buy one does not represent demand. Demand for a Mercedes Benz is represented by the people who want it, have the money to buy it, and are willing to spend the money for it.

There is a relationship between price and demand. With increased demand, prices generally rise in the short run. Later, when demand decreases, prices generally fall. For example, if a new large-screen TV suddenly becomes popular, its price may rise. However, when the TV is no longer in high demand, its price usually drops.

The supply of a product also influences its price. **Supply** of a product refers to the number of like products that will be offered for sale at a particular time and at a certain price. If there is a current shortage in the supply of a product, its price will usually rise as consumers bid against one another to obtain the product. For example, if bad weather damages an apple crop and apples are in short supply, the price of apples will go

Stephen Frisch/Stock, Boston

up. When apples become more abundant, their price will go down. Thus, price changes are the result of changes in both the demand for and the supply of a product.

Generally, changes in prices determine what is produced and how much is produced in our economy. Price changes indicate to businesses what is profitable or not profitable to produce. If consumers want more sports shoes than are being produced, they will bid up the price of sports shoes. The increase in the price of the shoes makes it more profitable to make them and provides the incentive for manufacturers to increase the production of sports shoes. As the supply of the shoes increases to satisfy the demand for more shoes, the price of the shoes will fall. Since it is now less profitable to make sports shoes, manufacturers will decrease their production of them.

Prices, then, are determined by the forces of supply and demand; that is, prices are the result of the decisions of individual consumers to buy products and of individual producers to make and sell products. Therefore, consumers help decide what will be produced and how much will be produced.

Here is how supply and demand work in setting prices. Refer to Fig. 3-3 as you study this example of a producer planning to sell a new style of sweatshirt. As can be seen, the market price for the sweatshirt is shown where the supply line crosses the demand line. The market price is $30, which allows the producer to meet costs and make a profit. It is also the price at which consumers will buy an adequate supply of the product in order for the producer to make a profit.

ig. 3-3

Supply and demand for a producer's new style of sweatshirt.

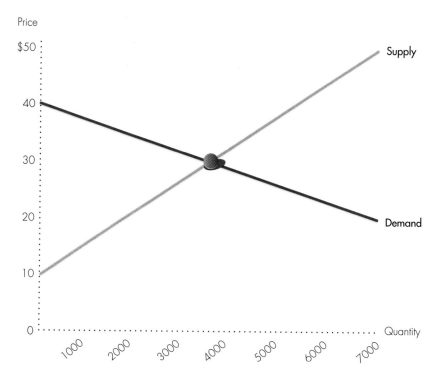

If demand drops, profit drops; but if demand increases, the producer's profits will increase. If the profit gets quite large, other producers will enter into production with similar sweatshirts, which will then increase the total supply and lower the price. If the supply and demand lines never cross, the producer will not make the goods because not enough consumers will want the product at the offered price and the profit reward disappears.

COMPETITION

In our free enterprise system, sellers try to make a profit and buyers try to buy quality goods at the lowest possible prices. This conflict of interest between buyers and sellers is settled to the benefit of society by competition. **Competition** is the rivalry among sellers for consumers' dollars.

Competition in a free enterprise system benefits society in many ways. To attract customers away from other sellers, a business must improve the quality of its products, develop new products, and operate efficiently in order to keep its prices down. Thus, competition serves to insure that consumers will get the quality products they want at fair prices.

In addition to benefiting consumers, competition benefits the country because it tends to make all businesses use our scarce productive resources efficiently. If a business firm does not operate efficiently, it will fail because customers will buy lower-priced or higher-quality products from a firm that is operating efficiently. Often these competing firms are from foreign countries. Competition in our economic system also provides the chance for people to go into business for themselves and to share in the profits being made by those already in business.

One aspect of competition is price competition. Price competition occurs when a firm takes business away from its competitors by lowering prices. Today, however, more and more competition takes place in the form of non-price competition. For example, a company attracts customers away from other sellers by providing products that have better quality or by adding something to the product that competitors do not have. Or, a company may attract customers away from competitors by unusual and colorful product packaging. Another company may conduct an extensive advertising campaign to convince the public that its product is better than all other brands. All these are effective devices used in nonprice competition.

Competition is the opposite of monopoly. *Monopoly* is the existence of only one seller who is able to avoid most of the elements of effective competition. For example, if a seller does not have to compete with other sellers for consumer dollars, profit can usually be increased by raising the price of a product. As you will learn in Chapter 7, legislation exists that encourages competition and discourages monopolistic practices.

INCOME DISTRIBUTION

Not only must all countries decide how scarce productive resources are to be used, but they must also decide how the goods produced will be divided among the people in the society. In a free enterprise economy, the share of goods produced that an individual receives is determined by the amount of money that person has to purchase goods and services.

People receive money—wages and salaries—by contributing their labor to the production of goods and services. Money is also received in interest on money that people lend to others, as rent for land or buildings that they own, and as profit if they are owners of businesses.

The amount of money an individual receives in wages or salary is determined by many factors, including personal traits and abilities. The same factors that determine the prices of goods are also important factors in determining wages and salaries; that is, the amount of wages paid for a particular kind of labor is affected by the supply of and demand for that kind of labor. The demand is low and the supply is high for unskilled workers. Thus, the price (income) of unskilled workers is low. On the other hand, the demand for brain surgeons is high in terms of the supply of brain surgeons and the services they provide; therefore, their price (income) is high.

MANAGING THE ECONOMY

The strength of a nation depends upon its economic growth. Economic growth is measured by an annual increase in the gross domestic product, increased employment opportunities, and the continuous development of new and improved goods and services. However, growth cannot always be at the most desired rate. As you will soon learn, when the economy grows too fast or too slow businesses and consumers suffer. Of concern to everyone is the promotion and measurement of such growth along with the identification and control of growth problems.

PROMOTING ECONOMIC GROWTH

Economic growth occurs when a country's output exceeds its population growth. As a result, more goods and services are available for each person. Growth has occurred and must continue if a nation is to remain economically strong.

The following are basic ways to increase the production of goods and services in order to encourage economic growth:

1. Increase the number of people in the workforce.
2. Increase the productivity of the workforce by means of improving human capital through education and job training.
3. Increase the supply of capital goods, such as more tools and machines, in order to increase the productivity of labor and management.
4. Improve technology by inventing new and better machines and better methods for producing goods and services.
5. Redesign work processes in factories and offices to improve efficiency.
6. Increase the sale of goods and services to foreign countries.
7. Decrease the purchase of goods and services from foreign countries.

For economic growth to occur, more is required than just increasing the production of goods and services. More goods and services must also be consumed. The incentive for producing goods and services in a free enterprise economy is profit. If the goods and services produced are in demand and are profitable, business has the incentive to increase production.

Economic growth is basic to a healthy economy. Through such growth more and better products become available, such as a new drug that cures a disease, a battery that runs a small computer for weeks, and new ways to make fuel-efficient cars. More and better services also become available, such as those provided by hospitals, travel agencies, and banks. But more importantly, economic growth is needed to provide jobs for those who wish to work.

MEASURING ECONOMIC GROWTH

To know whether the economy is growing at a desirable rate, statistics must be gathered. The federal government collects vast amounts of information and uses a variety of figures to keep track of the economy. The gross domestic product (GDP) that was discussed in Chapter 1 is an extremely valuable statistic. Another is the Consumer Price Index.

The **Consumer Price Index (CPI)** indicates what is happening in general to prices in the country. It is a measure of the average change in prices of consumer goods and services typically purchased by people living in urban areas. The hundreds of items in the CPI include prices for food, gasoline, and housing. With the CPI, comparisons can be made in the cost of living from month to month or from year to year, as shown in Fig. 3-4.

Consumer Price Index (1983 = 100)

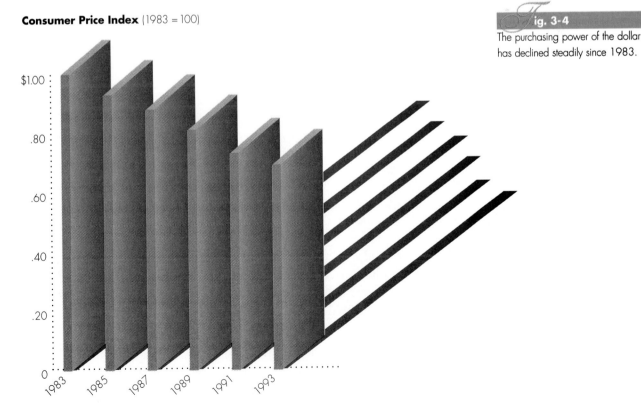

ig. 3-4

The purchasing power of the dollar has declined steadily since 1983.

CHINA'S ATTEMPT TO BUILD A MARKET ECONOMY

Questions:

1 What changes might China make in order to improve its chances of becoming a market economy?

2 Why do foreign firms appear to have more trouble succeeding in China than do Chinese firms? Explain.

3 Account for how a factory worker who is paid only $100 a month can have plenty of money left to buy consumer products.

4 Do you believe China can operate as both a market economy and remain communistic as well? Explain.

Source: *Adapted from* Louis Kraar's "Now Comes the Hard Part for China." *Fortune,* July 26, 1993, pp. 129–134.

Businesses around the world have a strong desire to sell products and services in a country that has 1.1 billion consumers. China, a huge country, has the third largest economy in the world. Only the United States and Japan have larger economies. Until recently, this Asian giant was a closed communistic society with a tightly controlled command economy. The government ran the businesses and everything else. For the most part, foreigners were excluded.

China is still communistic but the doors creaked open to outsiders as the country is attempting to move toward a market economy. Initially, few American firms were approved to operate branches in China. As China's political leaders welcomed more foreign firms, more foreigners opened factories. The outside firms have found, however, that adapting to China's version of a free enterprise system is anything but easy.

The problems vary as China attempts to remain communistic while shifting gradually to a market economy. The red tape is heavy. National and local authorities, for example, require numerous approvals and long delays for getting significant actions approved. Offering generous gifts to officials often expedites obtaining the required chops—stamps of approval. Bribing public officials seems to be a fairly common practice.

The government and its basic institutions, such as the banking system, are outmoded and not equipped to handle needed services. Central authorities are ineffective at controlling business activities that are, in part, overseen by regional and local governments. The central bank also lacks sufficient authority to regulate the economy adequately. The current top political leaders hesitate slowing growth and becoming unpopular, yet not to do so invites runaway inflation and eventually a major economic crash.

China does not have business codes for handling legal disagreements. Independent courts for settling disputes do not exist. International accounting rules are not followed. As a result, foreign firms entering the country without much knowledge of how things work get burned. A Beijing branch factory for Jeep pays factory workers $100 a month, but after allowances for housing, clothing, and food, the pay rate is close to $400 a month. Therefore, much of the $100 per month is available for consumer spending.

Foreign firms must also compete with state-owned companies. General Motors, for example, found that in addition to higher-than-expected labor costs, the sale prices of GM trucks made in China were above competing state-owned manufacturers once taxes and other government charges were added. In spite of hidden obstacles, some firms have profited from their ventures in China.

A small group of indicators for tracking the economy is shown in Fig. 3-5. When the CPI, GDP, and other statistics are examined each month by government economists, the condition of the economy is evaluated. If the growth rate appears to be undesirable, corrective action can be taken.

A Sample of Major Economic Reports Released Regularly By The U.S. Government

GROSS DOMESTIC PRODUCT

Measures the total goods and services produced. Released quarterly by the Commerce Department.

CONSUMER PRICE INDEX

Measures inflation at the retail level. Released monthly by the Department of Labor.

INDEX OF LEADING ECONOMIC INDICATORS

Measures the economy's strength for the next six to nine months using a variety of foward-looking indicators. Released monthly by the Commerce Department.

EMPLOYMENT

Measures the jobless rate and the number of jobs available. Released monthly by the Department of Labor.

RETAIL SALES

Measures consumer spending. Released monthly by the Commerce Department.

PERSONAL INCOME CONSUMPTION

Measures growth in personal income and consumer spending. Released monthly by the Commerce Department.

Fig. 3-5

The federal government issues many statistics each year to help determine whether the economy is growing or declining.

IDENTIFYING ECONOMIC PROBLEMS

Problems occur with the economy when the growth rate jumps ahead or drops back too quickly. One problem that occurs is a **recession**, which is a decline in the GDP that continues for six months or more. A recession occurs when demand for the total goods and services available is less than the supply. Decreased production and increased unemployment occur during recessions. In most recessions, the rate of increase in prices is reduced greatly and in some cases prices may actually decline slightly.

Les Moore/UNIPHOTO

Illus. 3-5

Unemployment grows during a recession or a depression, which means people are less able to buy goods and services. Why is this country more likely to have a recession than a depression?

Another problem arises when consumers want to buy goods and services that are not readily available. As revealed in the Consumer Price Index, this increased demand causes prices for existing goods and services to rise. **Inflation** is the rapid rise in prices caused by an inadequate supply of goods and services. In other words, total demand exceeds supply. Inflation results in a decline in purchasing power of money; that is, a dollar does not buy as much as it did before inflation. Retired people and those with fixed incomes are financially hurt the most because their incomes buy less. The effect of inflation on the purchasing power of the dollar is shown in Fig. 3-6.

Fig. 3-6

Inflation reduces the purchasing power of the dollar.

Dollars Needed to Buy an Item Costing $100 in 1983 (1983–1993)

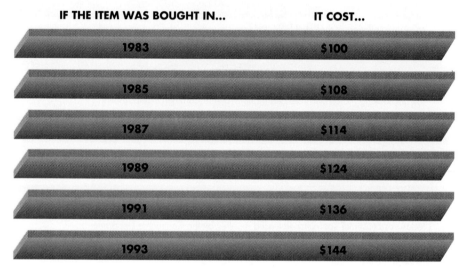

IF THE ITEM WAS BOUGHT IN...	IT COST...
1983	$100
1985	$108
1987	$114
1989	$124
1991	$136
1993	$144

Source: Council of Economic Advisers.

CORRECTING ECONOMIC PROBLEMS

Most major nations experience **business cycles**, a pattern of irregular but repeated expansion and contraction of the GDP. Business cycles, on average, last about five years, and pass through four phases as shown in Fig. 3-7. These four phases—expansion, peak, contraction, and trough—can vary in length and in intensity, with most lasting only a few years. Some, however, can be more severe than desired. When statistics show that the economy may be about to enter a recessionary period (a contraction) or an inflationary period (an expansion), certain actions can be taken by the government. Several specific devices used include controlling taxes, regulating government expenditures, and adjusting interest rates.

One way to control economic growth is to raise or lower taxes. Taxes are raised to slow growth and lowered to encourage growth. When taxes are raised, there is less money to spend, which discourages economic growth. When taxes are lowered, people and businesses have more money to spend, which encourages economic growth.

Business Cycle Phases

Fig. 3-7
Business cycles are irregular in length and in severity.

PHASE	EXPLANATION	POPULAR NAME
Expansion		Low inflation
	Modest rise in GDP, profits, and employment	
Peak		Modest to runaway inflation
	Growth reaches its highest level, as do profit and employment	
Contraction		Modest inflation
	Growth begins to decline, as does employment	
Trough		No growth, recession, or depression
	Lowest point in the cycle, with increased unemployment	

Government expenditures also influence economic growth. The federal government operates by spending billions of dollars each year to pay salaries and to buy equipment. Government can increase its spending to stimulate a slow economy or reduce spending to slow economic growth.

In addition, economic growth is regulated through interest rates, the money paid to borrow money. Borrowing by businesses and consumers generates spending. Spending stimulates economic growth. When interest rates are lowered, businesses are encouraged to borrow. This stimulates business activity and, in turn, the economy. When interest rates are raised to discourage borrowing, a slowdown occurs.

Through interest rates, government spending, taxes, and other devices, the rate of economic growth can be controlled somewhat. Control, however, is usually kept to a minimum in a free enterprise system. Furthermore, in a complex economic system the results of such controls are not always clearly visible in the short run. Economists do not always know exactly when control devices should be used, for how long they should be applied, or how effective they may be. While the nature of controls can be debated, some control is needed to prevent a destructive runaway inflationary period or a **depression**—a long and severe drop in the GDP. Such conditions not only affect U.S. citizens but affect the economic climate of foreign countries as well.

Because most nations engage in international trade and because of the impact of global competition on nations, a major recession or depression in one country usually impacts negatively on other countries. For example, during the first half of this decade the United States experienced a period of recession and slow growth. Japan, Germany, France, England, and other major nations also faced similar circumstances shortly thereafter. Economic aspects of international trade will be discussed in the next chapter.

CHAPTER REVIEW 3

B UILDING VOCABULARY POWER

Define the following terms and concepts.

1. economics
2. economic wants
3. noneconomic wants
4. utility
5. producer
6. factors of production
7. natural resources
8. labor
9. human capital
10. capital goods
11. capital formation
12. consumer goods and services
13. economic system
14. market economy
15. command economy
16. mixed economy
17. privatization
18. capitalism
19. socialism
20. communism
21. private property
22. profit
23. demand
24. supply
25. competition
26. economic growth
27. Consumer Price Index (CPI)
28. recession
29. inflation
30. business cycles
31. depression

→ Do For Tommorrow

R EVIEWING FACTS

1. How does an economic want differ from a noneconomic want? Give an example of each.
2. List the four most common types of utility and the four basic factors of production.
3. What is the difference between capital goods and consumer goods?
4. In relation to capital formation, what is one cause for the scarcity of consumer goods in China?
5. How is a market economy different from a command economy?
6. Compare capitalism, socialism, and communism as to (a) how each allocates scarce resources among alternative wants and (b) the existence of private property.
7. Is the profit earned by business usually overestimated or underestimated?
8. What special feature of a free enterprise system helps keep the prices of goods and services down?
9. How might a business attract customers from other sellers?
10. List three examples of nonprice competition.
11. Is the demand high and the supply low for unskilled workers?

12. Other than increasing the production of goods and services, what other element is required for economic growth?
13. List two ways used by government to measure economic growth.
14. List three problems that can occur within an economy when the growth rate is too fast or too slow.
15. List three devices used by the government to control economic growth.

DISCUSSING IDEAS

1. Discuss form, place, and time utility as they might apply to a small fast food pizza business that just opened in your community. See Fig. 3-1.
2. How is capital formation important to the creation of consumer goods?
3. Explain the immediate and long-range effects that the production of capital goods has on consumer goods.
4. Discuss how you might agree with the following statement: "Economic decisions in a capitalistic country are influenced by the federal government about 10 percent of the time; in a socialist country, about 50 percent of the time; and in a communist country, about 90 percent of the time."
5. A person who works for a local business firm made the following statement: "The company took in $500,000 last year. It is doing great." Is the firm necessarily doing great? If it were an average firm, estimate its profit.
6. Explain how supply and demand help determine the price for goods and services.
7. How do business firms know what products to make and how many to produce?
8. Your friend said: "The company I work for had a 10 percent increase in demand for its goods but the supply went up by 15 percent. Management should have raised prices if it wanted to make a bigger profit." Is your friend correct? Explain.
9. Discuss how economic growth that is too fast can cause people who are retired to be hurt financially.
10. If you were an economist working for the federal government, what would you do if you discovered the GDP and CPI were dropping at too fast a rate? Explain.

ANALYZING INFORMATION

1. Use the Consumer Price Index information provided in Fig. 3-4 to determine the following:
   a. By what percent did the CPI change between 1983 and 1993?
   b. If the CPI dropped by 10 percent between 1993 and 1995, what would the CPI be in 1995?

2. Use the following yearly gross domestic product figures to determine answers to the questions below:

1983	$3.5 trillion
1988	$5.0 trillion
1993	$6.3 trillion

    a. What was the percentage of increase between 1983 and 1988?
    b. What was the percentage of increase between 1988 and 1993?
    c. If the percentage of increase between 1983 and 1993 remains the same between 1993 and 2000, what will the GDP be in 2000?

3. Between 1990 and 1991, average yearly consumer price rises for selected countries follow: United States, 4.2 percent; Brazil, 440.8 percent; Israel, 19.0 percent; Portugal, 11.4 percent; and Switzerland, 5.8 percent.

    a. If you were on a fixed income, in which country would you fare the best? Worst?
    b. Over a five-year period, by what percent would prices rise in the United States if consumer prices rose by the same percentage?
    c. Which country was suffering from the greatest amount of inflation? By what percent would prices have increased in this country over a five-year period assuming the rate stayed the same?
    d. For the year shown, by what percent did Switzerland exceed the United States in the total increase in consumer prices?

4. From Fig. 3-5, select one of the economic indicators other than the GDP or CPI and collect statistics from a library for the past five full years. Then calculate the rate of change between the first and second year and the first and fifth year. Prepare a report for your class.

5.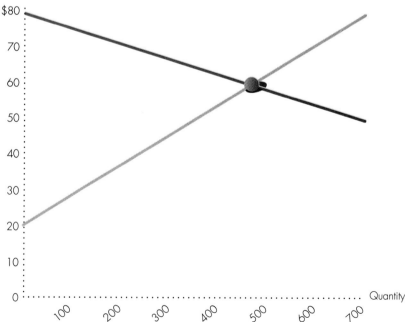

Using the preceding diagram, determine (a) the market price for the product, and (b) how many will be sold at this price.

Solving Business Problems

Case 3-1

Jay and Barry sat on the bench outside the entrance to the local mall chatting before going inside to their separate clerking jobs. The conversation turned to front page headlines that stared at them from an abandoned newspaper left at the end of the bench. "Castro Experiments with Capitalism," one headline read, while another shouted, "Headwinds in China's Nudge to Market Economy." "Brazil's Inflation Out of Control," read still another. Lower on the page could be seen, "CPI Inches Downward."

Silence ensued as Jay and Barry read. They were thinking about whether these stories had any bearing on their jobs and their lives. Finally, Barry broke the silence and the following conversation occurred.

Barry: Now I know why I never liked reading newspapers. The headlines don't make any sense—nothing in common. They jump all over the place, and most of the news is bad. And half of it is not understandable. Then we have to hear it again on TV and on the radio.

Jay: I try to read some of the articles, but many are unclear. For example, yesterday I saw "County Privatizes Trash Collection." The headlines aren't always clear, but fortunately things usually are explained in the stories. By reading each day, you learn more than you think you can, especially about economics.

Barry: The sports pages are what I read. You get the "stats" like team won/lost records and learn about how much the superstars are paid in contracts. Some of them make as much in one year as you and I will make in a lifetime. You don't have to worry about inflation when you make $2 million.

Jay: Today's headlines deal with economics and you're talking economics when you deal with how much people are paid. If you like "stats," you'll like looking at the economic indicators. You have a contract with your employer, Barry. Some day when you have more knowledge and skills to sell, your contracts will get larger, too.

Barry: Maybe I'll take this paper and read some of those headline details later . . . after I find out who won last night's big game between the Cowboys and the Bears. See you after work.

Required:

1. Is the headline that reads "CPI Inches Downward" good news or bad news? Explain your answer.
2. What did all the headlines have in common?

3. Tell Jay what the county did when it "privatized" the trash service.
4. What types of economics are found on the sports pages of a newspaper?

CASE 3-2

Workers in a small corporation were having an informal meeting one lunch hour to discuss wages in the company. One of the workers brought along the following chart, which was passed around.

*Average Weekly Earnings of
Full-Time Workers*

Managers	$1140
Sales workers	980
Clerical workers	520
Skilled laborers	700
Unskilled laborers	610

Some of the workers believed that the wages of all clerical and unskilled workers should be increased to match the amount earned by sales workers. Other workers believed that the clerical workers should be paid as much as the unskilled workers. Still a third group of workers believed that wages of each group of workers should be increased by the same fixed percentage. Shortly, a heated discussion ensued.

One of the workers present, Lisa, had taken several economics courses while in school. As yet, Lisa had not said a word, but now she was ready to give her opinion.

Required:

1. If you were Lisa, what would you say to the group about how wages are set in this country?
2. Would the suggestion of raising the wages of the clerical and unskilled workers to the level of wages earned by sales workers be more acceptable under capitalism or communism? Explain.
3. Which worker suggestion would probably least violate any economic principles dealing with supply and demand? Explain your answer.
4. If wages were to be increased by a fixed percentage for all workers as suggested by the third worker, how might the rate of increase be determined? Explain.

REVIEW

INTERNATIONAL ENVIRONMENT OF BUSINESS CHAPTER 4

After studying this chapter you will be able to:

4-1 Describe the nature, growth, and importance of international trade.

4-2 Explain two theories of international trade.

4-3 Discuss balance of trade.

4-4 Identify and explain key dimensions of international trade.

4-5 Discuss importing and exporting and give reasons why firms enter international trade.

4-6 Identify career opportunities in international business and factors related to selecting employees for overseas jobs.

*G*rant and Ashley graduated from a small-town high school in Montana. *Their parents' graduation gift to their twins was a two-week trip to London, Paris, and Rome. While Grant and Ashley once visited Canada and enjoyed it, anxiety could be read on their faces as they planned for this foreign adventure.*

Grant and Ashley had plenty of immediate questions: "How cold will it be this time of year in each of these cities? If it's 2:00 a.m. in Paris, what time is it here? Can I use my hair dryer or do I need to buy one for each country? Will everyone understand English or do we have to learn foreign languages? Is there a Disney World in Europe? How do we make hotel reservations? What happens if we get sick?" As the questions came to mind, they sought answers from friends, travel bureaus, and the library.

The anxiety did not disappear and the questions continued to flow, many of which were of a business nature: "Can we rent a car in London and drive to Paris and Rome? Will they carry American brands in the stores? Do we need an interpreter? How do we exchange dollars for pounds, francs, and lira? Can we use American credit cards and get cash from an automatic teller machine?"

The questions mounted and they found answers. The worried looks subsided but did not disappear. But the excitement of visiting three foreign nations kept happy smiles on their faces. When business people are transferred to foreign branch offices, they have similar questions and concerns.

llus. 4-1

The travel industry provides a major source of income for many countries. What three places would you most like to visit?

International business is not new; it has been taking place since the beginning of history. Greek and northern African merchants were sailing the seas to sell and buy products in distant lands long before recorded history. In 1600, the British East India Company was formed to establish branches and trade with countries in Asia. As Europeans discovered sea routes around the world, trade flourished among the nations of Europe and countries such as China, India, and Indonesia. American colonial traders began operating in a similar way.

Similarly, investing in factories and facilities abroad was also taking place. An early example of successful American investment abroad was a factory built in Scotland by the Singer Sewing Machine Company in 1868. By 1880, Singer had become a worldwide organization with several sales offices and factories abroad. During the 18th and 19th centuries, a great economic expansion occurred in the United States. Largely financed by foreign money, railway lines were constructed, mines were opened to extract coal and iron ore, and factories were built.

SIGNIFICANCE OF INTERNATIONAL TRADE

Although international trade and investment have long existed, it is only since the 1940s that they have become the object of much study and interest. The reasons are quite obvious. Foreign trade flourished. Companies grew rapidly and operated on a global scale. Transportation by airplanes and ships made it possible to move goods and people vast distances quickly and inexpensively. New technologies, especially computers and telephones, made it possible to communicate quickly. In addition, many countries experimented with new ideas and technologies and with new ways of running businesses. With constant changes, the world keeps shrinking.

EXTENT OF INTERNATIONAL TRADE

Look around and you see product names you are sure are foreign: Honda cars, Sony tapes, Benetton clothes, and Chanel perfume. But what about names such as Nescafé coffee, Shell gasoline, 7-11 stores, and Magnavox television? They are the brand names or products of foreign companies. See Fig. 4-1 on page 80 for a list of other common foreign brands. Similarly, think of familiar American companies such as McDonald's, General Motors, IBM, Coca-Cola, and Eastman Kodak. A bigger and bigger portion of their total sales takes place in foreign countries.

During the last decade of the twentieth century, business activities are no longer confined to one country but are global in scope. Foreigners buy American products (computers, wheat, airplanes) and services (banking, insurance, data processing) just as Americans buy foreign products (petroleum, cars, clothes) and services (vacations, shipping, construction). Americans make products in factories in foreign countries just as foreign companies make products in the United States.

IMPACT OF INTERNATIONAL TRADE ON AMERICA

International business typically refers to business activities that occur between two or more countries. Every country has its own laws and rules, its own currency, and its own business traditions. When a restaurant in North Carolina buys steaks from a meat processing plant in Nebraska, the rules of business are fairly uniform. However, when the restaurant in North Carolina buys codfish caught off Iceland and shipped immediately from the city of Reykjavik, the rules and regulations differ.

Most of the world's trade takes place among the developed countries of North America, Western Europe, and Japan. Over the past twenty years, countries on the western edge of the Pacific Ocean—referred to as the **Pacific Rim**—have emerged as important trading nations. These countries include

Fig. 4-1
Many products are made by foreign businesses.

Selected Products That Are Foreign Owned

BRAND NAME	PRODUCT	COMPANY	COUNTRY
Adidas	Footwear	Adidas	Germany
Benetton	Clothes	Benetton	Italy
Burger King	Fast Food	Grand Metropolitan	Britain
CBS Tape	Recorded Music	Sony	Japan
Close-up	Toothpaste	Lever Brothers	Britain
Fotomat	Film Processing	Konica	Japan
Hardee's	Fast Food	IMASCO	Canada
Magnavox	Television	Phillips	Holland
Michelin	Tires	Michelin	France
Nescafé	Coffee	Nestlé	Switzerland
O'Boisie's	Potato Chips	Keeblers	Canada
Shell Oil	Petroleum	Royal Dutch/ Shell Group	Netherlands/ Britain
10-K	Sports Drink	Suntory	Japan

South Korea, Taiwan, China, Hong Kong, and Singapore. A list of the major countries with which the United States trades is shown in Fig. 4-2.

Trade patterns have shifted from goods to services. More than one-fifth of the trading done internationally is represented by service industries. When service industries emerged as an important segment of the American economy, more and more trade and investments occurred in businesses such as tourism, banking, accounting, advertising, and computer services.

International trade and investment are dominant in the American economy. In a recent year, Americans sold over $400 billion of their products to foreign customers. Almost ten percent of all jobs depend on foreign trade, and four percent of American workers are employed by foreign companies operating in the United States. Foreign firms owned nearly ten percent of all assets and accounted for one-tenth of all sales. In Great Britain, for instance, foreigners owned 14 percent of the assets, employed one in seven workers, and accounted for one-fifth of all sales.

Leading International Trading Partners of the United States
(Listed in Order of Trade Volume)

CANADA

CHINA

FRANCE

GERMANY

JAPAN

MEXICO

NETHERLANDS

SOUTH KOREA

TAIWAN

UNITED KINGDOM

Source: Statistical Abstract of the United States, 1992.

Fig. 4-2
The United States trades with major nations worldwide.

EMERGENCE OF MULTINATIONAL FIRMS

With the evolution of international business, new terms have come into use. These terms apply to the many large firms that operate in other countries. While there are many ways to define these firms, typically a **multinational firm** refers to a business that owns or controls production or service facilities outside the country in which it is based. The **home country** is the country in which a multinational corporation has its headquarters. The **parent firm** is a company that controls another company. The foreign country where

Jeff Greenberg, Photographer

Illus. 4-2
Ships deliver products daily from other countries. And ships leave ports loaded with American goods headed for foreign destinations. What kinds of goods are likely to be sent by water rather than by air?

a multinational firm has production and service facilities is known as the **host country.** Foreign operations that are branches or are separately registered as legal entities are called **subsidiaries.** Most of the world's largest corporations are multinationals. Some of the largest multinationals are shown in Fig. 4-3 on page 82.

Fig. 4-3

Major multinational firms are found in Japan, the United States, and Europe.

The Top 15 Multinational Nonbank Firms by Foreign Sales in 1990 (in Billions of Dollars)

COMPANY	INDUSTRY	COUNTRY	TOTAL ASSETS	FOREIGN SALES	PERCENT OF TOTAL SALES
Exxon	Petroleum	U.S.A.	87.7	90.5	86
Royal Dutch Shell	Petroleum	Britain/ Holland	106.3	56.0	49
Ford Motor	Automobile	U.S.A.	173.7	47.3	48
British Petroleum	Petroleum	Britain	59.3	46.6	79
Mobil	Petroleum	U.S.A.	41.7	44.3	77
Mitsui	Trading	Japan	60.8	43.6	32
IBM	Computers	U.S.A.	87.6	41.9	61
Mitsubishi	Trading	Japan	73.8	41.2	32
General Motors	Automobile	U.S.A.	180.2	37.3	31
Nestlé	Food	Switzerland	27.9	33.0	98
Daimler- Benz	Automobile	Germany	48.8	32.7	61
Phillips	Electronics	Holland	30.6	28.6	93
Volkswagen	Automobile	Germany	41.9	27.5	65
Toyota Motor	Automobile	Japan	55.5	26.3	42
Asea Brown Boveri	Electrical	Switzerland	30.2	22.7	85

Source: "Survey: The Multinationals," *The Economist*, March 27, 1993, pp. 6–7.

THEORIES OF INTERNATIONAL TRADE

Economies of different countries have become interlinked through trade in ways so complex and extensive that most business is internationalized in one way or another. Two well-known theories help to explain much of what the experts find to be true.

COMPARATIVE ADVANTAGE THEORY

The **comparative advantage theory** states that to gain a trade advantage a country should specialize in products or services that it can provide more efficiently than other countries. For instance, because of climate and soil conditions,

France is better able to produce vintage wines as compared to Canada, whose soil and climate favors the growing of wheat. Each country would gain by specializing—France in wine and Canada in wheat—and then trading with each other.

What if one country can produce both wheat and wine at a lower cost than another country? The comparative advantage theory suggests that the focus should be on comparing the cost of producing both products in each country. For example, it is possible that France may be able to produce more wine than wheat for the same cost whereas Canada may find that it can produce wheat at a lower cost than it can produce wine. In such a case, Canadians should specialize in producing and selling wheat to the French and buy wine from France. Similarly, the French should produce wine and sell part of it to the Canadians to pay for the wheat they need. This theory explains why Americans produce computers and wheat, Hong Kong makes clothes, and Saudi Arabia extracts oil from the earth.

PRODUCT LIFE CYCLE THEORY

Another theory to explain trade and investment is known as the product life cycle. In Chapter 10 you will learn that a product or service goes through four stages: introduction, growth, maturity, and decline. Take black-and-white televisions, for example. In the introductory stage, only black-and-white TVs were sold. Soon, more and more people in the country started buying TVs—the growth stage. When many families owned a TV, sales leveled off—the maturity stage. Sales of these TVs then started falling off—the decline stage.

How does the product life cycle theory relate to trade and investment? When sales begin to slow in a country (the mature stage), Company A starts selling the television sets in foreign countries where the product may be in the introductory or growth stage. However, selling the sets to foreign countries is expensive because of transportation costs and taxes levied by foreign governments. Companies in the foreign country find it attractive to make and sell the sets at reduced prices. To counteract this action, Company A sets up a branch factory in the foreign country where it makes and sells the televisions.

Many American companies move to foreign countries when sales at home start lagging. Examples are fast food restaurants and soft drink companies. New products are constantly introduced. Their sales grow, then flatten, and eventually decline. To remain profitable, firms sometimes ship their products overseas, and later build factories abroad.

B ALANCE OF TRADE

The total goods and services sold abroad by American companies brings money to this country. Money also comes from foreigners who buy American companies or set up firms in the United States or lend money to Americans. At the same time, money leaves the country when Americans buy foreign products or vacation abroad or invest in foreign businesses. Countries keep records of all international transactions that are important for developing economic policies.

Business people and government officials make important policy decisions by looking at the **balance of trade,** which is the difference between money coming into and going out of a country. The balance of trade represents the total exports and imports of goods and services as well as the flow of money into and out of the country from investments. **Imports** represent goods and services purchased from other countries and **exports** represent goods and services sold to other countries.

When more money leaves a country than comes in, a **balance of trade deficit** exists. On the other hand, a **balance of trade surplus** occurs if more money comes into a country than goes out. A look at Fig. 4-4 shows that in 1980, the United States had a foreign trade surplus of $9.4 billion; but in 1991, there was a balance of trade deficit of $28.3 billion. In fact, over the past several years, the United States has had trade deficits every year. How long can a country continue to buy more than it sells? Not indefinitely, of course. However, the United States has an advantage because its currency is valued by countries everywhere. The U.S. dollar is valued overseas because its society is stable, its policies are pro-business, and its economy is the world's largest and richest. In addition, the government has a large reserve of money (like a savings account) to pay its deficits.

Some countries are less fortunate. Countries with prolonged trade deficits may not be able to pay their bills or may have to limit international trade or investment. In addition, restrictions may be placed on the outward flow of money or on the activities of foreign businesses in their countries.

Illus. 4-3

The United States has become a popular tourist attraction for many foreigners. How do foreign visitors help our balance of trade?

Jeff Greenberg, Photographer

United States' Balance of Trade With Other Countries (in Billions of Dollars)

	1980	1991
TOTAL EXPORTS	**343.2**	**676.5**
Goods	224.3	416.5
Services	47.6	144.7
Income from assets abroad	71.4	115.3
TOTAL IMPORTS	**333.8**	**704.8**
Goods	249.8	490.1
Services	41.5	106.8
Income on foreign assets in the U.S.	42.5	105.9
NET BALANCE OF TRADE	**9.4**	**-28.3**

Source: *Statistical Abstract of the United States, 1992.*

When balance of trade deficits occur, it means companies and individuals are demanding more foreign currency. For instance, if Americans buy more Japanese cars, the demand for Japanese currency—the yen—goes up because yen will be needed to pay the Japanese. When demand increases for yen, more dollars are needed to buy yen. Thus, the value of the dollar declines in relation to the yen. In turn, Japanese products become more expensive for Americans while American products become less expensive for the Japanese. Theoretically, at this stage, higher prices discourage the sale of Japanese products in America and lower prices encourage the sale of American products abroad. In this way, the trade deficits can be reduced and eventually eliminated.

DIMENSIONS OF INTERNATIONAL TRADE

Trade and investment differ in several ways in international and in domestic environments. Differences occur because of the nature of government policies toward foreign firms and products, the value of foreign currencies, the existence of international treaties and agreements, and the contrast of cultures.

GOVERNMENT POLICIES

Most economists who believe in competition prefer free trade. **Free trade** refers to the elimination of most trade barriers. Special occasions arise, however, when free trade barriers are necessary. To protect domestic industries and to earn revenue, governments often impose a **tariff**—a tax on foreign goods. For instance, assume that the United States government sets a tariff of 10 percent per pair of jeans made in Colombia, South America. If the jeans are valued at $30, the American customs department will collect a tax of $3 ($30 × .10), and the price per pair will rise to $33.

Tariffs are also imposed when a foreign supplier is guilty of "dumping" its products. **Dumping** refers to the practice of selling goods in a foreign market at a price that is below cost or below what it charges in its home country. When a company dumps, it is trying to win more customers by driving domestic producers out of the market. The government prevents dumping by setting tariffs that increase the price on goods being dumped. For example, if Japanese firms tried dumping computer parts in the United States, a tariff might be levied to sufficiently raise the price of those parts to permit domestic producers to compete successfully.

Another way governments may restrict the availability of foreign goods is to create **quotas,** which limit the quantity or value of units permitted to enter a country. For instance, the United States government could allow only 100,000 jackets to enter from Hong Kong annually, although many more jackets could be sold. Alternatively, the government could allow jackets worth up to $1 million into the United States from Hong Kong annually. In either case, quotas limit the number or dollar value of foreign goods that can be sold in a country. Quotas are designed to protect the market share of domestic producers. However, both tariffs and quotas increase the price of foreign goods to consumers.

In addition to tariffs and quotas, it may be difficult to sell goods and services abroad because of **non-tariff barriers,** barriers other than tariffs that restrict imports. In many cases, such barriers are not designed against foreign products, but have the practical effect of keeping them out. In some cases, barriers are deliberately created to protect domestic producers.

Non-tariff barriers of one sort or another exist in almost all countries. For example, in the United States, steering wheels are on the left side of motor vehicles while in New Zealand, the steering wheel is on the right side. Thus, before an American company can sell cars in New Zealand, it would have to make changes to the vehicle. Other examples of non-tariff barriers are a public campaign of "Be American, buy American," or the advertisements by labor unions to "Look for the union label." Both situations are clearly designed to discourage the buying of foreign goods and services. Non-tariff barriers are difficult to remove because they are often part of a country's culture and tradition.

While the advantages of international trade and investment are clear, anxieties arise because some nations are fearful about problems that might occur when foreign investors enter their countries. For example, as the amount of Japanese investment in the United States has grown over the past decade, there have been demands to regulate and restrict foreign investment here.

Governments may place restrictions on what companies and foreigners are allowed to buy or industries in which to make investments. For instance, in the United States, the government can stop a foreign company from buying an American business if it feels that the national security interests of the country might be endangered.

CURRENCY VALUES

International business involves dealing with the money, or currency, of foreign countries. Currencies have different names, such as yen in Japan and pound in the United Kingdom, but even more importantly, they differ in value. This is a key difference between doing business domestically and doing business internationally. The **exchange rate** is the value of one currency to another. The difference in value of each currency can change several times in a day, depending on many factors such as the demand for a particular currency, interest rates, balance of trade, inflation rates, and government policies. Major newspapers publish exchange rates daily for most currencies.

Managers must closely watch exchange rates, as they affect profits and investment decisions in a big way. For example, assume the value of one American dollar is equal to 150 Japanese yen. A camera made in Japan for 15,000 yen would be selling in the United States for $100 (15,000/150). If the exchange rate should change to 125 yen to the dollar, that same camera will then cost $120 (15,000/125).

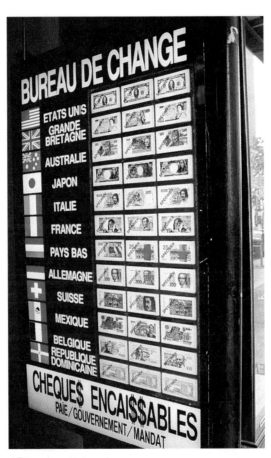

Jeff Greenberg, Photographer

INTERNATIONAL AGREEMENTS

Trading agreements are controlled by several major forces. One of these forces is represented by international treaties and institutions; another is the creation of trading blocs.

Treaties

International business is governed by agreements reached bilaterally (between two countries) or multilaterally (among several countries). In addition, there are international organizations such as the United Nations, and treaties such as the Patent Cooperation Treaty under which individual nations agree to respect the rights of those who invent new products.

One of the most important treaties that governs international trade is known as the General Agreement on Tariffs and Trade (GATT). Most of the world's major trading nations have signed this treaty. Since 1947, when the first GATT agreements were reached, there has been a huge cut in tariffs that countries had imposed on imported goods. GATT also provides a framework for resolving trade disputes between countries.

Two major international institutions are the International Monetary Fund (IMF) and the International Bank for Reconstruction and Development (popularly known as the World Bank). The IMF's main purpose is to help countries that have serious balance of trade deficits and thus have no money to pay for imports or to repay loans. The IMF provides low-cost loans and advice on how to manage the economy efficiently. The World Bank, on the other hand, provides low-cost, long-term loans to poor countries to develop their basic industries and facilities, such as roads and electric power plants. Both these international organizations are dominated by economically advanced countries.

Trading Blocs

Another major development in the international environment is the creation of trading blocs. A **trading bloc** is an arrangement between two or more countries to remove all restrictions among them on the sale of goods and services while imposing barriers to trade and investment from countries that are not part of the bloc.

There are many forms of trade blocs. The best example of an extreme form of trade bloc is the European Union (EU) which currently has 12 members (Belgium, Denmark, France, Germany, Great Britain, Greece, Ireland, Italy, Luxembourg, Netherlands, Portugal, and Spain). Since it was first formed in 1957 as the European Economic Community, the EU has gone beyond free trade among its members. It is trying to create a "United States of Europe" where there will also be free movement of money and people and where common economic and monetary policies would be followed.

In 1989, the United States signed a free trade agreement with Canada. Gradually, restrictions on the movement of goods and services between the two countries will disappear. In 1992, Canada and the United States signed a similar agreement with Mexico, called the North American Free Trade Agreement (NAFTA) which was later approved by Congress. NAFTA is the world's largest trading bloc. Tariffs and other trade barriers among the three nations will be removed.

Strong opposition to NAFTA came from labor unions, environmentalists, certain businesses, and countries outside of the trading bloc. Because Mexico has lower wage rates and weaker laws, NAFTA's opponents fear that businesses will move to Mexico, leaving behind unemployed workers and abandoned factories. And some countries fear that tariffs, quotas, or other restrictions will be placed on their products and services. However, NAFTA creates a huge trading area that includes two of America's biggest trading partners. It is believed that the three countries will benefit through increased trade and investment.

CULTURAL DIFFERENCES

International business may also involve understanding and coping with cultural values and traits in foreign countries that are different from ours. **Culture** refers to the customs, beliefs, values, and patterns of behavior of the people of a country or group. In many countries, especially large ones like India, Russia, and Canada, numerous cultural differences exist within their own populations. Likewise, in the United States there are cultural differences, such as among various racial and ethnic groups and between southerners and northerners and people from the east and west coasts.

As you will learn in Chapter 9, organizations also have cultures. Cultures consist of a combination of complex factors such as written and oral language; religion; attitudes toward work, authority, and family; practices regarding courtship, etiquette, gestures, and joking; and manners and customs. Some cultures may appear to be similar to America, such as the cultures of Canada and Great Britain; whereas other cultures appear to be very dissimilar, such as those of India and Thailand.

International business people need to be aware of cultural differences in order to be successful in their missions. For instance, McDonald's has been reluctant to set up their famous restaurants in India for a long time because beef is not eaten by Hindus, which is the religion of the majority of the people of India. The company is planning to sell "lamburgers" in Indian branches.

As Fig. 4-5 on page 90 suggests, even though English is spoken in Australia, there are terms and phrases that may not be familiar to an American. In a similar manner, French is spoken in many countries but each country adds its own words to the French language. A language is not always similar within a country. For example, in many parts of the United States a small container is called a "bag," while in other parts of the country it is called a "sack" or a "poke."

EXPORTING AND IMPORTING

When a company sells its goods and services to a foreign country, it is said to be **exporting.** Planes made by Boeing in the United States that are sold to British Airways is an example of exporting. **Importing** refers to buying goods or services made in a foreign country. When Americans buy French perfume, they are importing goods from France. Exporting and importing are usually the simplest and the first step a company takes in becoming an international business. The attraction to becoming an international business is that it requires limited resources and is relatively risk free.

The United States is the world's largest exporting and importing nation. Some of America's most popular exports are wheat, airplanes, computers, movies, and medicines. Among the products heavily imported into the United States are cars, clothes, gasoline, and electronic products such as televisions. More and more, companies are buying and selling services across borders, such as American accounting firms that provide tax advice to foreign investors.

Fig. 4-5

Australian English and American
English sometimes differ.

AUSTRALIAN ENGLISH	AMERICAN ENGLISH
Arvo	Afternoon
Biscuit	Cookie
Bloke	Man
Brolly	Umbrella
Cozzie	Bathing suit (also bathers or swimmers)
Crook	Sick
Entree	The appetizer, not the main course
Fair dinkum	The real thing
Footpath	Sidewalk
Jumbuck	Sheep
Jumper	Sweater
Lollies	Candy
Mate	Friend
Nought	Zero
Sandshoes	Sneakers
Serviette	Table napkin
Sweets	Dessert
Ta	Thank you
Takeaway food	Food to go
Taxi rank	Cab stand
Yank	An American

Source: Destination—Australia, Australian Tourist Commission.

Governments place restrictions on what goods and services can be imported
or exported. The goals again are to protect domestic businesses or citizens or
cultures and to ensure national security. Egypt prohibits the export of antiques;
the United States bars tuna caught with dolphins. American firms are required

to get special government licenses to sell high technology or military products abroad. Sometimes for political reasons, or as part of a multinational agreement, a government may bar companies from doing business with particular countries, which is known as an **embargo.** For instance, U.S. companies are barred from conducting business with Cuba.

Sanctions are a milder form of embargo where specific business ties with a foreign country are banned. For instance, it is illegal for an American company to sell nuclear technology to Pakistan.

R EASONS FOR ENTERING INTERNATIONAL TRADE

Why would McDonald's want to open a store in Moscow, or Motorola sell car phones in Japan, or Wal-Mart buy jeans from Hong Kong? Or for that matter, why would Volvo, a Swedish company, wish to sell cars in the United States? There are usually many good reasons why firms enter international business.

The main reason is profit. It may be that more profit is earned from foreign market sales or it may be possible to charge higher prices abroad than at home where competition could be more intense. When the cost of making goods is lower in foreign countries than in the home country, it then becomes cost effective to buy goods made abroad.

As the theory of comparative advantage suggests, some countries are endowed with specific resources and can produce certain goods more inexpensively and efficiently than others. A firm in a particular country might produce a unique product, like jade or coral jewelry. Thus, it would be cost effective and profitable to produce these goods at home and sell them abroad.

Managers may be enthusiastic about international business because they have traveled abroad or have grown up in foreign countries. If these managers are employed in small or medium-sized businesses, they may find that production costs can be lowered by entering a foreign market. When domestic and foreign sales are combined and mass production techniques are used, production costs should drop and profits should rise.

In many cases, a company goes international in reaction to what other companies are doing or because of changes in the domestic market. If some firms are making large profits by selling abroad, other companies may be encouraged to do the same. If a large foreign market opens up, as in China in recent years, an American company may lose the market to other firms if it does not act quickly.

Similarly, sales at home may be stagnant or declining while opportunities to sell abroad may be abundant. A company may have overproduced and the only way to possibly dispose of its surplus goods profitably is to sell them abroad. It could also be that a company is physically close to foreign customers and markets. For example, Turkish firms can sell easily to Greek firms because they are neighbors. It is quite natural for most European firms to sell to neighboring countries.

Global Perspective

THE LITTLE BOY WITH THE GNARLED KNUCKLES

Questions:

1 If you were the president of Jamshed Carpets, how would you defend your decision to sell carpets made by children in Pakistan?

2 How do you explain the action and logic of the human rights group?

3 If you were the Pakistani ambassador to the United States, how might you persuade the human rights group to call off its campaign?

4 Assume that the human rights group will succeed in its campaign. How can Jamshed Carpets or the Pakistani government prepare for this possibility?

J amshed Carpets sells fine hand-made carpets in its stores through-out the United States. Nearly 60 percent of its carpets come from Pakistan where they are handmade by children, many of them ten years in age or younger. The designs of these beautiful and very expensive carpets are of old Persian origin; and in creating them, the techniques and traditions of ancient times continue to be followed. Indeed, this is what gives these handmade wool carpets their value.

Small children are thought to be best suited to tie the little knots, thousands and thousands of them, that go into each of the carpets. They have small and nimble fingers, can work long hours and be bossed and controlled by elders and parents, and hardly need to be paid. In villages, after the sowing but before the harvesting season, the peasants organize the dyeing and weaving of the yarn and the tying of the knots for making the carpets. Given the long hours of work, the fingers become knotty and gnarled and before becoming teenagers, the children are no longer able to do a good job and are replaced by their younger brothers and sisters.

Jamshed Carpets buys the carpets and sells them in the United States. These handcrafted carpets contribute to nearly three-fourths of the company's profits. In its stores, Jamshed also carries a line of machine-made carpets, but this market is more competitive and profits are smaller.

Over the past year, Jamshed Carpets has learned that an American human rights group is campaigning to halt the sale of carpets made by "child labor" in Pakistan. Demonstrators protested in front of some stores in Washington, DC, and in New York City. The press reported the story. While sales have not yet been affected, Jamshed Carpets is worried that customers may turn away from buying the carpets or that the American govern-ment may impose a tariff or ban the imports outright.

Handcrafted carpets are a major export item from Pakistan, a poor South Asian country where the annual per capita income is less than $500. Pakistan uses the foreign currency—the dollars, pounds, yens, and marks it earns from selling the carpets—to build schools and electric supply plants and to buy machinery and fertilizers from abroad. A boycott of carpets in Europe and America would mean a major economic blow to the export earnings of Pakistan. Very few people in Pakistan, certainly not the youngsters nor their parents, can afford to own these splendid products.

Small businesses that look forward to entering the export business may find valuable assistance from a number of sources, including those listed in Fig. 4-6. Export trading and management companies may be hired to assist in selling a firm's products overseas.

EXPORT HOTLINE

A group of firms led by AT&T offers export help. Dial 1-800-USA-XPORT to request reports about types of products from specific countries.

STATE TRADE OFFICES

Many states offer services to entrepreneurs; helpful in making contacts abroad.

MAJOR BANKS

Subsidiaries of foreign banks or U.S. regional banks offer financial help.

U.S. COMMERCE DEPT.

Offers tips on trade shows and distributors. Located in major cities.

SMALL BUSINESS DEVELOPMENT CENTERS

Provide general advice on how to export.

Fig. 4-6
Budding exporters can use various resources for selling abroad.

CAREER OPPORTUNITIES

The phenomenal growth in international trade and investment has created many new types of jobs. In addition to those who work in foreign firms in the United States, there are over 150,000 Americans who work abroad for American or foreign firms.

Many people are employed in various aspects of international business such as in exporting and importing, teaching languages, translating services, administering trade laws, and working in international banking and insurance firms. Others work in international trade organizations such as GATT and the IMF, or in federal and state government agencies. As countries become economically interdependent, more and more jobs will require a knowledge of international business.

Most international companies hire host country employees at the entry level, but workers who are sent abroad are usually highly skilled, mature, and experienced. Studies show that the average salaries in foreign companies located in the United States are higher than for similar jobs in American companies.

In recent years, it has been reported that Americans, and especially women or blacks, have difficulty getting promoted above a certain level in foreign firms. Moreover, while working several years overseas is often seen as a plus in many companies, in others it may be a drawback since the person working abroad loses contact with people and developments occurring in the parent firm.

Jeff Greenberg, Photographer

Today, both private firms and government agencies recruit extensively for jobs that require skills that are tied to international business transactions. The required skills include not only a knowledge of business but also a knowledge of foreign languages as well as familiarity with specific foreign countries, cultures, and practices. Many colleges and universities provide course work and academic degrees in international business. Programs are also available that provide opportunities to study abroad as well as to work in foreign firms.

EMPLOYMENT OF INTERNATIONAL MANAGERS

The growth of international business has created a need for managers who can work successfully in a wide variety of environments. Such managers adapt readily to people from other cultures, are skilled and competent, are socially flexible, and are receptive to new ideas. Managers must also have the ability to keep track of events in foreign countries, to develop innovative problem-solving strategies, and to view the entire world as a potential market.

More and more managers are working in firms, whether American or foreign, that operate on an international scale. Usually firms rely on home country nationals (citizens) and host country nationals. Occasionally, other nationals (those who are neither from the home nor host country) are used to fill managerial positions overseas.

During the startup phase of foreign operations, firms tend to rely on home country managers sent from headquarters. Most supervisors and their managers tend to be staffed by host country managers as it is less expensive and many positions must be filled. Nationals from other countries are likely to be hired when they are exceptionally qualified or when host country managers are not available. Sending managers overseas is expensive because extra benefits and bonuses (like airfares for family and cost of living allowances) are usually provided.

In selecting managers, great weight is given to the ability to perform technical work, adapt to change, work independently with limited resources, and keep physically and emotionally healthy. Also, a manager headed for an overseas assignment needs a good education and language skills, a high degree of motivation, and support from the entire family.

While operating abroad, managers should recognize that their firms are bound by the rules and laws of the country in which they operate. Foreign governments have the right to seize foreign firms, with or without compensation, if such businesses are thought to be harmful to their national interests. As a result, managers should devise strategies to minimize the possibility of having restrictions placed on their operations. These include studying, anticipating, and preparing for political risks. The best way to defend a company's activities is to keep the host country informed of the value of the foreign company.

CHAPTER 4 REVIEW

BUILDING VOCABULARY POWER

Define the following terms and concepts.

1. international business
2. Pacific Rim
3. multinational firm
4. home country
5. parent firm
6. host country
7. subsidiaries
8. comparative advantage theory
9. balance of trade
10. imports
11. exports
12. balance of trade deficit
13. balance of trade surplus
14. free trade
15. tariff
16. dumping
17. quotas
18. non-tariff barriers
19. exchange rate
20. trading bloc
21. culture
22. exporting
23. importing
24. embargo
25. sanctions

REVIEWING FACTS

1. How does international business differ from domestic business?
2. How important is international business for the United States?
3. Explain the comparative advantage theory.
4. How does the product life cycle theory affect foreign trade?

5. What two policies can a government adopt to protect domestic businesses from foreign competition?
6. How do changes in foreign exchange rates affect international business?
7. What are the purposes of GATT, IMF, and the World Bank?
8. What countries are members of the North American Free Trade Agreement (NAFTA)?
9. Why has McDonald's been reluctant to open branches in India?
10. Give four reasons why firms might enter into international business.
11. For what types of jobs do international firms hire host country employees? For what jobs do they send employees abroad?
12. What qualities are needed by managers who work in foreign countries?
13. Under what condition is it likely for a country to take over a foreign company with or without permission?

DISCUSSING IDEAS

1. Explain the reasons for the growing importance of international business.
2. Would you like to work in a foreign-owned firm? Why or why not?
3. Identify six services that the United States exports.
4. Explain the situations under which a multinational firm will use home country, host country, and third country nationals in its foreign operations.
5. Select a product or service and show how the product life cycle theory applies.
6. If a country regularly has a balance of trade surplus, what will happen to its international business?
7. Why might a company dump its products abroad?
8. If the value of the German mark continues to rise in relation to the American dollar, what can a German exporter do to keep the price competitive of the goods it sells in the U.S. market?
9. Discuss several ways in which NAFTA might help the American economy.
10. Prepare a list of characteristics that you believe best describes the "American culture."
11. Why would it be expensive for an American firm to send a typical American to manage a business in Tokyo?

ANALYZING INFORMATION

1. The XYZ Electronic Corporation manufactures and sells video cassette recorders (VCRs). Since the product was introduced over ten years ago, nearly 90 percent of all American households have VCRs. Apply the product life cycle theory to answer the following questions.
   a. In what stage of the cycle are VCRs?
   b. What might XYZ do to increase sales and profits?

REVIEW

2. The Balance of Trade accounts of the nation of Utopia for the past three years are given below in millions of dollars.

	Year 1	Year 2	Year 3
Export of goods	$100	$120	$125
Import of goods	$175	$195	$205
Export of services	$ 80	$100	$150
Import of services	$ 40	$ 60	$ 80
Investment abroad	$ 30	$ 25	$ 40
Investment from abroad	$ 50	$ 70	$ 70

Given the above information, answer the following questions.
   a. Does Utopia have a deficit or surplus in its overall trade and investment in Year 1, Year 2, and Year 3?
   b. If you were the president of an American company, would you set up a business in Utopia? Why or why not?
   c. Suggest ways by which Utopia can reduce its deficit or increase its surplus.

3. An Australian sheep farmer who sells much of his wool in the United States has seen the exchange rate for the Australian dollar (AUD) go from U.S. $1 = AUD 1.20 to U.S. $1 = AUD 1.45 over the past six months. Answer the following questions assuming the sheep farmer sells 100 AUDS worth of wool.
   a. Will the new currency exchange rate help or hurt his sales in the United States?
   b. What may be some of the reasons for the drop in the exchange rate?
   c. Do American consumers gain or lose with the change in the currency rates?

4. You are planning to introduce your line of "SuperKids" comics in Thailand. In the United States the English-language comics, which are very popular with young girls, are sold mostly at supermarket checkout counters. You have just learned that most Thais cannot read English; books printed in color are very expensive; Thailand is not a wealthy country but the economy is growing rapidly; and supermarkets are very few and far between.
   a. Do you think your comics will be successful in Thailand? Why or why not?
   b. What modifications might you have to consider making for the Thai market?
   c. Given the information about Thailand, what do you think is the attraction for selling your comics in that country?

5. Country A has lots of wool and needs wheat. Country B has wheat and needs sugar. Country C has sugar and needs wool. Because of political

reasons, Country B has an embargo on trading with Country C. Country B has no money to pay for imports.

a. Given the above information, what form of international business may be the most successful for trading among these countries?

b. What sort of organizations are likely to be able to succeed in such situations?

SOLVING BUSINESS PROBLEMS

CASE 4-1

Morning Calm Industries is a huge South Korean company that has long exported to the U.S. market. The American market is very profitable not only to Morning Calm but to many other Korean businesses and the balance of trade has been in favor of South Korea for many years.

Morning Calm is in a wide variety of businesses including banking, automobile parts, and computers. Recently, the company learned that an engineering firm in Louisiana, Garden Pistons, was up for sale. Morning Calm decided to buy Garden Pistons, a manufacturer of specialty parts for high-performance automobiles, for $20 million and planned an additional investment of $15 million to modernize the equipment. Job security for existing employees would be assured, but no new employment would be created. Soon after Morning Calm announced its decision to buy Garden Pistons, state and local politicians, newspaper editors, and television commentators, as well as many members of the public, came out denouncing the proposed purchase.

Required:

1. Speculate on the reasons behind the hostility towards Morning Calm's plans to buy Garden Pistons.
2. Would reaction be different if the foreign company had been from Canada? Why or why not?
3. Would there be more support for Morning Calm if it had built a new factory instead of buying an existing American company?
4. What might Morning Calm do to ease the negative public and political opinion in Louisiana?

CASE 4-2

The recent economic changes in Hungary have led to private and foreign ownership of previously state-owned businesses. Bright Lights, an American lamp maker, has bought a majority ownership in a Hungarian electrical firm, Twinkle Stars. Bright Lights is anxious to integrate effectively the Hungarian unit into its American operations.

Several management issues have emerged as Bright Lights tried to assign several managers from the United States to go to Budapest for two-year periods during this startup phase. The cost of sending managers to Hungary

REVIEW

appeared to be extraordinarily high and some of the likely candidates said that they would go but wanted assurances of salary protection and career advancement when they returned from their tour abroad. In addition, a manager had just returned from Hungary, only three months into his assignment, complaining it was too "difficult" to work with the Hungarians. The vice president in charge of human resources, Mr. Ramon Santiago, was clearly facing important personnel issues and considered various courses of action.

Required:

1. Why might Bright Lights want to use U.S. managers and not Hungarian, or even third country nationals, to manage Twinkle Stars?
2. In selecting managers for Hungary, what abilities and qualifications should Bright Lights be seeking?
3. Why is there a concern about finding a proper place in the parent company when the manager returns from Hungary?
4. What can Bright Lights do to ease the reentry into the parent firm?

Unit Summary

1-1 *Describe the general nature and extent of business and how global competition affects business operations.*

The world of business has a language of its own. Therefore, since everyone comes directly into contact with business as employees and as customers, it is important to know the many terms used in the business world. Business also has a history of change that employees and customers experience as they work and see new products that continually appear. The size of the gross domestic product is testimony to the historic growth of business and to the well-being of America's people.

Foreign producers viewed America as a world of business opportunity. As a result, foreign producers slowly built sales in the United States. Competition intensified when more and more world producers crossed national boundaries to sell their domestic goods and services in foreign markets. Eager buyers bought diverse products from Japan and other Asian and European countries. Competition in the world marketplace became intense, forcing world competitors to streamline their operations by becoming as effective and as efficient as possible.

American businesses have been changing by becoming more committed to satisfying customers' desires by making better quality products. Many firms downsized, empowered employees, reorganized the way they operated, adopted total quality management practices, stepped up their use of technology, and experimented with innovative products and manufacturing processes. Their results have led to more productive and loyal employees and satisfied customers who bought superior products at competitive prices.

1-2 *Summarize key features of entrepreneurship, causes of failure, and the risks and opportunities that exist.*

Small businesses have contributed much to American business. In recent years, while major businesses were rebuilding themselves, small businesses continued to start and grow by the thousands. Small businesses add more employees to their payrolls than do large businesses. However, the ease of entering business has a downside. Some entrepreneurs start up at the wrong time, without adequate experience, or with inadequate capital. Nevertheless, many entrepreneurs experienced such great success that they converted their small thriving firms to

UNIT SUMMARY

create franchised businesses or converted to forms of business that would allow rapid growth.

Large firms also encourage entrepreneurship by inventing intrapreneurships that permit innovative employees to experiment with developing new products or new ways to provide goods or services. Employee stock ownership plans also add new incentives by allowing employees to become owners by sharing in the company's profits.

1-3 *Discuss how society's economic, social, and environmental problems influence business policies and practices.*

Every country has problems that directly impact on businesses. This country's problems are numerous. A major problem centers on a rapidly growing population that includes immigrants from other countries as well as a population that is moving westward and southward away from the Frost Belt to the Sun Belt. Many businesses follow population paths by relocating, leaving behind decaying cities, crime, homelessness, and poverty-stricken families. Families have downsized and both parents have joined the workforce to maintain or improve their standards of living.

Inequities among whites, black Americans, Asians, and Hispanic Americans exist. Poverty is higher among some groups and pay is unequal between males and females. Family patterns have changed. Children return to empty homes where no one greets them at the end of the school day because both parents are employed. Many youngsters are sent to day-care centers while grandparents are sent to elder-care centers. Increased numbers of people wanting more and more goods contribute to polluting the environment to the point where the air, water, and earth have contaminants that affect our health.

Businesses have responded to many social and environmental problems. Jobs were redesigned to make them more interesting and challenging. Improved health care benefits are often provided by employers. Businesses have adopted practices that benefit employees that range from no-smoking policies to assisting employees in overcoming weight and drug dependency problems. Businesses have also adapted to the changing needs of employees by offering telecommuting jobs, allowing family leave time for new parents, and by breaking the glass barrier that too often restricts the promotion of women and minorities.

Local and federal agencies and businesses are working together to control environmental problems. Businesses pollute less and work with communities to provide clean air, safe drinking water, and healthy crops. Natural resources are conserved by recycling them whenever possible.

1-4 *Explain basic social responsibilities and ethical issues as well as how ethics relates to business situations.*

Every business has a social responsibility to contribute to the well-being of society. Every business has stakeholders that include not only the owners and employees but also customers, suppliers, the local community, and the government. Most businesses are socially responsible, although not all authorities agree that businesses should be. When firms are socially responsible, they believe stakeholders will react in positive ways by showing loyalty to products and treating businesses favorably when passing laws.

Ethics relates to all people and all organizations, including business managers and employees. Ethics comes into play when laws do not exist. What is right or wrong is determined by a person's values, which are influenced by one's family, religious beliefs, and workplace environment. Acceptable and unacceptable behavior varies among individuals, businesses, and societies. Ethical decisions are based upon what is good for the greatest number of stakeholders. Businesses are constantly faced with ethical dilemmas. As a guide to assist in making ethical decisions, employers often establish codes of conduct that provide guidelines for employees as well as managers. However, the most critical support for good ethics comes from the efforts of top management.

1-5 *Identify basic economic concepts and problems, fundamental principles of capitalism, and economic-political systems.*

The economic wants that individuals and organizations can afford form the basis for creating the demand for goods and services that businesses attempt to provide. To create useful goods and services, businesses use natural resources, land, labor, capital goods, and management. Because no nation has enough resources to satisfy everyone's wants, an economic system helps decide answers to basic questions such as what goods and services will be made, how they will be made available, and who will get them.

The two types of basic economic systems are market and command economies. The main market economy is capitalism, which is found in various countries including the United States. The primary command economy is communism. In communism, deciding who gets what goods and how they get them is done by a central government agency that makes the decisions. Socialism is a combination of market and command economies, where some of the economic decisions are made by customers and others by government.

Capitalism contains fundamental principles, one of which is the right of people to own, use, and sell private property. Other principles include the right of business owners to earn a profit and the right to set prices on the goods sold. Another important principle is competition, which sets no limits on the number of sellers and buyers. Competition satisfies customers because it generates the highest quality products at the lowest possible prices. The final principle of capitalism is determining who will get the goods and services provided by businesses. Citizen income distribution is decided by the money that people and organizations earn. For example, workers with limited skills are numerous. As a result, employers can hire them at low wages, which limits what they can buy. People with scarce but valuable skills, however, are paid the most and can buy numerous and expensive goods and services.

No economic system operates without problems. The role of government is not only to measure economic growth, but also to promote growth during recessions and depressions and to control growth. The federal government restricts growth when the economy becomes overly inflated. Measurement is accomplished through the collection of data that is provided in such reports as the Gross Domestic Product and the Consumer Price Index. Growth is promoted by a variety of government actions, such as by increasing government expenditures and lowering taxes. Growth that is too rapid can be slowed by such actions as decreasing government expenditures and raising interest rates.

1-6 *Outline the importance, dimensions, and theories of international business, especially on how it impacts on the balance of trade and on importing and exporting operations.*

Growth in international trade has been rapid in recent years. Many of the products and services customers buy today are made in other lands. Trading with giant multinational firms is common, and trading by small businesses in other countries is becoming fairly common as well. Each country attempts to find a competitive trading advantage by utilizing its specialized resources or other strengths to produce desired goods and services at low cost. This theory of competitive advantage is matched by the product life cycle theory, which states that sales can be increased by selling the same efficiently made product in other countries.

Nations must be concerned about the balance of trade. If imports exceed exports in value, a negative balance of trade exists, which weakens a country over an extended period. Therefore, a positive balance of trade is desirable. If a wide discrepancy in the balance of trade exists, the value of a country's currency can be affected. For example, the value of the dollar has declined because U.S. imports have exceeded exports for some time, whereas Japan's exports have exceeded its imports by a large margin. Consequently, the value of the yen has risen while the value of the dollar has fallen, which has raised prices paid for foreign goods and services.

Governments protect themselves by regulating imports and exports through various strategies. Tariffs, for example, are imposed on foreign goods to restrict imports. Quotas that limit imports are also imposed to protect domestic producers. Nations establish embargoes to restrict firms or industries from operating in their countries, and nations also create sanctions that bar a country from selling certain items to other countries. On the other hand, treaties such as the European Community treaty and the North American Free Trade Agreement are developed with one or more countries to resolve problems.

Firms sell to other nations to improve their earnings. Help is available from state and federal governments as well as from banks and private agencies. Career opportunities are quite good for those who wish to work in international business. Multinational firms, some banks, and numerous federal agencies are sources for finding employment. Managers and others seeking international opportunities should prepare themselves to live and work in other countries.

Forms of Business Ownership and the Law

"The new information society has created new markets and new business opportunities. And in this new environment, individual entrepreneurs hold a key advantage over corporations: They can act faster. Entrepreneurs can respond to rapid technological change without wading through layers of bureaucracy."

John Naisbitt
Patricia Aburdene
RE-INVENTING THE CORPORATION, 1986

OBJECTIVES

2-1 Identify the characteristics of entrepreneurs and the process to follow when starting a business.

2-2 Discuss the advantages and disadvantages of sole proprietorships and partnerships.

2-3 List the basic features and pros and cons of the corporate form of business ownership.

2-4 Distinguish among several specialized forms of business organizations.

2-5 Describe how business is both protected and regulated by government.

2-6 Discuss reasons for taxes, types of taxes, and the effect taxes have on business decisions.

Professional Profile

A LEADER IN BUSINESS DEVELOPMENT

Managing one company is a significant challenge. Leading two major companies while providing ongoing help to thousands of other business owners requires special abilities. Over the years Earl G. Graves, President and Chief Executive Officer of the company that publishes *Black Enterprise* Magazine and of Pepsi-Cola of Washington, D.C., has demonstrated his talents as a successful entrepreneur and business owner.

Earl Graves has published *Black Enterprise* magazine for over 25 years. The magazine is an important source of business, technical, and career information for African American business owners and managers. In addition, many people who are considering starting their own businesses or entering business careers look to *Black Enterprise* for guidance and for role models. The magazine profiles entrepreneurs and executives each month. Readership of each issue totals more than 2 million people.

With former basketball star Earvin "Magic" Johnson, Mr. Graves purchased a Washington, D.C., Pepsi-Cola franchise in 1990. His organization is the largest minority-controlled Pepsi-Cola franchise in the United States, ranking among the top 20 of all U. S. black-owned businesses.

Mr. Graves graduated from Morgan State University in Baltimore, MD, and completed a distinguished military career as a captain in the Special Forces unit of the Green Berets. He is active in community service and business organizations and serves on the board of directors of many corporations. Mr. Graves is a model for his belief that you should "give back" to your community and aid in its improvement. His outstanding record of awards includes the Dow Jones & Company award for entrepreneurial excellence, the Free Enterprise Award of the International Franchise Association, and the highest award for volunteer service from the Boy Scouts of America.

Earl G. Graves, President and Chief Executive Officer, Black Enterprise Magazine

INSPIRATIONAL IDEAS

"You are your own limitation. Enjoy yourself. Love what you do. When you make mistakes—and surely you will—learn from them and move forward. Envision yourself doing what it is you want to do and being the person you want to be."

Photo courtesy of Earl G. Graves, Ltd.

PROPRIETORSHIPS AND PARTNERSHIPS

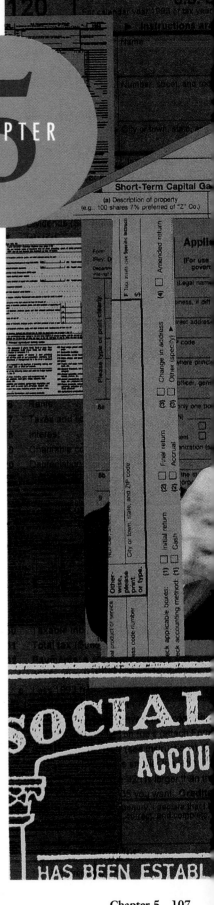

After studying this chapter you will be able to:

5-1 Describe characteristics of successful entrepreneurs.

5-2 Outline responsibilities of owning your own business.

5-3 List advantages and disadvantages of proprietorships.

5-4 List advantages and disadvantages of partnerships.

5-5 Describe legal points to consider when selecting a name for a business.

Maria Maldonado wondered about the rest of her life as she sat on the step outside the town's library. Was she too young to even consider starting her own business? Was the whole idea of opening a small corner grocery store absurd for a nineteen-year old? "My father would be proud if he knew that I was thinking of investing some of the money he left me for opening a neighborhood store," she muttered to herself. "If he were only here to show me what to do. Fortunately, the library has plenty of books on how to get started."

Maria continued thinking to herself. "I've learned plenty during the last several weeks reading and talking with my neighbor who runs the local Taco Bell fast food business. Working as a stock clerk and cashier in the Grand Union while in high school also gave me experience. Yet, there is so much I don't know. I never hired anyone or kept the books. But the idea is so exciting. Will people stop at . . . Maria's Market . . . to buy those groceries that people so often run out of but don't want to drive across town to the supermarket to get?" Maria got up to reenter the library. "Did I just name my store?" she said, smiling to herself.

Many people have dreamed about owning their own businesses. The idea may have crossed your mind, too. These dreams often start as simple ideas. Some of the dreamers with practical ideas do form businesses. That is how many well-known founders of large businesses got started.

Most businesses begin with one owner. But some firms start with two or more owners. One person, or a group of people, invest in a business with the hope of becoming successful owners. This chapter will examine the basic elements, advantages, and disadvantages of starting a business alone or with others.

CHARACTERISTICS OF ENTREPRENEURS

You learned earlier that an entrepreneur is a person who assumes the risk of starting and operating a business for the purpose of making a profit. Although individuals form businesses to earn a profit by providing consumers with a desired product or service, months and years of hard work are often needed before a profit is earned. About half of all new businesses fail within the first five to six years. Failures are often for financial reasons, but many closings of young firms occur because the owners are not well-suited to be entrepreneurs. But while successful entrepreneurs are all uniquely different, they also have some common personal characteristics.

Some people would rather work for others, while other people prefer to work for themselves. Entrepreneurs who prefer self-employment enjoy the freedom and independence that come from being their own bosses and from making their own decisions. Even when their businesses are not immediately successful, they do not give up. In fact, some entrepreneurs who are eventually successful often experienced unsuccessful business start-ups. However, they learned from their mistakes and started over.

Entrepreneurs are self-starters who have plenty of energy and enjoy working on their own. They like to take charge of situations and usually work hard and for long periods in order to meet their goals. Entrepreneurs are also good thinkers, often coming up with new ideas and new ways to solve problems. Most successful small business owners like people and people like them. As a result, they are often community leaders.

Successful entrepreneurs have other common characteristics. Generally, they obtain work experience in the types of businesses they launch. The person who starts a computer store, for example, will usually have taken some computer courses and will have worked for a business that makes, sells, or services computers. In addition to appropriate work experience, successful business owners are also well-informed about financial, marketing, and legal matters.

There is no magic age for starting a business. Teenagers, parents of teenagers, and retirees have all started successful businesses. In recent years, increasing numbers of women, Asian-Americans, Hispanics, and African-

Illus. 5-1
Well-known entrepreneurs—Walt
Disney, creator of Disney World; and
Steven P. Jobs, one of the founders of
Apple Computer Inc. What did these
two entrepreneurs accomplish since
starting their businesses?

S.S./SHOOTING STAR   *Photo courtesy of NeXT, Inc.*

Americans of all ages have opened their own firms. To start your own business, you need adequate funds, a general knowledge about business, some work experience, and a business opportunity.

One of the very first things a budding business owner must decide upon is the legal form of ownership. The form of ownership selected depends on several factors, such as the nature and size of the business, the capital needed, the tax laws, and the financial responsibility the owner is willing to assume. Two legal forms of business ownership—the proprietorship and the partnership—are presented in this chapter. Also presented in this chapter is the selection of a legal name for a business. But first, it is important to investigate the challenging responsibilities that entrepreneurs face.

GETTING A BUSINESS STARTED

The decision to enter business is not an easy one to make. The tasks to be performed are many. A single owner has more responsibilities than an ordinary employee. Assume, for example, that you are employed as a delivery person. Your duties include making pickups and deliveries. After obtaining several years of valuable work experience, you decide to start your own delivery service. You need to create a plan and to develop an awareness of your responsibilities as the owner of a business.

PREPARE A BUSINESS PLAN

Before starting a business, you need to prepare a business plan. A **business plan** is a written guide that helps the entrepreneur during the design and startup phases of the business. The business plan requires a great deal of careful thought. Most plans include those items shown in Fig. 5-1.

Fig. 5-1

Elements of a business plan.

NATURE OF THE BUSINESS

- Detailed description of products and/or services
- Estimation of risk based on analysis of the industry
- Size of business
- Location of business
- Background of entrepreneur(s)

GOALS AND OBJECTIVES

- Basic results expected in the short and long run
- Results expressed in terms of sales volume or profits

MARKETING PLAN

- Customers and their demand for the product or service
- Prices for the product or service
- Comparison of product or service with competitors

FINANCIAL PLAN

- Investment needed to start and maintain the business
- Projected income, expenses, and profit
- Cash start-up and cash flow needs

ORGANIZATIONAL PLAN

- Legal form of ownership
- Legal factors—licenses, leases, contracts
- Organization chart
- Job descriptions and employee skills needed
- Physical facilities—buildings, equipment, tools

A well-developed business plan helps you decide whether you should assume the risks of starting your business. It also generates the confidence needed to start a business. Others with whom you deal will also have confidence in your ability to succeed if you have a well-designed plan. Bankers, for instance, will ask to see your plan if you wish to borrow startup funds. They will have greater assurance when they see how carefully you have considered potential problems and solutions before launching your new enterprise. Equally important will be your own conviction that your business will thrive.

ASSUME THE RESPONSIBILITIES OF BUSINESS OWNERSHIP

By developing an excellent business plan, entrepreneurs become aware of their risks. As a result, they may be able to anticipate problems and take preventive action. The business plan also causes the aspiring business owner to become more realistic about the responsibilities of ownership.

As the owner of your new delivery service, your duties not only include pickups and deliveries, but also include many other duties. Even if you run the business from your home, you will have added expenses for an office, a garage, an answering machine, or perhaps a telephone answering service. You must find customers, persuade those customers to pay a fair price for your services, and collect from those customers. Furthermore, you must assume responsibility for damage that may occur to your merchandise. Fees for various licenses, taxes, insurance premiums, gasoline, van repairs, and other operating expenses must be paid. Additionally, it may be necessary to hire, train, and supervise employees.

Ownership responsibilities cannot be overlooked when one considers opening a business. These responsibilities may be seen as disadvantages by some people, but as advantages by others. People who enjoy being leaders and also enjoy making decisions find great satisfaction in owning a business. Opportunities to make decisions and to experience other rewards are found in business ownership. Some of these rewards will be identified in the section that follows.

P ROPRIETORSHIP

The most common form of business organization is the proprietorship, of which there are over 13 million in this country. A business owned and managed by one person is known as a **sole proprietorship**, or a **proprietorship**, and the owner-manager is the **proprietor**. In addition to owning and managing the business, the proprietor often performs those day-to-day tasks that make a business successful. Under the proprietorship form of organization, the owner furnishes money, management, and perhaps part of the labor. For assuming these responsibilities, the owner is entitled to all profits earned by the business.

Provided that no debts are owed, a proprietor has full claim to the *assets*—property owned by the business. If the proprietor has business debts, however, **creditors** (those to whom money is owed) have first claim against the assets. Fig. 5-2 presents a simple financial statement of Jennifer York, who is the proprietor of a small retail grocery store and fruit market.

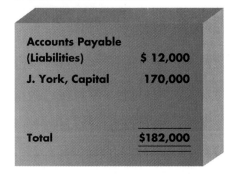

ASSETS

Cash	$ 14,800
Merchandise	26,400
Equipment	20,800
Land and Building	120,000
Total	$182,000

CLAIMS AGAINST ASSETS

Accounts Payable (Liabilities)	$ 12,000
J. York, Capital	170,000
Total	$182,000

Fig. 5-2
Jennifer York's balance sheet.

This simple financial statement, known as a *statement of financial position,* or *balance sheet,* shows that the assets of the business are valued at $182,000. Since York has *liabilities,* money owed by a business, amounting to $12,000, the balance sheet shows her capital as $170,000 ($182,000 – $12,000).

In accounting, the terms *capital, net worth,* and *equity* are interchangeable and are defined as assets less liabilities. If there are profits, York gets the total amount. She must also absorb losses. Since she owns the land and the building, she does not have to pay rent, although she must pay the cost of maintenance and taxes for the property.

ADVANTAGES OF PROPRIETORSHIPS

The fact that almost three out of four businesses are proprietorships indicates that this form of organization has definite advantages. Can you list any of the advantages before reading further?

Owner Is Boss

When a person is the only owner of a business, a great deal of pride and satisfaction exist in being one's own boss and being responsible only to oneself. The proprietor feels there is a better chance to be inventive and creative in working out ideas. This feeling stimulates the owner to work hard to make the business a success.

Owner Receives All Profits

Very closely related to this first advantage is the fact that all the profits belong to the sole proprietor. As a result, the owner is more likely to work overtime and to think continually of how the business can operate more efficiently.

Owner Personally Knows Employees and Customers

Because most proprietorships are small, the proprietor and the employees know one another personally. This relationship can lead to mutual understanding and interest between employer and employees. These same benefits should also result from the close ties that the proprietor has with customers.

Owner Can Act Quickly in Decision Making

The sole proprietor is not blocked in making decisions. As there is no need to consult others, the owner can act promptly when the need arises. If an unusual opportunity to buy merchandise or equipment occurs, or if the owner wishes to change the location of the business or to sell on credit terms rather than on a cash basis, there are no dissenting partners to stop such action. Thus, the management of a proprietorship is flexible and can adjust itself rapidly to changing conditions.

Owner Is Free from Red Tape

A sole proprietor can usually begin or end business activities without legal formality. It is not usually legally necessary to go through a large amount of red tape in order to organize a proprietorship. In some types of businesses, however, such as a restaurant, it is necessary to obtain a license before operations can begin.

Owner Usually Pays Less Income Tax than a Corporation

In most sole proprietorships, the income tax is usually less than in the corporation type of business, which is explained in the next chapter.

DISADVANTAGES OF PROPRIETORSHIPS

There are many advantages to owning your own business. However, there are also some disadvantages facing the sole proprietor.

Owner May Lack Special Skills and Abilities

Each person usually has a special aptitude or ability. One person may be able to sell merchandise. Another person may be more talented at purchasing goods or keeping records. Still a third person may have the ability to supervise employees. All of these activities are important to the success of a business, but the proprietor is likely to be weak in one or more areas. It is, therefore, easy to understand why many proprietorships end in failure within a short time.

Owner May Lack Funds

Additional funds (capital) are often needed for emergencies. Financial assistance on a large scale may be difficult to obtain by a single owner. Therefore, the expansion of the business may be slowed because of the owner's lack of capital.

Owner Bears All Losses

A proprietor assumes a great deal of risk. It is true that a sole owner receives all the profits of the business; but, too, a sole owner bears all the losses if the business fails. Should this happen and the owner is unable to pay the debts of the business, the creditors have a claim against any assets of the owner. The owner may therefore lose not only the money invested in the enterprise but also personal possessions such as a car or home.

Illness or Death May Close the Business

It is possible that the owner of a business could become ill. If the illness lasts for a long time or results in death, the business would have to close.

BUSINESSES SUITED TO BEING PROPRIETORSHIPS

The kind of business that is primarily concerned with providing personal services is well-suited to the proprietorship form of organization. Dentists, accountants, auctioneers, landscape gardeners, carpenters, painters, tourist camps, barbers, beauty salons, shoe repair shops, and television and appliance service centers are examples of businesses frequently organized as proprietorships.

Another type of business that seems to be well adapted to the proprietorship form of business is the one that sells merchandise or services on a small scale. Newspaper and magazine stands, roadside markets, fast food and family restaurants, flower shops, gasoline stations, small grocery stores, fish markets, clothing stores, parking lots, and dry cleaners are examples. In general, the type of business that can be operated suitably as a proprietorship is one that (a) can be managed by the proprietor or by persons hired by the proprietor, and (b) does not require a great amount of capital.

PARTNERSHIP

Jennifer York, who operates the proprietorship mentioned earlier, is faced with the problem of expanding her business. She is now 33 years old and has operated the business successfully for over ten years. She sees new opportunities in the community for increasing her business, but she does not wish to assume full responsibility for the undertaking. She realizes that the expansion of the business will place on her considerable financial and managerial responsibilities. She also realizes that in order to expand the business she needs additional capital, but she does not wish to borrow the money. Because of these reasons, she has decided that it will be wise to change her business from a proprietorship to a **partnership**, a business owned by two or more persons.

Robert Burton operates an adjoining bakery where he bakes fresh bread and pastries daily. He is younger than Jennifer York and has proved to be honest and to have considerable business ability. Combining the two businesses could result in more customers for both groceries and fresh baked goods. Customers who have been coming to the bake shop will possibly become grocery customers also. And those who have been buying at the grocery and fruit market may become customers of bakery products. A discussion between Jennifer and

Illus. 5-2

Well-known partners in American business: Ben Cohen and Jerry Greenfield (Ben and Jerry's Homemade, Inc.). Can you name another national or local business that was started as a partnership?

Photo courtesy of Ben & Jerry's Homemade, Inc.

Robert leads to a tentative agreement to form a partnership if a third person can be found who will invest enough cash to remodel both stores to form one large store and to purchase additional equipment. The financial statement of Burton's business is shown in Fig. 5-3.

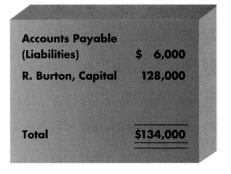

ASSETS

Cash	$ 8,800
Merchandise	3,000
Equipment	22,200
Land and Building	100,000
Total	$134,000

CLAIMS AGAINST ASSETS

Accounts Payable (Liabilities)	$ 6,000
R. Burton, Capital	128,000
Total	$134,000

Fig. 5-3
Balance sheet for Robert Burton.

The net worth of Burton's business is $128,000. In other words, after deducting the amount of his liabilities ($6,000) from the total value of his assets ($134,000), he has a net worth of $128,000. According to Jennifer York's balance sheet in Fig. 5-2, her business is worth $170,000. In order to have an equal investment in the partnership, Burton must invest an additional $42,000 in cash.

They find Lu Chan, a person with accounting experience, who has $120,000 and is able to borrow the remaining $50,000 to become an equal partner. The partnership agreement, shown in Fig. 5-6 on page 117, is then written and signed by York, Burton, and Chan.

Jeff Greenberg, Photographer

Illus. 5-3
A partnership agreement needs the signatures of all the partners. Why do you think the signing of such an agreement would be considered important?

Once the partnership is formed, a statement of financial position (balance sheet) must be prepared. This statement shows the total assets, liabilities, and capital of the owners at the start of the business. The partnership's balance sheet is shown in Fig. 5-4.

ig. 5-4

Balance sheet for York, Burton, and Chan at startup.

ASSETS		CLAIMS AGAINST ASSETS	
Cash	$235,600	Accounts Payable (Liabilities)	$ 18,000
Merchandise	29,400	J. York, Capital	170,000
Equipment	43,000	R. Burton, Capital	170,000
Land and Building	220,000	L. Chan, Capital	170,000
Total	$528,000	Total	$528,000

In operating the partnership, York, Burton, and Chan divide the responsibilities. York supervises the grocery department, Burton supervises the bake shop and meat department, and Chan handles the finances, inventory, and records.

During the year the three partners combine the stores, remodel them, and buy new equipment. The financial statement at the end of the year, shown in Fig. 5-5, is prepared to display the status of the partnership.

ig. 5-5

York, Burton, and Chan's balance sheet at year's end.

ASSETS		CLAIMS AGAINST ASSETS	
Cash	$ 48,000	Accounts Payable (Liabilities)	$ 16,000
Merchandise	93,000	J. York, Capital	188,000
Equipment	93,000	R. Burton, Capital	188,000
Land and Building	346,000	L. Chan, Capital	188,000
Total	$580,000	Total	$580,000

Has the partnership had a successful year? Each partner has received a salary of $4,000 a month (according to the terms of the partnership agreement); in addition, the capital or net worth of each partner has increased from $170,000 to $188,000 as a result of profits made during the year. This increase in the total capital from $510,000 ($170,000 × 3) to $564,000 ($188,000 × 3) amounts to $54,000 and is an increase of over 9 percent. Chan, who borrowed some of the money for his investment, had to pay 8 percent interest. His investment in the partnership brought him a return that is more than the interest on his loan.

ADVANTAGES OF PARTNERSHIPS

Many businesses are organized as partnerships at the very beginning. Fig. 5-6 shows a partnership agreement. There are over 1.5 million businesses operating as partnerships in the United States. While most partnerships have only two or three partners, there is no limit set on the number of partners. Some businesses have as many as ten or more partners. Some of the advantages of partnerships are discussed on the next two pages.

Partnership Agreement

Fig. 5-6

A clearly written and understood partnership agreement can prevent problems later.

This contract, made and entered into on the first day of June, 19-- by and between Jennifer L. York, of Buffalo, New York, party of the first part, Robert R. Burton, of Buffalo, New York, party of the second part, Lu Chan of Niagara Falls, New York, party of the third part:

Witnesseth: That the said parties have this day formed a partnership for the purpose of engaging in and conducting a retail grocery-fruit-meat market and bakery under the following stipulations, which are made a part of the contract:

First: The said partnership is to continue for a term of ten years from date hereof.

Second: The business shall be conducted under the firm name of Y, B, & C Fine Foods, at 4467 Goodson Street, Buffalo, New York.

Third: The investments are as follows: Jennifer L. York: Cash, $14,800; Merchandise, $26,400; Equipment, $20,800; Land and Building, $120,000; Total Assets, $182,000, less Accounts Payable, $12,000, equals Net Investment, $170,000. Robert R. Burton: Cash, $50,800; Merchandise, $3,000; Equipment, $22,200; Land and Building, $100,000; Total Assets, $176,000, less Accounts Payable, $6,000, equals Net Investment, $170,000. Lu Chan: Cash, $170,000.

Fourth: All profits or losses arising from said business are to be shared equally.

Fifth: Each partner is to devote his or her entire time and attention to the business and to engage in no other business enterprise without the written consent of the others.

Sixth: Each partner is to have a salary of $4,000 a month, the same to be withdrawn at such time as he or she may elect. No partner is to withdraw from the business an amount in excess of his or her salary without the written consent of the others.

Seventh: The duties of each partner are defined as follows: Jennifer L. York is to supervise the grocery-fruit-vegetable departments. Robert R. Burton is to supervise the bakery and meat departments. Lu Chan is to manage finances, inventory, and records.

Eighth: No partner is to become surety for anyone without the written consent of the others.

Ninth: In case of the death, incapacity, or withdrawal of one partner, the business is to be conducted for the remainder of the fiscal year by the surviving partners, the profits for the year allocated to the withdrawing partner to be determined by the ratio of the time he or she was a partner during the year to the whole year.

Tenth: In case of dissolution the assets are to be divided in the ratio of the capital invested at the time of dissolution.

In Witness Whereof, the parties aforesaid have hereunto set their hands and affixed their seals on the day and year above written.

In the presence of: .... (Seal)

.... (Seal)

.... (Seal)

Skills and Abilities Pooled

A partnership is likely to be operated more efficiently than a proprietorship because two or more persons share management duties. One partner may have special sales ability; another may have an aptitude for buying the right kind, quality, and quantity of merchandise. One partner may propose a change in the business, and another partner may be able to point out disadvantages in the plan and suggest changes that were not apparent to the partner who made the original proposal. The combined abilities of the partners should result in a more efficient operation than would be the case if each were conducting a business as a sole proprietor.

Sources of Capital Increased

When a business is started, more capital can be supplied through the investments of two or more people than can ordinarily be obtained by one person. Some business firms require a greater amount of capital for equipment and merchandise than one person may be able to supply; but enough beginning capital can be obtained if several persons enter into a partnership. Generally, the additional capital needed for expansion is obtained more easily if there are several partners.

Credit Position Improved

The partnership usually has a better credit reputation than the sole proprietorship. This is usually true because more than one owner is responsible for the ownership and management of the business.

Contribution of Goodwill

Each partner is likely to have a large personal following. Some people will be more likely to do business with the newly formed partnership because they know one of the owners. This is known as goodwill.

Increased Concern in Business Management

Each owner of the business will have a greater interest in the firm as partners than as employees. Much of this is due to the greater financial responsibility each person has as a partner.

Less Tax Burden than Corporations

Partnerships usually have a tax advantage over corporations. You will learn more about this in Chapter 6. Partnerships prepare a federal income tax report but do not pay a tax on their profits as do corporations. However, partners must pay a personal income tax on their individual share of the profit.

Elimination of Competition

Two or more proprietors in the same line of business may become one organization by forming a partnership. This move may substantially decrease, or even eliminate, competition.

Retirement from Management

A sole proprietor may wish to retire. However, the proprietor may not want to close the business. In such a case, the owner may form a partnership and allow the new owner to manage the business.

Operating Economies

It is often possible to operate more efficiently by combining two or more business firms. By combining firms it is possible to reduce certain operating expenses, such as advertising, supplies, equipment, fuel, and rent.

Jeff Greenberg, Photographer

Illus. 5-4

A ribbon-cutting ceremony often accompanies the opening of a new business. Have you ever attended a ribbon-cutting ceremony? What impressions did you have of the event?

DISADVANTAGES OF PARTNERSHIPS

While there are many advantages of partnerships, there are also disadvantages. The following discussion points out some of the disadvantages of the partnership form of business organization.

Unlimited Financial Liability

According to law, each member of the partnership has an **unlimited financial liability** for all the debts of the business. Partners are responsible for their share of the business debts. But, if some of the partners are unable to pay their share, one partner may have to pay all the debts.

Management Close-Up

BEN AND JERRY'S HOMEMADE, INC.

Questions:

1 At the outset, was Ben and Jerry's business typical for a new business? Give reasons for your answer.

2 Why did Ben and Jerry want to remain a small firm?

3 Did the value of employees decline as the firm got larger?

4 If the lowest-paid employee earned $15,000 a year, what would the maximum salary be for the highest-paid manager? What reason would you give for this high-level manager to be unhappy with this rule?

On May 5, 1978, Ben Cohen and Jerry Greenfield formed a partnership to open an ice cream parlor in a renovated gas station in Burlington, Vermont. The two former seventh grade buddies, who used top-quality ingredients, were delighted by their early success. Yet, to survive in those initial days they needed to improve sales to cover expenses that included repair to that old ice cream truck that kept breaking down.

With the rapid growth that followed came a major concern. Both were afraid of getting too large and losing the rewards of working alongside employees when making and experimenting with new products. Job enjoyment satisfied them more than profits. And they had both during the early years when the firm was small.

Their fears of growth became a reality when the firm got big enough to make Ben and Jerry feel as if they were losing control. In fact, they tried to resist further expansion but knew the business either had to grow or fade away. Jerry decided to retire, and Ben later decided to put the company up for sale. It wasn't fun anymore. Another entrepreneur, however, convinced Ben that he could still live his dream of serving employees and the public while continuing to expand. Jerry returned to join Ben in building a bigger business that could support the two goals.

Ben and Jerry's has grown to about four hundred employees and produces enough flavors to satisfy the taste buds of millions of customers. The company makes, distributes, and sells super-premium ice cream and low-fat frozen yogurt to supermarkets, restaurants, and over ninety franchised and company outlets in 47 states. Sales now exceed $140 million yearly as they expand into foreign countries.

While the business continues to grow, Ben and Jerry continue to remain committed to their employees. National recognition has been received for developing a proud and productive workforce. The emphasis given workers is reflected in the "7 to 1" rule that prevents any employee—including managers—from earning more than seven times what the lowest-paid employee earns. Recently, however, the 7 to 1 rule made the pay of top executives too low to attract qualified candidates. As a result, the rule became flexible.

Their social responsibility goal is met in many ways. For example, there is a Ben and Jerry's franchise in Harlem, New York, that earmarks profits to help the homeless. Donations to charities, art, and public musical concerts are common. Many other social causes have been strongly supported. Ben and Jerry—an unusual pair of innovative partners—have created a unique style of doing business.

Source: Adapted from company reports and Eric Larson, "Forever Young," *Inc.,* July 1988, pp. 50-62.

Suppose that the partnership of York, Burton, and Chan should fail and that, after all the business assets have been changed into cash, the amount due the creditors of the partnership is $18,000 more than the amount of available cash. Each partner should contribute $6,000 ($18,000 ÷ 3) to the partnership so that there will be enough money to pay the remaining business debts. The creditors, however, may choose to enforce their claims only against York because she may own more property outside the partnership than the other two partners. If York pays the entire $18,000, she then has a $6,000 claim against each of the other two partners.

Disagreement Among Partners

There is always danger of disagreement among partners. The majority of the partners may want to change the nature of the business but are unable to do so because of the refusal of one partner. For example, a partnership may have been formed for the purpose of conducting a retail audio gear business selling sound receivers, speakers, tape decks, and compact disc players. After a while, the majority of the partners may think it wise to stop selling audio gear and handle small home appliances instead. The change may be highly desirable. However, as long as one partner disagrees, the partnership cannot make the change. Furthermore, partners sometimes feel that they are not properly sharing in the management. This situation may cause disagreements that could hurt the business. Such a condition may be partly prevented if the partnership agreement states the duties of each partner.

Each Partner Bound by Contracts of Others

Each partner is bound by the partnership contracts made by any partner if such contracts apply to the ordinary operations of the business. There is always the possibility of friction and ill will between partners if one partner makes a contract that turns out to be unprofitable to the partnership.

Uncertain Life

The life of a partnership is uncertain. Sometimes when the contract for a partnership is drawn up, a definite length of time, such as ten years, is fixed for the existence of the business. Should one partner die, however, the partnership ends. The deceased partner may have been the principal manager, and, as a result of his or her death, the business may suffer. The heirs of the deceased partner may demand an unfair price from the surviving partners for the share of the deceased partner. Or the heirs may insist upon ending the partnership quickly to obtain the share belonging to the dead partner. In the latter case, the assets that are sold usually do not bring a fair price, and, as a result, all the partners suffer a loss. (Insurance on the life of a partner can be carried to provide money to purchase the interest of a partner who dies.) Under the laws of most states, the bankruptcy of any partner or the entrance of a new partner are other causes that may bring a sudden end to the partnership. To make matters worse, this type of situation could occur just at a time when the business is beginning to do well.

Limited Sources of Capital

The amount of funds that a partnership may obtain is limited by the contributions of the partners, the earnings of the business, and the money that can be borrowed. It is difficult for a partnership to obtain enough capital to operate a large business unless each member of the partnership is wealthy or unless there are many partners. Too many partners, however, may be the cause of inefficient operations.

Unsatisfactory Division of Profits

Sometimes there is not a satisfactory distribution of the partnership profits according to the ability and efforts of the individual partners. The profits are shared on the basis of the partnership agreement, such as 60 percent to one partner and 40 percent to the other. If no provision is made in the agreement, the law requires an equal division of the profits.

Difficulty in Withdrawing from Partnership

If a partner wishes to sell his or her interest in a business, it may be difficult to do. Even if a buyer is found, the buyer may not be acceptable to the other partners.

LIMITED PARTNERSHIPS

In an ordinary (general) partnership, each partner is personally liable for all the debts contracted by the partnership. The laws of some states, however, permit the formation of a **limited partnership**, which restricts the liability of a partner for the amount of the partner's investment. When this situation occurs, not all partners have unlimited financial liability for the partnership debts. However, at least one partner must be a general partner who has unlimited liability. In many states, the name of a limited partner may not be included in the firm name.

Usually the law requires that a certificate of limited partnership be filed in a public office of record and that proper notice be given to each creditor with whom the limited partnership does business. If these requirements are not fulfilled, the limited partners have unlimited liability in the same manner as a general partner.

The limited partnership is a useful form of business organization in situations where one person wishes to invest in a business but does not have the time or interest to participate actively in its management. Any business that is formed as a proprietorship can usually be formed as a limited partnership.

BUSINESSES SUITED TO BEING PARTNERSHIPS

The partnership form of organization is found in many businesses that furnish more than one kind of product or service. Each partner usually looks after a specialized phase of the business. For example, car dealers often have sales and service departments. One partner may handle the sale of new cars, and another partner may be in charge of servicing and repairing cars. Still another partner could be in charge of used car sales or of the accounting and financial side of the business. Similarly, if a business operates in more than one location, each partner can be in charge of a specific location. Businesses that operate longer than the usual eight hours a day, such as the retail food business advertised in Fig. 5-7, find the partnership organization desirable. Each partner can be in charge for part of the day.

Partnerships are often found in the same types of businesses that are formed as proprietorships, particularly in selling goods and services to consumers. Good faith, together with reasonable care in the exercise of management duties, is required of all partners in a business.

Fig. 5-7

An advertisement used to announce the opening of the Y, B, and C partnership.

BUSINESS NAME

A proprietorship or a partnership may be conducted under the name or names of the owner or owners. In many states, the law prohibits the use of *and Company* or *& Co.* unless such identification indicates additional partners. For example, if there are only two partners, it is not permissible to use a firm name such as Jones, Smith & Co., for that name indicates at least three partners. The name or names comprised in the term "company" must be identified by registration at a public recording office, usually the county clerk's office. Usually one can do business under a trade, or artificial name, such as The Superior

Shoe Store or W-W Manufacturing Company. Likewise, proper registration is usually required in order that creditors may know the person or persons responsible for the business. Operating under a trade name, therefore, does not reduce the owner's liability to creditors.

CHAPTER 5 REVIEW

BUILDING VOCABULARY POWER

Define the following terms and concepts.

1. business plan
2. sole proprietorship (proprietorship)
3. proprietor
4. creditors
5. partnership
6. unlimited financial liability
7. limited partnership

REVIEWING FACTS

1. What are two common legal forms of business ownership?
2. How will a good business plan help someone who plans to open a new business?
3. What types of people enjoy the responsibilities of business ownership?
4. List the major advantages of proprietorships.
5. List the major disadvantages of proprietorships.
6. Which kinds of businesses are most suited to the proprietorship form of business?
7. List the major advantages of partnerships.
8. List the major disadvantages of partnerships.
9. Under what types of situations is a limited partnership useful?
10. Why is it necessary for proprietorships and partnerships to register their company names with local authorities?

DISCUSSING IDEAS

1. Your friend followed your advice and made a business plan to create a new business called Crunchy Cookies. You noticed she did not include a marketing plan and you mention it. She then says: "Everyone likes cookies. My prices depend on how much it costs to make each type of cookie. And there isn't a cookie store within three blocks of where I plan to locate my

business. How could I go wrong?" List questions that should appear in the marketing plan that would make your friend give more thought to her decision.

2. You have been working part-time and summers at a local service station during your school years. You have performed just about every major task from pumping gas to repairing cars and even handling some of the bookkeeping. Discuss how your responsibilities as an employee will change if you become the owner of the station.

3. The sole proprietor is not hindered by partners when making decisions. What disadvantages could result from not having partners help in the decision-making process?

4. If a proprietorship needs additional capital but the owner cannot furnish it from personal funds, from what sources might capital be secured?

5. Why is it a good plan to include in a partnership agreement a clause such as the fifth clause shown in Fig. 5-6?

6. Why is it a good plan to include in a partnership agreement a clause such as the seventh clause shown in Fig. 5-6?

7. Why should a partnership agreement be in writing?

8. A partner signed a partnership contract for television advertising while the other two partners were on vacation. Upon returning, the vacationing partners claimed that the partnership was not bound to the contract because both of them disapproved of television advertising. Was the partnership legally bound?

9. What effect is there on the life of a partnership when (a) a partner dies, (b) a partner quits, and (c) a new partner is added?

10. Why are proprietorships much more popular than partnerships?

ANALYZING INFORMATION

1. Assume you are planning to open a business of your own by using your home computer to prepare designs and slogans that can be printed and ironed on T-shirts. You already have the computer but need a few other items. What you are not sure about is whether you really want to start such a business. To help you decide, make two columns on a sheet of paper: Why I *Would* Like Running My Own Business and Why I *Would Not* Like Running My Own Business. Fill in all your reasons. When you finish, study the two lists and write a paragraph indicating whether you have the essential characteristics of a successful business owner.

2. Adams invested $40,000 and Cook invested $30,000 in their partnership business. They share profits and losses in proportion to their investments. What amount should each receive of the $16,800 profit earned last year?

3. Carlton and Baker had invested equal amounts in a partnership business. Later the business failed with $40,000 in liabilities (debts) and only

$15,000 in assets (property). In addition to a share of the assets of the business, Baker had $35,000 of other personal property at the time of the failure, but Carlton had only $5,000 of additional personal property. Other than the partnership property, what amount will be required of each partner to pay the debts of the partnership?

4. Juan Delgado plans to go into business for himself. He wants to own a men's clothing store. He believes that he has adequate experience in this area, having managed a clothing department in a large local department store for several years. Juan thinks that he has sufficient capital, but it may be a little tight financially getting through the first year of operation.

    Cristina Mentor, a long-time friend of Juan's, is also planning to open a business. Her women's clothing store will be located next to Juan's in the same busy shopping area. Although Cristina has almost no experience in the clothing business, she did work part-time one summer in a fashion shop. And now she has a degree in finance from the local university. Her uncle is willing to lend her the money needed to start the business.

    Both Cristina and Juan have learned of each other's plans. The idea of forming a partnership has been mentioned, but they are not quite sure what to do. Form a committee of three to five students in order to (a) discuss the situation, and then (b) prepare a summary of your committee's recommendations to the two people involved.

5. Assume that the balance sheet of the partnership of Davis and Miller at the time they closed the business appeared as follows:

Assets

Cash	$ 9,000
Merchandise	20,000
Fixtures and Equipment	12,000
Land and Building	54,000
Total	$95,000

Claims Against Assets

Accounts Payable (Liabilities)	$ 5,000
B. S. Davis, Capital	45,000
T. C. Miller, Capital	45,000
Total	$95,000

When selling the assets, the merchandise was sold for $16,000, the fixtures for $9,000, and the land and building for $55,000. After paying their debts, what amount of the remaining cash should each partner receive?

REVIEW 5

Solving Business Problems

Case 5-1

John Willis, who is 27 and single, had just completed his fifth year of employment as a carpenter for a very small home builder. His boss, the sole owner of the company, is Ed Young. A few days ago, Ed asked John if he would like to become a partner, which he could do by contributing $70,000. In turn, John would receive 40 percent of all profits earned by the business. John had saved $30,000 and could borrow the balance needed from his grandmother at a low interest rate, but he would have to pay her back within 15 years.

John was undecided about becoming a partner. He liked the idea but he also knew there were risks and concerns. To help him make up his mind, he decided to talk to Ed at lunch. Here is how the conversation went.

John: I have been giving your offer a lot of thought, Ed. It is a tough decision, and I do not want to make the wrong one. So I would like to chat with you about some of the problems involved in running a business.

Ed: Sure. I struggled with the same problem about 15 years ago. When you own your own business, you are the boss. No one can tell you what to do or push you around. You can set up your own hours and make all the decisions. I enjoy the feeling of ownership.

John: I do not know if I am ready to become part owner of a business. I am still young and single, and I like working for you. I am not sure I want all those responsibilities—getting customers, paying bills, and buying tools and lumber. You say you set your own hours, but I know you are already working when I arrive each morning, and you are still here when I leave in the evening. I know you spend some nights in the office, because I see the lights on when I drive by.

Ed: Well, I do put in many hours. That goes with the territory. But I don't mind all those hours because I like making decisions. And, when you join me as a partner, we will share the work.

John: Then I will be working longer hours. Both of us could go to work for that big new contracting firm on the other side of town. They could struggle with all the problems and decisions. Then we could work shorter hours and have more time to relax.

Required:
1. Do you think John is seriously ready to become a partner? Explain your answer.
2. If you were in John's position, how would you decide? Explain.
3. If John decides to accept Ed's offer, what action should be taken?

CASE 5-2

Below are two balance sheets: one for Iris Daner and one for Dana Dell. Each operates a women's clothing store side-by-side on Main Street in their home town. They have chatted on many occasions about forming a partnership. Because you work part-time in Ms. Daner's store, she has asked you to study her balance sheet and that of Ms. Dell's. You have been given the following questions. When you get answers, they want to meet with you.

Required:

1. Which business looks to be in the best financial condition right now? Explain your answer.
2. What would their combined balance sheet look like if they formed a partnership?
3. How should they share any profits? Explain your answer.

**Iris Daner's
Balance Sheet**

Assets:	
Cash	$ 10,000
Merchandise	50,000
Equipment	20,000
Land and Building	150,000
Total:	**$230,000**
Claims Against Assets:	
Accounts Payable (Liabilities)	$ 30,000
I. Daner, Capital	200,000
Total:	**$230,000**

**Dana Dell's
Balance Sheet**

Assets:	
Cash	$ 20,000
Merchandise	80,000
Equipment	10,000
Land and Building	160,000
Total:	**$270,000**
Claims Against Assets:	
Accounts Payable (Liabilities)	$ 70,000
D. Dell, Capital	200,000
Total:	**$270,000**

REVIEW 5

CORPORATE FORMS OF BUSINESS OWNERSHIP

CHAPTER 6

After studying this chapter you will be able to:

6-1 Explain the basic features of a corporation.

6-2 Describe how a corporation is formed and organized.

6-3 List some of the major advantages and disadvantages of the corporate form of business.

6-4 Describe several specialized forms of business organizations.

A bbie Chawan came to this country from Nepal ten years ago and earned a business degree from a well-known college. Because he enjoyed being in the United States, he decided to stay. After graduation he found a management job in a small firm, where he learned a great deal. After five years, the job became less challenging even though he earned a very good salary. He wondered about opening his own business with the money he had saved, but that seemed too risky.

Surely there was some way to be in business but not have to assume so much responsibility alone or even with a partner. The partnership idea sounded acceptable, but the fear of lawsuits from creditors and customers if he did not do well kept haunting him. Nevertheless, his fears of those unlimited liabilities did not stop him from thinking about starting a business.

On his way home from work the next day, Abbie stopped to get his hair styled. He overheard two other customers talking about changing their small partnership to a corporation. One said, "We would pay higher taxes." The other responded, "But our financial liability would be less than in our partnership." Abbie was listening intently now but said nothing until after the first person said, "But we can't expand our successful business unless we can raise more money." By now

Abbie could no longer restrain himself. "Excuse me for listening, but I have an idea if you would like to hear it. I am a manager and have a degree in business, but more importantly, I'm looking for an opportunity to become a business owner." The two men looked at each other and nodded. "Let's hear your idea," one said with enthusiasm.

"There is a special type of corporation that permits you to be a corporation but allows you to pay taxes as if you were still a partnership," Abbie replied. "And if you are looking for another stockholder who can invest some money and help expand the business, I would be very interested in talking with you." After the introductions and handshakes, they scheduled a luncheon meeting for the next day.

In Chapter 5 you learned about proprietorships and partnerships as legal forms of organizing a business. This chapter will deal with the features and formation of regular corporations. In addition, special organizational structures will be examined that include joint ventures, S-corporations, nonprofit corporations, and cooperatives. If you were to join the three people in the opening story at their luncheon meeting tomorrow, you would need to understand the contents of this chapter.

CORPORATIONS

Corporations are towers on the business landscape. While proprietorships are many in number, they are generally small in size. In comparison, corporations are few in number, but generally large in size. Because corporations tend to be large, they play a powerful role in the economy of our country. For example, corporations employ millions of people and provide consumers with many of the goods and services they need and want. In a recent year, corporate sales of

Illus. 6-1

For less than $50, a person can become a stockholder in any one of hundreds of major corporations and may attend annual meetings. Even though many people buy stock in a corporation, is it likely that owners with just one share would attend meetings of stockholders?

Richard Pasley/Stock, Boston

goods and services were over fourteen times more than sales from proprietor-ships, and over twenty times more than sales from partnerships.

Not all corporations are large. While corporations such as Exxon, General Electric, and Pepsi are known to almost everyone, many small corporations also exist. Small corporations are popular for reasons you will discover in this chapter.

Because the corporation plays a vital role in American business, we need to understand its basic features as well as its advantages and disadvantages. To gain a knowledge of the basic features of the corporation, we can follow York, Burton, and Chan as they consider incorporating their fast-growing food store partnership, which they launched in the last chapter.

BASIC FEATURES

Karen Ritter, a lawyer, helped York, Burton, and Chan prepare the partnership agreement under which they now operate. As their attorney, she has been asked by the partners to describe a corporation. She stated that a **corporation** is a busi-ness owned by a group of people and authorized by the state in which it is located to act as though it were a single person. To get permission to form a corpora-tion, a charter is needed. A **charter** (often called a **certificate of incorporation**) is the official document granted by a state giving power to run a corporation.

A corporation is, in a sense, an artificial person created by the laws of the state. A corporation can make contracts, borrow money, own property, and sue or be sued in its own name. Any act performed for the corporation by an authorized person, such as an employee, is done in the name of the business. For example, the treasurer of a corporation has the power to borrow money for the business. An unauthorized employee, such as a receptionist who was hired to answer the phone and greet visitors, could not borrow money for the corporation.

Ritter further explained the important parts played by three key types of people in corporations: stockholders, directors, and officers.

Stockholders

Stockholders (often called **shareholders**) are the owners of a corporation. Ownership is divided into equal parts called **shares**. A person who buys one share becomes a stockholder. Therefore, thousands of people can own a corporation. Each stockholder receives a certificate from the corporation, which shows the number of shares owned. Stockholders have a number of basic rights, including the following:

- To transfer ownership to others.
- To vote for members of the ruling body of the corporation and other special matters that may be brought before the stockholders.
- To receive dividends. **Dividends** are profits that are distributed to stock-holders on a per share basis. The decision to distribute profits is made by the ruling body of the corporation.
- To buy new shares of stock in proportion to one's present investment should the corporation issue more shares.

■ To share in the net proceeds (cash received from the sale of all assets less the payment of all debts) should the corporation go out of business.

A stockholder does not have the same financial responsibility as a partner; that is, there is no liability beyond the extent of the stockholder's ownership. If the corporation fails, a stockholder may lose only the money that is invested. Creditors cannot collect anything further from the stockholder.

Directors

The **board of directors** (often shortened to **directors** or the **board**) is the ruling body of the corporation. Board members are elected by the stockholders. Directors develop plans and policies to guide the corporation as well as appoint officers to carry out the plans. If the corporation is performing successfully, its board is content to deal with policy issues and monitor the progress of the company. However, if the corporation's profits fall, or if it experiences other serious difficulties, the board often steps in and takes an active role in the operation of the business.

In large firms, most boards consist of 10 to 25 directors. A few board members are top executives from within the corporation. The majority of the directors are from outside the corporation and are usually executives from other businesses or people from nonprofit organizations, such as college professors. Often, directors are stockholders who hold many shares. But directors need not be stockholders. People who hold few or no shares are sometimes elected to the board because they have valuable knowledge that is needed by the board of directors in making sound decisions.

Officers

The **officers** of a corporation are the top executives who are hired to manage the business. They are appointed by the board of directors. The officers of a small corporation often consist of a president, a secretary, and a treasurer. In addition, large corporations may have vice presidents in charge of major areas, such as marketing, finance, and manufacturing. The titles of these officers are often shortened to letters. For example, the top officer is called a CEO (Chief Executive Officer) and the head financial officer is referred to as the CFO (Chief Financial Officer).

FORMATION OF CORPORATIONS

Over several months the partners asked their attorney, Karen Ritter, many questions. Only after careful thought did York, Burton, and Chan decide to form a corporation. Ritter was again consulted. She told them that there were basically three steps involved. First, a series of decisions had to be made about how the corporation would be organized. Second, the proper legal forms had to be prepared and sent to the state office that handles such matters. And third, the state would review the incorporation papers and issue a charter if it approved. The formation of a new corporation for York, Burton, and Chan is now presented in detail.

Preparing the Certificate of Incorporation

Each state has its own laws for forming corporations. No federal law exists. To incorporate a business, it is necessary in most states to file a certificate of incorporation with the appropriate state office. Ritter prepared the certificate of incorporation for York, Burton, and Chan as shown in Fig. 6-1.

Fig. 6-1

A certificate of incorporation includes information about the organizers of a corporation.

Certificate of Incorporation of
York, Burton, and Chan, Inc.

Pursuant to Article Two of the Stock Corporation Law.

State of New York
County of Cattaraugus } ss.

We, the undersigned, for the purpose of forming a Corporation pursuant to Article Two of the Stock Corporation Law of the State of New York, do hereby make, subscribe, acknowledge and file this certificate for that purpose as follows:

We, the undersigned, do hereby Certify

First.—That all the undersigned are full age, and .... all .... are citizens of the United States, and .... all .... residents of the State of New York.

Second.—That the name of said corporation is York, Burton, and Chan, Inc.

Third.—That the purpose for which said corporation is formed is to operate a retail food business.

Fourth.—That the amount of the Capital Stock of the said corporation is Eight Hundred Thousand Dollars ($ 800,000) to consist of Eight Thousand (8,000) shares of the par value of One Hundred dollars ($ 100) each.

Fifth.—That the office of said corporation is to be located in the City of Buffalo, County of Cattaraugus and State of New York.

Sixth.—That the duration of said corporation is to be perpetual.

Seventh.—That the number of Directors of said corporation is three.

Eighth.—That the names and post office addresses of the Directors until the first annual meeting are as follows:

Jennifer L. York 1868 Buffalo Street, Buffalo, NY 14760-1436

Robert R. Burton 1309 Main Street, Buffalo, NY 14760-1436

Lu Chan 4565 Erie Avenue, Niagara Falls, NY 14721-2348

Ninth.—That the names and post office addresses of the subscribers and the number of shares of stock which each agrees to take in said corporation are as follows:

Names	Post Office Addresses	No. of Shares
Jennifer L. York	1868 Buffalo Street Buffalo, NY 14760-1436	1,880
Robert R. Burton	1309 Main Street Buffalo, NY 14760-1436	1,880
Lu Chan	4565 Erie Avenue Niagara Falls, NY 14721-2348	1,880

Tenth.—That the meetings of the Board of Directors shall be held only within the State of New York at Buffalo.

In Witness Whereof, we have made, subscribed and executed this certificate in duplicate the tenth day of September in the year One thousand nine hundred and ninety-six

Jennifer L. York
Robert R. Burton
Lu Chan

Ethical Issues

TROUBLE IN THE BOARDROOM

Questions:

1 What defensive actions have CEOs taken that might cause boards of directors to perform their jobs improperly?

2 What happens when boards and CEOs do not adequately represent stockholders?

Experts generally agree that top management greatly influences the extent to which ethics are practiced in corporations. Top management includes CEOs and boards of directors. Shareholders usually assume that their elected directors are ethical, but that is not always the case.

The relationships between shareholders, boards, and CEOs should be as harmonious as possible. In practice, however, CEOs sometimes manipulate boards. As a result, employees, retirees, customers, and shareholders often suffer.

For example, CEOs know that the boards who hire them can also fire them. As a result, CEOs want to build relationships with board members that will keep them from being terminated. CEOs in firms that are not doing well are often motivated to take defensive action. One such defense is to get elected as chairperson of the board. In this way, CEOs set meeting agendas and thereby control topics that are discussed. CEOs can also recommend friends as nominees to the board for stockholders to elect via proxy statements. Directors might also be paid high fees for attending meetings. Through such actions, CEOs are able to build a group of loyal followers.

On the other hand, directors who are elected by shareholders and who are loyal to CEOs may be disloyal to the stockholders they represent. A condition like this creates problems. For example, CEO salaries may be raised despite poor performance. Strategic plans submitted by CEOs may be approved without adequate review. In good economic periods, the damage may be minor. But during tough competitive periods when a firm has difficulty making a profit or must go out of business, everyone is hurt. That's when employees get fired and stockholders lose money.

Employees get hurt in another way when employee pension funds are invested in corporations by the fund managers. Pension funds are pools of money set aside for employee retirement benefits. When corporations do poorly, managers of large pension funds try to see that changes are made within these companies. Changes made in recent years as the result of action taken by pension fund managers include these examples. First, boards now select more directors from outside firms who are more critical of poor CEO leadership. Second, more boards take greater care in selecting and evaluating the performance of CEOs. Finally, boards are now beginning to pay CEOs based upon the quality of their performance.

Ethics in boardrooms have been improving gradually. Now more boards listen to stockholders and no longer permit CEOs to control them. Rather, good boards control CEOs. And good CEOs encourage frank discussions with their boards and stakeholders, such as large pension fund managers.

Notice the general type of information called for in the certificate of incorporation. In addition to the firm name, purpose, and capital stock, information about the organizers is requested.

Naming the Business. A business is usually required by law to have a name that indicates clearly that a corporation has been formed. Words or abbreviations such as Corporation, Corp., Incorporated, or Inc. are used (see Figure 6-2). Taylor Co., Incorporated, and Bell Company, Inc., are examples. The organizers have decided to name their corporation York, Burton, and Chan, Inc.

York, Burton, and Chan, Inc.

Chan, Burton, and York, Inc.

Burton, York, and Chan, Inc.

Fig. 6-2
Organizers must select a name for the business to be recorded on the certificate of incorporation.

Stating the Purpose of the Business. A certificate of incorporation requires a corporation to give its purpose clearly. Figure 6-1, Article 3, precisely states the purpose of the corporation: "to operate a retail food business." It allows the corporation to expand into new food lines, but it does not allow the corporation to start nonfood operations. For major changes in purpose, a new request must be submitted and approved by the state.

Investing in the Business. The certificate of incorporation could not be completed until York, Burton, and Chan decided how to invest their partnership holdings in the corporation. They agreed that the assets and debts of the partnership should be taken over by the corporation. They further agreed that their capital (net worth or equity) of $188,000 each should be invested in the corporation. **Capital stock** is the general term applied to the shares of ownership of a corporation.

Here is how the details were worked out. The organizers requested authorization from the state to issue $800,000 in capital stock, as can be seen in Fig. 6-1. Shares were valued at $100 each at the time of incorporation; there were 8,000 shares in all ($800,000 ÷ 100 = 8,000). York, Burton, and Chan agreed to purchase 1,880 shares each as shown in Fig. 6-3.

The 2,360 unissued shares, the difference between the 8,000 authorized shares and the 5,640 shares bought by the organizers, can be sold at a later date and can be used to expand the business.

Paying Incorporation Costs. Usually, a new business must pay an organization tax—based on the amount of its capital stock. In addition, a new business usually pays a filing fee before the state will issue a charter entitling the business to operate as a corporation. In some states, the existence of the corporation begins when the application or certificate of incorporation has been filed in the Department of State.

Division of shares held by York, Burton, and Chan, Inc.

York	1880 shares x $100 per share	=	$188,000
Burton	1880 shares x $100 per share	=	$188,000
Chan	1880 shares x $100 per share	=	$188,000
Total			**$564,000**

Operating the New Corporation

York, Burton, and Chan, Inc., received approval to operate as a corporation. Their attention was next turned to getting the business started.

Getting Organized. One of the first steps in getting the new corporation under way is to prepare a balance sheet or statement of financial position. The new corporation's balance sheet is shown in Fig. 6-4.

Fig. 6-4

Balance sheet of York, Burton, and Chan, Inc.

ASSETS

Cash	$ 48,000
Merchandise	96,000
Equipment	90,000
Land and Building	346,000
Total	**$580,000**

CLAIMS AGAINST ASSETS

Accounts Payable (Liabilities)	$ 16,000
Capital Stock	564,000
Total	**$580,000**

The ownership of the corporation is in the same hands as was the ownership of the partnership. The ownership of the corporation, however, is evidenced by the issued capital stock. The former partners have each received a stock certificate indicating that each owns 1,880 shares of stock with a value of $100 a share.

The three stockholders own the business and elect themselves directors. The new directors select officers. York is appointed president; Burton, vice president; and Chan, secretary and treasurer. An organization chart of the new corporation is shown in Fig. 6-5.

Handling Voting Rights. The owners agreed that each owner will have 1,880 votes on matters arising in the meetings of the stockholders. Voting stockholders usually have one vote for each share owned. However, if Chan, for instance, sold 944 of his shares to Burton, Burton would own 2,824 shares, or more than 50 percent of the total 5,640 shares of stock that have been issued. Then Burton could control the corporation.

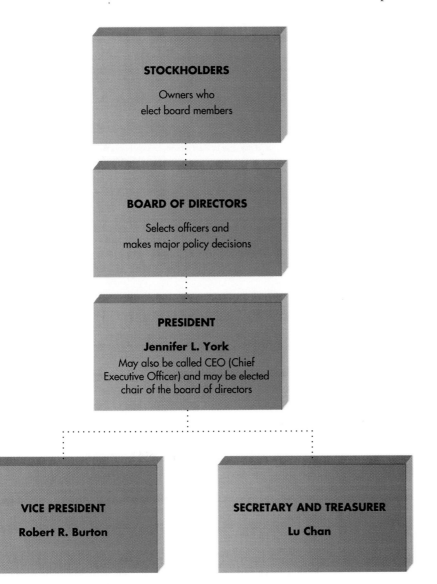

Fig. 6-5
An organization chart of a corporation.

The officers of the corporation were told by their lawyer that they must send each stockholder notices of all stockholders' meetings to be held. Even stockholders with just one share must receive notices of meetings. If stockholders cannot attend the meetings personally, they may be represented by a proxy. A **proxy** is a written authorization for someone to vote in behalf of the person signing the proxy. It is common practice for a proxy form to be enclosed with the letter that announces a stockholders' meeting. One example of a proxy that a corporation might use is shown in Fig. 6-6 on the next page.

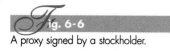

Fig. 6-6

A proxy signed by a stockholder.

Brumway Eastmont Power Corporation – Proxy – Annual Meeting, Nov. 7, 19--

The undersigned hereby appoints Henry T. Brumleve III, Dean G. Rehme, D.A. Dromboski, and Donald F. Stark, and any of them, proxies of the undersigned, with power of substitution, to vote at the Annual Meeting of Stockholders of Brumway Eastmont Power Corporation, at Kenwood, Ohio, on November 7, 19--, at 11:00 a.m., and at any adjournments thereof.

This Proxy is Solicited by Management

(1) FOR ☒ or NOT FOR ☐ the election of a Board of Directors;

(2) FOR ☒ or AGAINST ☐ the proposal to increase the number of authorized shares of Common Stock; and

(3) for the transaction of any other business property brought before the meeting.

Dated *October 25, 19--*

RAYMOND L COOKE
349 MIDPINES DRIVE
BUFFALO NY 14202-4449

Raymond L. Cooke

Signature of Stockholder

If no preference is indicated, this proxy will be voted FOR items (1) & (2).

(Please give your full title when signing as attorney, trustee, executor, administrator, or guardian, etc.)

CLOSE AND OPEN CORPORATIONS

A **close corporation** (also called a **closely held corporation**) is one that does not offer its shares of stock for public sale. It is owned by just a few stockholders, some of whom may help run the business in the same manner as partners operate a business. York, Burton, and Chan, Inc., is an example of a close corporation. The three former partners own all the stock and operate the business as well.

In most states, a close corporation does not need to make its financial activities known to the public. Its stock is not offered for general sale. It must, however, prepare reports for the state from which it obtained its charter. And it must, for tax purposes, prepare reports for all states in which it operates.

An **open corporation** (also called a **publicly owned corporation**) is one that offers its shares of stock for public sale. Figure 6-7 shows a newspaper ad announcing the sale of common stock to the public. A company must file a registration statement with the Securities and Exchange Commission (SEC) containing extensive details about the company and the proposed issue of securities. A condensed version of this registration statement, called a **prospectus,** must be furnished to each prospective buyer of newly offered stocks (or bonds).

Open corporations often have a large number of stockholders, some with hundreds of thousands or more. Many of the stockholders in large corporations own only a few shares. But because of the great number of stockholders, such a corporation has a large amount of capital. Naturally, these large corporations are not as simple in organization as York, Burton, and Chan, Inc.

Illus. 6-2

Cincinnati Microwave is an open corporation. What is an open corporation?

Eric Von Fischer/Photonics

2,530,000 Shares

GALACTICA, INC.

Common Stock

....
Price $18 a Share
....

Copies of the Prospectus may be obtained in any State from only such of the undersigned as may legally offer these Securities in compliance with the securities laws of such State.

Morgan Stanley & Co. Incorporated	**Hambrecht & Quist** Incorporated
Goldman, Sachs & Co.	Cowen & Company
Donaldson, Lufkin & Jenrette Securities Corporation	Kidder, Peabody & Co. Incorporated
Merrill Lynch & Co.	Montgomery Securities

Fig. 6-7
An open corporation must offer its shares for sale to the public.

ADVANTAGES OF CORPORATIONS

The corporation has a number of advantages as compared with the proprietorship and partnership. Four such advantages follow.

Available Sources of Capital

The corporation can obtain money from several sources. One of those sources is the sale of shares to stockholders. This special privilege helps to raise enough capital for running large-scale businesses. Because corporations are regulated closely, people usually invest more willingly than in proprietorships and partnerships. Also, corporations usually find borrowing large sums of money less of a problem than do proprietorships or partnerships.

Limited Liability of Stockholders

Except in a few situations, the owners (stockholders) are not legally liable for the debts of the corporation beyond their investments in the shares purchased. Thus, people—whether they have only a few dollars to invest or whether they have thousands of dollars—can invest in a corporation without the possibility of incurring a liability beyond their original investment.

Permanency of Existence

The corporation is a more permanent type of organization than the proprietorship or the partnership. It can continue to operate indefinitely, or only as long as the term stated in the charter. The death or withdrawal of an owner (stockholder) does not affect its life.

Ease in Transferring Ownership

It is easy to transfer ownership in a corporation. A stockholder may sell stock to another person and transfer the stock certificate, which represents ownership, to the new owner. When shares are transferred, the transfer of ownership is indicated in the records of the corporation. A new certificate is issued in the name of the new stockholder. Millions of shares are bought and sold every day.

DISADVANTAGES OF CORPORATIONS

Although there are several distinct advantages to the corporation, there are also disadvantages. A discussion of some of the major disadvantages follows.

Taxation

The corporation is usually subject to more taxes than are imposed on the proprietorship and the partnership. Some taxes that are unique to the corporation are a filing fee, which is payable on application for a charter; an organization tax, which is based on the amount of authorized capital stock; an annual state tax, based on the profits; and a federal income tax.

The federal income tax rate for corporations is based on taxable earnings (total yearly receipts less allowable deductions). As shown in Figure 6-8, a corporation with taxable earnings of $90,000 will pay $18,600 in federal income taxes.

Another tax disadvantage for corporations is that profits distributed to stockholders as dividends are taxed twice. This double taxation occurs in two steps. The corporation first pays taxes on its profits as just described. Then it distributes some of these profits to shareholders as dividends, and the shareholders pay taxes on the dividends they receive. Most other major countries do not permit double taxation on corporate profits. (Small close corporations with few stockholders may avoid double taxation by becoming an S-corporation, which you will learn about later in this chapter.)

Government Regulations and Reports

A corporation cannot do business wherever it pleases. To form a corporation, an application for a charter must be submitted to the appropriate state official, usually the secretary of state. York, Burton, and Chan, Inc., has permission to

Corporate Tax Rate Schedule

Fig. 6-8
Corporate tax-rate schedule.

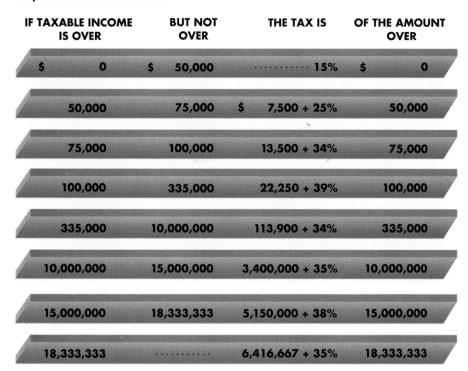

IF TAXABLE INCOME IS OVER	BUT NOT OVER	THE TAX IS	OF THE AMOUNT OVER
$ 0	$ 50,000	.... 15%	$ 0
50,000	75,000	$ 7,500 + 25%	50,000
75,000	100,000	13,500 + 34%	75,000
100,000	335,000	22,250 + 39%	100,000
335,000	10,000,000	113,900 + 34%	335,000
10,000,000	15,000,000	3,400,000 + 35%	10,000,000
15,000,000	18,333,333	5,150,000 + 38%	15,000,000
18,333,333	....	6,416,667 + 35%	18,333,333

conduct business only in the state of New York. Should it wish to conduct business in other states, each state will probably require the corporation to obtain a license as a **foreign corporation** and to pay a fee to do business in that state. State incorporation fees are not very expensive. The attorney's fee accounts for the major costs of incorporating. Each state has differing laws that govern the formation of corporations.

The regulation of corporations by states and by the federal government is extensive. A corporation must file special reports to the state from which it received its charter as well as in other states where it conducts business. The federal government requires firms whose stock is publicly traded to publish financial data. As a result, an increased need arises for detailed financial records and reports.

Stockholders' Records

Corporations that have many stockholders have added problems—and expenses—in communicating with stockholders and in handling stockholders' records. By law, stockholders must be informed of corporate matters, notified of meetings, and given the right to vote on important matters. Letters and reports must be sent to stockholders on a regular basis. In addition, each time a share of stock is bought or sold and whenever a dividend is paid, detailed records must be kept. Keeping records for the thousands of stockholders of General Electric, for example, is a time-consuming and costly task.

Charter Restrictions

A corporation is allowed to engage only in those activities that are stated in its charter. Should York, Burton, and Chan, Inc., wish to sell hardware, it would be necessary to go to the state to obtain a new charter or change the old one. As a partnership they could have added the other department without government approval.

BUSINESSES SUITED TO BEING CORPORATIONS

Even though the corporation has major disadvantages, a survey of business firms shows that almost every kind of business exists as a corporation. The corporate form of ownership is especially suited to certain types of firms. The following types of businesses most frequently organize as corporations:

1. Businesses that require large amounts of capital, such as airlines, construction firms, auto manufacturers, and steel firms. To start a 500-room hotel, for example, requires millions of dollars for buying land and for constructing and furnishing the hotel.

2. Businesses that may have uncertain futures, such as mining companies, amusement parks, publishers of new magazines, and makers of novelty goods. The publisher of a new magazine, for example, takes a great risk in assuming that the magazine will be popular enough to make a profit. Organizers of firms with uncertain futures do not wish to assume the added financial risks that fall upon a proprietor or a partner in case the business fails.

Illus. 6-3

Firms requiring large sums of capital often are organized as corporations. How might owners of this hotel get millions of dollars to build another one like it?

Boston Marriott/Copley Place, Courtesy of Marriott Corporation

Each form of business organization has special advantages to owners of different types of businesses. While the corporate form of organization is suited to firms that have uncertain futures or that require large amounts of capital, the partnership is especially suited to small, growing business firms. The proprietorship, in comparison, has great appeal to the person who wants to run a small business. In addition to sole proprietorships, partnerships, and corporations, there are still other legal forms of organizations.

SPECIALIZED TYPES OF ORGANIZATIONS

You have now become familiar with sole proprietorships, partnerships, and corporations. Still other ways in which organizations can be legally formed include joint ventures, S-corporations, nonprofit corporations, and cooperatives.

JOINT VENTURES

At times businesses want to join forces in order to achieve an important objective. A **joint venture** is an agreement involving two or more businesses to make and/or sell a good or service. The legal formation of the business is not important. For example, a sole proprietorship and a corporation could agree to work together. Each partner in the joint venture is expected to bring management expertise and/or money to the venture. Many major corporations today have learned that alone they may not have all the expertise or capital needed.

An example of a joint venture might include an agreement between two major contractors to connect two cities by building a tunnel for cars under a river. A company working alone may not have the capital to build the tunnel, and each may lack special equipment or skills that the other firm has. By forming a joint venture, they can acquire the expertise to build the tunnel that they could not complete alone. Joint ventures often include business partners from foreign countries. For example, Ford Motor Company produces cars in a joint venture with Mazda.

Because organizations must adapt quickly to compete effectively, an advanced form of the joint venture, the virtual corporation, is evolving in the world of business. The *virtual corporation* is composed of joint ventures in which alliances with other businesses are formed quickly to take advantage of fast-changing market conditions. The virtual corporation may include a large number of business partners—even competitors—in order to take advantage of special opportunities. Alliances may last for short or long periods as well as involve few or many partners. Virtual corporations rely heavily on trust among business partners and on the use of computers to coordinate efforts among diverse firms.

An example of a virtual corporation might include the following situation. Company A wishes to rush to market a new sophisticated computer but needs special parts that it does not produce. Company A learns that Company B produces one part and Company C produces the other needed part. Unfortunately, none of the three companies have customers who would likely have an interest in the new computer. After searching, the firms find that Company D sells computers to customers with special needs. Ultimately, all three companies agree to join with Company A to market the new computer. This virtual corporation situation, which is shown in Fig. 6-9, makes it possible for all four companies to benefit when no one company could have made and marketed the new computer quickly on its own.

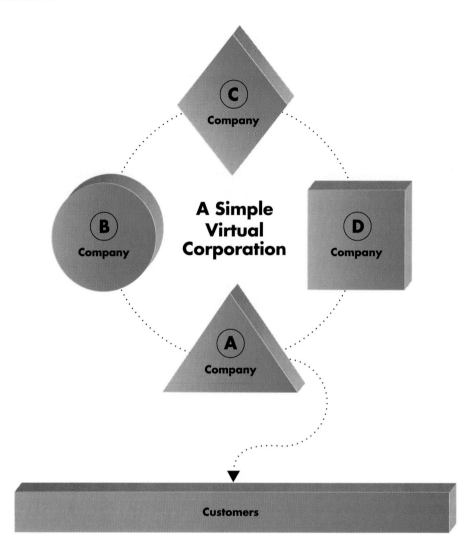

S-CORPORATIONS

Small but rapidly growing businesses are attracted by an S-corporation form of ownership. An **S-corporation** is a special type of corporation that is taxed as if it were a partnership. The S-corporation name comes from Subchapter S of the Internal Revenue Code. Two factors make S-corporations popular. First, a major weakness of a partnership is unlimited liability whereas a strength of a corporation is its limited liability. Second, a major strength of a partnership is its lower income tax rate whereas a weakness of a corporation is a higher income tax rate than that paid by partnerships. Stockholders also have to pay personal income taxes on dividends distributed by a corporation (double taxation). The S-corporation provides an ideal solution—lower taxes and limited liability. In addition, the profits from the corporation go directly to the stockholders who then include the profits on their individual income tax returns. Double taxation is avoided. York, Burton, and Chan, Inc., would qualify for this special tax advantage.

However, not all companies are eligible for S-corporation status. A few important rules determine eligibility. First, a firm must have no more than 35 stockholders. Second, the business cannot own 80 percent or more of the stock of another corporation. Third, not more than 25 percent of the income of the corporation can be from sources other than for the purpose(s) stated in the charter. And, fourth, all stockholders must be individuals who are permanent citizens or residents of this country. Large corporations and multinational firms do not meet these qualifications. Many partnerships, however, do qualify and find the S-corporation to be highly favorable.

NONPROFIT CORPORATIONS

Close and open corporations, as discussed on page 138, are businesses that operate mainly to make a profit for their owners. A **nonprofit corporation**, on the other hand, is an organization that does not pay taxes and does not exist to make a profit. Organizations that manage cities or operate schools are examples of nonprofit corporations. Because a nonprofit corporation is not established as a profit-making enterprise, it does not pay dividends to shareholders. Otherwise, it operates much like a close or open corporation. The Rotary Club, Boy Scouts, United Way, and most local hospitals are other examples of nonprofit organizations.

In this country, nonprofit corporations provide nearly one-third of the GDP. However, in most other countries, nonprofit corporations contribute much more to the GDP. The principles of business and management provided in this text apply equally to managers who run profit-making as well as nonprofit corporations.

Jeff Greenberg, Photographer

Ilus. 6-4
Nonprofit organizations do not make a profit for distribution to stockholders. Do you think a nonprofit organization would be allowed to raise money by asking the public for donations?

QUASI-PUBLIC CORPORATIONS

A business that is important, but lacks the profit potential to attract private investors, is often operated by local, state, or federal government. Government financial support (called a subsidy) may also be required. This type of business is usually described as a **quasi-public corporation.** Government imposes regulatory controls over quasi-public corporations.

The Tennessee Valley Authority, a rural electrification program started in the 1930s by the federal government, was one of the first quasi-public corporations. The Massachusetts and Pennsylvania turnpike authorities are state-owned quasi-public corporations. At the local level, examples of quasi-public organizations include water and sewer systems, parking garages, and civic and cultural facilities. The Los Angeles County Museum of Art is a government-owned cultural organization.

COOPERATIVES

A **cooperative** is a business owned and operated by its user-members for the purpose of supplying themselves with goods and services. The members, who are much like stockholders in a corporation with the protection of limited liability, usually join a cooperative by buying shares of stock. The members elect a board of directors, which appoints officers to run the business. Much like a corporation, a cooperative must also obtain a charter from the state in which it is organized in order to operate. Some types of cooperatives need authorization from the federal government.

The purpose of cooperatives is to provide their members with cost and profit advantages that they do not otherwise have. For example, a group of blueberry growers believes that individually they can save money and make more profit by forming a cooperative for the purpose of selling their berries. Once the business is organized and operating, the members (owners) sell their berries through the cooperative. The cooperative markets the berries. In turn, the growers earn more than if they tried to market the berries on their own. In addition, as owners they share in the profits of the business.

With almost 19 million businesses in the United States, only a small portion are cooperatives. This small number, however, does not reduce their importance. Cooperatives are popular in agriculture for buying and selling crops. And many employees belong to credit unions where they can invest and borrow money at low interest rates. Many insurance firms are formed as cooperatives. Apartment buildings are often formed as cooperatives as well.

CHAPTER 6 REVIEW

BUILDING VOCABULARY POWER

Define the following terms and concepts.

1. corporation
2. charter (certificate of incorporation)
3. stockholders (shareholders)
4. shares
5. dividends
6. board of directors (directors or board)
7. officers
8. capital stock
9. proxy
10. close corporation (closely held corporation)
11. open corporation (publicly owned corporation)
12. foreign corporation
13. joint venture
14. S-corporation
15. nonprofit corporation
16. cooperative

REVIEWING FACTS

1. Which form of business is fewest in total number but highest in terms of total sales of goods and services?
2. What are the five basic rights of stockholders?
3. How does one become a stockholder in a corporation? a director? an officer?
4. What steps must be taken to form a corporation?
5. By what means can stockholders vote on matters affecting the corporation even when they cannot be present at meetings?
6. How does a close corporation differ from an open corporation?
7. Give four advantages of corporations.
8. Give three disadvantages of corporations.
9. Why would a business want to form a joint venture?
10. What is the purpose of cooperatives?

DISCUSSING IDEAS

1. Why can a corporation be described as an artificial person?
2. Compare the financial responsibility of owners of a corporation with that of owners of a partnership.
3. Fig. 6-6, page 138, shows a proxy. If the person receiving the proxy only signed the card but did not vote for or against the numbered items, would the proxy be valid?
4. In its certificate of incorporation, why would a corporation request more shares of capital stock than are needed to get started?
5. The following people own all the shares of stock in the same corporation: Brower, 100; Garroway, 70; Forcina, 30; and Hall, 10. If all have an interest in running for the board of directors, how could it be possible that the largest stockholder does not get elected?
6. Under what conditions would you be able to buy stock in York, Burton, and Chan, Inc.?
7. Explain how a joint venture could be valuable in a situation in which Corporation A has expertise in one area and Corporation B has expertise in another.
8. What conditions should exist before York, Burton, and Chan, Inc., consider becoming an S-corporation?
9. Discuss whether the Girl Scouts organization meets the qualifications for operating as a nonprofit corporation in light of the fact that it sells large volumes of cookies each year.
10. Why are cooperatives popular in agricultural regions?

A NALYZING INFORMATION

1. George Fernandez purchased stock in the Elie Manufacturing Co., Incorporated, for $76 a share. Last year he received quarterly dividends of $1, $1, $1, and $.80 on each share. His total dividends for the year amounted to what percentage of the price he paid for each share?

2. A corporation's taxable earnings for federal income tax purposes amounted to $195,000 for a recent year. Use the tax rates shown in this chapter to answer the following questions.
   a. What was the total federal income tax for the year?
   b. What was the profit after taxes that could be available as dividends for distribution to stockholders?
   c. What percentage of the total earnings was the total federal income tax?

3. The board of directors of Melby Company, Inc., decided to distribute $40,950 as dividends to shareholders. There are 27,300 shares of stock held by stockholders.
   a. What is the amount of the dividend to be distributed on each share?
   b. John Taylor owns 240 shares. What amount will he receive in dividends?

4. On the statement of financial position of the Fenwick Company, the assets have a value of $117,000; the debts are listed as $37,000; and the capital stock as $80,000. The company decided to go out of business. The assets are converted into $97,000 cash. What amount of cash will the stockholders receive?

5. The net profit of a retail cooperative is $4,000, and the purchases made by members amount to $100,000. If the profit is divided in proportion to the purchases, how much should be given to a member who made purchases of $1,000?

S OLVING BUSINESS PROBLEMS

CASE 6-1

Kim Benitez owns 15 shares of stock in the Shale Oil Company, a large corporation that deals with oil and gas products. Tom Breslin, a friend of Kim's, owns 20 shares. Today they both received an invitation to attend the annual stockholders' meeting in Chicago, which neither can attend. This conversation occurred during the evening when they were having dinner at a local restaurant:

Kim: Since I cannot attend the meeting, I am going to sign the proxy card and answer "for" regarding the two proposals that are to be voted upon. Of course, I do not know any of the board members who are up for election, but they must be OK. I wish they could distribute more dividends, though.

Tom: You should not just give your vote away to management, Kim. You should elect one of the candidates to be an outside board member. That person could then shake things up a bit, get some changes made. You probably also don't know anything about the other item asking for approval to increase the number of shares of stock that can be sold.

Kim: I do not have time to do homework on the company. Shale Oil Company always makes a profit; therefore, it deserves my vote.

Tom: Too many stockholders do not do their homework on the company, and not many go to the meetings. So, management always has its own way. Why bother sending a proxy statement at all? I am not going to waste my time sending the proxy back.

Kim: I am still going to vote, Tom. Besides, the company pays the postage.

Tom: You are doing what everyone else does. Management always wins. But since you are going to vote, I will too. The difference is that I am going to vote against the two items . . . no, on second thought, I will just sign the proxy. That will really confuse them.

Required:

1. Whether they vote "for" or "against" the proposals listed on the proxy statement, how many votes can Kim and Tom cast?
2. If the proxy statement is like the one shown in Fig. 6-6 and Tom signs it but does not mark "for" or "against" the two proposals, how will management use the proxy?
3. If Tom or Kim wanted an important proposal to be made known and voted upon by the stockholders, how could they achieve their goal?
4. Should Kim and Tom have received information about each of the proposals from management that would enable them to vote with adequate information?
5. What might an outside board member do that an inside member might not do?

CASE 6-2

Melissa Steinert, Ed Parretta, and Cathy Robinson all own different types of businesses. Melissa, a sole proprietor, operates a catalog company and sells small kitchen appliances at discounted prices. Ed and his partner own a trucking firm. They haul merchandise in two very large trucks and several small ones that they own. The partners make deliveries to all parts of the United States, Canada, and Mexico. Cathy's firm creates and makes special-purpose cards, solely for several national greeting card firms. She is the president of a small corporation with a total of five stockholders.

Soon after Cathy had enlarged her staff, she learned that one of the two major buyers was planning to drop her greeting card line. Rather than lay off any of her very creative employees, she prefers to distribute her high-quality cards herself under her own brand name: Cathy's Cards.

She has hired you for advice on how she can market her cards. Her goal is not only to create her unique and personal greeting cards but also to increase distribution on as wide a basis as possible. The faster she can get the new business plan launched, the less likely she will have to lay off any of her workers.

Required:

1. How might you advise Cathy to reorganize the business so that her idea can be achieved?
2. Explain how Cathy's business might fit into Melissa's plan. How might Ed's business fit into Cathy's plan?
3. What type of organization have you created for Cathy?
4. If Cathy qualifies as an S-corporation, how might the profits be reported to the Internal Revenue Service?

REVIEW

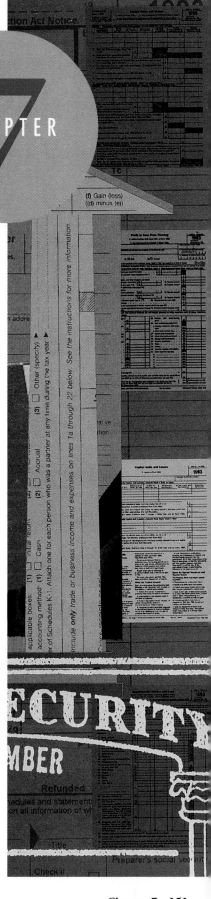

LEGAL ASPECTS OF BUSINESS

CHAPTER 7

After studying this chapter you will be able to:

7-1 Explain how federal laws help control and promote competition.

7-2 Tell how patents, copyrights, and trademarks are beneficial to business.

7-3 Offer examples of how the government protects the public.

7-4 Provide three methods used by state and local governments to regulate business.

7-5 Discuss the nature of taxes and the fairness of progressive, proportional, and regressive taxes.

7-6 Identify and explain the most common types of taxes that affect business.

Apollo Kane owns a small taxi business in his hometown. His lawyer, Kathleen Hess, joined him today for lunch. He wanted to discuss several matters that had occurred during the past several weeks. While waiting for lunch, Kathleen said, "You seem quite upset."

Apollo sat back and replied, "I am, Kathleen. Here are the new tax forms that need to be filled out. And that's the easy part."

After lunch was served, Apollo continued, "Would you check with the town officials, Kathleen, to see why they want to review my franchise before I buy another cab? Also, while you're at the Town Hall, see what you can do to prevent those officials from giving another taxi firm a license to operate. This town isn't big enough for two taxi companies. I'll get less business, and it will probably force down my *fares. If there is a chance of going bankrupt, I should probably move my business across the river. The income tax rate in that state is much lower."*

"Don't do anything drastic," said Kathleen. "Let me see what I can find out from our government officials. I'll get back to you in a few days with both your tax forms and with the answers to your questions."

Apollo Kane, like other business owners, must operate within the law. Laws that regulate business cover both products and services, and they govern general relationships of businesses with competitors, consumers, employees, and the public. Apollo Kane's taxi business is no exception. He currently benefits from being the only taxi company in town, but he now feels threatened. The town may, indeed, allow someone else the right to open a competing firm. So what can Apollo do?

Illus. 7-1

Government regulates large and small businesses. Do you think all businesses such as Apollo's like being regulated by government? Why or why not?

Jeff Greenberg, Photographer

In the following pages you will learn how government helps to encourage a free enterprise system by controlling monopolies and promoting competition. You will also learn how the government protects the general public as well as business. Like Apollo, you will learn about taxes and how taxes influence business decisions.

REGULATIONS MAINTAINING COMPETITION

Competition is the rivalry among companies for the customers' dollars. Competition, however, does not always operate smoothly by itself. To provide for fair competition, government has passed laws and created regulations to enforce the laws. These laws and regulations grow out of a need to preserve competition, which is done, in part, by controlling monopolies and unfair business practices. Firms that cannot survive in a competitive atmosphere either go out of business or face bankruptcy.

CONTROLLING MONOPOLIES

A **monopoly** exists when competition is lacking for a product or service, or when producers are in a position to control the supply and price of goods or services. By controlling the supply of an item, a single producer can set a price that will generate the greatest profit. In business situations such as Apollo Kane's taxi company, where a monopoly exists, prices are generally higher than where competition exists.

In actual practice, however, there are few business monopolies because of the effectiveness of competition. To illustrate, assume a business offers a new product that no other business has. The product suddenly becomes quite popular. Other companies now enter the market to help meet the demand. A temporary monopoly will exist until those competitors can produce and sell similar products. Usually, through competitive pricing, the more efficient companies will attract the greatest number of purchasers while the less efficient may struggle for survival or go out of business. Even if some competitors fail, however, a monopoly will not exist as long as there are at least two or more producers.

There are situations, however, where monopolies may be preferred over competition. These situations usually involve providing public services, such as public utilities, which have a fairly stable demand and which are costly to create. A natural gas company, for example, must build hundreds of miles of pipeline along streets and roads in order to deliver gas to homes and industries to fuel furnaces, stoves, and equipment. If two or three gas companies incurred these same costs to sell gas to a relatively fixed number of customers, the price of gas would be higher than if only one company existed. Also, installing and maintaining so many pipelines would create nuisance problems along crowded streets and highways. In these types of situations, therefore, a monopoly is more desirable than competition. When the government grants a monopoly to a company, it usually regulates the prices that can be charged and influences other company policies.

Greg Pease/Tony Stone Images

Illus. 7-2

Deregulation of airlines and other industries has helped benefit consumers through lower prices and improved services. Are passenger fares on commercial airlines regulated?

Until recently, the federal government had approved of closely regulated monopolies, such as the postal system, utility companies, railroads, and communication firms. However, the trend has shifted from approving of monopolies to weakening or eliminating them in order to encourage competition. No longer, for example, are passenger fares on commercial airlines regulated. As a result, fares have generally dropped. Even telephone service, the trucking industry, and railroads have been deregulated. Firms offering new communication services at competitive prices now freely compete with American Telephone and Telegraph (AT&T). The result overall has been that consumers pay lower prices and have more services from which to select.

Promoting Fair Competition

One way to promote competition is to limit the number of monopolies created and controlled by government. Monopoly conditions arise when businesses compete too harshly or too unfairly. A large, powerful business can lower its prices deliberately to drive out competitors, thereby discouraging competition.

Thus, the federal government attempts to establish and implement business practices that encourage competition and discourage monopolies. To achieve this goal, important laws have been passed and agencies created to enforce the laws.

Sherman Act. The first major law promoting competition was the Sherman Antitrust Act of 1890. Though somewhat dated, the law is still very much alive and enforced. One of its primary purposes is to discourage monopolies by outlawing business agreements among competitors that might tend to promote monopolies. For example, agreements among competitors to set selling prices on goods are unlawful. If three sellers met and agreed to set the same selling price on the same product each sold, they would all be violating the Sherman Act.

Clayton Act. Like the Sherman Act, the Clayton Act of 1914 was in part also aimed at discouraging monopolies. The Clayton Act contains several important features. One part of the law forbids corporations from acquiring ownership rights in other corporations if the purpose is to create a monopoly or to discourage competition. Corporation A cannot, for example, buy over half the ownership rights of its main competitor, Corporation B, if the aim is to reduce or eliminate competition.

Another section of the Clayton Act forbids business contacts that specify goods that a buyer must purchase in order to get other goods. For example, a business that produces computers cannot require a buyer also to purchase supplies, such as paper and disks that are needed to run the computer.

Robinson-Patman Act. A portion of the Clayton Act dealing with the pricing of goods was amended by the Robinson-Patman Act of 1936. The main purpose of both provisions in these laws is to prevent **price discrimination**—setting different prices for different customers. For example, a seller cannot offer a price of $5 a unit to Buyer A and sell the same goods to Buyer B at $6 a unit.

Different prices can be set, however, if the goods sold are different in quality or quantity. Buyer A is entitled to the $5 price if the quantity purchased is significantly greater or if the quality is lower. The same discounts must then be offered to all buyers purchasing the same quantity or quality as Buyer A.

Wheeler-Lea Act. In 1938, the Wheeler-Lea Act was passed to strengthen earlier laws outlawing unfair methods of competition. Unfair or deceptive acts or practices, including false advertising, were made unlawful. **False advertising** is defined as advertising that is "misleading in a material respect," including the failure to reveal facts about possible results from using the advertised products. Under the Wheeler-Lea Act, it is unlawful for an advertiser to circulate false advertising that can lead to the purchase of foods, drugs, medical devices, or cosmetics, or to participate in any other unfair methods of competition.

Federal Trade Commission

The Federal Trade Commission (FTC) was created as the result of many businesses demanding protection from unfair methods of competition. The FTC administers most of the federal laws dealing with fair competition. Some of the unfair practices that the FTC protects business firms from are shown in Fig. 7-1.

1. Any act that restrains trade.
2. Any monopolies except those specifically authorized by law, such as public utilities.
3. Price fixing, such as agreements among competitors.
4. Agreements among competitors to divide territory, earnings, or profits.
5. Gaining control over the supply of any commodity in order to create an artificial scarcity.
6. False or misleading advertising.
7. Imitation of trademark or trade name.
8. Discrimination through prices or special deals.
9. Pretending to sell at a discount when there is no reduction in price.
10. Offering so-called free merchandise with a purchase when the price of the article sold has been raised to compensate for the free merchandise.
11. Misrepresentation about the quality, the composition, or the place of origin of a product.
12. Selling secondhand or reclaimed merchandise as new merchandise.

Fig. 7-1
Types of practices prohibited by the Federal Trade Commission.

Other Federal Agencies

In addition to the FTC, other federal agencies have been created to administer laws that regulate specialized areas of business, such as transportation and communication. Some of the more important agencies are listed in Fig. 7-2.

ig. 7-2
Laws promoting fair practices that benefit business firms and consumers are enforced by government agencies.

Some Federal Agencies That Regulate Business

AGENCY AND REGULATION

Federal Aviation Administration

Safety standards, airplane accidents, and take-offs and landings

Federal Communications Commission

Radio, television, telephone, telegraph, and satellite communications

Food and Drug Administration

Foods, drugs, medical devices, cosmetics, and veterinary products

Nuclear Regulatory Commission

Nuclear power plants

Securities and Exchange Commission

Stocks and bonds

PROVIDING BANKRUPTCY RELIEF

All firms face the risk of failure. The free enterprise system permits unsuccessful businesses to file for bankruptcy as a means of protecting owners and others. **Bankruptcy** is a legal process that allows selling assets to pay off debts. Both businesses and individuals can file for bankruptcy. If cash is not available to pay the debts after assets are sold, the law excuses the business or individual from paying the remaining unpaid debts. In such a case, all those to whom money was owed would very likely receive less than the full amount.

A bankruptcy judge can permit a company to survive bankruptcy proceedings if a survival plan can be developed that might enable the firm to recover. As a result, after starting bankruptcy proceedings, many firms are able to survive. Should bankruptcy become finalized, however, disadvantages exist. The credit reputation of the business is blemished. All unpaid debts stay on file for ten years and those involved are not permitted to file for bankruptcy again for six years. As a result, obtaining credit is more difficult than usual.

REGULATIONS PROTECTING BUSINESS AND THE PUBLIC

Government regulations may be examined in terms of what the laws stress. One set of regulations stresses the manner in which competition is conducted while another set of regulations is concerned with the actual goods and services the business system produces. The previous section of this chapter dealt mostly with regulations that help to make the economic system work more effectively. Now we turn to regulations protecting those who create goods and services and those who use them.

PROTECTING BUSINESS

The federal government has passed laws to protect the rights of everyone who creates new products and new ideas. Specifically, intellectual property rights are granted to inventors, authors, and creators of distinct symbols and names for goods and services (see Fig. 7-3).

Intellectual Property

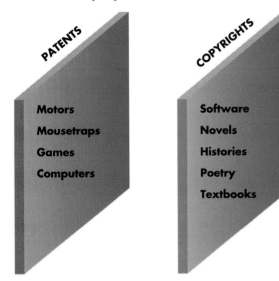

Fig. 7-3
Special property rights are granted by federal, state, and local governments.

Patent

A patent is an agreement in which the federal government gives an inventor the sole right for 17 years to make, use, and sell an invention. No one is permitted to copy or use the invention without permission. This protection is a reward for the time and money invested to create the new product. An inventor may allow others to make or use a product by giving them a license to do so. Many foreign firms obtain licenses from American firms that invent new products.

In a sense, through the Patent and Trademark Office, the government gives the inventor a monopoly on newly invented products, designs, and processes. This encourages manufacturers to establish research departments to develop new ideas. These research departments have produced many inventions. For example, Polaroid created and patented cameras that take and develop pictures within seconds. International Business Machines (IBM) has many patents on computer equipment.

Even synthetic tissue and plant life are patentable. For example, insulin used by diabetics that is made from human hormones and a new rot-resistant tomato are a result of using biotechnology (biology plus technology) to produce new products.

Unfortunately, stealing patents is an acceptable practice in some countries that do not honor the U.S. patent law. As a result, American firms lose millions of dollars. By tightening trade agreements with these countries, this great loss

Ethical Issues

THE PRICE OF A TRADE SECRET

Questions:

What would you do if an angry worker from a competitor's firm offered your business a similar trade secret? Would you:

1 Do nothing—ignore the situation?

2 Have your research department analyze the product and give you a report?

3 Call your competitor and tell the firm's CEO about the letter and the enclosed sample of the product?

4 Notify the police or the FBI (Federal Bureau of Investigation)?

Source: Adapted from Kevin Kelly and Joseph Weber, "When a Rival's Trade Secret Crosses Your Desk . . . " *Business Week,* May 20, 1991.

The Minneapolis-based 3M Co. makes various tapes that stick to just about everything, including Scotch Tape. In 1985, one of 3M's discontented employees helped create a tape used in setting casts for broken bones. The employee decided to make a few dollars for himself on the side. To do this, he illegally mailed four samples of the tape to four competitors. He also included a letter promising to explain the technology for $20,000.

Johnson & Johnson (J&J), a highly respected New Jersey-based competitor that makes medical products and supplies, received one of the letters. At the same time, J&J was also interested in developing a new casting tape. It was alleged that J&J analyzed 3M's tape to discover its chemical secret and thereafter developed a similar tape using 3M's trade secret. Of course, 3M was stunned to learn that its chief competitor had developed a comparable product.

In the meantime, the CEO of a small cast-making company had learned of the incident and notified 3M. 3M then sued the employee and J&J for unauthorized use of its trade secret. In 1991, an official of a Minneapolis court ordered J&J to pay $116.3 million to 3M for violating its patent rights. J&J plans to appeal the decision. However, the 3M employee was sentenced and served 22 months in prison.

To avoid such problems, more than 90 percent of U.S. companies have a written code of ethics. Such codes generally address topics such as confidentiality of corporate information, conflicts of interest, misappropriation of corporate assets, bribes and kickbacks, and political contributions.

For a code of ethics to make a real difference, employees must be aware of the code. A recent survey showed that only about two-thirds of all companies that have codes distribute them to employees. If a code is to be observed by all employees, a company must stand behind the code and make it available. Many companies hold meetings with employees to review and clarify their code of ethics. In some companies, ethics is an important part of management development programs.

Whether employees behave ethically depends largely on the actions and attitudes of top management. How employees are rewarded or punished for their actions influences whether they are likely to violate the ethics code in the future. Companies should make sure that the code includes fair procedures for handling violations. The procedures should be uniformly enforced. Also, the code should be revised when changes occur in a company's product line or competitive practices.

to American firms may begin to decline. On the other hand, patent laws differ worldwide. For example, Japan's patents promote technology sharing whereas U.S. patents protect inventors.

Copyright

A **copyright** is similar to a patent in that the federal government gives an author the sole right to reproduce, publish, and sell literary or artistic work for the life of the author plus 50 years. No one may publish or reproduce copyrighted work without permission of the copyright owner. However, the law permits occasional photocopying of copyrighted material. While a teacher could copy a business magazine article to distribute to students, articles from the same magazine could not be copied and distributed weekly throughout the school year without obtaining permission.

New electronic methods for distributing creative work are also covered by copyright laws. Creators of video and audio tapes and computer software programs, for example, are protected. Duplicating tapes, disks, and programs for distribution to others is usually illegal. When an employee makes a personal copy of a computer software program for use on a home computer, the employee violates the copyright law. Furthermore, if a warning is not publicized that copying creative work such as a software program is illegal, the employer is also guilty.

Copyrights are regulated by the federal Copyright Office. Like a patent, a copyright is a special type of monopoly granted to authors, publishers, and other creators of original works. An example of a copyright notice appears on the back of the title page in the front of this book.

Jeff Greenberg, Photographer

Illus. 7-3

Patents, copyrights, and trademarks are intellectual property rights protected by government for their owners. Would an artist like the one shown apply for a patent, a copyright, or a trademark?

Trademark

Trademarks are like patents because they are special types of monopolies. A **trademark** is a distinguishing name, symbol, or special mark placed on a good or service that is legally reserved for the sole use of the owner. Many nationally known products have trademarks that most people recognize, such as the games of Monopoly and Scrabble or the well-known symbols of major corporations. Trademarks, like patents, are regulated by the Patent and Trademark Office.

PROTECTING THE PUBLIC

While the federal government protects the legal rights of those who create new products and ideas, it also protects those who consume goods and services. One major emphasis of legislation is on ensuring safe products for consumers and preventing the misuse of information.

Food and Drugs

Products related to the human body are closely regulated. The Food and Drug Administration administers the Federal Food, Drug, and Cosmetic Act and other similar laws. These laws prohibit the sale of impure, improperly labeled, falsely guaranteed, and unhealthful foods, drugs, and cosmetics. Producers of cosmetics, for example, must show that products will not be harmful when used. Should a product cause harm, the Food and Drug Administration may require the producer to stop its sale or to notify the public of its possible danger.

Nonfood Products

Legislative activity dealing with the safety of nonfood products has increased in recent years. Labels are now required on many products if possible danger exists from using the product. A health-warning message, for example, must appear on cigarette packages. For the purpose of reducing death and injury, auto and highway safety laws have been passed.

The Consumer Product Safety Act of 1972 sets safety standards on many items. When it is found that products already sold have a dangerous defect, businesses are legally required to recall, repair, or stop selling the products. Dangerous toys, for example, have been removed from the market. And massive recalls have occurred with such products as cars and television sets. A federal Warranty Act requires sellers to specify carefully what will or will not be done when a product is defective. Many product liability laws also exist at the state level.

Information

Increased protection of individual rights in the marketplace is a result of many factors. In particular, our economy has shifted away from primarily producing goods to primarily producing services. Most large service businesses need massive amounts of information. This need has resulted in the heavy use of computers to manage data. Vast amounts of information from many sources are collected, processed, stored, and distributed by computer. As a result, it is necessary to protect individuals and businesses from the wrongful use of private information.

Often, information is needed by other businesses, such as by stores to check credit card balances and government to check income tax reports. Only correct information should be entered and made available, and highly personal information should be available only in special situations to authorized people.

Therefore, businesses that extensively use computer information must handle information carefully to protect the rights of individuals and organizations. When information is handled carelessly, the concept of **information liability** applies—the responsibility for physical or economic injury arising from incorrect data or wrongful use of data.

Information liability is similar to product liability. If someone is injured by a defective product, the injured party can sue the producer of the product. Similarly, if a person's credit reputation suffers because a social security number is incorrectly keyed onto a credit record, the business is liable for creating the problem.

Also, a company not directly involved in collecting or recording incorrect information may be held liable for distributing it. For instance, if a store gives an incorrect credit balance to a bank that results in the refusal for a loan, the bank is as liable as the store that provided the incorrect information.

Occasionally, someone tampers with computerized data. Two federal laws passed in 1986— the Electronic Communications Privacy Act and the Fraud and Abuse Act—make it a crime for any unauthorized person to access a major computer system and view, use, or change data. These and other laws help protect the public from the wrongful use or misuse of information.

Jeff Greenberg, Photographer

Illus. 7-4

A business must protect its records from anyone who might steal and wrongly use information about its customers. Would it be wrong for a school employee to obtain a list of names, addresses, and telephone numbers of all the students and sell the list to a business that would then call or send advertising to the students or parents?

STATE AND LOCAL REGULATIONS

The federal government regulates interstate commerce while the individual states regulate intrastate commerce. **Interstate commerce** is defined as business operations and transactions that cross over state lines, such as products that are produced in one state and sold in other states. **Intrastate commerce,** on the other hand, is defined as business transacted within a state. Most small service firms are involved mainly in intrastate commerce, since they usually sell to customers located within the same state. Because most large companies are likely to be involved in both interstate and intrastate commerce, they are subject to state and federal regulations.

Moreover, each state has a constitution that allows it to create other governing units, such as cities, towns, and counties. These units also regulate business transacted within them. Large business firms especially are subject to local, state, and federal laws.

Many state and local laws are related to federal laws. Most states, for instance, have laws that promote competition, protect consumers and the environment, safeguard the public's health, and improve employment conditions. In addition, however, state and local governments regulate business by issuing licenses, franchises, and building codes, and by passing zoning regulations.

LICENSING

State and local governments have used **licensing** as a way to limit and control those who plan to enter certain types of businesses. In order to start a business that requires a license, an application must be filed. If the government believes there is a sufficient number of these kinds of businesses, the application can be refused.

Business is regulated not only by the granting of licenses but also by regular inspections by government officials to see that the company is operated according to the law. If it is not being properly operated, it can lose its license. For example, a licensed restaurant is inspected from time to time for cleanliness. Failure to pass inspection may mean the license is withdrawn and the restaurant must close.

Licensing laws vary from place to place. In some cities, business firms of all types must obtain licenses while in other communities only certain types need licenses. It is particularly common to license restaurants, beauty salons, health and fitness centers, barber shops, and other types of service firms that may affect the health of customers. In most states and in many cities, licensing laws regulate the sale of such items as liquor and tobacco.

Businesses may also license the use of property. For example, a computer software company may give a business a license to use and copy a software program in return for a fee. Likewise, for a fee a business may license another firm to make a product using its patented device. Even firm names are licensed. For example, Walt Disney Productions licenses its animal characters for use on clothing and other products.

PUBLIC FRANCHISING

Another way for state and local governments to control business is through public franchises. A **public franchise** is a contract that permits a person or organization to use public property for private profit. No individual member of society, however, has a right to use public property for profit except through a special grant by society. Cities often grant public franchises to companies to operate bus lines, or to install electric power or cable television wires.

BUILDING CODES AND ZONING

Local governments may regulate business through **building codes,** which regulate physical features of structures. Building codes may specify such things as the maximum height, minimum square feet of space, and the types of materials that can be used.

Not only do local governments regulate the types of buildings permitted but also regulate where they may be built. **Zoning** regulations specify which land areas may be used for homes and which areas may be used for different types of businesses. A business must obey all local regulations relating to zoning and construction.

BUSINESS TAXES

While government uses many different ways to regulate business, no way is more important than taxes. The types and amounts of taxes levied influence business decisions that, in turn, can influence the total amount of business activity for a region and for the nation.

Both business firms and individuals pay many kinds of taxes to local, state, and federal governments. Taxes collected by the federal government account for 56 percent of all taxes collected, while various state and local taxes account for the remaining 44 percent. Most corporations pay nearly one-half of their profits in various kinds of taxes.

GENERAL NATURE OF TAXES

Taxes are levied for different reasons. When government decides to levy a particular type of tax, the question of fairness to taxpayers must be considered.

Reasons for Taxes

Taxes are used by government for a number of reasons. Governments use taxes mainly to raise revenue (money) to fund new and ongoing programs. Governments also use taxes to regulate business activity.

Governments set goals that must be reached in order to provide the various services desired by the public. Examples of these services range from law enforcement and road building to providing for the military defense of the country. It is costly for government to provide the many services required. To pay for these services, therefore, revenue is raised by levying taxes.

Taxes are also used to control business activity. Economic growth can be quickened by lowering taxes and slowed by raising taxes. The federal government also taxes certain foreign goods that enter this country in order to encourage consumers to purchase American-made rather than foreign-made products. Governments at the state and local levels also control business activity through taxation. For example, taxes are often high on alcoholic beverages and tobacco, in part to discourage customers from purchasing these products.

Fairness of Taxation

It is difficult for government to find methods of levying taxes fairly and in sufficient amounts to meet government expenses. The question of fairness has always caused much debate. One problem is the determination of who will, in fact, pay a tax that is levied by government. For example, a firm may have to pay taxes on the goods it manufactures. But, since the tax is part of the cost of producing the product, this cost may be passed on to the customer. Another problem of fairness is whether those with the most assets or most income should pay at a higher rate than those who own or earn the least. Different solutions to the fairness problem are represented by whether a government adopts a proportional, progressive, or regressive tax policy.

Proportional Taxation. A **proportional tax**—sometimes called a **flat tax**—is one in which the tax rate remains the same regardless of the amount on which the tax is imposed. For example, in a given area the tax rate on real estate per $1,000 of property value is always the same regardless of the amount of real estate owned by the taxpayer. The total dollar amount of the tax paid by someone with a $400,000 home will differ from that paid by the person with a $175,000 home in the same area, but the rate of the tax is the same for both owners. A flat state tax of 6 percent on income is also proportional. Those with higher incomes pay more dollars than those with lower incomes. But the tax rate of 6 percent stays the same.

Progressive Taxation. A **progressive tax** is a tax based on the ability to pay. The policy of progressive taxation is a part of many state and federal income tax systems. As income increases, the tax rate increases. As a result, a lower-income person is taxed at a lower rate than a higher-income person.

Some local and state governments have combined the policies of proportional and progressive taxes. For example, a flat tax of 5 percent may be applied to incomes up to $20,000, and 6 percent on all incomes over $20,000.

Following the federal Tax Reform Act of 1986 and later changes, a combination of progressive and proportional tax was created. Many tax exemptions and deductions were eliminated and the number of tax brackets reduced. In a recent year, a 15 percent tax was levied on taxable income up to $36,900 on a joint return. On taxable income over $36,900 and up to $89,150, the rate jumped to 28 percent. The rate then jumped to 31 percent, 36 percent, and 39.6 percent, respectively. For singles, the rate was 15 percent on the first $22,100. However, while taxable income over $22,100 and up to $53,500 was 28 percent, the rate then jumped to 31 percent, 36 percent, and then

39.6 percent, respectively, for people having higher taxable incomes. Because people with higher incomes pay more than those with lower incomes, the tax is considered fair.

Regressive Taxation. The third type of tax policy is represented by a **regressive tax,** wherein the actual tax rate decreases as the taxable amount increases. While general sales taxes are often thought to be proportional, they are actually regressive because persons with lower incomes pay a larger proportion of their incomes in taxes than those with higher incomes. Suppose, for example, that A and B live in a state that levies a 6 percent general sales tax. As shown in Fig. 7-4, Person A with an annual take-home pay of $15,000 pays a 6 percent tax rate while Person B with an annual take-home pay of $45,000 pays only a 5.7 percent tax rate. Because the sales tax applies to purchases rather than to income, the general sales tax is regressive. For a less regressive sales tax, some states exclude taxes on such purchases as food and clothing. These exclusions are usually items on which low-income families spend a high percentage of their income.

Fig. 7-4
People with very high incomes often prefer regressive taxes.

	PERSON A	PERSON B
Take-Home Pay	$15,000	$45,000
State Sales Tax	6%	6%
Amount Not Spent	0	$2,000
Amount Spent	$15,000	$43,000
Tax Calculation	($15,000 × .06)	($43,000 × .06)
Tax	$900	$2,580
Tax Rate Calculation	($900 ÷ $15,000)	($2,580 ÷ $45,000)
Effective Tax Rate	6%	5.7%

Erik Von Fischer/Photonics

KINDS OF TAXES

Taxation has become so complicated that the average business person spends a great deal of time filling out tax forms, computing taxes, and filing various reports. In many business firms, various taxes reduce a great percentage of the income. The three most common types of taxes affecting business firms and individuals are income taxes, sales taxes, and property taxes. Figure 7-5 gives examples of the types of taxes that a business operating in only one state may be required to pay.

Fig. 7-5

The most common business taxes.

Assessments	Payroll taxes
Corporation taxes	Property tax—intangible property
Federal excise tax	Property tax—merchandise
Federal social security tax	Property tax—personal
Federal income tax	Property tax—real estate
Franchise tax	Sales tax
Gasoline tax	Severance tax
Licenses	State income tax
Local income tax	State unemployment tax
Motor truck licenses and taxes	State workers' insurance tax

Income Tax

The federal government and most state governments use the income tax to raise revenues. An **income tax** is a tax levied against the profits of business firms and against earnings of individuals. For individuals, the tax is based on salaries and other income earned after certain deductions are allowed. For business firms, an income tax is usually levied on net profits (receipts less expenses).

The income tax is the largest source of revenue for the federal government. While individuals pay about 70 percent of the total federal income taxes collected, businesses pay nearly all of the remaining 30 percent. The cost of collecting individual income taxes is, in part, shared by businesses. Every business is required to withhold income taxes from employees' earnings and turn it over to the government. Thus, business performs an important tax service for government. Fortunately, taxes paid by firms and individuals in the United States are less than in most other nations, as shown in Fig. 7-6.

Major Taxes for Selected Countries (in Percent)

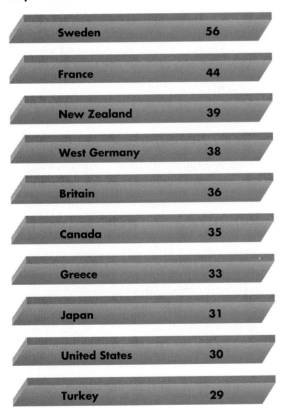

Country	Percent
Sweden	56
France	44
New Zealand	39
West Germany	38
Britain	36
Canada	35
Greece	33
Japan	31
United States	30
Turkey	29

Source: Statistical Abstract of the United States, 1992.

Fig. 7-6

U.S. tax rates are relatively low in comparison to other nations.

Sales Tax

A **sales tax** is a tax levied on the retail price of goods and services at the time they are sold. A general sales tax usually applies to all goods or services sold by retailers. However, when a sales tax applies only to selected goods or services, such as gasoline, it is called an **excise tax.**

Sales taxes are the main source of revenue for most states and some cities. Although state governments do not administer sales taxes in a like manner, in most cases the retail business collects the tax from customers and turns this tax over to the state government. A business must be familiar with the sales tax law of the state in which it operates so that it can collect and report the tax properly. From time to time, federal officials have considered charging a national sales tax. State officials, however, strongly oppose a national sales tax.

Property Tax

A **property tax** is a levy on material goods owned. While the sales tax is the primary source of revenue for most state governments, the property tax is the main source of revenue for local governments. There may be a real property tax and a personal property tax. A **real property tax** is a tax levied on land and buildings. A **personal property tax** is a tax on such items as furniture, machinery, and equipment. In many states there is a special property tax on raw materials used to make goods and on finished goods available for sale.

A tax on property—whether it is real property or personal property—is stated in terms of dollars per hundred of assessed valuation. **Assessed valuation** is the value of property determined by tax officials. Thus, a tax rate of $2.80 per $100 on property with an assessed valuation of $180,000 is $5,040 ($180,000 ÷ 100 = $1,800; $1,800 × $2.80 = $5,040).

EFFECT OF TAXES ON BUSINESS DECISIONS

Many major decisions that affect business firms are in one way or another related to taxes. Taxes may influence the accounting method a business selects to calculate profits and the method used to pay managers. Often, taxes are used as a basis for deciding where to locate a new business or whether to move a business from one location to another.

For example, assume that a producer of garden tools is trying to decide in which of two cities to locate a new factory. City A is located in a state that has a low state income tax and low property taxes. City B is located in a state that has no state income tax but has high property taxes. After weighing all the factors, the producer has decided to locate in City A. City A, which has both an income tax and a property tax, has been selected mainly because the total tax cost each year is less than in City B. Decisions of this nature are made every year by many businesses.

BUILDING VOCABULARY POWER

Define the following terms and concepts.

1. monopoly
2. price discrimination
3. false advertising
4. bankruptcy
5. patent
6. copyright
7. trademark
8. information liability
9. interstate commerce
10. intrastate commerce
11. licensing
12. public franchise
13. building codes
14. zoning
15. proportional tax (flat tax)
16. progressive tax
17. regressive tax
18. income tax
19. sales tax
20. excise tax
21. property tax
22. real property tax
23. personal property tax
24. assessed valuation

REVIEWING FACTS

1. When does a monopoly exist?
2. What is the name of the first major law promoting competition and in what year was it passed?
3. Which federal law forbids corporations from acquiring ownership rights in other corporations if the purpose is to create a monopoly or to discourage competition?
4. What is the main purpose of the Robinson-Patman Act of 1936?
5. Which act makes it unlawful for an advertiser to circulate false advertising that can lead to the purchase of foods, drugs, medical devices, or cosmetics, or to participate in any other unfair methods of competition?
6. How is it possible for a business to continue to survive even though it has filed for bankruptcy?
7. Name five federal agencies that regulate business activities.
8. What type of agreement gives an inventor the sole right for 17 years to make, use, and sell an invention?
9. How are patents and trademarks alike?
10. Name the federal agency that protects the consumer from dangerous food and nonfood products.

11. How is product liability like information liability?
12. Give two reasons why taxes are levied.
13. Would the federal income tax be considered a regressive tax?
14. In which tax policy does the actual rate of taxation decrease as the taxable amount increases?
15. What are the three most common types of business taxes?

DISCUSSING IDEAS

1. Discuss how a business that has a monopoly on a good or service can keep its prices unreasonably high.
2. Why is it necessary for the federal government to pass laws promoting fair competition?
3. Determine whether the following situation violates one of the antitrust laws and, if it does, which law is violated. Pinter, Inc., makes one type of flashlight and sells it to retail stores. Most of its flashlights are sold to large retail stores. For Stores A, B, and C it sells in about the same quantity at the same price. It also sells to Store D in about the same quantity but at a much lower price because it has been doing business with Store D longer.
4. Name at least three different kinds of practices that are prohibited under the laws administered by the Federal Trade Commission.
5. Explain how a computer software program might be both copyrighted and licensed.
6. What must a business do to protect itself from possible lawsuits if many of its employees have personal computers at home?
7. Sundial Products placed an advertisement in the local newspaper stating that its latest suntan lotion would give a deep suntan within 24 hours, without any danger to one's health. Within a week, ten persons were badly burned by the product.
   a. In what unfair practice did Sundial engage?
   b. Discuss how the federal government might control this company and its new product.
8. Monica Lopez wants to start a sewing shop business in her home where she can alter clothes and sell sewing supplies. Discuss whether the local zoning law that forbids her from using her home as a business is fair or unfair.
9. Which do you think is the fairest kind of tax—a proportional tax, a progressive tax, or a regressive tax? Provide reasons to support your answer.
10. Discuss how a local community can attract or discourage new businesses through property taxes and other controls.

REVIEW 7

ANALYZING INFORMATION

1. Three manufacturers that sell nationally discuss prices of a product that they all manufacture but which has become unprofitable to each. They believe that it is foolish to sell at a loss. They all agree to raise prices, but they do not agree on how much each will charge. Do you consider this action illegal? Explain.

2. Two of your friends were working in the school's computer lab one day. Because they received a failing grade on a major test, they figured out how to break into the school's computer containing student grades. Your friends were about to raise their grades and then asked you which grades you wanted changed.
   a. Discuss the ethics of changing grades.
   b. Discuss the legality of changing grades.
   c. If a student's grades were lowered, causing the student to be rejected by a specific college, how might a judge decide if the student sued the school?
   d. Can the school sue the students who changed the records?

3. You live in a state that has the following tax schedule:

Taxable Income	Rate
$0-$6,999	no tax
7,000-14,999	5%
15,000-24,999	6%
25,000 and over	7%

   Your state permits everyone to have $2,000 of exemptions from total income to arrive at taxable income. Your income this year is only $12,000 because of work lost due to illness. Your friend's income is $19,000.
   a. What is your tax this year? What is your friend's tax?
   b. What is the actual tax rate you and your friend paid this year based on your total incomes?

4. If the real estate tax rate is $3.40 per $100 of assessed valuation:
   a. What is the tax per $1,000 of valuation?
   b. What is the tax on real estate valued at $150,000?
   c. Using your local tax rate, compute the real estate tax on real estate valued at $150,000.

5. A married couple filed a joint return and had a taxable income of $45,000 after allowable deductions were taken.
   a. Under the federal income tax law described in this chapter, calculate their tax.
   b. Calculate their tax rate if their total annual income before deductions had been $50,000.

SOLVING BUSINESS PROBLEMS

CASE 7-1

Jason Romulus owns and operates a hardware store in a community of 50,000 people. The nearest town is at least 25 miles away but there are two competitors in the area who often run weekly advertisements.

Today, a customer he had never seen before came into the store. "I certainly hope you carry Weaver tools," the customer said. "The other stores in town don't carry the Weaver brand."

"Sure, we carry Weaver's," answered Jason. "It is one of my best lines."

The customer looked happy and relieved, and went to his truck to get the old tool he wanted to replace. While the customer was outside, Jason had a chance to think about what the customer had said. Now Jason knew why the Weaver brand was so popular in his store. As a result, he decided to raise prices on Weaver tools by tomorrow morning. Also, he could promote Weaver tools in next week's advertisements. A smile crossed Jason's face as the customer returned.

"Here is the tool," said the customer. "I hope you can replace it. As you can see, it is quite different from the other brands."

"I can see that it is different," Jason responded. "You are lucky to get it at this low price. The price will be going up in the very near future."

Required:
1. Does Jason have a monopoly on Weaver tools in his community?
2. If Jason raises his price by very much, what might happen?
3. Is raising the price suddenly (and for the reason given) an unfair business practice? Discuss.

CASE 7-2

Lori Lane is a computer operator for Crenshaw Associates, a data gathering firm used by local businesses. Data are obtained from many sources. One source is the local newspaper. On this particular day, Lori was handed a report regarding a Mary Ann Johnson who was arrested on a drug charge. Lori knew someone by the name of Marianne Johnston. As she keyed the information into the computer, she subconsciously keyed in the information under Marianne Johnston's name.

Two months later, Lori's boss called her into his office and said, "Because of your carelessness, Ms. Marianne Johnston failed to get a mortgage on a home she was planning to buy. She's suing the bank and us for your error. I sincerely hope you don't end up in jail." He then left, leaving Lori quite worried.

REVIEW 7

Required:

1. Can the bank be sued for Lori's error when it did not create the error? Explain.
2. Can Crenshaw Associates be sued if the error was not deliberately made by Lori? Explain.
3. Did the bank or Crenshaw Associates have a legal responsibility to check on the accuracy of the information Lori put into the computer? Explain.

Unit Summary

2-1 *Identify the characteristics of entrepreneurs and the process to follow when starting a business.*

Entrepreneurs are special people because they possess characteristics that others do not have. For example, they are cautious risk takers who like working hard in making their dreams come true. Entrepreneurs prefer working for themselves rather than for others. The independence of being their own bosses has special appeal for these self-starters. Furthermore, business failures do not block their desires to learn from mistakes and start new businesses.

Most successful entrepreneurs usually gain valuable work experience in a field directly related to the businesses they start. Men and women of all ages, races, and nationalities open new businesses every year. Before starting a business, however, it is wise to develop a plan that carefully describes the business in detail. A well-developed business plan establishes the specific goals, marketing and financial strategies, and organizational structure for the new enterprise.

2-2 *Discuss the advantages and disadvantages of sole proprietorships and partnerships.*

The sole proprietorship is the primary form of organization for launching a small business. The number of proprietorships far exceeds all other forms of business formations. A primary advantage is the ease of starting a proprietorship. No special agreements or business papers are required except for various licenses that might be needed to protect the public.

The attractiveness of sole proprietorships is also reflected in the owner being the only boss and the only person to receive whatever profits are earned. With smallness comes the opportunity for the entrepreneur to know all angles of the business and all of its employees. As a result, business problems can be resolved quickly, paperwork is limited, and taxes are often lower than with most other forms of business.

Problems exist, however. A sole proprietor may not possess all of the special skills needed to run a successful business. In addition, a sole proprietor suffers all losses alone. And when added capital is needed, it is much more difficult for a sole proprietor to raise capital. Furthermore, if the sole proprietor becomes seriously ill, the business may have to close indefinitely or permanently.

UNIT SUMMARY

2

The partnership is another popular form of business ownership. Partners generally hire lawyers who prepare a contract called articles of copartnership. Articles of copartnership usually help minimize problems that could occur during the life of the partnership.

A partnership can offset some of the disadvantages of the sole proprietorship. For example, two or more partners can usually obtain credit and raise capital with greater ease than the sole proprietor. Also, by pooling their skills and talents, several partners can usually help the business run more smoothly than the sole proprietor. For these reasons, partnerships are often larger than sole proprietorships, and the illness or death of a partner need not close the business.

The partnership also has disadvantages. One of the most critical weaknesses is that each partner has unlimited liability for the debts of the entire business. That means their personal assets can be taken away to pay debts owed by the partnership. Another critical weakness arises when partners disagree on basic issues that are difficult to resolve. Moreover, when a partner quits, the partnership legally ends. Remaining partners must form a new partnership.

Each partner is also bound by contracts that other partners make, even if they had no say in the contracts. Partners may agree on the division of profits before launching a business, but thereafter may not feel that the division of profit is fair in relation to the division of work. This too can lead to disagreements that can cause closing an otherwise profitable business.

2-3 *List the basic features and pros and cons of the corporate form of business ownership.*

While the corporate form of business ownership is not as popular as the sole proprietorship, it is the formation used by most large businesses. However, forming a corporation is far harder than forming a sole proprietorship or partnership. Stockholders are needed who elect a board of directors to represent their interests and who select officers to run the corporation. The board also sets general policies to guide the operation of the firm.

Forming a corporation requires a charter that is usually prepared by a lawyer and approved by the state in which the firm is organized. The charter includes the number of shares of stock authorized, the incorporators' names and the amounts of their initial investments, and the purpose for which the business is formed. If the purpose changes, formal approval must be obtained from the state.

The corporation has several key advantages. First, the owners have limited liability, which limits stockholders' losses to amounts invested. Second, large amounts of capital can be raised by selling stock to thousands of stockholders. The funds acquired can be used to expand the business as needed. Stock can be bought and sold much more easily than ownership shares in partnerships. And the corporation does not close when investors sell their shares.

The downside of corporations is that their tax rates are usually high and the paperwork is rather extensive. Filing reports required by the government and keeping track of stockholders' investments are time-consuming processes.

2-4 *Distinguish among several specialized forms of business organizations.*

Special forms of incorporation include nonprofit corporations such as private schools and charitable organizations. Cooperatives also exist that benefit user-members such as owners of cooperative apartments.

Joint ventures have also become popular between companies for large or special business undertakings. These joint ventures are beneficial when two firms, each with special and different strengths, find it mutually beneficial to work together to produce a product or service that neither alone could provide. An advanced variation of the joint venture, known as the virtual organization, has emerged. When quick action is needed to take advantage of a business opportunity on short notice, the value of the virtual corporation becomes evident. Many large American firms have found it highly desirable to create joint ventures on short notice to compete successfully in a global marketplace.

2-5 *Describe how business is both protected and regulated by government.*

Our free enterprise system has operated successfully for many years but not without basic rules for fair play. Early laws such as the Sherman Act and Clayton Act helped set the stage for creating guidelines for fair competition. A later law established the Fair Trade Commission (FTC). The FTC enforces many general laws and regulations. Other federal agencies were created to regulate specialized business areas such as power, food, drugs, communications, and aviation.

The federal government also regulates monopolies through the FTC. In some cases, such as with utility companies that must install pipelines and wires along roadways, monopolies are practical. In the past, businesses such as airlines and trucking were regulated heavily but were later deregulated. Deregulation creates open competition, which often leads to lower prices and improved customer services.

Free competition has a downside, however, and that is the inability to compete successfully. Federal legislation permits failing firms to file for bankruptcy. By doing so, firms may be excused from paying some of their debts. With the help of a bankruptcy judge, some firms are able to survive.

In addition to regulating successful and unsuccessful firms, the federal government also aids firms by protecting their inventions and other creations. Through patents, copyrights, and trademarks, the creators are given intellectual property rights that make it unlawful for others to use their creations for various periods of time.

The federal government protects consumers as well as businesses from unsafe foods and drugs, from damage to the physical environment, and from misuse of private information needed to conduct business. State and local regulations often reinforce and strengthen federal laws and regulations that protect consumers and businesses. Licensing and franchising of certain businesses are often required. Building codes and zoning laws are other examples of how communities and states control business conduct.

2-6 *Discuss the reasons for taxes, types of taxes, and the effect taxes have on business decisions.*

In order for the government to regulate businesses and to perform its many other activities, it must obtain revenue. The primary source of revenue comes from taxes. Some of the most common taxes are income taxes, sales taxes, and property taxes. Special types of taxes are common. Examples include taxes on special products such as gasoline, alcohol, and tobacco. The total local, state, and federal taxes paid by firms and individuals in the United States is significant, yet is still less than that paid in most of the world's industrialized countries.

Fairness is the most important consideration when a government decides to levy taxes. Three choices exist. A progressive tax levies a higher tax rate on higher profits than on lower profits. With a regressive tax, those who earn the most money have a lower tax rate than those who earn less money. And with a proportional tax, everyone has about the same tax rate. Arguments can be made for and against each tax choice.

Communications Systems

INFORMATION

Information and Communication Systems

OBJECTIVES

3-1 Describe the hardware, software, and telecommunications aspects of computers.

3-2 Discuss the technological, management, and systems aspects of electronic technology.

3-3 Explain basic communications concepts and the relationship of communications to corporate culture.

3-4 Identify problems related to organizational conflicts, international communications, and other organizational communication problems and offer solutions.

"Not every manager has to be an orator or a writer, but more and more kids are coming out of school without the basic ability to express themselves clearly. I've sent dozens of introverted guys to Dale Carnegie at the company's expense. For most of them it's made a real difference.

I only wish I could find an institute that teaches people how to listen. After all, a good manager needs to listen at least as much as he needs to talk. Too many people fail to realize that real communication goes in both directions."

Lee Iacocca
with William Novak
IACOCCA: AN AUTOBIOGRAPHY, 1984

Professional Profile

A LEADER IN BUSINESS DEVELOPMENT

Businesses engage in thousands of transactions with customers every day. Those transactions need to be processed accurately and efficiently. Traditional methods in which business documents are prepared and sent by mail no longer measure up to the pace of business transactions nor the demands of worldwide commerce. Automated methods of preparing and transferring paperwork and funds are now used by most companies.

Hatim A. Tyabji leads VeriFone, a company that manufactures systems and develops software to handle payment processing and other transactions for retailers, health care providers, and government agencies. Degrees in electrical engineering and business administration earned in India and the United States combined with over 25 years of business experience prepared Mr. Tyabji for his position as head of VeriFone. Under Mr. Tyabji's direction, VeriFone has grown from a small company serving customers only in the United States to one generating well over $200 million in revenues each year from worldwide operations.

Millions of VeriFone's transaction automation systems are being used today in businesses in more than 80 countries. The equipment is manufactured and maintained by a workforce located in facilities throughout the world. Those employees share the common values described by Mr. Tyabji, which include "recognizing the importance of each individual, promoting a team spirit, fostering open communications, strengthening international ties, and working ethically."

INSPIRATIONAL IDEAS

Hatim A. Tyabji, Chairman, President, and Chief Executive Officer, VeriFone

"Lead by example. You are the role model for those around you. Set standards of excellence and measure your performance against them. Demand the best. Be tough but fair. How you relate to people means everything. Toughness starts with your own standards, your own performance, and the example you set. Fairness is the other side of the coin. Judge others as you would judge yourself—fairly and consistently."

Photo courtesy of VeriFone, Inc.

TECHNOLOGY AND INFORMATION MANAGEMENT

CHAPTER 8

After studying this chapter you will be able to:

8-1 Describe computer hardware.

8-2 Discuss different types of computer software.

8-3 Identify technology for processing information.

8-4 Explain telecommunications and its importance in the computer world.

8-5 Describe technological and other management problems related to changes that organizations and people must address.

8-6 Discuss information management systems and the role of information managers.

efore flicking off his desktop computer at ten in the evening, Jon Johanssen composed several brief messages to let customers know their shipments would be sent out tomorrow. He faxed the messages over his modem and went to bed. At 7:00 a.m. he put his notebook-sized computer into the corner of his briefcase. While driving to visit a new customer, he used his car phone to call several of his fellow sales representatives to arrange a meeting for later that afternoon. Then he stopped at a coffee shop. While sipping his beverage, he recorded the late afternoon meeting on his computer calendar. Then he plugged in a CD player where he checked a street map to locate the new customer's address. He also called up a computer file to review the customer's first purchase order. Now he was organized to handle his busy day.

Through the ages, discoveries and inventions have had major impacts on society. No invention in recent years has had a greater impact on society than the computer. The personal work lives of Jon Johanssen and millions of other workers have profoundly changed.

Since the first practical computer was created, the processing of data has gradually shifted from manual to electronic systems by using computers and related technologies. Computers became popular because data could be processed rapidly and accurately. But the full potential of the computer still has not been fully realized even though much progress has been made in recent years.

Apple's Newton Courtesy of Apple Computer, Inc.

The traditional business office, for example, operates with filing cabinets, typewriters, and stenographers. Traditional offices like these are very labor intensive when compared to today's modern electronic office. The electronic office has little need for filing cabinets and stenographers because workers use computers rather than paper to process information. Simple business transactions that once took days—even weeks—are now processed in seconds by using up-to-date technologies.

Whether an office is in a bank, a factory, or a day-care center, it still is necessary to collect, process, store, retrieve, and distribute data. Despite its location, the modern electronic office is an information center operated by **knowledge workers**—people who work with information. Clerks, supervisors, and upper-level managers are all knowledge workers who handle data and information. **Data** are the original facts and figures that businesses generate, while **information** is data that have been processed in some useful way.

In this chapter you will learn about computers and how modern technology has changed the way data and information are handled. You will also learn how computers affect people, jobs, and organizations. And, finally, you will learn how information systems help managers make sound decisions by getting the right information in the right form at the right time.

COMPUTERS AND TECHNOLOGY

The introduction of computers into an organization involves understanding the basic elements of a computer system. One basic element is **hardware**—the equipment that makes up a computer system. A second basic element is **software**—the special instructions computers are provided to perform tasks. A **computer system** is a combination of related elements (hardware and software) working together to achieve a common goal.

We will discuss the fundamentals of hardware and software. Discussed first is the small device that is the most important part of the computer—a chip.

COMPUTER CHIPS

Computers can be compared to motor vehicles. The basic operating part of a car or truck is its engine. Similarly, the part that runs a computer is a chip. A computer **chip**—also referred to as an **electronic chip**, **microprocessor**, and **integrated circuit**—is a sliver of silicon containing circuits (transistors) through which electricity passes in order to process and store data. The first chip was rather large and could store only a modest amount of data. Today, a chip smaller than a baby's fingernail has enough memory to operate a small computer. Scientists are continuing to experiment with newer, lightning-fast chips, which further boost the power of computers. While chip sizes shrink, processing speeds increase, as shown in Fig. 8-1. Thanks to the tiny chip, today's small computer is more powerful and more reliable than the first computer developed in 1945 (the ENIAC) that measured 30 by 40 feet.

The Development of Microcomputer Chips

CHIP NAME	INTRODUCTION DATE	MILLIONS OF INSTRUCTIONS PER SECOND	NO. OF TRANSISTORS
8086	1978	0.3	29,000
286	1982	1.2	130,000
386	1985	6.0	275,000
486	1989	20.0	1,200,000
Pentium	1993	100.0	3,100,000

Fig. 8-1

New chips are constantly being developed by Intel Corporation and others to process data at faster speeds.

COMPUTER HARDWARE

As shown in Fig. 8-2, computer hardware is made up of three elements: input devices, the central processing unit, and output devices. *Input* refers to data fed into the computer system, such as the names of customers to be alphabetized or a math problem to be solved. An **input device** receives data and feeds it to the processor. Commonly used input devices include keyboards. The second element of a computer system is a **central processing unit (CPU)**, which both stores and processes data in addition to controlling operating procedures. The third element of a computer system, an **output device**, records, prints, or displays information in usable form. *Output* refers to processed data. Output may take different forms, but often it is a paper document prepared using a printer that is directly connected to a CPU. The most common output devices are the television-like screen and the printer.

Fig. 8-2

Computers contain three basic elements—input devices, the central processing unit, and output devices.

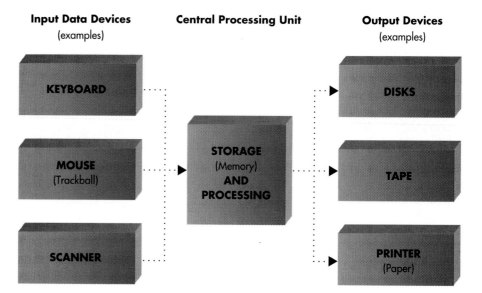

Input Data Devices (examples)	Central Processing Unit	Output Devices (examples)
KEYBOARD	STORAGE (Memory) AND PROCESSING	DISKS
MOUSE (Trackball)		TAPE
SCANNER		PRINTER (Paper)

The most common way to input computer data is to key (type) it on a keyboard. A computer keyboard resembles a typewriter but has additional keys that send instructions to the CPU. A television-like screen that immediately displays data is called a **monitor**, or **video display screen**. By viewing data on the monitor when it is entered, errors can be detected and corrected easily before printing or storing. A keyboard plus a monitor (with or without a CPU) is called a **terminal**. Data created on terminals are most commonly stored on disks or tapes rather than in the CPU, although other storage devices are also used. Some examples of common storage devices are shown in Illus. 8-2.

Of the various size computers that exist today, the microcomputer is by far the most popular. This desktop computer is also known as a personal computer or PC. The typical PC, shown in Illus. 8-2, consists of a keyboard, monitor, printer, and CPU that contains a disk drive. A **disk drive** is a device used to store and retrieve data on disks. The desktop is only one of many types of computers. The various types are described in Fig. 8-3.

Common Business Computers by Size

PORTABLE

Smaller than microcomputers and designed for portability; range from pocket size to briefcase size. Common among these are notebooks, subnotebooks, and palmtops, all of which use batteries and fit into small areas such as briefcases or pockets.

MICROCOMPUTER

A desktop computer used extensively in business offices; not usually designed for travel purposes.

MINICOMPUTER

A computer that is larger than a desktop and which can serve a number of users. Desktop PCs are often connnected to a minicomputer for sharing and storing common data.

MAINFRAME

For many years this was the most commonly used large computer in major corporations. Often used like minicomputers to store and share information among many desktop computer users in an organization. Supercomputers are like mainframes but are much more powerful and are often for research purposes.

Fig. 8-3
Computers are designed to meet different needs of users.

COMPUTER SOFTWARE

Computer equipment does not function alone. Software programs are needed to provide instructions for tasks that are performed by the hardware. In short, software directs the hardware to carry out the necessary procedures to accomplish tasks.

There are two general types of software. The first, called **system software**, is composed of procedures and routines that serve the general purpose of operating the computer hardware, such as directing the CPU to calculate numbers, to store information, and to find information stored on disks. The most common system software is a disk operating system, typically called DOS. A computer cannot process information without it. That is why it is always the first software to be installed when a new computer is obtained.

The second type of software, **applications software**, consists of instructions for performing various types of tasks. Many kinds of applications software

Illus. 8-2
The desktop computer has a keyboard, monitor, printer, and CPU with built-in disk drives. In which piece of equipment is the computer chip located?

exist. One fast-growing type of software that serves as a link, or bridge, between the disk operating system software and applications software is called a graphical user interface. A **graphical user interface (GUI)** is a software management package that uses symbols to select and shift among varied software applications and provides common desktop tools, such as a notepad, calculator, clock, and calendar. A GUI allows users to load programs easily, move from one software program to another, and transfer information among programs. The flexibility offered tends to imitate actions performed by office workers in a traditional office. However, the use of symbols (icons), a pointer device, and common computer commands among all programs improves the productivity of computer users over traditional office workers.

The most common software application programs that can be used—with or without a graphical user interface—are word processing, database management, and spreadsheet application programs. Other popular business programs are described in Fig. 8-4.

Word Processing

Word processing software is designed primarily to handle alphabetic (text) data and is the most widely used of all software programs. That popularity is not likely to change in the future because much of American business is transacted by means of written communications. Letters, memos, reports, manuals, and contracts are a few examples.

Word processing has distinct advantages over a standard typewriter. Unlike typewriters, word processing software electronically stores, moves, corrects, and changes text that is keyed into a computer. The primary advantage is the time saved by not having to rekey entire documents when changes are made. Dictionaries and grammar checkers built into word processing programs also improve the accuracy

Illus. 8-3

The most critical part of a computer system is the human element. Are writing devices like pencils and pens likely to be replaced by computers or other electronic devices?

REAL LIFE ADVENTURES by Gary Wise and Lance Aldrich

3-18 WISE/ALDRICH

SOFTWARE

WORD PROCESSOR

HARDWARE

PRINTER

© 1993 GarLanCo/Distributed by Universal Press Syndicate

REAL LIFE ADVENTURES Copyright 1993 Garlan Co. Reprinted with permission of UNIVERSAL PRESS SYNDICATE. All rights reserved.

Other Common Types of Software Applications Programs

TYPE AND APPLICATION

Fig. 8-4
Each business must decide on the most appropriate types of applications software programs.

ACCOUNTING

Maintain general and specific accounting records such as accounts receivable, accounts payable, and general ledger.

COMMUNICATIONS

Send and receive information from other computers and send fax messages.

DESKTOP PUBLISHING

Create high-quality newsletters, brochures, manuals, advertising and other special documents combining text, photographs, and graphics.

FORMS

Provide standard business forms such as invoices and purchase orders but allow for the modification of forms and the creation of entirely new forms.

GRAPHICS

Prepare diagrams, organization charts, line and bar graphs, pie charts, and other kinds of illustrations.

SCIENTIFIC

Calculate mathematical formulas, ratios, averages, and other statistics from data.

TUTORIAL

Teach employees about various topics, including how to use computers, how to supervise workers, and how to prepare a talk.

UTILITIES

Aid other software to work more effectively, such as providing a variety of type styles for printers, recovering lost files, reducing keystrokes needed to start a software program, and recovering data accidentally removed from the CPU.

of written documents. Sophisticated programs include graphics and desktop publishing features as well. The original word processor that appears in Illus. 8-3 can be used when a computer "crashes" or breaks down.

Database Management

Computers were initially used for **data processing**—electronically handling data that consist mostly of numbers and symbols but could also include a limited amount of text. The use of computers for data-processing purposes is widespread. Computers process financial, production, purchasing, and similar kinds of data from which reports are written.

A major type of software program used worldwide to process primarily numerical data and to provide summary reports is database management software, or DBMS. DBMS software is used extensively with mainframes and minicomputers. These programs are popular with microcomputers, too.

Spreadsheet

A spreadsheet software program consists of columns and rows into which data are placed and then analyzed for decision-making purposes. An example of a spreadsheet with an accounting financial statement is shown in Fig. 8-5. Mathematical formulas can be included to obtain such calculations as totals, percents, and profit. Spreadsheet programs are used often to develop budgets and prepare financial statements.

Fig. 8-5

Spreadsheets are used to prepare financial statements and other documents.

Cartright Corporation Comparative Income Statements

	Year 1	Year 2	Percent of Change
Sales	$58,000,000	$59,000,000	1.7
Cost of Goods Sold	30,000,000	32,000,000	6.7
Gross Profit on Sales	28,000,000	27,000,000	-3.6
Operating Expenses	12,000,000	11,000,000	-8.3
Administrative Expenses	10,000,000	9,000,000	-1.0
Net Profit Before Taxes	6,000,000	7,000,000	16.7

Spreadsheets and other software programs are prepared by **programmers**—persons trained to prepare detailed instructions that direct computers to perform desired tasks in a specified manner. While programmers help businesses create special software to meet specific purposes, many basic software programs are readily available from computer stores.

TECHNOLOGY FOR PROCESSING INFORMATION

Technology changes constantly. New computer technologies follow the information processing cycle: input, processing, output, storage, and distribution. The last stage, distribution, is discussed later under telecommunications.

INPUT

The typical way to input is to key data into the CPU from a keyboard. Data previously keyed and saved on a disk, for example, can be recalled and changed at any time without rekeying. Newer and faster or improved ways to input or manipulate data are a mouse, pen, scanner, and touch screen.

A popular input device to give commands is a mouse. A **mouse** (or **trackball**) is a small hand-controlled device that guides a marker (pointer) to a list of commands that appears on the monitor. When the marker is placed at a selected command, a button is pressed to execute the command. The mouse has become widely used as a result of graphical user interface software programs.

The newest device, which has not yet become as popular, is a marking pen, which allows using a special device to write notes that appear on the monitor. Notes are easily sent to others. Marking pens are preferred by people who dislike using a keyboard or need to input data when moving about. The pen is especially valuable to engineers and inventors who want to share diagrams or quick notes with others.

A **scanner** is a computer input device used to read and store handwritten, typewritten, printed, or graphic material. Retail stores use optical character readers (OCRs) at checkout counters to scan (read) bar codes stamped on products, which reveal product names and prices. Banks use scanners to process checks. Image processing occurs when a scanner plus software and special equipment are used to record, store, and retrieve records and important business documents, many of which might contain special photos, pictures, diagrams, graphics, or signatures.

Another device that aids computer users is the touch screen. By merely touching the monitor with a finger or other object, commands for performing tasks are received by the CPU. However, a special type of monitor is needed. Some retail stores use touch screens with computerized cash registers. Executives often prefer this convenient way of working with information. Data cannot be entered, however, by touch.

The ideal way to input data is by voice. The technology is available but problems exist. Differences in accents, pronunciations, and other speech characteristics are examples of problems. As a result, voice input devices are not sufficiently reliable for general use. Breaking the barrier for wider use is likely to occur during this decade.

PROCESSING

Data entered into computers can be processed in many ways to produce useful information. Improved chips enable computers to perform varied tasks that were not possible to perform with earlier chips. For example, commands can be executed simultaneously from several software programs. When two or more software programs work simultaneously in the CPU, the process is called **multitasking**. When multitasking occurs, computer users become more productive because several tasks are performed at once, thereby eliminating wait time between tasks.

OUTPUT

Output (information that has been processed from a computer) takes several different forms. For example, output could be stored on disks or tapes, or printed on paper. Printers come in a wide range of prices and performance. Common types of printers are described in Fig. 8-6. The least expensive printer is a dot matrix printer, which is sometimes used for accounting and statistical information distributed inside organizations. The more expensive and higher-quality laser printer is nearly always used for important documents inside firms and for most documents sent to outsiders such as to customers, suppliers, and government officials.

Fig. 8-6

Computer printers use different technologies and serve different purposes.

Common Printers Used with Computers

DOT MATRIX

Prints characters by forming dots as small pins strike paper. Prints graphics also. Somewhat noisy.

INK JET

Creates high-quality text quietly and quickly by spraying ink on paper to form characters. Prints graphics also.

LASER

Uses laser beam technology to print excellent graphics as well as text of high quality. Operates quietly and rapidly.

STORAGE

The fourth step in the information processing cycle is storage. Data not stored but processed in a CPU can be stored on a hard disk and/or a floppy disk as described in Fig. 8-7. Data needed infrequently can be stored away from the work area on floppy disks or tape reels. **Tape reels** contain one-half inch wide magnetic tape used primarily by mainframe computers for processing information sequentially and/or as backup of data stored on disk.

Fig. 8-7

Disk storage technology with increasing capacity continues to evolve.

Disk Storage Devices

DISK

A sealed, magnetically coated, thin "floppy" disk platter made of plastic and metal and available in different diameters, the most common of which are 3 $\frac{1}{2}$ and 5 $\frac{1}{4}$ inches.

HARD DISK

A thick disk usually measuring 5 $\frac{1}{4}$ inches in diameter which stores much more data than a floppy disk and usually is permanently built into a disk drive device. However, some firms use portable hard drives that can be moved from terminal to terminal.

COMPACT DISC

A hard unsealed disk on which huge amounts of data can be stored and read only by computer. Data storage capacity is well in excess of one thousand floppy disks.

OPTICAL DISK

A large glass or plastic disk that uses a laser technology to scan, record, and play back images appearing on documents, including graphics. Compresses vast amounts of information on a single disk.

VIDEODISC

A shiny disk that records, reads, and stores numbers (data), text, audio, and video data by using laser technology.

While tape technology has not changed much in recent years, disk technology changes keep evolving. To safeguard data, some firms provide managers with disks that hold vast amounts of data that can be removed from the computer and used wherever needed. By using removable disks, computer hackers are prevented from obtaining data electronically over telephone lines. As seen in Fig. 8-7, some types of disks have vast memory storage capacities.

TELECOMMUNICATIONS

Telecommunications (**data communications**) refers to a system involving the electronic movement of information from one location to another location. Information is communicated among computers by such means as wire and satellite. Sending messages over short and long distances is a critical need in today's computer world. A few of the major technological links among end users include local area networks and electronic messages.

NETWORKS

When microcomputers first became widely used, a special problem arose. Because each machine is an independent computer system, microcomputers could neither communicate with one another nor with large computers. Unlike a mainframe or a minicomputer, which has many keyboards and monitors connected to a single CPU, the microcomputer's inability to share information created a major obstacle to efficient business operations.

A special technology was developed known as a **local area network (LAN)**, an electronic system that allows computer information to move over short distances between or among different computers. A wiring system connects computers within a building or in nearby buildings. A computer such as a minicomputer acts as a server to the individual PCs that are seen as clients. The server stores software application programs that computer user clients obtain and also stores data created by the users. LANs are extensively used in business and have dramatically changed the former role of mainframe computers.

While many businesses install local area networks, national and international firms often utilize wide area networks (WANs). WANs use telephone and other communication companies to share information from different computer systems with branch computers in other states and in other countries. Even different companies share computer information with one another.

COMMUNICATIONS TECHNOLOGY

Today the communications process combines telephone and computer technologies to send or receive computer messages, paper documents, and voice messages from one point to another. Data communications marries the technologies of computers and communications to provide information-processing services wherever a business operates. Computer messages, printed documents, and voice messages can be sent to equipment located a few buildings away or many miles away.

Electronic Mail (E-Mail)

Electronic mail transmits and stores documents through a data communication system without the printing of hard copy. The most common use of electronic mail occurs when computer users send messages from one computer to another.

Many electronic mail operations occur within as well as among businesses. Assume, for example, that a regional sales manager located in Florida wishes to tell his national sales manager that orders for a new toy product cannot be filled because of lack of inventory. The regional sales manager could immediately key a computer message describing the situation and the need for the toy. The message would appear on the monitor of the national sales manager, who could immediately take action. This manager may first, however, send electronic messages to other regional sales managers to find whether the new toy is selling briskly elsewhere.

A message to all regional sales managers might read, "How are sales of the new toy in your territory? Respond immediately." Responses would then be used to make decisions about whether to contact the manufacturing division to request an increase in production or to ask the warehouse manager in an area of low sales to send a quantity to the Florida warehouse.

Facsimile

Data communications is also used to send copies of important documents quickly. Assume, for example, that a research department designs a new product and wants to know what various managers think about certain design features. A sketch of the product is sent electronically from the research department to other departments by facsimile. A **facsimile**, more commonly known as **fax**, is a machine that transmits a copy of a document from one location to another over telephone lines. A document is placed in a facsimile machine that includes a telephone. After dialing a fax telephone number at another location, the document is scanned and transmitted to the receiving fax machine. Fax machines can be stationed anywhere. Facsimile is used extensively because it is quick, easy to use, and inexpensive.

Voice Messaging (Voice Mail)

A third use of data communications is **voice messaging**, which allows spoken messages to be received by special telephone equipment that records, stores, forwards, and plays back. Employees are assigned voice mailboxes so that callers can leave messages when employees are away from work stations. Voice messaging systems have many valuable features. For example, recorded calls can be saved temporarily, listened to several times, and even transferred to another person. Voice messaging systems reduce the time receptionists spend answering phones, writing messages, and distributing messages. Voice messaging also allows more control over when employees respond to phone messages.

Managing Technology and Information

Running organizations that have been bombarded with a variety of new computer technologies, with new manufacturing methods, and with a workforce that constantly needs retraining is not an easy task. Various forces are at work within the computer field that add a variety of concerns to administrators who manage knowledge workers. Those concerns center on three areas: technology, information systems, and managing change.

Technology Issues

Basic technological issues that modern managers must address include never-ending pressures by competitors to fulfill needs of consumers in the field of multimedia, the need for information superhighways, and the need for systems compatibility.

Multimedia

The potential for consumer uses of electronic technology is still virtually unlimited. Current interest is particularly strong in the field of multimedia. **Multimedia** refers to the convergence of text, data, voice, and video through a microprocessor. Possible business applications are endless. Computer training programs, for example, might include animated cartoon characters, videotaped instructional materials, and background music as well. Managers can create reports with increased effectiveness by integrating text with graphics. A spreadsheet showing a corporate balance sheet could also be accompanied by the voice of the chief executive officer. A special dimension is added to computer-generated information when audio, video, and graphics are combined. The convergence of these elements may be delivered through a home television set, a desktop computer, or a new device yet to be invented.

Major television networks are developing extensive and exciting uses of multimedia on cable stations. For example, some major department stores sell merchandise on cable TV. Customers use a phone or a remote control device to place orders from their living rooms. It is also possible for film viewers to control the plot of a story as it unfolds.

The computer industry is fast developing the hardware and software needed to meet the demands of businesses that hope to attract customers by providing multimedia services. Desktop computers are already equipped to prepare, send, and receive multimedia messages. New directions for multimedia are still somewhat uncertain, but multimedia growth is inevitable. Changes in multimedia leave managers unsure about the purchase of computer systems to meet future needs.

Information Superhighways

Although everyone benefits by connecting computers to telephones and other technologies, increased uses of new technologies have created problems. One

AT&T—Calling All Countries

Questions:

1 Why is AT&T in a strong position to be the world's leading telecommunications company by the year 2000?

2 What makes competing with government-owned telecommunication companies difficult?

3 Because AT&T was a large bureaucratic monopoly until 1984, do you think it was wise for the court system to force it to give up being a monopoly?

Source: Adapted from David Kirkpatrick's "Could AT&T Rule the World?" *Fortune,* May 17, 1993, pp. 55-66.

Telecommunication superpowers are at work shaping our futures in terms of sending and receiving messages. One of the top world players is the American Telephone and Telegraph Company (AT&T). Other big players include Canada's Northern Telecom Ltd., France's Alcatel, Germany's Siemans, Sweden's Ericsson, and Japan's Nippon Telegraph & Telephone Corp. These and other serious rivals are all seeking to be the world's number one telecommunications company by the year 2000. That's not easy when in the past many government-owned telecommunication organizations tended to contract most or all their business to their nation's firms. Heated international competition will soon change that situation if AT&T has its way.

AT&T leads the pack of global competitors at this point for several reasons. First, under CEO Robert Allen, AT&T converted a traditional bureaucratic monopoly into a dynamic and flexible organizational structure with strong employee loyalty. Second, many government-owned firms cannot offer the many new technologies that other firms can. Third, AT&T has been aggressive in the development of new technologies—products and services—due, in part, to its world-renowned research arm, Bell Labs.

As a result, AT&T has positioned itself well in such areas as two-way video, messaging systems, voice recognition, computer-telephone machines, and mobile cellular phones. Moreover, its long-distance telephone share of the market is about sixty percent in spite of tough competitors like MCI and Sprint. Competitors are not likely to surrender to AT&T's strong initiatives. AT&T, however, is also developing new forms of technical equipment that will switch batches of phone messages from one system to another as messages cross national boundaries.

A key priority for AT&T is to raise total revenues in the international arena from the current 24 percent to at least 40 percent or more by the turn of the century. Spreading costs over many countries will help raise large sums of capital needed for research and other capital-intensive pursuits. Plenty of capital will be needed for achieving its goals, including being a key player in building a major part of the world's fiber optic data transmission superhighways.

problem exists with providing the best way to transmit exploding amounts of information on electronic devices across national boundaries. Voice messaging, international telephone calls, electronic mail, and multimedia demand more data routes than are available. One solution is to install fiber optic cables. A **fiber optic cable** is composed of hair-thin glass wires that simultaneously handle thousands of two-way voice, text/data, and TV transmissions at extremely fast speeds. Fiber optic cables greatly exceed the limited capacity of copper wires that are currently used.

Building fiber optic information superhighways, often referred to as data transmission highways, is a national priority that will take many years to complete. With fiber optic highways, it will be possible to read books or newspapers from home computers and select educational video programs at any hour of the day. Like a social security card, you might eventually have one phone number for your entire life that can be used wherever you might live.

By the turn of this century, a single electronic device will hold a computer loaded with software programs, multimedia hardware, a television monitor, a picture-phone, and a fax machine. This relatively small, sophisticated computer will also be portable so that it can be used at work, at home, and while traveling. Advances in data transmission are critical to the future of multimedia and all other electronic technologies.

Systems Compatibility

A major computer problem stems from the lack of standardized hardware and software systems. Each major producer tends to create its own system, which means users with different hardware or software systems cannot readily interact. When a business invests heavily in one producer's hardware and software, it cannot easily change to another system. Because computer systems control how a computer functions, the initial decision of selecting a computer system is critical. Otherwise, a lack of compatibility exists, which affects efficiency. As a result, when determining the present and future needs of a firm, managers must answer basic questions. A few of those questions are:

- Which computer chip should be selected?
- Which operating system should be selected?
- Which graphical user interface should be selected?

For each question, numerous choices are available. For example, does a manager select MS-DOS, Macintosh, OS/2, Unix, ProDos, Mach, or some other operating system? The answer depends somewhat upon which computer chip is selected. Confusion of this type restricts the free exchange of information from one computer system to another.

The solution to purchasing different system configurations is for producers to provide open systems. An **open system** allows for the relatively free interchange of information among a variety of hardware and software systems. Major producers of closed systems have much to gain if large buyers can be attracted to use closed, rather than open, systems. However, open systems are emerging because many of America's largest organizations will no longer purchase closed systems. Until open systems become more widespread, computer managers and end users will remain somewhat frustrated with closed systems.

INFORMATION SYSTEMS

An information explosion exists in organizations. Traditional methods of handling data have been replaced by computerized methods. Many managers suffer from information overload, the existence of more data than needed. Information overload leads to needless costs and inefficiencies. As a result, the necessity of managing information effectively is vital.

Illus. 8-4

Information overload can be stressful and cause health problems. What might one do to control information overload?

In fact, information is viewed as an asset in most organizations. Information that is well-managed contributes to a firm's financial health while information that is poorly managed becomes a liability. If information is not timely or is not presented clearly, managers are handicapped when making decisions. The development and management of effective information systems are critical to success.

When a computer system is used to process data for the purpose of generating information from that data, it is called an **information system**. Five types of information systems exist: operational information system, management information system, decision support system, expert system, and integrated information system.

Operational Information System

An **operational information system (OIS)** provides supervisors with information needed to make decisions about day-to-day business operations. Most of the important data are collected and processed in different departments of a company. The daily transactions are recorded as they occur, such as preparing purchase orders and recording sales. As transactions occur, they are entered into computers and processed. OIS provides all the basic information about the operations of a business. From this gathered and stored information, supervisors make daily operating decisions and send reports to managers.

Management Information System

A **management information system (MIS)** provides upper-level managers with information needed to control the overall operations of an organization. The OIS provides much of the information for the MIS. In a management information system, upper-level managers review what is happening at lower supervisory levels and suggest changes as needed. The MIS enables upper-level managers to control current operations at the supervisory level and provide information top-level managers need. Management information systems produce information needed for effective and efficient decision making.

Decision Support System

Today, the concept of the MIS has yielded to an idea that puts more control of data and information-processing activities in the hands of key decision makers. A **decision support system (DSS)** provides top-level executives with information needed to make decisions affecting the future goals and direction of an organization. Information used in the decision support system is gathered from the OIS and MIS. The set of files thus maintained for decision making is known as the **database**. Also used, however, is outside information that affects the company, such as information regarding competitors, the state of the economy, and government policies. With information from inside and outside the organization, top managers make long-term decisions that help a business grow.

Expert System

A special-purpose system, called an expert system, can be used by managers at any level. An **expert system** consists of software programs that help nonexperts make intelligent decisions. Commercial software has been developed, for example, that is of assistance when individuals make personal investment decisions, lawyers prepare solutions to legal problems, and doctors select treatments for rare diseases. Expert systems software programs are developed by asking experts how they arrived at the best decisions when solving problems in their specialized fields of study.

The expert's knowledge and problem-solving techniques are used when developing a software program to assist others to make reasonably sound decisions. Expert system software, therefore, can help managers solve business problems, such as finding the best location for a new factory, selecting the best promotional medium to market a new product, and choosing the best applicant for a particular job.

Integrated Information System

An **integrated information system (IIS)** is an organized way to capture, process, store, retrieve, and distribute information for decision-making purposes for an organization. Because IIS satisfies the needs of all decision makers within an organization, it includes OIS, MIS, and DSS. The three components of an IIS are shown in Fig. 8-8. Each system relies on the effective interrelationships among four key elements—people, hardware, software, and procedures. Building an integrated information system requires close attention to all key factors.

Developing any type of integrated information system requires careful planning. The cost and the quality of information are two of the most significant factors to consider.

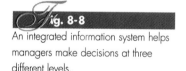

Fig. 8-8

An integrated information system helps managers make decisions at three different levels.

The Components of an Integrated Information System

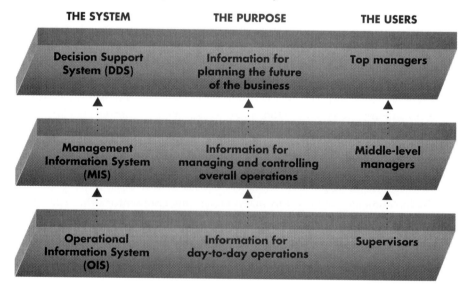

Information processing is costly whether a computerized or traditional system is used. The benefits received from a good computerized system generally justify the costs. However, costs are increased if unnecessary or unreliable data are gathered. Not collecting or processing needed data, however, is costly also. With inadequate data, poor decisions are made. IIS planning is successful when all managers specify the organization's objectives in detail and identify current and future information needs.

The cost factor is directly related to the quality of data. As noted earlier, information must be complete, accurate, timely, and concise. If information cannot meet these standards, computers will not be of much value. But if information is complete, accurate, timely, and concise, the organization will benefit from the quality of the decisions.

Designing an integrated information system may take as long as several years. Many actions must occur in developing the database, management information, and decision support systems for an IIS to operate effectively and efficiently. When developing an IIS, the specific data and information needs of the employees and managers must be known. To make certain this happens, basic steps should be followed. The more important steps include the following:

1. Appoint a director in charge of systems design. The director in turn appoints project teams. Each team concentrates on specific tasks such as developing a personnel or inventory system. From the information supplied by the project teams, the information needs are identified.
2. Decide upon the hardware and software to buy, methods and procedures to use, and personnel to train.
3. Install and test the hardware and software.
4. Put the new IIS into operation gradually while the existing information system continues. During this period, identify and correct problems.
5. Operate the system, observe it carefully, and identify and correct problems.
6. Evaluate the new system after a reasonable period as to whether the organization's goals and needs of managers are met.
7. Reevaluate the system and make further changes if necessary or adopt the system and make it totally operational.

While developing the IIS, employees are hired. Data entry workers are needed to input data. A **systems analyst** reviews current and proposed changes and determines whether a new or modified computer system will be beneficial. Computer programmers and database administrators are needed as well as an information systems manager. By the time the new system becomes fully operational, the system is ready to run for the

UNIPHOTO

Ilus. 8-5

Different types of computer jobs are found in organizations. Would you rather be a database manager, a data entry worker, a systems analyst, or a programmer?

entire organization. As the managing of information takes on added importance, the role of information specialists and managers takes on added importance. In major corporations, the top computer executive is called the **chief information officer**, or **CIO**. The CIO must not only be deeply knowledgeable about computers but must also possess expert management skills.

MANAGING CHANGE

Computers have affected our lives as consumers and as workers. As pointed out earlier, the work of employees has changed because of new technological devices and because firms have commenced restructuring the ways in which they operate. Computers have forced changes in the way individuals perform work tasks, which in turn has caused anxieties in people about their jobs, about computers, and about electronic devices that may affect their health.

A new and major role of today's managers, therefore, is to manage change. The rapid rate at which changes occur can be disruptive. To survive, businesses must be adaptable and employees must change to meet the needs of employers. The job of deciding how to change organizations matches the challenge of motivating workers to make changes in their work lives.

Reorganization of Work

Technological changes in business during the last several decades were made without changing how typical firms organized and operated. In recent years, businesses realized that sophisticated equipment cannot be fully utilized unless procedural changes are made.

For example, when a secretary gets a computer to replace a typewriter, the job changes. However, the secretary still answers the phone, receives callers, and keys documents using word processing software. Likewise, job changes occur when managers compose memos on their computers, send them to others, and respond to E-mail messages. The lines of work flow begin to merge. It becomes obvious that jobs and procedures must be restructured if new equipment is to pay dividends in increased productivity.

Using modern electronic equipment requires organizations to change the way they operate. **Reengineering** occurs when traditional operating procedures are replaced by more efficient methods. Computerized systems have made possible entirely new production methods in manufacturing, communications, transportation, and in nearly every other type of firm.

Office work has been affected as well as manufacturing operations. One major corporation, for example, permits customers to order by computer. The information is converted to computerized invoices, with limited need for rekeying data. Suppliers are permitted to review the firm's computerized inventory records and send merchandise when the inventory falls below a designated level. The number of forms used dropped from about 5,000 to 1,500, departments were combined or eliminated, employees were reduced by twenty percent, and the volume of business increased. The result was that this firm and similar firms need well-educated end users who have excellent computer skills.

Impact of Change on Employees

Other changes with which managers must deal are the effect of computers on employees concerning their jobs in general and on their health in particular. While many people see the information revolution as a blessing, others fear that society is not ready for it. They voice apprehension about misuses of data banks and invasions of privacy. People who worry about technological change often suffer from **cyberphobia**, the fear of computers.

Employee Anxiety. Most workers worry about job security, especially during periods when a shortage of work exists or when major changes occur in equipment or systems. Those worries are heightened when new procedures and new equipment are introduced, such as when a firm reengineers itself.

Usually, concerns about using new equipment are overcome when managers introduce changes carefully. Effective strategies are to notify workers well in advance of changes, seek feedback from them, explain how activities will be performed more efficiently, and provide proper training. Employees should also have the opportunity to ask questions and make suggestions before and after the installation of new equipment.

In highly computerized businesses, managers must be concerned about employees who become unhappy about job changes. Unhappy workers can be destructive by removing or modifying data. Good managers must recognize differences in attitudes when introducing new equipment or procedures. A thorough orientation and provision for open communication helps to reduce concerns displayed by troubled employees who adapt slowly to change.

Employees also fear that jobs will be eliminated when computers are installed or replaced. Computers have, indeed, eliminated some jobs. On the other hand, computers have also created many jobs. Computer programmers, writers of software manuals, computer operators, computer repair specialists, and computer salespeople represent new employment areas. Firms that use computers often do not discharge employees who are willing to learn new skills. As older employees retire, however, replacements may not be needed.

Employee Health. Certain complaints arise among workers who mainly use computers and other automated equipment. Employees may complain about eyestrain, cancer-causing radiation, backaches, and hand-muscle problems. Eyestrain is likely to occur when computer operators view monitors for long periods. Usually, eyestrain can be reduced or eliminated by adjusting light intensity on screens, shading screens from glare, wearing glare-reducing glasses, and requiring work breaks every few hours. Back problems are usually caused by sitting in uncomfortable chairs for long periods. Hand problems are often the result of improper keyboard or chair heights. Proper chair design with good back support helps, as do special exercise routines and designed breaks from being seated for long periods.

Employees may also be concerned about radiation. Many types of electronic equipment such as watches, televisions, and computers give off modest amounts of radiation. Some studies have shown that the amount of radiation is small and, therefore, does not cause job injuries or ill health. However, other studies claim computer radiation is harmful. Pregnant women are especially concerned. Many businesses assign women to noncomputer jobs during pregnancy to overcome possible harm from radiation.

The science of adapting equipment to the work and health needs of people is called **ergonomics**. Ergonomic experts study the relationships between people and machines. For example, they work with engineers to design more comfortable chairs and to produce lighting that reduces eye strain. In recent years, ergonomic experts have been spending much time making computer hardware, software, furniture, and lights adjustable, practical, and comfortable. Awards are now given yearly for the best newly designed or redesigned products in the United States. Well-designed products yield happier employees and improved productivity.

CHAPTER
REVIEW

BUILDING VOCABULARY POWER

Define the following terms and concepts.

1. knowledge workers
2. data
3. information
4. hardware
5. software
6. computer system
7. chip (electronic chip, microprocessor, or integrated circuit)
8. input device
9. central processing unit (CPU)
10. output device
11. monitor (video display screen)
12. terminal
13. disk drive
14. system software
15. applications software
16. graphical user interface (GUI)
17. data processing
18. programmers
19. mouse (trackball)
20. scanner
21. multitasking
22. tape reels
23. telecommunications (data communications)
24. local area network (LAN)
25. electronic mail (E-mail)
26. facsimile (fax)
27. voice messaging
28. multimedia
29. fiber optic cable
30. open system
31. information system
32. operational information system (OIS)
33. management information system (MIS)
34. decision support system (DSS)
35. database
36. expert system
37. integrated information system (IIS)
38. systems analyst
39. chief information officer (CIO)
40. reengineering
41. cyberphobia
42. ergonomics

REVIEWING FACTS

1. Why have computers become popular?
2. How is a chip important to a computer?
3. What are the three elements of a computer?
4. What is a terminal?
5. Name the five stages of the information processing cycle.
6. What are the three types of software application programs most commonly used by businesses?
7. Why is inputting data into a computer by voice not yet popular?
8. What is the least expensive type of printer that may be used inside organizations to prepare financial and statistical information?
9. What type of disk can record, read, and store numerical data, text, video, and audio data?
10. What type of computer problem was solved by local area network technology?
11. Name three ways that information is sent and received electronically.
12. What three areas concern administrators who manage knowledge workers?
13. Why do jobs have to be restructured when businesses decide to use computers extensively?
14. What two major concerns do employees have when change is brought about by new technology and work reengineering?
15. Name four types of health problems that computer users face.

DISCUSSING IDEAS

1. Shannon, the owner of a wholesale business that sells dolls to over 100 retail stores, is trying to decide whether to buy a computer and software to help with her busy operation. She has three employees. (a) Discuss whether you think such a small business needs a computer. (b) What type of computer would you recommend? (c) What two types of application software programs would you recommend if a computer were to be purchased?
2. An administrative assistant for a large company is trying to decide whether to replace an old typewriter with an electronic typewriter or a microcomputer. What points should be considered in making the decision?
3. Discuss the difference between disk operating system software, graphical user interface software, and application software.
4. A new business owner who just bought a computer plans to run a business preparing newsletters and manuals for local businesses. What type of applications software program and what type of printer should be purchased?
5. Would a scanner be helpful for preparing newsletters and manuals? Explain.

6. Explain how the idea of multitasking would be helpful to a manager who is writing a report on a PC. Assume the report involves collecting data on the number of departments that use computers and the types of software programs they use.

7. Discuss why telecommunications has become important in the computer world.

8. Why do major corporations prefer open hardware and software systems whereas major manufacturers prefer closed systems?

9. Explain why the installation of an integrated information system requires so much time.

10. Assume you manage ten workers in an office, each of whom performs a different task in a straight line work flow. You plan to replace the computers with updated machines and to reengineer how work is to be done in order to increase productivity. Your boss hopes you will be able to reduce the number of workers needed for this work by one or two after all the changes have been made. Discuss how you would go about making the changes so that employee anxiety would be kept to a minimum.

ANALYZING INFORMATION

1. Craig and Debbie Williams obtained prices from the following companies for a microcomputer system for their new business.

	Computer House	EZ-Electronics
CPU and keyboard	$1,400	$1,200
Monitor	600	625
Fax machine	400	350
Printer	900	850
Software programs	1,050	1,150

a. Which company has the best total price and by how much?

b. If the Williams' purchased each item from the company with the lowest price, what would their total cost be? How much would they pay each company?

2. The Onyx Corporation estimates it spends $25,000 annually to process data by using its traditional methods and equipment. A proposed computer system would cost $75,000 for equipment, software, installation, and training. In addition to depreciating the equipment at the rate of $15,000 per year, the company would spend $12,000 annually to process data.

a. During the first year after installing the new computer, would it cost more or less to process data? By how much?

b. How many years will it take to fully depreciate the equipment?

c. What will it cost to operate the computer system during the sixth year?

REVIEW 8

d. If the computer system is installed and lasts seven years, how much will Onyx spend in total for the computer system and how much will be saved or lost if the computer system is installed?

3. Poll ten students, or other people, who use personal computers at home or at work. Obtain the following information for your report.
   - What size computer is used (see Fig. 8-3)?
   - What brand of computer is used?
   - What type of disk is used (see Fig. 8-7)?
   - What type of printer is used (see Fig. 8-6)?
   - What types of applications software programs are used (see Fig. 8-4)?
   - What software program is most used?
   - What is liked most about using a computer?
   - What is liked least about using a computer?

4. A computer user took ten seconds to calculate a spreadsheet of financial figures. It took a bookkeeper 25 minutes to make the same calculations without a computer. However, the bookkeeper made an error that took an additional five minutes to find and correct. The data processing manager estimated a 25 cent cost when the calculation was done by computer. The only cost to consider for the bookkeeper is the $12.00 per hour of wages.
   a. How much faster was the computer over the bookkeeper in seconds? In percent?
   b. How much money was saved when a computer was used to perform the calculations?

5. Talk with several computer users to determine what ergonomic improvements they can recommend regarding their monitors, CPUs, keyboards, printers, chairs, or desks. Then list the two best recommendations made, giving reasons for your selections.

SOLVING BUSINESS PROBLEMS

CASE 8-1

Greg Rubick inherited his father's dairy farm nearly ten years ago. During that time, he had done well—doubling the number of cattle. Two years ago, he purchased the latest farm equipment when interest rates were low on farm loans. However, milk prices have fallen recently, and the farm's financial statements show small profits.

Greg has an idea, however, that may help increase milk production. He plans to purchase a computer and several dairy farm application software programs. He also learned that an electronic information system is available to farm managers. By subscribing to the service, he can obtain daily prices on milk, cow feed, and other farm items. Even short- and long-range weather forecasts are available. Equally important, Greg could learn from area farmers about other agricultural matters such as controlling insect invasions and stemming animal diseases.

The computer would also help Greg calculate the milk production from each cow. He could experiment, for example, with feeding different types and amounts of grains to determine the effect on milk production and costs. Poor milk-producing cows would be identified quickly, sold, and replaced. He might even consider putting financial data into the computer.

The information the computer system would provide, Greg believes, is important because it might lead to better profits during these highly competitive times. His main problem, however, is obtaining the cash to buy the computer system with sophisticated software and desk plus chair, which he estimates will cost $6,500. To obtain it, he will have to sell one of his cows. That would decrease production and lower profits in the short run. He wants to decide soon. His daughter, a computer science major in college, will be able to help him install and operate the system between semesters.

Required:
1. Should Greg further identify his farm management needs before buying the computer system? Why or why not?
2. Use the steps listed on page 199 and discuss the steps Greg might follow in designing his information system.
3. Use Fig. 8-8 and discuss how the proposed integrated information system for Greg's farm differs from that of a large corporation.
4. Do you believe Greg could increase his profits by purchasing a computer? Explain.

CASE 8-2

Alexis Wells and Marty Lane are both employed at the Waterford Company, a small life insurance firm. Both Alexis and Marty have been with the business for over ten years but are now quite upset by recent events. The office manager announced yesterday that all employees must attend several all-day training sessions on two changes being made. The old computer system is being replaced by a new one and jobs are being restructured.

Currently, when a sales representative sells a new policy, the work follows a long-established procedure. First, Carol keys information about the customer and policy into the computer. Second, the policy is prepared and then keyed in and checked over by Marty. Third, the policy is printed and mailed to the customer by another employee. And for the last step, an accounting department worker prepares an invoice and sends it to the customer. Other than the salesperson, four people are involved as work moves through the pipeline. Delays at certain stages are natural and expected, but the process is usually completed within two months. If customers have questions, they call their salespersons. The salespersons, however, often have trouble finding in whose hands the processing of the order is at the time of the call. Thus, they tell the customers it will be several weeks before an answer can be obtained.

The new organization of work will have each person in the office doing all of the tasks now done separately. The training will prepare them to do every-

REVIEW 8

one else's work, but all work will be done on the computer. To even the workload, all ten standard insurance policies will be in the computer and employees and salespersons will be assigned specific customers on an alphabetic basis. Then, when a salesperson calls with questions, the designated office worker can find the answers immediately.

The new computerized system has been installed but will not be used until the employees are all trained. They have just returned from the first day's training session. The following conversation took place:

Marty: I don't know about you, Alexis, but this change is just like coming to an entirely new job. I am very unsure about how all of this is going to work out.

Alexis: We should have at least been told about this in advance, rather than have it come as a complete surprise. We could easily get a job at another insurance company. Maybe we should quit. The company is not willing to give us more money to learn all the new procedures, new software, and new computers. With our experience, we should not have any trouble finding a new job.

Marty: Hold on, Alexis. We should not be too hasty. We make good money here. I agree, however, that they should have told us about this so we could have been doing some reading and getting ourselves ready for the change. If the system works well, our jobs will be more secure. Other insurance companies are changing their ways of doing things, too.

Alexis: From what we learned today, we could certainly make the company sorry that they did not get our opinions before deciding to change computers and how we work.

Required:

1. Describe what mistake the management of the Waterford Company made in replacing a new computer system.
2. In what ways could Alexis make the company regret not involving the employees in the decision? Explain.
3. If the new computer system and restructuring of the work is to be successful, will it be because of reengineering the work, installing a new computer system, or both? Explain your answer.
4. If the new changes are successful, how will the salespeople and customers benefit?

ORGANIZATIONAL COMMUNICATIONS CHAPTER 9

After studying this chapter you will be able to:

9-1 Describe the communication process.

9-2 Identify communication barriers and means for overcoming barriers.

9-3 Explain how corporate culture influences formal and informal communication networks as well as work teams.

9-4 Describe how to handle conflicts and how to run productive meetings.

9-5 Explain the types of communication problems that can occur when conducting business in foreign countries.

9-6 Identify ways to improve communications in organizations.

Erica Sakura, one of many managers for an international book company, sat at her desk looking at tomorrow's schedule. In the morning, she would review the new organization chart for her department that would appear in the employees' manual. Later, she would meet with two other managers and her boss to resolve a conflict. She dreaded the shouting match that was sure to occur between two people who never agreed on anything.

The afternoon would include interviewing a new employee and giving her best worker instructions on how to perform a new assignment. Then Erica would write a few business letters. She also had to finish her computerized monthly report for the division manager, which would be sent over the local area network. If the morning meeting did not drag on, Erica might also have time to return phone calls that *came in while she was dealing with a customer relations problem. Perhaps she could also squeeze in a call to Andrea in Accounting to learn more about a rumor regarding the sudden resignation of the vice president.*

Just before leaving the office she flipped the calendar page ahead a few days. In large letters she saw: "Meet with Mr. Yamamoto." She was not sure how to best deal with the major problems this manager had running the Tokyo office. At least she could recall a few Japanese words from earlier days when her family lived in Kyoto.

As she closed the office door, she smiled and waved to the evening cleaning person arriving for duty. On the way to her car she thought, "Tomorrow will be a busy day."

Erica is a somewhat typical manager because much of her time is spent communicating—speaking, listening, writing, and reading. Managers communicate in person, by phone and fax, by computer, and by paper documents. Communications are also handled through other means such as a smile, a frown, or a wave.

Communications are vital in running organizations. Communications provide a link between employees and customers and between employees and managers. In fact, it has been estimated that managers communicate more than two-thirds of each work day, as shown in Fig. 9-1.

Fig. 9-1

Many of a manager's hours are spent communicating, especially listening and speaking.

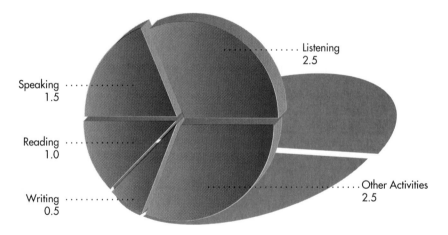

Listening
2.5

Speaking
1.5

Reading
1.0

Writing
0.5

Other Activities
2.5

In this chapter you will learn about basic communication concepts, corporate communications, and communication problems. You will also learn what businesses and managers do to improve communications.

COMMUNICATION CONCEPTS

For Erica Sakura to be an effective manager, she must understand some basic communication concepts. In this section, you will learn what communication involves and how barriers interfere with communication. You will also learn about communication channels.

THE COMMUNICATION PROCESS

Communication refers to the sharing of information, which results in a high degree of understanding between the message sender and message receiver. This meaning includes more than the passing along of factual data. It includes the sharing of ideas, beliefs, and opinions. The meaning further suggests that communication must involve more than one person—it is a *two-way process* between senders and receivers.

Communication is referred to as a process because it involves a sender who has information that must be put into clear words and a receiver who understands the message. If the receiver does not fully understand the message or if information is lacking, the receiver must request more information for clarification. Thus, feedback is critical to effective communication. **Feedback** is a receiver's response to a sender's message. The response may be in the form of taking action or asking questions to clarify the full meaning of a message. The communication process and the role of feedback is shown in Fig. 9-2.

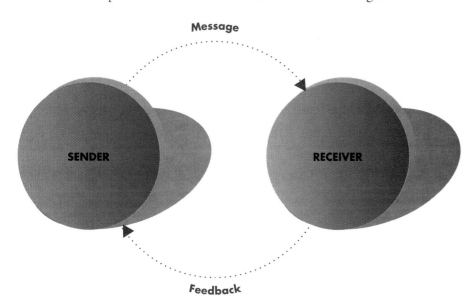

Message

SENDER

RECEIVER

Feedback

Fig. 9-2

The communication process involves a sender, a message, and a receiver. Feedback is also desired for effective communications.

COMMUNICATION BARRIERS

The meaning of communication is simple to understand. Yet, poor communication is one of the biggest problems managers face. Poor communication has been known to lead to disagreements, faulty work, delayed performances, and major industrial accidents. Barriers exist that interfere with the communication process. Two major barriers are distractions and distortions.

Distractions

Interruptions occur all too often while communicating. Anything that interferes with the sender's creating and delivering a message and the receiver's getting and interpreting a message is a **distraction**. Distractions are potential causes of communication problems. Two workers who whisper to each other during a meeting create a distraction that may cause a nearby worker to miss a point made by the manager. It may also cause the manager to forget to mention a point. Ringing phones, grammar errors in messages, and loud noises are other examples of barriers to communications.

Because distractions affect messages, some managers learn to work with various interruptions while others try to keep interruptions to a minimum. For example, some managers place telephone calls or write messages during specific times of the day when interruptions are less likely to occur.

Ilus. 9-1

A speaker can be distracted when others talk among themselves during a presentation. When two workers chat during a meeting, can other employees as well as the speaker be distracted?

Distortions

When messages are created, the sender must select the information to be included in each message. It is usually not necessary to include every bit of data surrounding an idea, an event, or situation. The sender selects only that information that the receiver needs to understand the message. Depending upon the information selected, though, the message can become distorted. **Distortion** refers to how people consciously or unconsciously change messages.

Distortion is usually not deliberate. People unconsciously pass along only information they feel others need. Often they leave out important data. Distortion may be deliberate, however, for self-enhancement or self-protection. For example, an employee may tell a supervisor about a machine breakdown but not admit that the machine was not oiled regularly. Or a manager may give an employee a very good rating when the worker may only be average. Distortions, whether deliberate or not, are serious communication barriers.

CHANNELS OF COMMUNICATION

In business the three major channels through which people communicate are oral, written, and nonverbal. All three channels are used extensively.

Oral Communication

In the opening story we learned that Erica's schedule for the next business day is nearly filled with oral communications. Speaking with employees, attending meetings, and receiving and making telephone calls consume a great deal of a manager's time. Day-to-day communications require frequent contact with people on a one-to-one basis. That contact may be formal, as when Erica interviews a potential employee, or it may be informal, as when she chats with another employee about the weather. Giving employees oral instructions is an especially common and significant task. How well managers communicate determines in great part how high they rise on the management ladder.

Written Communication

Written business communications take many forms. The most common are short memos, formal reports, and letters. Some common uses of business letters may be seen in Fig. 9-3. Other written communications include such documents as manuals, invoices, telegrams, and telephone messages. Other forms of written communications include documents commonly sent by facsimile (fax) machines over telephone lines or by computer.

Some Uses for Business Letters

- request credit from suppliers
- give and refuse credit to customers
- collect overdue accounts from customers
- request product catalogs from suppliers
- order merchandise from suppliers
- send information customers requested
- acknowledge and fill orders from customers
- ask for and make adjustments in customers' orders
- refuse adjustments in customers' orders
- persuade others to take action
- convince others about an idea
- sell goods and services
- congratulate others
- thank people for tasks performed
- request information about job applicants
- request interviews with job applicants
- hire or reject job applicants

Fig. 9-3
Business letters can be used for many types of messages.

How written communications are handled is extremely important. To communicate effectively, messages must be clear and well-written. They should also be concise. Long, unclear, or unnecessary messages contribute to information overload. In turn, information overload slows decision making and becomes an obstacle to effective use of one's working time. Written messages may also include the use of psychology. For example, good news should appear early in a message, and bad news should be delayed until an explanation can be provided. Good written communication skills are required for all managers.

Nonverbal Communication

Delivering messages by means other than speaking or writing is called **nonverbal communications**. Flashing lights, stop signs, and sirens are examples of physical ways to communicate. Even colors such as in traffic lights (green, amber, and red) signal messages. Nonverbal communication also appears in written documents in the form of charts, diagrams, and pictures. People also give nonverbal messages through body movements. "Body language," as this is sometimes called, may appear in many forms such as frowns, smiles, and avoidance of eye contact. Facial expressions are used extensively in oral communications as when Erica Sakura waved and smiled at the cleaning person who entered the building.

Illus. 9-2

Body language may get the message across better than the spoken word. What expression is the person in this illustration sending to the speaker?

Howard Grey/Tony Stone Images

Managers should be aware of messages that others give nonverbally. These messages are often given unconsciously. Sometimes a nonverbal message confirms or contradicts a verbal message. For example, what impression would Erica get if tomorrow's job applicant says "I am extremely interested in the position" but came unprepared for the interview and did not want to take the time now to fill out the application blank? As this job applicant has shown nonverbally, "Actions speak louder than words."

CORPORATE COMMUNICATIONS

Organizations develop internal conditions that set the stage for how communications occur. In each business, a formal organizational system is created that reflects an atmosphere that determines the extent and nature of communications. In this section, you will learn how organizations create an environment for encouraging or discouraging communications. You will also learn how communication network systems control the communication process.

CORPORATE CULTURE

Culture involves the shared values, beliefs, and behavior existing in an organization. The organization may be a corporation, a nation, or any other organized group. An organization such as a corporation develops a type of personality that is influenced by such factors as type of business, type of leaders who run the company, and type of operating procedures established. These and other factors affect the culture of the company. Each organization has its own culture, which members should understand.

The culture of a corporation influences the communication climate. Cultures differ widely among firms. Cultures may be very closed, very open, or somewhere in between. A closed culture is one that relies on top-down decision making and adheres to numerous rules and strict disciplining for violating established procedures. Distrust and secrecy often exist while creativity and decision making at lower levels are discouraged. In such organizations, communications are kept quite formal. Experts refer to this type of organization as having a closed communication system.

When trust and confidence prevail in employees, an organization is said to have an open communication system. Creativity and problem solving are encouraged at all levels. In such a setting, communications and information sharing are strongly supported. Trust, supportiveness, risk taking, and decision making influence whether an employee will like or dislike working for a company. In turn, these factors help determine how productive employees will be.

Most organizations will have neither a fully open nor closed culture. Sometimes, a business may change its culture. A comfortable culture for one person, however, may not be comfortable for another. Some employees prefer a culture with primarily an open communication system, while others prefer a culture with primarily a closed communication system. Employees often change jobs in search of an organization that has a set of beliefs, values, and practices suited to their needs.

COMMUNICATION NETWORKS

A **communication network** refers to how information flows through a business. Information flows through an organization in either a formal or an informal way.

Formal Networks

A **formal communication network** is composed of different levels of management with information flowing upward, downward, and across an organization in a prescribed manner. Typically, certain information such as budget allocations flows downward from top-level managers to lower-level managers. Other information such as requests for budget expenditures flows from the bottom to the top of the organization.

Upward communication includes oral and written reports from lower-level to upper-level managers. Usually, upper-level managers rely on lower-level managers for information that deals with new or unusual problems, the quality of employee performance, and the way employees feel about their jobs and the company.

Organizations with closed, rather than open, communications are less likely to benefit from upward communication. Upward communication is subject to distortion, especially in corporate cultures that are relatively closed. Supervisors, for example, might withhold or distort passing information upward when problems appear to reflect negatively on their performance. On the other hand, a supervisor might exaggerate information about successes. In a closed culture, employees often fear revealing negative information and avoid making honest criticisms.

Downward communication in organizations occurs mainly by memos, reports, and manuals. To be effective, this information should be timely and clear. In organizations with closed communications, there is often no opportunity for feedback because information does not flow upward easily. However, in open cultures, downward flowing information is presented to employees at meetings where feedback is encouraged.

Lateral communication flows horizontally or across the organization. For example, the production manager in one plant might want to know what problems other production managers face. Perhaps common problems could be solved jointly. However, many organizations do not have easy and fast channels for such communications. In a business with an open corporate culture, lateral communications are more likely to exist.

One communication expert has estimated that 80 percent of poor management decisions occur because of ineffective communications. Frequently, the causes for poor decisions can be traced to ineffective upward, downward, and lateral communications. That is why many major corporations such as Federal Express, IBM, Motorola, and Goodyear Tire & Rubber have promoted good employee communications programs.

Informal Networks

While a formal communication network exists in all businesses, an informal network also exists. An **informal communication network** consists of unofficial ways of sharing information in an organization. The most common informal networks include small informal groups and the grapevine. Informal networks rely heavily on interpersonal communications.

A great deal of communicating occurs among small informal groups, especially among employees who get along well together. These employees may or may not have the same supervisors, but often they do. They share information about the organization, assist one another in solving work problems, and look after one another. Members may even support one another when conflicts arise with other employees. Most employees belong to a small informal group.

Managers should not ignore informal groups. Often informal groups have more influence than managers over the behavior of individual workers. It is extremely important that informal groups support the efforts of the entire business. If they do not, informal groups can interfere with business goals and, in turn, hurt morale and decrease productivity. Managers often work closely with informal group leaders to obtain support and to test new ideas.

An extensive amount of organizational communications occurs in an unofficial way through interpersonal relationships. Employees working side by side, for example, generally talk about their jobs and about personal matters. These conversations are normal and usually do not interfere with work. Often these conversations deal with attitudes and opinions about their work, about other employees, and about supervisors.

The informal communication system that develops among workers is called the **grapevine**. Informal messages travel quickly through the grapevine and are often subject to distortion because they are often based on unofficial, partial, or incorrect information. That is why grapevine messages are often labeled rumors. Very often, however, grapevines convey accurate messages. For example, when a formal memo announces that a manager has just retired for "health reasons," the grapevine may provide the actual reason. The manager may have been asked to quit but was given the opportunity to resign voluntarily. When she calls Andrea in Accounting, Erica Sakura may also learn that the rumor about the vice president's resignation is true.

Generally, managers should not interfere with grapevines. Grapevines often fill the social needs of workers to communicate about their work lives. Only when a grapevine message is inaccurate and negatively affects company business should managers attempt to correct the situation.

WORK TEAMS

Global competition has required American firms to change from outmoded to updated organizational arrangements in order to remain competitive in international markets. Traditional practices no longer work as well as they once did. New organizational changes initiated by leading companies in recent years include important factors directly related to creating open cultures and improved communications.

One of the changes has been to involve more employees in the decision-making process. Increased decision making requires employees to possess more skills and knowledge, often provided through special training. Employees must also be able to gather timely and appropriate information from networking with other employees and through a firm's computer systems.

A second change includes the formation of employee work teams. While many forms of special-purpose teams exist, the most effective is a self-directed work team. A **self-directed work team** is a group of skilled workers who are completely in charge of handling a significant component of a well-defined segment of work. The work must be of vital importance and not a small, narrow task. A self-directed team has full authority over planning, performing, and evaluating its work. For feedback, the team may talk to other departments and customers who receive its work. In addition, the team is expected to talk to providers of raw materials or services to get feedback from inside or outside the firm. The team decides who will do which types of work and how it will be done. Each worker must be able to perform the tasks of most other team members when absences occur. Team members train other team members, hire and fire workers, evaluate performance, and handle most of the tasks performed by managers. The role of managers is to meet the needs of the team and to concentrate on higher-level management tasks. Some differences between self-directed work teams and traditional work groups are shown in Fig. 9-4.

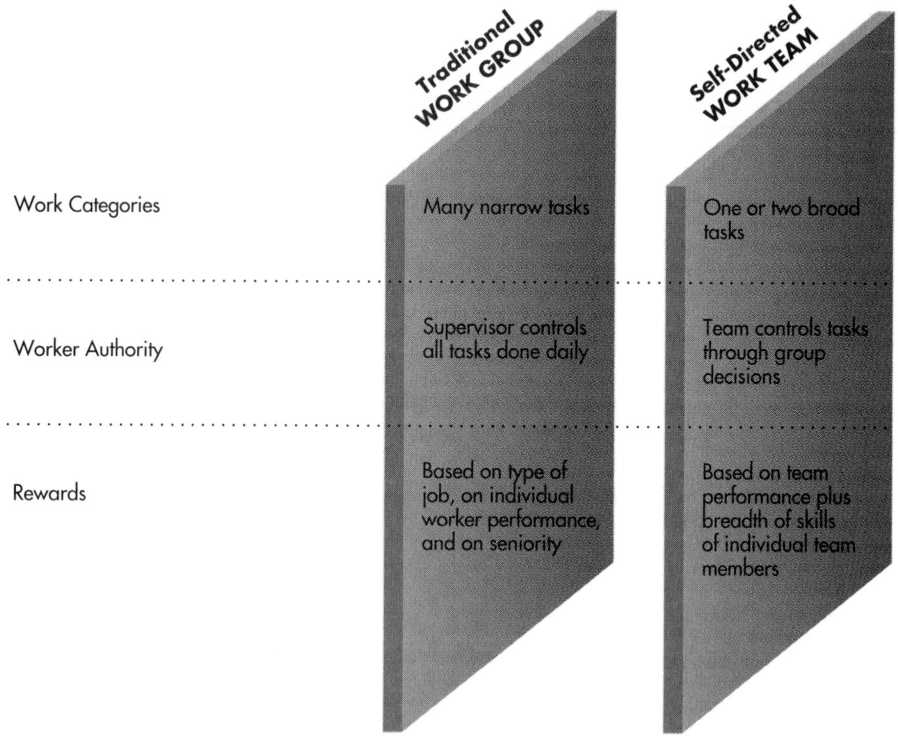

Fig. 9-4

How traditional work groups differ from self-directed work teams.

	Traditional WORK GROUP	Self-Directed WORK TEAM
Work Categories	Many narrow tasks	One or two broad tasks
Worker Authority	Supervisor controls all tasks done daily	Team controls tasks through group decisions
Rewards	Based on type of job, on individual worker performance, and on seniority	Based on team performance plus breadth of skills of individual team members

Effective work teams score impressive gains. Productivity increases dramatically over traditional work groups. Teams work harder than ever to improve the quality and quantity of work. Work is sometimes completed ahead of schedule. Customers are happier, absences decline, employee turnover drops, and team members are highly motivated.

Self-directed work teams require certain ingredients for success. Managers must support the idea and assist the teams as needed. Team members must become competent in three areas. The first ingredient for team members is technical job skills. The second requirement involves interpersonal skills, such as writing, speaking, discussing, and negotiating. Members must also be frank, outgoing, and trustworthy. The third competency area for team members is administrative skills, such as leading meetings, thinking analytically, and maintaining records. Teams that do not get adequate top management support and that do not possess the needed skills fare poorly. That is why smooth working teams usually take two to five years to reach their full potential. An open culture with excellent communication networks helps shape successful self-directed teams.

COMMUNICATION PROBLEMS

Managers deal with a variety of problems. Several important problems that challenge the communication skills of managers involve resolving conflicts, conducting successful meetings, and handling international communications effectively.

DEALING WITH CONFLICT

At times, people disagree with each other. Most job-related disagreements are likely to be temporary and are easily settled. Disagreements become a concern to a business when they lead to conflict. **Conflict** is a situation that develops when one person interferes with the achievement of another person's goals. Conflicts usually occur between two people, but they may also occur between an individual and a group, or between groups. Because conflicts are sometimes an obstacle to job performance, managers must be aware about conflicts.

Desirable Conflict

A small amount of conflict is sometimes beneficial because it may challenge employees and may stimulate new ideas. For example, the advertising manager may decide to budget as little as possible to advertise a particular product, while the sales manager may have decided to

Illus. 9-3

If handled properly, conflicts can be beneficial and productive. How do you handle conflict with another person?

try to boost sales for that particular product through increased advertising. At this point conflict exists because the goals set by each manager differ. However, this type of conflict can lead to a healthy discussion of how much to spend on advertising and how best to advertise to produce the highest sales at the lowest advertising cost. The result can lead to the achievement of a goal that is best for the business.

When conflicting goals are discussed and resolved, the organization can benefit. However, when conflicting goals are not changed, long-term problems often result. If the sales and advertising managers went ahead with their individual plans, money would be wasted and sales would be lost.

Undesirable Conflict

While some conflict in organizations may be healthy, too much conflict can be harmful. Undesirable conflict results when the actions of any person or group interfere with the goals of the organization. If, in the preceding example, the sales manager became resentful of the advertising manager and undermined the company's budget goals by deliberately overspending the amount agreed upon for the product, undesirable conflict would result. Employees who dislike others and carry grudges often cause problems for an organization. Therefore, most conflicts should be resolved as soon as possible.

Resolving Conflict

Conflicts can be resolved in various ways. Since each situation differs, it is necessary for the manager to decide which type of strategy will best resolve each conflict.

Avoidance Strategy. One strategy used to resolve conflict is to take a neutral position or to agree with another person's position even though it differs from your personal belief. This approach avoids the conflict. One manager may decide to accept the goal of another manager, or to avoid expressing an opposing opinion about the goal. When a conflict is relatively unimportant, the avoidance strategy may be the best approach. However, if a disagreement involves important issues, an avoidance strategy may not be advisable. It can often lead to resentment.

Compromise Strategy. A second way to resolve conflict is to seek a compromise. Everyone involved in a conflict agrees to a mutually acceptable solution. Often, a compromise grows out of a thorough discussion of the goals and the best way to achieve those goals. This strategy is preferred because it usually leads to a workable solution, since everyone involved personally contributes to the decision. Also, people are more likely to support a compromise strategy that they have helped to develop.

Win/Lose Strategy. The most dangerous approach used to resolve conflict is a win/lose strategy. A win/lose strategy is one in which no one compromises, thereby resulting in one person winning and one losing. A win/lose strategy is never acceptable to everyone, although people often engage in such a strategy. Win/lose strategies interfere with the achievement of organizational goals because they often (a) take time and energy away from the main problems and issues, (b) delay decisions, (c) arouse anger that hurts human relationships, and (d) cause personal resentment, which can lead to other problems.

Because win/lose situations are destructive, managers attempt to prevent them. Setting clear objectives that are understood and agreed upon, stressing the need for cooperation in reaching objectives, and working for group decisions when special problems or disagreements arise are ways managers can avoid win/lose strategies.

CONDUCTING EFFECTIVE MEETINGS

Meetings are a common way for employees to share information, discuss problems, and make decisions. Managers often prefer meetings because open communication encourages discussion and yields feedback that helps in decision making. Employees enjoy providing ideas and discussing them because it makes them feel important. However, meetings also have disadvantages. The chief disadvantage is the excessive time meetings take. Good managers overcome this weakness by careful planning and by following suggestions such as those shown in Fig. 9-5.

1. Have a good reason for calling a meeting.
2. Develop a specific agenda and stick to it.
3. Decide who should and who should not attend.
4. Schedule the meeting at a convenient time and place.
5. Start and stop the meeting on time.
6. Encourage communications by arranging the seating so that participants face one another.
7. Summarize the results at the end of the meeting.

Fig. 9-5
Suggestions for running effective meetings.

A second major problem with meetings occurs with those who attend the meetings. Differences among people may create problems. For example, an outspoken person may tend to dominate while a quiet person may say nothing. Neither situation is desirable. The person who leads the meeting should encourage but control discussions so that all ideas are heard, discussed, and summarized.

Two methods used to encourage group thinking and problem solving are the nominal group technique and brainstorming.

Nominal Group Technique

The **nominal group technique (NGT)** is a process a leader uses to involve all group members to solve a difficult problem that may create conflicts among members. Assume a manager has had a long-standing problem to which a solution is needed. The manager begins by stating the problem and following the steps described in Fig. 9-6.

The NGT encourages each group member to think about the problem, and it gives the quiet person and the outspoken person equal opportunity to be heard. Private voting encourages employees to choose the best solutions rather than spend time defending their own suggestions. As a result, this technique has been very effective.

Fig. 9-6

Steps in using the nominal group technique.

1. **Present the problem to be resolved to group members.**
2. **Distribute blank cards and, without discussion, ask members to write possible solutions by using a different card for each solution.**
3. **Read solutions from the cards and display for all to see.**
4. **Discuss each solution listed.**
5. **Distribute blank cards and ask members to write their three best solutions on separate cards.**
6. **Tabulate and display results.**
7. **Select the solution receiving the most agreement and present it to the group leader.**

Brainstorming

Problems arise in business for which prior solutions do not exist or are no longer acceptable. One technique for handling such situations is by brainstorming. **Brainstorming** is a group discussion technique used to generate as many ideas as possible for solving a problem. A group leader presents a problem and asks group members to offer any solution that comes to mind. Even wild and

Ilus. 9-4

A brainstorming session seeks to obtain new ideas for solving a problem—the more ideas the better. How many ideas can you think of for recycling chalk dust found in classroom chalkboard trays?

Bruce Ayres/Tony Stone Images

unimagined ideas are encouraged. No attempt is made to judge the goodness of any ideas while brainstorming is under way. Only after all possible ideas have been presented are they judged for usefulness. Often, an idea that appeared to be impractical or unusual when first presented may become the solution to the problem. Brainstorming is frequently used to deal with special types of problems where many solutions are desired, such as when generating new product ideas.

COMMUNICATING IN OTHER COUNTRIES

No aspect of international business is more troublesome than communicating. Written, oral, and nonverbal communication practices differ among countries. Just as organizations have cultures, so too do countries. The values, beliefs, and practices of people differ worldwide. Because nations differ greatly, some of the types of barriers that managers face when doing business abroad are created by language, cultural, and nonverbal differences.

Language Differences

Not enough American managers speak a foreign language fluently. However, speaking a foreign language fluently does not solve all problems. Although Americans, Australians, and the British all speak English, accents and peculiar word usage cause problems. Some differences between words used to describe the same things by American and British people are shown in Fig. 9-7 on page 225.

The people of most nations realize that learning a new language is often difficult. But they are more than willing to help foreigners learn. They are especially impressed when someone who does not know their language makes a noble effort to learn. Many corporations now provide intensive language training for managers assigned to foreign branches. Knowledge of the social customs and education, legal, and political systems are included in the instruction.

Joint ventures between American and foreign firms often reveal language problems. A successful joint venture between Ford Motor Co. and the Japanese Mazda Motors Corp. provides an example of overcoming language difficulties. The president of Mazda estimates that twenty percent of the meaning of a conversation with Ford leaders is lost between him and the interpreters. Another twenty percent is lost between the interpreters and the Ford leaders. Working with only about two-thirds understanding, the Mazda president tries extra hard to make sure his message is getting through. He especially believes people should meet face-to-face and talk freely. Successful products like the Ford Escort and the Mazda Protege are testimony to foreigners overcoming language barriers to build a strong international auto team.

Cultural Differences

People from other countries place different values on such things as family, status, and power. Countries value families differently. In India, for example, providing jobs for male family members in a business is more important than

Ethical Issues

ONLY ENGLISH SPOKEN HERE!

Questions:

1 Does an American business have the right to declare English as the official language within the company? Explain.

2 Do you believe the employees should be given a chance to learn the language before implementing the policy? Explain.

3 Was a written memo the appropriate delivery channel? What other choices would you recommend?

4 Why should employees and managers have an opportunity to provide feedback on the policy before it is implemented?

The Marxon Antique Corporation surprised employees by announcing a new policy stating that the official language of the company is English. "Effective immediately, all communications regarding business matters must be spoken and written in the English language."

The official memo included an explanation for the policy. Because so many different languages are spoken within the company, confusion exists from time to time. An American company should conduct business in one language. Employees may use their native languages during rest breaks (mid-morning and afternoon) and with customers who cannot speak English. At all other times, English must be spoken. Supervisors are expected to monitor the new policy carefully and report all violators to the human resources department. Employees who violate the policy more than twice will be required, at company expense, to attend company-sponsored English language training classes during nonwork hours—evenings and Saturdays.

Nearly two-thirds of all workers are first- or second-generation immigrants. The two primary languages spoken are Chinese and Spanish. Some speak Japanese and Italian. A few of the workers who only speak English reported feeling uncomfortable hearing so many languages. Errors have occurred that were blamed on miscommunication. Some employees have unthinkingly written memos in their own language.

The Marxon Corporation has a diverse workforce. "It is not our intent to be biased toward other languages or cultures. Rather, we wish to reduce the number of misunderstandings and errors caused during translations. The policy should also reduce feelings of exclusion on the part of some employees. One official business language is in the best interests of the company and the employees."

Many of the employees were upset by the policy. A few did not think they knew English well enough; they quit. Others demanded English training before the policy took effect. Still others believed it was a violation of free speech in a country that touts freedom so highly. Some managers feared that the different language groups would unify and exert strong pressure against management, such as by forming a union or bringing a lawsuit. Negative press coverage might also make it more difficult to hire new workers.

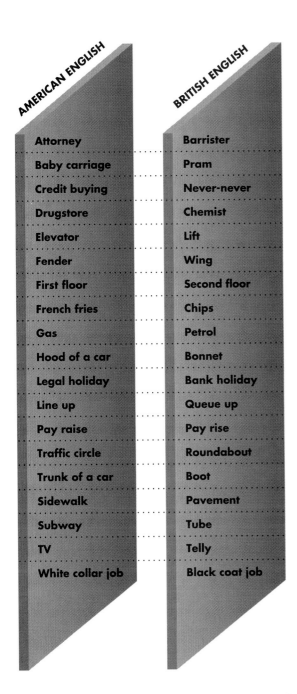

Fig. 9-7

How British English differs from American English.

AMERICAN ENGLISH	BRITISH ENGLISH
Attorney	Barrister
Baby carriage	Pram
Credit buying	Never-never
Drugstore	Chemist
Elevator	Lift
Fender	Wing
First floor	Second floor
French fries	Chips
Gas	Petrol
Hood of a car	Bonnet
Legal holiday	Bank holiday
Line up	Queue up
Pay raise	Pay rise
Traffic circle	Roundabout
Trunk of a car	Boot
Sidewalk	Pavement
Subway	Tube
TV	Telly
White collar job	Black coat job

earning a profit. Humor differs worldwide, too. In addition, accepted practices in one country may be impolite elsewhere. For example, American business people generally like to start and end meetings on time. In Japan and certain other countries, this practice would be considered rude rather than businesslike.

Nonverbal Differences

Great differences exist in the area of nonverbal communications, especially body language. For example, how close one stands when talking to someone else differs from one country to another. For most conversations, Americans stand two to three feet apart whereas Middle Eastern people stand much closer. Even colors have different meanings. In Western countries, black is often associated with death, but in Latin American countries, death is represented by white and purple. A handshake also varies from place to place. In Spain, it should last from five to seven shakes but the French prefer one single shake.

Because differences exist among nations, executives prefer to conduct extremely important business transactions in a formal manner. Usually, that means greater use of written reports and expert translators. For oral translation services by phone, AT&T provides an 800-number to assist callers. However, for day-to-day international operations, managers must learn to understand the cultural and communication practices of other nations.

IMPROVING ORGANIZATIONAL COMMUNICATIONS

Good managers are usually good communicators. They are effective managers because they understand human behavior. They also practice effective communication skills, some of which are discussed next.

ENCOURAGE TWO-WAY COMMUNICATIONS

Small businesses provide for plenty of two-way communication situations between owners and employees. As companies get larger, however, a shift to one-way communications often occurs for efficiency purposes. When this happens, problems arise because valuable feedback from employees and customers is reduced. Good managers establish plans to obtain feedback even when they are extremely busy. Some managers, however, discourage two-way communications because they feel uncomfortable with it and because it is time-consuming. Organizations that encourage managers to consciously engage in two-way communications, however, are often more successful than those that do not.

LISTEN ACTIVELY

Two-way communications assure feedback. Effective listening results in effective feedback. Frequently, employees have questions and encounter problems when doing what has been asked. They need to talk to someone who listens carefully. A distinction exists between hearing and listening. Most people are able to hear when someone speaks but they may not pay attention to the message. Listening involves hearing and understanding. A good listener makes every effort to practice the rules shown in Fig. 9-8 to make certain that messages have been received accurately.

FACILITATE UPWARD COMMUNICATION

In large organizations, upward communication is sometimes neglected. Managers may not want to hear complaints or deal with suggestions because they require time. To make certain upward communications occur, some businesses ask managers to use certain techniques.

Rule and Reason Behind the Rule

Fig. 9-8
Ten rules for good listening.

1. Stop talking!

You cannot listen if you are talking.

2. Put the talker at ease.

Help a person feel free to talk; create a permissive environment.

3. Show a talker that you want to listen.

Look and act interested; listen to understand, not to oppose.

4. Remove distractions.

Don't doodle, tap, or shuffle papers; shut the door if necessary to acheive quiet.

5. Empathize with talkers.

Try to see the other person's point of view.

6. Be patient.

Allow plenty of time; do not interrupt; do not start for the door or walk away.

7. Hold your temper.

An angry person takes the wrong meaning from words.

8. Go easy on arguement and criticism.

These put people on the defensive and may cause them to "clam up" or become angry. Do not argue—even if you win, you lose.

9. Ask questions.

This encourages a talker and shows that you are listening. It helps to develop points further.

10. Stop talking!

This is first and last, because all other guides depend on it. You cannot do an effective listening job while you are talking. Remember that:

- Nature gave people two ears but only one tongue, which is a gentle hint that they should listen more than they talk.
- Listening requires two ears, one for meaning and one for feeling.
- Decision makers who do not listen have less information for making sound decisions.

Source: Adapted from HUMAN BEHAVIOR AT WORK: Organizational Behavior, Ninth Edition, by John W. Newstrom and Keith Davis. Copyright © 1993 by Keith Davis. Used with permission of McGraw-Hill Publishing Company.

One technique is called "management by walking around." Managers leave their offices from time to time and make trips through the working areas. While doing this, they chat with employees about various problems and conditions.

A somewhat similar, but older, practice is for managers to encourage employees to meet with them when they have concerns. To control the time

Jeff Greenberg, Photographer

this "open door policy" takes, some managers restrict the practice to one hour per week when employees can make appointments. Suggestion boxes have been used for many years and have great value for encouraging communications.

No technique is better than regular meetings with employees. Some firms select a certain number of employees from different departments and organizational levels to meet with top managers on a regular basis. The manager informs them about important company matters and invites questions and ideas. Studies have shown that employees who are informed about their companies have stronger positive feelings than those who are not. These top-level managers benefit by getting feedback from people throughout the company.

SELECT COMMUNICATION CHANNELS CAREFULLY

When managers want to communicate with others, they should carefully select an appropriate communication channel. Generally, when a manager must reprimand an employee or settle a dispute, the oral communication channel is best. The oral channel is needed to explain the reason for the reprimand or to work out an acceptable solution to a dispute.

The written communication channel is best when managers want to communicate information requiring future action or to communicate information of a general nature. Such matters should be put in writing for later reference. Following up on information provided in writing is desirable under most circumstances because it serves as a reminder that the information is important and it provides an opportunity for the receiver to ask questions.

In today's computer world, E-mail is used often because it is fast, easy to use, and provides immediate feedback, but it is impersonal and not suited to lengthy topics. The strength of E-mail, therefore, is in the delivery of concise and candid information to co-workers.

In some situations, it may be desirable to use two channels of communication—first oral and then written. Using both channels is preferable when (a) an immediate order must be given, (b) a new policy is announced, (c) a supervisor is contacted about work problems, and (d) an employee is complimented for excellent work. In most of these situations, the information is best delivered orally on a one-to-one basis, which personalizes it and allows for immediate feedback. The written channel then allows for reinforcement and creates a record of the event.

Improving the communication process in business requires the efforts of everyone. Effective speaking and listening, as well as effective writing and reading, are the responsibilities of both message senders and receivers. People need to communicate for social and work purposes. How well they communicate is determined by their jobs, personalities, and cultural backgrounds. The communication process is improved greatly when communication strengths are understood and weaknesses are corrected.

CHAPTER REVIEW

B UILDING VOCABULARY POWER

Define the following terms and concepts.

1. communication
2. feedback
3. distraction
4. distortion
5. nonverbal communications
6. culture
7. communication network
8. formal communication network
9. informal communication network
10. grapevine
11. self-directed work team
12. conflict
13. nominal group technique (NGT)
14. brainstorming

R EVIEWING FACTS

1. How much time do managers spend each day communicating?
2. Why is communications referred to as a process?
3. Name three problems that can occur in a business when poor communications exist.

4. What are two major barriers to communications?
5. Name the three major channels used in business for communicating.
6. What is "body language"?
7. What are some characteristics of a business that has a closed culture?
8. One management expert has stated that 80% of poor management decisions are a result of poor communications. What are three causes for this?
9. Are messages that flow through the grapevine often incorrect?
10. What three strategies can a manager use to resolve conflicts?
11. Give five suggestions for running an effective meeting.
12. Would the nominal group technique or brainstorming be more effective in solving a troublesome work problem that is likely to create conflicts among employees?
13. List three types of differences about which American managers must be aware when transacting business in other countries.
14. Name four skills that good managers use to build effective communications.
15. In what types of situations would it be desirable to use both oral and written channels of communication?

D ISCUSSING IDEAS

1. Discuss the importance of feedback in two-way communications.
2. Explain how a grammar error in a memo might be considered a distraction and thus a barrier to communications.
3. Distortion is not always unconsciously done. Discuss how conscious distortion can be harmful if an employee regularly distorts information to a supervisor.
4. Describe the psychology behind why good news should be stated early in a written message and why bad news should be delayed somewhat.
5. A manager was enjoying giving a talk to a group of young people about business. An audience member asked the manager whether he believed in open communications. The manager looked uncomfortable with the question, snapped a fast "yes," and quickly said, "Any other questions?" Compare the oral and nonverbal message of the manager.
6. Discuss the main factors that help to determine the culture for an organization.
7. Discuss how small, informal groups can be helpful or harmful to a manager.
8. Present the negative factors that would have to exist for a self-directed work team to fail in a business.
9. Discuss what strategy you would use to help resolve a conflict situation between two employees who always disagree on how a task should be handled.
10. Even though English is spoken in the United States and in Britain, communication problems could occur for a business with branch offices in the

REVIEW 9

two countries. Discuss possible problems that might occur between an American manager and a British manager.

11. Although cultures differ from country to country, how can cultures differ within a country such as the United States?

12. How might busy managers in a business follow a policy of encouraging effective listening?

ANALYZING INFORMATION

1. From Fig. 9-1, determine the percentage of time managers spend each work day (a) listening, (b) speaking, (c) reading, and (d) writing. Also, determine the total percentage of time that is spent in communicating and in other activities.

2. The nonverbal communication channel involves the use of body language. When your teacher directs you, demonstrate five different messages by using only your hands and/or arms.

3. With the help of your teacher, complete the following activities that show communication breakdowns. Find a picture from a magazine that shows action, such as someone running, dancing, or playing a musical instrument. Then, ask for three, four, or five volunteers. Tell one volunteer to stay at the front of the class and ask the other volunteers to go beyond hearing and viewing distance. Now follow these steps:

   a. Explain to the first volunteer that you will allow one minute to study the action picture, which must then be described to the second volunteer. (Show the picture for one minute to the volunteer and then conceal the picture.)

   b. Call in the second volunteer and ask the first volunteer to describe the picture in as much detail as possible. Two-way communications are acceptable.

   c. Call the third volunteer and ask the second volunteer to relay the description just received. Continue this process until all volunteers have had a chance to listen to the description and repeat what they heard.

   d. Show the picture to the volunteers and the class and ask if the scene is what they thought was being described.

   e. Summarize by a discussion or written report what you learned about the communication process and how communication breakdowns occur.

4. Assume that you are working for a business that has many new young part-time workers. Many workers are often late or absent. As a result, other employees must work longer hours and are often called in on weekends. The manager and the workers are concerned and want to solve this problem.

   Follow the directions of your teacher and use the nominal group technique to solve this problem. Present your best solution to your teacher, who will serve as the manager of the work group. When done, discuss how well the NGT worked.

5. Clark put the following idea in his company's suggestion box: "Rather than hire a new full-time worker at $12.00 per hour to handle our increased business, hire two half-time workers at $8.00 per hour. Then if business slows later, we can cut back to one half-time worker or no workers."

   a. As the manager, write Clark a note saying his suggestion has been accepted and he will earn 20 percent of one year's saving for the idea.

   b. Assume one year went by and that one half-time employee worked 860 hours and the second worked 600 hours. A full-time employee would have worked 2,000 hours. How much will Clark receive for his suggestion?

S OLVING BUSINESS PROBLEMS

CASE 9-1

As a former regional manager for Jorgeson International, Ray Wheeler was promoted and transferred to the Philadelphia headquarters several years ago. A close friend, Curtis Van Vlack, manages the company's regional office in Atlanta. Curtis arrived in Philadelphia this afternoon along with other regional managers. At tomorrow's meeting, new procedures for submitting monthly reports will be explained by the new top managers. Ray called Curtis and invited him to dinner this evening, at which time he expressed his concerns about changes going on. After dinner the following conversation occurred:

Ray:　Tomorrow's a big meeting. The new president and the two new vice presidents will be present to explain the new reporting procedures.

Curtis:　Was something wrong with the old method? It worked fine for my office. We do the reports according to the rules. We only hear from headquarters when something isn't done right.

Ray:　The new managers are different. They like meetings and lots of contact with employees. They even stop by my office every few weeks to chat. They seem friendly . . . even invited me to stop by their offices if I have a problem. Nothing like the former managers! You never saw them and never heard from them unless something went wrong. Then threatening memos would come from all directions.

Curtis:　Is that why most of the regional managers kept clear of headquarters? The person I replaced warned me not to break any of the rules. "Just keep your nose clean," she said. "If you don't bother them, they won't bother you."

Ray:　That's the main reason why the Board of Directors changed the top managers. The new managers expect good work but they also seem to want the employees and managers to discuss problems. They even want us to suggest solutions. Imagine that! Some of us aren't sure

REVIEW

whether to trust them yet. We're afraid if we make one mistake, we'll be fired.

Curtis: They seem to be practicing what they preach, Ray. The Houston regional manager stuck her neck out and made a suggestion, and a vice president flew down to talk with her. The grapevine said he made a real big thing over the idea. Her picture is in the new newsletter that just came out. The newsletter has plenty of information about the business and about her suggestion.

Ray: That's what I mean, Curtis. The way these new people operate . . . it's different. I'm not sure I like it. The new monthly report even has a place in it where you can state complaints and make suggestions. They're going to get an earful when the next month's forms are returned. That's no way to run a business.

Curtis: Let's give them a chance, Ray. At least they're willing to listen, which is more than you could say about the departed managers. Maybe they would even let me manage an office one day in Denmark. My family came from there, you know!

Required:

1. Indicate whether the corporate culture changed between the old and new top management. Explain.
2. What evidence is there that the new top management will encourage or discourage upward communication?
3. Did the vice president who flew out to see the Houston regional manager regarding a suggestion for improvement use more than one channel of communication? If yes, how?
4. Did the old or the new top managers place more stress on two-way communications? Explain.
5. Will Ray be as comfortable as Curtis with the new managers? Explain your answer.

CASE 9-2

Linda Harley is the promotion manager for the First Commercial Bank of Indiana, a bank that is rapidly expanding. Because the bank is planning to open four new branch offices during the next three months, Linda needs new ideas to consider for promoting the bank and its services. She is especially concerned about doing a good job with the next branch, which will open in the city of Bedford.

In order to obtain new ideas, Linda called a meeting to be held before opening hours at the bank's main branch. She invited all of the bank tellers. At the meeting she told the tellers that she needed two kinds of suggestions. One type of suggestion was for a catchy slogan, such as "The first bank in Bedford is the First Commercial Bank." The second type of suggestion was for a promotional activity to use during the first week of the bank's opening. She said to the tellers, "Let's work on suggestions for a promotional activity first.

For the last branch we opened, we gave each new customer a beautiful rose. While that worked very well, we need other ideas to attract customers to our Bedford branch. What ideas do you have?"

Linda waited a few minutes for suggestions, but none were offered. However, one bank teller said, "Linda, we should brainstorm these ideas. We did it at another bank I worked for and it was fun. Not only that, but it really worked. Let's try it."

Required:

1. Assume that you are one of the bank tellers. Offer as many ideas as you can for a promotional activity to use to open the bank.
2. With a small group of students or your entire class, use brainstorming to come up with a slogan for the new branch bank.
3. What guidelines should be heeded when brainstorming?

Unit Summary

3-1 *Describe the hardware, software, and telecommunications aspects of computers.*

Computers are complex pieces of equipment that help process data and information used by businesses. Computers contain chips that control CPU (information processing) operations. Data are entered by keyboards and other input devices such as a mouse, pen, voice, and scanner while output is primarily in printed form using a variety of printers (dot matrix, ink jet, and laser). Information appears on a monitor through which it can be manipulated, stored on disks or tapes, retrieved, and sent to others via local and wide area networks.

Software, which provides general instructions for enabling computers to perform tasks, is composed of a disk operating system, graphical user interface, and specific application software. Word processing, spreadsheet, and database are the "big three" application-specific software packages. Many others exist, however.

As computers became widely used in the work world, new technologies became available to further expedite information processing. Electronic mail, voice messaging, fax machines, cellular phones, and handheld computers evolved. Still other enhancements evolved, including multimedia and data transmission using fiber optic cables to create information superhighways.

3-2 *Discuss the technological, management, and systems aspects of electronic technology.*

Managers have had to deal with difficult computer decisions and people decisions. Computer decisions influence which chip, which disk operating system, and which graphical user interface to purchase that will be least troublesome when exchanging data among computers. Vendors have problems, too, in being nudged by large corporate users into offering open rather than closed systems.

Organizations need specialists to aid managers. Programmers, systems analysts, database managers, and others help create an integrated information system supported by three subsystems: data processing, management information, and decision support systems. Systems specialists help managers by establishing procedures for making system changes that will aid decision makers. Most of all, managers want the right information, in the right form, at the right time, and in the right place.

UNIT SUMMARY

Managers found that managing rapid change is a difficult problem because new technologies evolve so quickly. After many years, it became clear that productivity did not improve by merely purchasing new technology. New technologies require restructuring how work is done. Once a firm reengineers itself, productivity usually improves.

Computers plus reengineering, however, result in human problems: fear of job loss as well as health-related complaints caused by using computer terminals extensively. Because of the varied problems, ergonomics has become a fast-growing science.

3-3 *Explain basic communications concepts and the relationship of communications to corporate culture.*

Because managers spend about two-thirds of their work days communicating, they need communication knowledge and skills. Communication means sharing information, which means a sender and a receiver interact. The quality of the information shared is improved when there is opportunity for feedback. But barriers often exist between senders and receivers in the form of distractions (noise and grammar errors, for example) and distortion of data (deliberate or unconsciously done). Managers can also make mistakes if they do not select the most appropriate channel for obtaining the desired results when sending messages. Oral messages are best when feedback is needed to add emphasis to the importance of the message. Written messages are needed for permanent records. Nonverbal messages often confirm or deny spoken messages.

The culture of an organization—its shared values, beliefs, and behavior—influences strongly how communications are conducted and viewed by its members. The leadership styles and form of organizational structure of a corporation point towards a cultural climate that is open or closed. An open climate encourages communication; a closed climate discourages it. An open climate is evidenced by open door policies, self-directed work teams, small informal meetings, mechanisms for encouraging employee ideas, and high morale.

Closed organizations exhibit few of these characteristics. Instead, an atmosphere prevails with formal networks, primarily a downward flow of information, an overly large number of management layers, a higher rate of employee turnover, and a greater distrust of managers. The evidence is clear that superior organizations tend to have open cultures.

3-4 *Identify problems related to organizational conflicts, international communications, and other organizational communication problems and offer solutions.*

Conflicts are normal within organizations. While some conflicts are healthy, others can be destructive, especially when employees undermine the goals of the organization. Three basic strategies can be employed to resolve conflict:

avoidance, compromise, and win/lose solutions. For minor conflicts, the avoidance strategy is often acceptable. A win/lose strategy permits the winner to boast of a personal conquest while the loser may harbor anger and a desire to undermine the winner. Consequently, the compromise solution is often the best overall strategy.

Often, meetings provide a way to resolve conflict by discussing problems openly. Problem-solving ideas can be generated by employing two effective techniques, brainstorming and the nominal group technique. Effective meetings generally call for planning, such as providing an agenda and sticking to it. Otherwise, meetings can be nonproductive and time-consuming.

Problems can also arise outside the firm, especially when communicating with people and organizations from other countries. Language is one common problem, as are cultural differences that lead to confusion and misunderstandings. The metric system, for example, confuses Americans who travel abroad. Even nonverbal differences such as head and hand movements often relay different messages, which create misunderstandings. Errors can alienate message receivers.

Whether communicating in German, Japanese, or English, some practices cross national boundaries for improving communications. Listening actively, promoting interpersonal communications, stressing upward communications, fostering open cultures, and nurturing work teams all appear to result in desirable outcomes.

ACME ROBOT

SPINNING DOODAD

REMOTE CONTROL
GRASPING
HANDS

Marketing

Distribution

PRODUCT SI...

Acme Robot

Respondent _____

Age   18-25   25-34   35-45   45-...   60

How did you first hear about the rob...

Did advertising play a part in your ... purcha...

How many members of your house... ... with the

If the robot could be any color what color ... uld you

How did you first hear about the robot?

4

Production and Marketing Management

"One can be a successful marketer only if one has adopted the proper marketing mind-set. This means having a clear appreciation for what marketing comprises and what it can do for the organization. More important, it means developing a philosophy of marketing that puts the customer at the center of everything one does. Marketing is not intimidation or coercion. It is not 'hard selling' and deceptive advertising. It is a sound, effective technology for creating exchanges and influencing behavior that, when properly applied, must be socially [beneficial]."

Philip Kotler
MARKETING
MANAGEMENT:
ANALYSIS,
PLANNING, AND
CONTROL, 1987

OBJECTIVES

4-1 Describe major marketing activities and how businesses make effective marketing decisions.

4-2 Identify the factors considered when developing a product for sale.

4-3 Diagram alternative channels of distribution and show the activities involved in moving products through the channel.

4-4 Discuss the procedures used by businesses to purchase products and to establish prices for resale.

4-5 Explain several methods that can be used to promote products and services effectively.

Professional Profile

A LEADER IN BUSINESS DEVELOPMENT

You can start from the bottom and end up on top. Frieda Caplan is the first woman in the United States to start a successful produce wholesaling company. She learned the produce business by first working for another company as a salesperson and bookkeeper. While selling, she saw that many customers were interested in unique types of vegetables and exotic fruits. Because other businesses were not meeting that need, Ms. Caplan started her own company in 1962. As a result of her expert leadership, Frieda's, Inc. now has gross revenues in excess of $20 million a year.

From the beginning of the business, Ms. Caplan has worked diligently with retailers to overcome skepticism of the unusual products and to build customer demand. Frieda's, Inc., uses a variety of carefully developed marketing strategies. The company works with retailers by offering merchandising strategies, setting up displays and demonstrations in stores, and giving recipes and product information to consumers. Ms. Caplan knows that if the retailers improve their produce operations, her company's products will have a higher sales volume. Because of those efforts, items once unknown to many consumers, such as California brown mushrooms, spaghetti squash, shallots, and kiwifruit, are now successful products.

Frieda Caplan's business leadership and community service have earned her numerous awards. They include the first woman to be named Produce Marketer of the Year, Outstanding California Woman In Business, and the first recipient of the Harriet Alger award from *Working Woman* magazine recognizing her as a role model for women entrepreneurs.

Frieda Caplan,
Chairman
and Founder,
Frieda's, Inc.

INSPIRATIONAL IDEAS

"Operate at all times with an open mind and an open door. Some of the greatest resources in business come from people who have real off-the-wall ideas or approaches that are different from their contemporaries. Aim to be ethical and recognize the needs of the people you deal with. The needs of everyone you work with are an integral part of successful leadership."

Photo courtesy of Frieda's, Inc.

NATURE AND SCOPE OF MARKETING

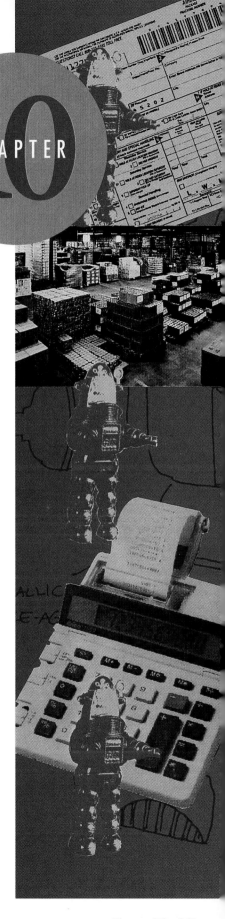

CHAPTER 10

After studying this chapter you will be able to:

10-1 Discuss the importance of marketing and its role in the economy.

10-2 List the activities that are a part of marketing.

10-3 Define basic marketing concepts and the four elements of the marketing mix.

10-4 Explain the four stages of the product life cycle.

10-5 Identify the consumer goods classifications.

Supply and demand is an economic concept that has no practical value in your daily life—or does it? You are shopping in a supermarket, discount store, or bank and have to wait in line because there are too few cashiers or tellers. You go to a 4:00 p.m. showing of a movie and find that only four other people are there to see the film with you. After your favorite group performs a concert in your city, the music stores are unable to stock their latest CD. Each of these examples describes a situation where supply and demand are not in balance. There are not enough store personnel to serve the number of customers; the number of movie-goers will not fill the theater seats; the music stores will miss out on the opportunity to sell a large number of CDs.

IMPORTANCE OF MARKETING

In our private enterprise economy, it is not always easy to match production and consumption. Individual business people make decisions about what they will produce, and individual consumers make decisions about what they want to purchase. For the economy to work well, methods must be available to assist producers and consumers with their decisions so the desired type and amount of goods and services will be produced and consumed.

Marketing activities, when performed well, help to match production and consumption effectively. As you learned earlier in the book, marketing is used to get goods from producers to consumers. That very basic definition may make you think that marketing is simply the transportation of products. However, it is much more than that. Products must be packaged, brand names must be developed, and prices must be determined. Often, products must be stored until customers are ready to purchase or use them. Someone must finance the product until it is sold. Most products require some type of promotion. Marketing is involved in all of these activities and many more. Much time and effort must be spent by firms in marketing their goods and services.

A more detailed definition will provide a better description of modern marketing. The American Marketing Association defines **marketing** as *the process of planning and executing the conception, pricing, promotion, and distribution of ideas, goods, and services to create exchanges that satisfy individual and organizational objectives.* Because marketing is the key tool in matching supply and demand, it can be viewed in another way as well. If marketing is successful, businesses will be able to sell their products and services and consumers will be able to obtain the things they want to purchase. Therefore, the goal of effective marketing is to create and maintain satisfying exchange relationships.

Every consumer comes into contact daily with marketing in one form or another. Whenever you see an advertisement on television or in the newspaper, notice a truck being unloaded at a warehouse, or fill out a credit application to purchase a product, you are exposed to the marketing efforts of business. Each retail store location, each form of advertising, each salesperson, and even each package in which a product is sold is a part of marketing. A great deal of business activity centers on marketing.

Millions of businesses worldwide are involved in marketing as their primary business activities. Those organizations include **retailers**—businesses that sell directly to final consumers, and **wholesalers**—businesses that buy products from businesses and sell them to retailers or other businesses. Many businesses that sell services, rather than products, are also included. In addition, companies such as advertising agencies provide promotional services, finance companies offer loans and other financial services, and transportation firms handle and move products. Each of these types of business as well as many others that support the marketing efforts of other businesses are directly involved in marketing.

Many manufacturing firms have marketing departments with employees involved in marketing jobs. For example, employees are hired to work on

Jeff Greenberg, Photographer

market research, to help in the design of products, and to sell the products. There are many other types of marketing jobs, such as advertising and sales promotion, customer service, credit, and insurance. The many jobs range from clerk to vice president in charge of all marketing activities. Well over one-third of all people employed in the United States are working in a marketing job or a marketing business.

NATURE OF MARKETING

When many people think of marketing, they think only of advertising and selling. However, many marketing activities must occur before a product can be advertised and sold. To better understand marketing, we will examine the major marketing activities, the cost of marketing activities, and the role of marketing in business.

MARKETING ACTIVITIES

The most common marketing activities are shown in Fig. 10-1 on page 244. They include:

Buying   Obtaining goods to be sold. This activity involves finding suppliers who can provide the right goods in the right quality and quantity at a fair price.

Selling   Providing personalized and persuasive information to customers to help them buy the goods they need.

Transporting   Moving goods from where they were made to where consumers can buy them.

Storing   Holding goods until needed by consumers, such as on shelves, in storage rooms, or in warehouses.

A number of marketing activities are necessary to get products and services from producers to consumers.

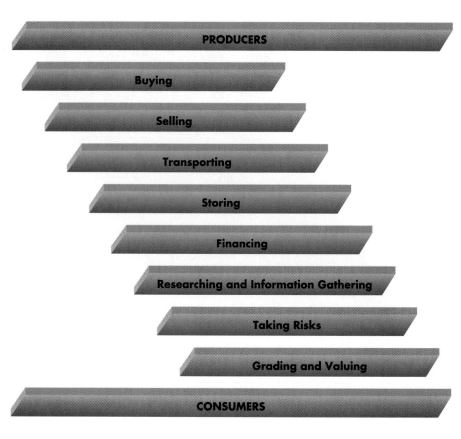

Financing	Providing money that is needed to perform various marketing activities, such as obtaining credit when buying and extending credit when selling.
Researching and information gathering	Studying buyer interests and needs, testing products, and gathering facts needed to make good marketing decisions.
Risk taking	Assuming the risk of losses that may occur from fire, theft, damage, or other circumstances.
Grading and valuing	Grouping goods according to size, quality, or other characteristics, and determining an appropriate price for products.

COST OF MARKETING

Whether the product is paper clips for offices or huge generators for utility companies, all eight marketing activities just described are normally performed as the product moves from producer to customer. Because performing these activities requires many workers and special equipment, the cost of marketing a product is sometimes higher than the cost of making that product. According to one study, all marketing activities cost the customer on the average of 42 to 59 cents for each dollar spent. There does not appear to be any major difference in marketing costs whether producers sell directly to consumers or whether they sell through retail stores and other businesses. Although this amount may appear to be high, the marketing dollar that is well spent contributes much to

Jeff Greenberg, Photographer

Illus. 10-2

The cost of marketing fragile or perishable items can be very high. What marketing activities will be particularly expensive for these products?

the success of products and businesses as well as to the satisfaction of customers. If marketing is not performed well, the product or service will not be available to customers when and where they want it. If that is the case, even a small cost will not make the product a value to the customer.

ROLE OF MARKETING

Marketing has not always been an important part of business. In the early 1900s, business conditions were much different than they are now. Customers had only a few products to choose from and a limited amount of money to spend. Usually, only a few producers manufactured a product, and the manufacturing process was not very efficient. Demand for most products was greater than supply. As a result, most producers concentrated on making more kinds of products in greater quantities. Firms were **production oriented**; that is, decisions about what and how to produce received the most attention. Business people did not have to worry a great deal about marketing.

As production became more efficient and more businesses offered similar products, competition among businesses increased. Each business had to work hard to sell its products to customers when those customers saw they had many choices. Companies began to emphasize distribution to get their products to more customers. In addition, advertising and selling became important marketing tools as businesses tried to convince customers that their products were the best. Production was still considered to be the most important activity, but it was not enough for businesses to be successful. Businesses had become **sales oriented**; that is, they emphasized promotion in order to sell the products produced.

However, with time, consumers realized that they had many choices of products and services to purchase. Many businesses were competing with each other to sell the same product. Customers could demand products that met their needs and a company would usually produce them. Companies began to realize it was not enough just to produce a variety of products; they had to produce the right products. Those companies that produced what customers wanted and made it easier for customers to buy were more successful than those that did not.

Since about 1970, more and more businesses have become very concerned about customer needs. They have become **customer oriented**; that is, they direct company activities at satisfying customers. Keeping the needs of the consumer uppermost in mind during the design, production, and distribution of a product is called the **marketing concept**.

A company that has adopted the marketing concept will have a marketing manager who is part of top management and involved in all major decisions, as shown in Fig. 10-2. Marketing personnel will work closely with the other people in the business to make sure that the company keeps the needs of customers in mind in all operations. The company's success will be determined by more than the amount of profits made. While profit is important, success is also based on the satisfaction of the company's customers.

Fig. 10-2

When a company is customer oriented, the marketing manager is a part of top management.

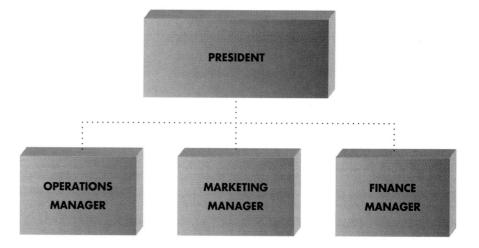

MARKET DETERMINATION

Before a producer decides to make and distribute a product to consumers, it is necessary to determine the market to be served. Here, **market** refers to the types of buyers a business wishes to attract and where those buyers are located. All companies need to clearly identify their markets.

Whom to Serve

A company has many potential customers for every product. Some people may be searching for the product, while others will have to be convinced to buy it. Some people will be very easy to reach, while others will be located long distances from the company. For cost reasons, it is usually unwise to attempt to reach all potential customers. Therefore, a business tries to identify groups of potential customers and then decide which group or groups will be the best markets for a product.

Population characteristics, such as age, gender, family status, education, income, and occupation, are often used to group consumers. A clothing manufacturer, for example, could handle women's clothing or men's clothing, clothing for children or adults, casual clothing or formal clothing, and so on. The producer of a calculator may want to attract students, engineers, or accountants. Businesses can decide to serve one or more markets. The market chosen is based on the opportunities available, including the competition that exists, the number of customers and their needs, the amount of money they spend, and other factors.

Where to Serve

Producers often limit the scope of their business operations to certain geographic areas. Marketing managers study sections of a region, country, or continent to determine whether a product might sell more successfully in one area than another. Climate, for example, may cause a small producer of air conditioners to concentrate its marketing efforts on countries with hot and humid climates for its markets, whereas the maker of skis may concentrate on areas where there is an abundance of cold weather and mountains. Some products may sell better on the coasts rather than the middle of the country, or in rural areas better than cities. Finding the best marketing locations enables a business to operate more efficiently.

David Schultz/Tony Stone Images

Illus. 10-3

Some products are clearly developed for a specific geographic area. Where would manufacturers of irrigation systems look to locate markets in other countries?

CHARACTERISTICS OF GOOD MARKETS

Companies find it easier to produce goods and services that meet the needs of consumers if they know who their customers are, where they are located, and what the customers' wants and needs are. Many companies spend a great deal of money on market research before they begin to develop products. **Market research** is the study of the people who buy a company's products or who may buy a new product.

Market research is used to identify target markets. **Target markets** are groups of customers with very similar needs to whom the company can sell its product. If a company can find a group of people with very similar needs, it will be much easier to produce a product that will satisfy everyone in the group. On the other hand, if people in the group have needs that are quite different, it will be almost impossible to develop a product that will satisfy each of them.

Imagine developing a product like a bicycle. It can be made in a variety of sizes and shapes with a number of special features. There is not one bicycle that will satisfy everyone's needs. Long-distance racers will want something very different than the weekend rider. A teenager may want a much different design and style than a ten-year-old. However, if you could find a group of people with very similar needs, you could successfully design a bicycle for that group. If several groups are identified as in Fig. 10-3, each with unique needs for a product, the company can design a different product for each group it decides to serve.

Fig. 10-3

Possible target markets for bicycles.

A company that has adopted the marketing concept will use research to identify markets before products are developed and marketing is planned. The research can help the company determine who the best possible customers are, what their needs are, and where they are located. That information should allow companies to make better production and marketing decisions.

ELEMENTS OF MARKETING

Marketing managers have many decisions to make. These decisions usually center on four elements of marketing: product, price, place, and promotion. Developing each element involves a series of important questions that need answers. For example, assume that you want to market a new product. You will need to answer the following questions related to the four elements of marketing: (a) Will the product be made in one size and color, or in several? (b) Will the product be high-priced, medium-priced, or low-priced? (c) Will newspaper, radio, or television advertising be used? (d) Will the product be sold door-to-door or through retail stores?

The blending of all decisions that are related to the four elements of marketing is called the **marketing mix**. The marketing mix for a new product may be to design an item for young adults that will be low-priced, sell through retail stores, and be advertised on the radio. Or it could be to produce a medium-priced item to be advertised on television and sold door-to-door to senior citizens.

The marketing mix used by several companies marketing the same product can be quite different because many different decisions are possible. Furthermore, these decisions need to be reviewed frequently because conditions are constantly changing. Changes in general economic conditions, changes in consumer needs, and the development of new or improved products by competitors are factors that may require a change in the marketing mix. Because the four elements of marketing and the decisions related to them are so important, we will review each element individually.

PRODUCT

The first marketing element is the product. **Product** can be defined as everything offered by a business to satisfy its customers. It includes services as well as physical products. A principal question relating to the product is: What do customers want? Product planning and development activities deal with finding answers to that question. Marketers examine consumer behavior and use special marketing research techniques to help with product planning.

By knowing the market or markets for a product and knowing what customers want, the production department can manufacture a better item. Market information can help the people involved in product planning make such decisions as:

- The *number* of items to produce.

- The *physical features* the product should possess, such as the size, shape, color, and weight.
- The *quality* preferred by the target market.
- The *number of different models and the required features of each model* needed to serve the various markets the company is trying to attract.
- The *packaging features* of the item, such as the color and the shape of the package, as well as the information printed on the package.
- The *brand name* to be used.
- Product *guarantees* and *services* the customers would like.
- The *image* to be communicated to customers by the products, features, packaging, and brand name.

PRICE

The second element around which marketing decisions are made is price. **Price** can be defined as the monetary and the perceived value of the product or service. Price is influenced by the many decisions that are arrived at during the development of the product. First, the costs of producing and marketing the product must be determined. If a decision is made to manufacture a high-quality product, the price is likely to be higher than that for a low-quality product. The prices and number of competing products, the demand for the product, and the credit terms to be offered are some of the many factors that influence price decisions.

When making price decisions, a company must do more than just set a price that customers will pay for the product. Decisions must be made about prices to charge to retailers and wholesalers who buy and resell the product. Will the company extend credit to customers? Will customers be allowed to bargain for a lower price or trade in a used product for a new one? As you can see, pricing is not an easy marketing decision.

PROMOTION

The third marketing mix element for which decisions must be made is promotion. **Promotion** is providing information to consumers that will assist them in making a decision to purchase a product or service. The major methods of promotion are advertising and personal selling. There are other types of promotion that we will study in a later chapter, including publicity, sales promotion, and product displays (showing or exhibiting goods).

Promotional decisions for a camera might involve selecting the kind of advertisements to use and deciding whether to advertise on television, radio, or in magazines. Decisions will be made on when to advertise and how frequently the advertisements should be seen. Then it must be decided whether to use sales demonstrations in stores, displays of the camera, or both. Decisions will also be needed about the type of information to communicate to consumers and whether to promote to large or small numbers of people with individualized or more impersonal messages.

Promotional decisions, of course, are influenced by the type of product and its price. The strategy for promoting an expensive piece of jewelry is likely to be much different from that of promoting tennis shoes.

While the product and its price provide general guides for promotion, many other factors must be consid-

UNIPHOTO

ered before developing the actual promotions to be used. For example, only a certain amount of money will be available to use for promotion. A business must decide when to spend the money, and how much to spend for advertising, displays, and other types of promotion. The company must consider what promotions competitors are using, and what information consumers need in order to decide to buy.

PLACE

The fourth and final element around which marketing decisions are made is place. This marketing decision refers to place utility as discussed in Chapter 3, which means the product must be in a place where it is needed or wanted by customers. **Place** (or **distribution**), therefore, deals with the methods of transporting and storing goods, and making them available to customers.

Decisions must be made regarding the types of businesses that will handle products as they move from the producer to the consumer. Relatively few consumers buy directly from manufacturers. The various paths or routes that goods follow and the places where they are sold are important marketing decisions.

MARKETING DECISIONS

It is difficult for a business to keep track of all the marketing decisions that must be made. To help deal with the problem, most businesses develop a marketing plan. The **marketing plan** is a detailed written description of all marketing activities that a business must accomplish in order to sell a product. It describes the goals a firm wants to accomplish, the target markets it wants to serve, and the marketing mixes it will use. It identifies the ways marketing will be evaluated to determine if the activities were successful and the goals were accomplished. The marketing plan is written for a specific time period (often one year).

The marketing plan is developed by the top marketing executive, who needs to get assistance and information from many other people. Market research will be very important in developing a marketing plan. Once a written plan is completed, it can be used by all of the people involved in marketing activities as they make decisions about each of the marketing mix elements and complete the planned activities.

THE PRODUCT LIFE CYCLE

The concept of a product life cycle implies that successful products move through rather predictable stages. They are introduced, then their sales and profits increase rather rapidly until a point at which they level off. Eventually, both profits and sales will decline as the old product is replaced by newer ones. The **product life cycle** predicts the combined sales and profit performance of all competing brands of a product. There are four stages in the life cycle of a product: introduction, growth, maturity, and decline. A typical life cycle is shown in Fig. 10-4.

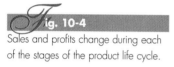
Fig. 10-4
Sales and profits change during each of the stages of the product life cycle.

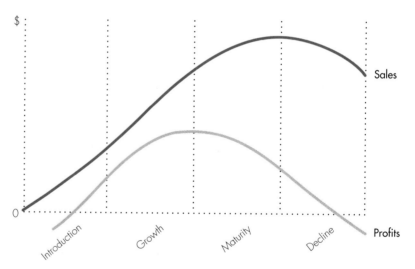

INTRODUCTION

In the **introduction stage**, a brand-new product enters the market. At this time there is only one brand of the product available for consumers to purchase. The new product is quite different from, and hopefully better than, products customers are currently using. While every product has gone through the introduction stage at some time, examples of products that were recently in that stage include digital audio tape (DAT) and virtual reality video games.

When a product is being introduced, the company is concerned about getting it distributed and informing customers about the brand-new product and its uses. There is no competition from the same type of product, but customers will probably be using other older products. The customers must be shown how the new product is better than the products they are currently using.

The costs of doing so are high, very likely resulting in a loss or very low profits for the firm.

GROWTH

When several brands of the new product are available, the market moves into the **growth stage** of the life cycle. If customers like the new product, they will begin buying it regularly. When competitors see the success of the new product, they also will want to get into that market.

In the growth stage, each of the brands is trying to attract customers. Companies try to improve their brands by adding features that they hope will satisfy customers. Profits should begin to appear and increase in this stage. Examples of products that have been in the growth stage recently are notebook computers, compact disc players, and cellular telephone services.

MATURITY

A product in the maturity stage has been purchased by large numbers of customers and has become quite profitable. The **maturity stage** has many competing brands with very similar features. Customers have a hard time finding important differences among the brands.

In this stage, companies emphasize the promotion of their brand name, packaging, a specific image, and often the price of the product. Competition is very difficult for many businesses. Money is being spent on promotion, prices are often being reduced, and customers have many brands from which to choose. Profits usually fall even though sales may still increase. Products in the maturity stage include automobiles, televisions, laundry detergents, and many other products that you use regularly.

One way that businesses respond to the maturity stage of the life cycle is to look for new markets. The move into international markets is often begun as businesses find competition increasingly difficult in their home countries. As the fast food industry found fewer and fewer attractive locations for new stores in the United States, they began to open outlets in Canada, Europe, and Mexico. Now expansion is occurring in South America, and even China and the countries of the former Soviet Union.

DECLINE

Many products stay in the maturity stage of the life cycle for a long time. However, sooner or later most products move into a decline stage. The **decline stage** occurs when a new product is introduced that is much better or easier to use, and customers begin to switch from the old product to the new product. When a product is in the decline stage, it has to be improved or it will lose sales and profits rapidly. Most older products cannot be improved enough to compete with the new products, so they will usually drop from the market after a short time.

Some companies have been able to move old products out of the decline stage by finding new uses for them. For example, baby oil is now being used as a suntan product, baking soda is used to remove odors from refrigerators, and miniature-sized black-and-white televisions are now available.

If a product cannot be saved from the decline stage, the company will attempt to sell its remaining products to the customers who still prefer them. However, companies will spend as little money as possible while marketing them and certainly will not produce any more.

TYPES OF CONSUMER PRODUCTS

When making marketing decisions, executives need to understand how customers shop for and use products. Products can be classified as either industrial goods or consumer goods. **Industrial goods** are products that are to be used by another business. Frequently, industrial goods are purchased in large quantities, are made to special order, or are sold to a selected group of buyers located within a limited geographic area. Examples of industrial goods include bricks purchased by a building contractor, steel purchased by a machine manufacturer, and computers and computer supplies purchased by accounting firms. Many, but not all, industrial goods are used to produce other products or are incorporated into the products being produced. Some are used in the operation of the business.

Consumer goods are produced for sale to people for personal use. Toothbrushes, chairs, fruit, aspirin, and combs are some of the many products used by consumers. Consumer goods require careful marketing attention because there are so many products and brands available and so many possible customers located throughout the world.

Illus. 10-5

Some businesses such as Sam's Club sell to both business and final consumers through the same store. Would their products be considered industrial goods or consumer goods?

Jeff Greenberg, Photographer

Depending on who buys the goods, however, certain merchandise may be both a consumer good and an industrial good. Gasoline and computer paper, for instance, may be purchased by consumers in small quantities or by business firms in large quantities.

Consumer goods can be categorized to help make marketing decisions easier. There are four categories of consumer goods: convenience goods, shopping goods, specialty goods, and unsought goods. The categories are based on (1) how important the product is to the customer, and (2) whether the customer is willing to spend time to compare products and brands before making a decision to buy.

CONVENIENCE GOODS

Convenience goods are inexpensive items that consumers purchase regularly without a great deal of thought. Consumers are not willing to shop around for these products because they are purchased often and customers have many choices. Therefore, convenience goods need to be sold through many retail outlets that are conveniently located close to where people work and live. Products that are usually treated as convenience goods are candy, milk, soft drinks, pencils, soap, and many other inexpensive household items.

SHOPPING GOODS

Products that are purchased less frequently than convenience goods, that usually have a higher price, and that require some buying thought are called **shopping goods**. Customers see important differences between brands of these products in terms of price and features. Therefore, they are willing to shop at several businesses and compare products and brands before they make a purchase. Shopping goods do not have to be sold in as many places as convenience goods. They need effective promotion so customers can make informed decisions. Cars, furniture, large appliances, and houses are all examples of shopping goods for most people.

SPECIALTY GOODS

Specialty goods are products that customers insist upon having and are willing to search for until they find them. The customer who has decided that only one product or brand is satisfying will shop until that brand can be found and purchased. Specialty goods are found in fewer businesses within a shopping area, can be priced higher than competing brands, and may need very little promotion. Examples of specialty goods for many consumers are designer clothing, expensive jewelry, and certain brands of stereo equipment or automobiles.

UNSOUGHT GOODS

There are certain products that many customers will not shop for because they do not have a strong need for the product. Such products are known as **unsought goods,** and they present a difficult marketing problem. Life insurance, encyclopedias, and funeral services are unsought by most consumers.

Global Perspective

SUITING A TARGET MARKET

Changing to a marketing mix that has never been tried is risky, especially when another mix has been very successful in a large market for many years. In Japan, one of the most traditional products in a conservative market is the sale of suits to businessmen. Japanese men have been willing to pay high prices and shop in the most exclusive downtown department stores to get well-tailored suits and very personal service. Because businessmen have been purchasing the same types of suits from the same retailers for years and seemed quite satisfied with the product and price, few people expected a new strategy could be successful. But Goro Aoyama was aware of changes in shopping behavior and economic conditions that offered him an opportunity.

The Japanese economy experienced a slowdown in the early 1900s. The economic change was unusual in the country and experienced businesses were not prepared to adjust. People were adjusting to the economic downturn by cutting back on personal spending wherever possible. At the same time, Japanese families were moving into the suburbs, farther and farther from the central shopping districts.

Aoyama believed that the growing middle class of businessmen was ready to purchase a basic suit at a lower price. To be able to offer the value, Aoyama buys basic suit styles in bulk from manufacturers; he does not use traditional distributors. The suits are sold in much higher volume from store locations in the suburbs. These stores have much lower rents and operating costs than the expensive city locations of the traditional department stores. Inventories are watched carefully and Aoyama makes sure that customers can select from several basic styles in their sizes whenever they visit the store. The new strategy emphasizes price and cuts back on expensive promotions and services.

Many business people are not impressed by the new approach to selling suits and continue to buy the more expensive suits from the large downtown department stores. But Mr. Aoyama is not attempting to sell to everyone. He has identified a target market of the average business person who is more concerned about price than style and does not really enjoy shopping. His suits sell for 20,000–30,000 yen (about $200 U.S.), which is often about half the price of competitor's suits.

As a result of his strategy, the Aoyama company now sells about 10% of the suits sold in Japan. In a market that sells over 10 million suits each year, that means sales of almost 120 billion yen a year for the company. Because costs are controlled, profit margins for the company are among the industry's highest.

Questions:

1. What philosophy seems to be demonstrated by Aoyama—production-oriented, sales-oriented, or customer-oriented?

2. While it is always risky to try a marketing strategy that other businesses have not used, what factors suggested the new marketing mix might work?

3. Is it possible for both the traditional method of selling suits in Japan and Aoyama's method to be successful in the future? Why?

Adapted from: Far Eastern Economic Review, February 18, 1993, p. 57.

A company marketing unsought goods will usually have to go to the customer and use personal selling to discuss the need for the product. Unless the customer recognizes a need that can be satisfied with the product, the product will remain unsold.

SUCCESSFUL MARKETING STRATEGIES

Marketing managers cannot afford to guess about the types of marketing mixes to use. Marketing is too expensive and customers have too many choices for businesses to risk making mistakes. Concepts such as the product life cycle and consumer goods categories can be used to plan effective marketing mixes. For example, if a product is in the growth stage, the mix will be quite different than if it is in the maturity stage. If consumers view a product as a specialty good, different mix elements will be emphasized than if it is a convenience good. Marketers study markets and competition and use their knowledge of marketing to make decisions that will satisfy customer needs and result in a profit for the company.

Many of the complaints consumers have about businesses today involve marketing activities. Misleading advertisements, poor customer service, high prices, and poor delivery are all marketing problems. Businesses must be as careful in making marketing decisions as they need to be in producing a quality product. In the next four chapters, we will examine each part of the marketing mix in more detail. You will learn how businesses plan products and use marketing activities to satisfy customers and attract them from competing businesses.

BUILDING VOCABULARY POWER

Define the following terms and concepts.

1. marketing
2. retailers
3. wholesalers
4. buying
5. selling
6. transporting
7. storing
8. financing
9. researching and information gathering
10. risk taking
11. grading and valuing
12. production oriented
13. sales oriented
14. customer oriented
15. marketing concept
16. market
17. market research
18. target markets
19. marketing mix
20. product
21. price
22. promotion
23. place (distribution)
24. marketing plan
25. product life cycle
26. introduction stage
27. growth stage
28. maturity stage
29. decline stage
30. industrial goods
31. consumer goods
32. convenience goods
33. shopping goods
34. specialty goods
35. unsought goods

REVIEWING FACTS

1. What are the two major categories of businesses that are involved in marketing as their primary business activity?
2. List five types of companies that provide special marketing services to support other companies.
3. What are the eight common marketing activities?
4. On the average, what percent of the consumer's cost of a product applies to marketing costs?
5. Why have businesses had to change from a production orientation to the customer orientation?
6. What two questions must a firm answer about its customers when identifying a market to serve?
7. How can marketing research improve production decisions for a business?
8. Identify the four elements of the marketing mix.
9. How can marketing decisions about a product and its price influence decisions about how the product will be promoted?
10. What should be included in a marketing plan?

11. How does the amount of competition change during the stages of the product life cycle?
12. List several products that are both industrial goods and consumer goods.
13. What are the two factors that determine the categories of consumer goods?
14. Why do companies have problems marketing unsought goods?
15. What are some consumer complaints about business that relate directly to marketing?

DISCUSSING IDEAS

1. How can transportation firms, finance companies, and insurance businesses be considered marketing establishments?
2. Before a producer decides to make and distribute a product, how is the market to be served determined?
3. Explain how valuing and grading are used in the marketing of food products.
4. For what types of products would you expect the cost of marketing to be well over 50 percent of the total cost of the product?
5. Do you believe the number of businesses directly involved in marketing will increase or decrease during the next five years? Why?
6. Identify several products that would sell well only in specific geographic locations.
7. Why should companies that have adopted the marketing concept be more successful than those that have not adopted it?
8. How can a product's package be used to satisfy customers?
9. Discuss a number of the products used in your own home that could be classified as industrial goods as well as consumer goods.
10. How do convenience goods differ from shopping goods?

ANALYZING INFORMATION

1. Select any product that you use regularly. Using the eight marketing activities listed in the chapter, give an example showing how each of the activities was completed between the time the product was produced and the time it was purchased.
2. Use the same product that you selected to answer the previous question. Describe how each of the four elements of the marketing mix (product, price, place, promotion) has been developed for the product.
3. Jan Shepard produced 100 bushels of potatoes for sale. She could have sold them in their ungraded condition to a city wholesale produce business at $4.00 a bushel. That would have required one trip to the city and four hours of her time. Instead, she decided to sell them door-to-door in the city. It took Jan 12 hours to sort, grade, and put the potatoes into

bushel baskets. She had to make one trip to the city (2 hours) to purchase the baskets, which cost $1.00 each. Jan spent 15 hours more traveling to the city and selling the potatoes. She sold 80 bushels of large size potatoes for $6.00 per bushel, and the remainder for $5.00 per bushel. Assume that the cost of driving a truck to the city was $20.00 for each trip, and Jan's time is worth $3.50 an hour. Did she receive more or less by marketing the potatoes directly than she would by selling them to the wholesaler? How much?

4. Go to a department store or discount store. Identify two products that you believe fit into each stage of the product life cycle. What evidence can you see in the store that supports your decision for each product?

5. Interview ten people to determine how they purchase jeans. Ask each of them the following questions:
    a. Where do you usually buy your jeans?
    b. What product features are important to you when you are deciding to buy?
    c. Is there one brand that you usually buy?
    d. Do you usually look in several stores before you buy a pair of jeans? Based on each person's answers, determine whether he or she is treating jeans as a convenience, shopping, specialty, or unsought good. Write a short report discussing your findings and your conclusions.

S OLVING BUSINESS PROBLEMS

CASE 10-1

Sandy and Beth wanted to buy a video cassette recorder to attach to their television set. They had seen advertisements for VCRs but they knew very little about them. Sandy suggested that they go to several stores and look at all of the brands available before making a decision. Then they could buy the one they believed had the best features for the price. Beth felt that the machines had so many differences that it would be hard for them to determine which brand to buy. She suggested that they buy the same brand as their television. The television had performed well for them for five years, and Beth thought they could trust that brand better than others they had not used before.

Required:
1. Which goods classification best describes Sandy's method of buying the VCR?
2. Which classification best fits Beth's buying method?
3. Describe how customers would shop for a VCR for each of the remaining goods classifications not described in questions 1 and 2.
4. Do you believe Sandy and Beth should be included in the same target market?

REVIEW 10

CASE 10-2

The Willomette Company manufactures small household appliances. The company was started by Ron Willomette twenty years ago as a sole proprietorship. Initially, Mr. Willomette reconditioned and resold used appliances. Now he has incorporated and has two manufacturing plants. The Willomette Company has a full line of nearly 100 products that are sold throughout the United States.

In the past five years, Willomette's executives have seen an increase in the competition from foreign companies in the small appliance market. While it hasn't hurt Willomette yet, they don't want to wait until sales and profits start to decline. One of the vice presidents has recommended that Willomette begin a program of international marketing. She believes the demand for household appliances would be very strong in Europe, South America, and several North African countries. Because there has been strong customer acceptance of the company's products in the United States, Willomette should have no trouble selling the same products in other countries.

Required:

1. Which of the major marketing activities would have to be performed if Willomette sold its products in international markets?
2. How does the marketing concept relate to the decision Willomette must make about entering international markets?
3. Do you agree that products that are successful in the United States will also be successful in other countries? Explain.

PRODUCT AND SERVICE PLANNING

CHAPTER 11

After studying this chapter you will be able to:

11-1 Identify several sources of ideas for new products.

11-2 Describe two categories of research used by business to develop new products.

11-3 Discuss the differences among manufacturing processes.

11-4 Suggest several important factors that should be considered when locating a manufacturing business and organizing the production process.

11-5 Identify the characteristics of services that make them different from products.

For many years, U.S. automobile manufacturers have been criticized for not building products that equaled the quality of those built by Japanese and European manufacturers. Consumers suggested that the manufacturers were more concerned about the automobile's style and features than its basic design. As a result, the share of automobile sales held by the U.S. manufacturers fell dramatically.

Managers of each of the major manufacturers developed plans to respond to the criticism. Ford developed improvements in quality control and involved employees in a program called "quality is job #1." Chrysler used a process called benchmarking in which it analyzed competing brands to find the best design for each part. It then incorporated those top designs into its new products. General Motors took the most dramatic step by developing an entire new division to design and produce a brand new automobile—the Saturn.

The initial customer acceptance of Saturn automobiles as well as growth in sales and profits of the other automobile manufacturers suggests product planning and production are critical to the success of companies. Automobile manufacturing demonstrated the efficiency of the assembly line system in the early 1900s. Today, the industry's success depends on the effective use of new methods and procedures that must be regularly evaluated and improved.

Illus. 11-1

The success of a new business depends on effective use of new methods and procedures. What makes a Saturn automobile different from those produced by American manufacturers in the past?

Jeff Greenberg, Photographer

NEW PRODUCT DEVELOPMENT

As consumers, we are offered a number of choices of products and services to satisfy our wants and needs. Businesses also have a choice of what products or services to sell. Businesses are most successful when they (1) are able to offer products or services that consumers want to purchase, and (2) can produce them at prices that consumers are willing to pay.

The development and manufacture of new products is a very difficult and expensive task. For example, a national fast food restaurant spent over a million dollars on research to determine the best type of bun to use for a new sandwich. In addition, it cost several million dollars more to add the new sandwich to the menu in all of its restaurants. While that investment was successful, other companies have spent that much money and more only to find the product was not acceptable to consumers. All of the money spent to develop the product was lost.

Only a small number of new products developed by businesses ever reach the market. Even for those that do, over half will not survive in the market for five years. Therefore, a producer or manufacturer risks a large amount of money in buildings, equipment, materials, and personnel in order to provide the product that we consume.

Product development is the process of creating or improving a product or service. As a result of many factors, products are continuously changing—old products go out of use or are improved, and new products are developed. You can expect that most of the products you will be using within ten years are not even available today. For a company to survive, it must continually search for ways to improve even its most successful products and regularly consider the development of new products.

Ideas for new products can come from many sources. People inside and outside the company may suggest new product ideas. A company may get ideas from salespeople and production personnel, from other business people, and from research projects. Many companies employ people whose primary responsibility is to create and test new products.

One of the best sources of new product information is a company's customers. They have used the company's products and know what they like and do not like. Customers can give useful information on how to improve products and on the types of new products they would like to see. There are many ways companies can get this information from customers. Some companies send questionnaires to people who recently bought a product asking for their opinions. Other companies have telephone numbers that customers can call when they have questions or problems.

If a company wants to get a great deal of information from consumers about possible new products, it might form a **consumer panel**—a group of people who offer opinions about a product or service. The panel consists of several people who have bought or are likely to buy the company's products. The panel members meet regularly with the company representatives or trained interviewers to discuss their feelings about new products and to tell the representatives what they think the company can do to improve its current products.

Salespeople can also be used to gather information from customers. Since salespeople regularly talk to customers, they collect valuable information that can help the company improve its products. Salespeople should be encouraged to learn as much as they can about customer likes and dislikes. Many companies have specific procedures and forms for salespeople to use when they gather important information from customers. The procedures insure that the information is communicated to the people responsible for product development.

PRODUCT DEVELOPMENT RESEARCH

No matter what the source of new product ideas, it is very risky for a company to go ahead with the development of a new product without completing some research. **Research** is the systematic search for and interpretation of facts in an effort to solve problems. A company must invest a great deal of money, time, and other resources in a new product.

Most companies are not willing to invest without being sure that they can successfully produce the product, and that there are customers who will buy the product. Business now spends billions of dollars a year on research. In addition, universities and the federal government are continually conducting research that results in new products. On the average, about four percent of a firm's annual sales is spent on new product research in the United States. That figure has increased in the past few years when it was only about two percent, but still lags behind the average research investments of businesses from other countries. As you can see in Figure 11-1, some industries spend much more on research and development than that average.

Several types of research can be done to help firms decide whether to produce and sell new products. Two broad categories are product research and marketing research.

Fig. 11-1

Examples of research and development expenditures in U.S. industries.

INDUSTRY	% OF SALES
Health care	10%
Leisure products	6%
Food products	1%
Office equipment	8%
Electronics	6%
Telecommunications	3%
Housing	2%
Average of all U.S. industries	3.7%
Average of foreign industries	4.5%

Source: Business Week, June 28, 1993, p. 102.

PRODUCT RESEARCH

Product research is research done to develop new products or to discover improvements for existing products. Researchers need to create products that customers will prefer over the products of other companies. Therefore, companies will try to use information about the needs and wants of potential customers while new product research is being conducted. There are two types of product research—pure research and applied research.

Pure Research

One type of product research is called **pure research**—research done without a specific product in mind. Scientists and researchers in many companies are continually searching for new processes, materials, or ideas. They are experts in specific areas such as biology, chemistry, robotics, electronics, or energy sources. They conduct experiments and tests in order to make discoveries that might lead to new products.

Many products we use today have been developed as a result of such research. The latest computer technology, life-saving drugs, energy efficient appliances and homes, and improved food products have resulted from pure research projects. Many of the products we consume have been changed and improved through chemical research. Some examples are low calorie sweeteners, meat substitutes made from soybean products, and vitamin-enhanced soft drinks. Insulation used in beverage coolers and non-stick surfaces on cooking utensils and razor blades are products that have been developed through research conducted by scientists involved in the space program.

Universities, medical research facilities, and government-sponsored research programs are heavily involved in pure research. Because of those efforts, we will likely see products developed in the near future that use energy more efficiently, apply laser technology, provide more effective treatments for diseases, and result in improved prediction and control of the weather. An interesting technology being studied is the use of a special type of metal wire that expands and contracts when exposed to slight temperature changes. It might be used in thermometers, automobile engines, air conditioners, and other products to replace expensive electronic components.

Applied Research

Applied research studies existing product problems or possible design improvements for current products. For example, automobile manufacturers are using plastics in body parts to reduce weight for fuel efficiency and to cut the cost of repairs. Fiber optics allow thousands of voice and data communications to move rapidly with no loss of quality on one transmission line. Refrigerators and air conditioners are being redesigned to eliminate the use of environmentally damaging chemicals. All of these improvements are the result of ongoing applied research.

Changes and improvements in products are necessary if the products are going to be successful for a long time. Many types of improvements result from product research. Changes can be made in the physical product, or new features can be added to existing products. It is possible that new uses for the product can be discovered or ways to make the product easier to use. Sometimes changes in the package can improve a product. Such improvements include aluminum and plastic soft drink containers, tamper-proof seals on medicine containers, and packing materials that use air to prevent product damage during shipping.

MARKETING RESEARCH

Marketing research is the study of all activities involved in the exchange of goods and services between businesses and consumers. Many companies have developed products that were well-designed and manufactured and were needed by consumers, but were not successful. The failure resulted from poor marketing planning.

Jeff Greenberg, Photographer

Many factors contribute to the success or failure of a product. Those factors include the many marketing decisions that determine the best ways to sell the product to consumers. Effective marketing decisions are as important to a product's success as are product decisions. Marketing research is conducted to assist business managers in making those decisions. Some common types of marketing research are shown in Fig. 11-2.

Fig. **11-2**

Common types of marketing research.

MARKET RESEARCH

The study of the people or businesses who buy a company's products or who may buy a new product. Market research is used to locate and describe potential customers.

MOTIVATION RESEARCH

The study of consumer buying behavior. Motivation research helps businesses determine why people buy and what influences their decisions.

ADVERTISING RESEARCH

Research done to test advertisements and the media that carry advertisements. It is used to determine if the company's advertising is effective in informing the public of available products and services.

Think of all the decisions that have to be made when marketing a product: Who will buy the product? What are the buyers' needs? What companies offer competing products? What brand name should be used? How should the product be packaged? Where will it be sold? What price should be charged for the product? What type of advertising will be most effective? The list is almost endless, but each of these questions must be answered. Marketing research can provide information to help answer such marketing questions.

PLANNING A NEW PRODUCT

Planning, producing, and marketing a new product must be approached carefully by a business. All of the major units in the business including production, finance, human resources, and marketing should be involved.

The product should be designed to meet the needs of the customers. Customers should be able to identify features of the new product that are different from and better than those of competing products. Also, products need to be safe and easy to use.

If marketing research shows that a company has a new product idea needed by enough customers to make it successful, the company can begin to design the product. In this step, engineers and researchers build models of the product and test them to be sure that a quality product can be produced. Once a model has been built, it can be used for additional market research, as well as for determining what resources the company will need to produce larger quantities of the product. At this time, the firm may decide not to produce the product at all, especially if consumer reaction has not been favorable or if the product cannot be produced and sold profitably.

If the new product has survived the research and testing process, the company can begin producing and marketing it. This will usually be an expensive step. Manufacturing facilities may need to be built or remodeled; raw materials will need to be purchased; enough employees must be available and trained to produce the product; and the product must be promoted, distributed, and sold. However, if the product has been carefully planned and produced, it has a better chance of being successful, and the company will be able to make a profit when the products are purchased by customers.

TYPES OF MANUFACTURING

The word production is used in the sense of making things. In a broader sense, *production* is the creation of goods or services desired by customers, as you learned in Chapter 1. **Manufacturing** is a special form of production in which raw and semifinished materials are processed, assembled, or converted into finished products.

Manufacturing is a complex process even if only one product is being produced. Look carefully at any product you have purchased recently. Very likely, it is made of several smaller parts or pieces. Those parts either have to be manufactured by the company or purchased from other companies. The manufac-

Illus. 11-3

Effective manufacturing requires careful planning and coordination. What do you think is meant by the term *world class manufacturing?*

Charles Gupton/Tony Stone Images

turer needs to store the parts until they are needed. Then the parts need to be assembled by machinery or people. Once assembled, the product will usually be packaged. Many products will be packed together for shipping and then stored in a warehouse for delivery to the places where the product will be sold.

In addition to the activities just discussed, many other things must happen during the manufacturing process. Equipment must be maintained and repaired, supplies must be available, and people must be trained to operate the equipment.

As you can see, manufacturing just one product is a complicated process. Often, manufacturers produce many products at the same time. So you can easily understand how complicated it can be to operate a manufacturing business.

When you think of a manufacturing business, you may have an image of a large factory with a long assembly line (mass production). Workers perform specific activities on the assembly line as the product moves past. Many products, all looking exactly alike, are produced on the assembly line each day. While assembly lines are one way to manufacture products, there are many other methods.

CUSTOM MANUFACTURING

Often there is a need to build only one or a very limited number of units of a product. The product may be very large or complex and take a long time to build. This type of product is often designed and built to meet the specific needs of the purchaser. Houses, buildings, bridges, and highways are all examples of custom projects. If a company needs a special piece of equipment built, a custom manufacturer must be used.

A custom project manufacturer must be able to work with a customer to develop a unique product. The company must be flexible enough to build a different product each time, and it may need to build part or all of that product at a new location each time.

MASS PRODUCTION

Earlier, you read about companies that use assembly lines to produce products. **Mass production** is an assembly process in which a large number of products is produced, each of which is identical to the next. Many products you use are assembled through mass production procedures. Automobiles, cameras, calculators, appliances, and wristwatches are examples of mass-produced items.

Mass production allows companies to manufacture products at a low cost and in large quantities. But many changes have occurred in mass production procedures since they were first used in the early 1900s. Now, assembly line workers are often trained to perform many activities. Groups of workers and supervisors meet regularly to identify problems and develop solutions. Computers are used to monitor the assembly process to insure that needed parts and materials are available at the right time and right place. Robots are used at many places on assembly lines to complete tasks such as painting, welding, and product testing.

CONTINUOUS, REPETITIVE, AND INTERMITTENT MANUFACTURING

Raw materials usually need to be processed before they can be consumed. Companies that work with raw materials to make them more usable are involved in *continuous processing*. Steel mills, for example, convert iron ore into steel to be used by other manufacturers. Oil refineries change crude oil into a variety of petroleum products including gasoline and oil. Cereal manufacturers process many different kinds of grain into the cereals you eat for breakfast. Production runs may last days, weeks, or months without equipment shutdowns.

Some companies manufacture a product using a repetitive activity. They do the same thing over and over to produce a product. The activity is usually rather simple and can be completed in a short time. The *repetitive process* uses modules, premade parts or units, in the assembly process. For example, the repetitive process is used to produce washing machines. First, the motor is assembled as a separate module, and then it is installed in the frame, which has been assembled separately. Controls, hosing, and other features may be added in yet another process.

With the *intermittent process*, short production runs are used to make batches of different products. The most common form of intermittent processing is the *job shop*, in which products are manufactured or assembled to an individual customer's purchase order or specifications. An example of a business using intermittent manufacturing is a printing company. Each printing job varies in quantity, type of printing process, binding, color of ink, and type of paper.

REDESIGNING TRADITIONAL PRODUCTS

Source: *Business Week*, July 15, 1993, pp. 78-81; *Fortune*, January 11, 1993, p. 77.

Questions:

1 Why should the largest appliance manufacturer in the world be concerned about research?

2 Why is it possible for a technology such as touchpad controls to be successful now when it was not successful several years ago?

3 Which appears to be most useful to Whirlpool—marketing research or product research?

New products are exciting, but what do you do if you are responsible for redesigning products that have been around for years and seem to have few ways that they can be changed or improved? Consider the challenges faced by companies that manufacture major appliances—stoves, refrigerators, washers, and dryers. Are there new colors, new styles, new features? Examples from Whirlpool show how effective product development procedures can be successful even with traditional products.

Whirlpool conducts an annual Standardized Appliance Measurement Satisfaction survey of nearly 200,000 households. The survey asks consumers to rate their appliances on very specific qualities. The results allow Whirlpool to compare its brands with competitors' products. If a competing brand is rated higher on a feature, Whirlpool design personnel study that brand to see why it is superior.

When a new product or product feature is designed, the company develops prototypes of the product for consumer testing. Most testing is done in the company's Usability Lab where consumers are brought in to try out the product's features. As they use the appliances, the consumers are videotaped so their reactions can be studied. If new appliance controls are being developed, a computer simulation may be prepared so consumers can see how the controls will look and perform. A prototype of a new appliance may be set up in a mall so it can be evaluated by actual appliance shoppers.

This comprehensive marketing research allowed Whirlpool to redesign its cooktop range to use electronic touchpads rather than the traditional knobs. An earlier prototype had failed because the technology was not as advanced. However, recent consumer feedback suggested consumers wanted controls that were easier to operate. The touchpad technology was redesigned and simplified. When consumers tried the new controls, they indicated a high level of satisfaction. The new design has now been incorporated into Whirlpool's product line and has proven to be one of the fastest-selling features ever introduced.

Another approach to product design is the use of pure and applied research to solve problems. Refrigerator manufacturers are competing to develop products that are both environmentally friendly and energy efficient. Refrigerators use about 20% of the electricity in an average home. At the same time, cooling comes from the use of fluorocarbon, a substance banned because of its effect on the ozone. Whirlpool's engineers have worked to discover better insulation materials, alternatives to fluorocarbons, and more energy-efficient electrical systems for their refrigerators.

ORGANIZING A MANUFACTURING BUSINESS

When a new manufacturing business is organized, a number of important decisions must be made. The company must be able to get the materials needed to build products. Buildings, machinery, and equipment must be purchased and arranged so that quality products can be produced rapidly and at a low cost. People must be hired with the skills to operate the business. If people with the proper skills cannot be found, others must be trained. Finally, after the products are completed they must be distributed and sold.

LOCATING THE BUSINESS

One of the first decisions of the manufacturing company is where to locate the business. While it might seem that a business could locate anywhere it wants to, it is a very complicated procedure to find the best location. A discussion of several factors that influence the decision follows.

Availability of Raw Materials

If a company uses a large quantity of raw materials, it must make sure they are available at a low cost. The owners, therefore, may choose to locate close to the source of the raw materials to make them easier to obtain and to keep the cost of transporting the raw materials as low as possible. Furniture and textile manufacturers, steel mills, and food processing companies are examples of industries that are located close to the source of needed raw materials.

Transportation Methods

A company must decide how to obtain needed materials and how products will be shipped to customers. The choice of transportation method can determine whether raw materials are received and products are delivered on time. The major transportation methods include air, rail, truck, water, and pipeline. Each has specific advantages based on time, cost, and convenience.

Supply and Cost of Energy and Water

The costs and supply of energy used by manufacturers is an important consideration in production planning. The company must be able to have an uninterrupted supply of energy at a reasonable cost.

Mark Wagner/Tony Stone Images

Illus. 11-4

Transportation of materials is a major consideration in business location decisions. What types of businesses usually locate close to major airports?

There have been times in recent years when the supply of several types of energy, including electricity and gasoline, has been in short supply. As a result, companies had to switch to other forms of energy or reduce operations. Prices of most energy sources have increased a great deal in recent years. In many parts of the country, water supplies are limited. Access to water as well as the requirements for treatment and discharge of waste water are carefully controlled. A company must be sure to locate where it will have enough energy and water to be able to operate for many years in the future.

Land and Building Costs

While some companies can operate in small buildings, others may need several hundred acres of land. Land and buildings can be purchased or leased. As a business grows, it must plan for possible future expansion. Many companies have had to expand several times since they started business. Expansion is easier if enough land is available close to the existing buildings and buildings are designed to be flexible.

Labor Supply

Well-trained employees are an important part of most manufacturing companies. In selecting a location, a company should look at the supply of workers, the training that might be necessary, and the cost of labor. It will make a big difference whether the company needs highly skilled employees, or if it can use unskilled labor. Few businesses can operate effectively today without well-educated employees. The days of easily available and inexpensive labor providing the skills a company needs are over. Businesses are working with government agencies, colleges, and universities to design training programs so they will have a competitive workforce.

Location of Customers

Just as some companies need to locate near the source of raw materials, others may consider the location of their customers. Manufacturers that supply parts for the auto industry usually locate near the automobile production facilities. Some companies locate near seaports if they have important markets in other countries. Soft drink bottlers have plants in most cities to reduce transportation costs. The location of a firm's customers is an important factor when most of them can be found in one part of the country, when they need products regularly and rapidly, or when transportation costs of the finished products will be very high.

Economic and Legal Factors

A company should consider the type and amount of taxes that must be paid in a given location. Some cities offer reduced tax rates or may even remove some taxes for several years to encourage new businesses to locate there. Most towns and cities today also restrict the location and operation of businesses. Zoning laws identify where specific types of businesses can operate. Environmental regulations control the use of water and other resources.

Factory Layout

Facilities, equipment, and materials all must be organized so products can be produced efficiently. Products must move through the building, parts must be added, and employees must be able to work on the product easily and safely. Raw materials, parts, and supplies must be received and stored. Once products are finished, they need to be stored or loaded for shipment.

The type of layout used by a manufacturer will depend on the product and the assembly process. One company that builds tractors has a continuous assembly line that is nearly a mile long. Many of the parts have to be stored long distances from the place they are needed. The parts are delivered to the assembly line with overhead conveyor belts and chains.

Another small company that builds electric motors has all of the needed parts brought to each assembler's work area. The assembler puts all of the parts together to finish the motor. The motor is then moved to the shipping area to be packaged and stored for delivery.

In addition to the type of product and the assembly process used, other factors influence the layout of the business. Products and people must be able to move around the building. Product testing may be needed. The layout should be designed to make product assembly easy and safe.

Companies should be able to build products rapidly and keep costs down. For most companies, the layout should be flexible so new machinery and equipment can be added. Also, the layout may need to be expanded if the company grows or changed if new products are developed.

Production Planning

Developing a production plan could be compared to planning a meal. All ingredients must be available in the right quantities and at the right time. Cooking utensils need to be assembled. Since some foods require longer cooking times than others, preparation of each item must begin at the correct time. If scheduled and completed correctly, all foods can be served at the same time.

When planning production, a company estimates the need for all of the resources required to produce a product, when each will be needed, and in what quantity. Because production occurs over a period of time and in a sequence, not all resources are needed at once. If materials are available before they are needed, the business will have to use both space and money for storage. On the other hand, if resources are not available at the time needed, production will be delayed and money will be spent for employee time and materials that cannot be used until the necessary materials are delivered.

Three important activities are a part of production planning. **Inventory management** determines the quantities of materials and supplies needed for production and the amount of finished products required to meet customer orders. **Human resource planning** determines the types of jobs that are required for each part of the production procedure and the number of people needed for each job. **Production scheduling** identifies the steps required in a manufacturing process, the time required to complete each step, and the sequence of the steps. Sophisticated planning systems are used by managers to help them develop production schedules. Computers are very useful in scheduling production and insuring that production schedules are being followed.

IMPROVING PRODUCTION PROCESSES

Improving quality and productivity has been one of the most important challenges facing businesses in the last decade. Increasing global competition has resulted in a larger number of products from which customers can choose. Businesses have found that customers will buy the best product available, resulting in increased pressure to improve quality and customer service.

For many years, companies were more interested in production efficiency than in quality. As early as the 1950s, an American management expert, Dr. W. Edwards Deming, was encouraging businesses to focus on quality as the most important company goal. His suggestions for operations were largely ignored by U.S. businesses but were implemented by Japanese firms.

Today, because of the success of companies that have adopted Deming's ideas, principles of quality management are used by most manufacturers. **Quality management** develops standards for all operations and products and measures results using those standards. For quality management to be successful, the company must believe that no defects are acceptable and that all employees are responsible for quality. Everyone must be able to identify problems and take responsibility for correcting them. Rewards need to be based on achieving the quality standards rather than meeting a certain level of production.

To encourage American companies to improve quality, Congress created the Malcom Baldridge National Quality Award in 1987. To win the award, a company must demonstrate that it has implemented a quality management program. Competing for the Baldridge Award is a very difficult and expensive process. Companies compete for the award because it demonstrates their commitment to quality and is one of the top honors available to businesses.

Technology has contributed to the improvement of manufacturing for many years. Computers have changed manufacturing procedures, dramatically improving the quality of production, speeding production, and reducing costs. Robots now complete many of the routine and repetitive tasks previously done by low-skilled employees. Fewer people are now needed to accomplish the same level of production. However, the people needed must be skilled in computer operations and modern production processes.

In addition to routine tasks, computer technology also provides the capability to accomplish very difficult and challenging tasks. One type of computer application is known as CAD (computer aided design). Computers are used by engineers to design and test products before they are even built. With a computer, a design can be viewed from various angles, modifications can be studied, and products can be tested for strength and durability.

The most extensive use of computers is a fully developed system known as computer integrated manufacturing. With **computer integrated manufacturing**, all manufacturing systems are designed and managed using computers. Design work, planning and scheduling, resource management, and control are all tied together through computers. When a change is made in one area, information is communicated to all other areas on the impact of the change.

The manufacturing of products is an important part of our economy. However, nearly half the money spent by consumers today is used to pay for services. Just as manufacturers must carefully plan the production of products, service businesses need to develop effective procedures. In the next section, we will examine the operation of service businesses.

SERVICE BUSINESSES

Service businesses are the fastest-growing segment of our society. It is predicted that over two-thirds of the United States labor force will be employed in service-producing businesses within the next decade. Nearly half of every consumer dollar will go for the purchase of services. Therefore, the United States is changing from the world's leading manufacturing economy into its leading service economy. While many service businesses are quite small and employ only a few people, others have total sales of millions of dollars each year and employ thousands of people.

NATURE OF SERVICES

Services are activities of value that do not result in the ownership of anything tangible. There are many types of service businesses such as theaters, travel agencies, beauty and barber shops, lawn care businesses, and insurance agencies. Services have important characteristics that make them different from products. These characteristics result in unique operating procedures for service businesses.

Form

Services are intangible. They do not include a physical product, they cannot be seen or examined before they are purchased, and they do not exist after the consumer uses them.

Availability

The service cannot be separated from the person or business supplying it. Dental care requires a dentist, a concert requires a performer, and tax preparation cannot be done without an accountant. People who purchase services are also purchasing the availability and the skill of the person performing the service.

Quality

The quality of the service depends on who provides it as well as on where and when that service is provided. Knowing these factors makes it much easier for a business to control the quality of services and insure that customers get the same quality time after time. A service provider who is tired, untrained, or unconcerned about the customer may not provide the same quality of service each time.

Timing

A service cannot be stored or held until needed. After a movie starts, it is no longer available in its complete form until it is replayed. If the courts in a tennis club are full, no one else can play tennis at that time. Likewise, the owner of a taxi company must have cars and drivers available even if no one is using a taxi at a specific time.

OPERATING A SERVICE BUSINESS

Each of the characteristics of services creates problems for the owner of a service business. By understanding the unique characteristics of services, those in charge of planning services can do a better job of meeting customer needs.

Illus. 11-5

Owners and employees of a service business must realize that customer satisfaction determines how well the business performs. How can the owner and employees of this service business insure that customers will be satisfied?

Jeff Greenberg, Photographer

Because a service is intangible, the service provider must find ways to describe the service to prospective customers. It is often necessary to demonstrate how the service will be provided and the benefits the customers will receive. To help overcome this problem, a product is sometimes also provided to customers as a part of the service. Insurance companies provide easy-to-read policies and leather cases to hold the policy, tour services provide travel bags, and hotels provide small gifts in their rooms.

The service must be available and must be provided in an acceptable way to the customer. A client visiting a barber shop may want the services of a specific barber. A person completing a banking transaction may want to talk with a teller rather than use an automatic banking machine. Airline travelers may want to check their luggage free rather than pay an additional fee for baggage handling.

The persons providing the service must be well trained. They must be able to work with customers, identify needs, and provide the appropriate service. They must recognize that customer satisfaction is directly related to how well they perform. In turn, customers will expect the same quality of service each time they purchase it.

The supply of a service must be matched to the demand. If it can be anticipated that a large number of customers will ride city buses on the Saturday of a home football game, more buses may need to be scheduled. If a snowstorm is anticipated, companies that clear parking lots and driveways may need to find additional equipment and operators. On the other hand, if a summer is particularly cool and rainy, the operator of a swimming pool will probably need to schedule fewer lifeguards and pool assistants.

CHANGES IN SERVICE BUSINESSES

Just as manufacturers have seen major changes occur in the ways they produce products, service businesses have also looked for better ways of providing services. Some of those methods include more careful hiring and training of employees, carefully planning how services will be provided to maintain quality standards, and using technology to improve the delivery and availability of services.

Franchises for service businesses are becoming quite common. Franchising allows a service to be provided in a variety of locations while maintaining a consistent image and level of quality. Examples of franchised service businesses include car repair, video movie rentals, tax preparation and legal services, telephone answering, and house-cleaning businesses.

Service businesses are responding to the specific needs of customers. Extended hours, more service locations, a greater variety of services, and follow-up activities with customers to ensure satisfaction are all ways that businesses are attempting to meet customer needs. Managers of service businesses are learning that the same care and procedures used in planning manufacturing must be used in the operation of service businesses. In both cases, customers expect quality delivered in a timely fashion at a fair price.

CHAPTER REVIEW

REVIEWING FACTS

1. Why is new product development important to a successful company?
2. Identify four sources of new product ideas for a business.
3. How is pure research different from applied research?
4. Give three examples of marketing research.
5. Why should a company produce a model of a new product before it begins to produce large quantities of the product?
6. What is the difference between custom manufacturing and mass production?
7. Why is it desirable for some businesses to locate close to the source of raw materials?
8. When would a company want to locate a business near its customers?
9. Explain the importance of a well-organized factory layout for a manufacturer.
10. What are three tools that can be used to improve production management?
11. How can management of manufacturing benefit from computer integrated manufacturing?
12. Give four examples of service businesses.
13. What four characteristics make services different from products?
14. Why is employee selection and training so important to a service business?
15. What is the importance of anticipating demand for a service business?

DISCUSSING IDEAS

1. Why should companies study customers' needs, likes, and dislikes before they begin to develop a new product?
2. Some estimates suggest that at least five of every ten new products introduced will never be successful. In your opinion, what are several reasons for this high rate of failure?
3. Why would a company invest money in pure research rather than applied research?
4. Under what circumstances might a company decide to go ahead with the production of a new product rather than spend time developing and testing a model?
5. List several examples of businesses that use each of the major types of production processes: repetitive, continuous, and intermittent.
6. In addition to the factors listed in the chapter, what should an owner look for when selecting a specific location for a new business?
7. Identify several ways that computers can be used to improve the process of manufacturing products.
8. Why are the number and size of service businesses increasing in the U.S. economy?
9. How does the concept of production scheduling apply to a service business?
10. What changes can you predict for the economy of the United States as the service sector continues to grow in relation to the manufacturing sector?

ANALYZING INFORMATION

1. The Hi-Tech Corporation spent $337,250 on research last year. Ten percent was spent on pure research, 25 percent on marketing research, and the remainder on applied research. The annual sales of the company for the last year were $9,500,000.
   a. What percentage of sales was spent on research?
   b. How much was spent on each of the three types of research by Hi-Tech?
2. The Autostart Company manufactures automobile batteries. During one year it produced 46,000 batteries and had the following expenses:

Materials	$320,000
Labor for production	$112,000
Equipment	$ 51,000
Depreciation	$170,000
Utilities	$175,000
Insurance	$ 69,000
Marketing costs	$483,000

a. What was the total cost of producing and marketing the batteries?
    b. What was the cost per unit?
    c. What percentage of total costs was spent on marketing?
3. A business is considering making changes to one of its products—
    a microwave oven. The business wants the product to be more efficient
    and durable and have features that make it very easy for people to operate.
    a. Identify several ways that the business could study its old product to
        find improvements.
    b. If the company cannot make the product more efficient and durable,
        should it continue to sell its old product?
4. Develop a chart that lists the three types of production processes: repeti-
    tive, continuous, and intermittent. Under each of the headings, list as
    many products as you can identify that are manufactured in that way. After
    you have completed the chart, identify the differences among the prod-
    ucts that indicate the type of production that was used.
5. Interview the owner or manager of a service business. Find out what the
    manager does in order to develop the service for the customers. Then
    write a short report comparing those activities to the activities that would
    be completed in producing a product.

S OLVING BUSINESS PROBLEMS

CASE 11-1

Gene and Levi were discussing their company's efforts to test new products
before the products were introduced into the market. Their conversation went
like this:

Levi: I cannot believe we have already spent almost $500,000 on research for
        the new computer.
Gene: It does seem like a lot of money for a product we believe is needed.
Levi: Much of the consumer research seems to be wasted. Most of the people
        told us they did not know enough about the new computer features to
        tell us what they did or did not like.
Gene: The research by our engineers shows that our computer is faster than
        most others and that it is easier to service and repair. That should be
        enough to convince people to buy our brand.
Levi: Now they say we have to put the computer into three test markets
        before it can be sold nationwide. That will take another four months.
Gene: The last time we used a test market for a product, one of our competi-
        tors got their brand into the national market before we did. Does the
        company want that to happen again?

Required:
1. Is $500,000 too much to spend on research for a new computer? How
    could a company determine the amount to spend?

2. What could be done with the information the company learned from the consumer research?
3. Is the information gathered from the engineers' research more useful than the consumer research?
4. What is meant by the term test market? What are some of the advantages and disadvantages of using a test market?

CASE 11-2

Fran and Jason Walker vacation with their family each summer on an island just off the coast of North Carolina. The island is a popular tourist area with several large hotels and a ferry boat that brings people from the mainland to the island for day-long visits. Fran and Jason began to think about ways they could use their time to make money during the summer. They thought about the needs of the tourists visiting the island, and they decided to begin a guide service for those people who wanted to explore the hills and forests of the island.

They spent some time planning two different tours. The short tour would last for one hour. It would be for those people who wanted to see some of the beautiful spots on the island but were not prepared for extensive hiking. The long tour would take a half day and would include hiking over five miles. It was designed for the more experienced outdoors person who wanted to study the plants, trees, and wildlife unique to the island. The short tour would be provided to groups of ten to fifteen people at a rate of $2.00 per person. The long tour would serve four to eight people and would cost $10.00 per person.

After planning, Fran and Jason developed small posters and some business cards that described their guide service, listed the days and hours the tours were available, and gave the Walker phone number. The materials were distributed to the hotels and restaurants on the island and the mainland.

Required:
1. Do you think Fran and Jason have done effective planning for their service business? What are some additional things they may want to consider before beginning the business?
2. Suggest ways that the Walkers can (a) help prospective customers understand the type and quality of their service, (b) ensure that customers get a high-quality service each time, (c) provide the service to customers at an appropriate time and location.
3. During the second summer, the Walkers' business became extremely successful, and more tours were requested than they could personally lead. Now they are considering hiring other teenagers who also vacation on the island to lead the tours. What recommendations would you make on the qualifications and training of the new employees?

DISTRIBUTION PLANNING CHAPTER
AND ACTIVITIES

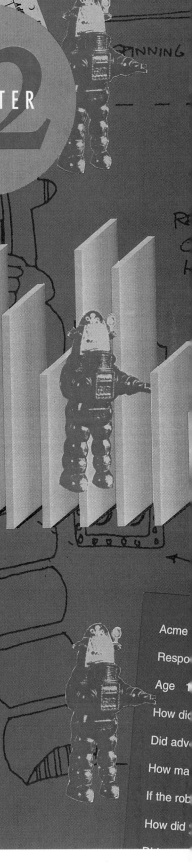

After studying this chapter you will be able to:

12-1 Describe how distribution is used to improve marketing of products and services.

12-2 Explain the differences among common channels of distribution.

12-3 Discuss the important factors to be considered when selecting channels of distribution.

12-4 Describe the characteristics of major forms of transportation used to distribute products.

12-5 Give examples of product-handling procedures that improve product distribution.

When a distribution system works well, consumers will not likely be aware of the many people and activities involved in that system. However, failures in the distribution system can cause real frustration for customers. Some of the following situations may seem familiar to you.

Customer A: *This is the third store in which I've looked and everyone seems to be out of the new Fudgey Snacks. I hope you have some.*
Clerk: *We don't carry that brand.*

Customer B: *I can't find the display of televisions your store advertised in Thursday's newspaper.*
Salesperson: *We didn't get the supply we expected from our warehouse. We are sold out and will not have more until next week.*

Customer C: I would like a refund on this plant stand. When I tried to assemble it, two of the pieces were missing and it doesn't look like the model pictured on the package.

Customer Service Representative: We can't give a refund. You will have to send it back to the manufacturer.

Our economic system relies on the successful exchange of the products and services between businesses and consumers. As we just saw in the three examples, consumers will become very frustrated if they are unable to satisfy their needs. Businesses, too, will suffer if they are unable to get their products to customers. Successful exchanges are not easy. In fact, most of the problems consumers and business people face in our economy occur during the exchange process.

Economic discrepancies are differences between the offerings of a business and the requirements of a consumer. Marketers are concerned about four important economic discrepancies. Those discrepancies include the types and quantity of products and services produced, and the location and timing of production and consumption. Producers develop large quantities of one or a very few products; consumers want small quantities of a variety of products. Products are produced at a specific time and in a particular location; that time and location does not typically match the place and time consumers need the product. Distribution systems are designed to get the products customers want to where they want them, when they want them, and in the quantity they want them. In this chapter, we will examine how businesses can make decisions about product distribution that will satisfy customers and allow the business to make a profit.

CHANNELS OF DISTRIBUTION

The routes products and services follow, including the activities and participating organizations, while moving from the producer to the consumer are called **channels of distribution** or **marketing channels**. Businesses that participate in activities transferring goods and services from the producer to the user are called **channel members**.

The most common types of channel members are retailers and wholesalers. As we learned in an earlier chapter, a retailer sells directly to the consumer. A wholesaler, on the other hand, primarily works with other channel members rather than selling to final consumers. Wholesalers also sell to organizations, institutions, and government agencies. Wholesalers, retailers, and other channel members serve important and specific roles in the exchange process.

Determining the number and type of businesses and the activities they will perform in a channel of distribution is an important decision. Adding businesses to the channel makes the channel more complex and difficult to control. However, using businesses that have particular expertise in transportation, product handling, or other distribution activities may result in improved distribution or actual cost savings.

The activities that need to be performed as a product moves from producer to consumer will help to determine the number and types of businesses in the channel. Remember that all of the marketing activities we studied in Chapter 10 are usually performed during the exchange process. Those activities are reviewed in Figure 12-1. If the producer or consumer is unable or unwilling to perform some of the activities, other businesses will be needed.

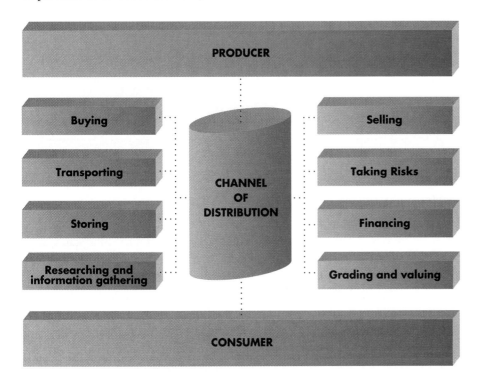

PRODUCER

Buying

Transporting

Storing

Researching and information gathering

CHANNEL OF DISTRIBUTION

Selling

Taking Risks

Financing

Grading and valuing

CONSUMER

Fig. 12-1
All of the major marketing activities need to be performed by businesses or consumers when an exchange is made.

Customers influence the development of a marketing channel. When developing a channel of distribution, businesses must consider the location of customers, the number of customers wanting the product, and the ways in which customers prefer to purchase and consume the products.

Connie Geocaris/Tony Stone Images

Illus. 12-1
Careful development of a channel of distribution is necessary for products that require special handling. What are some of the important distribution activities for a florist?

COMMON TYPES OF CHANNELS

Distribution channels are needed for products sold to final consumers and for products used by businesses. The channels that products follow may be quite simple and short or long and complex. The shortest path is for the producer to sell directly to the user; the longest path can include a retailer, a wholesaler, and even other businesses, as shown in Fig. 12-2. The most common types of trade channels are described next.

Fig. 12-2

Common types of marketing channels for consumer goods.

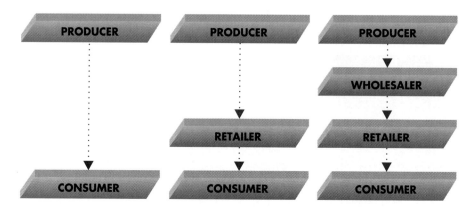

Producer Directly to Consumer

Certain producers prefer to sell directly to consumers rather than through other businesses. A farmer can sell fruits and vegetables at a roadside stand, an airplane manufacturer can sell planes directly to airlines, and a publisher can sell books through the mail to readers. When producers sell directly to the ultimate customer, it is called **direct marketing**. When distribution takes place through channel members, it is called **indirect marketing**.

Direct marketing is accomplished in a number of ways. One way is for sales representatives to call on users in person. Direct selling is a primary method used by businesses when selling to other businesses. Salespeople travel to businesses in order to make personal presentations to important customers. Door-to-door selling has also been popular in the past for reaching final consumers who were unable to make frequent shopping trips or who were not eager to buy particular types of products. For instance, door-to-door selling has been used successfully by cosmetic, insurance, and encyclopedia companies. In recent years, that type of direct marketing has been used less frequently and has been replaced by other forms.

A popular form of direct marketing is the use of mailings. Letters and advertising brochures or catalogs are sent to prospective customers through the mail. Customers can use a mail-order form or telephone to buy products. Mail-order companies have operated for many years selling a variety of merchandise. Many companies use some type of direct marketing through the mail even if it is not their most important method of selling. Mail order seems to be most successful with specialized types of merchandise. One of the largest mail order-companies, Sears, has decided to end its catalog business after over a century of operation because it was too expensive to manage sales of the thousands of products available. At the same time, Land's End, L.L. Bean, Spiegel, and other specialty merchandisers are very successful with catalog sales.

Today, one of the most popular methods of direct sales is telemarketing. **Telemarketing** combines telephone sales with computer technology. Salespeople at computer terminals make and receive calls to and from prospective customers. Some telemarketing simply involves taking orders from customers who have seen merchandise advertised on television or through direct mail advertising. When making a sale, the salesperson completes an order form displayed on the terminal screen. In other cases, the telemarketer is responsible for a complete sales presentation. The presentation is often made from a prepared script. Telemarketing is an extremely efficient method of direct marketing.

Many producers of business products sell directly to users, whereas fewer producers of consumer goods sell directly to the final user. Consumer goods are usually sold to large numbers of customers in many locations. Most customers will buy only one or a very few products at one time, which makes marketing very difficult. Most manufacturers avoid the expanded operations necessary for the direct marketing of consumer goods. In fact, only a small percentage of consumer goods go directly from the producer to the consumer. Manufacturers that want to serve a large number of consumers will typically use some type of indirect channel.

Producer to Consumer Through Retailers

When a producer cannot or chooses not to perform all of the marketing activities, the need for an indirect channel arises. Manufacturers can simplify many of their marketing operations by selling to retailers. Fewer salespeople will be needed because there will be a smaller number of retail customers than final consumers, and retailers buy in large quantities. Advertising can be shared with the retailers and retailers will be responsible for much of the product storage, consumer credit, and other activities. The retailer specializes in marketing activities, which allows the producer to specialize in manufacturing activities. As you learned in Chapter 1, specialization leads to improved efficiency, which benefits consumers through lower prices and added or improved services.

Retailers benefit consumers in several ways. Unlike producers, retailers can be conveniently located near consumers and can provide the products of many manufacturers in one place, thereby permitting consumers to make comparisons among a variety of types and brands of products. Furthermore, a retailer can offer several kinds of products that consumers may need, making it possible to complete shopping at one or a few locations. Convenient shopping hours, credit terms, merchandise exchanges, and other special services are often offered by retailers to encourage customers to shop in their businesses.

There are many different types of retailers. Retailers are classified by the types of products they sell and the services they provide. Some of the important types of retail stores that serve consumers are shown in Fig. 12-3. In addition, there is a growing number of types of non-store retailers. Products are sold to customers in a number of ways that do not require a shopping trip to a store. Those ways include vending machines; direct marketing by retailers through telephone, catalog, or computer-ordering services; in-home parties and sales presentations; and shopping channels on cable television.

Fig. 12-3
Common types of retail stores.

CONVENIENCE STORES

Small stores located in neighborhoods or at convenient shopping locations that handle a variety of inexpensive, regularly purchased products such as foods, beverages, health care, and household products.

DEPARTMENT STORES

Generally large full-service stores that carry many types of products for the home, such as furniture, appliances, clothing, and other household items.

DISCOUNT STORES

Stores that offer a range of common items for a broad set of customers. Items typically include apparel, household goods, hardware, toys, and nonperishable food. The products sell for less than the prices at which they may be sold in other types of stores because of the volume of products sold and fewer services provided.

SPECIALTY STORES

Stores that handle one category of products, such as shoes, jewelry, hardware, clothing, or furniture, but offer a wider choice of colors, sizes, and brands, and usually a high level of customer service.

SUPERMARKETS

Large stores that are well stocked with a variety of frequently purchased household products, with a primary emphasis on food items.

FACTORY OUTLETS

Combination discount and specialty stores that are owned by the manufacturer. Outlets are used to sell merchandise that cannot be sold through the normal marketing channels. They offer only the brands of that manufacturer in a limited number of locations.

Producers prefer to sell products to those retailers who buy in large quantities, such as department and discount stores and supermarkets. Smaller retailers are usually not able to deal directly with the manufacturer so they must buy from other channel members.

Producer to Consumer Through Wholesalers and Retailers

To increase sales volume or to reach varied target markets, some manufacturers may want to sell their products through many types and sizes of retailers in a variety of locations. The distribution of some products is very complex and requires a great deal of time and special services. Many manufacturers are not prepared to do an effective job of distribution under those circumstances. In those cases, manufacturers will use a longer channel.

The most commonly used marketing channel for consumer goods involves the use of wholesalers and retailers. Many producers distribute goods to a wholesaler, who then distributes the goods to retailers. Think of the types of activities that need to be performed in a channel of distribution. Products are bought and sold, promoted, financed, stored, and transported. Some wholesalers provide all of those activities while others specialize in one or a very few types of marketing activities. Wholesalers are classified by the types of marketing activities they perform. Some common types of wholesalers are described in Fig. 12-4 on page 292.

In certain cases, a product may even go through two wholesalers. For example, a small leather belt producer may distribute belts first through a leather goods wholesaler who then distributes them to a larger wholesaler who sells a variety of products including leather. The larger wholesaler then distributes the belts to retailers.

Jeff Greenberg, Photographer

Illus. 12-2
An auction company sells thousands of automobile dealers' used cars to other dealers. Why would an auto dealer choose to use a wholesaler for some of its cars?

Wholesalers provide valuable services that producers may not provide. They sell to retailers in small quantities and can usually deliver goods quickly. In addition, many wholesalers offer credit terms to retailers and provide help in planning promotions and sales strategies. These special services make wholesalers a popular part of many distribution channels.

Wholesalers are used to sell business products as well as consumer products. Many small businesses are unable to purchase in the quantities required by large manufacturers or to meet their terms of sale. They will seek the service of a wholesaler, often called an industrial distributor, to purchase the products they need.

For a time, the number of wholesalers declined as the size of manufacturers and retailers increased. The larger firms believed they could complete the wholesalers' activities more efficiently. However, the importance of wholesalers is again being recognized as new and small businesses attempt to compete and as businesses try to expand their markets and improve their services. Through specialized activities, up-to-date procedures, and the use of technology, wholesalers are able to participate effectively in product distribution. Wholesalers are an important part of international marketing today. Those who have developed

Fig. 12-4

Common types of wholesalers.

MERCHANT WHOLESALER

A wholesaler who takes legal title to goods, offers credit to retailers, and provides other services, such as help with advertising and displaying merchandise.

CASH-AND-CARRY WHOLESALER

A wholesaler who operates much like a merchant wholesaler, except that the buyer must pay cash and transport the product from the wholesaler's business. This type of wholesaler is often used by retailers who buy in small quantities.

RACK JOBBER

A wholesaler who takes legal title to goods and who usually works through large retail stores, especially food stores that carry nonfood items. These wholesalers furnish racks or displays, stock shelves, price products, fix displays, and keep inventory records. The retailer only provides space for the product, for which a fee or percentage of sales is paid.

SPECIALTY WHOLESALER

A wholesaler who specializes in one or only a very few types of merchandise—grocery items, automotive products, apparel, and the like.

MANUFACTURER'S AGENT

An independent salesperson who is given the sole privilege of selling a business's product in a given geographic area. An agent usually has the authority to set the price or the terms of sale for the product and to make arrangements for delivery of orders, but does not take title to or possession of the goods.

international customers and distribution systems offer an effective way for companies to enter those markets. The international wholesalers are also able to import products from other countries to sell to their customers.

The importance of wholesalers is indicated by the fact that in a recent year there were over 300,000 wholesaling establishments employing more than three million people in the United States. These businesses handled thousands of different products ranging from convenience goods, such as food and drug items, to other types of consumer and industrial goods. While consumers generally do not come into contact with them, wholesalers are an important part of marketing.

INTEGRATED MARKETING CHANNELS

Usually the businesses involved in a channel of distribution are independent businesses. Those businesses make their own decisions and provide the activities they believe their customers want. It is not unusual for businesses in a channel of distribution to have conflicts with each other. One of the challenges in distribution planning is to develop cooperative relationships among channel members.

One of the ways for channels to work more effectively is for a large business in the channel to take responsibility for planning, coordination, and communication. The business organizes the channel so each participant will benefit and helps the other businesses to complete their responsibilities successfully. A channel in which one organization takes a leadership position to benefit all channel members is known as an **administered channel**.

Cooperation is difficult among businesses that operate at different levels of a channel and have very different responsibilities. Some very large businesses attempt to solve that problem through channel integration. **Channel integration** occurs when one business owns the organizations at other levels of the channel. A manufacturer may purchase the businesses that provide wholesaling or retailing functions. A large retailer may decide to buy a wholesaler or even several small manufacturing businesses. Each business can still provide the specific functions needed for a successful channel, but having one owner for all businesses avoids the conflicts that occur in other channels.

DEVELOPING A CHANNEL OF DISTRIBUTION

From the available channels of distribution shown in Fig 12-1, producers must decide which channel or channels will best fit their needs. Producers generally prefer to use as few channels and channel members as possible. Sometimes it is necessary to use more than one channel if the product is to get the widest distribution. Goods such as razor blades, candy, pens, and soap are purchased by many people in a variety of locations. Such items will require several channels to reach all of the possible consumers. The manufacturers may actually sell directly to national discount stores that will be able to sell large quantities of the product. To reach other markets, they can sell to large merchant wholesalers who will in turn sell to supermarkets, convenience stores, rack jobbers, or other types of retailers and wholesalers.

Selling to different types of customers will result in varied channels of distribution. For example, a magazine publisher may sell magazines through retail stores, news agencies, newsstands, and magazine subscription agencies, as well as directly through the mail to subscribers as shown in Fig. 12-5.

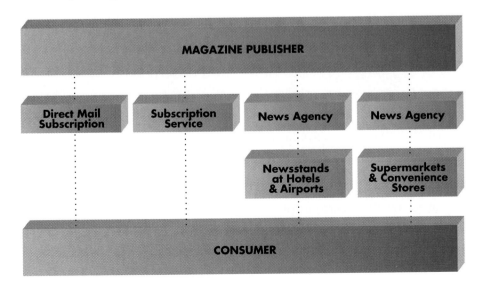

Fig. **12-5**
Four possible channels for the sale of magazines to consumers.

Many factors must be considered by a producer in deciding which channel or channels to select for distributing the company's products. Some of the main factors are:

- **Perishability of the product.** Highly perishable articles require rapid and careful handling. Those products, such as bread, fresh flowers, and ice cream, are usually marketed directly to the consumer or through very few channel members.

- **Geographic distance between the producer and the consumer.** Many products are now sold internationally as well as throughout the country in which they are produced. If the market is very close to the point of production, there is less need for channel members. There will often be more businesses involved in handling a product as the distance increases from producer to consumer.

- **Need for the special handling of the product.** If the product requires costly procedures or equipment for handling, it is likely to pass through as few channel members as possible. Gasoline, which requires pipelines, special tanks, and trucks for handling, is moved from the refiner to the retailer as directly as possible. Some gasoline retail outlets are owned by the refiner. Products that are highly complex in nature and which need experts to install and repair also require short channels. Manufacturers of large computer systems, for example, sell directly to users.

Illus. 12-3

Moving petroleum products from the point of production to the final consumer is a challenging distribution problem. What are some of the methods used to transport those products from the oil well to the gas pump?

Tony Stone Images

- **Number of users.** The greater the number of users of a product, the more channel members there probably will be. For instance, the manufacturer of steel is likely to sell directly to a few large users, whereas a shoe manufacturer may sell to wholesalers who will in turn distribute to a variety of retail businesses.

- **Number of types of products manufactured.** A producer who has only one product, such as pottery, will probably sell to a wholesaler. It is too expensive to maintain a salesforce large enough to contact all retailers in the country. But if a producer has a large number of electrical products, such as coffee makers, clocks, heaters, and toasters, it might sell directly to large retailers who will handle all products. The marketing costs can be distributed over many products.
- **Financial strength and interests of the producer.** Large companies that are strong financially are better able to perform the marketing activities required to move goods from producer to consumer through the least number of channel members. They may find it more profitable to handle the marketing activities within the company rather than using other businesses. It also gives them more control over the channel rather than relying on others to perform many of the activities.

Channel decisions, like other marketing decisions, require careful study and are subject to change. Changes in technology, in transportation and storage facilities, and in retail methods are reasons why producers are constantly looking for more efficient ways to market their goods.

DISTRIBUTION METHODS

Selecting the channel members who will help sell the product to the consumer is only one of the distribution decisions a company must make. One of the most important decisions is how the products will be moved from the producer to the consumer.

Several common problems related to the transportation of products must be faced by the buyer or the seller. One of these problems deals with the types of products to be shipped. Factors to consider in shipping include the size, shape, and weight of the goods. Also, certain goods are fragile and may need special care in handling. Transporting 100 tons of steel, for example, requires much different treatment from that required for moving a carton of glassware.

Another transportation problem is the time needed for delivery. Some buyers expect or need shipment within a matter of hours, and others may not need or expect delivery for several weeks. Still another shipping problem is cost. In addition to the basic transportation charges, there are the costs of packaging products for shipment, insurance, and often storing products before, during, and after delivery to the buyer. Those companies that do not perform their own shipping activities must first decide on the requirements that must be met in distribution. Then the transportation method is selected along with the company or companies that will handle the products.

Both consumers and business people are concerned about the quality of products when they are purchased. They also want to have products available where and when they need them and at a reasonable cost. The procedures used in distribution affect all of those concerns. **Distribution planning** is used by businesses to ensure that all important factors are considered when deciding on appropriate distribution methods and procedures. To deal effectively with distribution planning, it is necessary to be familiar with transportation methods, handling small shipments, and methods of storing and handling products during distribution.

The most commonly used methods of transporting goods are by railroad, truck, and airplane. A business may find that it is feasible or necessary to use more than one type of transportation, depending on the requirements for the shipment.

RAILROADS

Railway transportation is one of the most common forms of shipping in the United States. Over a third of the volume of products shipped in the United States is moved by rail car. The principal advantage of rail transportation is low cost for moving heavy and bulky items long distances. However, products move slowly on long train routes because of the need to drop off cars that have arrived at their destination or are being routed in another direction or to add cars to the train. Furthermore, only a limited number of communities are now served directly by rail freight services. Through the use of trucks, however, shipments can be delivered from almost any location to one where rail service is available. Also, attempts are being made in some parts of the country to reestablish rail services through new, short-distance railroads serving high-volume regional markets.

The cost of rail freight shipments is cheapest when a full carload can be shipped at one time. There are transportation companies that will build carloads of freight by combining the shipments of two or more companies, thereby providing cost savings to each company. The rates charged by railroads are typically based on the quantity and distance shipped, the amount of handling required, and the value of the products shipped.

TRUCKS

Trucks are the most frequently used transportation method for short-distance shipping. Trucks are essential to smaller communities and rural areas that are unserved by other methods. Industries such as agriculture, mining, and lumber are dependent on trucks to move products from the source of production to the location of processing.

Much long-distance shipping is also done by truck. For products that need to be moved rapidly, in smaller quantities than can be economically shipped by rail, or where rail is not accessible, trucks are the typical transportation choice. Some transportation companies load truck trailers and place them on railroad cars to be shipped close to the final destination. This service is called **piggyback service**. Shipments of manufactured products made by truck generally are picked up at the shipper's place of business and delivered directly to the receiver's place of business.

Jeff Greenberg, Photographer

Illus. 12-4

"Truck-trains" increase the amount trucks can carry, making them more valuable for long-distance transportation. Why have some states refused to allow these vehicles on their highways?

Truck shipment rates are usually based on the weight of the shipment and the distance to be transported. In most cases, the rates are higher than those charged by railroads. Trucks have dramatically increased the volume of freight transported in the past several years. This has occurred because of the improved highway system in the country, the size of trailers that are allowed on most highways, and the deregulation of the trucking industry. Additionally, many trucking companies are now using computer systems to track customer orders and reroute trucks for rapid pickup and delivery. This is important for businesses that are trying to keep inventories low while maintaining high service levels.

AIR SHIPMENTS

The shipment of products by air has grown rapidly. Hundreds of different products are shipped by air every day. Airplanes provide the most rapid form of transportation but their rates are much higher than other methods. Air shipments can move products quickly over long distances. Items can move across a country in a few hours and around the world in a day if necessary. The majority of air shipments are for items of relatively small bulk, high value, or quick perishability. Packages and mail are moved regularly on passenger airlines as well as through air parcel companies. Airlines are also used for shipping cut flowers, high-fashion clothing, seafood, film, and jewelry. Air shipments are very important for items needed in emergencies, such as medicine and blood, parts for machines needing quick repairs, or important documents and records.

Increasingly, large and bulky items are being moved by air through the use of special cargo planes. The planes have been designed for easy loading and unloading. Regional air freight terminals are being constructed so products can be moved rapidly into and out of airports without interfering with passenger travel. As rapid and efficient transportation is more important to businesses and consumers, air shipments are being used more often even though the cost is higher. People pay more for the transportation that meets their requirements. It is possible to pay more for the transportation but reduce the overall cost by following efficient procedures in storage, packaging, or handling.

OTHER TRANSPORTATION METHODS

Water transportation (ocean, lake, and river) is the slowest method of transporting goods. However, it is also the cheapest for bulky goods such as coal, iron ore, oil, lumber, grain, and cotton. Those are the principal items transported by water. Many products that are produced in large volume for international markets, such as automobiles and large pieces of equipment, are shipped across the oceans. If you have visited any large harbor on a coast you can see hundreds of types of products being loaded and unloaded from ships.

In the United States, as well as in many other countries, networks of thousands of miles of pipelines have been built. The principal items transported are petroleum and natural gas. In many countries, however, pipelines are important methods of moving water for irrigation and for human consumption.

One way of improving shipping services is through **containerization**. Products are packed in large shipping containers at the factory and are then shipped using a number of transportation methods before being unpacked. The containers can easily be loaded and unloaded from trucks to rail cars, ships, and cargo planes, and back to trucks. This reduces the amount of product handling and product damage.

When an order for goods involves only a small quantity of a product or when the product itself is very small, businesses must use a different type of shipment. The shipment of such small packages is usually called a **parcel shipment**. Various delivery services are available for sending these small packages by air, rail, bus, or truck. The speed of delivery ranges from one to a few days. The cost can vary a great deal depending on the carrier selected. In most cases, there is a limit to the size or weight of a parcel that will be accepted for shipment. Shippers must contact individual carriers to obtain shipping rates and requirements.

Some parcel services require that packages be delivered to their business. Also, the person or business ordering the merchandise may need to pick up the package upon arrival. Most parcel services now offer delivery to customers, and door-to-door service is typical for business-to-business parcel deliveries.

Several companies as well as the United States Postal Service provide express service for small parcels as well as important letters and documents. **Express service** guarantees the sender that the shipment will arrive before a designated time. Express services usually provide overnight delivery, but some offer same-day service.

PRODUCT HANDLING

Products that are lost during distribution, arrive late, or are damaged are of little value to customers. Product-handling procedures are an important part of the distribution process. Most products are handled several times from the time they are produced until they are delivered to the customer. Each time a product is handled adds to the cost of distribution, increases the amount of time needed for distribution, and increases the opportunity for damage to occur. Businesses evaluate their product-handling procedures to find ways to improve the process. Product-handling procedures used by businesses include improved packaging, the use of efficient procedures for packing and unpacking products, and specific equipment for handling and storing products.

Jeff Greenberg, Photographer

Ilus. 12-5

Warehouse stores use very different methods from those of other retailers to display products. How do those methods affect the amount of product handling required?

TRACKING PRODUCTS

An important part of product handling is keeping track of products. Businesses and customers want to know where products are located and when they will be delivered. The recordkeeping required is often a very time-consuming task. Bar coding is now used to track most products during distribution. **Bar codes** are product identification labels containing a unique set of vertical bars that can be read using computer scanning equipment. Each product or container has a bar code. The scanning equipment can read the codes at any time during distribution so the product can be tracked. This system is much faster and more accurate than the older systems where people read product codes and recorded them on paper.

Management Close-Up

A Real Marketing Channel

It gives the term "couch potato" a whole new meaning! People go on shopping sprees without leaving their homes. What is the fastest-growing form of retailing today? It's shopping by television.

Products have been available for sale on television for many years. You could order records and tapes, books, and even small appliances through mail-order companies that advertised on television. But in the 1970s, a new form of television retailing was introduced—the home shopping networks on cable television. By 1990, product sales from the television retailer had reached over $2 billion a year and were growing by 20 percent each year. This was during the same time that traditional retail stores were struggling to maintain their sales volume from year to year.

The two largest cable retailers have been QVC, reaching nearly 50 million consumers, and Home Shopping Network, reaching over 60 million people. The two networks merged in 1992 and now reach over two-thirds of all U.S. households. Through agreements with several satellite broadcasting companies, the networks are beginning to broadcast into Europe and South America. They will expand the satellite system until they are a true worldwide retailer.

Cable shopping offers advantages for both businesses and consumers. Distribution costs are much lower than when products are sold through stores. There is no longer a need for the traditional retail stores, equipment, personnel, and services. All inventory can stay in warehouses, orders are taken at one location by telemarketers and processed immediately, and all advertising and selling is done through the presentation of products in a television studio.

Consumers can tune in at any time during the day and can shop for a few minutes or several hours. Product ordering is as simple as a telephone call. Products usually arrive in a few days and usually can be returned for a full refund if the customer is not satisfied.

There has been a belief that home shopping would not appeal to most consumers. There was a stereotype of the home shopping customer as older, less educated, and easily influenced to buy lower-quality products or pay too much for their purchases. Market research has proved those assumptions to be wrong. Television shoppers are very much like the average shopper. They are somewhat younger, have almost equal education levels and incomes, and are more fashion- and value-conscious than the typical person buying in a retail store. Television shoppers are almost equally divided between men and women.

Questions:

1 In what other ways are products currently sold through television?

2 Do you believe that sales through shopping networks will continue to grow as rapidly as they have in the past?

3 What are reasons that many businesses and consumers prefer to use the traditional methods of retailing even though television retailing is convenient and less expensive?

Source: Business Week, July 26, 1993, pp. 54-60.

PRODUCT STORAGE

Storage is an important part of the marketing process. Usually, consumers do not buy products as soon as they are produced. Producers and channel members may want to accumulate a large quantity of products to make shipping more efficient. Some products are purchased more during one time of the year than another. Lawn mowers, air conditioners, snowmobiles, and skis are examples of such products. Most companies will produce those products throughout the year to make production more efficient. The products will be stored until they are to be distributed and sold.

Buildings used to store large quantities of products until they can be sold are known as **warehouses**. Warehouses are usually large buildings with racks, shelves, or bins for storing products. They may be controlled for temperature or humidity if products need special protection. Products must be carefully handled and stored to prevent damage. Accurate records must be kept so that products being stored can be located. Many companies are using computers to keep those records. When an order is received, the computer is used to determine the quantity of a product available and the location of that product in the warehouse.

Many changes have occurred in the way warehouses are operated. It is expensive to handle products several times and store them for a long time. There are many opportunities for products to be damaged while they are being stored. Many companies now use mechanical equipment and robots to handle the products in their warehouses. Computers control both the equipment and the robots as products are moved into storage and subsequently removed for shipment. The use of equipment in the warehouse has reduced the cost of storage as well as the amount of product damage.

Large wholesalers and retailers that handle a variety of products and sell them through a number of outlets have replaced the traditional warehouses with distribution centers. A **distribution center** is a large building designed to accumulate and redistribute products efficiently. A wholesaler or retailer usually buys products from a number of manufacturers. These products are shipped from each manufacturer to the distribution center in large quantities. They are then repackaged into smaller quantities, combined with products from other manufacturers, and shipped to a store where they can be sold to consumers. Distribution centers can save a great deal of money for a business. Transportation and storage costs are reduced and individual stores have the products they need quickly. Individual stores can order smaller quantities than if they had to order merchandise from each manufacturer, so products will not become outdated as easily.

ORDER PROCESSING

When customers want to purchase a product, they expect their orders to be handled accurately and efficiently. Planning must be done to ensure that effective procedures are in place and employees are well trained to complete customer orders.

Orders can be placed in person or by mail, telephone, and even computers or facsimile machines. When an order reaches the business, the paperwork must be processed so that the order is filled and the customer is billed for the product. If there are questions or problems with the order, they must be handled in a friendly and courteous fashion. Someone in the business must be responsible for tracking the order until it reaches the customer to make sure the customer receives what was expected.

Most companies have now automated some or all of the order processing system using computers. Many people are involved in order processing from manufacturing, to accounting, marketing, and customer service. If the order is entered into a computer system, it can be easily tracked by all parts of the business. Some companies now make computer records available to channel members and customers so they can also track orders at any time from their own computers.

CHAPTER REVIEW 12

BUILDING VOCABULARY POWER

Define the following terms and concepts.

1. economic discrepancies
2. channels of distribution (marketing channels)
3. channel members
4. direct marketing
5. indirect marketing
6. telemarketing
7. convenience stores
8. department stores
9. discount stores
10. specialty stores
11. supermarkets
12. factory outlets
13. merchant wholesaler
14. cash-and-carry wholesaler
15. rack jobber
16. specialty wholesaler
17. manufacturer's agent
18. administered channel
19. channel integration
20. distribution planning
21. piggyback service
22. containerization
23. parcel shipment
24. express service
25. bar codes
26. warehouses
27. distribution center

REVIEWING FACTS

1. Name four ways in which distribution can help satisfy customers' needs for a product.

2. Identify the two most common types of channel members between the producer and the consumer.
3. What is the difference between a direct and an indirect channel of distribution?
4. Why do producers of business products generally use direct channels more than producers of consumer products?
5. What advantages does a producer gain by selling products through a retailer?
6. What is the most typical channel for consumer goods?
7. Give an example of a possible marketing channel where two wholesalers and a retailer could be used by a producer.
8. Why might a producer choose to use more than one channel of distribution?
9. List several characteristics of a product that would indicate the need for a direct or a very short channel of distribution.
10. Explain how railroads and trucks combine their services in providing freight transportation.
11. What types of items are more likely to be shipped by air?
12. Suggest ways in which the use of containerization can reduce the cost of products for consumers.
13. What are the usual methods of shipping small parcels?
14. What are the ways that technology is used to improve product handling?
15. In what ways is the operation of a warehouse changing?

DISCUSSING IDEAS

1. Three producers make the same type and quality of cosmetics for sale. Producer A sells through wholesalers to retailers; Producer B sells to retailers; Producer C sells through door-to-door sales representatives. Why will the selling price be about the same even though the channels of distribution are different?
2. How can methods of distribution affect the form in which a consumer receives a product?
3. Provide examples showing that the ways in which consumers purchase a product influence the type of marketing channel used.
4. How can catalog sales be a part of an indirect channel?
5. Why might a manufacturer choose to sell products through a department store rather than a discount store?
6. What are some reasons that businesses are more concerned about transportation today than they were in the past?
7. Why would a company choose to use a truck to haul products from the East Coast to the West Coast when railroad shipping is available and is cheaper?

8. Make a list of products you purchased that were probably stored for a length of time before they were purchased. Then make a similar list of products that were not stored or were stored only a short time before they were purchased. Discuss the differences among the products.

9. In what ways could the procedures used in a warehouse help to reduce the prices of products to consumers?

10. Discuss the ways computer technology is changing order processing.

A NALYZING INFORMATION

1. The Better Bakers Business manufactures a line of cookies, cakes, and pies that it distributes directly to retail grocers within a 60-mile area with its own trucks. The company is considering doubling its baking facilities and marketing its products over a 200-mile area.

   a. If the distribution area is going to be much wider, will the Better Bakers have to use an indirect channel of distribution? List the advantages and disadvantages of an indirect system.

   b. What outlets, other than retail grocers, can be used for the company's products?

   c. Does the number of outlets help determine whether a direct or indirect channel is better?

2. The common types of trade channels used to distribute consumer goods are (a) producer directly to the consumer, (b) producer to the consumer through retailers, and (c) producer to the consumer through wholesalers and retailers.

   a. For each of the three types of trade channels listed, identify two products sold in your community that are distributed through that type of trade channel. You may need to interview business people or complete some research in the library to identify the products.

   b. Study the products you have identified for each of the trade channels. Discuss the advantages of each of the trade channels for distributing the products identified.

3. An appliance store can purchase a certain brand of electric heater for $35.00 from a firm in City A or for $35.50 from another firm in City B. The transportation cost from City A is $3.88 per heater. From City B, the transportation cost is $2.77 per heater. How much money will be saved if 50 heaters are purchased from the firm in City B?

4. A company located in Utah manufactures children's toys and games. Its potential customers are located throughout the world. Identify ways in which it can use each of the following distribution procedures to improve its customer service or profitability: (a) telemarketing, (b) containerization, (c) express parcel service.

REVIEW

5. A product weighs 30 pounds and needs to be delivered to a place 500 miles from your community. Identify three ways the product could be shipped. Then, compare the cost and time it would take for delivery using each method.

S OLVING BUSINESS PROBLEMS

CASE 12-1

John Allen is an artist who specializes in sketches of flowers, fruit, and small plants. People hang the sketches in their homes or apartments. By limiting his work to a dozen of the most popular sketches, he is able to produce about two original sketches each day, or about ten a week.

Until now, he has sold the sketches to his sister, Carla Allen, who sells them in her women's clothing shop. Because he now has a fairly large inventory of sketches on hand, John feels that selling to his sister is not the best method of distribution. He has been thinking about (a) opening his own small shop where he could continue to sketch and also wait on customers, or (b) selling the sketches in quantity to a friend who owns a retail art shop.

Required:
1. Describe the current channel of distribution.
2. Select the type of store shown in Fig. 12-3 that John's friend operates.
3. Are sales of sketches likely to increase over current sales if John distributes through his friend's shop? Explain.
4. If John opens his own shop and sells directly to customers, will he be performing more or fewer marketing activities than he does by selling to Carla Allen or his friend? Explain.
5. Would you recommend that John Allen sell his sketches to his friend or open his own shop? Explain your answer.

CASE 12-2

The Elegant Affair is a specialty retail shop. It sells assorted gift boxes of various meats, cheeses, nuts, jams, and jellies. The business is located in a Midwest city and is facing declining sales due to the economic difficulties facing the city. One major manufacturing plant has closed, and layoffs from other businesses have caused many people to move from the area seeking new jobs.

The president of the company has been studying telemarketing as a way to increase sales without having to move the store or build a new store in an area with a more attractive economic climate. She believes that by using salespeople and a computerized telemarketing system that she can sell the gift boxes to people throughout the United States. She also believes that the cost of those sales will actually be lower than selling the products to people who come into the store.

Required:

1. What types of activities will be required for the Elegant Affair to start a telemarketing system?
2. How can prospective customers be identified in order for the telemarketing salespeople to call them?
3. Identify two distribution methods that might be used by the Elegant Affair for products sold through telemarketing. What are the advantages and disadvantages of each?
4. Develop a brief script for the telemarketing salespeople to use to introduce the company and its products to prospective customers.

REVIEW 12

PURCHASING AND PRICING CHAPTER 13

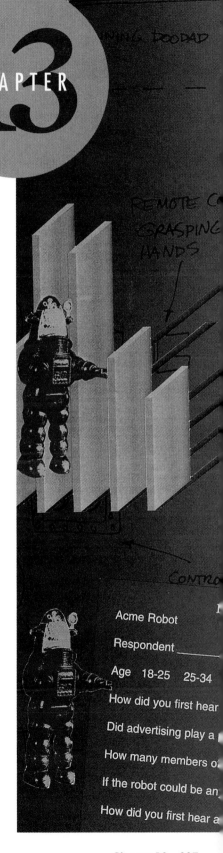

After studying this chapter you will be able to:

13-1 List four common purchasing decisions a business must make.

13-2 Identify the steps involved in ordering and receiving merchandise.

13-3 Explain the major terms and discounts related to purchasing.

13-4 Describe five methods of establishing product prices.

13-5 Discuss three important purchasing and operating problems that result in higher prices.

Roberta and Jason walked out of Windzors, a sporting goods store that had just opened in the new Regency Park shopping plaza.

"I can't believe that store will be successful," said Roberta. "I've never seen sports equipment priced that high!"

"The products really were expensive," agreed Jason. "It certainly isn't a normal sporting goods store. The salesperson said they would help design your own set of personalized golf clubs and that you would get five hours of work with the golf pro at the Regency Sports Centre if you purchased a set of clubs."

"Did you see the area where they sold downhill skis?" asked Roberta. "They had a moving slide area like an escalator where you could actually ski. They also had a machine that formed molds around your feet for custom fitting ski boots. They sponsor a ski club and organize vacations to the mountains in the United States and even to other countries. I've never seen that in a sporting goods store."

"Why would people want to pay that much?" Jason wondered. "Sure, they have the top brand names and unique services. But you can get the same type of products for forty to fifty percent less at other stores."

"I don't know," agreed Roberta. "The owners had better hope there are a large number of people who are willing to spend money for recreation."

Purchasing is the activity that brings buyers and sellers together and determines if they will be satisfied with the exchange. Both consumers and businesses are regularly involved in purchase decisions. To be successful, businesses must offer the type and quality of products and services that meet the needs of their customers. The products must be priced so they are considered an appropriate value by the buyer. The products and services offered by the Windzors sporting goods store described above will need to be viewed as valuable by a group of customers if the store is to be successful.

Whether buying goods for resale, raw materials for use in manufacturing, equipment to operate a business, or products and services for individual use, the buyer must make careful purchasing decisions. Before goods can be sold, a price and method of payment must be agreed upon by both the buyer and seller. The procedures and problems of purchasing and pricing are discussed in this chapter.

PURCHASING

When planning a purchase, buyers actually make several specific decisions. They must decide what to purchase, when to purchase, how much to purchase, and from whom to purchase.

WHAT TO PURCHASE

To be successful, a business must keep the right kind of products in stock. Manufacturers buy products to be used in the production of products to be sold to their customers. Wholesale or retail businesses purchase products for resale or for use in the operation of their businesses. In all cases, the most important consideration in making purchases is their customers' needs. If customers are not satisfied, the business will not be successful. Several specific factors must be considered in making decisions about the types of products to be purchased.

Quality

Some buyers hurt their businesses by thinking more about quantity than about quality in order to sell more products than their competitors. They do not consider the importance of the quality of their products. They believe that price is so important to customers that the customers will accept lower quality in order to save money.

The confidence of customers is the principal factor in the success of any business. While customers often have different expectations of quality, they will not put up with inferior quality. Customers may be fooled for a short time, but when they find that a product is not as good as expected, they look for another product to buy. There are normally several levels of quality available to customers for most products. Customers match quality with the prices that they are willing to pay.

Brand Names

The person who is just beginning a business is confronted with the problem of deciding what brand or brands of products to handle. Well-known **manufacturer brands** (brand names established by manufacturers of products for sale to a large market through a variety of businesses) are probably the best for a new business. Customers are more aware of the manufacturer brands and are willing to buy those brands from a new business rather than brands with which they are not familiar. After the business is well established and has earned a good reputation, customers might be willing to try **private brands** (brand names established by the individual business—usually a wholesaler or retailer—for sale to its customers), which usually yield a larger profit per item for the business.

A business must also decide how many different brands of similar products to carry in stock. For instance, a supermarket must decide on the number of brands of cereal to carry. A study of the customers and the competition could help in making this decision. If the business decides to carry three or four brands instead of two, a larger amount of capital will have to be used for inventory. For some products, only one brand will need to be carried. For other products, customers will expect a choice of two, three, or even more brands.

Jeff Greenberg, Photographer

Illus. 13-1

Some businesses have been successful with generic products where no brand name is used. Are you familiar with any generic products?

Product Assortment

A business must determine the assortment of products to be handled. Should a new men's clothing store handle only suits, or should shoes, shirts, underwear, socks, and neckties also be stocked? There are two factors that influence that decision. The type of competition is very important. If there are a number of nearby clothing stores, the owner of the new store will want to determine what items to handle in order to be competitive. It will be difficult for a new store to attract customers if it carries the same products or brands of already successful businesses. If none of the nearby stores sell leisure or sports wear, the new business may want to consider emphasizing those products.

The second factor to consider in reaching a product assortment decision is the financial ability of the business. It costs a great deal to keep a wide selection of products available. A limited variety of products can be stocked while still allowing customers a good selection of the few types of products carried. Product variety is a very difficult decision because the business needs to handle items that customers want and yet that can fit the financial capability of the business.

Because many items come in different sizes, the business person has to decide which sizes of various items should be stocked. For example, should a supermarket carry soft drinks in twelve-ounce, sixteen-ounce, or one- and two-liter containers? The quantity that is expected to be sold in each container size must also be determined so that an adequate supply is available without being overstocked. Similarly, the manager of a shoe store must determine the sizes and quantities of each shoe style and color that should be purchased and the purchasing agent for a manufacturer must determine the sizes and quantities of various parts needed in the manufacturing of the company's products.

GUIDES IN DETERMINING WHAT TO PURCHASE

Assistance is available for business people to help them determine what to purchase. Catalogs and salespeople are valuable tools. Trade associations and their publications can also help. Businesses should listen carefully to their customers in determining what to purchase. Two information sources readily available to every established business are company records of past purchases and sales and comparison studies.

Company Records

An important guide to buying is found in the records of past purchases and sales. If accurate and complete records are maintained, they will even show factors that affected sales in past years. Records can be used to determine differences in sales to various customers and how factors such as the time of year or the level of competition affected purchases and sales. Those records must be interpreted in connection with new circumstances, but they can be important guides for planning future purchases.

Comparison Studies

Understanding competitors' activities and consumers' reactions also helps a business make purchasing decisions. A study of the products and services offered by competing businesses can be helpful. Some retailers have research departments that study the quality of various brands of competing products. Many also ask consumers to evaluate products and brands to provide information on how each satisfies their needs. Market research firms, some consumer groups and organizations, and even government agencies provide product and brand comparison information.

WHEN TO PURCHASE

The determination of when to purchase is influenced by the type of products, the type and location of the supplier, and other factors such as style and price trends. Products must be available when they are needed for manufacturing or a business will not be able to maintain the production schedule. For product to be sold, an adequate supply must be available when customers want to buy or sales will be lost. Orders often have to be placed well in advance so that products will be available when they are needed. For example, orders for shoes that will be sold in the summer are usually placed in January or earlier. Toys for sale in November and December may have been ordered six to nine months in advance. A manufacturer must schedule purchases to be sure raw materials are available when they are needed to meet production schedules.

If a fashion item is selling slowly, the buyer may delay purchasing to determine whether it will remain in style. On the other hand, an item that is predicted to be very popular may be ordered well in advance to insure it is available when demand is high. Should buyers believe that prices for certain goods are likely to be much higher in the near future, they may wish to place the order for the goods before the price rises. In the same way, if prices seem to be falling, as has happened frequently with high-technology products such as computers, the business may want to delay purchasing as long as possible to take advantage of lower prices.

HOW TO PURCHASE

Through trade associations, magazines, and contacts with sales people and other industry personnel, a buyer should be able to obtain information about important sources of supply. The commonly used methods of buying are (1) ordering from sales representatives, (2) making buying trips, (3) ordering through buying offices, and (4) ordering by catalog or computer.

Sales Representatives

Many manufacturers and wholesalers and some retailers use sales representatives to contact prospective customers. The representatives can provide product information, demonstrate how products are used, and help the customer select appropriate merchandise. A salesperson usually is employed by one company to sell its product. However, some sales organizations represent several manufacturers and sell a variety of non-competing products. Most large manufacturers and retailers purchase from sales representatives who visit their businesses.

Buying Trips

The buyers for many small- to medium-sized wholesale and retail businesses make major purchases for each sales season by making buying trips to a merchandise market. A **merchandise market** is a city where several major manufacturers are located or where those manufacturers have brought their new merchandise for display and sale. By traveling to the markets, buyers have a chance to visit several suppliers at one time and to compare their merchandise before ordering. Usually, the buyers order the merchandise needed for an entire season during one buying trip. There are many national and regional markets located throughout the United States. Examples include fashions in New York, appliances and other consumer products in Chicago, and furniture in North Carolina.

Buying Offices

For some products, buyers can visit a buying office. A **buying office** represents the products of many manufacturers and assists buyers in making purchases. A buying office is useful for small manufacturers or for manufacturers located in a different geographic area. Many export and import sales are made through a type of buying office called international trade centers. Those centers are often located in the largest city of a state or the state capital. They may be privately owned but are often organized and staffed by the state government. The purpose of the trade center is to encourage exports by representing the products of the state's manufacturers to foreign buyers.

Ordering by Catalog or Computer

Repeat orders of regularly purchased goods are most often made through catalogs. Catalogs are best for supplies or products that are low priced and that are purchased by a large number of companies on a regular basis. Orders are placed by mail or telephone. In some cases, they are placed through the use of a computer linked by telephone to a computer at the office of the manufacturer or wholesaler.

Some printed catalogs have actually been replaced by a computer diskette or CD-ROM sent to a customer or by an on-line computer database that can be accessed by the customer through a computer and modem. Using the database, a buyer can select the products and quantities needed, confirm the current prices, and place the order through the computer. The databases have several advantages over catalogs. The cost of maintaining and updating the database is usually less expensive than the costs of printing, distributing, and reprinting catalogs. The speed of order processing is increased. The computer can be used for direct communications if the buyer or seller has questions or problems.

CHOICE OF SUPPLIERS

Most business firms have several different suppliers from whom they can make purchases. Therefore, the decision of which supplier or suppliers to choose can pose a problem. One of the most important considerations is the reputation of the supplier in such areas as dealing with customers, filling orders rapidly and exactly as requested, and providing necessary services. Other considerations are the price and credit terms that a supplier will provide.

A business must decide whether to make purchases from a few suppliers or to spread the orders among many suppliers. Most business firms find it practical to concentrate their buying among a few suppliers. This plan usually develops better relationships between the suppliers and the purchaser. Better prices and better credit terms, as well as better service, are also likely to result.

Sources of supply do not remain the same. Some firms go out of business. New businesses start up. Some businesses develop new products or improve old ones. The successful business will be constantly looking for better sources from which to buy. A business that relies on only one supplier may run into problems if the supplier changes products, increases prices, or goes out of business.

HOW MUCH TO PURCHASE

After deciding what to buy, when to buy, how to buy, and from whom to buy, someone in the business must determine how much to buy. A business should have sufficient products available to meet customer demand. If customers cannot be supplied with the merchandise they want when they want it, sales will be lost. If the business is engaged in manufacturing and the necessary raw materials and parts are not available when needed, the manufacturing process is delayed.

If a business has a much larger inventory of goods than is usually needed, large amounts of money will be tied up in inventory. The large inventory also requires extra storage space. If only small quantities are kept in stock, the danger of loss from spoilage, changes in design, or changes in demand will be small. When it comes to buying small quantities, however, the transportation costs should be considered. Transportation costs for a small amount of a product may be as much as or, in some cases, even more than the cost of shipping a larger quantity. Transportation companies may give discounts for full trucks or railroad cars and charge higher prices when smaller quantities are shipped.

The length of time required to replenish the stock is another important consideration. If the suppliers are located nearby or can supply products rapidly, there is less need for the business to purchase large quantities. Demand can affect the quantity purchased. If the demand is seasonal—garden tools, antifreeze, snowblowers, or summer clothes—the merchandise should be purchased in quantities that can be completely sold by the end of the season.

The amount and kind of storage space that is available limit the quantity that can be purchased. If a store that has sold small appliances decides to sell refrigerators, a large storage area will be required. Special storage facilities are needed for frozen foods, dairy products, chemicals, and plants.

Businesses today operate on much lower inventory levels than in the past. How can businesses reduce inventories while still maintaining a high level of sales?

Jeff Greenberg, Photographer

A study of the records of previous purchases and sales of an item can help determine the correct quantity to reorder. The economic outlook also affects the quantity of merchandise that should be ordered. A favorable economic outlook encourages more purchases, while a poor outlook discourages customers from purchasing. If a business owner decides to offer a new product for sale, it may be wise to buy only a small quantity on the first purchase. If the product proves to be a good seller, larger quantities can be purchased later.

PURCHASING PROCEDURES

In a small business, the purchasing is usually done by the owner or one of the partners. In larger businesses, a purchasing department is usually used with several people participating in the purchasing function. In each case, it is necessary that the procedures involved in purchasing be organized carefully.

A business that has a well-organized purchasing procedure obtains and keeps detailed information on inventory, sales or usage, quality, and prices. For each product that is purchased, there should be information on sources, product descriptions, quantities purchased in the past, time required for delivery, prices, price trends, and so forth.

THE PURCHASING DEPARTMENT

When a business has a department that handles all purchases, people with special purchasing skills will be hired or will be trained to complete those specialized duties. The person in charge of the purchasing department is known as the **purchasing agent**. The procedures involved in the purchasing and receiving of goods also involve departments other than the purchasing department. The relationships among the departments that result from the purchase and receipt of goods in one large company are shown in Fig. 13-1. Fig. 13-2 on page 316 describes each of the steps in the purchasing process.

REQUESTING DEPARTMENT

- completes purchase requisition
- uses purchases

PURCHASING DEPARTMENT

- receives purchase requisition
- prepares purchase order
- receives receiving report
- approves payment

RECEIVING DEPARTMENT

- receives purchase order
- receives and checks shipment
- prepares receiving report
- unpacks and transfers products

ACCOUNTING DEPARTMENT

- receives purchase order
- receives invoice
- makes payment

Fig. 13-1

Several departments within a firm may be involved in the purchasing process.

ORDERING AND RECEIVING PRODUCTS

Two important parts of the purchasing process are ordering products and receiving the order from the vendor. Typical procedures used by businesses to order and receive merchandise are described next.

Placing the Order

Managers or people responsible for the inventory of specific departments or products must watch the stock to determine when additional orders should be placed. For products that are purchased over and over, an amount of inventory should be set that identifies when reordering is necessary. For businesses that keep current inventory records on a computer, the inventory program used should identify when the minimum inventory point is reached.

When it is determined that an order is needed, the process for placing an order should begin. In small businesses, the owner or a designated employee will likely be responsible for the entire ordering process. It is impossible for the owner or even the purchasing department of a large business to know when all products should be ordered. For that reason, purchase requisitions are needed. **Purchase requisitions** are forms requesting the purchasing department to buy the items listed. A stock clerk or other employee usually fills out the purchase requisition, which may need to be signed by the department head. The original is sent to the purchasing department, and one copy is kept by the department requesting the purchase.

The purchasing department uses the information from the purchase requisition to complete a purchase order. A **purchase order** is a form that lists the

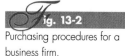

Who Performs the Task and Steps Taken to Accomplish the Task

INDIVIDUAL DEPARTMENTS

1. Prepare purchase requisition.
2. Send purchase requisition to purchasing department.

PURCHASING DEPARTMENT

3. Collect purchase requisition and prepare purchase order.
4. Send copies of the purchase order to the following:
   - requisitioning department
   - accounting department

SUPPLIER

5. Upon receipt of purchase order, supplier will do the following:
   - prepare invoice and send to accounting department of the purchaser
   - ship products with packing list to receiving department

RECEIVING DEPARTMENT

6. Receive goods—count items and check quality using packing list; prepare items for distribution to ordering department.
7. Prepare receiving report and send to purchasing department.

PURCHASING DEPARTMENT

8. Compare receiving report with purchase order as to quantities and prices.
9. Send completed purchase order and receiving report to accounting department with approval for payment of invoice.

ACCOUNTING DEPARTMENT

10. Receive approval for payment together with purchase order and receiving report from purchasing department.
11. Compare purchase order with the supplier's invoice.
12. Send payment to supplier.

merchandise being ordered from a supplier. Several copies of a purchase order are made by the purchasing department. The original is sent to the **vendor**, the company from which goods are being ordered. One copy is kept in the purchasing department files, and another copy is sent to the department that prepared the purchase requisition to indicate that the products have been ordered. A copy may be sent to the receiving department so it will have a record of when the products are received, and another copy is sent to the accounting department.

Handling Incoming Goods

When the purchase order is received by the vendor, the order will be filled. It will be packed and shipped to the ordering company along with a **packing list** that lists the packages or containers being shipped and their contents. When the shipment arrives, several operations must be carried out in preparation for the resale or use of the products.

All incoming shipments should be received at a specific place in the business and a complete record of the products received should be made there. Before signing the receipt of the transportation company, the receiving clerk should examine each carton or container to see if the goods are damaged and if they match the description on the packing list. If the shipment appears to be damaged or incomplete, a statement of the condition in which it is received should be written on the receipt provided by the transportation company. This will aid in establishing a claim for damaged or lost merchandise.

The next step in the receiving process is unpacking and checking the merchandise. The products should be counted and checked against a copy of the purchase order. In some firms, the checker does not receive a copy of the purchase order for comparison with the contents of the shipment. Instead, the checker lists the contents on a form. One copy of the form goes to the purchasing department and one to the department that placed the order. This list is then checked against the **invoice**, which is a form prepared by the vendor listing the goods shipped, the price, and the terms of sale. The invoice is sent to the purchasing company to request payment. After the purchasing department determines that the merchandise received meets the purchasing requirements, the accounting department is notified to make payment. The accounting department returns a copy of the invoice with payment to the supplier.

After merchandise is received and checked and the paperwork is completed, the products are readied for use or sale. Some items are moved immediately from the receiving area to the sales floor or department where they will be used. Others are held in a storage area until needed. Products for sale may need to be organized, repackaged, or prepared before they are displayed for the customer. Prices must be determined and price tags prepared. For equipment or other items used in the business, the descriptions of the products and inventory numbers will be entered into inventory records. All of this work may be completed in the receiving department or may be the responsibility of employees in the department that ordered the products.

TERMS OF SALE

The prices paid for products are affected by the terms of sale offered by the supplier. The terms of sale identify delivery conditions, when invoices must be paid, and whether credit or discounts are available to the purchaser. Since the terms of a purchase offered by sellers vary a great deal, a business should be familiar with those most commonly used. Choosing the best payment terms can have an important effect in reducing the cost of products.

DELIVERY TERMS

When purchases are made, a location is indicated by the seller that determines responsibilities for shipping costs and transfer of title for the products shipped. Ordinarily, products are bought **FOB (free on board) shipping point**. This means that the seller pays only the costs of delivering the products to the transportation company, such as a railroad, in the city in which the seller is located. **FOB destination** means that the seller will pay the transportation charges to the location of the purchaser.

Illus. 13-3

Transportation can have a major impact on the cost of a product. How can FOB be used by a seller that is located a great distance from a customer to compete with a local vendor?

Jeff Greenberg, Photographer

To see the effect of the FOB location, consider the following case. A manufacturer located in Buffalo, New York, orders a machine from a Chicago business. The price is $3,000 FOB Chicago (the shipping point). The transportation charges from Chicago to Buffalo are $450. The purchaser must pay $3,000 to the vendor as well as the transportation bill of $450. If the company had been able to purchase the machine for $3,000 FOB Buffalo, it would not have to pay the transportation cost.

There is another important point in connection with these two situations that the buyer should keep in mind. In the first situation, when the purchase is FOB shipping point, the title to the machine passes to the buyer as soon as the seller delivers the goods to the transportation company in Chicago. If the machine is damaged enroute to Buffalo, the loss would be the responsibility of the buyer unless the damage was the fault of the shipping company. In the second situation, however, when the machine was sold FOB destination, the title and the risk of damage remain with the seller until the time the machine reaches Buffalo.

PAYMENT TERMS

Companies that extend credit to customers list their credit terms on the invoice. A common way for the credit terms to be stated is **net 30 days**, which means that payment is to be made within 30 days from the date on the invoice. The date on the invoice is usually the date of shipment of the goods. Some businesses offer longer terms, such as net 60 days. The longer the terms, the better for the buyer, who will then have a chance to sell some or all of the goods by the time payment is due or can earn interest on the money that otherwise would have been paid to the vendor.

Another form of credit dating is EOM (end of month). **EOM** means that the date for payment is computed from the end of the month in which the merchandise is shipped. If an order is shipped on May 14 with terms of EOM 30 days, payment need not be made until June 30.

DISCOUNTS

Business firms may be offered discounts on products that they purchase. **Discounts** are reductions from the price of the product to encourage customers to buy. Common types of discounts are trade discounts, quantity discounts, seasonal discounts, and cash discounts. Discounts are usually subtracted from the **list price** (price quoted in price lists and catalogs of the vendor).

Trade Discount

A **trade discount (functional discount)** is a special deduction from the list price that is given to certain types of buyers, such as wholesalers or retailers, because the buyers perform certain functions for the seller. For example, a manufacturer may give retailers a 30 percent discount but may give wholesalers a 45 percent discount from the list price (or 15 percent more than retailers). In this case, it is expected that the wholesalers will be performing additional marketing activities for the seller than would be expected from retailers. Sometimes, a series of trade discounts may be offered. For instance, in a manufacturer's catalog, a particular article may be quoted as $40, less 25 percent, less 10 percent. The net cost would be figured as follows: $40 less $10 (25 percent of $40), or $30; less $3 (10 percent of $30), or $27. The retailer would be expected to pay $30 and the wholesaler $27 dollars.

The use of a trade discount serves as a simple method of adjusting prices. For example, when prices are rising, the manufacturer can drop one or more discounts from a series or replace a larger discount with a smaller one, without publishing an entirely new price schedule or catalog. Likewise, when prices are falling, manufacturers can adjust prices by increasing the rate of discount.

Quantity Discount

A **quantity discount** is used by sellers to encourage customers to buy in large quantities. One kind of quantity discount applies to individual shipments. For example, a retail paint store that orders 200 gallons of paint from a wholesaler is charged a certain price per gallon. However, if the store orders 1,000 gallons at one time, the price per gallon is lower. The manufacturer can afford to sell the larger quantity for a lower price because that sale reduces the cost of inventory, the amount of storage space needed, the insurance costs, and the administrative costs of product handling.

Another kind of quantity discount applies to the total purchases by a business over a period of time. If individual purchases are small but the number of orders result in a large quantity purchased during the year, the supplier may want to reward the purchaser with a quantity discount. This encourages the purchasing company to continue to buy from the same vendor time after time. Quantity discounts may be based on the number of units purchased or on the dollar value of the order.

Seasonal Discount

A **seasonal discount** is given to the buyer for ordering or taking delivery of goods in advance of the normal buying period. It encourages the buyer to purchase earlier than is really necessary or at a time when orders are normally low. An example is a discount offered on snowmobiles if they are purchased in the summer. The seasonal discount is a way the manufacturer attempts to balance production and inventory levels throughout the year for products that are normally purchased at one or a few specific times during the year.

Illus. 13-4

Seasonal discounts apply to services as well as products. What other types of service businesses often offer a seasonal discount?

Wolinsky/Stock, Boston

Cash Discount

To encourage early payments, many businesses offer a cash discount. A **cash discount** is given if payment is received by a certain date. A cash discount can be a specific dollar amount, but is usually stated as a percentage of the purchase price (for example, 2 percent). It may be offered with various dating and credit terms. For example, the terms of a purchase may be net 30 days with a 1 percent discount for payment within 10 days. If the invoice is dated May 1, the buyer will be permitted to deduct 1 percent off the total price of the purchase if payment for the merchandise is made on or before May 11; otherwise, the full amount must be paid by May 31. It is customary in business to express such terms as 1/10, n/30.

A 1 percent discount may seem so small as to be unimportant. However, when businesses order hundreds of thousands and even millions of dollars of products and services during the year, the total may be very important. Most businesses analyze cash discounts carefully because they may offer important cost savings. In some cases, it benefits a business to borrow money to take advantage of a cash discount. The savings may be at a rate higher than the cost of the interest on the borrowed money.

PRICING TERMS AND PROCEDURES

The prices charged for products and services are very important. The price must be viewed as a value by the customer, must be competitive with prices of competitors' products, and must be high enough that the business will make a profit on the sale. Establishing an effective price for a product is one of the most challenging business decisions. Knowing the general factors that affect prices is helpful, but this knowledge alone is not enough to enable a business person to set fair and profitable prices. The person must also be familiar with many specific pricing terms and procedures.

TERMS USED IN PRICING

There are many terms and concepts that need to be understood in order to determine the price to charge for a product. Several of the most important terms are discussed in this section. Figure 13-3 illustrates the makeup of the selling price of an item.

Selling Price

The **selling price** is the actual price paid for a company's products by the customer. The selling price is determined by subtracting discounts from the list price. Businesses often set prices for products much higher than the actual price at which they end up being sold. If the business fails to consider that the selling price may be lower than originally planned, it is likely that there will be no profit on that sale or the business may even lose money.

Cost of Goods Sold

The basic factor in determining the minimum price at which a product can be sold is the cost of goods sold. The **cost of goods sold** is the actual cost of the product to the selling company. For manufactured products, the cost of goods sold is the total cost of the materials and activities used in producing the product. For a product purchased for resale, it is the price of the product when delivered from the vendor, including the transportation costs. For example, if the invoice price of an item is $55 and the transportation charge is $5, the cost of goods sold is $60.

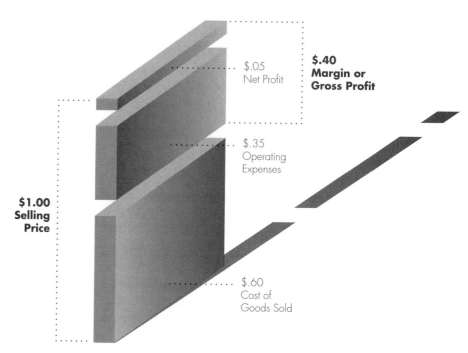

Fig. 13-3
Component parts of the selling price of the customer's sales dollar.

$.05
Net Profit

**$.40
Margin or
Gross Profit**

$.35
Operating
Expenses

**$1.00
Selling
Price**

$.60
Cost of
Goods Sold

Operating Expenses

Operating expenses are the costs of operating a business. They do not include costs involved in the actual production of products, which would be a part of the cost of goods sold. Most regular costs of running a business fall into this category. Some of the more common operating expenses are listed in Fig. 13-4.

Margin

Margin is the term used to indicate the difference between the selling price and the cost of goods sold. Sometimes it is called the *gross profit*. In Fig. 13-3, the margin is 40 cents. Margin is the term frequently used when referring to the percentage of sales a business has available to cover operating expenses and allow for a profit. For example, a business may operate on a 25 percent margin. If operating expenses are more than 25 percent of sales, the company will lose money.

Net Profit

Net profit is the difference between the selling price and all costs and expenses of the business. Net profit can be expressed in the following formula:

Net profit = selling price – cost of goods sold – operating expenses

Fig. 13-4
Some common operating expenses.

Rent	Taxes
Interest paid on borrowed money	Repairs and maintenance
Salaries, wages, and benefits	Supplies
Telephone service	Inventory losses due to theft, spoilage, or breakage
Depreciation expense	Customer service expenses
Furniture, fixtures, and equipment	Advertising
Uncollected accounts and collection expense	Donations
Delivery costs	Utilities
Insurance	Cost of business services

Markup

Markup is the amount added to the cost of a product to determine its selling price. It is similar to margin. When both are spoken of in dollars and cents, they are identical. For example, in Fig. 13-3, the markup is also 40 cents. The markup may be expressed as a percentage of the cost or as a percentage of the selling price. Thus, the markup in Fig. 13-3 is 66 2/3 percent (40 cents ÷ 60 cents) if expressed as a percentage of the cost. If the markup is expressed as a percentage of the selling price, it is 40 percent (40 cents ÷ 100 cents). It is, therefore, very important that business people are certain of the exact meaning intended when these terms are used.

Markup is the term often used when referring to a given product rather than to the entire business. While the business may operate on a 25 percent margin, the markup on the business' products may range from 5 percent to 50 percent. Some consumers confuse the percentage of markup with profit. They believe that if a business has a markup of 50 percent, it is making a profit of 50 percent of the selling price of its products. People who understand pricing realize that markup must cover the operating expenses of the business. If the business with a 50 percent average markup on its products has operating expenses of 45 percent of sales, it will have a profit of 5 percent.

Markdown

Markdown is any amount by which the original selling price is reduced before an item is sold. Markdowns are used when inventory is not being sold at a satisfactory rate. Markdowns are actual reductions in the selling or list price and do not include discounts. More will be explained about markdowns on page 329.

ANALYZING PRICES

In order for a business to determine effective prices and control expenses, a system must be developed to make it easy to compare figures that are related to sales. A common base for all computations is necessary. If salaries are figured as a percentage of cost of goods sold and the net profit is figured as a percentage of sales, an accurate comparison cannot be made. Since selling price includes everything (cost of goods, operating expenses, and net profit), it is generally used as the base, or 100 percent. Then the cost of the goods, the various operating expenses, the net profit, the margin, and practically all financial items can be stated as percentages of the sales of the business. When they are calculated on a common base, they can be compared with each other, with figures from previous operating periods, and even with competitors' figures or industry averages if available. The percentages are particularly valuable when budgeting and planning prices for the future.

The cost of selling different kinds of merchandise varies. Competition and other factors, which are discussed later in this chapter, affect the prices that can be charged. These factors make it difficult to have the same margin on all items. It is necessary, therefore, that the business keep records of sales and operating expenses by departments or by types of products. Only when such information is available is it possible to price each kind of product so that it will be sold profitably.

PRICING DECISIONS

The products and services of a business must be priced for resale to the business' customers. Since a business is operated for profit, the owner must set prices very carefully so that customers will be attracted to the business and will buy its products. In this section, we will discuss pricing methods and policies that businesses use to determine the prices of products and services.

A company may establish prices of products so high that very few of them are sold. As a result of that decision, the firm may make very little profit or may actually lose money. On the other hand, some businesses establish very low prices, believing that practice will result in very large sales. The result may be very high operating expenses to handle the high volume, so little or no profit is made. It is not possible to suggest that a high or low price is best for a product. Consider the following two examples:

Example A: An article that costs a business $50 is offered for sale at $100. The company sells four of these in a month, making a gross profit (revenue minus cost of goods sold) of $200.

Example B: Another business, selling the same item, attempts to sell a greater quantity at a lower price. This company offers the item for $80. During a month, six of these are sold at a gross profit of $180.

If we assume that all other factors are equal, the company in Example A makes a greater gross profit than the one in Example B, although each may fail to make a net profit (revenue minus cost of goods sold and operating expenses). In many cases, more expense will be involved in selling six items than in selling four items. The operating expenses, therefore, will be greater when the larger volume of business is handled.

Businesses must be careful about setting extremely high or extremely low prices. At one extreme, prices are set so high that a sufficient quantity will not be sold to yield a net profit; at the other extreme, prices are set so low that a sufficient gross profit will not be made. Between these two extremes there is a reasonable price that satisfies customers and allows a reasonable profit. But there are many factors that influence the choice of that price. Businesses can make better pricing decisions if they understand their customers, competitors, and the costs of operating the business.

PRICING TO MEET COMPETITION

The amount of competition among companies handling similar goods or services is an important factor in establishing prices. If one company has much higher prices than competitors, some of the company's customers are likely to buy from the competitors. Even business firms in separate locations may be influenced by competition. If prices are too high in one area, many people will travel to nearby communities to purchase goods or services. For example, if a service station in one neighborhood is selling a certain brand of gasoline for $1.10 a gallon and a station two miles away is selling the same brand for $1.00, a customer may travel to buy where the price is lower.

Illus. 13-5

Some businesses engage in intensive price competition. Is it possible for consumers to be harmed when businesses are forced to reduce prices because of competition?

Jeff Greenberg, Photographer

A business may need to offer some of its merchandise at a price lower than a fair profit because a competitor has established an even lower price. However, it is not always necessary to have a lower selling price than competitors. If a company has a loyal group of customers and offers a product with some distinct advantages, or provides services that customers want and other companies do not offer, the company may be able to charge a higher price without losing customers. Remember that the cost of providing higher-quality products or more services may be expensive, so profits may not be higher just because prices are higher.

When competition is strong, a company will usually set prices at a level to cover only the actual costs of doing business. Net profits are made, therefore, only by the most efficient business firms. Even if there is little or no competition, a company that sets its prices too high finds that people will try to do without its products or services or find substitutes, rather than pay prices that seem to give that company an unduly large profit. For example, a car wash that asks too high a price for its services will find that many of its customers will wash their cars less often or will wash their cars at home.

When introducing a new product, the manufacturer should become acquainted with competitive products on the market and check their prices. Gaps in the prices of competing products may be discovered that can be filled by pricing the new product accordingly. For example, if a competing manufacturer is selling shoes in the $50 to $60 range, the new product may be designed to sell in the $30 to $45 price range or the $75 to $85 range, thus hitting a price bracket not being filled. Again, it is important to determine customer preferences for prices. It does little good to price products at a level that customers do not want to pay or do not believe is a value.

PRICING TO EARN A SPECIFIC PROFIT

When introducing a new product, many businesses base their selling price on a specific profit they want to make. The costs of producing and marketing the product, and all related operating expenses, are determined. The price is then set by adding an amount necessary to make a profit. This policy can help a company determine prices, but the actual profit earned will be influenced by how well customers like the product and by the prices of competing products. If the established selling price is too high, a markdown will have to be taken and the amount of profit will be reduced.

PRICING BASED ON CONSUMER DEMAND

The owner of a business that carries fashion merchandise knows that at certain times the products will be in great demand, and at other times the demand will be very low. A retailer will find that swimsuits sell quickly early in the season, but slowly late in the season, unless the prices are greatly reduced. Since the exact number of suits that a business will sell cannot be estimated accurately, the retailer will, at the beginning of the season, set a selling price that should ensure a net profit on the entire group of swimsuits, even though prices may have to be reduced drastically late in the season so that no suits are left in inventory.

Sometimes a business may buy a group of similar items at the same price, but because of variations in designs, colors, and styles, it may charge different prices for the various items. Since certain colors or designs are more attractive than others, customers are willing to pay higher prices for them.

A manufacturer of a product that suddenly becomes popular may want to sell at a high price while the demand is great. When new competitors enter the market or customers tire of the product and the demand begins to decline, the manufacturer will need to sell the product at a much lower price.

The introduction of new products in the market presents an interesting study in price decisions. When handheld calculators were first introduced, they sold for several hundred dollars. Within a few years, competitors entered the market and prices rapidly dropped to as low as $30 even though the calculators had more features than the original models. Very good calculators can now be purchased for $10 or less.

During the process of introducing a product of this type, a business needs to begin to recover the high costs of developing the product, and will use large amounts of money for advertising and promotion. In the early stages of a product's life cycle, there are few, if any, competitors. The price that is established at this time may, therefore, be the highest price at which the manufacturer can sell a reasonable quantity.

As the manufacturer increases production facilities and develops more economical methods of producing the item, the price can be reduced and, in many cases, gross profit can be increased. As new competitors come into the market there is usually a tendency to lower prices. The additional sales promotion of several competitors helps to create a greater total demand. With this greater demand, a larger volume of sales often results. But, in spite of the greater volume, a large reduction in price may decrease profits for many of the manufacturers. There are many products on the market today that reflect this trend of high to low prices.

PRICING TO SELL MORE MERCHANDISE

Products that are marked at higher prices usually sell more slowly than those that cost the same but are marked at lower prices. For example, an article that cost $40 may be sold at a price of $60, but remains in stock for nearly six months. Another article that also cost $40 may be marked at $50, but remains in stock for only two months. Because more of the second product can be sold, it may yield a larger net profit to the business at the end of the year. The business must be careful that the lower price is high enough to cover operating costs and still contribute to profit. Otherwise, using the lower price is a poor decision.

The number of times during a year that a business is able to sell its average inventory is known as its **inventory turnover rate**. Some businesses (such as discount stores) attempt to increase their rates of turnover by setting lower prices.

The following methods are used in computing the inventory turnover rate:
1. Divide the total cost of goods sold by the average inventory valued at its cost.
2. Divide the total net sales by the average inventory valued at its selling price.
3. Divide the total number of units sold by the average number of units in stock.

Ethical Issues

THE USE AND MISUSE OF PRICING

Questions:

1 A free enterprise economy is based on the principle of little government control. Should government stay out of price competition and let consumers and businesses decide what is a fair price? What are your feelings about the laws and regulations described?

2 How should other businesses react when they see a competitor continually using unethical pricing practices?

3 What experiences have you had with prices or the promotion of prices that you believe are unfair, unethical, or possibly illegal? How have those experiences influenced your buying behavior?

" We will beat any competitor's price or give you double the difference!"

"Prices so low we can't print them!"

Each of these statements is frequently used by some businesses to suggest that customers can expect to receive extraordinary values on the products sold there. They are used because business people have learned that advertising a very low price is an effective method to get the attention of many consumers and to influence their decisions. Because of the power of price, however, pricing is often misused.

One of the roles of government in a free enterprise economy is to regulate competition when it appears that businesses or consumers have an unfair advantage. Several types of laws have been developed by federal and state governments to control the prices that businesses can charge and how prices are communicated to customers. The following are some regulations that affect the pricing practices of some businesses:

- Businesses cannot discriminate in the prices offered to other businesses at the same level in a channel of distribution. If one business is offered a price, a discount, or specific credit terms, all of its competitors should have the same opportunity for that price.
- Businesses cannot price their products well below their costs if the purpose is to drive competitors out of business. The short-term use of below-cost pric-

ing is allowed to attract customers into a business. It cannot be continued if the intent is to cause competitors to leave the market and then increase prices to a very profitable level.

- Competing businesses in the same market cannot agree or cooperate in establishing prices so there is no price competition.
- A large channel member cannot require other businesses in the channel to sell products for a specific price. Channel members should have the freedom to charge any price that is appropriate and legal.
- Businesses cannot attempt to confuse or mislead customers on the price of a product by combining a large number of units at one price or pricing products in unusual package sizes. Businesses must provide information on the unit cost of the product based on a commonly used standard of measurement so customers can easily compare prices.

Even though there are laws and regulations that attempt to control the prices charged by businesses and the ways prices are promoted, there are still businesses that violate the law or use practices that may be legal but could be viewed as unethical. Two statements apply to consumers when they see businesses promoting unusually low prices:

"Let the buyer beware."

"If it seems too good to be true, it probably is."

If a business has a low rate of merchandise turnover, higher prices will need to be charged. The higher prices are needed to cover the cost of the inventory and the operating expenses of the business. For instance, many items in an exclusive jewelry store may be sold and replenished at the rate of once a year or less. The jeweler, therefore, finds it necessary to mark the retail price of the products very high in relation to its cost in order to make a reasonable profit.

PRICING TO PROVIDE CUSTOMER SERVICES

A business that has a policy of extending credit, offering free delivery, or providing 24-hour emergency service will have a much higher level of operating expenses than one that sells on a cash-and-carry basis. Higher operating expenses require a higher selling price to yield the same net profit as that earned by a business with lower expenses. If the customers of a business expect a high level of service, or if the business is using the extra service to appear different from competition, prices will have to be set higher in order to achieve a profit.

CONTROLLING PRICES AND PROFITS

Businesses are not always able to increase prices just because they are not making a profit. Costs of merchandise and operating expenses for the business often increase, while prices charged to customers cannot be increased due to competition. Businesses have to make careful purchasing and operating decisions to avoid unnecessary expenses. Three important areas that can affect costs are markdowns, damaged or stolen merchandise, and merchandise returns.

MARKDOWNS

In many cases, businesses are forced to sell some of their products at lower prices than they had planned. This can happen because companies purchase products that customers do not want, that go out of style, or that are damaged or soiled. Businesses also have to sell products at lower prices when too many products have been purchased or when competition increases or competitors lower prices.

Markdowns cannot be avoided totally, but they can usually be controlled. Careful purchasing can eliminate many markdowns. Proper product handling and marketing practices can also reduce the number of markdowns.

DAMAGED OR STOLEN MERCHANDISE

Some products may be damaged so much that they cannot be sold. Other products may be stolen through shoplifting or employee theft. These situations have a serious effect on profits.

Assume that a product with a selling price of $5.00 is damaged or stolen from a business. The product cost the business $4.00, and operating expenses amounted to $.75 for each product. Expected net profit was 25 cents. In order to recover the cost of the damaged or stolen product, the business will have to sell 16 more products than first planned (16 products × 25 cents = $4.00). Another three products will have to be sold to cover operating expenses. The business will not earn a profit on the sale of the 19 products if just one product out of 20 is damaged or stolen.

Companies that want to reduce the amount of damaged and stolen merchandise do several things to improve operations. Operating procedures are improved so merchandise is carefully handled and displayed, and places where merchandise can be easily stolen by employees or customers are eliminated. Employees are carefully hired and trained to reduce both types of losses. Businesses invest thousands of dollars in special equipment and security personnel to reduce losses.

RETURNED MERCHANDISE

If customers are not satisfied with their purchases, they may return the products to the business. This adds to expenses in two ways. If the merchandise can be resold, it will have to be sold at a reduced price, which lowers the selling price of merchandise. Also, many expenses are involved in handling and reselling the returned merchandise, which increases operating expenses.

If businesses fail to consider the expense of returned merchandise, they may well find themselves operating at a loss. A business should consider its record of returned merchandise when buying and pricing merchandise. The study of merchandise returns is another important type of marketing research. Careful purchasing to ensure that products are the type and quality that customers prefer will help reduce returns. Salespeople should be trained to sell products that customers need rather than attempting to convince customers to buy things they do not need. Offering customer service and support so that customers use products effectively and have their questions and problems resolved also reduces the amount of merchandise returns.

When business managers give close attention to the three problem areas of markdowns, damaged or stolen merchandise, and returns, it is possible to keep operating expenses at a minimum. As a result, profits can be maintained and the percentage of markup may be lowered. In that way, both the business and its customers benefit.

BUILDING VOCABULARY POWER

Define the following terms and concepts.

1. manufacturer brands
2. private brands
3. merchandise market
4. buying office
5. purchasing agent
6. purchase requisitions
7. purchase order
8. vendor
9. packing list
10. invoice
11. FOB shipping point
12. FOB destination
13. net 30 days
14. EOM

15. discounts
16. list price
17. trade (functional) discount
18. quantity discount
19. seasonal discount
20. cash discount
21. selling price
22. cost of goods sold
23. operating expenses
24. net profit
25. margin
26. markup
27. markdown
28. inventory turnover rate

REVIEWING FACTS

1. How can a business be hurt by thinking more about quantity than about quality when making purchasing decisions?
2. When is a business likely to be successful using private brands?
3. What sources of information are helpful to a business when determining what to purchase?
4. What types of products do businesses usually purchase by use of a catalog?
5. Why should businesses usually concentrate their buying among a few suppliers?
6. What are the disadvantages of buying products in very large quantities?
7. What is the value of a purchasing department to a large business?
8. How can a purchase order be used when products are received by a business?
9. How does the use of FOB affect the point at which the title to the goods is passed from seller to buyer?
10. Why is selling price typically used as the base when comparing pricing figures?
11. What must happen in order for a business to reduce the selling price of a product and still increase its gross profit?
12. In what situation can a business have a higher selling price for its products than the products of its competitors?

13. Why does the price for a new product often decrease very rapidly in the first few years it is on the market?
14. What effect does self-service usually have on prices charged by businesses?
15. Why are the amounts of markdowns, stolen merchandise, and returned merchandise important to a business manager?

DISCUSSING IDEAS

1. What types of businesses usually carry both manufacturer and private brands?
2. Why would a business want to use a buying office to sell its products?
3. Are there situations where a business should purchase a large quantity of a new product?
4. Why should a small business use a purchase procedure that is similar to that used by large businesses?
5. What should a firm do if the quantity of merchandise listed on the invoice is not the same as listed on the purchase order?
6. Should a business ever borrow money to take advantage of a cash discount?
7. How could a small grocery store successfully compete with a supermarket whose prices are lower?
8. A business has no competition in the same town. Therefore, it sets its prices quite high and makes a large profit. What will probably be the effect of this policy?
9. Why does the rate of inventory turnover affect profits?
10. Why might customers return merchandise to stores?

ANALYZING INFORMATION

1. The bookkeeper for the Downtown Store has the following invoices to pay today, November 30. For each invoice, determine (a) how much discount may be taken, if any, and (b) the amount the check should be made out for in payment of the invoice.

Invoice No.	Amount	Date	Terms
A-4371	$100	Nov. 17	1/10, n/30
A-8235	$450	Nov. 19	1/15, n/60
D-0071	$135	Nov. 2	2/10, n/45

2. A dress shop purchased 200 dresses at $50 each. The dresses were priced to sell at $75 each, and 100 dresses were sold at that price. For those dresses that weren't sold, the price was reduced to $56; 60 dresses were sold at that price. The remaining dresses were then sold for $35. What was the dollar amount of sales? What was the cost of goods sold? What was the gross profit?

REVIEW 13

3. Suppose a retailer estimates that sales in a year will be $1,000,000 and that operating expenses will be $200,000. (a) What will be the amount of the margin if a net profit of 5 percent of sales is expected? (b) What is the percentage of margin? (c) What percentage of the total sales is the cost of merchandise? (d) If an article costs $15, what should its selling price be? (e) What is the rate of markup on the cost?

4. During a year, a manufacturer sold 1800 kerosene heaters. The number of heaters on hand during the year was as follows: January 1, 220; February 1, 280; March 1, 360; April 1, 300; May 1, 420; June 1, 550; July 1, 500; August 1, 500; September 1, 480; October 1, 430; November 1, 660; and December 1, 700. What was the rate of turnover?

5. A hobby shop has been selling an average of 10 model airplane motors each month that cost $20 each. The regular selling price has been $28. By reducing the selling price to $24, the number of sales was increased to 15 each month. If the average monthly operating expenses were increased a total of $10 by the change, how much was the monthly net profit increased or decreased by the change in price?

S OLVING BUSINESS PROBLEMS

CASE 13-1

The Touring Bicycle Shop is currently selling a racing bicycle that costs $160 for $305. On the average, five of the bicycles are sold each month. The owner thinks that if the selling price were reduced $25, more sales and more profit could be made. The owner believes that operating expenses would not increase even if more bicycles were sold.

Required:
1. How many additional bicycles will have to be sold during the year at the lower price in order to keep the same amount of gross profit?
2. Does it seem reasonable that the owner could expect to sell the additional bicycles if the price was reduced by $25?
3. Comment on the owner's belief that operating expenses would not increase.

CASE 13-2

Kuen Young is planning to open a small convenience grocery store in a town of 50,000 people. The town also is served by two well-known supermarket chains. One chain is a cash-and-carry supermarket where customers must sack their own merchandise. The store offers no special services and stocks mostly private brands.

The second supermarket offers a selection of three or four national brands for most products. Its prices are much higher than the prices of the first chain, but it offers many customer services including check cashing, a place to pay utility bills, and a small package wrapping and mailing service.

Kuen's store will be located in a new housing development on the opposite end of town from the two supermarkets.

Required:

1. What type of grocery products and services should Kuen offer to compete with the two supermarkets?
2. Are there other products that Kuen might carry in addition to grocery items to attract customers from the supermarkets?
3. How should Kuen decide on the prices to charge for the products carried in the new business?

REVIEW **13**

PROMOTION CHAPTER 14

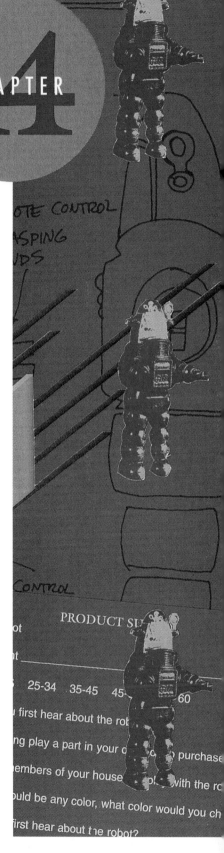

After studying this chapter you will be able to:

14-1 Identify the two major methods of promotion and three other promotional methods used by businesses.

14-2 Describe the five categories of advertising media and give examples of each.

14-3 Discuss how cost and timing affect the management of promotion.

14-4 Explain the parts of the selling process and how each is used to help customers make effective buying decisions.

14-5 List promotional methods businesses can use to have an immediate impact on sales.

14-6 Identify the types of penalties that can be applied to businesses that violate laws and regulations in their advertising.

J ackson Shey was interested in buying a new bicycle. He had saved nearly $300 and started to plan his purchase. He knew he wanted to buy a mountain bike so he talked with several of his friends who had purchased such a bike in the past year. Each had purchased a different brand, and they each seemed to like the brand they had purchased. Yet few of Jackson's friends could tell him very much about the differences among brands or what features made their brand better than the others.

Jackson watched television and looked in several magazines, but he didn't see many advertisements for bicycles. While he was in the school library, he looked for information to help him with his decision. The librarian showed him a consumer *magazine that had done a comparative study of the major brands. The study provided a great deal of information about the brands but didn't indicate which was the best.*

Next, Jackson went to a local discount store. He saw that the store had several choices of children's and ten-speed bikes but only two models of mountain bikes. The clerk in the sporting goods department really didn't know much about the bikes but showed him a brochure about each model.

Finally, Jackson went to a bicycle shop. There he found so many brands and styles of bicycles that he didn't know which to look at first. A very helpful salesperson showed him some of the common features on all mountain bicycles and how to judge quality differences in those features. Then she described the primary differences among the major brands. When Jackson indicated that he didn't want to buy that day, but was trying to learn enough to make a good decision, the salesperson showed him a copy of Cyclist *magazine. She said that the magazine contained articles for beginning as well as for experienced cyclists, and that each month it had a feature that evaluated equipment. She told Jackson that the public library had a subscription to* Cyclist, *so he could read back issues. While he paged through the magazine, he noticed many informative advertisements about the brands of bicycles. As Jackson was leaving the store, the salesperson told him about a 30-minute show on public television each Saturday about bicycling.*

P ROMOTION AS A MARKETING TOOL

Before a business can be successful, it must interest people in buying its products and services. Even though a company has a good product, the product will not be sold automatically. Consumers may not know the product is available or where it can be purchased. They may not easily see the differences among brands or be able to determine which brand will be the best in meeting their needs.

Consumers have varied needs and use different methods of gathering information to satisfy those needs. In the situation described above, Jackson Shey was gathering a great deal of information in a careful way before making a decision about which brand of bicycle to buy. Other consumers might not be as careful or use the same method. Therefore, an important responsibility of businesses is to provide appropriate information to help consumers make effective decisions.

Promotion is the primary marketing activity used to communicate with prospective customers. It is used to inform them about the features and benefits of the company's products and services and to encourage them to buy. There are many types of promotion. The two primary methods are advertising and personal selling. Other methods include sales promotion, displays, and publicity. In this chapter, we will examine the major types of promotion and determine how each can be used effectively to sell products and satisfy customers.

Effective promotion is based on planning effective communications. You learned about the elements of a communications model in the chapter on organizational communications. Those elements are shown in Figure 14-1. In promotion, the company that develops the promotion is the sender. The information in the promotion is the message and the method of promotion (advertising, personal selling, sales promotion) determines the medium to be used in communication. The prospective consumer is the receiver. Feedback from the receiver to the sender will help to determine if the promotion was successful or not.

Jeff Greenberg, Photographer

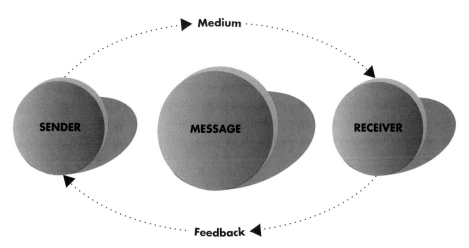

ADVERTISING

Advertising includes all forms of paid promotion that deliver a message to many people at the same time. Because the message is prepared for many people, it will be rather impersonal. However, since the message will be seen by thousands of people, the cost of communicating with each person is very low.

More money is spent each year in the United States on advertising than on any other type of promotion. Each year, the total expenditures for advertising by all businesses in the United States is well over $100 billion. Large companies such as Procter & Gamble and Sears alone invest more than $1 billion each year in advertising to persuade customers to purchase their brands.

While the average business spends less than 2 percent of total sales annually on advertising, some businesses spend over 20 percent of their sales each year on advertising. Companies in industries such as beverages, cosmetics, and electronics depend on advertising and spend a significant amount throughout the years to keep their brand names in front of consumers. While not every business uses advertising, there are many ways that advertising can help a business.

PURPOSES OF ADVERTISING

Advertising is a powerful tool because it can help a business accomplish a variety of objectives. Companies need to consider carefully what they want to communicate to consumers and plan specific advertising to ensure that a communication goal is accomplished. The major purposes of advertising are shown in Fig. 14-2.

Fig. 14-2

Advertising can be used to accomplish many communications tasks of a business.

1. **To inform and educate consumers.**
2. **To introduce a new product or business.**
3. **To announce an improvement or product change.**
4. **To reinforce important product features and benefits.**
5. **To increase the frequency of use of a product.**
6. **To increase the variety of uses of a product.**
7. **To convince people to enter a store.**
8. **To develop a list of prospects.**
9. **To make a brand, trademark, or slogan familiar.**
10. **To improve the image of a company or product.**
11. **To gain support for ideas or causes.**

ADVERTISING CATEGORIES AND MEDIA CHOICES

Most businesses use some form of advertising to attract prospective customers; however, the methods of reaching consumers, the advertising media, vary a great deal. **Advertising media** are the methods of delivering the promotional message to the intended audience. The most widely used forms of advertising media classified by categories are shown in Figure 14-3.

Fig. 14-3
Forms of advertising media by categories.

PUBLICATION ADVERTISING

newspapers, general and special interest magazines, business and professional journals, and directories

MASS MEDIA ADVERTISING

radio, network and local television, cable television

OUTDOOR ADVERTISING

billboards, signs, posters, vehicle signage, and electronic displays

DIRECT ADVERTISING

sales letters, catalogs, brochures, inserts, telemarketing, fax messages, and computer databases

DISPLAY ADVERTISING

window, counter, and aisle displays; special signage; self-service merchandising; trade show displays

Some large companies use practically all of these media, but many small or specialized business firms use only a few. For instance, a business in a small town may use only the local newspaper or radio station. Billboards and local radio and television programs are good methods of advertising for many local companies serving large numbers of customers. Such advertising is effective in attracting the public within a particular geographic area. It is doubtful, however, that a neighborhood retailer in a large city will find television advertising profitable. The cost is so great that the results would not justify the expense. Television advertising, in this case, is not effective because such a small percentage of the viewers are potential customers of the business. However, a supermarket chain in a metropolitan area might find television advertising profitable because a large number of its customers are served by several stores.

National advertisers in general spend the most money on television. National magazines and large city or regional newspapers are also used extensively. Newspapers and radio advertising are the media most often chosen by local advertisers.

Almost any business, particularly small or new businesses, can use forms of direct advertising. The cost and number of people reached with direct mail advertising can be easily controlled by adding to or eliminating people from mailing lists.

Media choices must be made carefully by businesses to use resources effectively while influencing consumer decisions. Characteristics of the major advertising media usually considered by advertisers are discussed next.

Radio

Radio is a very popular advertising medium because of the large number of radios available in homes, businesses, and cars. Because radios are portable, many people carry them for leisure activities as well.

Radio advertising is used extensively by local and regional businesses, but many national advertisers have begun to increase expenditures for radio advertising. It is possible to be quite creative in the development of radio advertising at a lower cost than television. Messages can be changed quickly if special needs arise so radio advertising can be very topical with immediate impact.

The large number of radio stations with specific content (talk, news, music) allows the advertiser to get messages to specific types of customers. Also, radio stations try to appeal to very specific groups of consumers (age, interest, etc.).

Advertising time is typically sold in 60-, 30-, or 10-second spots. The most expensive time on many stations is known as **drive time**. That is the time during the early morning and later afternoon when many people are in their cars going to and from work and are likely listening to the radio.

Television

Television is the newest of the major advertising media, having become available in most American homes only in the last forty years. Today, nearly 100 percent of all U.S. homes have at least one television and over half of those homes have two or more. Most people view television several hours each day.

Because of the mass appeal of television, it has become a very attractive advertising medium for many businesses. Television can communicate both sight and sound, making it a very creative and effective medium.

Regional and national advertisers whose products appeal to mass markets find television advertising to be inexpensive. Even though a minute of television advertising time may cost as much as several hundred thousand dollars, when reaching a national audience of millions of people the cost per person is low. The cost of television advertising depends on the number of people likely

Illus. 14-2

National sporting events provide valuable advertising opportunities for some businesses, even though the costs are extremely high. What types of products are best suited for those events?

Stephen Swinburne/Stock, Boston

to watch the show being telecast. Therefore, television networks and station executives are concerned about the programs they offer and the number of people who watch their shows.

There are two elements that are a part of the cost of advertising. Producing a high-quality television commercial can cost several hundred thousand dollars. Then the advertiser must purchase time on each network or individual television stations for the advertisement to be shown. The cost of television time can range from several thousand dollars on small stations or at times when there are fewer viewers to over a half million dollars for a major, nationally televised event such as the Super Bowl. In general, the most expensive time for television advertising is between 6 p.m. and 11 p.m., which is referred to as **prime time**. The time and money needed to prepare television advertising are major limitations in its use.

The growth of cable television offers another option for businesses using television advertising. It is expected that nearly 75 percent of all U.S. homes will have access to cable television by the end of this decade. Hundreds of cable channels are available to advertisers with most cable television companies providing specific channels for local programming. Cable channels are often viewed by groups of people with specialized interests such as health and fitness, sports, home improvements, or personal finance. Also, the cost of advertising on cable channels is often lower.

Two recent developments in television advertising are the shopping channels and infomercials. **Shopping channels** are television channels devoted exclusively to presenting merchandise for sale and accepting orders by telephone for direct shipment to customers. Shopping channels such as the Home Shopping Network and QVC have become very popular and successful methods of promoting and selling merchandise to customers worldwide. **Infomercials** are full-length television programs (30-60 minutes) produced to promote and sell a specific product. The program is carefully developed to look like an actual television program rather than an advertisement. The program content focuses on unique features of the product and its benefits to the consumer. Satisfied customers or celebrities often provide testimonials about the effectiveness of the product. During the program, viewers are provided with a telephone number and purchasing information in order to buy the product being promoted. The company sponsoring an infomercial buys the time from a television station to air the program.

Newspapers

Newspapers are read by over 75 percent of all people over the age of 18. Since people read newspapers daily and use the newspaper to get a variety of information, they are a good place for advertising. Most large city newspapers are published daily, so advertising messages can reach consumers frequently. Newspaper advertising can also be changed rapidly if needed. Newspapers published in smaller towns or specialty newspapers (entertainment, business) are published only once or twice a week.

The cost of placing an advertisement in a local newspaper is inexpensive when compared to other advertising media; therefore, it is used by many businesses. More advertising dollars are spent for newspaper advertising than for any other type of advertising. However, it is used much more by local and regional businesses than by national businesses. Types of newspaper advertising include display ads, classified ads, and specially printed inserts.

Magazines

Magazine advertising was the first type of national advertising. It was first used in the late 1800s when magazines were distributed on trains. Magazines have increased in popularity in recent years as more specialized publications have been developed. Today, many magazines are very specialized and often relate directly to their readers' occupations, hobbies, or interests.

The major advantage of advertising in magazines is the high quality of the advertisements. They are usually printed on heavy, glossy paper using several colors. Also, magazines are often read by more than one reader and each reader may see the ad several times since they read the magazine at more than one sitting.

Advertising in national magazines can be very expensive. However, advertising dollars spent in magazines has increased. Businesses have learned that magazine readers use the medium as an important and specific information source. A great advantage of magazines is that they can appeal to highly segmented audiences.

Outdoor (Billboards, Signs, and Posters)

Some of the oldest forms of advertising are included in this category. Businesses have long used carefully crafted signs outside their shops to attract customers. Billboards allow simple, brief messages to be presented to everyone who passes by. If the right location is chosen for an outdoor advertisement, thousands of people can see a business' message every day as they pass the billboard. The use of electronic displays and new billboard designs have increased the popularity of this form of advertising. Public transportation vehicles such as busses, taxis, and commuter trains are now popular locations for advertising messages.

Direct Advertising

Some promotions are sent directly to potential customers. **Direct advertising** allows a company to direct its message to specific people through the use of specially selected mailing lists or computer databases.

The use of mailed advertisements is the most common form of direct advertising. Because the consumer receives the advertisement through the mail, the message may get more attention than if it were placed in a magazine or newspaper. While some direct mail advertising is ignored, if it is prepared carefully and targeted to consumers interested in the product or service, consumers often will study the advertisement more carefully. Direct mail advertising can be used to provide detailed information to consumers about products or services.

There are many forms of direct mail advertising ranging from quite inexpensive to very expensive. A business can send a one-page flyer to all residents of a small town at a very low cost. A national retailer that sends a mail-order catalog to thousands of customers will spend a great deal of money on that form of advertising.

One-page advertising pieces can be placed in customers' packages or enclosed in the envelope containing the monthly statements mailed to credit customers. In these instances, however, the promotion will only reach current customers.

Newer forms of technology have resulted in additional opportunities for direct advertising. Many companies now have facsimile machines so letters and other information can be transmitted to them immediately. Some consumers with computers subscribe to information services or participate in special interest user groups. Some computer data services allow advertising messages to be sent to subscribers indicating an interest in particular products and services.

Telemarketing

A relatively recent development in advertising is telemarketing, or the use of the telephone as a sales and advertising medium. With a database of telephone numbers maintained in a computer and computer dialing equipment, a large number of people can be contacted in a short time. When telemarketing is used for advertising, a person reads from a prepared script or outline to inform the person called about a product or service. The message can also be recorded and the recorded message is played for the person answering the telephone.

Jeff Greenberg, Photographer

Illus. 14-3

Telemarketing is an important promotional tool but can be easily misused. What negative and positive experiences have you had with telemarketers?

Outbound telemarketing is used by companies to make direct contact with potential customers and inform them of products and services with the intent to sell the product or encourage the customer to take further action. Inbound telemarketing is the use of a special telephone number (often an 800 number) that customers can use to contact a business for product information or to place an order. Inbound telemarketing is combined with other forms of advertising media that are used to provide initial information to consumers.

Several concerns have been expressed by consumers, consumer protection groups, and businesses regarding the use of telemarketing for advertising. Because it can be annoying to receive telephone calls advertising products that are not of interest, there have been attempts in some states to place limits or controls on the use of computers and telephone dialing equipment for telemarketing.

However, telemarketing can be a very efficient and personalized advertising medium and one that is appreciated by potential customers when used effectively. Business-to-business telemarketing has become a very important and useful form of promotion. Business people have found they save both time and money when contacts can be made by telephone to gather or provide information. Businesses need to be aware of consumer needs and concerns and should use professional methods when choosing any new advertising medium such as telemarketing.

PLANNING AND MANAGING ADVERTISING

The preceding discussion shows that businesses have many choices of media to use to communicate information to customers. However, planning an advertising program involves much more that selecting the media. Advertising should be planned to support other promotion and marketing decisions. All advertising efforts need to be evaluated to see if they are effective. The marketing department should always be looking for a new or more effective means of advertising.

Most businesses that spend a significant amount of money for advertising and use advertising throughout the year develop an advertising plan. The plan outlines the communications goals and specifies a calendar of advertising activities, an advertising budget, and how evaluation of advertising will be accomplished. Responsibility for developing the advertising plan is usually given to the marketing manager or a person with the specific responsibility for managing advertising.

Small businesses often need help in developing their advertising plans and in writing their advertisements. A printing company may have specialists who will help in writing the copy and designing the advertisement for a direct mail piece. The people who sell advertising space may offer suggestions in preparing

Salespeople
Manufacturers
Advertisements of competitors
Trade associations
Exchange of ideas with business
    friends

Freelance artists, writers,
    and advertising consultants
Advertising agencies
Marketing and advertising
    instructors at schools and
    universities

Fig. 14-4

Sources of advertising assistance for businesses.

newspaper advertisements. Radio and television station marketing people might also help plan advertising. Other sources of help in planning and carrying out an advertising program are listed in Figure 14-4.

As the business grows, the owner has the option of hiring someone to handle the advertising or of placing all of the company's advertising planning in the hands of an advertising agency. Full-service agencies provide all of the services related to planning and producing advertisements for all media and buying the space or time for the advertisements in the media. Most agencies also offer research services to determine customers' product and information needs. For their services, advertising agencies usually charge a percentage of the total amount spent for the advertising, but may charge for the actual costs of developing and placing the advertisements.

Some very large companies have a complete advertising department that provides all of the functions of an advertising agency. Because of the amount of advertising done and its cost, it is more efficient for those companies to have their own advertising personnel than to pay an advertising agency.

THE ADVERTISING BUDGET

The amount that a business can spend for advertising should be determined when the company's budget is developed. Most businesses plan the advertising program for one year or less. Of course, emergencies may arise that require a quick decision; but unless some planning has taken place, the budget may be misused. If a new product is being developed, the company will usually prepare an advertising budget to support the new product's introduction into the market.

Separate advertising budgets in large businesses are often developed for new products, product lines, customer groups, or regions of a market. If specific budgets are developed, it is easier to determine the results of advertising on sales and profits.

A business person should know what constitutes a reasonable expenditure for advertising in the particular industry and type of business. Most trade associations provide information on average advertising expenditures for their types of business. Several publications are available in most business libraries that have up-to-date information on advertising expenditures for a variety of businesses. Advertising expenses range from 1 to 2 percent of sales in some businesses to 10 percent or more in others.

The amount spent by a specific business on advertising depends more on the characteristics of the product and target market than on the competition. A business with a loyal group of customers and a product that has been in the market for a long time may need to spend much less than a business with a new or very complex product or one that is in an extremely competitive market. A business that relies on advertising for the majority of its promotion will, of course, spend a larger percentage of sales on advertising than a business that has a balanced promotional program of advertising, personal selling, and sales promotion.

Firms that advertise nationally and internationally to very diverse markets will often spend the largest percentages on advertising. The high amount of advertising helps increase demand for the company's brands, which permits the company to sell low-cost products at a profit.

TIMING OF ADVERTISING

In almost every type of business there are certain times when advertising can be more effective. A company should determine the times when potential customers are most willing and able to buy the goods or services advertised. Many products and services are seasonal with the majority of sales concentrated in a few months of the year. It would be wise for a company to spend more advertising dollars during those times when consumers are considering the purchase of the product than during times when it is not likely the customer will buy. For example, advertising for ski resorts or ocean cruises is increased during the winter months while advertising for air conditioners and lawn mowers is emphasized in the spring and summer.

Occasionally, advertising can be used to increase purchases at times customers have not traditionally considered buying a product. Through an emphasis on new product development and advertising, turkey producers and processors have increased the sale of turkey products throughout the year. Those businesses had previously sold almost all of their products near the Thanksgiving holiday and one or two other holiday times during the year.

A continuing emphasis on advertising is usually needed by businesses. A single advertisement may produce temporary results, but regular advertising is important in building a steady stream of customers. If advertising does not appear often enough, customers tend to forget about a business or product. It is practical for most businesses to spread their advertising over the entire year, as shown in the advertising budget in Fig. 14-5. A company can use smaller and less expensive advertisements more frequently, rather than spend all advertising funds on a few expensive advertisements. Only when a company wants an immediate impact, such as for a new product introduction or for a special event, should a large, one-time expenditure be considered.

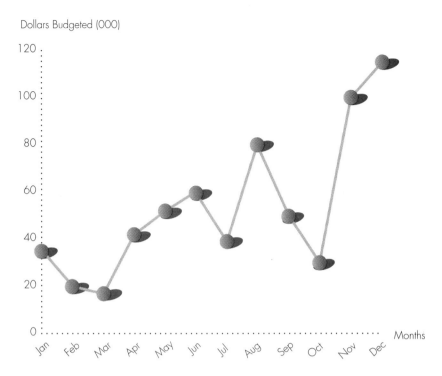

Dollars Budgeted (000)

PERSONAL SELLING

Personal selling is promotion through direct, personal contact with a customer. The salesperson usually makes direct contact with the customer through a face-to-face meeting. For retail sales, that contact often occurs in the salesperson's business; it is more likely to occur in the customer's business for business-to-business selling. Personal selling can also be accomplished by a personal letter or a telephone call. The most effective personal selling is through face-to-face contact, which better enables the salesperson to answer the customer's questions and to explain how goods or services can benefit the customer.

Four elements are a part of personal selling: the customer, the business, the product or service, and the salesperson. The salesperson bridges the gap between the customer and the business. The success of the business depends, to a great extent, on the quality and price of the goods or services, but its success is also very dependent on the selling skills of the salesforce.

What do customers like about a business? A customer survey identified seven factors customers believe to be important in retail business. Those factors are shown in Fig. 14-6 on page 348. Since Items 3 and 5 are directly related to the actions of salespeople and salespeople can be an important part of Items 4 and 7, it is evident that personal selling plays a very important part in the success of many businesses.

There are many types of customers, and a salesperson must be able to adjust to each. Some customers know exactly what they want. They do not want to listen to a long explanation about the product. Some customers may be attempting to satisfy several needs, so they may change their minds several times. Some

Fig. 14-6

Characteristics customers look for in a retail business.

> 1. **A sufficient variety of products from which to choose.**
> 2. **Prices comparable to the quality of the merchandise.**
> 3. **Pleasant and helpful employees.**
> 4. **Willingness to make adjustments in case of errors and returns.**
> 5. **Truthful statements about the goods and services.**
> 6. **Attractive premises (including lighting, ventilation, equipment, and arrangement).**
> 7. **Service features, such as delivery, credit, and parking.**

customers are in the early states of decision making. They are not interested in any particular article but are just gathering information. Some customers are talkative, some are quiet, some are irritable, some are suspicious of salespeople, and some always want a lower price. The successful salesperson must be able to understand and serve all types.

STUDYING THE WANTS OF CUSTOMERS

The salesperson who attempts to sell apparel to a fashion-conscious consumer by emphasizing its low price will not be successful. On the other hand, the salesperson who emphasizes the uniqueness and image of a specific item is more likely to make a sale simply because that salesperson understands the important reason the customer will prefer one brand of clothing to another. At the end of a season, a more cost-conscious customer may respond to an emphasis on price reductions. An individual who wishes to be successful in satisfying customers must study and understand consumer behavior. Why do people buy? What wants do they have? How can those wants be satisfied?

Buying motives are the reasons people buy. Many motives cause people to search for and buy products and services. Some of the most important buying motives of final consumers are listed in Fig. 14-7.

Fig. 14-7

Salespeople must be able to identify buying motives.

Status	Ease of use	Affection
Appetite	Love of beauty	Wealth
Comfort	Amusement	Enjoyment
Desire for bargains	Desire for good health	Pride of ownership
Recognition	Friendship	Fear

To be successful, the salesperson must determine what is likely to be the buying motive of a particular customer and then make the sales presentation appeal to that motive. In many cases, the salesperson can make appeals to more than one buying motive. For instance, a laundry company representative, in attempting to sell laundry services to a couple with three children and an income that is a little above average, may talk about the comfort and convenience of having the laundry done outside the home rather than doing it themselves. The salesperson may also explain that it is less expensive to send the laundry to a professional service because of all the expenses that are involved in doing laundry at home.

Suppose that this same laundry representative calls on the owner of a barber shop or beauty salon. Here the salesperson can place emphasis on the special sterilizing treatment given to towels, capes, and uniforms and the high degree of whiteness and cleanliness in the laundered items. Both the family and the business owner might find individually scheduled pickup and delivery services attractive.

If a customer has several buying motives, the salesperson can often make brief appeals to different motives and carefully observe the reaction of the customer. As soon as the most important motive is identified, the salesperson can spend additional time emphasizing it.

In other words, it is a sound policy in selling to determine a customer's wants and buying motives and then satisfy those motives with the product. Providing customer satisfaction through a sale is the ultimate goal of a salesperson. This method of selling does not require high-pressure selling; it requires intelligent customer-oriented selling.

PRESENTING AND DEMONSTRATING THE PRODUCT

Effective personal selling requires that the salesperson understand the wants or needs of the customer. In addition, it is necessary that the salesperson have a thorough knowledge of the company's products and services to suggest those that best fit the customer's needs and to be able to provide the information needed by the customer.

Jeff Greenberg, Photographer

Illus. 14-4

The product demonstration is an important part of the sales presentation. How do watching and participating in a demonstration affect a consumer's attitude toward the product and the salesperson?

Customers are interested in what the products or services will do for them and how they can be used. It is important that salespeople have a thorough knowledge of the various uses of products, advantages as well as their limitations, and how the products compare to those of competitors.

The primary uses of products that have been in the market for a period of time are usually known to the customer. The salesperson should be able to convince the customer that a particular brand is best suited for the customer's particular purpose. The salesperson can also point out the versatility of the product by explaining its secondary uses. For example, the primary use of a vacuum cleaner is to clean rugs and carpets, but a particular cleaner may also be used to clean curtains or upholstery and even to remove lint from clothing.

A thorough knowledge of the products is necessary so that the salesperson can comfortably provide information and answer questions. For example, customers might ask: "How much paint will I need for a bathroom six feet by eight feet?" "Which vinyl is best for a concrete basement floor?" "Can these slacks be laundered or do they need to be dry cleaned?" "Why is this pair of shoes $68 and that pair $55?"

One of the best ways for a salesperson to provide service to the customer is to obtain information concerning the kind, quality, cost, and source of materials used in making the product. These factors affect the price, quality, durability, appearance, uses, and care of an article. For example, the fact that a certain piece of clothing is made of specific fabrics determines the care that it should be given and how it should be cleaned. It also has a definite influence on the quality, appearance, and price. A salesperson should be aware of important information, such as knowing that certain products are handmade and that others have been assembled by robots.

Different types of information about the same product will be important to various customers. For instance, several fabric cycles on a washing machine will appeal to some people, while the simplicity of operation or the availability of a certain color of appliance may be more important to others. Salespeople should study the products they sell as well as the competition's products. They should always be prepared to explain why their products are worth the price. Some useful sources of product information are shown in Fig. 14-8.

Fig. 14-8

Salespeople can obtain product information from many sources.

Examination and use of the product

Booklets, circulars, and training provided by the manufacturer or company training programs

Magazine and newspaper advertisements

Representatives of the manufacturer or distributor

Technical books and magazines

Customers who have already had experience with the product

Other salespeople who are acquainted with the merchandise

Selling points that competitors make for their products

In addition to giving customers information, salespeople should effectively demonstrate the product and its use so customers can determine whether or not the product will fit their needs. It is usually a good idea for salespeople to show the product and its uses at the same time that they provide information about it. The customer's attention is then focused on the product as its features and advantages are being explained.

A product should be shown to its best advantage. By handling it carefully and showing respect for it, the salesperson enhances the value of the product in the customer's mind. For example, the value of a piece of jewelry is enhanced when the salesperson handles it very carefully and places it on a piece of velvet where its color and design are easily seen. In some cases, the value of the product is enhanced by demonstrating its durability. If the door panels of an automobile are built to resist dents and chips, the salesperson may want to demonstrate the durability by hitting the door.

An effective way of convincing the customer to buy an object is to show it in use as it would be used by the customer. A sewing machine may be demonstrated by sewing some samples for the customer; a furniture polish, by actually polishing a piece of furniture.

Whenever possible, the customer should be encouraged to participate in the demonstration—to operate the vacuum cleaner, to key material into a computer, to try on a coat, or to drive the automobile. When a customer is directly involved and becomes comfortable with use of the product, initial interest can change to the desire to own the product.

In certain selling situations, such as selling very large or bulky products or selling services, sales representatives demonstrate without having the actual product. They use such items as photographs, charts, catalogs, slides and video tapes, or computer displays. Such situations make it more difficult for the customer to get a true feeling for the use of a product, so the salesperson will have to rely on effective communications to increase understanding and desire to purchase the product.

Answering Customer Questions

It is usual for a customer to have many questions during the salesperson's presentation and demonstration. The salesperson should not be concerned by the questions but should view them as an opportunity to better understand the customer's needs and help the customer make the best decision. Customers who have a sincere interest in the product and believe that the salesperson has their best interests at heart will usually ask specific, important questions. They will expect direct answers to the questions from the salesperson. When their questions are answered, they will be able to determine whether the product will meet their needs or not.

When customers are not certain whether the product is suitable for them or when they have concerns about the salesperson's intentions, they may raise objections. **Objections** are concerns or complaints expressed by the customer. Objections may represent real concerns of the customer. However, they may not express the true feelings of the customer but may simply be an effort to avoid making a decision to purchase. Objections may be raised about the product, its price, the company, the salesperson, or information that has been provided to the customer.

It is difficult to try to second guess a customer to determine if the objection is real or not. It is best for the salesperson to listen carefully to the objection, and then make sure the customer recognizes that the salesperson wants to help the customer make the best decision. An effective salesperson welcomes the question or concern, and provides information directly and briefly that will satisfy the customer.

CLOSING THE SALE

For many salespeople, the most difficult part of the selling process is asking the customer to buy. Rejection is difficult for many people to deal with, and it is easy to believe that a customer who does not buy is making a statement about the salesperson's ability. Instead, the salesperson should recognize that a decision to purchase involves several steps and that each customer moves through those steps in a different way and at a different speed. The salesperson should be aware of cues that the customer is ready to buy. Body language such as nodding the head or handling the product may indicate that interest. Asking questions about minor product features, pricing or credit terms, or delivery schedules is also an indication that the customer is nearing a decision.

If the salesperson has involved the customer in the sales presentation and has listened carefully to the customer's needs, it should not be an uncomfortable situation to close the sale. Typically, effective salespeople give the customer the opportunity to buy several times during the sales presentation by asking for a decision on a specific model, color, price, or type of payment. If the customer continues to ask questions, the salesperson will answer the question and continue the discussion until it appears the customer is satisfied. Then the salesperson will attempt to close the sale again.

Many sales, particularly for expensive products, take several meetings between the salesperson and the customer. In business-to-business selling, teams of salespeople and specialists from the company may meet several times with teams of buyers from the customer's company. The final decision will likely be made by several people. Salespeople should continue to work with the potential customers until it is clear that they do not want the product or until the sale is made.

SUGGESTION SELLING

Have you ever had the experience of buying a pair of shoes and having the salesperson suggest that you buy polish or an extra pair of shoestrings? Or have you ever observed a man purchasing a shirt and the salesperson suggesting a necktie to match? Such activity on the part of salespeople is known as suggestion selling. **Suggestion selling** occurs when the salesperson calls the customer's attention to products that were not requested. Four common types of suggestion selling are:

- Suggesting an item related to the one the customer has just purchased.
- Recommending that a larger quantity be purchased.
- Suggesting a substitute item or brand.
- Calling attention to a featured item or a special purchase.

If the salesperson really uses suggestion selling to benefit the customer and does not attempt to force unwanted goods on the customer, then suggestion selling is an effective marketing strategy. Calling attention to products that are necessary for the effective use of the original purchase may save the customer from making an extra trip to the store later to buy the related article. It may also provide products that more closely complement the original purchase than those that could be purchased elsewhere. For example, a particular dress may have a complimentary purse or belt from the same designer. The customer may want to buy those items instead of looking in several other stores for similar items.

Other types of valuable suggestion selling include recommending the purchase of a large quantity in order to get a better value, suggesting high-priced merchandise when it means better quality, and suggesting a substitute brand when the initial request is not available. Each of these suggestions may be of value to the customer and should be considered part of the service a salesperson gives if they are done with the best interests of the customer in mind.

To a business, suggestion selling has great possibilities for increasing sales by getting customers to purchase related items now instead of buying them later from competitors. The increased sales should result not only in larger net profits, but also in a greater percentage of net profit because the additional sales cause only a little increase in overall expenses.

FOLLOW-UP

The selling process is not complete just because the customer agrees to purchase a product. Remember that effective marketing results in satisfying exchanges between a business and a customer. Therefore, selling is successful when the customer is satisfied.

Salespeople need to check with the customer to be sure the order is correct, the customer knows how to use the product, and that it meets the customer's needs. If there are problems, they can be corrected immediately. If the customer is satisfied, the salesperson's contact will remind the customer where the product was purchased so the customer is likely to use the same business for the next purchase.

Followup can be done in person, by telephone, or by sending a note or letter to the customer. Even if a sale was not made, the salesperson may want to followup with the customer to see if needs have changed or if the customer is interested in other products or services the business offers.

OTHER PROMOTIONAL METHODS

Businesses have other ways to promote their products in addition to advertising and personal selling. Some promotional methods are developed to encourage customers to make an immediate purchase decision. Others are designed to display the products in an attention-getting or attractive way to encourage sales. Several of these methods are discussed next.

COUPONS

Coupons are used extensively to promote the sale of consumer products. Coupons are an effective method of increasing sales of a product for a short time. They are used principally to introduce a new product or to maintain and increase a company's share of the market for established brands. Coupons usually appear in newspaper and magazine advertisements, but they are also distributed by direct mail. Some businesses now offer coupons to customers as a part of a product display. Coupon dispensers are placed in easy-to-see locations on store shelves. Customers can obtain a coupon and use it immediately to purchase a specific brand. Other businesses provide coupons to customers at the time of the sale based on the purchases they make. A coupon for a product the customer just purchased may encourage the customer to buy the same brand the next time. Or a coupon for another brand may encourage the customer to try it.

MANUFACTURER AND DEALER AIDS

Manufacturers often cooperate with wholesalers and retailers by providing certain materials to be used in promoting products. Some of these promotional materials, commonly furnished without cost or at a low price, include window displays, layouts and illustrations for newspaper advertisements, direct mail inserts, counter displays, and sales presentation aids.

Manufacturers and wholesalers benefit when they assist retailers with their promotional campaigns. Local retailers can tie their advertising and promotion into a national campaign by keeping themselves informed on advertising and advertising programs, and by obtaining all the free materials and suggestions that are available. For example, when a dealer who distributes cassettes and compact discs learns that a particular recording group is appearing on a national television program or is performing locally, it is a good opportunity to feature their recordings and obtain all the displays and other promotional materials that are available.

When producers are introducing a new product, they may distribute samples through the mail. The purpose of this activity is to familiarize people with the products to create a demand for them in local businesses. The samples are often accompanied by a coupon to encourage the consumer to go to a local store and buy the product.

Producers and distributors also cooperate with retailers by arranging special displays and demonstrations within stores. Samples are given to customers as they enter the store. This practice usually helps the retailers sell the new product. The retailer, of course, gives this merchandise a preference over other competing products. Sometimes distributors pay merchants for the privilege of giving demonstrations or offer special prices for the opportunity.

STORE DISPLAYS

Many prospective customers get the first impression of retail stores that are located in shopping malls or other central shopping locations by merchandise displayed in its windows; thus, windows are a very valuable part of a retail store. Using windows to display merchandise alerts a passerby that the store handles these items and presents an image of the store. The result should be an increase in the numbers of customers entering the store as well as increased sales of the items displayed. Stores have estimated increases of 30 to 50 percent in the sale of items that are effectively displayed in windows. To the small store located in a large shopping center, the window display may be the most effective method of promotion.

The interior of a business can be used for promotion as well. In planning an interior display, it is necessary to take into consideration the whole interior and not just an individual area. In order to obtain a harmony from displays, the interior planning should include the decoration of the store, layout, and merchandise. In the past, discount stores and supermarkets were not as concerned about interior displays as were department stores. It was believed that simply presenting the merchandise on well-organized racks and counters was enough to sell the lower-priced merchandise. Today, most businesses are reorganizing their interiors to group similar products, provide more space for shoppers, and present attractive displays of the merchandise.

Jeff Greenberg, Photographer

Illus. **14-5**

Attractive, spacious interiors result in increased sales for retail businesses. How have the retailers in your community changed the ways their products are displayed?

Ethical Issues

SOCIAL RESPONSIBILITY SELLS

Questions:

1 Do you believe social responsibility and environmental consciousness are fads or do they represent long-term consumer concerns?

2 Why do appeals such as those described above work for some people but not for others?

3 What companies and products are you aware of that use social and environmental responsibility as an important buying motive to promote their products or services?

Adapted from: Hemispheres, May, 1993, pp. 25-28.

The chairman in a Benetton ad says, "I want my clothes back," to encourage people to recycle. The president of another clothing manufacturer, Patagonia, says in a radio interview, "Buy fewer products, but buy excellent products that are going to last." While fewer items are sold to each customer, profits are high.

We have come to believe that marketing means sell as much of your product as you can. But a changing philosophy of careful consumption is resulting in success for companies that are targeting the growing number of consumers who are motivated by social and environmental responsibility.

Are you more likely to buy a product if the direct mail flyer promoting it is printed on recycled paper? Will an endorsement from Ralph Nader testifying that a company is pro-environment encourage you to switch brands? One telephone company promotes its long-distance service with the direct appeal, "Save money, change the world." They direct some of their revenues to environmental and consumer causes.

For many consumers, those appeals work. They do not want to be seen as the typical consumer who has to buy the latest fad or believes that everything is made to be thrown away. They are turned off by traditional promotional appeals and do not respond to the usual advertising media. That doesn't mean they do not buy. They are just interested in buying from companies that understand their motives and share their values.

How does a company attract that audience? Through the careful design and selection of products and direct promotional appeals. The Body Shop sells bath oils, soaps, and lotions. It promotes ecologically safe products and a commitment to "the cultural integrity of indigenous people." The Kapalua Land Company promotes travel packages to Hawaii as "eco-packages" where you can enjoy an island vacation "while helping to preserve the environment." Even one Crystal Pepsi promotion stated, "Only wildlife needs preserving."

Using socially responsible appeals does not guarantee a business' success. First, consumers must sort through the message to identify the product. Next, the consumers in this segment will want evidence that the company is sincere and that it means what it says. Finally, companies must be concerned about the effect of the promotions on other customers. Will the environmental appeal lose as many customers as it gains?

SELF-SERVICE MERCHANDISING

Modern store fixtures and packaging methods have resulted in such effective displays of merchandise that the use of self-service merchandise has increased greatly. In **self-service merchandising**, customers select the products they want to purchase, take them to a cashier or checkout counter, and pay for them. Self-service stores have only a few salespeople to aid customers in making selections. Most employees receive and stock merchandise in the store.

Marketing specialists generally agree that successful self-service merchandising requires products that do not need to be demonstrated or explained, that have well-known brand names, and that are packaged so that they can be easily handled. The display of merchandise in self-service stores should attract attention and make it convenient for the shopper to examine the merchandise. The labels on the merchandise should provide adequate information about the merchandise for the shopper.

TRUTH IN ADVERTISING AND SELLING

There has been a continuing belief by many consumers that advertisers and salespeople cannot be trusted. They feel that much of the information provided is misleading and that some is actually false. While most promotion is accurate and honest, there are examples of businesses who intentionally mislead consumers with their promotions. Businesses, consumers groups, and government are concerned about those practices.

The Council of Better Business Bureaus has established standards to be followed in selling and advertising. The Council is made up of businesses concerned about honest and fair practices. The purpose is to assist customers in resolving problems with businesses and to identify those businesses that regularly receive consumer complaints. Particular attention is given to misleading statements, misinformation, or lack of information necessary for making good purchasing decisions.

Laws and regulations exist that affect the promotional efforts of businesses. Nationally, the Federal Trade Commission and the Federal Communications Commission are responsible for the regulation of promotion. False advertising is a violation of the law. **False advertising** is defined by federal law as "misleading in a material respect" or in any way that could influence the customer's purchase or use of the product.

To protect consumers, advertisers are required to use **full disclosure**, providing all information necessary for consumers to make an informed decision. They must also use **substantiation**; that is, be able to prove all claims made about products and services in promotions.

If businesses violate laws and regulations in their advertising, they may face three types of penalties from the regulating agencies. They may be asked to **cease and desist**, which requires that the company stop using specific advertisements. In situations where consumers have been harmed by the advertising, the company may be required to use corrective advertising. With **corrective**

advertising, the company must use a specific amount of its advertising budget to run new advertisements correcting the misleading information. In unusual situations, the company may have to pay a fine to the government or to consumers harmed by illegal advertising.

Long-term business success is built on honesty and fair practices. A business person may occasionally be tempted to exaggerate or to imitate a competitor who seems to be stretching the truth. In the long run, however, it does not pay to destroy the confidence of customers. If customers do not get what they believed was promised to them in advertisements or by salespeople, they will likely not return to the business again. On the other hand, a satisfied customer is often an important source of promotion for a business.

CHAPTER REVIEW 14

BUILDING VOCABULARY POWER

Define the following terms and concepts.

1. advertising
2. advertising media
3. drive time
4. prime time
5. shopping channels
6. infomercials
7. direct advertising
8. personal selling
9. buying motives
10. objections
11. suggestion selling
12. self-service merchandising
13. false advertising
14. full disclosure
15. substantiation
16. cease and desist
17. corrective advertising

REVIEWING FACTS

1. Name five categories of advertising and give two examples of media for each category.
2. Compare newspaper advertising with direct advertising.
3. Explain the importance of frequency of advertising.
4. Explain why consumers and businesses are concerned about telemarketing.
5. What are some of the most common buying motives?
6. List five sources of assistance available to small businesses for planning advertising programs.
7. What are the four elements of selling?
8. Where can a salesperson obtain information about the products he or she sells?

9. Name four kinds of suggestion selling.
10. What should a salesperson do when a customer asks a question?
11. Describe the importance of followup as a part of personal selling.
12. What is the purpose of coupons?
13. List five promotional aids that manufacturers often provide for retailers.
14. How are most employees used in self-service merchandising?
15. What types of penalties can be applied to businesses using illegal advertising?

Discussing Ideas

1. Why is the cost for television advertising between 6 p.m. and 11 p.m. the most expensive?
2. Name some types of business firms that could benefit from advertising in a school newspaper.
3. Announcements in newspapers of engagements and approaching weddings could be a mailing list source for what kinds of businesses?
4. Discuss several characteristics that you believe would be desirable in a salesperson and give a specific example of the importance of each.
5. Explain how a salesperson's lack of knowledge about products can cause problems for a company.
6. What should the training of salespeople include?
7. Why are some stores using less self-service merchandising and more personal selling today?
8. Why are coupons an effective booster of sales?
9. Why should manufacturers and wholesalers help retailers with promotions?
10. Describe some types of promotional practices you think are unfair.

Analyzing Information

1. A book and gift store that has average annual sales of $700,000 spends 3 percent of its sales for advertising. The store's advertising budget is divided as follows: catalogs, 30 percent; calendars and other sales promotions, 7 percent; window displays, 15 percent; newspaper advertising, 15 percent; direct mail, 20 percent; and miscellaneous, 13 percent.
   a. How much is the average annual advertising budget?
   b. What is the amount spent on each type of advertising?
2. Obtain a sample of direct mail advertising. Evaluate it concerning its effectiveness in the following areas: (a) attractiveness, (b) ability to attract attention, (c) specific information, and (d) effectiveness of promotion.
3. From a local newspaper office find out (a) what types of help they will provide for a business in preparing advertising, and (b) the costs of advertising in the newspaper.

4. Assume that you are a salesperson in a furniture store. Explain how you can make appeals to several buying motives when selling a sofa sleeper to a customer.

5. For an upcoming school activity, develop an effective plan for using tele-marketing to inform and interest people in the activity.

S OLVING BUSINESS PROBLEMS

CASE 14-1

Anthony and Fontella were discussing how companies use advertising. Their conversation follows:

Anthony: Companies spend too much money on advertising. If they would spend less, the prices of products would be a lot lower.

Fontella: Advertising is used to get people to buy products they don't want. Companies should not have to advertise good products.

Anthony: The worst thing about advertising is that businesses can say anything they want to about products, even if the statements are untrue. You won't know what is wrong with the product until you have bought it, and then it is too late.

Required:
1. Do you believe product prices would decrease if companies did not advertise? Explain.
2. Do good products need to be advertised?
3. What types of controls are there on what a business can say in its advertising? Can customers do anything if they have been misled by advertising?

CASE 14-2

Korie Wager is manager of the Denim Duds Shop, a retail store in a shopping center that specializes in selling jeans and related clothing to young people. The town is served by a daily newspaper, three radio stations, and one television station. Ms. Wager has budgeted $8,000 to be spent on advertising for the year.

Required:
1. Identify the method or methods of advertising Ms. Wager should use and give reasons for your choice.
2. If Korie is going to use radio advertising, how should she select the radio station to use?
3. Suggest one idea for a window display that would encourage young people to come into the store.
4. List the types of training Korie should provide for her salespeople.

REVIEW 14

Unit Summary

4-1 *Describe major marketing activities and how businesses make effective marketing decisions.*

Many people who are not involved in marketing have a narrow view of marketing activities. They may think of advertising or selling as having the same meaning as marketing. Marketing is much broader than that. It involves all of the activities that occur as products and services are exchanged between a producer and consumer.

The major marketing activities include buying, selling, transporting, storing, financing, research and information gathering, risk taking, and grading and valuing. Each of the activities must be performed as products and services are exchanged. Effective businesses determine the best and least expensive ways to complete the marketing activities. Often, many businesses are involved in marketing as products move from the place they are produced to the consumer.

Marketing has changed a great deal as businesses have become more competitive and as consumers become more aware of choices. No longer will most customers accept whatever a business wants to provide. Businesses must study customer needs and respond with the right product, in the right place, at the right time and right price.

4-2 *Identify the factors considered when developing a product for sale.*

Developing an effective product is a real challenge for businesses. The production and manufacturing process must be carefully developed. Some products are individually developed for a specific customer while others are mass produced on an assembly line. Many new products are created each year, but only a small percentage are successfully sold for a long period of time.

Businesses must look at a number of factors when planning products. They study customer needs, the products offered by competitors, and economic conditions before deciding whether to produce or sell a new product.

Research is an important part of new product planning. Engineers and scientists design and test new product ideas. Marketers complete consumer research and market tests to determine customer needs and reactions to new product ideas.

UNIT SUMMARY

After a decision is made to produce a product, the business needs to organize the procedures for manufacturing and marketing. Suppliers of raw materials and other parts and supplies must be identified. Equipment needs to be purchased and personnel trained. Budgets are prepared to insure that needed resources are available.

4-3 *Diagram alternative channels of distribution and show the activities involved in moving products through the channel.*

A channel of distribution is the businesses involved in moving a product from the producer to the consumer. In a direct channel of distribution, only the producer and the final consumer participate. In an indirect channel of distribution, other businesses in addition to the producer are involved in performing some of the marketing activities. The common types of businesses in an indirect channel are wholesalers and retailers.

Markets for most products are located throughout the country and even throughout the world. Product transportation is an important marketing activity. Businesses must determine the requirements for transportation including how rapidly products need to be moved, the product handling and storage requirements, and the cost of each method. Common methods of transportation include truck, railroad, airplane, ship, and pipeline.

Product-handling procedures are an important part of the distribution process. If products are mishandled, orders can be lost, can arrive late, or can be damaged. Product handling includes order processing, appropriate buildings and equipment, and training the people who are responsible for product-handling activities.

4-4 *Discuss the procedures used by businesses to purchase products and to establish prices for resale.*

Just as consumers make purchases, businesses also must buy products and services. Those purchases are used in the production and manufacture of products, in the operation of the businesses, or for resale to customers. Because most businesses operate in a very competitive environment, purchasing must be done carefully in order for the business to make a profit.

Specific procedures are designed and followed for purchasing. Most large businesses have a specific purchasing department and specific people responsible for completing purchasing activities. That department works closely with the department needing the products, with the accounting department, and with the company selling the products during the purchasing procedure.

Once products are purchased for resale to customers, prices need to be set. Again, pricing procedures are important so that a price is set that is satisfying to customers, is competitive, and provides a profit for the company. The people responsible for pricing decisions must understand pricing terms and various methods of determining prices. Managers and employees need to be aware of the factors that lead to increases in costs and to markdowns in prices. Keeping costs and markdowns as low as possible also increases the profits for a company.

4-5 *Explain several methods that can be used to promote products and services effectively.*

Even if a business has a good product, it still may not be successful. Customers must be aware of the product and see how the product will satisfy their needs better than alternative products. Promotion is the marketing activity that businesses use to communicate with the customer.

The two major types of promotion are advertising and personal selling. Advertising is used to communicate a common message to a large number of people. Personal selling is used when the business wants to communicate more specific messages with one or a very few customers at a time.

There are many advertising media from which a business can choose. Types of media can be grouped into five categories: publication, mass media, outdoor, direct, and display media. Media are selected based on the audiences they reach, their ability to communicate specific messages, cost, and timing.

Professional salespeople are often among the highest-paid employees of a company. Effective salespeople understand the wants of the customers and their buying motives. They then use product information to translate the product information into buyer benefits. They demonstrate the product so the customer understands how the product is used. The customer is involved in the demonstration to become comfortable with the product and to increase interest in owning it. The salesperson observes and listens to the customer and answers any questions. When the customer appears satisfied with the product, the salesperson will attempt to close the sale. Suggestion selling and followup are important procedures after the sale to insure customer satisfaction.

Several other promotional methods are available to businesses in addition to advertising and personal selling. Each has a specific purpose. Coupons attract customers into a business to take advantage of a special price reduction. Manufacturer and dealer aids are display and promotional materials provided to retailers that call attention to specific brands and featured products. Businesses use window and interior displays to create a positive image and to attract customers' attention to products that can be found in the business. Businesses that use self-service merchandising must be particularly effective with promotional tools since customers are responsible for locating and evaluating products.

Many of the complaints of consumers toward businesses result from dishonest or misleading advertising and promotion. Business organizations, consumer groups, and the government attempt to control the misuse of promotion. Businesses who misuse promotion can be required to correct the misleading information and can even be fined.

INSURANCE

Financing

Tax Guide for
Small Business

5

*F*inancial Management

OBJECTIVES

5-1 Describe types of records, record systems, and budgets needed in running a business.

5-2 Discuss the need for and use of such financial tools as the income statement, balance sheet, working capital, and cash flow.

5-3 Distinguish among three major kinds of capital (owner capital, borrowed capital, and retained earnings) and among various types, sources, and procedures for obtaining capital.

5-4 Explain the characteristics of bank and nonbank financial institutions and the financial instruments provided to investors.

5-5 Identify and describe credit plans, credit cards, credit policies, collection procedures, and credit analysis methods.

5-6 Discuss the significance of insurance to businesses, common types of policies, and how noninsurable risks can be reduced.

"From the time I took out my first bank loan—the $1,800 to buy that ice cream machine for the Ben Franklin down in Newport—I was never really comfortable with debt. But I recognized it as a necessity of doing business, and I had gotten pretty good at accumulating it. For a while, I would just go down to the local bank and borrow whatever I could to build a store or buy something we needed to grow the business. That practice had gotten me in debt to practically every bank in Arkansas and southern Missouri. They believed in what we had done up to that point, and they believed we would pay them off. I always did . . . , but sometimes I would borrow from one to pay the other . . . ."

Sam Walton
MADE IN AMERICA:
MY STORY, 1992

Professional Profile

A LEADER IN BUSINESS DEVELOPMENT

Can a career in the United States Secret Service prepare you for business management? Dario Marquez, Jr., spent eight years as a special agent. After years of ignoring minorities for employment, the Secret Service became more active in recruitment and promotion. Mr. Marquez credits those efforts for his interest in becoming an agent and the opportunity to be hired.

Because of the expertise gained in the Secret Service, he has given expert testimony to the U.S. Senate Committee on Terrorism and has made presentations to many corporations and law enforcement groups on criminal behavior, terrorism, and security operations. He later formed a security services company with two other agents.

MVM, Inc., works with other businesses to help them protect their resources. The company provides security management services, executive protection, security planning, and security personnel training. In 1992, the company was ranked 29th on Inc. magazine's list of the 500 fastest-growing businesses. Its annual sales put the company in the top 100 of the Hispanic Business 500, a list of the largest Hispanic-owned businesses. With over 1,000 employees, the company is in the top 10 of the largest employers on the same list.

Throughout his career in private security, Mr. Marquez has seen a reluctance among many managers in the United States to deal with companies that are not headed by white males. He believes, however, that business executives value success. Minority-owned companies that are able to establish a reputation for quality and effectiveness will ultimately be accepted.

INSPIRATIONAL IDEAS

Dario O. Marquez, Jr.
Cofounder and
President,
MVM, Inc.

"I believe in five principles that contribute to business success. The first is strength of will—the courage of your convictions. The second is vision—a clear focus and direction. Next is judgment —to make sound, high-quality decisions in a timely fashion. Communication enables a leader to inspire, motivate, guide, direct, and listen. The final factor is values or business ethics—the belief system a business person uses to deal with others that reflects his or her character."

Photo courtesy of MVM, Inc.

FINANCIAL RECORDS IN A BUSINESS

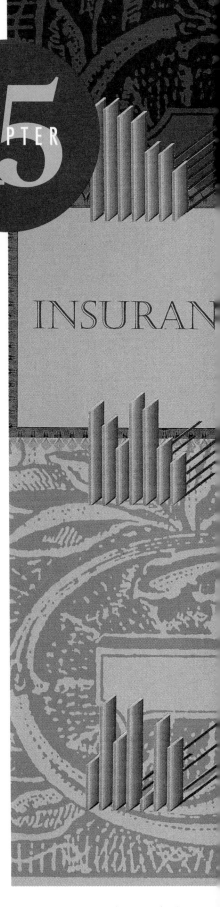

CHAPTER 15

After studying this chapter you will be able to:

15-1 Discuss recordkeeping systems needed in different businesses.

15-2 Identify and discuss types of records used in business.

15-3 Define depreciation, obsolescence, and other accounting terms.

15-4 Give two reasons why assets should be safeguarded against damage or loss.

15-5 Describe different types of business budgets.

15-6 Explain how budgets are used to run businesses efficiently.

J amie walked the two blocks from his three-year-old car rental business to the bank. He always liked going to the bank with his deposits. Of course, his favorite teller, Marcia, often scolded him for not doing the paperwork. But then, she always did it for him.

This morning was different, however. His business had done so well this past week, he felt uneasy carrying today's large deposit. While most of the deposit wasn't cash, he still thought he needed a better way to keep track of receipts and payments. As he walked inside the bank, he recalled that his accountant had told him last month to keep better records.

"Good morning, Marcia," said Jamie. "I've got a stack for you today!" Marcia greeted Jamie, but she looked unhappy. "Jamie, that stack will take me forever to

*complete. Haven't you gotten someone to help you with your books?" "Not really,"
Jamie replied, "but I'm thinking about it." Marcia smiled. "You've been thinking
about it for over a year. How do you know if you're really making any money?
Last month you overdrew your account. And you're overdrawn again. My boss
wants to see you right away."*

*Jamie knew he had to keep better records, but thought nothing could cloud his
image of today's big deposit. Clearly, the most tangible reward that any business
owner gets is profit.*

Ilus. 15-1

Businesses must keep accurate records.
Why do you also need to keep
records for your personal needs?

Without profits, it would be impossible for companies to remain in business.
Some method, therefore, is needed to determine how a business is doing financially. **Accounting records** are financial records of the transactions of the business. Because accounting information is used to make numerous important
decisions, these records must be carefully kept. Some valuable information
obtained from accounting records includes:

- Kinds and values of assets.
- Amounts of various debts owed by the business.
- Amounts owed to the business.
- Cash balance in the bank and cash on hand.
- Amount of cash sales and credit sales.
- Kinds and amounts of expenses.
- Merchandise bought and sold.
- Profit or loss.
- Trends in sales, expenses, profits, and net worth.
- Comparisons with other similar businesses.

Financial records are handled in various ways. The business owner can keep the records personally, employ a full-time or part-time accounting clerk, use an accounting service organization, or establish an accounting department. The way records are handled is determined, in part, by the record system adopted by the business.

RECORD SYSTEMS

Systems for keeping accounting records may be simple or complex, and they may require no equipment or be highly computerized. Regardless of the type of record system a company selects, the system must be easy to use and must be designed to provide timely and accurate information. The type of record system used is based on the nature of the business. Therefore, we will look at manual and computer systems and at systems for small and large businesses.

MANUAL SYSTEM

Accounting records are not difficult to keep. Standardized forms can be purchased at office supply stores. Trade associations, such as those of service stations and hardware stores, supply their business members with standard forms. Model sets of records are also available from some cash register manufacturers. In these systems, no special equipment is generally needed; the records are usually kept by hand. When a business has only a small number of records, manual systems can be practical and rather inexpensive to maintain.

COMPUTER SYSTEM

In many offices, computers are used to perform tasks that were formerly done manually or by simple machines. Whenever it is necessary to perform repetitive clerical operations and to store large amounts of information, computers are useful because they handle these operations quickly and at a lower cost. Depending on the volume of information to be processed and the way information is to be used, a business must decide whether to process information manually, purchase computer equipment, or hire the services of a data processing service center.

A **data processing service center** is a special type of business that processes data for other businesses for a fee. A business delivers data to the service center on a daily, weekly, or monthly basis. In return, the service center processes the data and prepares reports that the business needs. Many business firms use a data processing service center to perform such tasks as preparing bills for customers, keeping track of inventory bought and sold, and preparing payroll records and checks. A business can have many routine operations processed efficiently by a service center.

Various types of computers and computer-like equipment are available. A discussion of computers and data processing is found in Chapter 8.

Illus. 15-2

Many businesses use computerized accounting systems. Can you think of any types of businesses that can run efficiently without computers?

Phil Cantor/UNIPHOTO

SYSTEMS IN SMALL BUSINESSES

Small business firms, especially retail stores, do not need elaborate records. Many such businesses use a cash register as a basis for obtaining most of the information for their financial records. An example of a financial record that might be kept by a small retail business is shown in Fig. 15-1. If a business uses a cash register that shows detailed kinds of transactions, needed information can be taken from the cash register tape (or audit strip) and copied on the daily balance form.

A special form listing the daily cash payments should be kept. Many cash registers show these amounts on the daily audit slip. In the absence of an adequate cash register, a written record of all types of sales and other receipts and payments should be made throughout the day.

SYSTEMS IN LARGE BUSINESSES

Advanced systems for keeping records are generally required in large firms. Accounting departments usually maintain these records. An accounting department is commonly divided into several sections. Each section is typically responsible for handling one or more phases of accounting, such as cash records, receipt and payment records, depreciation records, and tax and payroll records.

Most large firms, and many small ones, use cash registers that are connected to computers. Such a register is called a **point-of-sale terminal**. When cashiers use bar code scanners to record sales, for example, each item sold is subtracted from the inventory recorded in the computer. The computer calculates when merchandise reordering is necessary (based on predetermined inventory needs)

DAILY BALANCE FORM

Store Name .... O.A. ......   Prepared by .. Hal Vogel ....   Date Mar. 8, 19---

	RESET TOTALS OF REG. (SALES)	RESET TOTALS OF REG. (RETURNS AND VOIDS)	NET REGISTER TOTALS
DEPT. 1 Meat	7,020. 00	108. 00	6,912. 00
DEPT. 2 Produce	2,106. 00	54. 00	2,052. 00
DEPT. 3 Deli	1,404. 00	-0-	1,409. 00
DEPT. 4 Grocery	21,060. 00	81. 00	20,979. 00
DEPT. 5 Frozen food	2,808. 00	27. 00	2,781. 00
DEPT. 6 Household	702. 00	13. 50	688. 50
DEPT. 7			
TAX			
TOTAL			
CASH	35,100. 00	283. 50	34,816. 50
CHARGE	675. 00	-0-	675. 00
TOTAL	35,775. 00	283. 50	35,775. 00
ACCT. NO.	CH0079		
REC'D ON ACCT.			
CASH			
TOTAL			
CASH RETURNS	(X Reed Cash Total) ⟶		OTHER INCOME
ACCT. NO.			TOTAL
LAYAWAY PAYMENTS REFUND	(X Reed R. A/C) ⟶		
TOTAL			
PAID OUTS		RETURNS AND VOIDS / MDSE. AND EXP.	( )
CASH TO BE ACCOUNTED FOR			34,816. 50
ACTUAL CASH			34,816. 50
CASH OVER OR SHORT			-0-

PAID OUTS TO DR. & CR	$ KEPT ON RET.	P.O. AMOUNT	D.R. CODE	ACCOUNTS RECEIVABLE CONTROL	
#1				BEGINNING ACCTS. RECEIVABLE	
#2				NET CHARGES TODAY	675. 00
#3				TOTAL	675. 00
#4				LESS: NET REC'D ON ACCT. TODAY	
#5					
#6				ENDING ACCTS. RECEIVABLE	675. 00
#7				• DATA PROCESSING NO.	
#8				• TODAY'S DATE	
#9				• CASH SHORT DR. ___ CR. ___	-0-
CREDIT CODE	CR MISC. INC.			• CASH OVER DR. ___ CR. ___	-0-
AUDITOR'S CREDIT •				•	
MARK DOWNS OR UNITS					
PURCHASES AT RETAIL OR SALES AT COST					
Register Totals					

Fig. 15-1

The cash register often provides the information shown on this daily balance form.

and provides other valuable information for management. With point-of-sale terminals, scanners electronically read product codes stamped on merchandise, thereby speeding the checkout service for customers. Most large retail stores today use scanners to make their accounting systems more efficient.

TYPES OF RECORDS

Accounting records in all types of businesses have many similar characteristics, but they differ in some respects because of the nature of each business. The kinds of records that a business uses also depend on the size of the business. Some of the most common records kept by all businesses are discussed next.

Management Close-Up

VIKING OFFICE PRODUCTS INC.

Questions:

1 What are three types of firms from which a business can purchase office products?

2 What features attract small- and medium-size firms to buy office products from Viking?

3 By what percent did sales increase over the last three years?

4 What will total sales be next year if the projected sales of 41 percent are met?

Source: Annual Reports and Thompson Financial Networks Inc., 1993.

For decades, the traditional approach to buying office products such as paper and desks was to find a local office supply store. Today there are two other choices. One may buy from a superstore that sells office products at substantial discounts. Office Warehouse and Staples are examples of superstore competitors usually found in highly populated areas. Another growing choice for businesses is to make purchases by phone from a catalog.

Viking Office Products Inc. is a direct catalog mail marketer that sells stationery, computer supplies, office furniture, fax paper, and general office supplies. Viking is the second largest and fastest growing direct marketer. With an 800-telephone number and a catalog of brand-name products, Viking has made its mark. Firms with under one hundred employees are its main customers. And cost and convenience are its strong selling weapons. Price discounts on brand name products range from 30 to 50 percent less than prices found in traditional office supply stores.

No delivery charges on orders over $25 and delivery within two business days have accelerated Viking's growth rate. Add to that a one-year guarantee, a 30-day free trial on all products, and free pickup of any merchandise returned, and the result is plenty of repeat customers.

Success is further attributed to superior customer service that is achieved, in part, through efficient business operations. A sophisticated computer system keeps track of all of Viking's sales records. That is not an easy task when you have 6,600 different items to sell to customers in the United States and Europe. An analysis of customer purchases permits Viking to tailor-make special catalogs and to offer special sales that attract new customers and retain repeat customers.

Sales of $132 million three years ago sounds good for any office supplier, but Viking's current sales have since grown to $320 million. Not only are sales up in the United States, but recent entry into foreign markets has speeded Viking's expansion. Sales in England and France have been rapid. Other European nations will soon add to Viking's accelerated growth. The sales budget for the next year is set to increase 41 percent. Low prices, outstanding customer service, and good management practices should allow Viking Office Products Inc. to meet or exceed its sales forecast.

ACCOUNTING FOR CASH

A cash register or point-of-sale terminal is used in most retail businesses for handling cash transactions. Regardless of whether a business employs a book-keeper or whether the records are kept by the owner of the business, similar procedures must be followed in accounting for cash. Several suggestions for the safe handling of cash are listed in Fig. 15-2.

ig. **15-2**

Suggestions for the safe handling of cash.

1. **A petty cash fund, adequate for small emergency payments, should be kept in a safe place with someone responsible for it. A written record of all money put into the fund and all money paid out must be kept. Receipts for payments should be obtained where possible, and the fund should be replenished by check to provide a further record.**
2. **If a cash register is used, small emergency payments can be made out of cash register funds instead of through a petty cash fund, but adequate records of payments must be made and receipts obtained.**
3. **If a cash register is used, there should be a daily change fund of a fixed amount, which is never deposited in the bank but is kept available to start each day's operations. This fund should be counted and verified daily.**
4. **All receipts should be deposited in a bank account.**
5. **Make payments by check for all items except small emergency payments.**
6. **Verify by a double check any cash overages or cash shortages in the daily transactions.**
7. **Do not keep any more cash in the office than is necessary and, if convenient, make more than one deposit in the bank daily.**
8. **Pay salaries by check instead of by cash.**
9. **Audit regularly the amounts received on account.**
10. **Audit regularly the receipts by comparing them with the bank deposits you have made.**
11. **Audit regularly the actual cash paid out by comparing the check stubs with bills paid.**
12. **Endorse all checks for deposit with a company rubber stamp or, when signing checks for endorsement, write "For deposit only."**
13. **Reconcile the monthly bank statement promptly and regularly as explained in Chapter 18.**

In accounting for cash, a special problem arises when a business wants to make payments of small amounts of money quickly. For example, a store may need a small box of paper clips that can be purchased at a nearby store. Businesses usually make small payments in two ways. When a cash register is used and there is no special petty cash fund, the usual practice is to take cash from the register and replace it with a petty cash voucher, such as the one

Jeff Greenberg, Photographer

shown in Fig. 15-3, in the cash register drawer. When money is put aside (often in a special box or drawer) for a petty cash fund, a petty cash record is kept that shows why cash was given and the reason for the payment.

It is very important to watch a bank account carefully in accounting for cash.

A bank normally provides a monthly statement that should be compared with the checkbook. If the checkbook balance does not agree with the bank's monthly statement balance, the reasons for the difference must be determined. The process of bringing the checkbook balance and bank statement balance into agreement is discussed in Chapter 18.

Fig. 15-3
A petty cash voucher.

PETTY CASH VOUCHER

NO. 6   DATE February 9, 19--

PAID TO Sims Computer Service

FOR Printer Ribbons   AMOUNT 28 50

CHARGE TO Miscellaneous Expenses

PAYMENT RECEIVED: Helen Jones

REED AND MALLOCH

APPROVED BY George Ajax

RECEIPT AND PAYMENT RECORDS

All business firms must deal with money that is received as a result of the sale of goods or services to customers. Because many businesses sell on credit, careful records must be kept showing what each customer owes and pays. This record is called an **accounts receivable record**. When a sale is made, the salesperson completes an appropriate form, such as the one shown in Fig. 15-4. The information on this form is transferred to the accounts receivable record. Money owed to the business and money received from customers is recorded daily on these records.

A record must also be kept to show money owed and payments made by a business. When a business buys such items as supplies and merchandise, it often does so on credit. As a result, an **accounts payable record** must be kept showing money owed and payments made by the business.

NO. 7382   DEPT. *Furniture*   DATE *Feb. 17*, 19 -- --

NAME *Barbara Linkenheimer Associates*

ADDRESS *Main Street*

CITY *Princeton, NJ 08540 - 1245*

SOLD BY		CASH	C O D	CHARGE	ON ACCT	MDSE RETD	PAID OUT	
		DESCRIPTION					PRICE	AMOUNT
4	1	Chairs, No. 75-A					450 –	1800	00
1	2	Table, No. 120-B					2500 –	2500	00
	3								
	4								
	5								
	6								
	7								
	8								
	9								
	10							4300	00
	11	Tax at 6%						258	00
	12							4558	00
	13								

CUSTOMER'S ORDER NO.	REC'D BY

REDIFORM
5S34   **KEEP THIS SLIP FOR REFERENCE**

DEPRECIATION RECORDS

Every business person should recognize the problems that result from a decrease in the value of property through use. For example, a service station owner buys a piece of equipment that costs $1,600. The owner knows from experience that at the end of five years the equipment will not be worth any more than its value as junk, about $100. It is estimated, therefore, that the equipment will wear out at the average rate of $300 a year:

$$\$1,600 - \$100 = \$1,500; \quad \$1,500 \div 5 \text{ years} = \$300.$$

When this asset loses its usefulness, it must be replaced.

Fixed assets, or **plant assets**, are material assets that will last a long time—land, equipment, and buildings, for example. Except for land, fixed assets tend to lose their value over time. Fixed assets are recorded on the books of a business when they are purchased. They become part of the property owned by the business. As they wear out or become less valuable, the business is allowed by law to charge the loss in value each year as an operating expense.

The general term that is applied to such a decrease in the value of an asset due to wear and age is **depreciation**. Property may also decrease in value because of **obsolescence**; that is, the asset may become out of date, or it may become inadequate for a particular purpose. For all practical purposes, however, any decrease in the value of an asset can be considered depreciation. A cash register, for instance, may wear out gradually, or it may become obsolete.

The loss due to depreciation is very real, although it usually cannot be computed with great accuracy. Any business that fails to recognize depreciation is failing to observe good business principles. The depreciation of assets is part of the cost of doing business. When equipment is worn out, it must be replaced. If money is not available to replace the equipment, the business may be seriously handicapped.

SPECIAL ASSET RECORDS

Financial statements provide information on such items as insurance, fixed assets, and real property, but they do not provide detailed information about these assets. As a result, a business must keep special records. For example, a business should maintain a precise record of insurance policies showing such details as type of policy, the company from which it was purchased, amount, premium, the purchase and expiration dates, and the amount to be charged each month as insurance expense. A detailed special record should also be maintained for all fixed assets, such as filing cabinets and forklifts, providing such information as asset description, date of purchase, cost, monthly depreciation expense, and **asset book value**—original cost less accumulated depreciation. Special records provide additional information that is helpful to management.

TAX RECORDS

The federal income tax law requires every business to keep satisfactory records so that its income and expenses can be reported. Preparation of an income tax return for a small business is relatively simple; however, both small and large firms use the services of tax accountants. The information needed for the income tax return of a business can be obtained from any good set of business records.

Employers are required to withhold a certain percentage of the wages of each employee for federal income tax purposes. Each employee is required to fill out a card regarding family status. From a table furnished by the Internal Revenue Service, the employer can determine the amount to withhold from each paycheck. Periodically, these withholdings must be paid by the employer to the Internal Revenue Service.

Most employers have to pay social security taxes for old-age benefits and unemployment compensation payments. The employer is also required to withhold taxes from each employee's wages for social security purposes. The business is required to pay to the federal government its own taxes and those withheld from employees.

PAYROLL RECORDS

In order to keep satisfactory payroll records to provide the information needed by the business owner and to satisfy federal and state authorities, businesses must keep complete records for all employees and show the hours worked, regular wages, overtime wages, and all types of deductions from wages for each employee. It is from these records that an employer makes regular reports. A simple set of payroll records is shown in Fig. 15-5.

This line may be used to write in earnings other than cash, such as meals furnished, etc.

Hours worked have been filled in here to illustrate how this line is used if employee is paid on an hourly basis or if employer desires to keep a record of the number of hours worked by each employee. Overtime work and pay may be recorded and computed in the line shown as "Additional."

Here you may account for cash advanced or for merchandise given in place of cash to employee.

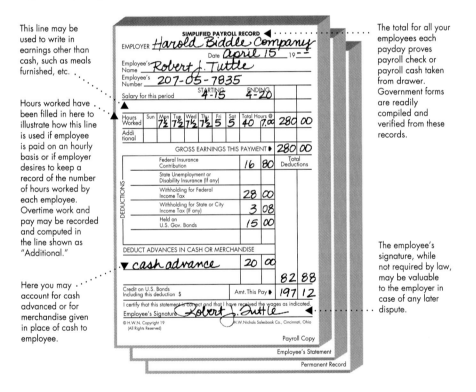

The total for all your employees each payday proves payroll check or payroll cash taken from drawer. Government forms are readily compiled and verified from these records.

The employee's signature, while not required by law, may be valuable to the employer in case of any later dispute.

A simplified payroll record.

USING AND KEEPING RECORDS

Business records should be accurately maintained and always up to date. A convenient filing system that permits quick and accurate storage and retrieval of financial records is essential. Common filing systems are arranged in one or more of the following ways: alphabetically, numerically, geographically, and by subject. Office supply firms and filing equipment companies usually recommend appropriate filing systems for various kinds of businesses.

The financial records, including the accounts of customers and all other vital information, should be protected from such hazards as fire and theft. Many records, such as the accounts of customers, might not be stolen but could easily be destroyed by fire. Every office, therefore, should have a fireproof safe or vault for such records. Fireproof filing cabinets are also available. Valuable documents, such as deeds, leases, and contracts, should be placed in safety deposit boxes if there is no adequate protection in the office.

Information stored in computers and in computer files should also be protected from damage or loss caused by various conditions. For example, computers are often placed in climate-controlled settings, such as air-conditioned offices. Backup generators and battery systems are often installed to protect computer information from electric power failures. Damage to computer information may also be caused by people who might steal, alter, or destroy data. For this reason, business firms usually restrict entrance to computer centers to authorized workers only.

B UDGET SYSTEMS

Budgeting is critical to financial success. A study conducted by the United States Department of Commerce reveals that stores that budget their financial operations are more successful than stores that do not budget. The stores that are most successful are those that (a) keep recommended accounting records, (b) have their accounts audited or checked by an experienced accountant, (c) take an inventory of merchandise more than once a year, and (d) operate under a financial budget. All new businesses should create a business plan, as pointed out in Chapter 5, that contains a financial plan and a budget for the first year or two of operations.

A **budget** is a financial plan extending usually for one year. A budget requires the setting of goals and the timely comparison of actual results with these goals. A budget helps a business manage and control operations. Often, a budget may help keep expenses in line with income. Overbuying can be prevented and borrowing can be anticipated.

Actual budgeting procedures depend on the type of business. For a small business, the process is mostly one of budgeting sales, expenses, purchases, and cash. For large businesses, budgeting is more complicated, as is indicated in Fig. 15-6.

Budgeting procedure for a manufacturing business.

1. The estimate of sales is based on past experience and future expectations. As will be explained later, there is more than one method of making this estimate.
2. The advertising budget is based on expected sales and on the amount that the company should spend to promote new products and open new territories.
3. The production plans should be based on the expected sales of the individual products. It is, therefore, necessary to take into consideration the production capacity of the business and the equipment needed.
4. The purchasing requirements are based on expected sales and production. Purchases must be made far enough in advance to allow time for delivery and production. It is, therefore, necessary to be familiar with the times of the year when sales are the greatest.
5. In a large manufacturing business, it is necessary to anticipate labor requirements. The labor budget must, therefore, be based on production requirements.
6. The budget of administrative costs, office costs, and costs of supplies must be based on all previously mentioned factors.
7. The complete budget is made up after all of the preceding budgets have been made.
8. The cash budget, which is explained later in this chapter, is a budget that shows the cash balance that can be expected at any particular time. Such a budget is necessary when a company anticipates borrowing.

TYPES OF BUDGETS

The final overall budget for a business is made up of several other budgets, such as the sales budget, the merchandising budget, the advertising budget, the cash budget, the capital budget, and the income statement budget. Most individual budgets are based on sales projections. At times, however, in some types of businesses, either the production capacity or the financial capacity must be determined first. Sales and all other estimates are then based on the ability to produce.

The traffic manager, the office manager, the employment manager, and the engineer in a large production plant must know about all of the individual budgets because their departments are affected by budget requirements. The small business obviously will not have such a detailed set of budgets as that described previously. It will, however, be concerned with budgeting sales, purchases, expenses, and cash.

Illus. 15-4

Managers from all departments develop and discuss budgets. Because budgets are based on estimates or projections, should managers give them much attention?

Tim Brown/Tony Stone Images

SALES BUDGET

The **sales budget** is strictly a forecast of the sales for a month, a few months, or a year. Estimated sales could be based on such areas as sales territories, sales representatives, branch offices, departments, or particular products or services. Sometimes, independent estimates are made on all of these bases and, after some discussion, a final sales budget is prepared. Sometimes, sales estimates are prepared with the idea of developing sales quotas or goals for sales representatives and territories. These estimates provide a goal for the sales department, as well as a basis for preparing the merchandising, purchasing, and other operating budgets.

Figure 15-7 shows sales estimates determined in two different ways for the same company. Since the two sets of estimated figures are not the same, someone must be responsible for combining them into one satisfactory estimate that can be followed.

Numerous factors influence sales estimates. General business conditions play an important part. Although one company may enjoy brisk sales, another, at the same time and under the same conditions, may suffer a decline in sales. If a good harvest and favorable prices for crops are anticipated in a certain section, there should be good prospects for selling farm machinery in that section. A retail store located in such an area should expect increased sales. A flood or drought may affect certain businesses unfavorably but others favorably. These are examples of some of the influences that should guide a manager in making a sales estimate.

The following is suggested as a checklist of factors to be used as a guide in preparing a sales budget:

- Previous sales
- Economic trends
- Changes in competition
- Factors such as weather conditions
- Population shifts
- Sales force
- Availability of merchandise
- Buying habits
- Season of the year

Budget Based on Analysis of Sales Representatives

Fig. 15-7
Two ways of budgeting sales.

SALES REPRESENTATIVE	YEAR 1 SALES (ACTUAL)	YEAR 2 SALES (ESTIMATE)
T. A. Nader	$ 356,720	$ 380,000
H. E. Loch	348,380	360,000
C. D. Heidel	471,240	440,000
J. H. Sharmon	442,940	440,000
C. F. Powell	426,980	440,000
J. G. Dunbar	408,360	400,000
Total	$2,454,620	$2,460,000

Budget Based on Analysis of Products

PRODUCT	YEAR 1 SALES (ACTUAL)	YEAR 2 SALES (ESTIMATE)
Washers	$ 642,840	$ 680,000
Dryers	202,320	200,000
Ranges	189,260	180,000
Lamps	209,360	200,000
Refrigerators	1,210,840	1,300,000
Total	$2,454,620	$2,560,000

When a person is starting a new business, it is advisable to investigate the experiences of other people in the same line of business and secure whatever information can be obtained from wholesalers, manufacturers, trade associations, and government agencies.

MERCHANDISING BUDGET

The **merchandising budget** is a means to plan and control the supply of merchandise to be sold to customers. If a business has too little merchandise, sales might be lost. On the other hand, if a business has too much merchandise, valuable cash may be tied up that could be better used elsewhere. Furthermore, excess merchandise has to be stored, protected, and insured. These expenses add to the cost of doing business. It is important, therefore, to manage properly the purchase of merchandise in relation to sales.

The business must determine the kinds of stock to have on hand at all times. Maximum and minimum inventory levels are set. Purchases are planned and information is given to the financial department so that cash needs can be estimated. Sources of supply are checked, and delivery dates are scheduled. The receiving department is notified of the delivery dates. Careful procedures must be set so that all departments and personnel are fully aware of the merchandise needed, on hand, and ordered.

ADVERTISING BUDGET

The **advertising budget** is a plan of the amount of money a firm should spend for advertising based on estimated sales. Advertising expenditures should be kept within reasonable bounds, for it is not true that sales will always be in direct proportion to advertising. In other words, if estimated sales are pretty well known, it is unwise to spend a large amount of money for advertising. Such a plan may result in a loss. On the other hand, a special advertising campaign, properly planned, may increase the sales of a certain product, if only temporarily; and the advertising budget will, as a result, have an influence on the sales budget. Merchandising and advertising budgets should, therefore, be planned together. Likewise, the finance department should be aware of the advertising budget in order to control those expenses and to have the necessary cash at the proper time.

CASH BUDGET

The **cash budget** is an estimate of cash received and paid out. Budgeting cash is a matter of making certain there is enough cash available to meet payments as they come due. Cash comes from either or both of two primary sources: (1) from the cash receipts of the business, and/or (2) from borrowing. When money is borrowed, it must eventually be paid back. In the cash budget, therefore, borrowed money should be included as a special item under receipts. When it is to be repaid, it should be included in the cash budget under payments.

The form in Fig. 15-8 can be used for the cash budget of a small business. A cash budget, however, should be prepared by every business, regardless of size. It should show the anticipated necessity of borrowing and the possibilities of repaying borrowed money. For instance, it is possible for a business to make a sizable profit; but at some particular time during the year, it may not have enough cash for its operations and may, therefore, have to borrow.

Cash Budget—for Three Months Ending March 31, 19--

Fig. 15-8
A cash budget.

	JANUARY	FEBRUARY	MARCH
NET SALES	$ 80,000	$ 80,000	$ 80,000
Beginning cash balance	33,500	4,000	7,000
Collections from customers	70,000	70,000	80,000
Total cash available	$103,500	$74,000	$87,000
Payments			
Accounts to be paid	45,000	45,000	60,000
Labor	9,500	12,000	16,000
Salaries and administrative expense	7,000	7,000	7,000
Sales expense	15,000	15,000	15,000
Other operating expenses	13,000	18,000	24,000
Purchase of fixed assets		10,000	10,000
Repayment of bank loan	10,000		
Total cash payments	$ 99,500	$107,000	$132,000
Expected cash shortage		33,000	45,000
Bank loans needed		40,000	50,000
Ending cash balance	4,000	7,000	5,000
End-of-month situation:			
Materials purchased	$ 45,000	$ 60,000	$ 80,000
Accounts receivable	150,000	160,000	170,000
Accounts payable	45,000	60,000	80,000
Bank loans		40,000	90,000

CAPITAL BUDGET

Every business that plans to continue in operation must give thought to replacing worn-out or obsolete fixed assets. For instance, a van used by a firm will have to be replaced at some future date. Also, if the business is highly successful, it is possible that the firm may wish to buy a second van. A plan must exist for replacing the old van or buying a new one.

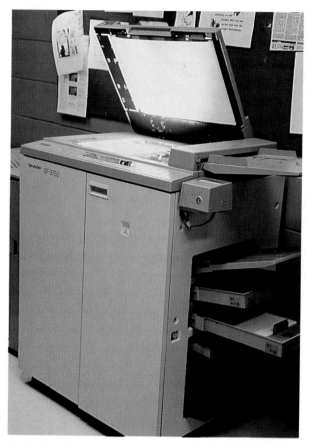

Jeff Greenberg, Photographer

A **capital budget** is a financial plan for replacing fixed assets or acquiring new ones. Capital budgeting is important because large sums of money are tied up for long periods of time. A wrong decision can be costly. For example, a decision to buy a new van that will last five years involves a large expenditure of money. The manager must plan well in advance if the money is to be available when the van is needed. Assume that the van is purchased based on a forecast that future sales will justify the need for the van. However, if sales do not increase as expected, profits will be lowered as a result of added costs related to the van.

INCOME STATEMENT BUDGET

An **income statement budget** is a plan showing projected sales, costs, and individual expense figures for a future period, such as for one month, three months, or a year. The projected total sales, less total projected costs and expenses, permit a business to estimate its net profit. Like other budgets, the income statement budget is based on past experience and many other considerations.

ADMINISTERING THE BUDGET

Because a budget is an estimate of what might happen, it usually cannot be followed exactly. Staying close to the amount budgeted is desirable. However, for various reasons beyond the control of managers, actual income and expenses may vary from the budgeted amounts. For that reason, managers of large organizations often prepare three budget estimates. The first estimate assumes that sales will be less than expected. The second estimate considers what most likely will occur. And the third estimate assumes sales will be better than expected.

The second estimate is used—the one most likely to occur—unless anticipated conditions change. If sales are less than expected, the business can shift immediately to the first (lower) set of budget figures. Should sales be better than expected, the business can shift to the third (higher) set of budget figures. Having more than one budget estimate allows for realistic flexibility during budget planning.

Whether a business is large or small or uses one or more budget estimates, the estimates must be checked against actual business conditions. The comparison determines whether the business is on, under, or over budget estimates. If expenditures exceed budgeted amounts, managers want to know why. Changes might be made that can be corrected easily, while in other cases changes may not be possible. For example, labor costs might exceed budget estimates because too many employees are poorly trained. A training program might help reduce the labor cost during the rest of the budget period. However, if labor costs increase because of a recent pay raise given to all workers, little can be done to lower those costs. Comparing budgets with actual operating conditions provides a basis for making timely and knowledgeable management decisions, which, in turn, leads to efficient and profitable business operations.

Figure 15-9 shows a comparison of actual sales for the first quarter of a year with estimated sales for the same quarter. If a comparison of actual operating performance with the budget estimates reveals that the business will not make the expected profit or will have a loss, the manager must review the expenses to determine what can be done to reduce them. Savings can result when businesses budget the inventories carefully to avoid buying unnecessary new merchandise and to reduce the quantity of old items in inventory. The difference

ITEMS	ESTIMATED SALES FIRST QUARTER	ACTUAL SALES FIRST QUARTER	VARIANCE	PERCENT OF CHANGE
Ranges	$27,300	$23,100	-$4,200	-15.4%
Refrigerators	$59,150	$60,350	+$1,200	+ 2.0%
Microwaves	$26,000	$26,200	+$ 200	+ 0.8%
Washers	$19,500	$24,000	+$4,500	+23.1%
Dryers	$31,200	$25,800	-$5,400	-17.3%

Fig. 15-9

A comparison of estimated and actual sales.

between the budgeted and actual figures, which is often called the variance, is generally considered acceptable if it is plus or minus five percent. If sales are considerably below the anticipated level, it may be necessary to make drastic adjustments, such as reducing delivery service, discharging a few workers, or canceling certain purchases.

The use of budgets and a budgeting system cannot guarantee the success of a business, but these management devices can help reduce losses or increase profits. The entire budgeting process is valuable in planning and controlling operations. But whether a business is a success or not can only be determined after the budget time periods have passed. A business measures past success by preparing and analyzing financial statements. A few of the most commonly used financial statements are discussed in the next chapter.

CHAPTER REVIEW
15

B UILDING VOCABULARY POWER

Define the following terms and concepts.

1. accounting records
2. data processing service center
3. point-of-sale terminal
4. accounts receivable record
5. accounts payable record
6. fixed assets (plant assets)
7. depreciation
8. obsolescence
9. asset book value
10. budget
11. sales budget
12. merchandising budget
13. advertising budget
14. cash budget
15. capital budget
16. income statement budget

R EVIEWING FACTS

1. Name at least five kinds of information that a manager or owner of a business should expect to obtain from the accounting records.
2. How can a business use a data processing service center?
3. What do many small business firms use as a basis for obtaining most of the information for their financial records?
4. Use the daily balance form of a small retail business shown in Fig. 15-1 and record the following information.
   a. What is the amount of cash sales?
   b. What is the amount of charge sales?
   c. What is the cash register total?
   d. What are the total cash returns?

5. Give at least three suggestions for the safe handling of cash.
6. Why is depreciation a part of the cost of doing business?
7. What kind of information is shown in an insurance record? in a fixed assets record?
8. Is an employer required by law to make income tax deductions from the wages of employees?
9. Name the types of information that must be recorded for social security and payroll tax purposes for each employee and for all employees as a group.
10. Name two ways in which information stored in computers could be damaged.
11. In what ways does a budget help a business?
12. List six types of budgets that are a part of the final overall budget for a business.
13. Name six areas on which sales estimates could be based.
14. Why can't budgets be followed exactly as prepared?

DISCUSSING IDEAS

1. Regardless of the type of record system a company selects, what features should the system have?
2. Discuss why the safe handling of cash is so important to a business.
3. How could a truck be a fixed asset? Under what circumstances would land not be a fixed asset?
4. Could a piece of equipment, such as a computer, both depreciate and become obsolete? Explain.
5. What are some of the advantages of keeping an insurance policy record?
6. What problems would be created if a business had a fire and all the records of customers were destroyed?
7. Why must the production manager know the estimated sales budget?
8. Explain why the advertising budget should be prepared at the same time that the sales budget is prepared.
9. Why is the cash budget so important from the viewpoint of the owner of a small business or the director of a large business?
10. Why is it valuable for managers to compare budgeted amounts with actual amounts spent?

ANALYZING INFORMATION

1. Study the following petty cash form, which is defective. Identify (a) what is wrong with the items included on this form and (b) identify items that should be added.

PETTY CASH SLIP

Date: _____ Month _____ Day   Amount: _____

Cash Given To: _____

Employee Giving Cash (print) _____

2. L. A. Hendricks has assets as follows: (a) a store building that was bought two years ago at a cost of $360,000, not including the value of the land; (b) store equipment that cost $54,000 and was installed when the building was bought; and (c) a used delivery truck that was bought two years ago for $12,000. Assume the following with regard to depreciation: (a) the building decreases in value at the estimated rate of 5 percent a year; (b) the store equipment decreases at the estimated rate of 10 percent a year; and (c) the truck will last one additional year and can be traded in then for $1,800. What is the depreciated value of the assets now?

3. A list of certain items kept by the Fine Fabrics Shop, a small retail store, follows. Decide where each item should be kept for safekeeping. Make three columns across a sheet of paper and place these headings at the top: Office Safe, Fireproof Filing Cabinet, and Bank Safe Deposit Box. Write the items below in the column where they best belong.
   a. Office lease
   b. Petty cash
   c. Customers' accounts
   d. Contracts
   e. Bills owed suppliers
   f. Checks received from customers and not yet deposited
   g. Insurance policies

4. The sales budget by product for the Gonzalez Supply Company for this year was estimated to be as follows:

Product A	$150,000
Product B	60,000
Product C	180,000
Product D	210,000

   a. What are the estimated total sales?
   b. If total sales the prior year were $480,000, what percentage of increase does the company expect this year over last year?
   c. What percentage of this year's total sales will Product A provide?
   d. The actual sales for this year for Products A, B, and D were as shown, but the sales for Product C were only 50 percent of the budgeted amount. What are the actual total sales for the year?

5. The following realistic yearly expense budget was presented by the budgeting director to the manager of a service business for final approval. After studying the figures, the manager asked that a flexible set of budget estimates be prepared because certain conditions might cause a 15 percent increase in sales, while certain other conditions might cause a 5 percent

REVIEW 15

decrease in sales. Assume, however, the amounts budgeted for rent and insurance will not change under any circumstances.

Sales Salaries	$300,000
Office Salaries	60,000
Supplies	80,000
Advertising	48,000
Rent	36,000
Insurance	8,000

a. Prepare a new flexible budget showing three columns of figures: 5 percent Decrease, Expected, and 15 percent Increase.
b. What is the total of each of the three budget columns?

SOLVING BUSINESS PROBLEMS

CASE 15-1

George Gorski operates his own restaurant, which is called George's Place. His accountant, Rosalind Quinn, is quite concerned about the way George handles cash.

Each morning before opening the business, George counts all the money in the cash drawer that was taken in the day before. He then leaves all the coins in the cash drawer so there will be enough on most days for making change. On days when the change runs low, he sends a worker to the nearby bank to get some. All the paper money in the cash drawer is put in a file cabinet that can be locked. When restaurant supplies are bought, George uses the money in the file cabinet to pay cash for them. On Friday of each week, the money in the file drawer is deposited in the bank.

George cannot understand why Rosalind Quinn is upset with his cash practices. "It has been working fine for years," he says.

Required:
1. Which of George's procedures are improper business practices? Why?
2. What methods should George follow to correct the improper business practices?

CASE 15-2

Karen Kline and Joe Kim are both accounting clerks in a medium-sized manufacturing firm called Electrical Home Products, Inc. The head accountant, Brooke Shenker, has just asked Karen to provide the sales budget for next month's annual budget meeting. Joe was asked to construct the cash budget. Neither was happy about the request, though neither complained directly to the head accountant. Karen did, however, let her feelings be known to Joe.

Karen: We spend weeks developing these budgets and all the budget committee does is argue for two days and change our estimates. It makes me wonder why they ask for our figures in the first place.

Joe: I agree. What is worse is that we never come in on target. Those credit sales projections are never right, and it makes me look bad because my cash budget is off.

Karen: Why don't they just agree to try to improve sales? The company should put a little more money in advertising expenses to help boost sales, and then hope for the best. I am sure that would be just as good a way to plan and everyone would be happier. I hate all that arguing that goes on.

Joe: Last year they argued for three days and look what happened. They were so far off budget that I heard Brooke say a child could have done a better job forecasting. Budgeting is a waste of time.

Karen: I will start on the sales budget tomorrow, but if I were smart my vacation would begin then, too!

Required:

1. If budget figures are prepared by Karen and Joe, why is it necessary for management to discuss them?
2. Do you agree with Joe that when budgeted amounts and actual figures do not agree, the budgeting process is not worthwhile? Explain your answer.
3. Do you agree with Karen that by increasing the advertising budget, sales will increase?

REVIEW 15

FINANCIAL ANALYSIS OF A BUSINESS

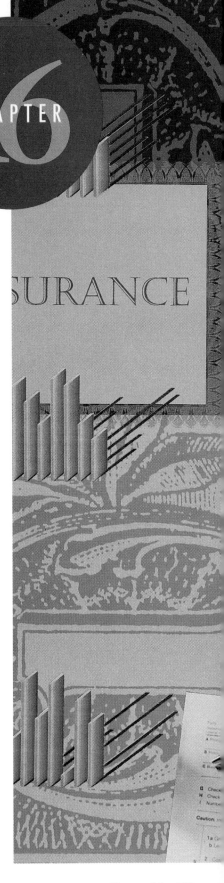

CHAPTER

16

After studying this chapter you will be able to:

16-1 Describe a balance sheet and explain how it can be useful to a business.

16-2 Point out the usefulness of the income statement in making business decisions.

16-3 Describe the importance of cash flow and working capital.

16-4 Explain several useful financial ratios.

16-5 Describe how various financial experts can assist business managers.

B rad Hyatt never liked visiting his accountant. She always talked about his *financial standing, ratios, and bottom line. Most of this made little sense to Brad, but he also knew understanding them was important to understanding his business.*

"Your current assets are either too low or your current liabilities are too high," Diana Sette had said to him on his last visit. "If you want to get that bank loan, you have to improve your working capital. Your inventory turnover is also too low to impress your bank manager."

"I'm going to take an accounting course at Bucks County College," Brad thought. "It seems Diana talks to me in a foreign language, and I've got to learn what she means. That bank loan is just too important."

Like many other business owners, Brad Hyatt never had an accounting course, even though he has great need for grasping the basics about his financial condition. A knowledge of accounting helps business owners make sound business decisions. Accounting is the language of business.

USES OF FINANCIAL REPORTS

Business activity is in large part measured in terms of money, and the amount of money a business earns is one way to judge its success. Because success is judged in dollar terms, every business must (a) keep thorough and accurate records, (b) prepare important financial reports on a regular basis, (c) interpret the financial information in the reports, and (d) make decisions that will affect future financial results.

While the importance of keeping good financial records was presented in Chapter 15, this chapter deals with financial reports and how to use information they contain. Though there are many types of financial reports, the two most used by business will be examined: the balance sheet and the income statement. These reports must be carefully understood if the best financial decisions are to be made. Like Brad Hyatt, you need to learn why financial reports are so important to business success.

Financial reports have many uses in the business world. Executives use financial reports on a regular basis as a means to run an efficient, profitable business. Suppliers, lenders, unions, governments, and owners also use financial reports when making various types of decisions about a business. The purposes for which financial information is needed by various users are shown in Fig. 16-1.

While a general understanding of financial matters is necessary for all users of financial information, there are times when it is necessary to hire experts who have special skills in handling financial matters. Some of these experts, such as accountants, are identified and discussed in this chapter.

Illus. 16-1

For most businesses, success depends on careful financial planning and reporting procedures. Is a budget one way to compare projected results or outcomes with actual performance?

UNIPHOTO

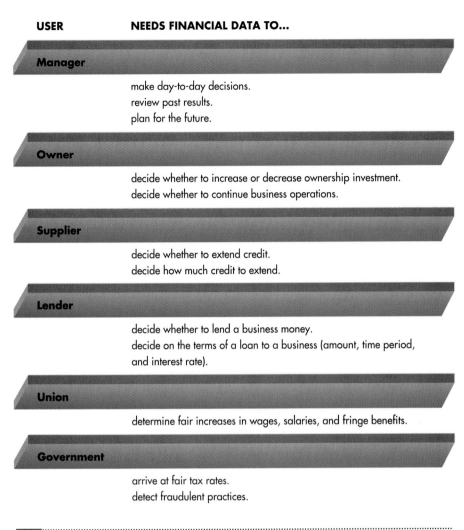

USER	NEEDS FINANCIAL DATA TO...
Manager	make day-to-day decisions. review past results. plan for the future.
Owner	decide whether to increase or decrease ownership investment. decide whether to continue business operations.
Supplier	decide whether to extend credit. decide how much credit to extend.
Lender	decide whether to lend a business money. decide on the terms of a loan to a business (amount, time period, and interest rate).
Union	determine fair increases in wages, salaries, and fringe benefits.
Government	arrive at fair tax rates. detect fraudulent practices.

Fig. 16-1
The financial reports of a business serve a variety of purposes.

FINANCIAL STATEMENTS

Financial statements are reports that summarize financial data over a period of time, such as a month, three months, a year, or even the life of the business. We now turn attention to the two most used financial statements—the balance sheet and the income statement.

BALANCE SHEET

You will recall that a **balance sheet**, or **statement of financial position**, lists the assets, liabilities, and capital of a business. **Assets** are those things owned, such as cash and buildings. **Liabilities**, on the other hand, are claims against assets or things owed—the debts of a business. And **capital** (also called **net worth, owner's equity, shareholders' equity**, or **stockholders' equity**) is what a business, an individual, or a not-for-profit organization is worth after subtracting the liabilities from the assets. The total of the assets equals the combined total of the liabilities plus capital. In fact, the **basic accounting**

formula is represented in the balance sheet as Assets = Liabilities + Capital. You may think of the basic accounting formula as an old-fashioned scale, as shown in Fig. 16-2.

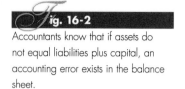

Fig. 16-2
Accountants know that if assets do not equal liabilities plus capital, an accounting error exists in the balance sheet.

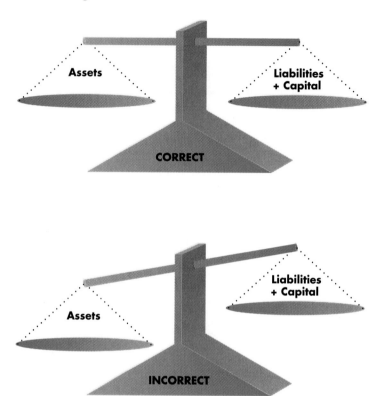

Each balance sheet has a heading that includes the name of the person or business, the title Balance Sheet, and the date. The information in the balance sheet presents a picture of the financial position of a business on the date shown in the heading. Balance sheets are prepared at least once a year. Some business firms, however, prepare balance sheets more often.

Because a balance sheet reveals the basic financial position on a given date, it is valuable to anyone who needs such information. Therefore, a balance sheet can be as useful to individuals as it is to businesses.

An example of a balance sheet for a jewelry store, the Crown Corporation, is shown in Fig. 16-3.

Kinds of Data

On December 31, the accountants for the Crown Corporation prepared a balance sheet. Everything the business owns and the value of each asset is listed under Assets. As shown in Fig. 16-3, the total assets are $536,000. The company debts—items purchased on account and the mortgage still owed on the land and building—are listed under Liabilities, which total $136,000. When the total liabilities were subtracted from the total assets, the accountants reported that the capital (net worth) amounted to $400,000.

Crown Corporation
Balance Sheet
December 31, 19--

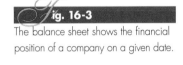
Fig. 16-3
The balance sheet shows the financial
position of a company on a given date.

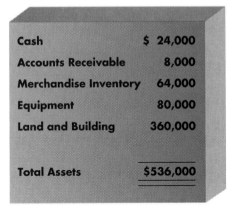

ASSETS

Cash	$ 24,000
Accounts Receivable	8,000
Merchandise Inventory	64,000
Equipment	80,000
Land and Building	360,000
Total Assets	$536,000

LIABILITIES AND CAPITAL

Liabilities:	
Accounts Payable	$ 32,000
Mortgage Payable	104,000
Total Liabilities	**$136,000**
Capital:	
Stockholders' Net Worth	400,000
Total Liabilities and Capital	**$536,000**

Two assets on the balance sheet need an explanation. The items are merchandise turnover and accounts receivable. The Crown Corporation purchases jewelry from a manufacturer, displays the jewelry in its store, and then sells it to customers. Until the jewelry is sold, it is listed as an asset called merchandise inventory. **Merchandise inventory** refers to goods purchased to sell to customers at a profit.

Illus. 16-2
An accurate worksheet is necessary when preparing a balance sheet. What would happen if a worker were careless about keeping a worksheet up to date?

The merchandise is sold on a cash or credit basis. For credit sales, the Crown Corporation allows customers 30, 60, or 90 days to pay for purchases. The amount owed by customers is an asset called **accounts receivable**. It is an asset because the business has a legal right to obtain cash for the goods sold and can sue customers who do not pay. The store will eventually collect cash from the customers.

In the same sense, the accounts payable item that is found under Liabilities on the balance sheet means the Crown Corporation owes money for purchases made on credit. Money owed for credit purchases is a liability called **accounts payable**. In this example, the store bought jewelry on credit from a manufacturer and may take up to a month to pay for it.

Value of Data

The balance sheet for the Crown Corporation provides a great deal of useful data. Specific types and amounts of assets and liabilities are listed. The balance sheet also shows that the business owns assets of $536,000, owes $136,000, and is worth $400,000 on December 31. The total figures on the balance sheet agree with the basic accounting formula as follows:

$$\text{Assets} = \text{Liabilities} + \text{Capital}$$

$$\$536,000 = \$136,000 + \$400,000$$

A careful look at the specific items reveals other valuable information. For example, the Crown Corporation cannot now pay the $32,000 that is owed under accounts payable because only $24,000 in cash is available. Hopefully, adequate cash sales will be made, and certainly some of those customers listed under accounts receivable will soon pay. Even though the money owed under accounts payable is not likely to become due all at once, the company could possibly have trouble meeting other day-to-day expenses. The company would be in trouble if a sudden emergency arose that called for much cash.

The Crown Corporation may use its balance sheet to compare financial results with prior time periods or with other companies. Because a yearly balance sheet is prepared, the business can review its financial progress by comparing this year's results with last year's results. It may find, for example, that the amount of capital increased over last year without an increase in liabilities. If the Crown Corporation wished to do so, it could also compare some information on its balance sheet with that of other business firms of similar size and kind. Published information is available from several sources, such as trade associations. With comparative figures, the business can make judgments about its success and perhaps even find ways to improve its financial picture in the future.

INCOME STATEMENT

The **income statement**, also known as a **statement of operations**, is a financial document that reports total revenue and expenses for a specific period, such as a month or a year. Income statements have three major parts:

1. Revenue—income earned for the period, such as from the sale of goods and services.
2. Expenses—all costs incurred that helped to earn the revenue.
3. Profit or Loss—the difference between total revenue and total expenses.

When the revenue is greater than expenses, a profit results. When the expenses are greater than revenue, a loss occurs. The income statement shows a picture of success or failure (profit or loss) for a specific period of a year or less. The balance sheet, on the other hand, shows the financial condition of a business at a particular point in time. Both types of financial statements serve useful but different purposes. An example of a business income statement is shown in Fig. 16-4. The period covered for the Crown Corporation is one year, as shown in the heading.

Crown Corporation
Income Statement
For the Year Ending December 31, 19--

The income statement shows profit or loss for a specified period of time.

Revenue from Sales	$800,000	
Cost of Goods Sold	440,000	
Gross Profit		$360,000
Operating Expenses		
Salaries and Wages	$160,000	
Advertising and Promotion	48,000	
Depreciation	32,000	
Utilities	20,000	
Supplies Used	12,000	
Other	8,000	
Total Operating Expenses		280,000
Net Profit (before Taxes)		$ 80,000

Kinds of Data

The revenue for the Crown Corporation comes from one source—the sale of jewelry. Total revenue for the year was $800,000. If the company earned other income, such as from the repair of jewelry, it would be listed separately under revenue.

WHAT WENT WRONG AT VILLAGE SHOES?

Questions:

1 What caused Danny Sullivan's accounts payable to get out of control?

2 Why was it unwise for Danny to ignore paying his taxes?

3 What did James Greenfield, the consultant, do to help Danny?

4 What did Danny Sullivan learn from his consultant?

5 Do you think Danny would have prevented bankruptcy proceedings if he had prepared and followed a cash budget? Explain your answer.

Source: Adapted from Jill Andresky Fraser, "Account-Ability," *Inc.*, March, 1991.

Danny Sullivan was in deep financial trouble. Early one summer day, authorities from the state of Michigan tax office appeared and closed his upscale retail shoe store located in the upper-class Detroit suburb of Grosse Point, Michigan. Danny had been paying neither his state taxes nor his federal taxes. He immediately contacted his lawyer and filed for bankruptcy.

What went wrong? Plenty, but the main cause of Danny Sullivan's problem was his inattention to accounts payable. He spent too much time worrying about how to increase sales. He also overstocked his shoe inventory during an economically slow period. Danny assumed that the recession would be short lived. It wasn't. As a result, he ended up with a cash flow problem that made it difficult to pay his invoices and his tax bills.

Before the slowdown, Danny did quite well. His business was well established, there were plenty of customers, and sales were brisk. When the downturn occurred, Danny did not cut back on adding to his inventory. But sales continued to slump as the recession failed to come to a halt. Fewer dollars were coming in and the bills did not cease. That's when Danny realized he had problems. Some suppliers allowed delayed payments but the state and federal tax authorities did not—penalties and interest continued to mount.

Filing for bankruptcy allowed the doors of Village Shoes to remain open. In addition to following the bankruptcy judge's instructions, Danny sought help from a customer who was a financial consultant, James Greenfield of the Wharton Resource Group Inc. Greenfield soon learned that most of Danny's suppliers would sell to him only on a cash basis. The consultant also learned that the initial $12,000 in overdue taxes had swelled to over $30,000 with penalties and interest. All of Danny's debts grew to $130,000.

Another cause of Danny Sullivan's problems was revealed. His recordkeeping system left much to be desired. No systematic plan for paying the 32 suppliers existed. With Greenfield's advice, he concentrated on paying taxes first. Then he negotiated terms for paying suppliers— the accounts payable.

In retrospect, Danny Sullivan is fast to agree with his consultant's advice. Pay attention to your payables; you know you are in trouble when overdue payables average 45 to 60 days. Pay bills such as taxes when due rather than pay penalties and interest. Use a good recordkeeping system that you can easily review and manage. Keep your vendors informed; communicate with them when you think a cash flow problem is beginning to occur. Like many entrepreneurs, Danny learned that cash management is critical.

In order to earn revenue in a retail goods business, goods are purchased from suppliers and sold to customers at a profit. As you learned in Chapter 13, the net price paid for merchandise bought and sold is called cost of goods sold. Generally, the cost of goods sold is a rather large deduction from revenue. To highlight the cost of goods sold, it is kept separate from other deductions and is used to arrive at gross profit. Gross profit should not be confused with net profit. Gross profit for the Crown Corporation is $360,000, which is found by subtracting the cost of goods sold ($440,000) from sales ($800,000). A firm that sells services only would not have cost of goods sold. An example of a firm that would not show cost of goods sold would be a photo developing business such as Fotomat Corporation.

Expenses needed to operate the business during the year are listed next on the income statement. When the total of these operating expenses, $280,000, is subtracted from the gross profit, $360,000, the net profit, $80,000, is obtained.

The net result of the business activity reported in the form of revenue, cost of goods sold, expenses, and profit on the income statement will appear in one form or another on the balance sheet. For the Crown Corporation, the assets and capital will each be increased by the amount of the profit, $80,000. The basic accounting formula will still show that assets equal liabilities plus capital.

Value of Data

The manager of Crown Corporation can learn a great deal about the business from the income statement. Specifically, the total deductions from the $800,000 in revenue are $720,000, which consists of cost of goods sold ($440,000) and operating expenses ($280,000). It can also be observed that the net profit before taxes—$80,000—is a rather small part of the total revenue.

The Crown Corporation can improve its financial controlling and budget planning by doing an item-by-item analysis of the income statement, such as that shown in the first two columns of figures in Fig. 16-5 on page 400. Each expenditure can be compared with the total sales to get percentage calculations. Once the percentages are obtained, they can be compared with similar figures from prior months and years.

For instance, the first and largest operating expense is $160,000 for salaries and wages. When $160,000 is divided by total sales, $800,000, and the answer is changed to a percentage, the result is 20 percent. If last year the total wages and salaries expense amounted to only 18 percent of sales, the business would know that this expense had increased in relation to total sales. If possible, the company can try to correct this 2 percent increase for the next year by trying to increase sales, raise prices, or reduce expenses in some way. The same type of calculation and analysis can be made for each of the remaining expenses on the income statement. In addition, it is possible to determine the percentages of gross profit and net profit in relation to sales.

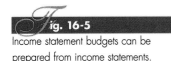

Fig. 16-5

Income statement budgets can be prepared from income statements.

Crown Corporation
Budgeted Income Statement
for 12 Months Ending December 31, 19--

INCOME, EXPENSE, AND PROFIT	AMOUNTS FOR PAST 12 MONTHS	PERCENTAGE OF SALES	AMOUNTS BUDGETED FOR NEXT 12 MONTHS	ESTIMATED PERCENTAGE OF SALES
Sales	$800,000	100.0%	$960,000	100.0%
Cost of Goods Sold	440,000	55.0	528,000	55.0
Gross Profit	360,000	45.0	432,000	45.0
Operating Expenses				
Salaries and Wages	160,000	20.0	182,400	19.0
Advertising/Promotion	48,000	6.0	58,560	6.1
Depreciation	32,000	4.0	32,000	3.3
Utilities	20,000	2.5	28,800	3.0
Supplies Used	12,000	1.5	14,400	1.5
Other Expenses	8,000	1.0	9,600	1.0
Total Operating Expenses	280,000	35.0	325,760	33.9
Net Profit	80,000	10.0	106,240	11.1

A NALYSIS OF FINANCIAL DATA

The financial statements that have just been presented are not always sufficient to enable the manager to interpret the condition of the business. Other information that can be used to assist in interpreting financial data follows.

CASH FLOW

Cash flow refers to the movement of cash into and out of a business. Money comes in immediately as a result of the sale of goods and services for cash and later from customers who buy on credit. Money goes out to pay for various costs and operating expenses. Because money does not always flow in at the same rate it flows out, cash needs must be budgeted.

Regardless of the size of a business, cash is both a short-term and a long-term concern. Businesses must have cash on hand to pay bills when they are due and to plan ahead for large cash payments, such as the purchase of equipment or the launching of a new product.

Jeff Greenberg, Photographer

Illus. 16-3
Some businesses have a cash flow problem when cash does not flow into and out of the business on a steady basis. Can you name other businesses that may have cash flow problems?

The planning of cash flow needs is shown in Fig. 16-6 by an example for a retail piano store. While some pianos are sold for cash, most are sold on credit. The bulk of piano sales occurs during the December holiday season. The need for cash is greatest during September, October, and November when pianos are purchased. Large sums of cash are needed to pay for the pianos, for sales promotions such as advertising, and for regular operating expenses. The cash flowing out of the company from October through December is greater than the cash flowing in. Large amounts of cash start to flow in during December from customers who pay cash for their purchases. Credit customers who pur-

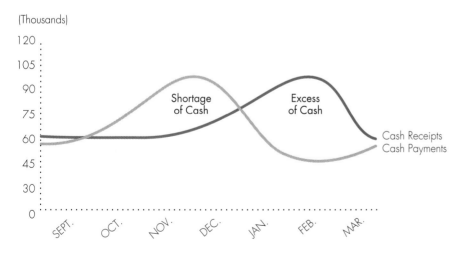

Fig. 16-6
Cash flow needs change each month. Businesses must plan their spending around their cash shortages and cash excesses.

chased in December, however, will make cash payments in January, February, and March. During these three months, the flow of cash coming into the business will be greater than the cash going out. Knowing the cash needs of the business enables the manager to plan accordingly.

WORKING CAPITAL

Closely related to cash flow is the concept of working capital. **Working capital** is the difference between current assets and current liabilities. The word *current* refers to assets and liabilities that have a life of one year or less. When current assets are much larger than current liabilities, business firms are more readily able to pay current liabilities. The amount of working capital is one possible indicator that a business can pay its short-term debts. Businesses with large amounts of working capital usually find it easier to borrow money than those with little working capital. The working capital for the Crown Corporation is shown in Fig. 16-7.

Fig. 16-7

Working capital can be obtained from the balance sheet by subtracting current liabilities from current assets.

Crown Corporation
Working Capital
December 31, 19--

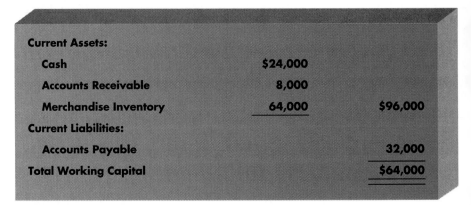

Current Assets:		
Cash	$24,000	
Accounts Receivable	8,000	
Merchandise Inventory	64,000	$96,000
Current Liabilities:		
Accounts Payable		32,000
Total Working Capital		$64,000

FINANCIAL RATIOS

Managers find ratios helpful when interpreting financial data and especially when comparing various items on financial statements. Some of the more important ratios and their uses are found in Fig. 16-8. Once a ratio is calculated for a business it can be compared with prior period ratios, with ratios from other firms, and with other types of ratios. Organizations such as Dun & Bradstreet, Inc., publish a standard list of average ratios for various types of businesses.

Frequently Used Financial Ratios

RATIO	CALCULATION	CROWN CORPORATION*	PURPOSE
Return on Sales	$\frac{\text{Net Profit}}{\text{Sales}}$	$\frac{80,000}{800,000} = 10.0\%$	Shows how profitable a firm was for a specified period of time.
Inventory Turnover	$\frac{\text{Cost of Goods Sold}}{\text{Ave. Mdse. Inventory}}$	$\frac{440,000}{64,000} = 6.88$	Shows whether the average monthly inventory might be too large or small.
Current Ratio	$\frac{\text{Current Assets}}{\text{Current Liabilities}}$	$\frac{96,000}{32,000} = 3.0$	Shows whether a firm can meet its current debts comfortably.
Return on Owners' Equity	$\frac{\text{Net Profit}}{\text{Owners' Equity}}$	$\frac{80,000}{400,000} = 20.0\%$	Shows whether the owners are making a fair return on their investment.
Return on Investment	$\frac{\text{Net Profit}}{\text{Total Assets}}$	$\frac{80,000}{536,000} = 14.9\%$	Shows rate of return on the total money invested by owners and others in a firm.

* See Fig. 16-4, 16-5, and 16-7 for sources of figures for calculations.

SECURING FINANCIAL INFORMATION

If a business needs general advice or special help with a financial problem, experts are available. Types of experts who are called upon to help solve financial problems are accountants, bankers, consultants, and the federal government.

ACCOUNTANTS

Accountants establish systems for collecting, sorting, and summarizing all types of financial data. They prepare and explain in detail the many figures found on financial statements. Accountants also help managers interpret financial data and make suggestions for handling various financial aspects of a business. Large firms have full-time accountants, while small firms usually hire accountants on a part-time basis. A firm may hire a **Certified Public Accountant**, or **CPA**, a person who has met a state's education, experience, and examination requirements. CPAs are hired to approve the yearly financial records of public corporations.

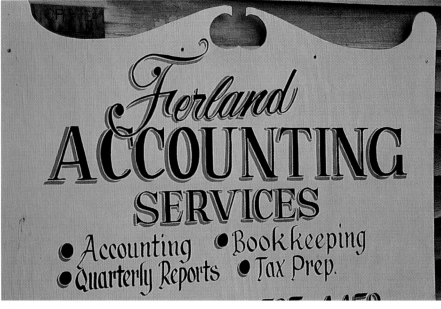

Jeff Greenberg, Photographer

BANKERS

Bankers also assist business organizations with financial decisions. Bankers are not only well informed about the financial condition of businesses, but they also provide advice on how and where to get loans. Since bankers frequently work with business firms, they are aware of businesses' problems and needs.

Jeff Greenberg, Photographer

CONSULTANTS

Consultants also assist businesses. A **consultant** is an expert who is called upon to study a special problem and offer solutions. Consultants usually are not employees. They are outside experts with specialized knowledge.

A financial consultant is valuable to persons thinking about starting a business. For example, consultants provide advice on the amount of money needed to get started and also provide advice on handling finances during the early years of operation. Professors of accounting, finance, and management at local colleges or universities often serve as consultants. There are even business firms that sell consulting services, such as large consulting firms. Large as well as small firms use the many services offered by consultants.

SMALL BUSINESS ADMINISTRATION

Still another source of financial information and advice is the federal government. Of particular value is the Small Business Administration (SBA). The SBA is an agency of the federal government that provides helpful literature on money matters and on other aspects of running a business. The SBA can assist small firms in getting loans under special conditions. And the SBA can also recommend consultants to businesses.

CHAPTER REVIEW 16

BUILDING VOCABULARY POWER

Define the following terms and concepts.

1. financial statements
2. balance sheet (statement of financial position)
3. assets
4. liabilities
5. capital (net worth, owner's equity, shareholders' equity, or stockholders' equity)
6. basic accounting formula
7. merchandise inventory
8. accounts receivable
9. accounts payable
10. income statement (statement of operations)
11. cash flow
12. working capital
13. Certified Public Accountant (CPA)
14. consultant

REVIEWING FACTS

1. For each of the following, state two purposes for which financial information is needed: (a) managers, (b) owners, and (c) suppliers.
2. What are the two most used financial statements?
3. Name the three parts to a balance sheet.
4. How is it possible that accounts receivable is listed on the balance sheet as an asset when customers have not yet been paid?
5. Give an example of what a business can learn by comparing one year's balance sheet figures with another's.

6. Name the three major parts to an income statement.
7. Does the income statement show results for the same period of time as the balance sheet?
8. Is net profit likely to be larger than gross profit?
9. How can a percentage be calculated for an income statement expense?
10. Why is cash flow a concern for most businesses?
11. If current liabilities are larger than current assets, is this an indication that a business might have trouble paying some of its debts in the short run?
12. How are ratios helpful to managers?
13. What do accountants do?
14. Why would a business want to use a consultant?
15. What is the SBA and what does it do?

D ISCUSSING IDEAS

1. Assume a business recently started and its balance sheet shows: Assets, $75,000; Liabilities, $30,000; and Capital $45,000. However, the owner forgot to include a $3,500 computer purchased for cash. How would this affect the total assets, total liabilities, and net worth?
2. If, in Fig. 16-3, all the customers paid their bills, which are shown in accounts receivable, what effect would it have on the total assets, total liabilities, and the stockholders' net worth?
3. Discuss the accuracy of this statement: The balance sheet tells you whether you made a profit or a loss for the year.
4. A net loss of $5,000 appears on an income statement. How would this loss affect the Capital section of the balance sheet?
5. From Fig. 16-5, which two operating expenses helped make it possible for the estimated total operating expenses to decrease from 35 percent to 33.9 percent?
6. If a business that previously sold on a cash basis now permits customers to buy on 30-day credit terms, how will the cash flow be affected during the first month of credit sales?
7. Discuss whether it would be possible for working capital to ever go below zero.
8. If the average return on sales for all jewelry stores reported by the trade association is 7 percent, how would you judge the success of the Crown Corporation? See Fig. 16-8.
9. What experts would you contact for help if you were planning to open a gift shop, but you were having trouble deciding where to get financial help and deciding how much to borrow?

REVIEW 16

A NALYZING INFORMATION

1. Use the following items to prepare a balance sheet dated today for the Starboard Corporation. Use Fig. 16-3 as a model.

Cash	$ 5,000
Accounts Receivable	8,000
Merchandise Inventory	15,000
Land and Buildings	120,000
Accounts Payable	12,000
Mortgage Payable	90,000
Stockholders' Net Worth	46,000

2. Use the following items to prepare an annual income statement dated today for the Portside Corporation. Use Fig. 16-4 as a model.

Revenue from Sales	$250,000
Cost of Goods Sold	80,000
Operating Expenses:	
Wages	$ 40,000
Advertising	13,000
Depreciation	10,000
Insurance	6,000
Supplies Used	3,000
Other	2,500

3. A friend asked you to help analyze her financial affairs. You agreed and obtained from her the following items and amounts:

Cash	$125
Clothing	450
VCR, Radio, & Tapes	600
Balance owed on charge	
accounts	700
Savings account balance	700
Checking account balance	200

  a. Prepare a balance sheet.
  b. Offer financial advice to your friend.

4. The following is a portion of an income statement for a local retail store. Calculate the percentage that each item represents of the total sales so that the manager can use the information to help prepare next year's budget.

Revenue from Sales	$500,000
Cost of Goods Sold	300,000
Gross Profit	$200,000
Operating Expenses:	
Wages and Salaries	$ 90,000

Advertising	15,000
Supplies Used	30,000
Other	20,000
Total Operating Expenses	$155,000
Net Profit	$ 45,000

5. Use the following information that was obtained from the balance sheet and income statement of the Waterwing Company to calculate the following financial ratios: (a) inventory turnover, (b) current ratio, (c) return on owners' equity, and (d) return on investment. See Fig. 16-8.

Revenue from Sales	$600,000
Cost of Goods Sold	320,000
Net Profit	25,000
Current Assets	36,000
Total Assets	200,000
Current Liabilities	15,000
Owners' Equity	150,000
Average Merchandise Inventory	20,000

S OLVING BUSINESS PROBLEMS

CASE 16-1

Katie Jackson finished the first year of operating her new dry cleaning business. Her accountant gave her an income statement and a balance sheet. The income statement showed that the total revenue from sales was $144,000 and the net profit was $5,760. The balance sheet follows and shows total assets, total liabilities, and capital.

While her profits were small, she was certain that she would do much better next year. "After all," she said, "there were extra expenses in getting started the first year; and now that people know me, I will be getting more and more business." Even so, she is concerned about her financial status. Because you are a friend and you have had some business training, she calls you as a consultant to answer a few questions.

Required:
1. What was the return on sales for the first year?
2. How much is Katie's working capital?
3. If she were to go to a bank to borrow $40,000 to expand the business, is the bank likely to give her the loan? Explain.

REVIEW 16

**Katie's Cleaners
Balance Sheet
December 31, 19--**

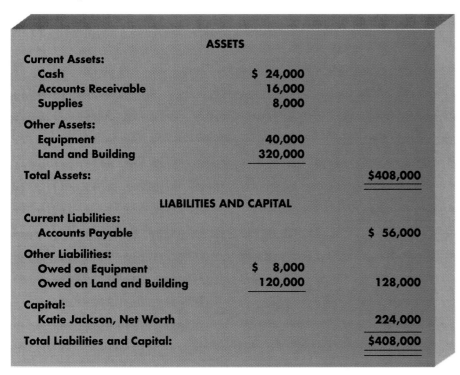

ASSETS		
Current Assets:		
Cash	$ 24,000	
Accounts Receivable	16,000	
Supplies	8,000	
Other Assets:		
Equipment	40,000	
Land and Building	320,000	
Total Assets:		$408,000
LIABILITIES AND CAPITAL		
Current Liabilities:		
Accounts Payable		$ 56,000
Other Liabilities:		
Owed on Equipment	$ 8,000	
Owed on Land and Building	120,000	128,000
Capital:		
Katie Jackson, Net Worth		224,000
Total Liabilities and Capital:		$408,000

CASE 16-2

For several years, Carla and Juan Sanchez have been making leather items, such as belts, purses, and wallets, in their home as a hobby. They have sold many items to friends and neighbors. Because Juan has just lost his regular job, he and Carla have decided to go into business full time making leathercraft items. The items will be sold to retailers and, perhaps later, to wholesalers. A great deal of money will be needed, some of which they have saved. Both agree that they know a great deal about how to make leather items, but very little about financial matters.

Carla believes they should hire a consultant before they do anything else to start the business. Juan, on the other hand, believes they should go to a bank to borrow as much as they can and then start the business. Juan believes that they can hire an accountant after they have gotten the business started. He does not believe the consultant will know enough about the leather business to give advice. "Besides," he adds, "consultants are too expensive."

Required:

1. Do you agree with Carla or Juan about whether a consultant is needed? Explain.
2. How could a consultant help them?
3. Could the Small Business Administration be of help? How?

DO REVIEW QS FOR 17 FOR TONITE

FINANCING A BUSINESS

After studying this chapter you will be able to:

17-1 Distinguish between owner capital, retained earnings, and creditor capital.

17-2 Describe three types of stock and explain how common stock differs from preferred stock.

17-3 List and discuss three sources of short-term and long-term creditor capital.

17-4 Describe bond terms, types of bonds, and how bonds differ from common stocks.

17-5 Discuss why and when capital might be needed and how it might be obtained.

The Video Shoppe opened for business in a popular mall a few years ago. Yolanda Diaz, its owner, used her entire savings to launch "The Shoppe," as she called it. After losing money the first year, she nearly closed down. But through hard work and creative marketing, The Shoppe has become quite successful. Furthermore, she left all the profits in the business except for a modest amount of cash for personal living expenses.

Today Kelly Graham, her accountant and friend, was in the back room balancing the books. As Kelly finished her work, Yolanda excitedly asked, "Can I open another shop with my current earnings?"

Kelly's shocked response was fast. "No. Your earnings are good but your balance sheet needs more muscle."

"But Kelly, my business sense tells me I could open other shops and begin making healthy profits right away. Don't tell me no. Tell me how. And let's not think of opening one shop. My idea is to have a chain of shops within the next two years."

Kelly, somewhat startled by Yolanda's bold plan, was momentarily speechless. "But how would you finance a chain?" Kelly asked.

"I was hoping you could give me some ideas," Yolanda replied. "For starters, I have an aunt who might be able to lend me some money. Perhaps my bank would provide a loan. Maybe my brother. . . ."

"Your family might help some," Kelly interrupted, "but you will need 'big' dollars. Right now, I have to see my next client. Until I return next week, think about forming a partnership with someone or a corporation so that you could sell stock to others."

After Kelly left, Yolanda sat wondering how she could raise the money to expand her business. "Strike now while the market is hot," again entered her mind as three steady customers walked in.

Illus. 17-1

When successful entrepreneurs want to enlarge their businesses, they often face the problem of raising large sums of capital. Other than from friends and relatives, where can a prosperous small retail store obtain large sums of money to enlarge or open branch stores?

Yolanda faces the same problem most successful business owners face—how to get financial backing. Capital is needed when a business is started and when a business wishes to expand. In financing a business, capital refers to the money and credit required to run a business. Capital comes from many sources. It can be provided by the owners, by those who lend money to the business, by credit extended to the business, and by earnings left in the business. Capital is used to acquire assets.

In this chapter, you will learn about the various sources of capital and about important matters to consider when deciding upon sources of capital. In addition, you will learn how stocks and bonds, which are called **securities**, are marketed to the public.

S OURCES OF CAPITAL

It is necessary to determine where capital will come from to start and to operate a business. First, money invested in the business by its owner or owners is called **owner capital**, or **proprietary capital**. This capital may be from personal funds, such as from accumulated savings, or borrowed using one's home or other property as security for the loan. Yolanda Diaz can consider such sources for expanding The Video Shoppe. As shown in Fig. 17-1, small businesses rely heavily on owner capital.

A second source of capital comes from retained earnings. **Retained earnings** are the profits that are put aside to run a business. A successful business, such as Yolanda's, generally uses retained earnings as a source of capital.

Sources of capital to start a new business.

Percentage of Businesses

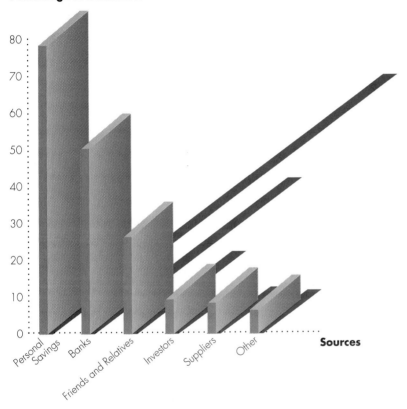

Source: *New Business in America, The NFIB Foundation.*

A third source of capital is **creditor capital**, or **borrowed capital**, which is capital loaned to a business by others. Banks and other types of lending institutions usually will not lend money to a business unless the owner capital exceeds the creditor capital. As a result, businesses in financial difficulty often have trouble getting creditor capital.

McGraw's Pet Shop, as shown in Fig. 17-2, might be able to get an additional loan from the bank because its liabilities are much less than its capital. However, if its liabilities were $240,000 and the capital were $160,000, the Pet Shop probably would not get the loan.

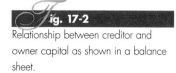

Relationship between creditor and owner capital as shown in a balance sheet.

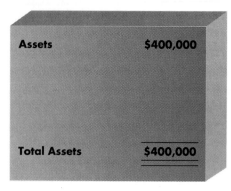
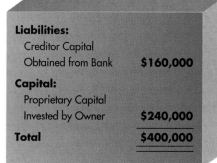

**McGraw's Pet Shop
Balance Sheet
July 31, 19--**

Assets	$400,000
Total Assets	$400,000

Liabilities:	
Creditor Capital Obtained from Bank	$160,000
Capital:	
Proprietary Capital Invested by Owner	$240,000
Total	$400,000

OWNER CAPITAL

To finance a business by acquiring owner capital, the individual proprietor has several alternatives. The owner can sell personal assets, borrow from an individual, mortgage the business property, or mortgage personal property.

The sole owner of a business can also obtain additional funds by (a) forming a partnership and requiring the new partner to invest money in the business, or by (b) forming a corporation and bringing in owners by selling stock. A business that expands in one of these ways might increase its sales and profits, but the profits must be shared among more owners. In the short run, the result may be less profitable for each owner. To raise capital, therefore, the business owner must estimate whether it will be more profitable to remain a sole owner or form a partnership or a corporation. Yolanda Diaz must deal with this question if she wishes to expand her Video Shoppe.

Assume that the proprietor decides to secure additional owner capital by incorporating and selling shares of stock. The two kinds of stock most frequently issued by a corporation are common stock and preferred stock.

Common Stock

Common stock represents a type of ownership that gives holders the right to participate in managing the business by having voting privileges and by sharing in the profits (dividends) if there are any. Holders of common stock, however, do not receive dividends until all other investors have been paid. Furthermore, the dividend rate on common stock can vary over time.

Preferred Stock

Preferred stock represents a type of ownership that gives holders preference over the common stockholders when distributing dividends or assets. Common stockholders receive dividends, if any remain, after the preferred stockholders are paid. A corporation must, of course, pay its regular debts and interest on borrowed money before distributing dividends. Holders of preferred stock usually receive a fixed dividend based on a stated percentage of the face value of the stock.

How does this plan work? Suppose that a corporation issues $100,000 of 7 percent preferred stock and $100,000 of common stock. Further assume that profits for the year are $10,000. The pre-

Jon Riley/Tony Stone Images

Illus. 17-2
Corporations obtain capital by selling stock. Can sole proprietorships and partnerships sell stock? Where would you go to buy a share of stock?

ferred stockholders would receive 7 percent of $100,000, or $7,000. Only $3,000 would be left for the holders of common stock. Their return on $100,000 would yield only 3 percent ($3,000 ÷ $100,000).

But what would happen if the same corporation earns $31,000 in profits during the following year? In this case, the preferred stockholders would be paid their fixed rate of dividends (7 percent of $100,000), or $7,000; and $24,000 would be left to distribute to the holders of the common stock. If the entire amount were distributed, subject to approval of the board of directors, the holders of the common stock would receive a dividend of 24 percent ($24,000 ÷ $100,000).

Normally, a good policy for a firm is not to distribute all of its profits. It is better to withhold some of its profits in reserve (retained earnings). If all of the profits are paid out in the form of cash, a company may later need to borrow money in order to carry on its operations. As shown in Fig. 17-3 on page 416, some corporations prefer to leave retained earnings in the business. In addition, if no profit is earned during a particular period, dividends could be paid out of retained earnings. If a corporation pays out all of its earnings and current year's profits, serious problems may arise if a loss is suffered in a later year.

Ordinarily, the preferred stockholders do not have voting privileges in managing the business. However, the ownership of certain types of preferred stock permits the stockholders voting privileges when dividends are not declared and paid regularly. Most kinds of preferred stock have priority over common stock with regard to claims against assets. For instance, if the corporation ceases operations, assets are first distributed to preferred stockholders and the remainder, if any, to common stockholders.

What would happen if a corporation with $500,000 of outstanding common stock and $500,000 of outstanding preferred stock ceased operating? After selling all of the assets for cash and after paying all of its creditors, assume further that $800,000 in cash still remains. The sum of $500,000 (the face value of the preferred stock) must be paid to the preferred stockholders because their stock has asset priority. As a result, the holders of common stock would receive only $300,000, which is 60 percent of the full face value of their stock

($300,000 ÷ $500,000). Had there been no preference as to assets, both common and preferred stockholders would have shared equally, with each group receiving $400,000.

When a corporation ceases operations, preferred and common stockholders seldom get much money from the assets. The assets that are sold often do not raise enough cash to pay the creditors, who must be paid before stockholders are paid.

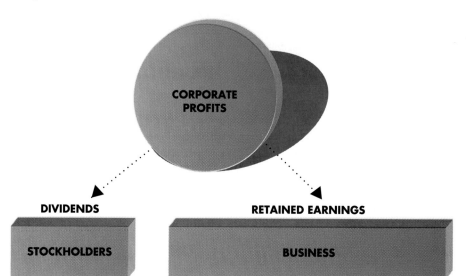

Value of Stock

Three special terms are often used in a discussion of the value of stock: market value, par or stated value, and book value.

The value sometimes shown on a stock certificate should not be confused with its **market value,** which is the value at which stock is bought and sold on any given day. When a share of stock shows a dollar value, it is referred to as its **par value** or **stated value**, which is an arbitrarily assigned amount that is used for bookkeeping purposes. These arbitrary amounts, such as $1, have little practical value because they do not indicate the current worth of the stock. A company whose stock shows a stated value such as $1, for example, may have a market value of over $100 depending upon how well it has performed financially. The real value of stock is not the stated value but the amount buyers are willing to pay for it.

Another term, book value, is often used in connection with the value of stock. The **book value** of a share of stock is found by dividing the net worth (assets minus liabilities) of the corporation by the total number of shares outstanding. Thus, if the net worth of a corporation is $75,000,000 and the number of shares of stock outstanding is 1,000,000, the book value of each share is $75 ($75,000,000 ÷ 1,000,000), regardless of the stock's stated value or market value. Book value is used in special situations, such as to help determine the value of an entire business that is about to be sold. Book value may also be used, in part, to estimate the amount of money to distribute to shareholders when a corporation is dissolved.

Kind of Stock to Issue

Corporations must determine the kind of capital stock to issue. The certificate of incorporation states whether all authorized stock is common stock or whether part is common and part preferred. Corporations can issue no other stock unless authorization is received from the government.

It is usually a good practice to issue only common stock when starting a business. Even though profits may be made from the very beginning, it is often wise to use those profits to expand the business, rather than to distribute the profits as dividends. Although a corporation often pays dividends to holders of common stock, it is not required to do so. When preferred stock is issued, however, the corporation is under an obligation to pay the specified dividend from its profits. If only common stock is initially issued and the corporation later wants to expand, it may then issue preferred stock in order to encourage others to invest in the business.

RETAINED EARNINGS

Rather than distribute all profits earned as dividends, a business should reserve some of its earnings to reinvest in the business. This is called "plowing back" earnings. A business plows back earnings for some or all of the following reasons:

- Replacement of buildings and equipment as the result of depreciation (wearing out).
- Replacement of equipment as a result of obsolescence (out of date).
- Addition of new facilities for expanding the business.
- Financial protection during periods of low sales and profits, such as recessions and tough competitive times.

Illus. 17-3

Businesses may choose to pay for expansion with retained earnings rather than through borrowing. How does a business obtain retained earnings?

Even when the business is not making a profit, it should plan to replace assets that decrease in value because of depreciation or obsolescence. For instance, a car rental company may start operations with new cars. The company may not make a profit, but there may be considerable cash available each month. If the owners of the business remove the retained earnings, funds will not be available with which to buy new cars when the present ones wear out.

Retained earnings are not kept in the form of cash only. Cash may be tied up in such current assets as inventories and accounts receivable, which are later converted to cash. Since retained earnings are a part of owner capital, the earnings can be used for investment purposes and for future expansion.

CREDITOR CAPITAL

Regardless of size, businesses often borrow capital to pay expenses, buy materials, or purchase equipment. Much of this capital is made available from the savings of individuals. Millions of people deposit their savings in banks and in other financial institutions that lend these funds to businesses. Since a business can borrow for as few as 30 days or for several years or longer, creditor capital is of two types: short term and long term.

Short-Term Capital

Short-term capital is creditor capital that must be repaid within a year, and often in 30, 60, or 90 days. Short-term capital may be obtained from a bank or other lending agency.

Obtaining Funds From Banks. Banks want to be certain that loans will be repaid. Some of the questions that may be asked about borrowers are listed in Fig. 17-4. If satisfactory answers are given to these questions, banks may grant loans or they may also grant an open line of credit. An **open line of credit** permits borrowing up to a specified amount for a specified period of time. For example, a business may be allowed a line of credit up to $50,000 for a year. Whenever it needs to borrow, it may do so up to the $50,000 limit. Should the business borrow $10,000, it could still borrow an additional $40,000 during the year.

When a business wants to borrow money from a lending institution, whether the business has a line of credit or not, a promissory note must be signed. A **promissory note** (see Fig. 17-5) is an unconditional written promise to pay a certain sum of money at a particular time or on demand to the order of the one who has obtained the note. The business or person who promises to pay the amount of the note is the **maker**. The person to whom the note (or check) is payable is the **payee**.

If there is some doubt about the ability of the firm to repay a loan, the bank may require the business to pledge its accounts receivable or merchandise inventory as security for the loan. If the loan is not repaid, the bank can claim the money collected from the accounts of customers or can reclaim the merchandise and sell it.

Questions That May Be Asked About a Borrower

1. Is the borrower of good character?
2. Is the borrower putting up enough cash?
3. What experience has the borrower had in this business?
4. Will the loan be secured properly? Will payments on debts be made from profits only?
5. Will financing be sound? (Lender will want to see the net worth to debt and the cash-to-cash needs ratios; also the debt payments to income ratio.)
6. Is enough cash being raised to supply needs:
   for repairs on buildings and equipment?
   for modernization, new equipment?
   to build up accounts receivable?
   for build-up of inventory expansion?
7. How good is the estimate of salaries, wages, utilities, advertising, supplies, taxes, insurance, and other expenses?
8. What are the terms of the lease or mortgage? What amount must be paid in taxes?
9. Does the borrower have good accounting knowledge?
10. Does the borrower keep proper accounting records?

Fig. 17-4

There are many questions lenders need to have answered before lending money to borrowers.

Fig. 17-5

A promissory note.

DUE August 10, 19--   NO. 528

$ 5000.00   MUNCIE, IND., May 10 19--

Three months AFTER DATE, WE, OR EITHER OF US, PROMISE TO PAY

TO THE ORDER OF J.J. McKissick

Five Thousand and 00/100 DOLLARS

WITH ATTORNEY'S FEES, NEGOTIABLE AND PAYABLE AT INDUSTRIAL TRUST & SAVINGS BANK OF MUNCIE, IND., FOR VALUE RECEIVED, WITHOUT RELIEF FROM VALUATION OR APPRAISMENT LAWS. THE DRAWERS AND ENDORSERS SEVERALLY WAIVE PRESENTATION FOR PAYMENT, PROTEST, NOTICE OF PROTEST AND NOTICE OF NON PAYMENT OF THIS NOTE WITH   8   PERCENT INTEREST AFTER DATE, AND NINE PERCENT INTEREST AFTER MATURITY UNTIL PAID.

1145 South High

T Oliver Ree
JB Burton

Obtaining Funds From Other Sources. Depending upon the type of business, there may be other sources of short-term capital. Owners with life insurance policies can borrow from funds paid to insurance companies. Funds are available at favorable rates from some states, cities, counties, and towns in order to encourage businesses to locate in a particular area or to encourage businesses not to leave.

In addition, **factoring companies**, or **factors**, specialize in lending money to businesses based on their accounts receivable. The usual practice, however, is that the factor will purchase the accounts receivable at a discount and then collect the full amounts when due.

In a similar manner, a **sales finance company** engages in purchasing install-ment sales contracts at a discount from businesses that need cash or that do not care to handle collections. A sales finance company may also lend money to a business and use the business' installment contracts as security for the loans.

Long-Term Capital

Long-term capital is capital borrowed for longer than a year. A business usually obtains such capital by issuing long-term notes and bonds.

Notes. **Notes** are a significant source of capital in modern business. Written for periods of 1 to 15 years, they are often called **long-term notes** or **term loans**. Because the term loans extend for a long period, lending institutions require the principal and interest to be repaid on a regular basis over the life of the note.

Long-term notes are often used to purchase equipment. Rather than borrow large sums of money to buy an expensive piece of equipment, however, a com-pany may prefer to lease it. A **lease** is a contract that allows the use of an asset for a fee. Leasing is a practical substitute for long-term financing, especially if capital is difficult to obtain. For example, large computers are often leased because they are costly, are constantly changing, and are soon obsolete. Even though a business does not legally own the leased asset, it has full use of it for the life of the lease. The maintenance of the asset is often included in the leasing agreement.

Bonds. A **bond** is a long-term written promise to pay a definite sum of money at a specified time. The issuer must pay the bondholder the amount borrowed —called the *principal* or *par value*—at the bond's maturity or due date. Bonds also include an agreement to pay interest at a specified rate at certain intervals. Bonds are usually issued in units of $1,000—for example, $1,000, $5,000, or $10,000.

Bonds do not represent a share in the ownership of a corporation; they are evidence of debts owed by a corporation. Bondholders, also called bond investors, are creditors who have a preferred claim against the earnings of a corporation. Bondholders must be paid before stockholders share in the earnings.

There are two general types of bonds: debenture and mortgage bonds. **Debentures** are unsecured. No specific assets are pledged as security. Deben-tures are based upon the faith and credit of the corporation that issues them. Public corporations, such as city, state, and federal governments, usually issue debentures when they need to borrow money. Reputable, successful corpora-tions usually find it relatively easy to sell debentures. However, relatively unknown and weak firms usually find it easier to attract investors when bonds are secured. **Mortgage bonds** are secured by specific assets pledged as a guarantee that the principal and interest will be paid according to the terms specified on the bond certificate. Property often used as security includes real estate, equipment, stocks and bonds held in other companies, and life insurance policies.

If principal and interest are not paid when due, creditors can take legal action against the firm to collect the value of the debt. Creditors can force property to be sold in order to recover the amount of the outstanding debt. Often, however, property cannot be sold for the amount of the loan. In some cases, a bond contract may have a provision that allows bondholders to claim assets other than the assets originally used as security.

Unsecured debentures and secured mortgage bonds are basic types of bonds that businesses might issue when funds are needed for an extended period. Special features may be attached to these bonds to attract investors. For example, a mortgage bond can have a convertible feature to make it appealing to bond buyers. A **convertible bond** permits a bondholder to exchange bonds for a prescribed number of shares of common stock.

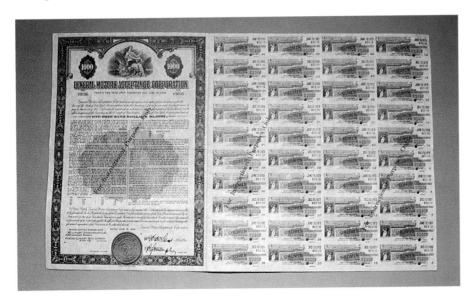

Illus. 17-4

Bonds are often used by corporations to borrow large sums of money. How does a debenture differ from a mortgage bond?

DETERMINING WHICH SOURCE OF CAPITAL TO USE

Three important factors should be considered when deciding the source from which capital should be obtained: (a) the original cost of obtaining the capital, (b) the interest rate, and (c) the authority exercised by the various contributors of capital.

COST OF CAPITAL

It can be costly for a business to obtain capital by selling bonds, long-term notes, and new stock issues. A new bond issue, for example, is expensive to launch. Forms must be filed, approvals obtained from government authorities, agreements made, bonds printed, buyers found, and careful records kept. These costs are usually so high that only large or highly successful firms even consider obtaining capital by issuing new stocks or bonds. It is far less costly to obtain capital from a simple mortgage or a note.

INTEREST RATES

As suggested in Fig. 17-6, interest rates can vary from week to week and from month to month. Borrowing when rates are low will cost less than borrowing when rates are high. If a business needs money when interest rates are high, it will usually borrow for a short time with the hope that rates will drop. If rates drop, long-term obligations such as bonds can then be issued, and a portion of the capital obtained can be used to pay off short-term obligations. In this way, a company has to pay high interest rates for only a short time. In following this plan, however, a business exposes itself to possible difficulty in obtaining funds when short-term obligations fall due, and to the possibility that interest rates may rise even higher.

Fig. 17-6

Because interest rates change frequently, the cost of borrowing also changes.

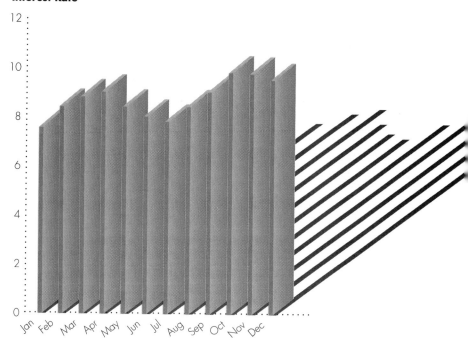

Interest Rate

AUTHORITY OF CONTRIBUTORS

If short-term creditors contribute capital, they usually have no control over the affairs of the business. If the obligations are not paid, creditors can take legal action to recover the amount due. Otherwise, owners of the business are in no way restricted by short-term creditors.

If capital is obtained from mortgage bonds, however, the holders usually have a lien (claim) on at least part of the assets of the company. This lien may impose limitations on the use of these assets, and the agreement under which the mortgage bonds were issued may limit the use of the income of the company.

If new stockholders or new partners contribute owner capital, they gain a voice in the management of the business. In most states, stock can be issued that does not have voting rights, but such stock may be difficult to sell. Of course, if existing stockholders or partners provide the additional funds, the control of the company will not be affected as long as the existing stockholders contribute in proportion to their past holdings.

If the number of shares is increased by selling new shares to stockholders, earnings must be shared with an increased number of shareholders. For example, when the number of shareholders increases from 2,000 to 2,500, the distribution of $130,000 in dividends changes from $65 per share ($130,000 ÷ 2,000) to $52 per share ($130,000 ÷ 2,500). The original owners may not wish to give up any of their profits or voice in management unless it is profitable to do so. An increase in shareholders would need to be offset by an increase in earnings.

OBTAINING OUTSIDE CAPITAL

When a business decides to obtain capital, sources must be found. Some common sources of capital are shown in Fig. 17-7. The particular source to be used depends, in part, on such factors as the amount of capital needed or the risk involved. Companies with poor reputations find it hard to sell stocks or to sell bonds to potential investors. A newly formed company also has similar difficulties in securing a loan. Many banks avoid doing business with these types of organizations because of the high risk involved. When they do assist such firms, interest rates and other charges will be much higher than for successful firms.

Sources of Capital

1. **Banks and related financial firms (the most poplular source of outside capital)**
2. **Small loan companies (firms that lend money to individuals and businesses that may involve more risk than other lenders might accept)**
3. **Venture capital firms (companies that lend large sums of money to promising new or growing businesses)**
4. **Commercial credit companies (companies that lend money on current assets, such as accounts receivable and notes receivable)**
5. **Sales finance companies (used primarily when installment sales are involved; these firms purchase installment sales contracts)**
6. **Insurance companies (portions of funds collected from policyholders may be loaned to firms)**
7. **Individual investors and investment groups**
8. **Pension funds (retirement funds collected from employees may be loaned to firms)**
9. **Investment banking organizations (firms that specialize in selling new security issues to the public)**
10. **Equipment manufacturers (firms that do not actually lend money, but will sell needed equipment on an extended-time payment plan)**

Fig. 17-7

Businesses can get capital from many sources.

Ethical Issues

PELEX, INC.

Questions:

1 What is the main means by which Pelex, Inc. makes its money?

2 Identify the primary accounting practice Pelex, Inc. used when purchasing Central Engineering that did not follow a generally accepted accounting rule.

3 Why does CEO Lauren Wells seemingly violate generally accepted accounting practices?

4 Is the practice of violating accounting and tax regulations unethical? Explain your answer.

Lauren Wells seemed to have launched a promising business in the early 1980s when she commenced building a large firm in the construction equipment industry. CEO Wells started out like many other successful entrepreneurs when she acquired her first floundering bankruptcy-ladened firm with $1,200. On nearly a yearly basis, she acquired other financially weak businesses with the hope of turning them around.

Wells' general strategy was to buy distressed firms at low prices and make them profitable. The means for making them profitable, however, may be Wells' undoing. Evidence indicates that her primary operating company—Pelex, Inc.—violates generally accepted accounting principles and perhaps Internal Revenue Service rules as well.

After buying a firm and before buying the next company, it is necessary to show investors and lenders that Pelex is performing well and is doing especially well with the most recent business acquired. To accomplish this, CEO Wells' company may have stretched accounting rules too far.

For example, the first company acquired was Central Engineering Co., which had a large inventory of construction equipment. Pelex, Inc. reported the value of Central's inventory on its balance sheet as zero, claiming the equipment was obsolete and worthless. However, this "valueless" equipment was later sold for substantially more than its purchase price, thereby generating inflated revenue. This practice is considered improper by the Financial Accounting Standards Board, which establishes generally accepted accounting rules. Properly reported earnings would have reduced the company's earnings by 50 percent. The high earnings made the company look profitable to investors and bankers, who agreed to provide capital for additional acquisitions.

Investors and lenders have become increasingly uncomfortable. The most recent purchase brought further troubles to Lauren Wells. Because of Pelex, Inc.'s weakened financial position, venture capitalists have refused to provide funds for new acquisitions. Pelex, Inc. has resorted to selling junk bonds at an interest rate of 13 percent. *Junk bonds* are high-risk, high-return bonds that are used to finance takeovers of other companies. Profits will need to rise substantially to pay junk bond obligations. Pelex, Inc. has not done well recently.

But the aggressive CEO has her followers, including many employees and board members. By using questionable strategies in the takeover of firms, Lauren Wells converted her original $1,200 to a company worth over $10 million. Previous employees—accountants and managers—however, do not speak well of her business practices.

INVESTMENT BANKERS

Typical banks found in most communities do not generally become involved in helping large organizations raise capital by selling stocks and bonds. Corporations that wish to sell stocks and bonds seek the services of **investment banking firms**—organizations that help businesses raise capital.

A major service provided by investment bankers is to help corporations raise capital by selling large issues of stocks and bonds. For example, if a corporation wishes to raise $50 million by selling bonds, it would seek the services of an investment banking firm. The firm would offer advice, buy the bonds at a price below the expected market value, and then sell the bonds to the investing public through its marketing channels. The firm's profit would amount to the difference between what it paid the corporation for the bonds and the selling price it received from the bond purchasers.

STOCK RIGHTS

Some corporations, on the other hand, may only wish to sell a small number of additional shares of stock. In such cases, a corporation can handle the sale itself. The sale of additional shares can be made attractive to current stockholders by using stock rights. **Stock rights** allow stockholders to buy one additional share of stock for each share owned at a price lower than the current market price. The lower price may attract more funds to the corporation without the additional expense of selling through an investment banker. If stockholders do not wish to take advantage of their stock rights, these rights can be sold to others within a stated period at a small gain. Employees may also be given the opportunity to buy stock at prices below market value.

Bob Daemmrich/Stock, Boston

Illus. 17-5
Venture capitalists such as Ross Perot provide large sums of money to someone who wants to start a new company. What do you think would most influence a venture capitalist's loan decision?

VENTURE CAPITALISTS

While relatives and private investors can provide limited sources of capital for new or unusual businesses, so can venture capitalists. A **venture capitalist** is usually a wealthy investor or investment group that lends large sums of money to promising new or expanding small companies. These investors expect many of the businesses to fail, but they accept the risks in expectation that some of the businesses will be successful enough to offset losses. The business plan (see Chapter 5 for details) must be well thought out and have potential for success. Venture capitalists, many of whom are former entrepreneurs, have helped many small firms become large successful firms.

CHAPTER REVIEW 17

BUILDING VOCABULARY POWER

Define the following terms and concepts.

1. securities
2. owner capital (proprietary capital)
3. retained earnings
4. creditor capital (borrowed capital)
5. common stock
6. preferred stock
7. market value
8. par value (stated value)
9. book value
10. short-term capital
11. open line of credit
12. promissory note
13. maker
14. payee
15. factoring companies (factors)
16. sales finance company
17. long-term capital
18. long-term notes (term loans)
19. lease
20. bond
21. debentures
22. mortgage bonds
23. convertible bonds
24. investment banking firm
25. stock rights
26. venture capitalist

REVIEWING FACTS

1. In financing a business, what is the meaning of capital?
2. List three sources of capital.
3. What is the difference between owner capital and creditor capital?
4. Are holders of common stock the first investors to get dividends?
5. Are preferred stockholders guaranteed a fixed dividend?
6. Do preferred stockholders ordinarily have voting privileges in the management of the business?
7. When a corporation goes out of business, are both preferred and common stockholders likely to get much money from the assets?
8. What is the relationship between the par value of stock and its market value?
9. How is the book value of a share of stock calculated?
10. List two situations in which book value might be used.
11. What are the types of questions that a borrower must be prepared to answer when applying for a loan?
12. List three ways that a corporation obtains long-term creditor capital.
13. What is the principal difference between mortgage bonds and debentures?
14. What three factors should be taken into consideration when deciding the source from which capital should be obtained?
15. What is the major service provided by investment bankers?

DISCUSSING IDEAS

1. Distinguish between types of owner capital and creditor capital.
2. Why do you think that the preferred stock of a corporation would probably cost more per share than its common stock?
3. Why should a business retain some of its profits as a reserve or surplus?
4. Why might a bank require a business to pledge its accounts receivable or merchandise inventory as security for a loan?
5. When might a business lease, rather than purchase, equipment?
6. Explain the importance of an investor's owning secured debt as opposed to unsecured debt in the event a company is forced to go out of business.
7. Assume interest rates are high but a corporation needs to borrow money. Give an advantage and a disadvantage of borrowing capital for a short time rather than for a long period.
8. Why would a corporation wishing to raise $75 million by selling bonds hire an investment banker rather than handle the matter itself?
9. How can venture capitalists make a profit, even though they often invest in firms that eventually fail?
10. Assume that you are starting a new business for the first time. What do you think your greatest obstacles will be in obtaining funds for the new venture? Why?

ANALYZING INFORMATION

1. The assets of the Rosemont Corporation are $750,000; the accounts payable, $45,000; bonds payable, $100,000; common stock, $350,000; and preferred stock, $150,000. Does the corporation have a surplus or a deficit? By what amount?
2. Refer to The Barker-Trowe balance sheet provided and answer these questions:
   a. If the par value of both common and preferred stock is $10 a share, how many shares of each kind are outstanding?
   b. If the preferred and common stock shares have equal claims, what is the book value of each share?
   c. If the directors decide to distribute $9,600 as dividends, how much will be paid to preferred stockholders and how much to common stockholders?
   d. If a stockholder owns 10 shares of preferred stock and 10 shares of common stock, how much of the dividends in (c) should the stockholder receive?

The Barker-Trowe Corporation
Balance Sheet
December 31, 19--

ASSETS

Cash	$ 37,000
Notes Receivable	1,000
Accounts Receivable	15,000
Merchandise	70,000
Equipment	16,000
Real Estate	96,000
Total Assets:	**$235,000**

LIABILITIES AND CAPITAL

Notes Payable		$ 2,000
Accounts Payable		7,000
6% Bonds Payable		50,000
Common Stock:		
Authorized	$100,000	
Unissued	20,000	
Outstanding		80,000
7% Preferred Stock:		
Authorized	100,000	
Unissued	20,000	
Outstanding		80,000
Retained Earnings		16,000
Total Liabilities and Capital:		**$235,000**

3. The net profit of the Ajax Corporation has averaged $60,000 a year. There are 12,000 shares of common stock authorized, but only 6,000 are issued and outstanding. More capital is needed and the owners might sell the additional 6,000 shares at $100 a share. It is estimated that the new capital will make it possible to increase the net profit to $90,000.
   a. What is the net profit per share now?
   b. What is the expected net profit per share if 6,000 new shares are sold?
   c. Does it appear to be a good action to take?

4. Don Cobb and Sudha Sanyal each own 2,000 shares of stock, representing all of the common stock outstanding in a rural bottled gas company, a product that customers buy to heat their dwellings. They need $20,000 and have three ways to secure the funds: (a) borrow $20,000 for a period of three months—April, May, and June—and again for a period of three months—October, November, and December—at a yearly interest rate of 9 percent; (b) sell 2,000 additional shares of common stock at $10 each to raise a total of $20,000 for permanent working capital; and (c) sell 2,000 shares of preferred stock at $10 a share with a dividend rate of 11 percent. In other words, these owners are faced with a need for cash to

REVIEW 17

finance their operations, and must decide whether to borrow the money, sell common stock, or sell preferred stock. Assume that the profit of the company is $36,000 a year without anticipating any interest charges.

   a. How will the interest on the borrowed money affect Don and Sudha's profits if $20,000 is borrowed as indicated?

   b. How will their profits be affected if 2,000 shares of common stock are sold?

   c. How will Don and Sudha's profits be affected if 2,000 shares of preferred stock are sold?

5. A venture capitalist company invested in five new businesses during the past year. The results at the end of the year were as follows:

Business A: Loss	$ 500,000
Business B: Loss	900,000
Business C: Loss	250,000
Business D: Loss	50,000
Business E: Profit	2,500,000

   a. What was the total loss for the year?

   b. What was the net gain or loss for the year?

   c. Is it possible that Businesses A, B, C, and D might earn a profit by the end of the second year? Discuss.

S OLVING BUSINESS PROBLEMS

CASE 17-1

Reiko Mori is a member of a four-person car pool. Morning conversations on the way to work often deal with what people did the night before. Reiko started the discussion today because she had attended a lecture last evening on investing in stocks and bonds. Selected parts of the conversation by car pool members follow:

Lou: What did you learn that we do not already know, Reiko?

Reiko: I learned that there are all kinds of stocks and bonds. There is something to meet everyone's needs. But it is all quite confusing.

Pedro: My broker suggested I buy some new debentures, but I did not understand what he was talking about. Did the lecturer explain these things?

Reiko: Not really. The lecturer spent nearly all the time talking about stocks. Maybe next week's talk will cover bonds.

Susan: My uncle gave Larry and me a mortgage bond for a wedding gift. We are going to keep it because the company has been doing great. I wish I had some stock in this company, too, but we cannot afford it right now.

Reiko: Susan, can you have lunch with me today? I did learn something about mortgage bonds that might be helpful.

Required:

1. Explain debentures to Pedro.
2. If you were having lunch with Susan, what would you tell her about the mortgage bonds she owns?

CASE 17-2

The manager of the Corner Appliance Store needs a new delivery truck. The desired truck has new, technologically advanced features that will improve the delivery process and reduce operating costs. However, the truck costs nearly $30,000.

   The manager is considering getting a loan or selling the accounts receivable. The store has $50,000 in accounts receivable, which it can sell to a factoring firm for 78 percent of the total amount the customers owe. Otherwise, the store can get a six-month 12 percent loan for $30,000 from a bank if it pledges the accounts receivable as security.

Required:

1. How much would the company receive if the accounts receivable were sold?
2. How much will the company receive in cash from the bank loan? How much will the interest be?
3. Discuss the advantages and disadvantages of each plan.
4. Is there any other way for the company to acquire the new truck?

REVIEW

FINANCIAL SERVICES CHAPTER 18

After studying this chapter you will be able to:

18-1 Distinguish between banks and nonbanks and the services provided by each.

18-2 Describe the impact of computers on banking.

18-3 Compare and select various types of investment instruments.

18-4 Identify practices related to the use of checks and other negotiable instruments.

18-5 Describe types of loans and practices related to obtaining a loan.

18-6 Discuss past and present changes in the financial world.

A mong his other duties, Jim Preston is newly in charge of office and financial matters for the small but growing firm of Kilgore Appliances, distributor for all types of kitchen gadgets. During the morning break, he planned to discuss the large balance in Kilgore's checking account with Sandra Dickens, the accountant. As they entered the nearby deli, Sandra expressed her frustration in balancing this month's checking account.

"You know, Sandra," Jim replied, "we should start thinking of other places to park the excess amount of cash building up in that account. That's money not working for us."

"I agree, Jim," Sandra said. "We make no money in a regular checking account. And during the next three months, I don't see any heavy payment drains. Why don't we put some into short-term investments?"

Jim paused and then remarked, "But we need answers to some questions first. Where can we put the money and earn the most on it? Is one bank any different from another? What investment opportunities exist for short- and long-time periods?"

"Jim, let's work together on this," Sandra replied. "Can you find time by lunch tomorrow to do some financial shopping? Then we can sort out our information and perhaps be ready to make a decision."

"Sounds like the right move to make, Sandra. I'll try the savings and loan association down the street and our own commercial bank. Do you want to contact the new mutual savings bank near your home and perhaps the investment company that has been running ads in the local paper?" Sandra nodded her approval, then added, "See you at lunch tomorrow."

All businesses rely on the services of financial institutions such as banks. A business like Kilgore Appliances must deposit cash, make payments by check, invest excess funds, and borrow money. Whether a business is small, large, new, or old, financial services are absolutely essential. A knowledge of the available types of financial institutions and the services they provide help managers like Jim and Sandra operate businesses efficiently.

FINANCIAL INSTITUTIONS

Financial institutions play a major role in the business world by handling transactions that deal primarily with money and securities. While banks provide many of the needed services, other financial institutions also provide essential services. In fact, each year it is getting more and more difficult to distinguish among the services provided by various financial institutions.

In recent years, financial institutions have expanded the services they offer. Banking laws, deregulation of banking, and computer technology have created intense competition and a variety of banking services.

Illus. 18-1

Competition among financial institutions is growing as the services offered become more similar. Can you name three financial institutions in your community from which you might obtain financial services?

Jeff Greenberg, Photographer

DIFFERENCES AMONG BANKS

Banks and nonbank financial institutions are common. As defined by Congress in 1970, a **bank** is an institution that accepts demand deposits and makes commercial loans. A **demand**

deposit is money put into a financial institution by depositors that can be withdrawn at any time without penalty. Checking accounts represent the most popular form of demand deposits. Money deposited for a fixed period is called a **time deposit**. A popular example of a time deposit is the standard savings account. Banks also provide commercial loans, which differ from consumer loans. A **commercial loan** is made to a business, whereas a **consumer loan** is made to an individual. If an institution offers only demand deposits or commercial loans, but not both, it is called a **nonbank bank**, or **nonbank**.

A bank is subject to more regulation by federal banking laws than a non-bank. As a result, nonbanks have gained a competitive advantage over banks. To avoid regulation, some banks become nonbanks by dropping commercial loans or demand deposits. Many corporations have added nonbanks to their operations, such as American Express, General Motors, and General Electric.

BANK INSTITUTIONS

In spite of the changes that occur in the financial world within banks and non-banks, financial services have improved greatly during the last several decades. The common types of banking institutions are shown in Fig. 18-1 on page 434. These institutions still offer the basic services provided in earlier years.

Today, the majority of banking institutions provide a host of services. None, however, is more complete or more valuable to business than a commercial bank. A commercial bank, which makes commercial and consumer loans and handles checking accounts, also rents safe deposit boxes and provides financial advice. Legal and tax advice are also often available, along with bill-paying and payroll-preparation services. Commercial banks can collect promissory notes, do insurance planning, and provide vault service as well. Many now also sell stocks and mutual funds. Because commercial banks provide a variety of services, they are referred to as full-service banks. The popularity of these banks is unquestioned. For every savings and loan association or mutual savings bank, there are nearly four commercial banks.

NONBANK INSTITUTIONS

Nonbank institutions have grown rapidly because of the many valuable financial services they offer. Stock brokerage firms, for example, not only buy and sell stocks and bonds for customers, but also offer checking privileges and credit card services. Credit unions provide many of the services available at banks—but on a smaller scale. Insurance companies loan funds in large amounts to eligible businesses for long periods. Pension funds created by businesses to benefit employees provide another source of funds for long-term loans.

Financial institutions are available in most communities.

Common Banking Institutions

COMMERCIAL BANK

Handles time and demand deposits, commercial and consumer loans, and many other special services.

MUTUAL SAVINGS BANK OR SAVINGS BANK

Specializes in handling passbook savings accounts and loans, particularly long-term loans such as mortgages.

TRUST COMPANY

Manages property such as securities, real estate, and cash as directed by its customers. May be a separate institution or a department within a commercial or savings bank.

SAVINGS AND LOAN ASSOCIATION

Specializes in savings accounts and home mortgage loans. Also known as S&L.

COMPUTERS AND BANKING

Remarkable changes have occurred in banking practices in recent years because of the extensive use of computers. Much of the work once done by clerks, such as processing checks, recording deposits and withdrawals, and keeping customer accounts up to date, is now done rapidly by computer. **Electronic funds transfer (EFT)**, transferring money by computer rather than by check, has enabled financial institutions to provide faster, improved services. The need for checks, for example, has been reduced by EFT transactions. Direct deposits, automatic teller machine transactions, and other forms of computerized banking are three common uses of EFTs. Debit cards, which are discussed in the next chapter on pages 460-61, are still another use of EFTs.

DIRECT DEPOSITS

Banks provide **direct deposit** services that allow businesses to electronically transfer employees' paychecks directly from the employer's bank account to employees' bank accounts. The use of direct deposit banking has increased in popularity. Employees who select this service receive immediate use of their earnings. They no longer have to wait in line to cash checks or make deposits. For each pay period, the employer must provide the employee with a record listing gross pay and all deductions. The Social Security Administration encourages retirees to use direct deposit. In this way, checks do not get lost or stolen, and senior citizens have ready access to their funds without making unnecessary trips to banks.

AUTOMATIC TELLER MACHINES

An **automatic teller machine (ATM)** enables bank customers to deposit, withdraw, or transfer funds by using a bank-provided plastic card. ATMs are located at banks and at other convenient places such as outside of banks and inside malls. ATMs are also found in many foreign countries. ATMs are widespread because they are quick and convenient to use and are especially valuable for people who do not wish to carry large sums of money. The appeal of ATMs is enhanced because cash can be withdrawn during nonbanking hours. Bank customers simply insert the bank's card and follow the ATM's instructions. Writing and cashing checks for small sums is quickly disappearing. Furthermore, banks with ATMs need fewer branch offices to serve their customers. By the year 2000, at least 15,000 branch banks are expected to be eliminated.

Financial institutions have adopted anti-crime devices for their ATM systems. One such device is to place a daily limit on the amount that a customer may withdraw. Another device is for banks to warn customers when they detect an irregular pattern of ATM withdrawals, which might suggest some unauthorized person is withdrawing cash. Many banks have located ATMs in well-lighted areas. Still other financial institutions have installed hidden cameras that may help police identify thieves.

UNIPHOTO

Illus. 18-2

Over the last decade, automatic teller machines have doubled in number. Where are the ATMs located in your community? How many of your friends and relatives use ATMs?

COMPUTER BANKING

Electronic banking speeds business activities. Firms conduct banking and other types of business activities quickly and conveniently through computers and telephones. Computer banking makes it possible for bills to be paid and for money to be transferred from one bank account to another. Of course, most banks charge fees for these services.

In the future, banks will be able to lower operating costs because fewer bank tellers and clerks will be needed. Banking by computer is almost like having one's own ATM, except that cash cannot be withdrawn.

INVESTMENT INSTRUMENTS AND DECISIONS

Businesses earn profits that are not entirely shared by owners. Profits are sometimes invested in the business or in financial instruments where further income may be earned. Investors, whether businesses or individuals, need to know about basic investment instruments and how to decide upon investment goals.

INVESTMENT INSTRUMENTS

Financial institutions are constantly seeking new and better ways to serve customers. With high technology in a highly competitive environment, many financial instruments have been created. From the wide variety of financial instruments, businesses and individuals can select the instruments that best fit their investment needs. Some of the primary financial instruments are shown in Fig. 18-2.

Fig. 18-2

Financial institutions provide many types of investment instruments.

Interest-Bearing Checking Accounts	**Treasury Bills**
Regular Savings Accounts	**Treasury Notes**
Certificates of Deposit (CDs)	**Treasury Bonds**
Money Market Funds	**Corporate Stocks**
Mutual Funds	**Corporate Bonds**

Interest-Bearing Checking Accounts

Many checking accounts provide opportunities to earn interest if account balances do not drop below a specified minimum, such as $500 or $1,000. If a balance falls below the minimum, service fees are charged by the bank. Investors with small sums of money find interest-bearing checking accounts a convenient way both to save and use funds to pay for items purchased. Because checking accounts are not primarily designed as savings instruments, however, they serve that purpose only to a limited extent and the interest rate earned is relatively small in comparison to most other investments.

Regular Savings Accounts

A **regular savings account**, or **passbook savings account**, allows customers to make deposits and withdrawals without financial penalties. Amounts invested can be small and usually earn low interest rates when compared with other investment instruments.

Certificates of Deposit

While the number of regular savings accounts has declined, certificates of deposit have increased. A **certificate of deposit (CD)** is a time deposit savings account that requires an investor to deposit a specified sum for a fixed period at a fixed interest rate. Many CDs must be for $500 or more and may be purchased for periods ranging from three months to five years. The length of time influences the interest rate earned. For example, the interest rate on a six-month CD will normally be less than on a two-year CD. Although CDs usually pay a higher rate of interest than passbook savings, a CD cannot be withdrawn before its stated time without penalty—a substantial loss of earned interest. Most financial institutions offer certificates of deposit.

Money Market Funds/Accounts

A **money market fund**, or **money market account**, is an account where investments are made mostly in securities that pay interest. Investors can select tax-free or taxable accounts. Deposits of investors are placed in fairly safe, interest-earning, short-term securities. Businesses often invest in money market funds when money will be needed soon or when businesses are not sure about forthcoming changes in interest rates on other investment opportunities.

Another reason for the popularity of money market funds is that depositors have check-writing privileges and can withdraw funds at any time without penalty. However, minimum deposits in money market accounts are often $1,000 or more and a check cannot be written unless it exceeds a minimum amount, such as $200 or $500. Businesses, as well as individuals, often invest in money market funds because the funds earn interest and checks can be written for large amounts.

Money market accounts are offered by banks, and money market funds are offered by investment companies. In recent years, investment companies, often referred to as mutual funds, have become involved in banking-type activities.

Mutual Funds

An **investment company** specializes in the sale of a variety of stocks and bonds. Most investment companies specialize in mutual funds. A **mutual fund** pools the money of many small investors for the purchase of stocks and bonds. Mutual funds are usually bought by people who prefer to invest in securities but do not wish to select individual stocks

CERTIFICATES OF DEPOSIT
WEEK OF 10 24
$1000 MIN. DEPOSIT

	RATE	ANNUAL YIELD
3 MONTHS	2.60%	2.63%
6 MONTHS	3.20%	3.25%
1 YEAR	3.94%	4.00%
18 MONTHS	4.67%	4.75%
2 YEARS	4.67%	4.75%
30 MONTH	4.67%	4.75%
3 YEARS	4.67%	4.75%
MONEY MARKET		2.50%

I R A

	3 85	3 91
18 MOS	4 45	4 52
24 & 30 MOS	4 45	4 52
36 MOS		

Jeff Greenberg, Photographer

Illus. 18-3
Banks offer many investment choices. What rates of interest can be earned on investments in savings accounts, CDs, and money market accounts at the bank nearest to your home or school?

and/or bonds. Professional fund managers select a variety of securities that have been carefully evaluated.

Treasury Bills

The United States government provides financial services by selling instruments for various government agencies such as the U.S. Treasury Department, which sells bills, notes, and bonds. A **treasury bill**, or **T-bill**, is a short-term (one year or less) security sold by the federal government to finance the cost of running the government. T-bills are sold in $10,000 to $1 million amounts and mature in 3 to 12 months. Like other government securities, they are considered one of the safest of all short-term investments.

Treasury Notes and Bonds

Treasury notes and **treasury bonds** are also U.S. government securities. Treasury notes are available in amounts of $1,000 up to $5,000 that generally mature in one to ten years. Treasury bonds are available in $1,000 to $1 million amounts with maturities ranging from 10 to 30 years. Businesses frequently invest in these securities because they are practically risk free and are readily bought and sold. Although the federal government taxes the interest earned, state governments do not.

INVESTMENT GOALS

Inexperienced investors frequently give little thought to determining their investment goals because they are too busy attempting to select a specific investment. For example, individuals often put all their funds into one type of account such as a savings account. Small business owners often make the same mistake. Investors need to make investment decisions based upon their investment goals, especially those that apply to liquidity, safety, and growth.

Liquidity deals with the speed with which the investor needs to convert an investment into cash. For example, Kilgore Appliances, described at the start of this chapter, is a small but growing business that may have a great need for cash on a regular basis. Therefore, excess cash should be invested for very short periods. Investment choices might be limited to money market accounts. Assume, on the other hand, that an established, profitable firm has a steady source of income and expenses. It, however, has a great need to replace equipment in about five years. Treasury notes and bills might be appropriate choices for this firm. Both firms have different objectives that will determine, in part, the investments selected.

A second investment goal depends upon the degree of safety desired. Some investors want maximum safety; they do not want to risk losing any of their money. They may accept earning less on an investment to obtain safety. Investment in savings accounts, money market funds, and government bonds appeal to them. Other investors like to take some risks if more money might possibly be earned. These investors might prefer to buy stock in a newly developed corporation, stock in a developing country, or junk bonds.

The third investment goal focuses on investors who invest primarily for growth purposes rather than for income. These investors do not need a steady income from investments and are willing to invest for long periods of time. They hope to see their investments grow faster than inflation. Substantial growth is their goal. Stocks with good long-term growth prospects are preferred. Bonds are not generally considered a good choice for growth.

Most experienced investors also suggest another rule that pertains to safety: "Don't put all your eggs in one basket." Spread your risks by placing money in different categories of investments, never in one alone. For example, a diversified investment plan might be to put one-third of one's investment money into bonds, one-third into stocks, and one-third into money market funds. To follow this rule further, not all investments in bonds should be in one company, nor should all stock investments be in one corporation. Diversity greatly reduces the risk factor.

CHECKS AS NEGOTIABLE INSTRUMENTS

Because few transactions involve cash, other devices are needed to conduct business operations. A **negotiable instrument** is written evidence of a contractual obligation and is normally transferable from one person to another by endorsement. Promissory notes, discussed in Chapter 17, are negotiable instruments that are frequently used. However, the most commonly used negotiable instruments are checks.

CHECKS

A vital service that many financial institutions offer is a checking account. Businesses make many payments by writing checks from checking accounts and money market accounts. Certain practices and procedures should be followed when paying by check, when accepting checks, and when balancing a checking account.

Paying by Check

A **check** is a written order on a bank to pay previously deposited money to a third party on demand. Businesses use special check-writing equipment that prints checks in proper form. Care should be taken when handwriting checks; see Fig. 18-3 on page 440. When writing checks, perform each of the following bank-recommended guides:

- Fill in completely the check record, or stub, *before* writing the check.
- Fill in all blank lines with a pen.
- Start writing at the far left of each blank line and draw lines through any unused parts to prevent alterations.
- Fill in the name of the payee (person to whom a check is written) and avoid making checks payable to "cash," which a finder or thief could cash.
- Do not write a future date on a check because banks will not cash postdated checks.

Fig. 18-3

Checks should be written with care.

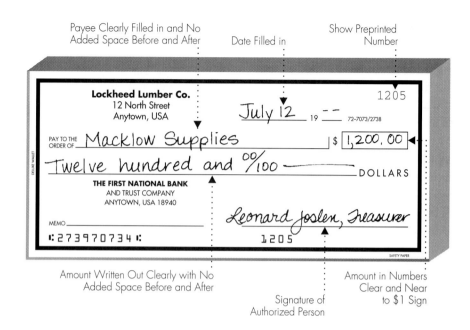

Payee Clearly Filled in and No Added Space Before and After

Date Filled in

Show Preprinted Number

Amount Written Out Clearly with No Added Space Before and After

Signature of Authorized Person

Amount in Numbers Clear and Near to $1 Sign

After a check has been issued, the **drawer** (the person who owns the account and signs the check) can direct the bank to refuse payment when the check is presented. For example, if a business discovers fraud or deception, it may issue a stop-payment order directing the bank to refuse payment when the check is presented. Stopping payment should be done only for protective purposes.

Accepting Payment by Check

Before accepting a check, precautions should be taken to avoid receiving checks that "bounce." A protective business practice is to ask for identification, such as a driver's license. For unknown customers, accepting a bank credit card such as Visa or MasterCard for payment may be safer than accepting a check. If a loss occurs, the credit card company—not the business—will be responsible. A business cannot be too cautious because losses from bad checks can be severe.

Checks received from customers should be deposited daily. When checks are deposited, they must be endorsed. An **endorsement** is the signature—usually on the back—that transfers a negotiable instrument. Endorsements should be prepared carefully and correctly. The most commonly used types of endorsements found on checks are shown in Fig. 18-4.

Balancing the Checking Account

To maintain a checking account, it is necessary to keep a record of all transactions, such as deposits made and checks written. Typically, each month the bank sends the customer a bank statement (see Fig. 18-5 on page 442) listing the monthly transactions. The ending bank statement balance, however, and the checkbook balance are usually different for many reasons. You must determine why the balances differ so that any necessary changes or corrections can be made to the checkbook balance. The bank must also be notified when a bank error is discovered.

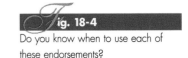

Fig. 18-4
Do you know when to use each of these endorsements?

TYPE	EXAMPLE	USE
Blank	*T.S. Mason*	Easiest to use, but not recommended because it can be cashed by anyone if lost.
Restrictive	*For deposit only* *T.S. Mason*	Limits the use of the negotiable instrument to one specified purpose only. Most often used to deposit checks.
Special or Full	*Pay to the order of* *Thomas Kune* *T.S. Mason*	Names the parties to receive the negotiable instrument. Recommended for general use for safety purposes.

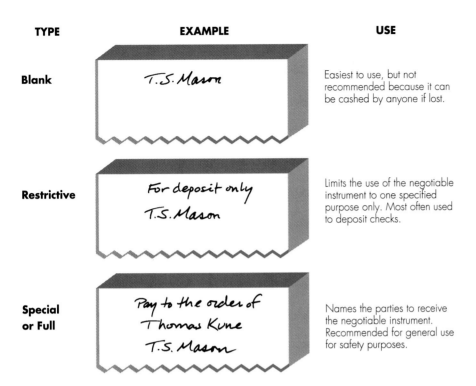

A **reconciliation statement** is a summary that reveals the causes for the difference between the checkbook balance and the bank statement balance, as shown in Fig. 18-6 on page 443.

SPECIAL CHECKS

At times, firms may not accept a regular check from customers. In situations where a customer is unknown or has a weak financial record, businesses may only accept certain types of negotiable instruments. As summarized in Fig. 18-7 on page 443, these types of checks may be preferred in certain situations.

LOANS

Bankers are usually eager to lend money, but they must lend it cautiously, even though at times they take reasonable risks. A business should not hesitate to borrow money if it helps the company make more money. Through borrowing, most businesses are able to grow. However, the banker will expect complete facts to be given before deciding whether the business will be able to repay the loan under the terms of the agreement.

REQUIREMENTS FOR OBTAINING A LOAN

In addition to personal characteristics of business owners, such as honesty and integrity, most lending agencies want other information when making a loan. Additional information includes the business ability of the borrower, past business experience, chances for continued success, personal investment in

Fig. 18-5

A bank statement.

The First-Mason Bank
MASON, OHIO 45040-0045

Elizabeth B. Gordon
1813 Baxter Street
Mason, Ohio 45040-0045

ACCOUNT NUMBER
108325-41

PAGE
1

DATE
June 2, 19--

BALANCE FROM PREVIOUS STATEMENT	NUMBER OF + CREDITS	AMOUNT OF DEPOSITS AND CREDITS	NUMBER OF DEBITS	AMOUNT OF WITHDRAWALS AND DEBITS	TOTAL ACTIVITY CHARGE	STATEMENT BALANCE
$1052	2	$660.00	10	$938.34	$4.05	$769.77

DATE	TRANSACTION DESCRIPTION	TRANSACTION AMOUNT	AMOUNT BALANCE
5-01	CHECK 932	27.63	1024.53
5-01	CHECK 933	234.00	790.53
5-08	CHECK 929	68.40	722.13
5-10	DEPOSIT	375.00+	1097.13
5-15	CHECK 931	48.60	1048.53
5-15	CHECK 936	158.79	889.74
5-20	CHECK 934	196.35	693.39
5-23	CHECK 935	98.25	595.14
5-23	CHECK 937	36.75	558.39
5-25	DEPOSIT	285.00+	843.93
5-29	CHECK 938	69.57	773.82
5-31	SERVICE CHARGE FOR MAY	4.05	769.77

the business, the need and purpose of the loan, and the probability of its repayment on time and in full.

KINDS OF LOANS

Most regular bank loans are short-term loans because they extend for 30, 60, or 90 days. These loans are often renewed and are either unsecured or secured.

Unsecured Loans

Under normal conditions, bank credit is widely extended on **unsecured loans** (nothing of value is pledged to the bank) merely by the signing of a promissory note. However, bank practices vary in this respect, and the type of business will often determine whether a bank will give an unsecured loan.

Character, capacity, capital, and conditions (explained in Chapter 19) are factors considered by bankers in giving unsecured loans. Unsecured loans are

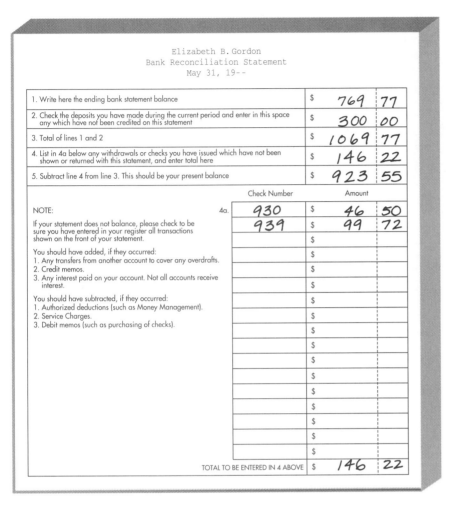

Fig. **18-6**
A reconciliation statement.

generally made for a shorter period than secured loans. Unsecured loans are ordinarily granted only to an established, successful business or to individuals in business who are well known by the lender.

Selected Negotiable Instruments

CASHIER'S CHECK

A check drawn on the bank that issues it, payable to the person designated by the purchaser of the check.

CERTIFIED CHECK

A check on which a bank certifies that a checking account customer's funds are being held specifically to pay the check when presented.

TRAVELER'S CHECKS

Checks purchased in fixed denominations by people who do not wish to carry large sums of cash. When cashed, a traveler's check is filled in and signed in the presence of the person accepting it.

Illus. 18-4
Businesses often receive traveler's checks from customers who are tourists or who travel extensively. Where would you go to buy traveler's checks? Is a fee paid for traveler's checks?

Jeff Greenberg, Photographer

Secured Loans

A **secured loan** is also called a **collateral loan**. For this type of loan the borrower pledges something of value to the bank as security. Collateral loans are usually the easiest to obtain because they give the banker protection. Therefore, a collateral loan is usually made at a lower rate of interest than an unsecured loan. The following types of security or collateral are commonly used:

- Accounts receivable and notes receivable
- Merchandise
- Bonds, stocks, and other marketable securities
- Buildings and real estate
- Machinery and equipment

A person can borrow money on real estate and grant a mortgage that gives the lender the right to take possession of the real estate if the loan is not paid. Any stock or bond that has a value can usually be used as collateral. A bank will ordinarily lend about 50 percent of the value of a good stock or a good bond.

INTEREST RATES

Although interest rates are governed to some extent by law, bank rates are largely based on the supply of and the demand for money. The lowest rate of interest is called the **prime rate**. This is the rate at which large banks lend large sums to the best-qualified borrowers. Small loans and loans to less-qualified customers are made at rates higher than the prime rate. Rates can vary from day to day and from month to month.

On short-term commercial loans, it is common for a bank to deduct the interest in advance. Interest deducted in advance from a loan is called **bank discount**. Suppose, for example, that a loan of $10,000 is needed for three months and that the bank charges 12 percent interest per year. As shown below, the borrower will receive $9,700. Inventory, bonds, or stocks with a market value of approximately $20,000 may be required as security by the bank.

Amount to be paid to bank in three months	$10,000
12 percent interest deducted in advance	300
Amount of cash given to borrower	$ 9,700

The formula for computing interest is:

$$\text{Interest} = \text{Principal} \times \text{Rate} \times \text{Time}$$
$$\text{Interest} = \$10,000 \times 12\% \times 3/12$$

In this example, the actual interest charge is slightly more than 12 percent because $300 is charged for borrowing $9,700 for three months. If the loan is not repaid in three months, the bank has the privilege of selling the securities to obtain the $10,000.

REPAYMENT OF A LOAN

Some borrowers have a tendency to borrow money without giving specific thought as to when and how it can be repaid. They assume that if they cannot repay a loan when it becomes due, they may renew it and continue to pay the interest without making payments on the principal. Borrowing without specific intentions and a specific plan for repaying the principal is a dangerous practice for both borrowers and lenders. Borrowers may be forced into bankruptcy, and lenders may be unable to collect debts. Generally, lenders have found that borrowers will pay long-term obligations with less difficulty if a provision is made for repaying loans at intervals instead of in one lump sum at the end of the loan.

A loan may be payable on demand (whenever requested by the lender), or it may be payable over a stated time, such as a month or year. The **maturity date** refers to the date on which a loan must be repaid. When borrowing money, it is important for an individual to set up a schedule of loan maturities based on a budget of cash as explained in Chapter 15. In estimating one's cash flow, a reasonable margin of safety should be allowed so that funds will be available to pay a maturing loan.

Ethical Issues

CONFLICTING INTERESTS

Questions:

1 Why might you leave a high-level and high-paying position in business to accept a high-level but low-paying position in government?

2 Identify ways in which the director of a government agency who buys equipment might become involved in a conflict-of-interest situation.

3 What regulation or law in your state exists that prevents conflict-of-interest situations from occurring in your state?

4 Except under special circumstances, why should cities and states require competitive bidding?

Governments and corporations must work together on business-related matters. For instance, local and state governments buy merchandise from firms, as does the federal government. Governments also buy services. For example, selling government bonds to the public is done through investment firms. Conflicts of interest, therefore, are possible in government-business relationships.

Occasionally, these relationships lead to situations where an official has to decide what is best for the public. Well-known people are often involved in these conflicts of interest. The U.S. Attorney's Office and the Securities and Exchange Commission are beginning to check into conflict-of-interest situations.

One such case involved an aide to the governor in the state of New Jersey. The aide was accused of helping a Wall Street investment firm obtain a contract to sell state municipal bonds. No one involved in the investigation admitted breaking any laws. And no laws may have been broken! State and municipal bond issuers are relatively unregulated.

As government officials establish relationships with businesses, businesses reward officials with campaign contributions. In turn, those officials sometimes reward businesses with government contracts, such as for underwriting the sale of city or state bonds. **Underwriting** means selling a new issue of a security, such as bonds, through an investment banking firm* for a specified fee. Responsible government officials are creating regulations to prevent questionable conflict-of-interest practices. An executive order signed by New Jersey's governor, for example, requires interested investment firms to bid competitively to underwrite state bonds. Tough laws regulating bond underwriters have been approved in Florida and elsewhere. Other cities and states are considering tough regulations as well.

---

*Investment companies, commonly known as mutual funds, must not be confused with investment banking firms. Mutual funds do *not* underwrite new security issues. The holdings of funds, called the portfolio, are diversified among banks, preferred stocks, and common stocks.

THE CHANGING NATURE OF FINANCIAL INSTITUTIONS

The financial world has undergone dramatic changes during the last two decades. While computer technology has caused some change, the major changes have been a result of legislation aimed at deregulating the banking industry. Legislation has led to extensive competition among banks and nonbanks.

In 1980, Congress passed the Depository Institutions Deregulation and Monetary Act. A major aim of the law was to increase competition among financial institutions. Prior to this law, many state and federal laws controlled what financial institutions could and could not do. The amount of regulation was extensive.

The 1980 law and a 1982 law allowed savings banks, savings and loan associations, and credit unions the right to offer services previously reserved for commercial banks. It also gave more freedom to financial institutions regarding interest rates set on savings accounts, certificates of deposit, and mortgages. Further, the law allowed nonbank institutions to extend the geographic area served.

Changes in laws have created competition among banks (commercial banks and savings banks, for example) and among nonbanks (stock brokerage firms like Merrill Lynch and investment companies like the Vanguard Group). Competition has also increased between banks and nonbanks, such as stock

Jeff Greenberg, Photographer

Ilus. 18-5

In recent years, failures of some banks and savings and loans prompted federal authorities to control and supervise the management of banks. Since 1985, has a savings bank or savings and loan failed in your area? What was the cause of the failure? Were investors reimbursed fully?

brokerage firms and savings and loan associations. While competition proved beneficial to customers, it, in turn, has created problems.

Small and financially weak banks were swallowed up in mergers while others were taken over by larger banks. The most troublesome situation, however, was the failure of many savings and loan associations. In order to survive, these institutions were forced to accept risky loans or invest depositors' funds unwisely. The Federal Savings and Loan Insurance Corporation, unable to pay depositors in the many failed savings and loans, collapsed. The federal government stepped in to protect investors.

The lesson learned was that deregulation encourages competition, but stronger controls and supervision over the practices of financial institutions are needed. The regulators were too lax in detecting the seriousness of problems in time to take corrective action. Certain precautions must be considered by Congress, however, in making any changes. Legislators and bank regulators need to be concerned that new laws do not undermine the soundness, safety, and stability of all our financial institutions. Open competition with stronger regulatory controls can lead to still more and better financial services. However, all competitors—banks and nonbanks—deserve fair and equal treatment by the federal government.

CHAPTER REVIEW 18

BUILDING VOCABULARY POWER

Define the following terms and concepts.

1. bank
2. demand deposit
3. time deposit
4. commercial loan
5. consumer loan
6. nonbank bank (nonbank)
7. commercial bank
8. mutual savings bank (savings bank)
9. trust company
10. savings and loan association
11. electronic funds transfer (EFT)
12. direct deposit
13. automatic teller machine (ATM)
14. regular savings account (passbook savings account)
15. certificate of deposit (CD)
16. money market fund (money market account)
17. investment company
18. mutual fund
19. treasury bill (T-bill)
20. treasury notes
21. treasury bonds
22. negotiable instrument
23. check
24. drawer
25. endorsement
26. reconciliation statement
27. cashier's check
28. certified check
29. travelers' checks

30. unsecured loans
31. secured loan (collateral loan)
32. prime rate

33. bank discount
34. maturity date
35. underwriting

REVIEWING FACTS

1. If Irene Day borrowed funds from a bank in order to buy a new cash register for her business, would she apply for a commercial or consumer loan?
2. If Irene went to a financial institution that handled checking accounts and commercial loans only, did she go to a bank or a nonbank bank?
3. Give two examples of corporations that have nonbank operations.
4. What type of bank would provide the greatest number of useful services to a business?
5. Do ATMs increase or decrease the need for checks?
6. List ten types of investment instruments.
7. What is an advantage and a disadvantage of certificates of deposit over regular savings accounts?
8. Name three important factors to consider when developing investment goals.
9. List three recommended guides when writing checks.
10. What type of identification should a business person request when someone pays by check?
11. From Fig. 18-4, what type of endorsement do most businesses use when making deposits?
12. From Fig. 18-7, what type of negotiable instrument should a business accept from a tourist?
13. Give at least three kinds of information or facts that a borrower will be expected to furnish when requesting a loan.
14. What is a major aim of the Depository Institutions Deregulation and Monetary Act?

DISCUSSING IDEAS

1. A financial institution handles CDs, money market accounts, personal car loans, home insurance, and home mortgage loans. As defined by Congress in 1970, is this institution a bank or a nonbank? Explain your answer.
2. Discuss the advantages and disadvantages of direct deposits for employees.
3. How is an ATM similar to and different from business or home computer banking?
4. This chapter opened with a problem faced by Kilgore Appliances of handling the "excess cash" that is currently building up in its checking account. Assume the excess cash amounts to $10,000 and the company

will continue to use its regular checking account to pay bills. What two investments would be safe as well as earn the highest rate of interest for a six-month period?

5. How are money market funds and mutual funds alike and how do they differ?

6. How are the following financial instruments alike and how are they different: treasury bills, treasury notes, and treasury bonds?

7. A new business has $15,000 to invest for 6-12 months, and it wants a safe investment that makes as much money as possible. Suggest an investment instrument or investment instruments to the owner and give reasons for your answer.

8. Explain what is meant by a reconciliation statement.

9. Business A, which is new, needs to buy equipment from Business B in another city. For safety reasons, Business B will not accept a regular check from Business A. What negotiable instruments mentioned in Fig. 18-7 could be used to transfer the money?

10. How do unsecured and secured loans differ?

A NALYZING INFORMATION

1. The Clemson Company has $30,000 to invest for a two-year period. The company has asked you to select the investments, but it specified that one-third of the investment should always be available every six months without paying a penalty. Also, the earned interest should not be invested. You have decided to invest in CDs. The annual interest rates for the following financial institutions were obtained:

	Months and Rates		
	6	12	24
Capitol State Bank	3.8%	4.5%	5.7%
First Savings & Loan	4.4%	4.9%	5.2%
Merchants Bank & Trust	4.6%	4.8%	5.4%

a. Select First Savings & Loan in which to make all investments and develop an investment plan.

b. Use the investment plan developed in (a) above and determine the total interest you would have earned for the company if the interest rates did not change.

c. Could you invest in more than one institution and earn more interest? If yes, prepare a plan that would provide the maximum interest.

2. Draw three rectangles about the shape of an average check. These will be used to represent the backs of actual checks. Use Fig. 18-4 to guide your endorsement selection for each of the following situations. Give a reason for the endorsement you select.

a. You walk up to the idle bank teller's window to cash your unendorsed paycheck.

b. You receive a check in the mail, which you are mailing to your bank for deposit along with other checks received.

c. You received a check from an investment company and went to your grocery store to cash it.

3. The ending balance shown on R. Mathew's monthly bank statement for November is $313.95. His checkbook balance showed $355.65. Two checks he had written have not yet been returned by the bank: #34 for $12.60 and #37 for $47.35. A deposit on December 1 for $100 does not appear on the bank statement, but a service charge for $1.65 does. Follow a procedure like the one shown in Fig. 18-6 and prepare a reconciliation statement.

4. As the financial manager for your company, you need to borrow $5,000 to purchase new equipment. The bank is willing to lend the money at 10 percent interest payable in four months, with interest deducted in advance.

a. What is the amount of the interest?

b. How much money will you receive from the bank?

c. How much must be paid to the bank at the end of 120 days?

5. Assume that you have an invoice for $1,153 on which the terms are 2 percent in 10 days, net 30 days. You wish to take the discount but find it necessary to borrow money at 8 percent until the end of 30 days in order to pay the invoice. You will need to borrow $1,000. How much money will be saved by borrowing the money for 20 days in order to obtain the discount?

S OLVING BUSINESS PROBLEMS

CASE 18-1

Jim Liu, owner of a delicatessen in a shopping center, often chats outside his business with Dan Hall, who owns the bakery next door. One weekday morning when business was slow, Jim mentioned that he needed to go to his bank in order to put cash in his passbook savings account. Jim was not that familiar with the American financial system. Dan asked Jim how much money he had in his savings account. Jim said he had a regular practice of putting 10 percent of his profits in the account each month. Jim was now concerned that perhaps he should start an account with another bank because the sum was getting quite large. The rest of the conversation follows:

Dan: You are losing money, Jim, by putting that much of your savings in a regular passbook account.

Jim: What do you mean? I came to this country ten years ago and opened this business. I have always believed that a savings bank was the best place to save money. Now you tell me I am losing money.

Dan: It is a place to save money, but the interest you are making right now is 2½ percent less than what you could make elsewhere. In fact, you should buy CDs and T-bills, or even put some of your money in a money market fund. You should shop at nonbank banks as well as at banks.

Jim: Wait. I do not understand these words you are using. But I do know that I do not want to lose my hard-earned profits in any risky investments.

Required:

1. Could Jim invest his money in other savings instruments at his savings bank? Explain.
2. Are T-bills and CDs considered risky investments? Explain your answer.
3. If Jim had $100,000 in his savings account, rather than in treasury notes earning 2½ percent more interest, how much money would Jim lose in a given year?

CASE 18-2

The Home Furnishings Company has borrowed all it can borrow on unsecured credit from its bank. It owns its own building. Many of its sales are on the installment plan, and the company has $60,000 outstanding on accounts receivable. Orders have been placed for a substantial amount of furniture for a special sale, but it is not expected that sufficient money will be available to pay the bills promptly and to take advantage of special discounts. The company wishes to protect its credit standing but needs additional cash.

Required:

1. Can the Home Furnishings Company borrow on an unsecured loan from another bank?
2. What are some ways in which the Home Furnishings Company can probably obtain the cash needed?

REVIEW 18

CREDIT AND COLLECTIONS CHAPTER 19

After studying this chapter you will be able to:

19-1 Explain three different types of consumer credit plans.

19-2 Discuss different kinds of credit cards.

19-3 Compare credit in the United States with credit in other countries.

19-4 Describe how credit decisions are made and how legislation influences these decisions.

19-5 Provide reasons and procedures for implementing sound credit and collection policies and practices.

19-6 State four ways in which credit sales can be analyzed.

Your old jogging shoes are about worn out so you decide to buy a new pair in your favorite sporting goods store. After you find the right size and color, the salesperson asks, "Cash or charge?" You would probably be surprised if that question were not asked. Of course, not all businesses sell on credit, but most do. Whether you buy those new jogging shoes in New York, Berlin, or Tokyo, cash or credit could be an option available to you.

If a business extends credit, the policies that determine how credit is extended and how collections are made will greatly affect the success of that business. Therefore, business owners must have an understanding of general principles and practices that apply to credit when establishing credit policies and collection procedures that they should follow.

Alan Brown/Photonics

CREDIT PRINCIPLES AND PRACTICES

Consumer credit is extended by the retailer to the consumer, whereas **commercial credit** is extended by one business to another business. While all forms of credit operate on the same general principles, consumer and commercial credit differ somewhat. Although some of the main differences are pointed out, the emphasis in this chapter is on consumer credit.

CONSUMER CREDIT PLANS

A business owner may extend credit to customers under any one of a number of different types of credit plans. The factors that most commonly influence the selection of credit plans are the credit practices in the community and the credit practices of competitors.

Regular Charge Credit

In **regular charge credit**, a customer can charge a purchase at any time but must pay the amount owed in full by a specified date. When a customer buys merchandise, the sale is charged to the customer's account. At the end of each month the customer is expected to pay within thirty days for purchases made during the month. A business usually sends each customer a monthly statement, which lists purchases made on credit and merchandise returned for credit during that month. A finance charge is levied if the total amount due is not paid on time.

While a regular charge account is often used for consumer credit, it is more commonly used for commercial credit. For commercial credit, the length of time allowed for payment may be longer and the dollar credit limit is often higher than for consumer credit. Commercial credit can also be for very large nonroutine, single-payment purchases as when expensive items are purchased. Discounts often accompany commercial credit as an incentive for prompt payment, and are much less common for consumer credit.

Installment Credit

Unlike regular charge account plans, an installment credit plan permits partial payments on a monthly basis. An **installment credit** plan is used when a customer makes a sizable purchase and agrees to make payments over an extended but fixed period of time. A principal difference exists between regular credit and installment credit plans. An installment credit customer is given a longer time in which to pay. In addition, the installment credit customer is usually required to pay an interest charge for the privilege of making monthly payments that might likely run for several years or more. Installment credit is commonly extended by retailers who sell expensive items that have a long life, such as cars, furniture, and major home appliances. Other types of installment credit purchases are shown in Fig. 19-1 on page 456.

Because installment credit extends for a long period and involves large sums of money, it is handled somewhat differently from regular charge plans. Usually, a customer makes a down payment for the purchase and signs a formal contract for the balance. An **installment contract**, or **conditional sales contract**, is the agreement under which the buyer promises to make regular payments until the goods are fully paid. With regular charge credit, legal ownership (**title**) passes to the buyer at the time of purchase. But with installment credit, title does not pass to the buyer until all payments have been made. The merchandise, such as a car, can be **repossessed** (taken back) by the seller if the buyer does not pay as agreed. These special conditions should be included in the installment credit contract and explained to the customer.

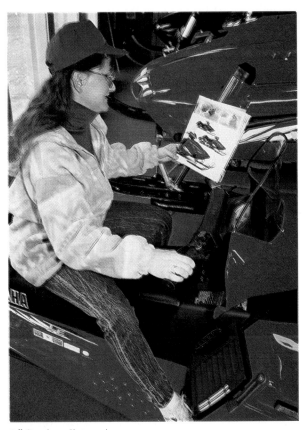

Jeff Greenberg, Photographer

Ilus. 19-2
Consumers often use installment credit when making expensive purchases. Payments are then made over a fixed period of time. What might you or your family have purchased on the installment plan? Might a snowmobile, jet-ski, dirt bike, or sailboat be purchased on the installment plan?

Fig. 19-1

Installment credit purchases far outnumbered noninstallment credit purchases in a recent year.

Consumer Credit (in Billions)

INSTALLMENT CREDIT		$729.4
Automobiles	$267.9	
Revolving	234.5	
Mobile Homes	19.1	
Other	207.9	

NONINSTALLMENT CREDIT	47.9

TOTAL CONSUMER CREDIT	$777.3

Revolving Credit

A very popular and special type of installment credit is revolving credit. A **revolving credit** plan combines the features of regular charge credit and installment credit. Legal title passes to the buyer at the time of purchase as with regular credit. Under the revolving credit plan, the customer is permitted to purchase on credit at any time, usually up to a specified amount. As with regular credit plans, the full amount may be paid by the end of the billing period without a finance charge. However, customers who do not wish to pay in full have the option of making partial payments each month. The minimum amount of a partial payment is dependent upon the amount of the unpaid balance in the account. A finance charge, stated as an interest rate, is added each month to the amount that is unpaid. An example of a revolving credit plan agreement is shown in Fig. 19-2.

Other Credit Plans

Layaway plans and budget plans, which are variations of other installment and revolving credit plans, are also offered by retailers. A **layaway plan** permits a customer to make payments on an item until the item has been fully paid; however, the store holds the merchandise for the customer until the last payment has been made. The layaway plan is especially practical for customers who may not have sufficient cash readily available but want the store to hold merchandise for them.

Still another credit plan is the **budget plan**, which is short-term credit usually covering a two- or three-month period. Department stores, furniture stores, and similar stores often allow customers to purchase major items on a 60- or 90-day credit plan, without additional charge. For instance, a store may permit a customer who has a good credit record to buy furniture amounting to $2,400 and allow the customer 60 to 90 days to pay without adding a service charge.

Dawn's Department Store

Once you use your card or sign a credit card sales slip, this Agreement will be in force. It covers repayment of purchases made with your card.

DAWN'S RETAIL INSTALLMENT CREDIT AGREEMENT

In this Retail Installment Credit Agreement ("Agreement"), the words "you" and "your" refer to any person who signs this Agreement, is issued a credit card, or is authorized to use this Dawn's Charge Account ("Account").

1. Promise to Pay: This Agreement and all charges on this Account are subject to our approval. This agreement shall not become effective unless and until you sign a sales slip evidencing a purchase by use of the credit card, as requested, and extending credit to you on this Account from time to time, you agree to pay for all purchases you charge to your Account, and all other charges mentioned below, in U.S. dollars, according to the terms of this Agreement.

2. Cost of Credit: Finance Charge not in excess of that permitted by law will be charged on the outstanding balances from month to month. There is no Finance Charge in any monthly billing period (a) in which there is no balance at the beginning of the billing period (the "Previous Balance" shown on your monthly statement) or (b) in which payments received and credits issued, within 25 days after the closing date shown on your monthly statement, equal or exceed the balance at the beginning of the billing period. If we do not receive the full amount due (the "New Balance" shown on your monthly statement) within 25 days after the closing date shown on your statement, we will impose a Finance Charge determined by applying a monthly periodic rate of 1.5% (ANNUAL PERCENTAGE RATE 18%) to the average daily balance. A minimum FINANCE CHARGE of $.50 will be imposed in any month in which the Finance Charge resulting from application of the above-stated periodic rate would be less than $.50.

3. Method of Computing Finance Charge: We figure the Finance charge by applying the above-stated periodic rate to the "Average Daily Balance" of your Account. To get the "Average Daily Balance" we take the beginning balance of your Account each day, add any new purchases and any other charges, and subtract any payments and credits. This gives us the daily balance. Then we add up all the daily balances for the billing cycle and divide the total by the number of days in the billing cycle. This gives us the "average Daily Balance."

4. Minimum Monthly Payment: You agree to pay a minimum payment each month equal to at least 1/10th of the "New Balance" shown on your statement, but at least $20.00, or the entire "New Balance" if that amount is less than $20.00. If you fail to pay any amount when it is due, your minimum monthly payment will include such past due amounts. If you pay more than the minimum monthly payment, but less than the New Balance, the excess amount will not decrease the next month's minimum monthly payment nor will it eliminate one or more subsequent minimum monthly payments. We can accept late payments or partial payments, or checks, or money orders marked "payment in full", without losing any of our rights under the Agreement. You may at any time pay more than the minimum monthly payment or your total New Balance.

5. Returned Check Fee: If any check you present to us is returned unpaid by your bank, we will charge you a processing fee of $20.00, or such lesser amount that is authorized by law, to cover our bank costs and processing fees, and you agree that we may add such fee to the balance due in your Account.

6. Late Fee: If the full minimum monthly payment is not received by us within 10 days after the due date shown on your monthly statement, we will impose a late fee of the lesser of 5% of the unpaid amount of the delinquent minimum monthly payment or $5.00, except no Late Fee under $.50 will be imposed.

7. Default: If you fail to pay any minimum monthly payment when due, if you die, or if you become subject to a bankruptcy proceeding, it will be a default, and, subject to any right you may have under state law to receive notice of and to cure such default, we may declare your entire unpaid balance due and payable. If the Account is referred to an attorney who is not our salaried employee, you agree to pay, in addition to the full amount you owe, reasonable attorney's fees up to 20% of the unpaid balance and court costs, but only to the extent authorized by applicable state law. If you successfully assert a partial defense or counterclaim in any action we bring, the court may withhold part or all of the attorney's fees we seek to recover from you.

8. Credit Investigation: We may request a consumer report from consumer reporting agencies in considering your application for this Account and later in connection with any update, renewal or extension of credit. Upon your request, we will tell you the name and address of any consumer reporting agency from which we obtained a report about you. You authorize us to investigate your credit history by obtaining consumer reports and by making direct inquiries of businesses where you have accounts and where you work. You also authorize us to report your performance under this Agreement to credit bureaus and others who may properly receive such information.

9. Canceling or Limiting Your Credit: We have the right at any time to limit or terminate the use of your Account without giving you notice in advance.

10. Credit Cards: All credit cards remain our property and, upon our request, you agree to return any credit card issued to you. If your card(s) is lost, stolen, or used by someone without your permission, you agree to notify the nearest store immediately and confirm the report in writing providing any information you may have about the card.

11. Change in this Agreement: We may change any term of this Agreement, including the rate of finance Charge, by furnishing you notice of the change in the manner prescribed by law.

12. Change of Address: You agree to notify us promptly in writing if you move. Until we receive such notice of your new address, we will continue to send monthly statements and other notices to the address you stated on the application for this Account. Upon receipt of notice that you have moved to another state, the terms of this Agreement applicable to the new state will apply to the entire balance in your account.

13. Governing Law: This Agreement is governed by the law of your state of residence, except if you live in a state where we do not have a store, this Agreement is governed by the law of the State of New York.

NOTICE: ANY HOLDER OF THIS CONSUMER CREDIT CONTRACT IS SUBJECT TO ALL CLAIMS AND DEFENSES WHICH THE DEBTOR COULD ASSERT AGAINST THE SELLER OF GOODS OR SERVICES OBTAINED PURSUANT HERETO OR WITH THE PROCEEDS HEREOF. RECOVERY HEREUNDER BY THE DEBTOR SHALL NOT EXCEED AMOUNTS PAID BY THE DEBTOR HEREUNDER.

NOTICE TO THE BUYER: 1. DO NOT SIGN THIS CREDIT AGREEMENT BEFORE YOU READ IT OR IF IT CONTAINS ANY BLANK SPACE. 2. YOU ARE ENTITLED TO A COMPLETELY FILLED IN COPY OF THIS CREDIT AGREEMENT. 3. KEEP IT TO PROTECT YOUR LEGAL RIGHTS.

A copy of this Retail Installment Credit Agreement along with information regarding your rights to dispute billing errors, will be delivered with your credit card if this application is approved.

RETAIL INSTALLMENT CREDIT AGREEMENT

Donald Vasil
....
Senior Vice President, Chief Financial Officer
Dawn's Department Store

x *Doris S. Bushey*   *Aug. 25, 19--*
....
Buyer Signs   Date

x
....
Co-Buyer Signs   Date

Dawn's Department Store

ig. 19-2

A revolving credit plan requires that the customer follow all of the terms included in the agreement.

CREDIT CARDS

Credit cards are often simply called "plastic" or "plastic money." Over the last 25 years, credit card purchases have grown steadily. The growth in credit card use is reflected in Fig. 19-3.

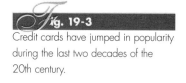

Fig. 19-3
Credit cards have jumped in popularity during the last two decades of the 20th century.

Credit Card Type and Growth in the U.S.

TYPE OF CARD	NO. OF CARDHOLDERS (in Millions)			AMOUNT SPENT (in Billions)		
	1980	1991	2000*	1980	1991	2000*
BANK	63.3	79.7	90.0	52.9	260.0	493.6
OIL COMPANY	68.5	79.9	91.1	28.9	26.5	53.5
PHONE	.....	98.0	111.6	.....	12.4	23.1
RETAIL STORE	83.0	95.0	108.9	74.4	76.4	135.2
TRAVEL & ENTERTAINMENT	10.5	23.1	26.4	21.2	89.4	146.6
OTHER	13.4	7.1	7.3	23.8	21.3	37.9

* Projected

Source: Statistical Abstract of the United States (1992).

Three out of four Americans have at least one credit card. Many individuals have five or more cards. Competition among credit card companies has been strong and will remain so. As a result, companies will continue to compete by offering creative credit card services.

Business Credit Cards

Large local department stores and especially large chain stores issue credit cards to customers who request them. These businesses operate their own credit departments. They seek credit card applicants, check whether the applicants qualify for credit, and issue cards. Most businesses that issue their own private credit cards allow customers to purchase on revolving credit plan terms. However, two major disadvantages to the business are the cost and inconvenience of operating the credit card system. The major disadvantage to the customer is that a separate credit card must be obtained from each business where credit purchases are made. Therefore, customers often must obtain a variety of credit cards.

Bank Credit Cards

Credit cards issued by banks overcome the weaknesses of the typical business credit card. Rather than each firm establishing and maintaining its own system, a bank operates the credit system. A customer obtains a credit card from a bank and uses it to purchase goods and services from any of thousands of participating businesses. In this way, one credit card takes the place of many separate cards. Both the consumer and the retailer benefit. Bank credit cards contributed greatly to the development of credit throughout the nation.

The two most-used bank credit card systems are Visa and MasterCard. Both systems operate in very much the same manner. Banks that are a part of either credit system invite qualified customers and retailers to participate in the system. Customers apply for credit through a bank, and each participating retailer sells on credit to customers who present a bank credit card. When a credit purchase is made, the retailer prepares a charge slip. Charge slips are then submitted to the bank for payment. After deducting a service charge, which is about 3 to 4 percent of the total charge sales, the bank pays the retailer and bills the customer who, in turn, pays the bank. The customer benefits by making one monthly payment even though purchases may have been made at many different stores. And the business benefits by selling on credit without operating its own credit system.

Nonbank Credit Cards

Nonbank credit cards have become quite popular in recent years because of the deregulation of banking. Nonbank financial institutions that include special financial divisions of major corporations entered the credit card market early in the decade of the 1990s. AT&T, for example, teamed up with Visa to offer credit card services. Ford and General Motors separately paired with MasterCard. Not to be outdone by nonfinancial institutions, Citibank of New York joined in the competitive game. As one of the nation's largest credit card issuers, Citibank responded to the growing strength of nonbank financial institutions with its Visa card and teamed up with MCI. Co-branding a credit card, as it is sometimes called, between a bank and a nonbank financial institution continues to attract new competitors to the fiercely competitive credit card industry.

Credit card competition has resulted in lower credit card interest rates, lower yearly fees, and even rebates. The largest credit card companies now offer special opportunities. For example, purchases made through the General Motors/MasterCard co-branded card may earn credits towards buying a GM car. Likewise, special telephone rates are available to joint Citibank/MCI cardholders. Other co-branded card issuers have offered incentives to attract credit card customers. Some of the largest credit card companies are shown in Fig. 19-4 on page 460.

Major credit card issuers and the estimated number of cards issued in a recent year.

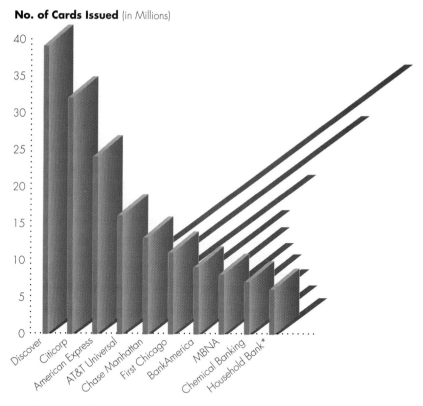

No. of Cards Issued (in Millions)

* Includes one million General Motors cards

Bank Debit Cards

Bank credit cards resemble bank debit cards except for certain differences. A **debit card** allows a person to make cash withdrawals from ATMs, pay bills by phone from bank accounts, and pay for on-site purchases such as foods and household items. Debit card users, however, do not actually write checks because computers are used extensively to handle debit card transactions.

A debit card operates much like a bank or nonbank credit card from a retailer's point of view. The card is presented to the retailer when a customer makes a purchase. By using a point of sale terminal, funds are electronically deducted from the customer's bank account and added to the retailer's bank account. Retailers no longer send sales slips to the bank and the bank no longer bills and collects from customers. The bank, however, sends monthly summaries of transactions to retailers and customers. Fees are charged, of course, for debit card services.

Through the use of debit cards and credit cards, the amount of cash and the number of checks handled are greatly reduced. Paperwork is also greatly reduced. While debit card use is over fifteen years old, it represents only one half of one percent of the way payments are made. Why? Retailers were unhappy because high fees were charged and large retailers were unhappy because debit cards were not national in scope. However, in a joint effort and a publicity campaign, Visa and MasterCard made debit cards national in scope. This added incentive will likely expand the popularity of the debit card. The extensive consumer use of credit cards plus ATM debit cards and the growing acceptance among retailers should increase debit card use throughout this decade.

A new way to use debit cards is growing rapidly on college campuses. Students can pay a fixed amount in advance for a debit card. The card can be used to pay for a variety of low-cost goods and services, such as school supplies, photocopying, snack-bar foods, soft drinks, and even laundry and dry-cleaning services. Because this form of "prepaid" debit card greatly reduces carrying cash, which can be lost or stolen, students like the convenience of this new service.

Not long ago, it was predicted that a "cashless" and "checkless" society might soon develop. While that situation is not likely to occur, people are using less cash and fewer checks to purchase goods and services.

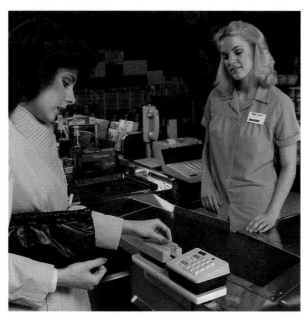

Courtesy of NCR Corporation

Ilus. 19-3
Debit cards have become an increasingly popular way to pay for purchases at grocery stores and other retail outlets. Does someone in your family have a debit card? What types of good are purchased with the card?

Smart Cards

Another newly created service is the smart card. A **smart card** is a credit and debit card with a memory that stores financial, health, credit, and other kinds of data that can be read by computers. Unlike credit cards that contain only one line of data on a magnetic strip, smart cards hold several pages of information. Smart cards will likely replace regular cards for several reasons. First, because the card provides up-to-the-minute account balances after every transaction, bad debts should shrink. Second, because lost or stolen cards cannot be used without first knowing the cardholder's personal identification number, fraud should decrease. Smart cards may eventually reduce credit and debit card use because all essential data can be put onto a single smart card.

Major credit card companies are actively involved in developing and expanding ways to use smart cards. Sears created a form of smart card—the Discover card—for credit, savings, electronic banking, investments, insurance, and financial-planning purposes. Smart cards are used by hospitals and doctors for recording medical information, by financial institutions for recording investments sold, by banks for recording ATM transactions, by transportation companies for recording tickets sold, as well as by libraries and supermarkets. Businesses have the opportunity to learn about customers' purchasing habits from the computer data found on cards. Smart cards are, indeed, all-purpose cards.

Prestige Cards

In addition to bank credit cards, other types of credit cards are available, such as Carte Blanche, Diners Club, and American Express. Such cards are sometimes referred to as travel or entertainment cards. All three cards, however, cater to people in search of status. "Prestige cards," as these cards are often called, charge higher annual fees but provide added services and allow higher credit limits than standard cards. Excellent credit ratings are expected of card applicants.

The original American Express Green Card, for example, was designed to attract high-income cardholders. Its popularity lead to the creation of the Gold Card and the Optima Cards for those seeking even greater status. The popularity of the American Express Gold Card prompted general credit card firms to add their own status cards. Business executives and other professional people often seek prestige and other special purpose cards.

CREDIT IN OTHER COUNTRIES

While the United States is ahead of other countries in using credit cards, Europe is ahead of the United States in using smart cards. Unique problems arise when promoting credit in some countries. For example, in some countries banks are not permitted to offer revolving credit. Regular charge cards, therefore, require that all account balances must be paid in full each month. Even though revolving credit may not be permitted, credit card usage continues to grow, especially among the younger generation.

Of the billions of credit cards held worldwide, Americans own more than half. While foreign consumers purchase on credit, the majority transact business mostly on a cash basis. In recent years, however, the increased use of "plastic" in Europe, Japan, and other countries has been gaining momentum.

The growing popularity of credit cards by foreigners came about, in part, by international competition from American credit card companies. American firms with extensive credit card experience continue to expand successfully in many markets overseas by attracting new customers. In turn, foreign credit card companies, especially banks, have taken steps to offer their credit plans. Credit purchases worldwide will continue to grow as international competitors offer more and better services.

In most foreign countries, the older generation still tends to make cash purchases. In fact, few elders even have checking accounts. For the younger generation, however, the number of checking accounts and charge cards continues to grow. American firms such as Visa, MasterCard, and American Express are drawing the Japanese, Europeans, and other cultures into a globally "plastic" society.

DETERMINING CREDIT STANDING

A business needs a policy and a system for approving credit for customers. Two methods commonly used for checking the worthiness of credit applicants are the four Cs of credit and the point system.

The Four Cs of Credit

To determine the creditworthiness of people or organizations, businesses often apply the "four Cs" of credit: character, capacity, capital, and conditions. The C factors help to determine the answers to two basic questions: Will the customer pay? Can the customer pay?

Character reflects one's moral obligation to pay debts. It includes honesty, integrity, morality, and attitude toward indebtedness. Credit-granting businesses check an applicant's credit reputation, payment habits, and job stability. The applicant who is always late in making payments or who is frequently changing jobs will not likely be approved for credit. Character is considered the most important factor in approving credit.

Capacity is earning power and refers to the potential to pay based on current income. For consumer credit, capacity refers mainly to steady employment, income, and credit obligations. For commercial credit, capacity includes technical know-how, management skill, and a sound performance record as revealed in financial statements.

Capital, the third measuring factor, applies to the credit applicant's current financial worth, or financial ability to pay for credit purchases. For an individual, capital means having assets such as savings, a car, or a home. For a business, capital means a healthy balance sheet—far more assets than liabilities. Capital is especially important when people lose jobs or when businesses suffer losses. With capital, individuals or businesses can still pay for credit purchases. Assets can also be used as collateral.

Conditions, the last of the four Cs of credit, relate to economic and other matters such as the economic health of a community or nation and the extent of business competition that affects credit decisions. The local economy, for example, may be depressed. As a result, many people would be unemployed. Inflation, wars, and recessions also affect credit decisions. These types of conditions influence the availability of credit.

Point System

A point system for making credit decisions has become popular. Points are assigned to the important C factors just discussed. These factors are found in the form of questions on credit applications. Answers are assigned a specific number of points. To receive credit, an applicant must earn a predetermined score. Some factors that are rated and assigned points include the type of job, the length of time the applicant has held the job, the applicant's income and savings, and the total debts owed by the applicant. The higher one's income, for example, the higher the number of points assigned. No points will be assigned if one's income is too small.

No matter what credit determination system is used, credit experts agree that the best single measure of whether to grant credit is one's past credit paying record. For that reason alone, credit applicants need to build and maintain excellent credit records.

SOURCES OF CREDIT INFORMATION

After selecting a method for making decisions about credit applicants, it is necessary to collect information about applicants. Much of the information is obtained directly from applicants and from credit agencies.

Applicants

Retail stores that operate credit departments obtain information directly from applicants who complete credit application forms such as the one shown in Fig. 19-5. The application requests information about the applicant's job, years employed, and salary. The applicant is also asked to list debts, other charge accounts, and bank accounts. After the retailer reviews the credit application, the applicant is either rejected or approved temporarily for a limited amount of credit. At this point, the business seeks additional information from one or more consumer credit agencies. These agencies also provide information when credit customers make requests to raise credit limits or when customers have difficulty making payments for credit purchases.

Commercial credit applications require more elaborate business data, including financial statements. Unlike consumer credit, commercial credit decisions are often delayed until a complete credit check is made, especially when the amount to be charged is rather large. From the completed application, the business seeks additional information from such sources as references, banks, and credit agencies. Once the information has been checked, the applicant is informed of the credit decision.

Credit Agencies

In general, there are two types of credit agencies—one that provides consumer credit information about individuals and another that provides commercial credit information about businesses.

Private credit agencies, or bureaus, collect data and publish confidential reports for their subscribers, who are usually retailers. While there are over one hundred credit agencies, most local credit bureaus are associated with three national credit reporting firms, namely, TRW, Equifax, and Trans Union. Each national agency shares with its local agencies vast amounts of computerized data about millions of customers. A business subscriber, therefore, can get information quickly for making credit decisions. Without credit agencies, credit decision making would be a slow process indeed.

Subscribers contribute information about charge customers to credit agencies. Agencies gather additional information from sources such as public records, which include court decisions, death notices, and other factual data.

Problems among businesses differ from problems encountered by retailers who transact business with consumers. An important source of information on the credit standing of retailers, wholesalers, and manufacturers is Dun & Bradstreet, Inc. As a service to subscribers, D & B regularly publishes and sells credit ratings. The service covers the entire United States. In addition, a subscriber can obtain a special report on any business or professional person from

Dawn's Department Store

To find out about changes in the information in this application for credit you may call us at 1(800) 555-1111.

APPLICATION FOR CREDIT

FOR OFFICE USE ONLY

☒ **Individual Account** – Is based on your own creditworthiness. Complete sections A, B, C, E. You may designate one authorized user, for whose payments you will be responsible, by writing only his/her name and relationship in section D.

☐ **Joint Account** – Is based on the creditworthiness of both parties, and both will be responsible for payment. Complete sections A through E.

STORE	ASSOCIATE NO.	DATE

Section A – Tell us about yourself

LAST NAME: BUSHEY FIRST NAME: DORIS MIDDLE: S SOCIAL SECURITY NO.: 081 329 482 AGE: 32

HOME ADDRESS: 1400 WALNUT STREET APT.

CITY: PHILADELPHIA STATE: PA ZIP CODE: 17094 HOME PHONE: (215) 555-2337

☐ OWN ☐ ROOM & BOARD ☐ LIVE WITH PARENTS ☐ OTHER TIME AT THIS ADDRESS: YRS. 2 MOS. 3
☐ RENT FURNISHED ☒ RENT UNFURNISHED ☐ MOBILE HOME MONTHLY RENT OR MORTGAGE PAYMENT $ 1,150 —

PREVIOUS HOME ADDRESS (IF LESS THAN 3 YEARS AT PRESENT ADDRESS): 237 LANTERN RD., BOSTON, MA 02153 TIME AT PREVIOUS ADDRESS: YRS. 3 MOS. 6

NAME AND ADDRESS OF NEAREST RELATIVE NOT LIVING WITH APPLICANT: JENNIE NUDO, 5 CREEK RIM DR., TITUSVILLE, NJ 08632 RELATIVE HOME PHONE ( ) NOT LISTED

Section B – Tell us about your employment

BUSINESS OR EMPLOYER: WANAMAKER'S TYPE OF BUSINESS: DEPARTMENT STORE BUSINESS PHONE: (215) 555-1820 EXT. —

BUSINESS ADDRESS: CENTER CITY CITY: PHILADELPHIA STATE: PA ZIP CODE: 19107 EDUCATION: ☐ ELEMENTARY ☒ HIGH SCHOOL ☐ POST COLLEGE ☐ COLLEGE

POSITION OR TITLE: ASSISTANT BUYER HOW LONG WITH THIS EMPLOYER: YRS. 2 MOS. 2 ANNUAL SALARY $ 22,800

IF SELF EMPLOYED, PLEASE GIVE YOUR BUSINESS BANK REFERENCE AND ACCOUNT NUMBER DRIVER'S LICENSE NO. E1793218B

PREVIOUS BUSINESS/EMPLOYER (IF LESS THAN 3 YEARS AT THIS JOB): FILENE'S HOW LONG: YRS. 3 MOS. 1 POSITION OR TITLE: STORE CLERK

OTHER INCOME: ALIMONY, CHILD SUPPORT, OR SEPARATE MAINTENANCE INCOME NEED NOT BE REVEALED IF YOU DO NOT WISH TO HAVE IT CONSIDERED AS A BASIS FOR REPAYING THIS OBLIGATION. ANNUAL AMOUNT $ – 0 – SOURCE

Section C – Tell us about your credit and banking relationships

BANK REFERENCES – NAMES OF BANKS AND BRANCH LOCATIONS	ACCOUNT NUMBERS		
1. GERMANTOWN SAVINGS BANK CENTER CITY	4239-0071-4443	☐ CHECKING ☒ SAVINGS ☐ NOW/MONEY MKT. (CHKG. & SAVINGS)	
2. FIRST CENTRAL BANK CENTER CITY	7284-7771-3	☒ CHECKING ☐ SAVINGS ☐ NOW/MONEY MKT. (CHKG. & SAVINGS)	

CREDIT REFERENCES – ACCOUNTS WITH DEPT. STORES, BANK CARDS, OIL COMPANIES	ACCOUNT NUMBERS	BALANCE
1. STRAWBRIDGE & CLOTHIERS	821-932-4691	$ 75 00
2. VISA CORE STATES NEWARK, DELAWARE	472-938-8543-21	$ 160 00
3.		$

OUTSTANDING LOANS (NAME OF CREDITOR/CREDIT UNION/FINANCE COMPANY)

OTHER CREDIT REFERENCES HAVE YOU EVER HAD ANOTHER DAWN'S ACCOUNT YES ☐ NO ☒ ACCOUNT NUMBER (IF KNOWN)

Section D – Information regarding joint applicant or authorized user

LAST NAME FIRST NAME MIDDLE SOCIAL SECURITY NO. AGE

BUSINESS OR EMPLOYER TYPE OF BUSINESS BUSINESS PHONE ( )

BUSINESS ADDRESS CITY STATE ZIP CODE EDUCATION: ☐ COLLEGE ☐ ELEMENTARY ☐ HIGH SCHOOL ☐ POST COLLEGE

POSITION OR TITLE HOW LONG WITH THIS EMPLOYER: YRS. MOS. ANNUAL SALARY $

RELATIONSHIP TO APPLICANT OTHER INCOME: ALIMONY, CHILD SUPPORT, OR SEPARATE MAINTENANCE INCOME NEED NOT BE REVEALED IF YOU DO NOT WISH TO HAVE IT CONSIDERED AS A BASIS FOR REPAYING THIS OBLIGATION. ANNUAL AMOUNT $ SOURCE

Section E – Optional Accountgard Credit Insurance Plan

Please enroll me in the Credit Insurance Plan providing the coverages described and at the cost set forth on the reverse. I understand it is not required to obtain credit and will not be provided unless I sign below and pay the additional cost disclosed on the reverse.

☐ YES ___initial___, I want ___/___/___birthdate___ ☒ NO _DB_initial_, I do not want Accountgard Credit Insurance

Section F – Please sign here and on reverse side

I (We) agree to terms of the RETAIL INSTALLMENT CREDIT AGREEMENT on reverse side.

I (We) understand that you may investigate my (our) credit record and may report information concerning the credit experience of the Account for individual and joint accountholders and authorized users to consumer reporting agencies and others.

APPLICANT'S SIGNATURE: x *Doris S. Bushey* DATE: 8/16/--

Fig. 19-5

To apply for credit, an application form must be filled out.

any part of the country. The reliability of this agency has been established through many years of effective service to all types of business and professional people.

Dun & Bradstreet checks on the credit reputations of businesses throughout the country. How is D&B likely to provide a business in your community with information about another business?

Jeff Greenberg, Photographer

CREDIT LAW

Credit is governed to a great extent by state and federal laws. Some of the laws that relate directly to credit are examined next.

State Credit Laws

All fifty states have laws that regulate credit transactions. The legal profession created the Uniform Commercial Code and the Uniform Commercial Credit Code. Both codes have been adopted by the majority of states. These model laws cover credit conditions relating to credit terms, negotiable instruments, and installment sales contracts. Companies with credit departments often obtain the advice of an attorney on credit matters and usually hire credit managers who have a knowledge of the appropriate state and federal laws.

Federal Credit Laws

Federal credit laws have been passed that affect credit relationships between retailers and consumers. These laws apply to such areas as fair and equal credit rights, the cost of credit, and the process for correcting errors on credit transactions.

Equal Credit Opportunity Act. The Equal Credit Opportunity Act of 1974 makes it illegal to deny applicants credit because of age, sex, marital status, race, national origin, religion, or public assistance income. The age of the applicant, however, may be used to deny credit if it affects the financial soundness of a business transaction. Legally, credit may be denied a person too young to sign contracts or too old to carry out long-term credit agreements. For example, a person aged 65 who requests a 30-year mortgage to buy a home may be denied credit because the person may die before the debt is completely paid. However, a person aged 65 with a good credit history who requests credit terms for five years, for instance, should not be denied credit solely on the basis of age.

Jeff Greenberg, Photographer

Women are entitled to the same credit rights as men. At one time, single women were often denied credit. Today, the law prevents unfair credit treatment of single males or females. In the past, when a husband and wife obtained credit, only the husband's name appeared in credit records even though both spouses could make credit purchases. This situation became especially unfair under certain conditions. When the husband died, for example, the wife was often refused credit because she had no established credit record. No longer is it legal in such situations for only the husband's name to appear on shared credit accounts and in credit records. Both husband and wife have the right to open separate accounts with the same creditor if both are creditworthy.

Still another provision of the Equal Credit Opportunity Act is that an applicant must be notified by the creditor within thirty days of the decision made on the credit application. If credit is refused, the applicant must be notified in writing. Furthermore, the applicant has the right to know why credit was refused. A specific reason, such as not being employed at a job long enough, is acceptable, but a vague reason, such as stating that the applicant is not worthy of credit, is not valid.

Truth-in-Lending Act. The Consumer Credit Protection Act, passed in 1968 and better known as the Truth-in-Lending Act, had a major impact on credit practices. The law and its later amendments contain many provisions protecting consumers who buy on credit. Some of the noteworthy features of the law are shown in Fig. 19-6. In addition, a Truth-in-Leasing Act was passed to help consumers more readily compare the cost and terms of one lease with another, and with the cost and terms of buying for cash or on credit.

Truth-in-Lending Act Requirements

Fig. 19-6

Consumer credit requirements for business firms under the Truth-in-Lending Act.

1. The total dollar cost of obtaining credit must be shown on forms and statements as the finance charge.
2. The finance charge must be shown on forms and statements as an annual percentage rate.
3. The total cost of credit and the finance charge must be displayed prominently on credit forms and statements.
4. If a credit card is lost or stolen and is used by an unauthorized person, the maximum credit loss to the customer is $50. The customer is subject to no loss if the business is notified of the missing card before unauthorized purchases are made. If a debit card is lost or stolen and not reported within two days, the maximum loss may be as high as $500. And if not reported within 60 days of receiving a bank statement showing unauthorized withdrawals, there is no maximum loss limit.
5. A business cannot send a credit card to a person unless that person has requested or applied for it.
6. If a business advertises credit terms, it must include all information that might be needed by a buyer who wishes to compare similar terms among competitors. These terms generally include the down payment and the number, amounts, and dates of payments.
7. Business firms must allow a customer three business days to cancel credit purchases on which the buyer's home is used as security.
8. Business firms must notify customers in writing about the required procedure for challenging possible errors on forms and statements. The customer, who must submit the challenge in writing, must receive a response from the business within 30 days; and within 90 days the challenged amount must either be corrected or the customer must be provided with an explanation as to why the business believes there is no error.

Fair Credit Reporting Act. Credit agency files contain a great deal of information about consumers. This information is usually obtained from retailers, employers, banks, and other sources and is used as a basis for giving or refusing credit. Due to the large amounts of information credit agencies process, occasional errors occur. To protect consumers from inaccurate or out-of-date information appearing in credit agency files, the Fair Credit Reporting Act was passed in 1970. Under this law, a person has a right to see information in credit agency files and to have any errors in the files corrected.

CREDIT POLICIES AND COLLECTION PROCEDURES

Any business that extends credit to customers is concerned about losses from uncollectible accounts. In some firms there are practically no bad debt losses; in others, the losses run rather high. Surveys show that the losses from uncollected debts usually run 1 to 2 percent of net sales. However, when economic conditions are poor, bad debt losses can increase greatly. During such times, large numbers of uncollectible accounts can lead businesses to bankruptcy. If bad debt losses are to be kept to a minimum, it is necessary to establish effective credit policies and collection procedures.

CREDIT POLICIES

Whether a business operates on a credit basis depends more on competition than on cost factors. If competing firms extend credit, it is almost necessary that a similar business also extend credit. The chief disadvantage of offering credit is higher operating costs because of increased recordkeeping and bad debt losses. The chief advantage is that credit increases the volume of sales. With proper attention given to credit sales, the increase in sales volume should lead to increased profits.

If a business decides to sell on credit, a number of important policy decisions must be made to create an effective credit system. The simplest credit system for a small retailer to use is to participate in a national credit card service such as Visa, MasterCard, or AT&T Universal. However, if the business chooses to start its own credit department, one of the first decisions to be made is the selection of the type of credit plans to offer, such as a regular charge account, revolving credit, or installment credit. A credit application form must be designed that meets state and federal requirements. Also, the business should decide whether to use the services of a credit agency to help make wise credit decisions about each applicant.

While making policy decisions, a firm must also set up specific credit terms, finance charges, and a billing schedule. For example, a department store that uses revolving credit may allow customers 25 days in which to pay accounts in full, and charge 1½ percent interest on account balances that are not paid within the billing period. It may further decide that the maximum amount of credit will be $500 for new customers and $1,500 for customers who have established good credit records.

A business should also consider establishing a billing policy. Retailers with many charge account customers find it convenient to use cycle billing. In **cycle billing**, monthly statements are sent to certain customers on one day of the month and to other customers on other days of the month. The billing cycle is usually determined by the alphabetical arrangement of customers' names.

Global Perspective

A British Bank Sells Credit Cards in Germany

Questions:

1 Were German banks prepared to compete globally in the credit card field?

2 What service does Barclays' card in Germany offer that American credit card issuers generally do not offer?

3 Why do you think that competition from foreign credit card competitors has been nearly nonexistent in the United States?

4 Is it likely that Visa would co-brand a card with MasterCard such as was done with the MasterCard/Eurocard?

Banks in the past were very conservative institutions. Until recently, that was especially true in Germany. Thanks to Great Britain, German banks are fast learning that international banking in the credit card arena does not allow for "doing things as usual." One of Britain's major bank players in the credit game is Barclays Bank. And it is giving the mighty German banks the credit card wake-up call.

Not many years ago, Germans carried few credit cards in comparison to the British and Americans. Most were regular charge cards as opposed to revolving credit cards. Today, Germans have greatly increased their holdings of plastic. That shift was caused by British, American, and other European firms competing for the German credit card market.

Barclays' Bank entered the German market with a revolving credit card somewhat like that of Visa and MasterCard. German customers showed a strong preference for the revolving card over the regular charge card that requires paying in full rather than allowing a partial monthly payment option. The Barclays' card also permits German credit cardholders to make deposits and receive substantially more interest than similar German bank credit cards.

Barclays has challenged German banks in other ways. For example, it offers its German customers a combined Barclays/Visa and the popular Eurocard. The competitive challenge caused German banks to offer a combined card—MasterCard/Eurocard. Barclays retaliated with a lower annual credit card fee. Barclays also helps large German department stores develop private credit cards.

Other players in this hot plastic market are American Express and Visa. One thing is certain, stuffy banking practices in Germany and throughout Europe have changed greatly in just a few short years. Germans and other Europeans are winners in the international plastic war.

Source: Adapted from "Germany's Credit Cards: A Boost from Barclays," *The Economist*, April 13, 1991, p. 77.

For example, customers whose last names begin with A through H are sent statements on the 10th of the month, I through R on the 20th of the month, and S through Z on the last day of the month. In cycle billing, a customer may be required to pay the account balance within 10 to 15 days after the date shown on the statement. The major advantage of cycle billing is that all charge accounts do not become due on the same day of the month.

Management also must decide how to collect from customers. This is an extremely important function, especially when it involves overdue accounts.

COLLECTION PROCEDURES

When establishing collection procedures, the credit manager must collect the amount due and retain the goodwill of the customer. Both objectives can be met when a systematic procedure is used.

The usual collection procedures include sending a statement at the end of the billing period, followed by impersonal reminders at 15-day intervals. Stickers such as those shown in Fig. 19-7 are often used. If payment is not received within a reasonable period thereafter, no further credit is extended. The final collection step is to bring legal proceedings against the customer. Managers must remember that the longer the accounts are overdue, the less likely the chances are for collecting the overdue accounts.

During the collection process, an effort should be made to find out why overdue accounts are not being paid. Most people are honest and plan to pay. Therefore, it is important to learn why an account is overdue in order to provide a means for working out a revised payment plan. Part of the reason for overdue accounts may be that too much credit was extended too easily. Overextension of credit is as much the fault of the seller as it is of the buyer.

Sticker 1

Sticker 3

Fig. 19-7

Collection stickers, which are placed on copies of monthly statements, can be purchased from office supply businesses.

Sticker 2

Sticker 4

The length of the collection period may be as short as a few months and as long as six months. When a credit manager makes every possible effort to collect and a customer still has not paid, several choices remain:

- Bring legal action through an attorney.
- Sell the account to a factoring agency as described in Chapter 17.
- Hire a credit collection agency to collect the amount owed.

Each of the above choices is expensive. In some situations, the credit manager may take no final action to collect, especially if the amount due is small or the customer is financially unable to pay. With installment credit plans, however, the final collection step may be to repossess the merchandise purchased on the installment plan.

Whichever method is used, the law must be observed when collecting overdue accounts. Under the Fair Debt Collection Practices Act passed in 1977, collectors cannot use abusive, deceptive, or unfair collection methods. Under most state laws, if an account has not been paid within a specified number of years, collection is no longer legally possible. Fig. 19-8 indicates the chances of collecting an overdue account.

Fig. 19-8

Possibility of collecting accounts that are overdue.

AGE OF ACCOUNT	POSSIBILITY OF COLLECTING
60 DAYS OR MORE	90%
6 MONTHS OR MORE	50%
12 MONTHS OR MORE	30%
24 MONTHS OR MORE	25%
36 MONTHS OR MORE	15%
4 TO 5 YEARS	ALMOST NONE

ANALYZING CREDIT SALES

In every business, it is important to watch accounts receivable (the debts or money owed to the business) in order that the total does not get out of proportion to the amount of credit sales. For example, if credit sales are not increasing but accounts receivable are gradually growing larger each month, an effort should be made to collect accounts more efficiently.

The total accounts receivable may not show the true picture. For instance, an analysis of the accounts receivable record may show that most of the accounts receivable are only 30 or 60 days old, while only a few are 90 days old or older. The situation may, therefore, not be unusual. On the other hand, if an analysis of the accounts receivable record shows that most of the accounts receivable are 90 days old or older, it may prove necessary to have some of the customers sign notes, to place some accounts with a collection agency, to start lawsuits for collection of some accounts, and to strengthen and speed up the collection procedure so that accounts will not become so old in the future.

One of the most common methods of studying accounts receivable is referred to as **aging the accounts**; that is, analyzing customers' account balances within categories based upon the number of days each customer's balance has remained unpaid. The form in Fig. 19-9 is an example of aging accounts.

The amounts owed by the Adams-Jones Company and the Artwell Company are not overdue. However, one balance owed by Brown and Brown, $82.23, has been due for more than 60 days but less than 90 days; $120 has been due for more than 30 days but less than 60 days; and $157.50 has been due less than 30 days. The $228.18 owed by Custer Stores has been due more than 60 days but less than 90 days. And the amount due from A. Davis, Inc. has been due more than 90 days. The form shown in Fig. 19-9 enables the manager to see clearly the status of the accounts receivable and to plan carefully any corrective action that might be needed.

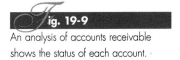

Fig. 19-9
An analysis of accounts receivable shows the status of each account.

ANALYSIS OF ACCOUNTS RECEIVABLE

DATE January 2, 19--

NAME AND ADDRESS	1 TO 30 DAYS	31 TO 60 DAYS	61 TO 90 DAYS	OVER 90 DAYS	TOTAL	EXPLANATION
Adams-Jones Company Cincinnati, Ohio...	$705.00				$705.00	
Artwell Company, Chicago, Illinois..	$1279.53				$1279.53	
Brown and Brown, Gary, Indiana......	$157.50	$120.00	$82.23		$359.73	They wrote "will clear up account this month."
A. Davis, Inc. Detroit, Michigan..				$525.00	$525.00	Account in hands of attorney.
Custer Stores, Granville, Ohio....			$228.18		$228.18	Now on COD basis.

A second method of analyzing accounts receivable is to determine what percentage of the accounts outstanding is collected each month. For example, if the total amount outstanding is $10,000 and collections are $8,000, 80 percent of the accounts receivable have been collected. Each business must decide for itself what percentage collected is acceptable.

A third method of measuring the efficiency of collections is to compute the percentage of delinquent accounts in relation to the total outstanding accounts. For example, if 10 percent of the accounts in January are delinquent, 15 percent are delinquent in February, and 20 percent are delinquent in March, this indicates an unfavorable trend.

A fourth method of determining the efficiency of collecting accounts is to compute the bad debt losses. If a business had $200,000 in net sales and $4,000 of uncollectible accounts, then the bad debt loss is 2 percent ($4,000 ÷ $200,000). Even though most bad debt losses are generally 1 to 2 percent of net sales, a business must compare its loss rate with those of similar businesses. Industry averages are available from credit agencies such as Dun & Bradstreet, Inc.

By carefully analyzing credit sales, a business can learn which policies and procedures are most effective for increasing total sales and for keeping uncollectible account losses to a minimum while increasing net profits.

CHAPTER REVIEW 19

BUILDING VOCABULARY POWER

Define the following terms and concepts.

1. consumer credit
2. commercial credit
3. regular charge credit
4. installment credit
5. installment contract (conditional sales contract)
6. title
7. repossessed
8. revolving credit
9. layaway plan
10. budget plan
11. debit card
12. smart card
13. character
14. capacity
15. conditions
16. cycle billing
17. aging the accounts

REVIEWING FACTS

1. Is a regular charge plan more commonly used for consumer credit or commercial credit?
2. Give examples of items that are commonly purchased on installment credit.
3. When does title pass to customers when purchasing on the following credit plans: (a) regular charge credit, (b) installment credit, and (c) revolving credit?
4. For what type of merchandise might the budget credit plan be used?
5. Give two reasons why a business may not want to operate its own credit card system.
6. Which two bank credit cards are most used?
7. List three ways that customers benefit from competition among credit card issuers.
8. Do Americans or foreigners make the greatest number of credit purchases?
9. Of the four Cs of credit, which is considered the most important in approving credit?
10. From what two sources do retailers obtain information about their credit customers?
11. What law makes it illegal for a retailer to refuse credit to a person receiving public assistance income?

12. Name four decisions that a retail business will have to make when creating an effective credit system.
13. What are the two major objectives of the person who is placed in charge of collection procedures?
14. List the usual collection procedures for a business.
15. What percentage of net sales is usually lost from uncollected debts?

DISCUSSING IDEAS

1. How does installment credit differ from a regular charge account?
2. Discuss whether a budget plan is more like a revolving credit or a regular charge credit plan.
3. Why could it be better for a small retail store to use a bank credit card system for selling on credit than to establish its own business credit card system?
4. How does a "debit" card differ from a "smart" card?
5. Discuss the importance of character, capital, and capacity in a decision to grant credit to a young person who has just started a full-time job but has never had credit before.
6. Discuss the differences in how an application for credit would be processed for (a) a consumer who applies for credit in a department store and (b) a small retail business that applies for credit with a wholesaler.
7. Under the requirements of the Truth-in-Lending Act, as shown in Fig. 19-6, discuss how it could be possible for a consumer to lose no money should a thief steal a credit or debit card and use it.
8. Although the use of credit usually leads to increased sales for retailers, when could credit sales actually lead to decreased profits?
9. What would you do as a retail store owner if a customer paid very slowly and you found that the person's credit rating and credit reputation ranked very high?
10. Both Charm, Inc. and Cats Claws have $10,000 in accounts receivable, yet Charm has more trouble than Cats Claws in collecting accounts. Discuss how Charm, Inc. can find out more about its overdue accounts in order to improve its collection process.

ANALYZING INFORMATION

1. Use Fig. 19-1 and calculate answers to the following questions:
   a. What percentage of total consumer credit is installment credit?
   b. What percentage of total consumer credit is noninstallment credit?
   c. By what percentage is installment credit for automobiles greater than revolving credit?

2. Item 7 of Fig. 19-2 shows what might happen if a customer defaults on an installment contract. Assume that a customer owes Dawn's Department Store $1,500. The store tried to collect and could not, so it hired an attorney to collect. Dawn's is charging the maximum amount allowed plus court costs of $150. What is the total amount that the store should collect from the customer?

3. Your local hardware store does business on a cash or credit basis. A bank credit card system is used. Each week all credit card slips are sent to the bank, and the bank credits the hardware store's account for the proceeds after deducting a fee amounting to 3.8 percent of total credit sales. Cash sales last week were $4,575.87 and credit sales totaled $5,820.53. What is the amount of total sales for the week after deducting the bank credit card service fee?

4. Use the following information to prepare a credit report dated November 30 on the accounts receivable for a business that offers only 30-day open credit terms. The report should contain (a) an analysis of accounts receivable similar to the one shown in Fig. 19-9 and (b) the percentage of delinquent accounts in relation to the total outstanding accounts receivable.

   Sykes purchased $600 of goods on November 15.
   Sanford purchased $1,500 of goods on November 19.
   Jenkins purchased $2,100 of goods on November 12.
   Sanchez purchased $900 of goods on October 17.
   Godowski purchased $600 of goods on October 10.
   Yamamoto purchased $300 of goods on September 25.

5. Assume that you have been hired as the credit and collection manager of the Midwest Wholesale Hardware Company. You have been hired because the former credit manager retired. The owners of the business have discovered that there are many overdue accounts because of a poor collection system. Prepare a detailed plan and schedule for the mailing of monthly statements and overdue collection notices. Indicate when the final collection step will be taken and how the final collection step will be handled.

S OLVING BUSINESS PROBLEMS

CASE 19-1

Toni, a recent college graduate, has just been promoted from her part-time clerk's position to work in the credit department of a popular fashion-oriented clothing store. Toni feels that even though most customers can pay for their merchandise immediately by cash or check, credit is very convenient. Toni's friend, Ching-yu, works in the collection department of the same store. He has been involved in collections for some years and believes that a fashionable store

with well-to-do customers does not need credit. Further, too many of the store's customers are always late in paying bills. They never give a reason for being late other than the typical "Oh, I just forgot."

Toni always purchases items over $50 on credit herself, and Ching-yu has never purchased anything on credit. In fact, he does not have a single credit card. Ching-yu and Toni usually avoid discussing credit, knowing they disagree. However, Ching-yu approached Toni one day and told her that her uncle was now 30 days late in paying his bill for an expensive suit. Toni, not being aware of the situation, was embarrassed and shocked.

"I am sure it was just an oversight," she said.

"Not so," said Ching-yu. "We have sent him two notices 15 days apart by certified mail. It is no oversight." Ching-yu could not resist adding, "Now, do you still believe credit is so great for everyone? If the well-to-do cannot pay on time, I bet half of the poor people are always in debt and unable to pay their bills. Credit should be outlawed. It encourages people to buy over their heads. Without credit, everyone would be better off. Stores would not have to worry about collecting debts, and customers would only buy what they need."

By now Toni was really angry. "And you and I would not have a job. Credit is good for the country and the people. Many customers would not shop here without credit. Furthermore, anyone who does not like credit does not have to use it. Did it ever occur to you that my Uncle Henry might be away on a month's ocean cruise?" With that, Toni left the room and slammed the door.

Required:
1. What are possible advantages to credit?
2. What are possible disadvantages to credit?
3. Do you agree with Toni or with Ching-yu? Explain.
4. What might account for Ching-yu's attitude toward credit?

CASE 19-2

Marla Benitez was just hired as credit manager for a new branch of a well-known department store that has an excellent reputation for selling top-quality merchandise. However, as a result of sluggish local business conditions, losses on uncollectible accounts have jumped from 2 to 4 percent during the year. Marla was told to use a credit bureau to gather information about credit applicants as well as to obtain information from each customer through the store's standard credit application form.

On her first day on the job, Marla received three applications for revolving credit plans on which decisions had to be made immediately. Here is a sketch of the main points about each person:

Elena Alfonso: Age 15; baby-sits evenings while going to high school; lives with her parents; no prior credit record.

George Lorenz: Age 40; employed as a lawyer for a large real estate firm; married and owns his home; has credit with three other business firms and pays his bills on time.

Ichiro Tanaka: Age 66; retired early from his job as a dishwasher for a local restaurant because of a heart problem; married and rents an apartment; has credit with two other department stores; credit record is quite uneven, although he eventually pays his bills.

Required:
1. State whether you would grant credit to each person if you were Marla Benitez and give your reasons.
2. If one person had to be denied credit, which one would you select and why?
3. Should Marla Benitez consider the Equal Credit Opportunity Act when making her decisions to grant credit? Explain.

BUSINESS RISKS AND INSURANCE

CHAPTER 20

After studying this chapter you will be able to:

20-1 Identify the purpose of insurance and how insurance rates are established.

20-2 Describe five types of property losses that businesses can insure.

20-3 Discuss how health, life, and liability insurance protect the personnel and customers of a business from risks.

20-4 Provide four examples of insurance developed for specific business activities.

20-5 Offer examples of risks facing companies that are noninsurable and how each risk can be reduced.

f you have $5 in your pocket, there is a risk that you might lose it. While you might not want to lose the money, its loss would not be a serious problem. However, if you own a $300 bicycle, you may not be able to afford to replace it if it is stolen. You may choose to buy insurance to protect against the larger loss.

If you own a business, you may be faced with uncontrollable events that could result in financial loss. A fire could destroy the building; burglars could steal property and money; a customer or employee could get hurt at the business and sue you; or an important manager could die. These events may never occur for your business. If they do, however, the loss could be so great that the business would fail.

An important way for businesses to protect against the possibility of financial loss is to purchase insurance. Insurance enables a business to trade the possibility of a large, but uncertain, loss for a smaller, affordable loss (the cost of the insurance).

MANAGING TO REDUCE LOSSES

Just as you would not buy insurance to protect against the loss of a five dollar bill, not every possible financial loss of businesses can or should be insured. As a normal part of operations, businesses will have losses that are not very costly even if they do occur. For more costly losses, however, planning can prevent them from being large enough to hurt the business so much that it cannot continue to operate. A business should purchase insurance for the types of losses that would be difficult to overcome or could be very disruptive to business operations.

Most retailers know that a certain amount of shoplifting will occur. Rather than attempting to insure that loss, they take steps to prevent it, and, when possible, add a small amount to the retail price of products to cover expected losses from shoplifting.

Businesses can also lose money if employees do not show up for work. Because it is expected that some employees will be absent, businesses may have part-time workers available who can be called in on short notice. Some businesses may actually employ more people than necessary when expecting some absentees. Managers should watch absentee rates carefully and keep them as low as possible through policies, incentives, and penalties.

In most manufacturing processes, small amounts of materials are lost or damaged. To make sure that losses do not interfere with production, a company should keep a larger amount of those materials to have an adequate supply to complete production. Planning, training, and controls for production processes should also reduce the amount of material loss in the manufacturing process. In each of the cases described, the company is spending a small amount of time and money to prevent large losses. This may be a better strategy for the company than purchasing insurance for those losses.

INSURANCE OPERATIONS

Some important terms will help you understand insurance operations. Those terms are defined in Fig. 20-1.

It is difficult for any business to predict whether specific losses will occur or the amount of those losses. However, many businesses face the same types of perils. When large numbers of businesses are grouped together, the probability of a certain type of loss and the amount of the loss can be reasonably estimated. For example, by the use of historical records on fire losses for certain types of businesses, estimates of the probable amount of fire damage suffered among 10,000 businesses during a year can be made. While the actual amount of loss in a specific year might be different than the estimate, over a number of years, the estimates prove to be very accurate.

Insurance companies only insure against losses that are reasonably predictable. They spread the cost of losses across many firms or people. Each policyholder pays a regular premium to the insurance company. By paying

Fig. 20-1
Common insurance terms.

INSURER

A company that sells insurance.

POLICYHOLDER

The person or business purchasing insurance.

POLICY

The written agreement, or contract, between the insurer and the policyholder.

INSURED

The persons or organization covered by the insurance policy.

PERIL

The cause of a loss for a person or organization. Common perils are fire, accidents, sickness, death, and theft.

RISK

The uncertainty that a loss may occur.

PREMIUM

A payment by a policyholder to the insurer for protection against risk.

a premium, the policyholder is paying a smaller amount of money for protection against a larger possible loss.

The funds collected from policyholders are used by the company in somewhat the same manner as deposits are used by banks. With the funds paid by policyholders, insurance companies make investments that earn an income. Insurance companies must, of course, keep a reasonable amount of cash available to pay the claims of policyholders. In order to make a profit, the insurance company must earn more from premiums and investments than is paid out in claims by policyholders.

Sometimes, insurance companies lose money because they do not make wise investments or because there are many more losses among the policyholders than the company anticipated. For example, in a recent year, several large natural disasters (hurricanes, floods, and fires) occurred in several parts of the country at about the same time. Because of the number of disasters and the large amount of property in each area damaged or destroyed, insurance companies had to pay a much higher amount than expected. Some small insurance companies failed because of those events and larger companies increased their insurance rates in order to recover their losses.

Insurance Rates

An **insurance rate** is the amount charged for a certain value (such as $1,000) of insurance. Rates vary according to the risk that is involved. For instance, if a particular community has a large number of robberies, theft insurance rates are high in that community. If fire protection is poor, or buildings are not constructed in a way that makes them safer from fire, the fire insurance rates will be high in that community. Rates charged for insurance are based on the past experience of the insurance company with losses for the type of property that is to be insured. Therefore, the rates established for any particular year anticipate that the losses for that year will be essentially the same as those of previous years.

Rates for various kinds of insurance in each state are determined by the experiences of insurance companies. The same basic rates are usually charged by insurance companies for the same kinds of risks in the same locations within a state. Regardless of the basic rates, the charge made to any policyholder may be lower or higher than the basic rate depending on certain circumstances. For example, a new building that has an automatic sprinkler system and is located where there is good fire protection can be insured at a lower rate than an older building that does not have a sprinkler system and is located where there is poor fire protection. In many states, automobile rates vary from the basic rate depending on whether the driver has a good or bad accident record, the age of the person who drives the car, and the brand, model, and age of the car.

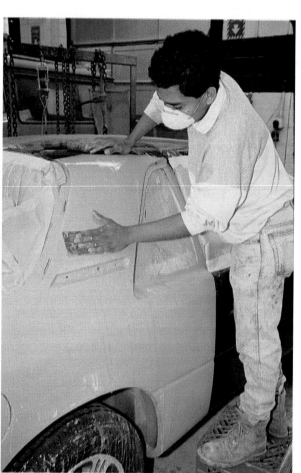

Insurance rates will be higher on the property of individuals who have made many claims. Why might insurance companies have differences in rates based on risks?

Jeff Greenberg, Photographer

Cancellation

The insurance policy contains information about how contracts may be terminated. Most property or liability insurance contracts may be canceled by the insurer or may not be renewed when they expire if the insurer believes the risk has increased. If insurance is canceled, enough notice must be given to policyholders to allow them to find another insurer. Generally, life insurance contracts may not be canceled by the insurer except for nonpayment of premiums.

Health insurance is very important to people because of the very high cost of health care. Insurance companies have been able to cancel health insurance in the past. It is difficult for people with health problems to get insurance from another company once their current insurance plan has been canceled. Some states have passed laws to prevent the cancellation of health insurance as long as premiums are paid.

Insurable Interest in Property

The policyholder must have an insurable interest in the property. An **insurable interest** is generally defined as the possible financial loss that the policyholder will suffer if the property is damaged or destroyed. A person who has purchased a piece of property but has not paid for it has an insurable interest. A person who uses a building as a warehouse has an insurable interest in the building, even though that person does not own the building. A person who has a mortgage on a piece of property has an insurable interest in the property. The interest in property to be insured must be specifically indicated in the policy.

Deductibles

Many insurance contracts include deductibles. Generally, a **deductible** is an arrangement that permits the insured to be responsible for part of the loss in return for a lower premium. Most deductibles are expressed as a dollar amount of any given loss that will not be covered by the insurer. For example, if an insured driver has a $100 deductible collision insurance policy and a $500 loss occurs, the insurer pays $400 and the insured bears the $100 loss. If the loss is only $100, the insurer pays nothing.

Often it is worthwhile for the insured to include a higher deductible in the policy. For example, the premium for a $200 deductible collision insurance policy on your auto may be $750 a year; the premium for a $500 deductible policy may be $600. Having the $500 deductible policy saves you $150 a year. Of course, if there is a loss you must pay $500 of it rather than $200. You purchase the higher deductible insurance because you believe you will not have an accident that requires you to pay the deductible. In general, if you can afford to pay the deductible amount if a loss occurs and there is a significant difference in the cost of the two policies, you should include the higher deductible in the insurance policy.

Coinsurance

Another method of sharing the risk of loss between the insurance company and the insured is **coinsurance**, sometimes known as copayments. It divides the loss between the insurer and the insured on a percentage basis. Coinsurance is often used in health insurance and property insurance policies where individual losses are quite difficult to predict and can be very expensive.

A typical coinsurance requirement in health insurance would make the insured responsible for 20 percent of the cost of a claim and the insurer responsible for 80 percent. If there was a covered expense of $10,000, the insured would have to pay $2,000 and the insurer would pay the remaining $8,000. With most coinsurance policies in health insurance, there is a cap placed on the total amount the insured must pay in one year. For example, the policy may require the insured to pay a maximum of $2,500 for each family member or a total of $6,000 for the entire family in a year. When that amount has been paid, the insurance company will pay the remaining total of covered expenses.

Coinsurance for property protection is a bit different. Insurance companies found that property insurance policies were often being purchased for much less than the actual cost of the property being insured. The people buying the insurance believed that any fire loss would not completely destroy the property. They could save money on premiums by reducing the amount of coverage and still be paid the full amount for their expected losses. Insurance companies use coinsurance to encourage policyholders to buy adequate property coverage. If the property is not insured for the required value under the coinsurance clause (typically 80% of replacement value), the insurance company will only pay a percentage of any partial loss that occurs. If the insurance coverage meets the coinsurance requirement, all partial losses will be paid in full by the insurer.

Coinsurance is a useful practice when losses are likely to be quite large or may occur rather frequently. Through coinsurance, the insured is encouraged to control the amount of loss in order to keep the amount paid through co-insurance as low as possible. The insurance company will be able to offer lower rates for the insurance since the insured will pay a percentage of the large losses.

Reinsurance

Insurance companies also have risks and must plan to be sure that losses are not so great that the business will be unable to continue. If policyholders have a large amount of claims in a short time, the company may not have enough money from premiums and investments to cover those claims. To protect against such a risk, insurance companies may use **reinsurance**. It is a method of reducing risk of a major loss by transferring part of the risk to another insurance company.

As an example of reinsurance, a company may insure a multimillion dollar building against fire loss. If there were a fire in the building, there is a chance a very large loss could be suffered and the insurance company would not be able to pay that amount. It can reinsure the building with a second insurance company by giving it a part of the premiums. Then, if a major loss occurs, the two insurance companies will each pay a percentage of the loss as described in the reinsurance contract.

How To Buy Insurance

Most insurance contacts are written by insurance agents. **Insurance agents** represent the insurance company and sell insurance to individuals and businesses. Some agents represent several different insurance companies and can provide many types of insurance for a business. Other agents represent only one company or may sell only one type of insurance, such as life or auto insurance.

In most communities there are many reputable agents offering all types of insurance. There are often differences in the policies and services offered by insurance companies and agents. A business person should discuss insurance needs with two or three insurance agents before selecting a company and the type and amount of insurance. Points to consider when choosing an insurance company and an agent are given in Fig. 20-2.

1. **Can the company that the insurance agent represents furnish the right kind of insurance?**
2. **Does the insurance agent have a proper knowledge of insurance?**
3. **Are the policies understandable?**
4. **Are the company's rates reasonable?**
5. **What kind of service does the agent furnish?**
6. **What kind of reputation does the agent have for helping when losses occur?**
7. **What reputation does the company have for settling claims?**
8. **Can the company help in reducing risks?**

Fig. 20-2
Points to consider in selecting an insurance company and agent.

In buying insurance, the primary objectives are (a) to get the proper coverage of risks and (b) to make certain that the claim will be paid in the event of loss. For example, a person who needs fire insurance wants to be sure that the insurance company that issues the policy will pay a claim promptly so that business activities will not be interrupted. A person who buys liability insurance wants to be sure that if a person is injured, the insurance company will help to determine the responsibility of the insured and make a fair settlement with the injured person.

A business person should consider the areas where major losses could occur when planning the purchase of insurance. Protection is needed for both property and people. The remainder of this chapter examines the major types of insurance as well as noninsurable risks.

PROPERTY INSURANCE

A business may obtain various types of insurance to fit its needs in protecting its property. The major types of property insurance that a business might have are (1) fire insurance, (2) business income insurance, (3) transportation insurance, (4) vehicle insurance, and (5) burglary and robbery insurance.

Billy Barnes/Stock, Boston

FIRE INSURANCE

Fire insurance provides funds to replace such items as buildings, furniture, machinery, raw materials, and inventory destroyed by fire. Fire insurance on a building may not cover the equipment, machinery, and materials in the building. Separate policies may be required to give a business full protection from fire loss. The owner of a building should be interested in insurance to protect his or her investment. The occupant of a rented building should be interested in insurance to protect personal contents in the building. You should know exactly what is covered by the policy when buying fire insurance.

Features of Fire Insurance Policies

When business people buy fire insurance they should know what they are buying and how they will be protected. They should give careful consideration to the amount of protection, the kind of protection, and special clauses in the policy.

There is no advantage in a business firm being overinsured. Insurance companies will pay no more than the actual value of the loss even if more insurance is carried. However, a business must be careful that it carries enough insurance. The value of some property increases from year to year. When an insurance policy is renewed, it should be revised in amount so that it covers the real value of whatever is being insured. It is, therefore, important to check the policy carefully before it is renewed. Some policies automatically increase the amount of coverage each year based on the rate of inflation. That type of coverage requires a higher premium.

In every fire insurance policy the property that is covered should be clearly identified by description and location. The property included in the policy and the property excluded should be clearly understood.

The standard insurance policy usually will not cover such items as business records (both paper and computerized), bills, money, and notes. This fact emphasizes the need for keeping such items in fireproof filing cabinets, safes, or buildings designed for storing and protecting those types of materials. It is difficult to establish a value for most records if they are lost in a fire. Since records are not covered by an ordinary policy, extreme care should be exercised in protecting them. Even if such items can be insured and their value is known, the difficulty of replacing them is a good reason for their protection.

Many businesses such as banks, investment firms, and insurance companies base their operations on records. The records are so valuable that the business could not operate if the records were damaged or destroyed. In this case, insurance is not adequate protection for the business. They must rely on safety and security of their records. They store them in well-protected, secure areas. They also keep duplicate records in a totally separate location, often in another city.

Another way businesses attempt to protect records is with a disaster plan. Businesses anticipate the types of disasters that could occur, the protection required, and ways to respond to the disaster. Each department in the company regularly practices the disaster plan. For example, without warning a manager may be asked to assume a fire has destroyed all of the records in a department. The department must recover and operate again as quickly as possible following the procedures developed in the disaster plan.

Extended Coverage

Some basic fire insurance policies may be extended to cover additional risks such as wind, hail, hurricane, or flood. Additional protection beyond the primary peril is called **extended coverage**. It is obtained by paying an additional premium and by adding a special clause to the contract. Of course, such coverage should not be added unless the peril is likely to occur and loss is suffered.

BUSINESS INCOME INSURANCE

Business income insurance (also known as business interruption insurance) is designed to compensate firms for loss of income during the time required to restore property damaged by an insured peril. For instance, after a fire in an office, a factory, or a store, the business suffers an additional loss because it cannot carry on its regular operations. Some of its expenses continue in spite of the fire. These are such expenses as interest on loans, taxes, rent, insurance payments, advertising, telephone service, and some salaries. The business may lose not only the normal income from sales but also could lose its customers, who may go to other sources and never come back. On the other hand, during the period that the business is shut down because of the fire, it may save on the salaries of certain employees and a few other miscellaneous expenses.

In determining the amount of business income insurance to carry, the business person should consult an insurance agent. It is advisable to prepare a list of items that are customarily considered fixed expenses and to make an estimate of the firm's normal profit, based on past experience and business plans. When such an estimate has been made, a record should be kept of the method of computing the estimate so that these figures can be submitted in justifying a claim if a loss occurs.

TRANSPORTATION INSURANCE

Protection against damage, theft, or complete loss of goods while they are being shipped is obtained by purchasing **transportation insurance**. While the transportation company may be responsible for many losses during the shipment of goods, some losses may be the responsibility of the seller or buyer. The owner of the goods may purchase insurance, or the company that transports the goods may provide insurance as a part of the cost of transportation. Most transportation companies insure all of their shipments through an insurance company. However, they may choose to assume risks themselves and pay for any losses rather than to carry insurance. Any time products are shipped, businesses should understand if insurance is provided for the goods and who is paying the cost of the insurance.

BURGLARY, ROBBERY, AND THEFT INSURANCE

Burglary, robbery, and theft insurance provides protection from loss resulting from people stealing money, inventory, and various other business assets. Because of the differences in types of businesses and methods of operating them, the risks vary considerably, as do premium rates. Burglary and robbery insurance does not cover losses of goods taken by employees or merchandise that is shoplifted. Separate insurance is available to cover these losses, but it is often very expensive. Businesses are taking special security efforts to prevent these types of losses from occurring.

VEHICLE INSURANCE

An individual or business may purchase several different kinds of vehicle insurance for protection against such losses as theft, property damage, or personal injury. Several parts of a typical automobile insurance policy are described next.

Collision Insurance

Collision insurance provides protection against damage to one's own car when it is in a collision with another car or object. This type of insurance is costly because of the number of accidents and the high cost of repairs. A way to reduce the cost of collision insurance is to buy it with as large a deductible as possible (described earlier in the chapter). For businesses insuring a fleet of cars, higher deductibles can result in considerable savings.

Jeff Greenberg, Photographer

Comprehensive Insurance

Most basic vehicle insurance policies include a coverage called **comprehensive insurance**. Insurance paid for under this clause usually includes loss caused by flying objects such as rocks or birds, fire, theft, storm damage, hail, water, or vandalism.

The most common practice in comprehensive coverage is to issue policies that state that the insurance company will pay claims based on the market value of the vehicle at the time of the loss. For instance, a new car may be insured on January 1 for its actual value of $19,200. If it is destroyed six months later, the amount that the insurance company is obligated to pay is only the market value of a used car of that particular age and model. That amount will be somewhat less than $19,200. When there is only partial loss, the insurance company pays for the amount of repairs.

Automobile Liability Insurance

Automobile liability insurance is a specific type of liability insurance that provides protection against damage caused by the insured's automobile to other people or their property. Property damage insurance and bodily injury insurance are usually sold together in the same policy. They are both important because the risks are unknown and the claims for damages may be very extensive.

The liability insurance section of a policy will state the maximum amount of damage that will be paid in case of an accident. Most states have a minimum amount of liability insurance that must be carried. For example, one state requires $10,000 of property damage insurance, $25,000 of bodily injury insurance if one person is injured, and $50,000 of bodily injury insurance if more than one person is injured. Because the costs of auto repair and medical care are increasing, the minimum amounts of liability insurance are not enough to cover the costs resulting from an accident.

Often, the amount of insurance carried by companies and many individuals is much higher than the minimum required amounts. Liability claims against companies and individuals can amount to large sums of money. If adequate insurance is not carried, the additional amount must be paid by the insured, so many will carry liability insurance of one million dollars or more.

Medical Payments Insurance

A common clause in an automobile insurance policy will cover medical, surgical, hospital, and related expenses caused by injuries to any occupant of the automobile, including the insured. These payments will be made regardless of the legal liability of the policyholder. This type of insurance is called **medical payments insurance**.

No-Fault Insurance

Normally, the insurance company of the person responsible for an accident must pay the costs of damages. However, some states have passed no-fault insurance laws. Under **no-fault insurance**, each insurance company is required to pay the losses of its insured when an accident occurs, regardless of who might have been responsible for the accident.

The laws governing such policies vary in different states. No-fault insurance was developed to eliminate the need for the victim to have a costly lawsuit or a long-delayed trial to recover for losses suffered in an automobile accident. The intent of no-fault insurance is to reduce the costs of automobile insurance that result from legal actions required to determine fault and obtain payment for losses.

INSURING PEOPLE

People are important to the success of all businesses. Owners and managers, employees, people working for suppliers or other businesses, and customers influence the financial success of the business. Because of this, there are economic risks that involve people. Insurance is available to protect businesses from those risks.

The primary types of insurance related to employees of the business are health, life, and disability insurance as well as employee bonds. Liability insurance covers risks related to both employees and other people who have contact with the business or its products and services. Those types of insurance are discussed next.

HEALTH INSURANCE

Health insurance provides protection against the expenses of health care. Typically, three categories of coverage are provided to the employees of a business. They are medical payments, major medical, and disability. *Medical payments* cover normal health care and treatment costs. Visits to physicians, treatments of minor illnesses and injuries, costs of medical services, prescription drugs, and other routine health care expenses are generally included in this type of health insurance. Some policies also cover dental expenses and eye care.

Major medical insurance provides additional coverage for more critical illnesses or treatments that are particularly extensive and expensive. Long hospital stays, major surgery, and costs of extended care can be very expensive. Major medical insurance provides protection for those types of expenses. Typically, major medical policies contain a coinsurance requirement in order to keep premium costs lower. Also, most insurance plans today contain a provision that requires preapproval of non-emergency services so the insurance company can determine if the service is needed and will be provided at a reasonable cost.

Disability insurance offers payments to employees who are not able to work because of accidents or illnesses. The employee's disability must be severe enough that it is not possible to continue to work or to obtain other employment for an extended period of time. The insurance coverage will provide monthly payments that may be as high as the employee's regular wage or salary while the employee is disabled.

Because health and wellness of employees is important both to the business and to the individual, the cost of health insurance is often shared by the employee and the business. Many businesses offer a **group insurance** policy. Under this type of plan all employees can obtain insurance at a reasonable cost regardless of their health, and the cost is typically lower than if the coverage was purchased individually.

Health insurance has become an important concern of American businesses, individuals, and government. Because of the high costs of medical care, insurance costs have increased to the point that it is not affordable for many individuals and even a large number of companies, especially small businesses. Alternatives have been considered to control costs and to provide basic coverage to as many people as possible.

One alternative to health insurance for employees is **health maintenance organizations (HMOs)**. An HMO is a cooperative agreement between a business and a group of physicians and other medical professionals to provide for the health care needs of the employees of the business. A regular payment for each employee is made to the HMO to pay for a complete set of medical services. The emphasis of the HMO is on preventing health problems and reducing the cost of treatment for health care rather than just paying for the treatment of medical problems when they occur. Many businesses that participate in HMOs have developed wellness programs, organized fitness centers, and provided employees with information and counseling on health care, diet, and exercise in order to reduce the costs of health insurance.

Some people prefer to receive health care services from a physician and hospital they select rather than from a number of health care practitioners in an HMO. An alternative health insurance program is know as **preferred provider organizations (PPOs)**. PPOs make health care available from a selected set of physicians and health care facilities through negotiated contracts between health care providers and the insurer. The insurance company negotiates with a number of physicians and hospitals for a full range of health care services. The contracts identify the costs of those services that will be paid by the insurer. Participants in the PPO can select any health care provider that has a contract with the insurance company so they maintain the choice they prefer. The contracted services usually result in cost savings.

Even though alternatives such as HMOs and PPOs have resulted in some savings, other methods of providing health insurance are being studied. Some people believe that the United States should offer a national health care system within which everyone would have a basic set of medical services paid by tax dollars. Others suggest employers should either provide health insurance for all of their employees or pay a tax that would be used to purchase insurance for those people who do not have an insurance plan.

Another proposed method of extending insurance coverage is to form large insurance pools of people in geographic areas of the country. Those pools could then develop contracts for health services with health care providers just as PPOs do now. The result would be more available health care and possible cost controls. Other plans for more accessible and affordable health care are sure to be developed and studied.

LIFE INSURANCE

Life insurance provides money that is paid upon the death of the insured to a person or people identified in the insurance policy. Those who receive payment of the life insurance are known as beneficiaries. Life insurance plays an important function in business. It is often included as a part of employee benefit plans. With life insurance, individuals can provide some financial protection for their families in the event the employee dies.

Life insurance is also purchased by many businesses for the owners and important executives of the business. In the case of a sole proprietorship, the owner will usually find it easier to borrow money if adequate life insurance is carried. An owner may carry life insurance so that in the event of death the proceeds from the insurance will pay any debts of the business, thereby permitting the business to be turned over free of debt to the owner's family. Some sole proprietorships are so dependent on the owner of the business that when he or she dies, it is difficult for the business to continue successfully. If the owner provides proper insurance, funds will be available to carry on the business until it can be sold or until someone can be found to manage it.

Life insurance has an especially important place in partnerships. Generally, a partnership is dissolved at the death of one partner. Each partner usually carries life insurance on the other partner so that when one partner dies the other will receive, as beneficiary of the insurance policy, sufficient money to buy the share of the partnership owned by the deceased partner.

Important executives of corporations are also usually insured. The theory behind this plan is that if a key executive dies, the progress of the corporation may be damaged; but the proceeds from the insurance will help the corporation make any adjustments that are necessary until a new executive can be found.

In a small corporation owned by just a few stockholders, there is also a practice of stockholders carrying insurance on each other. If one stockholder dies it is possible for the remaining stockholders to purchase the stock of the deceased stockholder and maintain ownership of the business within the small group.

Several types of life insurance are normally used by companies to protect against losses resulting from the death of an owner, manager, or key employee. **Term insurance** provides protection for a period of time specified in the policy. Payment is made only if the insured dies during that time. Term insurance is the most popular type of life insurance in employee benefits programs.

Whole life insurance maintains insurance coverage for the entire life of the insured as long as premiums are paid. As insurance premiums are paid, a cash value develops. *Cash value* is an amount that increases over the years and that a policyholder receives if the insurance policy is given up.

A newer form of life insurance is **universal life insurance**. Insurance companies developed this form of insurance to compete with investments that pay a higher rate of return than the interest rate on whole life policies. Universal life insurance combines protection with a savings and investment plan. The premiums are invested by the insurance company after deductions are made for insurance protection and the expenses and profits of the company. The policyholders' earnings depend on the investment skills of the managers of those funds who are employed by the insurance company to invest policyholders' premiums.

Karl Nemecek/MetLife

Ilus. 20-4

Insurance companies offer many choices of life insurance plans. How can you determine whether to buy life insurance and which type of insurance to purchase?

Ethical Issues

DO INSURANCE RATES DISCRIMINATE?

Questions:

1 Is the practice of setting rates based on gender discriminatory even if it can be shown by actuaries that on average life expectancies are different for men and women?

2 Insurance companies used to have different rates for life insurance based on the race of the insured. That practice has been stopped even though statistically there are differences in the life expectancy for people of different races. Why do you believe the practice was stopped while gender-based rates are still used by some companies?

3 Among the factors used in setting auto insurance rates are the age and gender of the driver. Based on those factors, males in their teens and twenties pay significantly higher rates than other groups. Do you believe this practice is discriminatory? Why or why not?

4 How would you suggest that insurance people establish insurance rates that reflect the losses a person or business is likely to suffer for a particular peril?

Insurance rates are set by evaluating the amount of losses suffered for a particular peril by a large number of people or businesses within a specific period of time. It is a very scientific process completed by people known as actuaries. *Actuaries* review records of losses, determine the number of people or organizations to be insured, and then use statistics to calculate the rates insurance companies must charge to be able to cover the cost of losses and make a reasonable profit. The rates charged will be based on the anticipated losses for a particular group. Some people believe that the way groups are identified in order to set insurance rates can be discriminatory. If so, it may mean that some people pay higher premiums than are needed to cover their potential losses while others pay less than is needed. Life insurance rates based on a person's gender illustrate the claim of discrimination.

For many years, men and women have usually paid different rates for the same type and amount of life insurance. The people who established the insurance rates for insurance companies grouped men and women into two different categories when they analyzed life expectancy. Life expectancy is the primary factor in setting life insurance rates. When the population was divided in that way, the evidence showed that men had a shorter life expectancy than women and so paid a higher rate for the insurance. On the other hand, when a payment schedule was calculated for making payments from the policies to policyholders or beneficiaries, women received lower payments because they were expected to live longer.

Consumer interest groups that study insurance rates suggest that many factors contribute more to the length of a person's life than gender. Lifestyle, occupation, heredity, and eating and exercise habits are all important. Therefore, a male can have a much longer life expectancy than average and a female a much shorter one based on those other factors. The consumer groups believe the gender-based rates are unfair and discriminatory and suggest that insurance companies base rates on factors that are more specific and controllable by the person purchasing insurance.

Some insurance companies have changed their rate structures and now have the same rate for men and women of the same age. Others argue that the gender differences exist and should at least be one of the factors used to calculate rates.

LIABILITY INSURANCE

Businesses face many risks that result from the operation of the business. People may get hurt while on the job, products may cause damage or injury, and employees of the business may do things that damage people or their property. **Liability insurance** provides protection for the risks to others that result from the products, services, and operations of the business. Automobile liability insurance was discussed earlier in the chapter. It is used to pay for damage caused by business vehicles and their drivers. A business usually needs other liability insurance to protect against risks such as customers being injured while in the business, damages resulting from the use of the business' products, and damage or injury caused by employees of the business or by operations of the business.

Professionals such as lawyers and physicians who provide personal services are in danger of being sued by clients. Malpractice claims are an important cost to professionals. Even if the business person is not guilty of malpractice, the legal fees can be very high. **Professional liability insurance** provides protection from the types of financial losses resulting from providing professional services.

A special type of protection available to businesses is bonding. **Bonding** provides payment of damages to people who have losses resulting from the negligence or dishonesty of an employee or from the failure of the business to complete a contract.

▌S▐PECIAL TYPES OF INSURANCE

In addition to the types of insurance already discussed, a business may sometimes need certain special types of insurance. The special insurance is based on specific business activities. Some of the more common types include credit insurance, credit life insurance, forgery insurance, and title insurance. Also, international business presents some unique insurance problems.

CREDIT INSURANCE

A company may purchase **credit insurance** to protect itself against losses on credit that is extended to customers. If the business cannot collect an amount due, the insurance company will pay the loss. However, the insurance company still has the right to try to collect from the customer. Unless businesses carefully control their credit accounts to limit losses, credit insurance will be very expensive.

CREDIT LIFE INSURANCE

Credit insurance should not be confused with credit life insurance. **Credit life insurance** is used by small loan companies, banks, and retail businesses that provide installment credit loans. The borrower or installment purchaser may be asked to buy sufficient life insurance to pay the balance of the debt in the event of his/her death.

FORGERY INSURANCE

Forgery insurance may be obtained by business people, individuals, banks, and other institutions to provide protection against loss caused by forged or altered checks and securities. Losses may occur as a result of a person altering a signature, altering an amount on a check, or the wrong person cashing a check. Business people are constantly exposed to these risks. Any business that regularly cashes checks or processes a large number of legal documents should carry this kind of insurance for protection from loss.

TITLE INSURANCE

When land or buildings are purchased, they may have been owned by several other persons or businesses in the past. **Title insurance** is purchased to protect against losses that could occur if title to the property has not been legally transferred sometime in the past. A company could suffer a large loss if it were forced, because of a problem with the title, to give up buildings or land it had purchased. While title insurance will not guarantee that the company can keep the property, the insurance company must pay for the losses that result from giving up the property.

INTERNATIONAL INSURANCE NEEDS

Many businesses operate or sell products in other countries. Insurance policies typically do not cover losses or liability resulting from those international operations. Special coverage may be available at additional cost within existing insurance policies. Business people need to remember that the insurance laws of the country where the business is operating must be applied. To encourage international business with developing countries, the United States government formed the **Overseas Private Investment Corporation**. The purpose of the corporation is to provide insurance coverage for businesses that suffer losses or damage to foreign investments as the result of political risks. **Export credit insurance** is also available to businesses; it covers losses suffered if the purchasers of exports do not pay for their purchases. Businesses shipping products to other countries must also be aware of the need for special transportation insurance.

NONINSURABLE RISKS

Businesses are also concerned with special types of risks for which there is no insurance. For instance, anyone who has operated a business has discovered that the needs and wants of people change. These changes cause serious business risks. Products are produced in anticipation of their sale. If the needs and wants of consumers change, however, the business is likely to suffer a loss on unsold goods.

Fashions, particularly in clothing, change frequently. Consequently, clothing manufacturers and retailers are sometimes overstocked at a time when styles change or customers look for new fashions. A company that is stocked with old merchandise, therefore, suffers a loss and probably has to sell the goods at a low price. A company should be careful to avoid overstocking.

Old equipment and lighting can also cause customers to avoid a business. A store with a modern interior and new lighting may attract customers away from an old, established store. Improved methods of transportation may give one type of business an advantage over another. For instance, private parcel services have injured the parcel business of the post office. Change is a constant factor in business.

Changes in the weather can cause serious business risks. For example, a long winter season may prevent manufacturers and retailers from selling spring clothing. A rainy summer may slow the business of resorts if people stay at home. A lack of rain or storms can result in crop failures for farmers who have invested large amounts of money in seed, fertilizer, and equipment. A lack of snow may reduce sales of skis and snowmobiles.

Changes in economic conditions present another serious risk. Increased unemployment rates cause people to be more careful when spending their money. This risk can be overcome to some extent by studying business forecasts and by planning carefully in anticipation of changes in the economy. Therefore, a knowledge of economics and business trends is valuable to business people.

Within any business community there are numerous local risks, such as the relocation of highways, which may cause customers to change their shopping behavior. The development of new highways may take customers to larger communities to do their shopping.

Jeff Greenberg, Photographer

Ilus. 20-5

There are certain risks for which there is no insurance. Losses due to slow sales are noninsurable. What are some other risks that are noninsurable?

Street improvements may make one location better than another and, therefore, draw customers away from an old location; street repairs or the establishment of no-parking zones may have a bad effect on certain types of businesses; and population changes and shifts in a community may make it necessary to move business firms. Against these and similar risks there is no insurance. Unless business people recognize trends and take action, they may find their businesses totally or partially destroyed. Noninsurable risks pose a great challenge to business managers.

CHAPTER REVIEW 20

BUILDING VOCABULARY POWER

Define the following terms and concepts.

1. insurer
2. policyholder
3. policy
4. insured
5. peril
6. risk
7. premium
8. insurance rate
9. insurable interest
10. deductible
11. coinsurance
12. reinsurance
13. insurance agents
14. fire insurance
15. extended coverage
16. business income insurance
17. transportation insurance
18. burglary, robbery, and theft insurance
19. collision insurance
20. comprehensive insurance
21. automobile liability insurance
22. medical payments insurance
23. no-fault insurance
24. health insurance
25. disability insurance
26. group insurance
27. health maintenance organizations (HMOs)
28. preferred provider organizations (PPOs)
29. life insurance
30. term insurance
31. whole life insurance
32. universal life insurance
33. liability insurance
34. professional liability insurance
35. bonding
36. credit insurance
37. credit life insurance
38. forgery insurance
39. title insurance
40. Overseas Private Investment Corporation
41. export credit insurance

REVIEWING FACTS

1. How are insurance rates established?
2. Describe what may be considered an insurable interest in property.

3. Name five business losses that can be covered by insurance.
4. Does a fire insurance policy on a building usually cover the equipment, the machinery, and the products in the building?
5. Is there any advantage in carrying fire insurance for a greater amount than the replacement value of the property?
6. Under a fire insurance policy with a coinsurance clause, why are the rates per thousand dollars of insurance lower than they are under an ordinary fire insurance policy?
7. What is the purpose of reinsurance?
8. Under an automobile insurance policy, on what basis is the value of the car determined when the insurance company pays for the loss?
9. How are HMOs different from traditional health insurance policies?
10. Why are alternatives to current health insurance plans being considered?
11. Why would a sole proprietor need life insurance?
12. In what way can a business obtain protection against possible loss due to theft by an employee?
13. What types of losses are covered by liability insurance?
14. Name some business risks for which it is impossible to buy insurance protection.
15. How can businesses protect themselves against noninsurable risks?

DISCUSSING IDEAS

1. A manufacturing plant is located in a modern building, but there is poor local fire protection. How will the fire insurance rates be affected?
2. Does a person who rents a building have an insurable interest in the building?
3. Why would a fire insurance company insist that you correct certain defects in your building before insuring the building for you?
4. Is it possible to carry too much property insurance? Explain.
5. Why is business income insurance so important to some corporations?
6. Many large corporations operating large fleets of cars driven by sales representatives do not carry collision insurance but maintain their own auto repair business. Why do these corporations believe that collision insurance is not a good value?
7. What are the advantages to a business that invests a large amount of money in a fitness center and wellness program for employees?
8. Assume that you are able to make what appears to be a very favorable contract with a new construction company. The contractor does not have much money and asks that you pay part of the cost of the construction in advance. Explain how you can protect yourself if the contractor does not perform the work.
9. If you operate a factory producing furniture, what are some of the possible claims for damages that might be brought by your customers?

10. Why is it important for companies offering credit on large purchases to ask customers to purchase credit life insurance?

A NALYZING INFORMATION

1. The following four examples provide information on insurance claims for fire insurance policies containing a coinsurance clause. Using the information in the table, indicate how much of the loss will be paid by the insurance company for each of the examples A, B, C, and D.

Example	Value of Property	Coinsurance Clause	Amount of Policy	Amount of Loss
A	$100,000	80%	$100,000	$80,000
B	40,000	90%	25,000	30,000
C	60,000	80%	48,000	30,000
D	20,000	90%	20,000	5,000

2. Obtain an automobile insurance policy and make a report on the different kinds of losses covered by the policy, the obligations of the policyholder, and the kinds of liabilities or losses that are not covered.
3. Contact an insurance agent to obtain the rates for term, whole life, and universal life insurance. Compare the annual premium costs for $50,000 of each type of insurance for a person (a) 20 years old, (b) 35 years old, (c) 55 years old.
4. Using library research, prepare a report on product liability for businesses.
5. For a business of your choice, make a list of the possible risks facing the business that could result in financial loss. For each risk, identify how the risk could be reduced and the type of insurance, if any, the business should purchase for protection.

S OLVING BUSINESS PROBLEMS

CASE 20-1

Carl and Judy Lockhart are making final plans to open a small antique shop. Most of their capital is tied up in inventory, display equipment, advertising, and a six-month advance payment on the rental of the store building. They plan to operate the shop themselves to save the cost of wages for employees. Judy has suggested that they consider buying a few insurance policies to protect themselves from various risks. Carl believes that because their capital is so limited they can do without insurance. "After all," he reasons, "we are renting the building so we do not need fire insurance. If there is a fire, the landlord's policy will cover us. And we do not have any employees, so there will not

REVIEW 20

be a need for health or life insurance. Why should we waste money on unnecessary insurance?"

Required:

1. If the landlord has a standard fire insurance policy, is it likely that the inventory will be covered in case of fire loss? Explain.
2. What minimum types of insurance policies should the Lockharts seriously consider? Give reasons for your answers.
3. Are there ways the Lockharts can reduce the cost of insurance needed to protect the business?

CASE 20-2

Jorden Alvarez purchased a used delivery truck two years ago that cost $9,500. Its present value is $7,800. He purchased an auto insurance policy from the Justright Insurance Company. Coverage included comprehensive insurance, $500 deductible collision insurance, $25,000 of property damage insurance, and $10,000/$25,000 of bodily injury insurance.

Jorden was involved in an accident, and he was at fault. As a result of the accident, the delivery van had $1,500 damage and the other driver's car received $3,000 damage. Jorden had $500 of medical bills. The driver of the other car was more seriously injured and had $12,000 of medical bills.

Required:

1. Determine how much the Justright Insurance Company would pay as a result of the accident for:
   a. comprehensive insurance
   b. collision insurance
   c. property damage
   d. medical bills
2. Would Jorden be responsible for paying any damages resulting from the accident? If so, how much?
3. If Jorden lived in a state with no-fault insurance, how much would the Justright Insurance Company pay?

Unit Summary

5-1 *Describe types of records, record systems, and budgets needed in running a business.*

In any business, financial records must be kept regarding assets, debts owed, cash available, revenue, expenses, and earnings. Various types of systems such as manual and computerized systems provide a basis for recording, processing, and retrieving data. Some of the more important types of records include those that account for cash, accounts receivable, accounts payable, depreciation, payroll, and taxes.

Budgeting systems are of particular significance. The first budget to be prepared is the sales budget because other budgets such as merchandising, advertising, cash, and the income statement budgets are all dependent upon projected sales. A capital budget is also important for planning to obtain funds to pay off major investments in fixed assets such as land, buildings, and equipment. For example, if a major expansion program is needed, funds must be obtained to purchase big-ticket items. Budgets also allow managers to control general business operations. Variances between planned and actual revenues and expenses often provide clues for needed corrective action.

5-2 *Discuss the need for and use of such financial tools as the income statement, balance sheet, working capital, and cash flow.*

Financial statements are prepared by accountants to serve the owners, managers, lenders, government officials, and others. One of the key statements is the balance sheet, which gives the financial status of the business at a given moment in time—a snapshot of the business. It shows a firm's assets, liabilities, and capital, with the total assets equaling liabilities plus capital. The relationship among these three items reveals other helpful data to accountants, such as a firm's ability to borrow funds and to pay its debts.

Another valuable financial report is the income statement. It reveals the total revenue earned, the total expenses, and the profit (or loss) earned for a specified period of time—usually one year. Finding relationships among these items allows managers to learn, for example, what the percentage of profit is to sales or what the percentage of each expense is to sales. These percentages provide assessments for how the firm performed during the most recent time period and what might be done to better control expenses.

From the balance sheet and income statement, accountants can also prepare other statements that provide helpful data—working capital, cash flow, and financial ratios. In addition to accountants, managers can also seek financial assistance from consultants, bankers, and the Small Business Administration.

5-3 *Distinguish among three major kinds of capital (owner capital, borrowed capital, and retained earnings) and among various types, sources, and procedures for obtaining capital.*

Three broad categories for seeking business capital are owner capital, borrowed capital, and retained earnings. Owner capital is that which comes directly from the owners themselves, whereas borrowed capital represents funds that come from others. Retained earnings are profits owned and kept by a business. Owner capital is usually the primary source of funds for starting a business. Ongoing businesses are more likely to use both borrowed capital and retained earnings.

Shares of stock are owner capital, of which there are two major types: common and preferred. The most realistic value of stock is market value, the price paid for a share of stock on any given day. In case of bankruptcy, however, book value takes on added importance. The book value represents the value of each share after liabilities are paid and assets are sold for division among all stockholders.

Borrowed capital may be obtained by selling a variety of types of long-term and short-term bonds and notes on which a stated rate of interest must be paid yearly. Bondholders lend firms money, whereas stockholders own a portion of the company.

Businesses must decide which source of capital is best by using such criteria as the cost of obtaining capital, interest rates, and whether to sell stock and thereby agree to share future profits with additional owners. Because interest rates vary as do stock prices, economic conditions often influence decisions. Firms can always use retained earnings to expand if adequate earnings have been put aside for this purpose.

5-4 *Explain the characteristics of bank and nonbank financial institutions and the financial instruments provided to investors.*

Two general types of financial institutions are banks, which accept demand deposits and make commercial loans, and nonbanks that either accept demand deposits or make commercial loans but not both. During the last decade, nonbank banks became a dominant force because of laws deregulating the banking industry. Deregulation and the extensive use of computer technology created intense competition, resulting in many financial services for businesses and at lower costs. Some banks, however, could not compete successfully and failed.

In addition to standard checking and savings accounts, banks and nonbanks offer a host of investment choices. Popular investment choices include CDs, money market funds, mutual funds, municipal bonds and notes, and interest-earning checking accounts. Selecting the best investment depends upon such factors as the investor's needs for safety, income, and growth. Bonds, for example, provide for safety and income whereas stocks offer growth opportunities.

Checks and other forms of negotiable instruments (notes, cashier's checks, drafts, etc.) are the primary financial instruments used in day-to-day business operations. Businesses must exercise caution when issuing and accepting checks and making loans. New forms of financial instruments will continue to be created in the years ahead to meet the needs of business and consumers.

5-5 *Identify and describe credit plans, credit cards, credit policies, collection procedures, and credit analysis methods.*

Because business operates on credit, good credit practices are needed. Both commercial and consumer credit policies must be established to assure financial success. Important business decisions must be made before offering regular charge accounts, revolving charge accounts, or installment credit plans. For those firms that want to sell on credit but prefer to reduce the problems related to managing credit sales, bank and nonbank credit cards are preferred among most small retailers.

Credit card use has grown rapidly in the United States as well as in foreign countries. As a result, competition among major issuers of credit cards has been keen. Customers benefit from lower interest rates and annual fees. Competition has also encouraged the increased use of debit cards and smart cards.

Credit agencies provide credit issuers a valuable service because they offer information about credit applicants and credit cardholders. Information about applicants enables firms to apply the four Cs of credit (character, capacity, capital, and conditions) to decide whether an applicant is an acceptable credit risk. When a customer flashes a credit card for a purchase, merchants are able to determine whether to accept or reject the credit request based upon the cardholder's prior paying record and approved credit limit.

Credit laws help protect credit applicants from unfairly being denied credit, from inaccurate information found in records, and from being mistreated by collection agencies when payments are overdue. To prevent losses caused by nonpaying or slow-paying customers, businesses need to keep accurate, up-to-date records, develop a sensible plan for collecting overdue accounts, and analyze customers' accounts receivables carefully.

5-6 *Discuss the significance of insurance to businesses, common types of policies, and how noninsurable risks can be reduced.*

A major loss of a building and its contents could force a business to fail. Losses caused by fire, tornadoes, and other uncontrollable events could strike any firm. Insurance is a means by which businesses can be protected from large, uncertain losses. Insurance rates, however, can influence whether to buy insurance or how much and what kind of insurance to seek. Certain losses, for example, may be uninsurable, such as drastically marking down merchandise that suddenly becomes obsolete. Other losses such as spoiled or damaged goods may be a regular recurrence or too small to justify insuring.

The types of standard insurance policies for businesses include fire, liability, vehicle, employee health and life, forgery, transportation, and credit. With each type of insurance, special provisions are provided, some of which influence the cost of insurance (premiums). For example, with fire insurance, a sprinkler system and nearness of a building to a fire department reduce premiums. Fire insurance policies require insuring about eighty percent of the total value of a building; otherwise, the insured must suffer some of the loss. Other provisions are often found in policies that also affect premiums. With car and health insurance, for instance, high deductible amounts lower premiums and low deductibles raise them.

The insurance industry uses many technical terms with which business managers must be familiar. A few such terms include insurable interest, reinsurance, coinsurance, extended coverage, no-fault insurance, peril, and risk. An informed insurance buyer must grasp these terms in order to wisely compare competitors' policies against an insurance-buying checklist.

R. Whitcomb

R. Whitcomb

Employee 12468

Career Planning

Human Resources

INSPECTED BY • INSPECTED BY

NUMBER 22

INSPECTED BY • INSPECTED BY

6

*H*uman Resources Management

OBJECTIVES

6-1 Describe the role of human resources management in an organization and the major activities performed by human resources personnel.

6-2 Outline the procedures used in employee selection, promotion, and termination.

6-3 Discuss the factors to be used in designing an effective compensation and benefits program for an organization.

6-4 Discuss the importance of employee training and development and the primary methods used for employee training.

6-5 Explain the purpose and characteristics of a career development program.

6-6 Justify the need for organizational development to improve employee productivity and motivation.

A LEADER IN BUSINESS DEVELOPMENT

"Six hundred dollars and a prayer" were used to start her first business at age 22. Since then she has founded four more companies. Theresa "Terry" Neese is currently CEO of Terry Neese Personnel Services which, along with her other companies, has found jobs for more than 9,000 people. Ms. Neese is a Cherokee Indian, married, and the mother of three children. She hosts a radio show on small business and has written many articles on the subject. Her involvement with many community organizations and knowledge of small business issues has resulted in numerous honors. She was the first woman nominated by a political party for the office of Lieutenant Governor in Oklahoma.

Terry Neese Personnel Services is one of the largest privately-owned professional placement agencies in the country. Her agency functions as the "personnel department" for many businesses offering such services as recruitment, out-placement for companies reducing employment, career counseling and planning, and wage and salary surveys. Ms. Neese recognizes that both the employee and employer must be happy when a person is selected for a job. Employee turnover is too costly for companies to make mistakes.

Values have guided Terry Neese through the challenge of starting and managing her businesses. Those values include consistency, integrity, leadership, self-motivation, and self-esteem. She has always remained focused on her vision and does not accept "no" for an answer. She credits much of her success to hard work and determination.

Ms. Neese's commitment to others is demonstrated through her continuing service to the March of Dimes, the Arthritis Foundation, and the Diabetes Foundation. She has also served on the National Advisory Council for Indian Education.

Terry Neese, Chief Executive Officer, Personnel Services

INSPIRATIONAL IDEAS

"This is the most exciting time in history to be a business leader. Remember, every adventure is a learning experience, even if you fail at that adventure. Learning from our failures is a success. To me, success means loving what you do so much that you would do it for free, but you do it so well, you get paid for it."

Photo courtesy of Terry Neese Personnel Services.

HUMAN RESOURCES PLANNING

CHAPTER 21

R. Whitcomb

yee 12468

After studying this chapter you will be able to:

21-1 Describe the types of activities that occur in a human resources department.

21-2 Outline the procedures to follow in identifying and selecting new personnel.

21-3 Identify when employees should be promoted, transferred, or released.

21-4 Compare three major types of compensation systems used by businesses.

21-5 Describe several common employee benefits provided by businesses.

21-6 Discuss how laws and regulations affect human resources management.

Jason has worked for the same small delivery service now for three years. He started as a part-time person packaging items for delivery while in high school. This is his first year of full-time employment since graduating. He feels that he is underpaid and unappreciated. While he has received three pay increases since he started work, they have totaled only twenty-five cents per hour. He is making less than several of his friends who work at a local factory and only began working this year. He has moved up to a full-time delivery job, but he doesn't really feel it is a promotion since he works harder now than he did before.

Here is what Jason told a friend about his feelings. "I believe the owner owes me a lot. I am one of the few young people who has continued to work for the business. Most quit after only a few months' work or at least by the time they graduate *from school. I seldom make mistakes on my deliveries but only hear from the owner when a customer complains. Since the company doesn't recognize how important I am to them, I make up for it. Sometimes when I'm making a delivery I might stop for a hamburger or soda and a short break. I even visit my girlfriend at her work if I'm in the area. I know that is against the rules, but I think I deserve it. I knock myself out for my salary. Where would the company be without me?"*

What do you think of Jason's statement? Do you think he is correct in his feelings? Would you feel the same way if you were the owner of the business? Do you believe Jason is a valuable resource for the company?

Of all the resources used by a business, probably the most important to the success of the business is people. People are responsible for the effective use of all other resources in the business. People make decisions, operate equipment, maintain records, and deal with customers. Because of their value to the business, a great deal of attention must be given to the effective management of people.

All managers work with people. However, ensuring that an adequate number of employees is available, that they are well paid and trained, satisfied with their jobs, and productive is a specific area of management known as **human resources management**, sometimes called personnel management. In the past, business managers did not always see the close relationship between selecting and hiring personnel, the training required, and factors such as employee motivation, productivity, or job problems. As a result, some organizations faced an increasing number of personnel problems ranging from difficulty in finding qualified employees, growing costs of training, employee dissatisfaction, poor performance, and a high employee turnover rate. Now most companies realize that they need programs to deal with a variety of issues related to making the best use of the people who work for the company and keeping them satisfied with their work.

Illus. 21-1

Managers are most successful in getting the best possible performance from employees when recruitment and selection are planned and coordinated with human resources personnel. In what ways can effective recruitment and selection techniques ultimately affect the training of employees?

Bruce Ayres/Tony Stone Images

HUMAN RESOURCES ACTIVITIES

Employees must be recruited, hired, and trained. Once on the job, they must have the necessary equipment and other resources to complete their jobs. Some employees need close supervision while others require very little supervision. Managers must be sure that employees are satisfied with their jobs and motivated to perform well. They need to be concerned about employee safety and health, working conditions, wages, and benefits. Managers need to recognize and reward those employees who are doing a good job and to improve the performance of those who are not. Managers must also possibly dismiss those employees who fail to improve their performance.

As you can see, there are many management responsibilities involved in working with people. Human resources management is involved with all of those responsibilities. Typical activities of the human resources department are shown in Fig. 21-1.

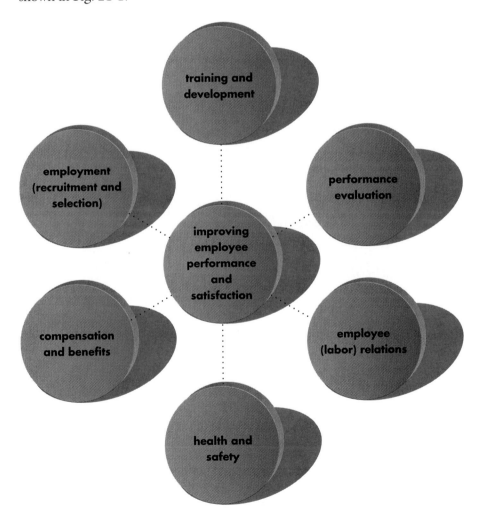

Fig. 21-1

The major activities in a human resources department.

In very small companies, the owner or an assistant handle all of the personnel activities. The procedures may be quite informal, although state and federal laws and regulations often require formal procedures to be followed in completing many personnel procedures. Large companies usually have a major department that is responsible for human resources management. It may have several specialized divisions within the department, each of which deals with a specific area in human resources. Some of the human resources activities may be performed in other departments across the organization but are planned and coordinated through the human resources department.

An example of the relationship of human resources to other parts of the organization is shown in Fig. 21-2. The dotted lines in the illustration indicate that the human resources department gives service and support to other departments in the company. Company managers regularly use the services of the human resources department as they work with the employees in their departments. A large human resources department will be organized into divisions reflecting the types of activities provided. Examples of human resources activities are described below.

Fig. 21-2

The relationship of human resources to other departments in an organization.

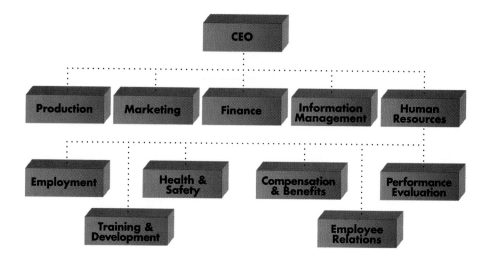

EMPLOYMENT

Employment is the one area most people associate with human resources management. Employment activities include determining the need for employees and skill requirements, recruiting applicants, evaluating qualifications, and hiring the most qualified to fill available jobs. In addition, transfers, promotions, retirements, dismissals, and other job changes must be processed by the division.

COMPENSATION AND BENEFITS

The amount a company spends for employee wages and benefits (such as insurance and vacations) is usually a major part of its operating budget. The level of wages and benefits helps to determine the quality of the personnel hired and their satisfaction. The productivity of the personnel (the amount of work produced) compared to the expenses of wages and benefits will determine whether the company can be profitable or not.

The division responsible for determining compensation classifies all jobs according to pay levels. When a person is hired, promoted, or given a pay increase, the division completes the procedures needed to ensure that the employee gets paid the correct amount.

It also is responsible for developing and managing the benefits program. This responsibility includes determining what benefits can be offered, determining the cost of each benefit, and providing information to employees about each type of benefit. Some companies offer employees choices of benefits, so helping employees make the best decisions and keeping track of each person's choices can be quite complicated. Once decisions are made, the necessary paperwork must be completed to ensure that employees receive the appropriate benefits. Each benefit program must be monitored to control costs and to ensure proper procedures are followed when employees receive the benefit.

TRAINING AND DEVELOPMENT

Several types of training are conducted in most businesses. Once an employee is hired, an orientation to the company and initial training is needed to prepare the employee for the job. Then as equipment or procedures change, training is needed to prepare employees for the changes. Finally, when evaluations indicate that an employee is not performing as well as expected, training may be used to improve his or her performance.

Often, employees are promoted or transferred to a new job in the company. Part of the process of ensuring that the employee is prepared for the new job responsibilities is training. Many companies allow employees to participate in education programs for their own personal development. Reimbursement for some or all of the costs of the education may be provided. Finally, if the company cuts back on the number of employees needed, eliminates a department, or has a major change in the type of business activity, it may provide training programs to help the employees who will be forced to leave prepare for new jobs.

EMPLOYEE RELATIONS

If a labor union is organized within a company, a very formal set of relationships exists between employees and management. The unit responsible for employee relations assists in negotiating the agreement with the union and deals with employee activities and problems that relate to the agreement. If employees are not represented by a union, the same types of activities are performed, but usually in a less formal way.

Effective management/employee relations have become an important concern for businesses today. Fewer managers are being used in many businesses, and employees are expected to take more responsibility for their work. Work teams made up of employees and managers are taking responsibility for many decisions once made just by managers. These decisions include hiring, deciding how work will be performed, and improving quality. Human resources personnel help to prepare people for their new responsibilities.

HEALTH AND SAFETY

If employees are unhealthy or injured, they may not be able to work. Also, the cost of health care and insurance will be higher than necessary. Expensive insurance is harmful to both the employee and the company. The health and safety division is responsible for safe work areas, procedures, and for helping employees to be healthy and productive. The division must also implement all local, state, and federal health and safety laws that apply to the business. Most companies provide safety training and monitor procedures to identify and correct possible safety problems. Some companies have organized wellness and fitness programs and some even have medical personnel on staff to give physicals to employees, treat injuries and illnesses, and help to maintain a healthy workforce.

PERFORMANCE EVALUATION

Employees must be able to perform their jobs well. Companies regularly evaluate personnel to determine how well they are meeting expectations. Areas of strength should be identified so employees can be recognized and rewarded. If performance problems are identified, managers need to be prepared to help the employee make the necessary improvements or determine if training is needed.

Often, each manager is responsible for evaluating employees and using the results of the evaluation to improve performance. The role of the human resources department is to develop the evaluation system and prepare the forms and materials needed. The department will train managers to be able to evaluate employees objectively, complete the evaluation forms, and conduct evaluation conferences with the employees. They will also help employees understand the procedures. The department may be responsible for maintaining the results of the evaluations in each employee's personnel file.

OTHER HUMAN RESOURCES ACTIVITIES

While the major activities performed by the human resources department have been described, others may be provided, particularly in very large companies. Some departments have administrative divisions responsible for maintaining all records, processing forms, and managing the large amount of data related to the firm's personnel.

Educational programs, counseling, day-care services, employee services, and many other activities are becoming a part of human resources management. Many years ago, making sure that all jobs in the company were filled may have been the only major responsibility of a personnel manager. Today, however, human resources management is a very broad and important function.

In the remaining sections of this chapter, we will examine procedures for identifying and hiring employees and for determining wages and salaries. Chapter

22 discusses employee training and development as well as other activities involved in improving the effectiveness of employees. Chapter 23 describes the process of maintaining effective organization and work environments.

SELECTING PERSONNEL

Hiring new employees is an important management activity. If selection procedures are effective and the right employees are hired for each job, many problems can be avoided. If poor selection procedures are used, people are hired who do not meet specific job qualifications. This results in higher training costs, dissatisfied employees, and many other personnel problems.

Not only is it illegal to discriminate in hiring employees, it is good business practice to search for the most qualified applicants. Managers or businesses that rely on stereotypes to automatically exclude women, people from specific racial or ethnic groups, older or younger workers, or other groups that have been subjected to discrimination will often lose effective employees who can con-tribute to the success of the business. They also are likely to become involved in lawsuits because of ille-gal practices that will cost time and money and harm the public image of the business.

A business must take the necessary time to find and hire the right people. This sec-tion discusses some of the essential proce-dures that should be followed in selecting personnel.

Illus. 21-2
Some businesses are reluctant to hire young people with limited work experience. What can an applicant do to try to overcome this type of age discrimination?

ESTABLISHING A NEED

As a first step in the process of hiring a new employee, it is necessary to estab-lish that a new employee is needed. Normally, the need develops to replace a current employee who has left the company, has been promoted, or has retired. If the company or department is growing, new employees will be needed to complete the extra work. Changes in the operations of a department or the use of new procedures or equipment may require that new employees be hired to perform those duties.

When a need has been identified in a department, the department manager will fill out an **employment requisition**, a form requesting that a position in a department be filled by the human resources department. An example of an employment requisition is shown in Fig. 21-3.

Fig. 21-3

A sample employment requisition.

THE SHEFFIELD COMPANY EMPLOYMENT REQUISITION

Job Title.... Receptionist .... Department.. Marketing ....

Duties . Greet visitors, operate switchboard, some data entry on microcomputer .....

Additional Position? .....Yes ..X.. No   Permanent .... Temporary ....

Replacement? ..X.. Yes .....No   Permanent ...X... Temporary ....

Rate of Pay... $5.60/hour   Hours of Work . 8:30 am - 5:00 pm, M-F .

Education... High School Graduate   Experience   Receptionist experience

                                                  desirable but not necessary

Number Needed ..1... Date Needed .. 7/12/--..   Date of Request .... 5/2/--...

Account No. 327XY ....   Signed .... Supervisor

                                                  Approved .... Dep't Head

Human Resources Record   #### Confirmation of Employment

Name ....   Supervisor...........................

Address................................   Date...............................

....

New Hire .... Transfer.........   Dept. Head ....

To Begin Work ....   Date ....

Wage Rate...............................   H.R. Mgr. ....

                                                  Date ....

To obtain an additional employee under normal circumstances, the need has to be justified and approvals obtained from top-level management. The amount and source of the new employee's salary and benefits must be identified within the department or company budget. After the employment requisition is completed, it is sent to the human resources department. The need for an employee should be anticipated as far in advance as possible so the human resources department has time to find a suitable replacement and the requesting department does not have an unfilled position for a long period of time.

An employment requisition does not contain complete information about the unfilled job. The human resources department must have detailed and accurate information about the position in order to do an effective job of screening and hiring the most suitable applicants. One of the best ways to obtain the needed information is to have detailed specifications prepared for each job in the company. A **job specification** (shown in Fig. 21-4) includes information on the nature of the work done in a particular job, the necessary qualifications needed by the employee to do the work, and where the job fits in the organizational and wage structure of the company. Job specifications are developed by specialists in the human resources department with the help of personnel in each department of the company. The specialists have been trained to observe jobs and analyze the work performed in order to develop a detailed description. The job specifications are kept on file or in a computerized record system in the human resources department and are updated regularly as job requirements and activities change. The information is used in a variety of ways, but in the selection process, it is used in deciding how to find qualified applicants for the job. After applicants are recruited, the information is used to determine which applicant is best qualified for the job.

Fig. 21-4
A job specification form.

THE GREENBOUGH CO.
Job Specification Form

Developed October 21   19--
By M. Fountrey
Revised ....

Job Title... Stock Manager   Department Receiving Warehouse

Duties

Responsible for filling all orders as received; reconciling received goods with invoices; maintaining stock records; completing physical inventory; reconciling physical inventory count with computer records; maintenance of inventory on a first in-first out basis; appearance of stock and warehouse; routine equipment maintenance.

Qualifications

Education: College ...... Technical School ...... High School .. X ..
Experience: Minimum of two years stock room or warehouse experience; familiarity with inventory record keeping.
Physical Requirements: Good health; able to lift bulky items of 50 pounds
Mental Requirements: Computer entry skills; analysis of inventory records; accuracy; limited mechanical ability

Career Information

Hours of Work: 8:00 a.m. - 4:30 p.m. Monday - Friday; limited overtime.
Compensation: $8.25/hour; semi-annual review; profit sharing based on individual evaluation and department performance.
Vacation: One week after one year; accumulates an additional day for each three months worked to three weeks total.
Benefits: Full benefit options for Schedule 1 employees
Promotion: Promotion review after 18 months; promotion based on job availability and recommendation of division manager; promoted to Warehouse Manager or Assistant Purchasing Agent.

Additional Information

....
....
....
....
....

RECRUITING APPLICANTS

After the human resources department has received an employment requisition and reviewed the job specifications, it must then identify applicants for the opening. Effective recruiting will result in a number of applicants from which a well-qualified person can be selected. If too small a number of applicants is available, the chances of finding someone who is well qualified decreases.

If too large a number of applicants is available, the process of selecting the most qualified will take longer.

Many sources of prospective employees exist. It is the responsibility of the human resources department to be aware of those sources and to use those most likely to locate qualified applicants. Some of the most often used sources of prospective employees are discussed next.

Current Employees

Often, a vacancy can be filled with a current employee from another job in the company. There are many reasons for using transfers. It may be a promotion for the employee, which can serve as an incentive to work harder. If it is not a promotion, allowing an employee to change jobs may provide better working hours or a better pay rate. The new job may match the employee's interests and abilities better than the old job. Sometimes placing a current employee in a job opening is useful for companies who are anticipating reducing the number of employees in another department. Many companies have a policy of posting all vacancies and giving current employees the first opportunity to apply.

Recommendations of Present Employees

Employees of the business may recommend people they know for employment. Specific job openings and requirements need to be communicated to employees so they can attempt to identify appropriate applicants. Procedures should be developed to allow employees to nominate qualified people for jobs and to be sure that those people are treated the same as all other applicants during the selection process.

Current employees are likely to identify people they know only if they are satisfied with their jobs and believe the company provides a good employment opportunity. They will often communicate their satisfaction to the person they nominate. Because the employee understands the company and the work required, they are more likely to nominate people who they believe will be happy working for the company.

Previous Applicants

A business that has a reputation as a good employer is likely to have people applying for jobs at all times. Most large companies take applications regularly, even though specific jobs may not be available at that time. The applications are kept on file and reviewed when openings do occur. Usually with this procedure, an initial screening of an application is done to determine if the applicant meets minimum job qualifications and to classify the application according to job categories in the company. Then the application is maintained in an active file for a period of time such as six months. Persons not hired by that time must reapply to keep their applications active.

Using a procedure of regularly accepting applications shortens the time it takes to identify qualified people when a vacancy exists. As long as the applications are screened and those not hired are removed from the file regularly, the pool of applicants will be up-to-date and of a reasonable size.

Education Placement Offices

Colleges and universities, vocational and technical schools, and an increasing number of high schools have placement offices to assist graduates in obtaining jobs. Businesses can use those offices to obtain lists of potential employees and, in some cases, to obtain resumes and other information about the school's graduates. The offices may provide assistance in scheduling interviews with a number of applicants to help the recruiting business. Because the applicants are graduates from the college or school, the employer will often be able to get detailed information about academic performance and school activities as well as specific references from teachers and counselors.

Professional and Labor Organizations

Many workers maintain memberships in professional associations or labor unions. Those organizations provide a variety of services for their members including career information, education and training opportunities, and information about the profession. Many of the organizations provide job search and placement help for members. Businesses can contact the organizations to obtain information on members who are seeking employment. The organizations will also notify members of available jobs through employment files, computer databases, or advertisements in their publications.

Employment Agencies

Employment agencies are businesses that actively recruit, evaluate, and help people prepare for and locate jobs. All states maintain an employment agency supported by state and federal taxes. Public employment offices are usually located in several cities throughout each state. They offer testing services, job listings, and help in preparing applications and in developing interviewing skills.

In some cases, employment agencies can help prospective employees with specific skill training if needed to qualify for a job. The public employment services will work with companies to complete initial screening and interviewing in order to provide a list of qualified candidates.

Private employment agencies work with both employers and individuals looking for jobs. They charge a fee for their services. In some cases, the employer pays the recruitment costs of the agency. At other times, the applicant must pay a fee for services provided or pay a percentage of the beginning salary once employed. Just as with state agencies, private employment agencies also offer a range of services ranging from resume and interview preparation to skills training.

Advertising

Advertising in newspapers or magazines is a popular method of obtaining job applicants. It is frequently used when a large number of workers is needed, or when they are needed immediately. Usually, the company that uses advertising does not have applications on file. Classified newspaper ads and ads in trade publications often get results. They can either be **open ads**, which give the name of the company, or they can be **blind ads,** which do not identify the company. Blind ads give a post office box or telephone number to be used by the applicant. Usually, open ads result in more applicants with better qualifications than do blind ads.

Advertisements must be carefully written. While advertisements are usually not lengthy because of the cost, they must be large enough to attract the attention of potential applicants. The advertisement must describe the job and company in enough detail that readers can determine the job requirements, necessary qualifications, and working conditions. In that way the company will receive applications from those people who are most likely to qualify for the job and want to work for the company if they are offered the job.

PROCESSING APPLICATIONS

Most business firms require applicants to fill out an application form. Questions should be asked that obtain specific information necessary to make the best selection for the job. The company must be careful that the form does not ask for information that can be considered discriminatory or that violates state and federal labor laws. A company gains nothing by asking for information that does not relate specifically to the applicant's qualifications for the job. Application forms should be reviewed carefully to eliminate inappropriate questions.

The following procedures are typically followed by human resources departments after applications for a job have been received:

1. Applications are reviewed to eliminate those people who do not meet minimum qualifications. Those qualifications would typically include level of education, specific training, certificates, or licenses. Applicants are often eliminated at this stage because they filled out the application form incorrectly, did not fully complete the application, or had very poor written communication skills.

2. Applicants are interviewed to confirm information on the application, to gather information on oral communications and human relations skills, and to provide more information to the applicant about the company and the job. The interviewer will typically have a specific procedure to follow and a set of questions to ask each person. Careful notes will be kept by the interviewer to help in deciding who will be hired.

3. Information supplied on the application form and through the interview is checked for accuracy. Schools attended and previous employers can be confirmed. References should be contacted with the permission of the applicant. Some employers believe that references are of no value because an applicant will not list a reference who is likely to give a poor recom-

mendation. However, all references should be contacted by telephone. Careful questioning of a reference can often reveal important information about particular strengths of the applicant, work habits, and the types of work experiences the person has had.

Stacy Pick/Stock, Boston

4. For applicants who have the necessary minimum qualifications and have successfully completed the interview and check of credentials, tests are often administered to determine if they have the needed knowledge and skills. Again, tests should be used only if they measure characteristics important for success on the job and if training programs are not available in the company to develop the needed characteristics. Some companies have been charged with employment discrimination because of the use of tests that had little relationship to the skills and knowledge required on the job.

5. The applicants still being considered are interviewed by the manager of the department that has the opening. In the interview, the manager can ask more specific questions related to the duties and qualifications for the job, provide detailed information about the job and the department, and answer questions the applicant may have. Some companies are now involving experienced employees from the department in the interview. They believe that employees understand the job and working conditions and can help select personnel who will be effective members of the work team.

As a part of the interview process, the prospective employee should have a thorough introduction to the job, the area in which the work will be performed, the equipment and procedures to be used, and co-workers.

By understanding the job and its requirements, the applicant will be in a better position to determine if he or she will be satisfied if offered the job. There are many examples of employees who quit a job soon after beginning it because it turns out to be quite different than they had anticipated. Providing the opportunity to learn about the job during the interview should help to reduce this problem.

6. The final selection is made by comparing information gathered during the application process with the job requirements as listed in the job specification. Since several people are involved in the procedures and many sources of information are used, the final selection may take some time. A decision-making process should be developed by the human resources department that is objective, considers all of the information collected, and eliminates the chance of employment discrimination. If done carefully, a well-qualified employee will be hired who is likely to be happy and successful on the job.

7. Before the final employment decision is made, many businesses require the prospective employee to pass a physical exam. The examination is done to see if the applicant is physically able to do the work. It may also protect the business if the worker later claims a disability as a result of the work. Some firms are now using the results of physical examinations to develop health and wellness programs for their employees in order to reduce sickness and absenteeism. Because of the increasing problems with drug abuse and its effects in the workplace, drug testing is also used to screen prospective employees.

8. When an applicant is hired, the necessary records are prepared for the employing department and for the human resources department. Procedures are then established to help the new employee begin the job. An important part of those procedures is job orientation and training for the new employee. Those activities will be discussed in the next chapter.

9. After the new employee has been at work for some time, the human resources department should perform a follow-up to see whether the right person has been selected. Consulting with both the department head and the employee will help the human resources department improve its selection procedures in the future.

PROMOTING, TRANSFERRING, AND RELEASING EMPLOYEES

The amount of time and money invested in recruiting, hiring, and training a new employee is very high. Most firms spend several thousand dollars on each new employee. To obtain employees with very specialized skills or to hire someone when there is only a small number of qualified applicants, a company may have to spend as much as $100,000.

Because of that expense, once a good employee is found, the company should attempt to keep that person as long as possible. Procedures for promotions and transfers are helpful. The company also needs to plan in order to deal with employees who are not performing satisfactorily. While efforts should be made to improve performance through effective supervision and training, the human resources department should develop procedures for discharging personnel.

PROMOTIONS

Promotion is the advancement of an employee within a company to a position with more authority and responsibility. Usually, a promotion includes an increase in pay and may include greater prestige and benefits. Promotion opportunities occur when jobs are vacated as a result of another promotion, retirement, resignation, death, dismissal, or when a new position is created.

Whenever possible, a business should have a policy of filling vacancies by promotion. Assuming that the company has an effective selection procedure, well-qualified people are working in the business. Those people will be ambitious and will look for new opportunities including advancement. If those opportunities are not available in the company, employees may not work as hard, may not take advantage of training opportunities, or may decide to move to other companies that can provide them with better job possibilities.

Promotion policies need to be carefully prepared and all employees need to understand the procedures. Every employee should have an equal opportunity to receive promotions for which they are qualified. Employees need to know the possible jobs where they can advance and the factors considered in promotion. Many companies now provide career counseling services for employees. Through career counseling, employees can plan career paths, determine the education and training required for the jobs in the career path, and develop plans to prepare for each of the jobs.

Most companies use two basic factors, ability and **seniority** (the length of time an employee has been with the company). The company should have policies to determine who is promoted if two or more workers have about the same abilities. In the past, some companies have had promotion practices that excluded some people from the possibility of promotion. They were excluded because of stereotypes about who would or would not perform a job well or because some people were selected for additional attention and training while others were not. Human resources departments regularly analyze promotion data to identify areas where possible employment discrimination is occurring. In those situations, they will make special efforts to encourage employees from underrepresented groups to prepare for and apply for promotions.

Generally, the decision as to whether a person should apply and be considered for promotion is made by the immediate supervisor and the employee. That information should be a part of the company's regular personnel evaluation procedures so that employees and supervisors can be aware of and discuss the possibilities for promotion. Some companies use tests or special application procedures for persons being considered for promotion.

TRANSFERS

Transfer is the assignment of an employee to another job in the company which, in general, involves the same types of responsibility and authority. Transfers are made at the request of the employee or the supervisor. There are many reasons for transfers: (1) employees being trained for management positions are transferred among several positions to gain experience, (2) employees are transferred to give them a better opportunity for promotion, (3) transfers are made to new departments or new company locations due to growth or reduction of the size of departments, (4) workers choose to transfer to jobs that better meet their current interests and needs, and (5) transfers are made to overcome difficulties resulting from poor employee performance or conflicts with other people on the job.

EMPLOYEE RELEASES

There are a few situations where employees are no longer able to work at a business. Some situations are permanent while others are temporary. They may result from a downturn in the business that requires fewer employees or from the unacceptable actions or unsatisfactory job performance of the employee.

A **discharge** is the release of an employee from the company due to inappropriate work behavior. In ordinary language, this means that the employee is fired. Discharges are unfortunate for both the employee and the employer because they usually indicate significant problems have been occurring for some time.

A **layoff** is a temporary or permanent reduction in the number of employees because of a change in business conditions. Those changes could include reduced sales because of competition or a poor economy, or the elimination of jobs because of changes in products, procedures, or equipment. After a layoff, employees may be called back to work when jobs become available. When a large number of layoffs is planned, the human resources department may be asked to help the employees plan for the layoff. That may include help in locating another job, personal counseling, or retraining.

In the 1990s, many companies found they needed to restructure their businesses to reduce costs and become more competitive with businesses from other countries. The result has been major layoffs of workers who may have worked for the company for many years. In some cases, companies like General Motors and IBM reduced their labor forces by tens of thousands of employees. It is not likely that most of those workers will ever be rehired by their former employers as more technology is used by the companies and fewer workers are needed to operate the business.

Decisions on both discharges and layoffs are usually made by management in consultation with the human resources department. Specific procedures are used to make a fair decision. If a discharge is anticipated, the human resources department may first counsel the employee or consider transferring the employee if a problem with job skill or relationships with co-workers is identified. The department must be sure that the problem is not one of lack of training or poor supervision. It would be inappropriate and inefficient to discharge an employee who just needed additional training or whose supervisor was not effective.

EMPLOYMENT TURNOVER

Employment turnover describes the extent to which people enter and leave employment in a business during a year. The rate of turnover is important to a business because the loss of experienced employees means that new employees need to be hired and trained. New employees will not be as productive as experienced workers for some time. Between the time when an experienced employee leaves and a new employee is hired, the remaining employees have to work harder to get the work done. A high rate of labor turnover usually results in lowering employee morale. Therefore, most companies watch their employee turnover rate carefully and make every effort to keep it low.

Two of the most common formulas for computing the rate of employee turnover are shown in Fig. 21-5.

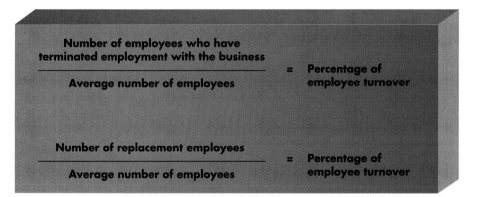

Fig. 21-5
Calculating the rate of employee turnover.

An example will illustrate the difference between the two methods. Suppose that during one year 150 employees left their jobs in a company. One hundred twenty new employees were hired to replace those who had left. The average number of employees on the payroll was 1,000. According to the first formula, the labor turnover was 15 percent (150/1,000). According to the second formula, it was 12 percent (120/1,000). It is important that the same formula be used by a company from year to year. That will make it easier to study trends in labor turnover.

EXIT INTERVIEWS

Whenever an employee leaves a company, it is important that the person be interviewed. A formal interview with an employee who is leaving a company to determine the person's attitudes and feelings about the company is known as an **exit interview**. The exit interview provides an opportunity to learn about the views of an employee towards the company's policies and procedures, management, and operations. Often, the employee can provide valuable information about problems, effective procedures, or other items that can lead to improvements in the company.

The exit interview is usually completed in person, but it may be done by telephone or with a questionnaire that the employee completes. The procedure should be conducted by a person skilled in personnel interviewing in order to make the employee comfortable and to obtain the most useful information. It should not be done by the employee's department head or supervisor because information about that department and its management will be needed.

COMPENSATION METHODS

One of the reasons people work is to earn money. The money and other benefits people receive for work is called **compensation**. The compensation received can be an important factor in determining whether an employee will continue to work for the company, will be satisfied with the work, and will do a good job. Therefore, a manager of human resources must develop a compensation system that is fair to all employees, satisfies them, encourages them to do a good job, and is affordable by the company.

The amount of compensation paid is affected by many factors: the skill required for the job, the conditions within which the work is performed, the amount of education and experience the person has, the supply and demand of that type of worker, economic conditions, and other factors.

In this section, we will study the types of compensation systems typically used by companies. We will also examine the policies and procedures used to manage compensation.

WAGE AND SALARY PLANS

Two terms are used to describe the type of employee compensation. **Wages** describes compensation paid on an hourly basis. **Salary** describes compensation paid on other than an hourly basis, such as weekly or monthly. Salaries are most often paid to executives, supervisors, professionals, and others who do not have a fixed number of hours to work each week. Most employees who are paid on an hourly basis are covered by the Fair Labor Standards Act (FLSA). Under the provisions of that act, employees who work more than 40 hours in a work week must be paid 1 1/2 times their regular pay rate for all hours over 40. Salaried employees do not have to meet that restriction since their work is not tied to a specific number of hours. If they work more than 40 hours in a week, the company does not have to provide additional compensation.

The Fair Labor Standards Act also prescribes a minimum wage that must be paid to employees in businesses that are covered by the Act. Those are typically larger businesses and businesses involved in interstate and foreign commerce. At time the FLSA was passed in the late 1930s, the minimum wage was set at $.25. In 1991, the minimum wage was increased from $3.80 to $4.25 per hour.

Because businesses vary a great deal in the types of work and the qualifications of employees, many methods are used to determine how employees are paid. Under some plans, workers with the same qualifications and experience are paid the same no matter what job they do or whether one produces more than another. Other systems determine pay by the type of work, the amount produced, or the quality of the work. Common compensation systems are described next.

Time Plan

The payment of a specific compensation rate for a specified period of time is probably the most common method of compensation. A **time wage** pays the employee a specific amount of money for each hour worked. In a similar way, a **straight salary** pays an employee a specific amount of money for a longer period of time worked (week, month). This plan is an easy system to administer because compensation is determined by multiplying hours or time worked by the rate of pay. However, it does not recognize or reward employees who provide extra effort or do outstanding work.

Commission Plan

Under the **commission plan** of compensation, employees—usually salespeople —are paid a percentage of the volume of business for which they are responsible. For example, a salesperson may be paid a commission of 5 percent on total net sales made each week. If sales were $10,000, the salesperson would earn $500. The commission system provides a direct incentive to the employee because the amount of work determines the compensation received. Also, the business can control costs because compensation relates directly to the amount of sales.

Illus. 21-4

Some automobile dealerships have ended the practice of paying salespeople commissions and have begun to pay them straight salaries. What do you see as the advantages and disadvantages of this change?

Piece-Rate Plan

A plan similar to the commission plan used for salespeople is also used for some production workers. The **piece-rate plan** pays the employee a fixed rate for each unit of production. How much individual employees are paid is often based largely on how well they do on the job. For example, if an employee earns 30 cents for each unit and produces 250 units a day, the amount of compensation for the day will be $75.

Although piece-rate plans were first used in factories, other types of employees may also be paid on the basis of units of work completed. Billing clerks may be paid based on the number of invoices processed; word processing and other data entry personnel may be paid according to the number of lines of material completed; and order pickers in a distribution center may be paid based on the number of items they pick from inventory to fill orders received.

Piece rates are usually established by a careful study of each job. If the study is well done and workers can control the amount of work they can do, piece-rate plans can be effective. The plan is difficult for beginning workers, however, and experienced employees may find shortcuts to increase their production, resulting in quality or safety problems.

There have been some negative effects of piece-rate plans in some businesses. When a number of people are working on the same piece-rate, there may be pressures placed on particularly fast workers to reduce the amount they produce so the standard for piece-rate work is not increased.

Base Plus Incentive Plan

To get the advantages of various types of compensation systems, some companies combine a smaller wage or salary with an incentive based on production or performance. That system is called a **base plus incentive plan** and can be used in combination with the other types of plans (straight wage, salary, commission, or piece rate). In each case, the employee is guaranteed a minimum amount of wage or salary. Employees can then earn an additional amount of money above the minimum based on their own production or on the performance of the department or company.

While the incentive can be in the form of a commission or a higher piece rate for additional production, one type of incentive used frequently is a bonus. A **bonus** is money paid at the end of a specific period of time for performance that exceeds the expected standard. Bonuses can be paid to individuals or to groups such as team members working on a specific project, employees in a department, the managers of one division or location, or even all employees in a company. Individual bonuses are often used as an incentive when managers are attempting to challenge each person to increase productivity. Group bonuses are better when the efforts of an entire group are needed to accomplish specific goals of the business.

While most bonuses are a specific amount of money, some bonus plans are directly tied to the performance of the company. Companies that offer **profit**

sharing provide a bonus to each qualified employee based on a percentage of the profits earned by the company. Other companies use **employee stock ownership** plans, where bonuses are in the form of shares of company stock rather than in cash. Both plans have been developed to encourage employees to be concerned about the profitability and success of the company. Employees benefit when profits and the price of stock increase in the companies using these plans.

The base plus incentive plan removes most of the disadvantages of the other plans. It provides a minimum salary so beginning workers do not have to worry so much about high levels of production, and all employees will receive some compensation. However, an incentive is provided for workers to be productive since they can increase the amount of their compensation that way. It is a more complex system for the company to manage, however, and the total amount of compensation paid by the company to employees is not easy to predict.

FACTORS AFFECTING COMPENSATION LEVELS

Determining the amount of wages and salaries of employees is an important management decision. In addition to the compensation plan, other factors to consider when determining wages and salaries include the abilities of the employees and their value to the company, the relative importance of the job compared to others in the company, the experience of the individual and the years worked for the company, the supply and demand of that type of labor, the prevailing wage rates in the community and in the industry, the type and value of employee benefits provided by the company, the current economic conditions, and certain federal and state labor laws. Two of the most difficult problems facing managers when determining compensation are the relative value of one job when compared with another in the company and the impact of cost of living on wages.

Establishing the Relative Value of Jobs

Great differences exist between the receptionist's and the president's skills, duties, responsibilities, and authority. There is also quite a difference in the receptionist's wage as compared to the president's salary. While those examples are obvious, there are a number of jobs in a business where it is more difficult to determine the differences in factors that might affect the amount of compensation.

Employees are naturally concerned about how much they earn when compared to others in the business. If Joan is earning less than Kathy, but believes that her work is of more value to the company, she may be upset. It could affect the quality or quantity of work. It is important for the company to have a compensation plan that fairly values each type of work to the company.

Job evaluation is the process of ranking jobs according to their value based on specific characteristics of each job. It should not be confused with the evaluation of individual employees' performance. In job evaluation, experts analyze each job in the company. They determine such things as the skills needed, the responsibility and authority, working conditions, and training required. The information is then used to develop a classification system that organizes all jobs according to their work characteristics and value to the company. Wage and salary rates are established for each job based on the classification. The classification system can be published so all employees are aware of the system used to determine compensation.

A common method used to rank jobs is a point system. Jobs are evaluated on common characteristics, and points are assigned using an objective rating system. Figure 21-6 shows a point system used to evaluate two jobs. In the example, the data entry job is responsible for entering data from marketing surveys into the computer. Based on an evaluation of job characteristics, it has a total value of 505. The second job is responsible for writing copy for print advertisements. The evaluation resulted in a value of 570. The job with a point value of 505 has a lower level of work characteristics and, therefore, should have a lower rate of pay than the job with a point value of 570.

Fig. 21-6

A job evaluation point system.

JOB CHARACTERISTICS	RATING	
	DATA ENTRY	COPYWRITER
Training Required	60	80
Experience Required	70	70
Creativity	30	65
Communications	40	50
Responsibility for Details	85	50
Responsibility for Quality	80	75
Supervision	20	45
Physical Effort	45	40
Mental Effort	35	60
Work Environment	40	35
TOTAL POINTS	505	570

Cost of Living

One of the factors that people use to determine whether the amount of compensation they receive is adequate is the amount of goods and services they are able to purchase. It is possible that employees may receive an increase in pay but are not able to purchase as much as they could in the previous year. This happens when the cost of living increases faster than the increase in compensation.

Real wages represent the amount of goods and services that money earned will buy. For example, assume that the monthly cost of purchases for the Martin family in 1994 was $2,000. If the same things were purchased today and cost $2,200, the Martins would have to earn $200 more each month in order to have the same standard of living as they had in 1994.

Employees will be dissatisfied if they are producing the same amount or more for a company but their wages will not buy as much as before. The cost of living is one of the important factors for managers to consider when determining how much to pay employees. Some wage agreements between companies and employee groups build in an automatic adjustment for increases in the cost of living. Such agreements need to be considered very carefully by both management and employees. If inflation is high, the costs of wages and salaries may increase so much that the company is unable to pay the amount agreed upon. They will then need to reduce the size of the labor force or cut costs in other areas. If inflation is low, salary increases may also be lower than employees typically expect.

EMPLOYEE BENEFITS

If asked why they work, most people identify money as an important reason. However, we have learned that money is not the only reason—or even the most important reason—for why people work. The amount of money earned does influence the satisfaction a person gets from a job, but full-time employees normally earn more than their salary or wages. Financial compensation in addition to salaries and wages is known as **fringe benefits**.

Fringe benefits can significantly increase the total compensation received by an employee. Because the costs of many fringe benefits are not easy to identify and are not reported regularly, employees often do not realize the actual cost to the employer. Many companies contribute between 20 to 40 percent of an employee's salary to pay for fringe benefits. Assume that a company employed 300 people at an average salary of $20,000. In addition to the $6,000,000 to pay the salaries, the company would have fringe benefit costs of $2,400,000. Some of the most common types of benefits are described next.

CUSTOMARY BENEFITS

Many businesses make it possible for their employees to obtain insurance at lower costs through group policies. In many cases, the company pays part of the insurance premium. Life, health, dental, and disability insurance are common types of coverage provided.

A valuable benefit for employees is profit sharing, which was discussed earlier in the chapter. Profit sharing is valuable because it encourages employees to do things that increase the profits for the business in order to obtain the benefit.

Because employees are retiring at an earlier age and living longer, they are concerned about retirement income. To meet that need, many companies have developed pension plans. **Pensions** are regular payments made to an employee after retirement. In companies with a pension plan, a percentage of all employees' salaries is put into a pension fund. The funds are invested and earnings are used to make pension payments to retired employees. In a few pension plans, the employer pays the entire cost of the pension, but in most plans the employee makes a contribution as well.

After employees have worked for a company for a time, often one year, they may be eligible for vacation days. Most companies pay the employees' regular salary for earned vacation days. In addition to earned vacations, some companies are closed for federal and state holidays and may pay their employees for those days. Similar benefits include allowing absences for personal illness, the illness or death of family members, the birth of a child, and other occasions.

HOURS OF WORK

To respond to the changing lifestyles of workers and the operating needs of businesses, some companies have experimented with changes in the standard 40-hour, five-day work week. One such change involves scheduling employees to work ten hours a day for four days per week. Another variation lets employees choose the hours they work during a day. This plan is called **flex-time**, in which some employees start early and leave early, while others start and finish late. A work week may also be staggered by having some employees start their week on days other than Monday. In this way, a business can operate seven days a week without having employees work more than five days, thereby obtaining maximum use of facilities and equipment while controlling labor costs.

Illus. 21-5

Flex-time gives employees options for scheduling their work time. Why would a person choose to work four 10-hour days in a week rather than the traditional five 8-hour days?

Jeff Greenberg, Photographer

Job sharing allows two people to share one full time job. Each person works half the time, either half days or alternate days of the week. Companies benefit with this plan by being able to hire people who cannot work full time. This is often the case with people who have very young families, who are attending school, or who are recovering from medical problems. It is particularly useful to the businesses when one of the employees is sick or on vacation. Arrangements can often be made to have the person who job shares to fill in for the other employee.

OTHER BENEFITS

The benefits described above are most common and are available to employees in many companies. Increasingly, businesses are providing other types of fringe benefits for employees. While they may not be as common as those already discussed, they may be very important to the employees of the business.

Many companies provide free parking facilities or parking at a low cost. Discounts on the purchase of products produced or sold by the company may be offered to employees. Food service and cafeterias are available in many businesses.

Some companies offer free or low-cost professional services to employees including financial and investment advice, lawyers, accountants, and counselors. An increasingly important benefit for employees with young children is the availability of day-care facilities. Finally, companies sometimes help employees by providing or contributing to the cost of educational programs.

CAFETERIA PLANS

As you can see, the range of fringe benefits is quite broad. New benefits are offered as employee needs change and as companies compete to attract and keep good employees. Since individual needs can be quite different, businesses have a difficult time providing the right set of benefits for each employee. Some companies have attempted to solve that problem by letting employees choose from among a number of available benefits. A fringe benefit program in which employees can select the benefits that meet their personal needs is known as a **cafeteria plan**. In this program, each employee is given choices among benefits with equal value or give up certain benefits and receive their cost as additional compensation.

OTHER HUMAN RESOURCES RESPONSIBILITIES

The goal of human resources management is satisfying and productive work. The department activities are developed to make sure that the people who work for the business are well trained, that their skills are used as effectively as possible in the business, and that they are satisfied with their work. In addition to the major human resources activities already discussed, several other areas are important responsibilities of human resources personnel.

Management Close-Up

INCREASING EMPLOYMENT OPPORTUNITIES THROUGH THE ADA

Questions:

1 Why do you believe it was necessary for the federal government to develop the ADA legislation?

2 If you were a business person, how would you respond to the ADA requirements?

3 Using this class as an example, in what ways can the facilities, equipment, and materials be modified to meet the needs of disabled students?

Many companies search to fill increasingly technical and complex jobs with qualified applicants. Some employment divisions report screening hundreds of applications to find one person that meets the necessary job requirements. At the same time, millions of Americans who have necessary job qualifications for many jobs are regularly overlooked by businesses. Why? They have disabilities that many employers believe will prevent them from performing job duties effectively.

Because of misunderstanding, stereotypes, and discrimination faced by disabled Americans in the workplace, a new employment law was enacted in 1990. The Americans With Disabilities Act (ADA) prohibits employment discrimination against individuals with physical and mental handicaps or chronic illnesses if the applicant is able to perform the basic functions of a job. Many disabled job applicants have been unable to demonstrate that they can perform a job because they are eliminated from consideration when the employer learns of their disability. Under the new law, employers must provide the opportunity for all disabled applicants who are otherwise qualified for the job to compete for available jobs. A qualified applicant is a person who has the required education and experience and can perform the work if the employer provides "reasonable accommodation."

Reasonable accommodation means that the employer must make facilities, equipment, procedures, and activities accessible and usable; restructure jobs and work tasks when possible; and provide access to the same benefits and privileges available to other employees. The word "reasonable" is used to ensure that employers do not have to make changes that result in a severe financial hardship for the business or that alter the job so required work cannot be completed. Studies in businesses that were done in preparation for implementing the ADA found that many accommodations for disabled employees could be accomplished at no additional cost if careful planning were done, and others changes were relatively low cost if creative solutions were considered.

Most organizations have charged the human resources department with developing options for meeting the ADA requirements.

While some organizations are concerned about the impact and cost of complying with the Americans With Disabilities Act, others have found that it has encouraged them to consider a group of productive employees they had previously ignored.

EMPLOYEE HEALTH AND SAFETY

Businesses should be concerned about the health and safety of all employees. If employees are expected to do their best work, they must be healthy. Illness and accidents are expensive for businesses. Not only do they have increased costs of insurance, but they also lose the services of the employee during the time of sickness or injury.

Large companies have specialists who work to protect and improve the health and safety of employees. Building inspections, review of training programs, work methods, and equipment operations are completed regularly to identify and eliminate dangers. First-aid equipment is available throughout the business and employees are trained to use it.

Programs have also been developed to help employees improve their fitness and health. Studies have shown that fitness and health programs are very cost effective because they reduce employee absences as well as the costs of insurance benefits. Most companies are now concerned about diet, exercise, smoking, drug use, and fitness.

EMPLOYMENT LAWS

As we learned earlier, the federal government has been concerned for years about employee/employer relationships and the protection of employees. Several specific laws have been passed to protect employees, improve their health and safety, and provide minimum employee benefits. Human resources departments are responsible for understanding the laws and ensuring that the business complies with the requirements of each. Some of the most important employment laws are described in Fig. 21-7 on page 536.

EQUAL OPPORTUNITY IN EMPLOYMENT

Throughout the history of business in the United States, it has been difficult for some groups to have the same opportunities for success due to discrimination. Women, minority races, older workers, and people with disabilities have often been prevented from entering and succeeding in many careers. To correct these injustices, laws have been passed to provide equal opportunity and to prevent inequalities.

In recent years, many businesses have taken positive steps to correct discrimination in employment. Those steps include the development of written affirmative action plans, a review of recruitment and selection procedures, improved access to job training to qualify current employees for promotions, diversity training for all managers and employees, and objective performance evaluation procedures. While not all discrimination has been eliminated from the workplace, companies that have taken a sincere and active interest in improving the diversity of the workforce and eliminating discrimination have found many of their efforts have been successful.

ig. 21-7

Laws providing benefits and protection for employees.

LAW AND PURPOSE

OCCUPATIONAL SAFETY AND HEALTH ACT

The law developed very specific safety and health standards for businesses. The Department of Labor enforces those standards through inspections of businesses and investigations of accidents.

FAIR LABOR STANDARDS ACT

The Act established a minimum wage that must be paid to employees by those businesses included in the law. The businesses must pay employees 1 1/2 times their normal wage rate for any hours above 40 worked in a week. The law places limits on the number of hours and times during the day when teenagers can work. It also prevents businesses from hiring people under 18 years old to work in hazardous occupations.

SOCIAL SECURITY ACT

The portion of the Social Security Act that provides pensions to retired workers and their families and provides benefits to disabled workers is known as Old Age, Survivors, and Disability Insurance. Medicare is a broad program of hospital and health insurance for people who have reached retirement age.

UNEMPLOYMENT INSURANCE

Unemployment insurance provides a fund to pay an income to certain unemployed workers. The unemployment insurance program is administered by each state. To be eligible for unemployment benefits, a worker must not be responsible for losing the job and must be actively looking for new employment.

WORKERS' COMPENSATION

All states have workers' compensation laws that require employers to provide insurance for death, injury, or illness resulting from employment.

VALUING HUMAN RESOURCES

Human resources management is very important in all types of businesses. Managers faced with improving the effectiveness and profitability of their business are increasingly looking at the ways that they can improve employee performance. The management of human resources has changed a great deal in the past several years as managers seek to improve relationships with employees and to involve employees more actively in making important decisions for the business. As employees' needs continue to change and as the cost of providing employee services and benefits increases, all managers will have to emphasize building and maintaining effective employee relations.

BUILDING VOCABULARY POWER

Define the following terms and concepts.

1. human resources management
2. employment requisition
3. job specification
4. open ad
5. blind ad
6. promotion
7. seniority
8. transfer
9. discharge
10. layoff
11. employment turnover
12. exit interview
13. compensation
14. wages
15. salary
16. time wage
17. straight salary
18. commission plan
19. piece-rate plan
20. base plus incentive plan
21. bonus
22. profit sharing
23. employee stock ownership
24. job evaluation
25. real wages
26. fringe benefits
27. pensions
28. flex-time
29. job sharing
30. cafeteria plan

REVIEWING FACTS

1. Why is human resources management so important to a company?
2. What are some of the management responsibilities involved in working with people?
3. What is the meaning of the dotted lines in the organizational chart shown in Fig. 21-2?
4. What effects do poor selection procedures have on a business?
5. How is a job specification different from an employment requisition?
6. What are the major sources of new employees for a job?
7. Why are job applicants asked to complete an application form before being interviewed?
8. What types of tests should be used in an application procedure?
9. Why should the human resources department perform a follow-up after a new employee has been at work for some time?
10. Why should a company attempt to do everything it can to keep an employee once the person has been hired?
11. What is the advantage of a policy of filling vacancies by promotion?
12. What are some of the factors that affect the amount of compensation paid for a job?

13. What are some examples of compensation plans that reward an employee's performance?
14. Why have modified work schedules become an important benefit for many employees and businesses?
15. What types of employment laws are of concern to human resources departments?

DISCUSSING IDEAS

1. Why have human resources departments grown in size and the number of activities performed in recent years?
2. Do you believe the employment division of a human resources department is the most important? Why?
3. Why is it necessary to get top management approval before a department hires a new employee if the department has adequate funds to pay the employee's salary?
4. Why should an applicant be eliminated if she or he does a poor job of completing the application form?
5. What alternatives rather than a discharge should be considered for an employee who is not performing well?
6. What problems may be indicated by a high rate of employee turnover?
7. If a salesperson receives a much larger commission for selling one product than another, what is likely to happen? Why would a company use different commission rates for products?
8. Offer some examples of jobs for which salaries have been affected by supply and demand for labor.
9. What are the advantages and disadvantages of a cafeteria plan of employee benefits for a company? for an employee?
10. What steps can a human resources department take to ensure that all people have an equal employment opportunity in the selection and promotion processes?

ANALYZING INFORMATION

1. A telemarketing firm has a complex pay structure for its salespeople. Each person is given a base salary and a quota (minimum expected sales). In addition to the base salary, the following commissions on sales are paid:

> 4 percent for all sales up to $50,000
> 5 percent for sales of $50,001-$100,000
> 6 percent for any sales above $100,000

Any salesperson who exceeds the assigned quota is paid a bonus of $3,000. Complete the following table using the information given.

REVIEW 21

Salesperson	Base Salary	Commission	Bonus	Total Salary
Edwards				
Vajesh				
Sing				

Edwards has a base salary of $17,000, sales of $70,000, and a quota of $65,000.

Vajesh has a base salary of $26,000, sales of $130,000, and a quota of $140,000.

Sing has a base salary of $29,000, sales of $220,000, and a quota of $200,000.

2. Jones and Jackson operate a used car business as a partnership. They want to hire salespeople who will do a good job of selling cars, but who will work to meet the customers' needs when selling and not simply try to get customers to buy the most expensive car. They are considering several options for paying the salespeople. The options are (a) to offer an attractive hourly wage, (b) to offer a small weekly salary and a reasonable commission for each car sold, (c) to offer an attractive commission for each car sold, and (d) to offer a reasonable monthly salary, a small commission on each car sold, and a bonus based on the satisfaction level of customers after they have purchased a car.

    Discuss the four options with a small group of students. Determine the advantages and disadvantages of each plan in meeting the goals of Jones and Jackson and on the financial success of the business. Report to the class on your decision about a compensation plan for the company and the reasons for it.

3. Obtain an employment application blank from a business or your teacher and fill it out. Which of the questions on the application do you think would be most helpful to the company in deciding whether to hire you? Are there any questions that do not seem to be useful or that could discriminate against some applicants?

4. As the manager of a supermarket, you are responsible for hiring a new checker/cashier. Answer the following questions:
    a. What sources would you use to find qualified applicants?
    b. What procedures would you use to select the new person?
    c. What would you do with the new employee to get him/her successfully started on the job?
    d. How would your procedures in (b) and (c) be different if your business had optical scanning equipment at the checkout counters, rather than cash registers where the checkers have to enter the information by hand?

5. The Jonesville Company has an average of 600 employees this year. The number of employees who left the company during the year was 40; the number of replacements was 30. During a prior year, the average number

of employees was 560 with 30 leaving and 20 replacements. Using both methods shown in the chapter, calculate the labor turnover rate for each of the two years.

SOLVING BUSINESS PROBLEMS

CASE 21-1

Charles Morgan was hired five weeks ago to work in the mail room of the Teletron Trading Corporation. His job was to collect mail twice daily from each office in the building, sort and process outgoing mail, deliver outgoing mail to the post office, and pick up incoming mail from the post office. He learned the job in one day by working with the outgoing employee, Tom Williams. Tom had been hired by another company and had only one day left by the time Charles was hired.

After one month, Charles thought that he was doing rather well. While some of the first few days had been rather rough, things seemed to be going more smoothly now and he seldom had any complaints. He seldom saw his supervisor, but when he did the supervisor always had a pleasant greeting.

A week later he received notice that he was being discharged next week at the end of his six-week probationary period. There was no explanation for the discharge, and Charles was not aware of the probationary period. He went to the human resources office immediately. The employment manager pulled a folder from the file and began reading notes that had been placed there during the past month. Charles responded truthfully to each item:

a. An hour late to work on May 15: "My car would not start, but I called to say that I would be in as soon as possible. I worked an extra hour at the end of the day to finish my work."

b. Two offices complained the mail had not been picked up on the second of the month: "It was my second day on the job and I couldn't remember all of the stops. After the second day, I made a schedule and I have not missed an office since."

c. The Research Department complained that an important document was sent by regular mail and it should have been sent by Express Mail: "I didn't know the policy for deciding when and how to send items until I was told I had done it wrong. I asked the supervisor, who gave me a procedures manual to study. Tom Williams had not told me about the manual."

Several other similar complaints were included in the file, each readily admitted to, but explained by Charles. According to the employment manager, Charles was being discharged according to company policy. The policy stated that any employee who received five or more complaints during the probationary period was automatically discharged.

REVIEW 21

Required:
1. What is your opinion of the company's discharge policy for new employees?
2. Are there any problems with the way new employees are prepared for their jobs in the Teletron Trading Corporation?
3. What recommendations can you make to improve the company's procedures?

CASE 21-2

Jonathan Wilkens and Torrey Walker were exercising on the stationary bicycles in the health and fitness center of the Wainwright Company. As they exercised, they discussed an article that had appeared in the company newsletter that day.

Jonathan: The article said that the average employee in this company makes $26,500 a year. I can't believe that. I think I'm close to the average in salary and I will only take home a little more than $18,000 this year.

Torrey: That's right. What they don't say is that we have a lot of money deducted from our checks each month for taxes, the company pension plan, insurance, and union dues.

Jonathan: As a matter of fact, the article says the company contributes an additional $6,000 on the average for each employee to pay for fringe benefits. That makes over $14,000 difference between what I take home and what the company says it pays me. I don't see any of those fringe benefits. There must be something wrong.

Torrey: Let's go to the Benefits Office when we get finished here. Maybe they can explain how there can be such a difference.

Required:
1. Do you agree that Jonathan never sees any of the fringe benefits for which the company pays? Explain.
2. If you were the benefits manager, how would you explain the difference in the salary and benefits the company says it pays and the amount of money Jonathan and Torrey take home in their paychecks?

TRAINING AND EMPLOYEE ORIENTATION

CHAPTER 22

After studying this chapter you will be able to:

22-1 Describe the value of training to businesses.

22-2 Identify seven types of training needs businesses must meet.

22-3 Describe four training methods businesses use.

22-4 Justify the importance of an orientation program for new employees.

22-5 List at least five characteristics of effective training programs.

22-6 Outline a procedure for conducting an employee evaluation conference.

Helen Stokes and Jeffrey Hinton, two supervisors for the Asco Printing Company, were walking to a conference room in the Training Department. They were both going to attend a seminar on effective employee evaluation. As they walked they chatted about a problem Jeffrey was having in his department.

Jeffrey: I really hated to have to let another new employee go yesterday. He's the third of the last ten employees we have hired who wasn't performing well enough at the end of the six-month probationary period.

Helen: Maybe you just can't find enough good people who want to operate printing equipment.

Jeffrey: That's not really it. The people look very good when we hire them. They are interested in the job, interview well, and even score high on the tests Human Resources gives them. That is why it is hard to fire them.

Helen: Then what kinds of problems do they have?

Jeffrey: They have a hard time meeting the standards we set for printing jobs. They aren't fast enough; and when we give them new types of printing jobs, they seem to have a large number of errors before the job is done correctly.

Helen: Maybe the training needs to be improved.

Jeffrey: We assign the new employees to our best and most experienced printers for a full month when they start working for us. Then we encourage the new people to go to the experienced printers for help whenever they have questions or problems. I would think that should be a good way to train them.

The supervisors are discussing a situation that occurs in many businesses. Employees who look very promising when they are hired either quit or must be fired later because they cannot perform the job successfully. The same problem can occur with experienced employees when job duties change or new equipment or procedures are introduced. The employee may not be able to perform as well as in the past. This results in an overall poor performance, an unhappy employee, and problems for the supervisor or manager.

When a new or experienced employee is unable to perform as well as expected, there is a need for training. While training can be expensive, there are many costs to businesses that do not have good training programs. Those costs come from employee turnover, low levels of speed and quality in performance, wasted supplies and materials, damage to equipment, and even injury to employees or customers when errors occur. It is not difficult to see that an effective training program can pay for itself.

NEED FOR TRAINING

Training is needed by most people in a business from time to time. Few people are hired for a new job with all of the necessary knowledge and skills. Therefore, all new employees should require some training.

Experienced employees can change from average to expert workers with additional training. Training allows them to improve methods and procedures, learn to operate new equipment, and prepare for a promotion. Sometimes training programs can remind experienced employees of information they may have forgotten, such as safety practices and techniques for improving the speed or accuracy of their performance. Important types of training provided by many businesses for their employees are listed in Fig. 22-1.

New employee orientation

New equipment and activities

Changed or improved procedures

Knowledge of company activities and performance

Correct errors or poor performance

Improve accuracy and efficiency

Preparation for advancement

Fig. 22-1

Important needs for employee training.

People are often promoted into supervisory positions because they have proven themselves as effective employees. It is not unusual for employees to begin work as supervisors with no training for the new position. Their new supervisory positions will be quite different than the work they had been doing before they were promoted. In order to be successful, they need to learn how to manage employees effectively and how to perform many other management responsibilities. Even the highest-level executives regularly need to update their knowledge about the company, learn more about customers and competitors, and improve their management skills by participating in management training programs.

Companies in the United States spend a great deal of money on activities designed to improve the productivity of their employees. Studies estimate that between 40 and 50 billion dollars is spent by businesses each year on formal training programs. Informal training (i.e., learning on the job, self study, coaching) may cost businesses as much as $150 billion each year. The cost of informal training is in addition to the amount spent by schools, colleges, and government to prepare people for jobs. The large amount of money for training can be justified if employees are able to perform more and higher quality work as a result of the training. Because of the high cost, businesses need to determine if training results in improved performance and reduces operating costs.

Evidence shows that employees receiving regular, effective training are more satisfied with their work and want to do a better job for their company. These employees believe their company is interested in them if training is provided, and they see themselves doing a better job, having greater job security, and having a greater possibility of promotion as a result of the training.

Companies in the United States are increasingly faced with competition from businesses in other countries. One of the advantages of many foreign companies is lower costs for salaries and wages. If U.S. firms are going to compete, their employees must be more productive to justify the higher wages. Businesses must also produce high-quality products to meet customer expectations. Employee development efforts in the future will emphasize training to allow the companies to compete in international markets.

UNIPHOTO

Jllus. 22-1

Effective employee training can provide the advantage needed by U.S. companies involved in international business. If training adds to the cost of producing a product, how can it result in an advantage?

Most businesses recognize the need for training but the amount and type of training varies from company to company. Some only offer a small amount of training when an employee begins work, while others provide regular training for all employees. One estimate indicates that companies spend approximately one percent of their total payroll costs on training. For an employee earning $25,000 a year, approximately $250 was available for training. Some companies spend much more while others spend almost nothing.

In the remaining part of this chapter, we will examine the major types of training provided by business and the characteristics of effective training programs. We will pay particular attention to an important type of training, new employee orientation. We will also see how employee evaluation is used to determine the need for training and to see if the training has been effective. By studying this chapter, you will learn how Jeffrey Hinton can use training to reduce the problem facing his department.

METHODS OF TRAINING

Both the amount and quality of training is increasing in business as managers realize the value effective training can provide. They see that the quantity and quality of work is improved and that employee morale is higher as a result of training. While training programs have existed in businesses for a long time, much of the training in the past has been informal. **Informal training** is provided without careful planning, management, or evaluation. It is usually accomplished by having a new employee work with an experienced employee, having a supervisor or expert demonstrate a new procedure, or by having the employee use manuals and written materials to learn a new procedure or how to operate new equipment.

Formal training is carefully planned, managed, and evaluated. When a company uses formal training methods, employees, their managers, or training specialists identify the training needs of the company. People from the training department or training experts hired from outside the company design training programs and procedures for employees based on the identified needs. Training personnel or managers carefully evaluate employee performance after the training to see if it was effective.

Formal training is most often conducted by people skilled in delivering instruction. Training departments spend a great deal of time planning training programs and preparing training materials in order to deliver effective training and to determine the best ways of helping employees once they have gone through the training and are back on the job.

A variety of methods are used in employee training. Training is very similar to teaching a class in school. Just as teachers use equipment, materials, and many activities to help you learn, trainers use those things to help employees improve their skills. Training methods are usually selected based on the needs of the employees and the resources available to the trainer. The primary methods of training are discussed next.

CLASSROOM TRAINING

Much of the formal training done in business is done in a classroom. **Classroom training** is instruction accomplished in a room designed for a variety of training programs that emphasize knowledge and attitude development. Training done in a classroom is usually short term, often one or two days in length. It is conducted much like the classes in your school with presentations, discussions, films, case studies, and other group activities. Facilities developed as training classrooms usually have comfortable chairs and tables and a variety of instructional equipment such as computers, film projectors, chalkboards, video recorders and television monitors.

The advantage of classroom training is that it is very flexible. It can be used for specific types of people and to meet a broad set of training needs. It is not particularly expensive for a business to develop a training classroom. The type of training is determined by the people planning the training rather than by the training facility.

LABORATORY TRAINING

Another type of formal training used by some businesses is laboratory training. **Laboratory training** is conducted in a special room designed to represent the equipment and procedures the employee will use on the job. Examples of

Management Close-Up

TRAINING TV

Source: Adapted from "Prime Time for
Videoconferences," Fortune, Dec. 28,
1992, pp. 88-95.

Questions:

1 What are some of the advantages and disadvantages of classroom training through videoconferencing for trainers and for trainees?

2 In addition to conducting training and holding meetings, what are other business applications of the video technology?

3 What type of planning would be needed to conduct an effective training session using videoconferencing?

Classroom training can be relatively inexpensive unless a company needs to train people in several locations across the country or around the world. A significant portion of training costs for companies that operate nationally and internationally is for airplane tickets, hotel rooms, meal expenses, and the time it takes people to travel to and from the training site. A new training tool now makes it possible for those companies to deliver training at any time, anywhere in the world, and neither trainers nor trainees have to leave the places where they work. The training tool is videoconferencing.

Videoconferencing is a meeting by satellite or telephone transmission. A business provides a television monitor and a video camera at each location where people will be participating in the meeting. If discussion among the participants is required, microphones and speakers are provided. The equipment can get more sophisticated, with computer screens or electronic drawing tablets and fax machines for developing illustrations and exchanging print information. Then each site is connected through a satellite link or a decoder that changes video and audio information into digital data that are transmitted across telephone lines.

Anything that can be done in a normal meeting or training program can be accomplished through videoconferencing. Participants can listen to speakers, view demonstrations, hold discussions, and evaluate the performance of others. Also, more people can participate than might normally be able to attend a meeting due to the reduced travel costs and the additional space from multiple sites.

Several companies are seeing direct benefits from the use of videoconferencing. One of the most sophisticated systems is used by United Technologies. They have developed a video system for each of their engineers' personal computers. Each engineer can communicate with any other engineer in all of the company's worldwide locations or join in on video conferences or training sessions without leaving their desks. The company is investing $30,000 in each of the computer video units but believes the investment will quickly pay for itself through improved communication and more effective use of their employees' time.

Even schools are now connected by video to deliver advanced classes to locations where a teacher is not available or to combine several small classes from rural schools into a large group. Evidence shows that students who participate in well-organized video classes learn as much and perform as well as the students in the more traditional classes.

companies that use this type of training are manufacturers who prepare people for work on assembly lines, businesses that prepare people to work with computers, telemarketing firms that train salespeople, customer service representatives, and other companies that use technical equipment.

Laboratory training is used to develop and improve the skills of employees without the pressures of performing directly on the job. They can make mistakes or perform slowly in the laboratory without affecting the quality and speed of production going on in the business. Laboratory training is usually longer than most classroom training. Employees may be involved in laboratory training for several days or weeks as they learn new procedures or develop skills on equipment.

Demonstrations and employee practice are used in laboratory training. Trainees often watch films, read procedures manuals, or observe experienced employees or skilled trainers before attempting the new skill. As they practice they will usually be videotaped or critiqued by trainers in order to improve their performance.

You can see that laboratory training can be expensive. The cost of equipment is high, and the equipment in the training room is not being used in production by the company. However, it is an effective method for companies that need to give employees technical training. After the employees have developed the skill in the laboratory, they can be very effective when they get to their workstation. If an employee is having difficulty performing a task, that person can be taken to the training room to improve performance without disrupting the regular business operations.

Companies that use laboratory training often save a great deal of money. Equipment is not damaged by employees who do not know how to operate it. Regular operations are not disrupted and employees are more

Mike Surowiak/Tony Stone Images

Ilus. **22-2**

Training laboratories can be very expensive, but can actually save money for the companies that use them. What are some of the savings that can result from the use of a training laboratory?

likely to remain with the company after training since they can successfully perform their job duties.

ON-THE-JOB TRAINING

On-the-job training is formal or informal training done at the employee's workstation. It is the most frequently used method of employee training in business. In on-the-job training, employees learn new procedures or improve their skills while performing their normal job duties. The training may occur informally by assigning a new employee to an experienced employee. The experienced employee helps the new employee learn the job through demonstrations and advice. This is the type of training used by the Asco Printing Company described at the beginning of the chapter.

Another way used to provide on-the-job training is through coaching by the employee's supervisor. **Coaching** involves regular observation of an employee by a supervisor or experienced employee with follow-up discussions on ways to improve performance. Finally, many businesses who do not recognize the value of formal training allow new employees to start working and simply improve by observing and practice. While this is informal training, it is the employees' responsibility to determine what they need to know and identify ways to learn the information or develop the skills. This type of on-the-job training often results in poor performance and unhappy employees.

Formal on-the-job training can be done by having a trainer work with a new employee at the workstation. The trainer uses training manuals or other materials that help the employee to learn, or has an experienced employee or supervisor follow a specific training procedure with the trainee.

A method of formal on-the-job training being used by many companies today is providing training information by computer. If an employee has access to a computer at the work site, training programs on the computer can be accessed when help is needed. Some of these programs provide only basic information. New programs now combine print, audio, and visual information in a multimedia format.

Using formal methods of training on the job may require additional time and may be more expensive than informal methods. However, the employee should learn faster and make fewer errors. The employee will also be more comfortable with formal rather than informal training.

On-the-job training is most useful when the company is hiring skilled or experienced employees that require little additional training. It is also appropriate for jobs requiring limited amounts of training. It appears to be a very inexpensive way to provide training but many of the costs are hidden until employees make serious mistakes or quit because they don't believe they have the necessary skills.

APPRENTICESHIP TRAINING

The oldest form of formal training is **apprenticeship training**. It is a specialized program for preparing skilled employees that is jointly organized and managed by labor unions and management and approved by the U.S. Department of

Labor. Apprenticeship programs are found in occupations such as carpentry, plumbing, printing, electrical work, and other trades requiring a high level of skill. Forms of apprenticeship programs have been used for hundreds of years to develop the skill of young people wanting to learn a trade. A master craftsperson selected an apprentice to work in the business and taught the apprentice the unique skills of the trade.

Today, people learning a trade through an apprenticeship program must apply and be accepted into a program offered through a local trade union. Then they go through formal training that includes both classroom instruction and on-the-job training lasting for several years. After successfully completing the apprenticeship program, the person is approved to practice the trade without supervision. Programs following the apprenticeship model are now being developed in non-union occupations. Some are being developed cooperatively between high schools, community colleges, and businesses or are a part of a government-sponsored job training program to reduce unemployment.

THE CHANGING NATURE OF TRAINING

Companies are increasingly using formal rather than informal methods of training. They are either employing training specialists full time to work in the company, or they are enrolling employees in programs offered by companies specializing in training. Many equipment manufacturers now provide training for the employees of their customers' companies when new equipment purchases are made.

New jobs are created in business because of training programs. In addition to people who actually conduct training programs, there are others who study employee performance to determine the need for training. Training specialists are used to develop training materials, including training manuals, films, computer programs, and others. Managers of training help other department managers determine needs for training, develop plans for training programs, and evaluate the effects of training on employee productivity.

NEW EMPLOYEE ORIENTATION

The first few hours on a new job are difficult ones for most people. A number of new employees may quit their jobs during the first week, and some may even quit during the first day. If a new employee is placed behind a desk or a machine without any idea of how to proceed or where to get help, that person may develop an immediate dislike for the company, the job, and for co-workers. That dislike results from the pressure of wanting to do a good job and to be accepted by other employees. Companies that help a new employee become comfortable when he or she starts a new job reduce the chance of losing the person because of poor adjustment to the job and company.

An **orientation program** is a carefully designed introduction to the company, the work, and co-workers, and preparation for the job. Large companies offer regularly scheduled orientation programs for groups of employees since hiring is occurring all of the time. Companies that hire infrequently also need to provide new employee orientation but may have to offer it to individual employees or very small groups.

Illus. 22-3

The first hours and days on a job are very difficult for most new employees. What can companies do to make their new employees comfortable?

Jeff Greenberg, Photographer

Most companies begin their employee orientation program with a film or slide presentation on the company and a brief welcome from a top-level manager. Then the new employees are taken on a tour of the business and are shown the locations of important areas such as medical facilities, parking, lunch and break rooms, and training areas. A general introduction to policies, work rules, and benefits is usually given as well.

New employees should be reintroduced to their department head and supervisor even though they may have met him/her while interviewing for the job. Then the work area can be toured, and the person's job explained in more detail. The employee should be shown where needed supplies and materials are located and how to obtain help or answers to questions.

Introductions to co-workers is an important part of the new employee orientation. A method should be used to make the person feel a part of the work group as soon as possible. If the company has an employee manual that explains policies and procedures, a copy should be given to the new employee. Important sections should be highlighted. If the employee will be participating in a training program, the training should also be explained. Finally, the new worker should be assigned to an experienced employee, training specialist, or supervisor who will be responsible for helping the person learn the new job. That person will provide detailed information and directions about the job duties and will be available to answer questions and offer help when needed. Figure 22-2 gives additional recommendations for developing a good employee orientation program.

1. **Set aside adequate time for the orientation. Do not rush through a great deal of information.**
2. **Do not use business language that a new employee is not likely to understand.**
3. **As you show the employee around the business, explain the importance of what the new employee is seeing.**
4. **If there is a lot to be learned, break the orientation into several sessions.**
5. **Whenever possible, provide materials for the employee to keep and study. Be sure to explain the materials, and be careful that the materials are not too difficult to read and understand.**
6. **Make sure the new employee understands the information. Ask questions and give plenty of opportunity for the employee to ask questions. Some things may need to be explained more than once.**
7. **Show the employee where to go with problems and questions. Reassure the individual that it is all right to ask questions at any time.**

Whether the training department is planning formal or informal training or is designing an employee orientation program, the training needs to be carefully designed to make sure it is effective. The characteristics of effective training are explained next.

CHARACTERISTICS OF EFFECTIVE TRAINING

As companies recognize the value of training, they are working to develop more effective training procedures. On the average, companies spend several hundred dollars on every employee each year for training. Therefore, they want to be sure the training is effective in improving employees' performance. There are many techniques used by trainers to improve employee performance. Several of the characteristics of effective training are shown in Fig. 22-3 on page 554.

DETERMINING EMPLOYEE TRAINING NEEDS

An important activity for all companies is determining the need for employee training. Some training needs are quite obvious. When new equipment is purchased or when a company begins new operations or introduces improved procedures, employees need to be trained for the changes. Typically, when new employees are hired or experienced employees are promoted to new jobs, they do not have all of the skills needed to begin work immediately. In these examples, managers should recognize the need for training and develop appropriate training programs.

Other training needs are not as obvious. In some instances, problems in getting work completed successfully are related to training needs. Conflicts among employees, areas of customer dissatisfaction, or work hazards and

Fig. 22-3

Characteristics of effective training programs.

TO BE EFFECTIVE, TRAINING SHOULD:

1. Be interesting to the trainee.
2. Be related to knowledge the trainee already has developed.
3. Explain why as well as how something is done.
4. Progress from simple to more difficult steps.
5. Let the trainee learn complicated procedures in small steps.
6. Allow plenty of practice time.
7. Let the trainee concentrate on becoming comfortable with a new procedure before worrying about accuracy.
8. Provide regular and positive feedback to the trainee on progress being made.
9. Be done in short time blocks using a variety of activities.
10. Involve the learner in training activities as much as possible.

employee injuries signal the need for training. Unless managers are aware of problems and try to determine whether training can help solve them, the problems probably will not disappear.

Many companies regularly evaluate operations to determine if training is needed. If performance is not meeting the company's plans, studies are done to determine reasons for the poor performance. If some of the reasons are related to the performance of employees, training is developed to improve performance.

When new operations are developed, new equipment purchased, or job procedures redesigned, there will be a need for training. Specialists from the training department will carefully analyze the new operations, equipment, and

Illus. 22-4

One use of employee teams is to identify the training needs of the group. How can the involvement of employee teams in determining needs improve the effectiveness of training?

Jeff Greenberg, Photographer

procedures to determine what knowledge and skills will be required of the employees. They will use that information to determine needed training and to design the training programs.

In some companies, each department has formed a problem-solving group made up of managers and employees. The groups meet regularly to identify problems and to suggest ways the company's performance can be improved. Those groups can be used to identify training needs as well. Because they work regularly with the equipment and the procedures of the department, the groups are in a good position to identify performance problems and to help design training.

DESIGNING TRAINING PROGRAMS

After the need for training is determined, a training program must be developed. Again, it requires special skill to design effective training programs. Many companies hire training designers to develop training programs specifically for the company. Others will purchase training programs that have been developed by companies who specialize in training design.

A training program consists of several components. First, objectives for training are written. Objectives identify the knowledge, skills, and attitudes that trainees will develop if they successfully complete the training. Objectives are important for two reasons. First, the objectives are used to determine the content of the training program. By identifying what the results of the training should be, the training content and activities can be directed at achieving those results. Second, the objectives can be used to evaluate the success of the training. At the end of the training program, trainees can be tested to determine if they have developed the needed knowledge, skills, and attitudes.

The next step in training program development is to identify the content of the program—what information will be presented. Trainers must be sure the content is accurate, up-to-date, and understandable. The people responsible for training design will often use expert employees, textbooks, and procedures manuals to identify the content for training.

After objectives and content have been identified, the trainers will determine the training methods to be used. They will decide whether training should be formal or informal and whether it can be best accomplished through classroom, laboratory, on-the-job, or some other type of training. Along with the method of training, specific training activities for each objective will be developed. Any necessary equipment and materials will be identified at the same time.

Plans must be made to identify the length of training and a training schedule. Trainers and trainees will be identified, the training facility will be scheduled, and information about the training program will be developed and sent to the trainees and their supervisors.

The final step in training design is to determine how training will be evaluated. If it cannot be determined whether training was effective or not, business will be unwilling to invest in training. Training designers must develop evaluation procedures and design evaluation instruments.

Evaluation should determine whether the training program was successful in accomplishing the objectives that were established at the beginning of the planning process. Training evaluation should be done both informally and formally. Informal evaluation can be completed by the trainees through discussions, through observing each other's performance, and by practicing the skills being developed. The trainer will also provide informal evaluations of trainee's performance through observations and discussions with trainees. Informal evaluation should be included frequently in a training program each time an employee learns important information or develops a new skill.

Methods of formal evaluation include tests, specific observations of trainee performance by the trainer or the employee's supervisor using rating scales or checklists, and the regularly scheduled employee evaluations that are a part of most jobs. Formal evaluation is done at the end of the training program and also should be completed several weeks and months after the employee has returned to the job. This will ensure that the employee can effectively use the training on the job.

EMPLOYEE EVALUATION

You have seen that employee evaluation can be used to identify training needs and to determine training effectiveness. Because employee evaluation is so important to training and because of the involvement of the human resources department in designing and managing employee evaluation systems, this topic will be examined specifically in this section.

One of the important responsibilities of all managers is to make sure employees are performing as well as they possibly can. The procedure used to determine how well employees perform their jobs is known as **performance appraisal**. Information obtained from performance appraisals is used for several purposes. One source of information used to determine promotions is an employee's current performance. Those employees with the best performance records are most likely to be considered for promotion.

Some companies use evaluation information to determine increases in wages and salaries. If the amount of compensation is based on an employee's performance, a system for evaluation is needed.

Finally, performance appraisal is related to training. Information obtained from evaluations can be used to determine when and what type of training is needed. When employee performance does not meet company standards, training needs to be provided.

After employees have completed a training program, evaluation should be used to determine if the training was successful. Measuring employees' performance before and after their participation in training will help managers to decide whether to continue to use that type of training.

EVALUATION PROCEDURES

All supervisors and managers are responsible for evaluating employees. However, the human resources department should develop procedures for evaluation, prepare evaluation forms and materials, and train managers in how to conduct the employee evaluations.

The first step in developing an evaluation procedure is to determine what to evaluate. Managers should look at those things related to successful job performance. In addition to the specific skills needed for the job, most employees are evaluated on their work habits (initiative, dependability, etc.) and their ability to get along with others on the job.

Next, the human resources department prepares an evaluation form. The form should be designed so all evaluations are as objective as possible. If supervisors are asked to rate employees' performance as below average, average, or above average, each supervisor may have a different definition of "average" performance. The same problem occurs if supervisors are asked to rate employee performance on a scale of 1-5. Each of the numbers can have different meanings to several supervisors.

Two methods of making evaluations more objective are shown in Fig. 22-4. The first method lists the skills needed for successful performance of a job duty.

Fig. 22-4
Objective methods for employee evaluation.

METHOD 1. LIST OF JOB SKILLS.

Selling

.... Approaches customers quickly and courteously.

.... Asks appropriate questions to determine customer needs.

.... Selects several products for discussion and demonstration related to customer needs.

.... Presents products to customers emphasizing benefits of product features.

.... Analyzes customer reactions and responses to guide the presentation.

.... Gets the customer involved in product demonstration.

.... Uses trial closes to determine customer commitment.

.... Successfully closes sale with qualified customers.

.... Suggests alternatives or follow-up when sale is not closed.

METHOD 2. DESCRIPTIONS OF PERFORMANCE LEVEL.

Employee Initiative

.... Does not need supervision; always looks for work to be done.

.... Frequently looks for additional work; occasionally needs supervision.

.... Proceeds with assigned work; reports to supervisor when finished.

.... Sometimes needs reminder of work to be completed; requires regular supervision.

.... Completes only one task and does not proceed; needs constant supervision.

The supervisor can observe the employee and check those skills the employee is able to demonstrate. Several managers observing the same employee should check the same items because the skills will either be demonstrated by the employee or they will not.

The second method provides specific descriptions for levels of performance by the employee. The supervisor selects the description that best matches the employee's performance. Again, if several people rate the employee using the descriptions of performance, they should give the same rating.

The supervisor or manager should conduct regular evaluations of all employees using the evaluation form. Companies should require formal evaluations of all employees in making promotion and compensation decisions. Those formal evaluations are usually done once or twice a year. The results are then discussed in an evaluation conference between the supervisor and the employee and entered in the employee's personnel file.

More frequent evaluations should be completed to help employees understand how well they are performing and how their performance can be improved. These evaluations can be more informal, but the results should be discussed with the employee.

CONDUCTING AN EVALUATION CONFERENCE

Whether an employee evaluation is formal or informal, it is important that the employee know an evaluation is being done. After the evaluation, the employee and supervisor should hold an evaluation conference. An **evaluation conference** is a scheduled meeting in which an employee and his or her immediate supervisor (or a human resources specialist) review the performance evaluation. Both managers and employees are often reluctant to participate in an evaluation conference. They are afraid the conference will focus on job problems and that they will not be able to agree on the evaluation results.

If it is carefully planned, an evaluation conference can be a very positive experience. The following steps are helpful in achieving that goal:

1. Schedule enough time for the conference and hold it in a quiet room where you will not be interrupted.

Ilus. 22-5

Effective communications between an employee and a supervisor are an important part of an evaluation conference. What types of planning and preparation should be done to make sure the evaluation conference is successful?

Jeff Greenberg, Photographer

2. Both the supervisor and the employee should plan for the conference by reviewing the evaluation form.
3. The purpose of the evaluation should be clear—if it is informal or formal (required) and whether the results will be used for salary or promotion decisions.
4. The discussion should focus on the employee's performance, not on the employee. It should be based on objective information obtained through the evaluation and not on opinion.
5. Discuss strengths as well as weak areas that need improvement.
6. Both participants should listen carefully to each other.
7. Identify ways the employee can improve performance and what will happen if improvement occurs.
8. Agree on specific activities and responsibilities for each person to work on after the conference.
9. End the conference on a positive note by offering encouragement to the employee.

The results of employee evaluations and other activities will identify the training needed by individuals or groups of employees. Evaluations conducted after training can help to determine if the training was effective. That information should be shared with training specialists in the human resources department in order to improve future training activities.

MAKING IMPROVEMENTS WITH TRAINING

If you review the employee problem discussed by Helen Stokes and Jeffrey Hinton at the beginning of the chapter, it appears that Helen's comment about training was correct. The training being provided to the new printers needs to be improved. Like many companies, Asco relies on informal on-the-job training. It is likely that a formal plan for on-the-job training or that the use of laboratory training might improve the employees' performance and reduce the number of employees fired at the end of the probationary period.

Because Jeffrey is the supervisor, he is concerned about employee performance and the expense of hiring employees and replacing them if they quit or are fired. He will want to work closely with the training department in his company to identify training needs of his employees and to develop effective training programs. He should involve training immediately to help solve the problem he is facing. It is likely that an effective training solution can be developed.

CHAPTER REVIEW

22

BUILDING VOCABULARY POWER

Define the following terms and concepts.

1. informal training
2. formal training
3. classroom training
4. laboratory training
5. on-the-job training
6. coaching
7. apprenticeship training
8. orientation program
9. performance appraisal
10. evaluation conference

REVIEWING FACTS

1. Why might experienced employees need training?
2. Costs associated with what factors are typical of businesses that do not have employee training programs?
3. What types of training are needed by people who are promoted to the job of supervisor?
4. On the average, how much training does an employee receive in one year?
5. How is informal training usually accomplished?
6. How are training specialists involved in formal training?
7. Why is training similar to teaching a class in school?
8. What are the advantages of using the classroom method of training?
9. Why do employees have less pressure in laboratory training than in on-the-job training?
10. What are some of the ways that formal training can be done on the job?
11. Why are the first hours and days of a new job so difficult?
12. What are several characteristics of effective training programs?
13. How can groups of employees and managers in departments be used to identify training needs?
14. How can information from performance appraisals be used by a company?
15. What are the steps in developing an evaluation procedure?

DISCUSSING IDEAS

1. In what ways can a business actually save money by investing in employee training?
2. If supervisors are selected from the best employees, why is supervisory training so important?
3. What are the major advantages and disadvantages of informal training?
4. List five jobs that would likely use laboratory training for new employees.

5. Why is on-the-job training used so frequently to train new employees?
6. What activities and experiences would you include in an orientation program to increase the chances that it will be successful?
7. How do the characteristics of effective training compare with effective classes in a school?
8. What types of skills are needed by people who work in training positions?
9. What information on employee performance would help managers determine if their employees need training?
10. What are some typical problems employees and managers have with conducting an evaluation conference?

A NALYZING INFORMATION

1. Locate the employment opportunities section of a major newspaper in your school or city library. Analyze the job opportunities in business and industry training. Prepare a written report describing those opportunities, including one descriptive chart that presents data you have collected.
2. A review of a report on the amount of formal training activities of Yarcho and Slayton, Inc. revealed the following data:

Date of Training	Number of Participants	Cost of Training	Department
2-4	45	$ 900	Marketing
7-26	26	3,120	Information
1-13	11	495	Management
4-05	58	870	
9-29	32	960	Operations
5-30	65	3,250	
11-08	29	435	Human
3-19	12	900	Resources
7-12	38	760	
12-01	19	855	

   a. Calculate the cost per participant of each training session.
   b. Determine the average cost of training per participant for the entire company.
   c. If Yarcho and Slayton has a total of 206 employees with 45 in Marketing, 58 in Information Management, 65 in Operations, and 38 in Human Resources, determine the average amount spent on each employee for training for each department and for the entire company.
3. Identify a specific skill that you have developed as a hobby or through a job. Develop a list of steps you would follow to help another person learn that skill. Identify how you would evaluate the training to see if it was effective.

4. Prepare a list of all of the training that occurs in your school that is not a part of regular classes. For each item on the list, identify whether it is formal or informal training.

5. Obtain a copy of an employee evaluation form from a business or use one provided by your teacher. Fill it out as if you were the supervisor. Make sure to identify both areas where the employee performs well and a few areas for improvement. Then use the form to role play an employee evaluation conference with another student in your class. When you have completed the role play, study the steps for completing an effective evaluation conference listed in the chapter. Discuss the steps with your partner to determine what you did well and what could be improved.

SOLVING BUSINESS PROBLEMS

CASE 22-1

Ari Lohmann has been a successful salesperson of industrial supplies for ten years. George Granger, the purchasing agent for one of Ari's largest accounts, has decided to open a new sales agency where the company will sell products for 15 to 20 small manufacturers who cannot afford to have their own sales force. George has hired Ari as the sales manager for the new company.

As sales manager, Ari is responsible for hiring and managing a sales force of 20 people. He has decided to hire people without sales experience in order to train them to sell the way he believes is most effective. New salespeople will need three types of training.

1. Effective selling procedures.
2. The use of a portable computer with spreadsheet, word processing, and database management software to manage their accounts.
3. Knowledge of the manufacturers' products the company will represent.

Ari believes experienced salespeople will need regular training to improve selling skills and to learn about new products as they are added.

Required:
1. For each of the training categories listed for new salespeople, identify whether formal or informal training would be most effective. Explain.
2. For each of those categories, indicate whether Ari should use classroom, laboratory, or on-the-job training. Explain.
3. Outline a plan for the regular training of experienced salespeople.

CASE 22-2

Jacki Knox had just left her workstation when her supervisor, Dorothy Trent, stopped her.

Dorothy: Do you have a few minutes, Jacki? I would like to go over your performance evaluation with you.

Jacki: I'm just ready to go on break.

Dorothy: That's where I'm going, too. Let's get a table together in the break room and review your evaluation form. It shouldn't take very long.

After they found a table in the corner of the break room, Dorothy removed an evaluation form from the folder she was carrying and handed it to Jacki.

Dorothy: I think you are doing a very good job, Jacki. Your ratings have gone from four to five in three categories, and that is the top rating. You have maintained fours in four other categories. You need to pay attention to the two categories where I gave you a three and really work on the area where you only received a two. Do you have any questions?

Jacki: Well, I haven't had a chance to look at the form, so I am not sure about questions. Is this my formal evaluation that will determine if I get a salary increase?

Dorothy: No. We will complete that in four more weeks. I just wanted you to see the form informally so we could discuss your performance before you had the formal evaluation.

Just then a receptionist came to the table and told Dorothy that she had a visitor in her department.

Dorothy: Jacki, why don't you spend some time reviewing the evaluation. Then we will schedule some time in my office to discuss it completely.

Required:
1. Compare Dorothy's action with the procedures for effective evaluation conferences described in the chapter. What were Dorothy's strengths and weaknesses?
2. Describe what Dorothy should do to improve the conference when she and Jacki meet again.
3. What should Jacki do to prepare for the next meeting with Dorothy?

CAREER PLANNING AND ORGANIZATIONAL DEVELOPMENT

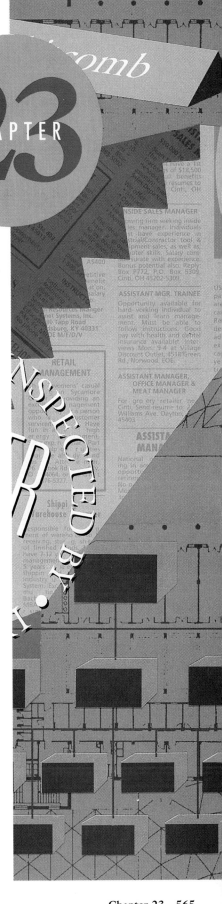

CHAPTER 23

After studying this chapter you will be able to:

23-1 Describe reasons why career development programs are important to businesses and individuals.

23-2 Explain the components of a career development program.

23-3 Define organizational development and the two important components of an organizational development program.

23-4 Discuss reasons that labor unions were formed and how labor/management relations have changed recently.

23-5 Identify several ways that organizations have changed the work environment to increase employee motivation, satisfaction, and performance.

Jo Wu has been a divisional merchandiser for Reighbroughs, a regional chain of department stores, for two and one-half years. Her career development had taken her from sales trainee to salesperson, jewelry department manager, assistant buyer, and now to divisional merchandiser. She has spent twelve years with Reighbroughs and is very satisfied with her current job and her career progress.

Jo had prepared from high school for a career in retailing. She enrolled in business and marketing courses for three years in high school. She completed a two-year degree in retail merchandising at the local community college. She began working for a small independent women's fashion store while in high school. After completing her community college program, she was offered the sales position at Reighbroughs and has worked there since.

After three years of full-time employment, Jo enrolled in State College and completed her bachelor's degree in Marketing Management as a part-time *student. Reighbroughs supported her by developing a work schedule that allowed her to attend classes and even paid part of her tuition costs. They entered Jo in the management training program as soon as she finished her degree. Everything seemed to be on track for a successful career.*

During the past two years, however, Reighbroughs faced increased competition and declining sales. They had to close two smaller stores and cut back on the number of employees by not replacing people who left the company.

Jo had not expected the meeting with her store manager. She was called in and told that Reighbroughs was going through a major organizational change to become more competitive and profitable. The company was going to reduce the number of employees by twenty percent. Jo was one of the people who would be terminated. Her manager was very clear that her termination did not reflect at all on her performance. On the contrary, her evaluations had always been very high and the company was pleased with her work. They had considered her one of their top merchandisers. However, the new organization plans eliminated the divisional merchandiser positions in all stores and combined the duties into a job that would be handled by personnel from the store's administrative center. There was not a position available for Jo in the new structure.

Jo was devastated. While she was not certain that her entire career would be spent at Reighbroughs, she had been very satisfied with the company and had not planned to leave in the near future. She had made no other career plans. Jo's manager was also disappointed. He would prefer to keep someone with Jo's talent but was required to reduce the number of employees. The company's performance left no room to keep people who might be useful in the future but for which there were no current positions available.

While Jo was terminated immediately, the company did provide four months' salary in severance pay and her benefits, including health insurance, remained in force for that time. In addition, the human resources department provided help for all terminated employees in seeking new employment.

THE NEW EMPLOYMENT ENVIRONMENT

While Jo Wu is facing a very difficult situation, it is not unusual. In the 1980s and 1990s, many companies faced the same pressures as Reighbroughs. Increasing competition, a slow economy, and rising costs forced companies to reconsider their organization size, structure, and operations. Many were forced to cut the number of employees as well as reduce other costs, a process known as **downsizing**. Other companies went through **restructuring**, which reorganized work and resources to improve the effectiveness of the organization. Some large companies reduced employment by thousands of people. Employees who had spent many years with the same company (some nearing retirement) suddenly found themselves without a job.

Jeff Greenberg, Photographer

Ilus. 23-1
Hundreds of thousands of employees lost their jobs as companies closed or restructured in the 1980s and 1990s. What roles do you believe human resources departments played in helping with the changes?

While much of the dramatic changes in organizations have now been accomplished, dealing with the result of those changes presents challenges to both employees and managers. Many former employees who lost their jobs when businesses cut back have been unable to find new employment. Some have had to accept employment in lower-level jobs or jobs that pay less or offer fewer benefits than those they held previously. Those who were able to keep their jobs are not certain of their **job security**, the likelihood that their employment will not be terminated in the future. They may distrust their employer, believing that the previous job cutbacks demonstrate a lack of commitment to employees.

Much of the pressure to reestablish a strong organization falls on the human resources department. This department is responsible for implementing many of the changes in the organization, terminating people whose jobs have been eliminated, and preparing people for their new roles. The human resources department will need to develop ways to motivate the remaining employees and restore their confidence in the company.

Two new major responsibilities have emerged for the human resources department in today's organizations. **Career development** is a program that matches the long-term career planning of employees with the employment needs of the business. **Organizational development** is carefully planned changes in the structure and operation of a business so it can adjust successfully to a competitive business environment. In the remaining parts of this chapter, these two human resources programs will be examined. You will learn how companies can use employee resources effectively while maintaining positive management/employee relations.

CAREER DEVELOPMENT

In the past, many companies were quite short sighted when they planned for their employment needs. When a vacant position developed they would begin the recruitment and selection process. If the company no longer needed employees, it was not unusual for the company to terminate those employees without considering the possibility of future employment needs. Those procedures were based on the belief that companies could easily find the employees they needed and that they had no real long-term commitment to the people they hired.

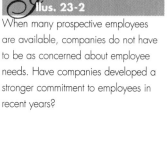

Illus. 23-2

When many prospective employees are available, companies do not have to be as concerned about employee needs. Have companies developed a stronger commitment to employees in recent years?

Rob Crandall/Stock, Boston

Companies now think differently about their relationships with employees. It is not easy to find the employees a company needs with the qualifications required. It is also very expensive to hire and train a new employee. A company that has made an investment in employees wants to get the greatest value from them. That occurs when the employees' skills can be matched as well as possible with the jobs in the company. As the company and its jobs change, employees need to learn new skills so they can fit into those changes and help the company be successful.

As an example, consider how some important activities have changed in businesses in a very short time. Fifteen years ago, most of the information in businesses was processed manually or by using typewriters and calculators. Today, the majority of information processing is done with computers. Auto mechanics relied on hand tools in the past but now use a variety of electronic tools, machines, and computerized diagnostic equipment. Every business has similar examples of the new skills that are required of employees. It is not possible to be successful with the old equipment and procedures. Also, businesses cannot simply fire employees with outdated skills and expect to replace them with people who have the needed new skills.

REQUIREMENTS FOR A CAREER DEVELOPMENT PROGRAM

A **career development program** provides a long-term focus on a company's employment needs combined with support for employees so they can prepare for future jobs in the company. While human resources personnel will be responsible for implementing the career development program, they will need the support of all parts of the company for the program to be successful. A career development program requires a long-term organizational plan, career paths, effective employee evaluation, career counseling, training, and development opportunities.

Long-term Plans

Career development starts with the job opportunities in a company. Companies need to determine what jobs will be available in the future, how many people will be needed in each job, and the knowledge and skills those employees will require. Companies develop long-term plans to identify business opportunities and changes in the organization. One part of those plans should identify employment needs. Then the human resources department can work with the plans to project specific job opportunities in each part of the company and the requirements employees must meet for each job.

Career Paths

A **career path** is a progression of related jobs with increasing skill requirements and responsibility. Career paths provide opportunities for employees to advance within the company, to make additional contributions, and to receive increased satisfaction from their work.

Typically, career paths move an employee from an entry-level position into management. However, career paths should be available in a company that allow employees to advance into non-management positions. Some people do not want to be managers and there are usually relatively few management positions in a company. Therefore, other opportunities must be available so employees do not get locked into one job if they choose not to become a manager or are not qualified for those positions. Examples of a management career path and a non-management path are shown in Fig. 23-1 on page 570.

A variety of career paths should be identified in a company. Each job should be a part of a career path and employees should be aware of the paths available to them from the job they currently hold. The Appendix on pages 685-690 includes a special section on Career Opportunities. The topics discussed are levels of employment, careers in international business, preparing for a business career, developing a career plan, and preparing a career portfolio.

Employee Evaluation

Employees and managers need accurate information on the skills and abilities of each employee to make effective career decisions. When an employee knows how well he or she is performing, the person can determine what skills need to be improved to meet the current job requirements or to qualify for another job in a career path. Managers that carefully evaluate employees' performance can identify those that need additional training and those who are prepared to advance in the organization. The results of employee evaluations should be compared to new job requirements as the company makes changes so employees can prepare for those changes.

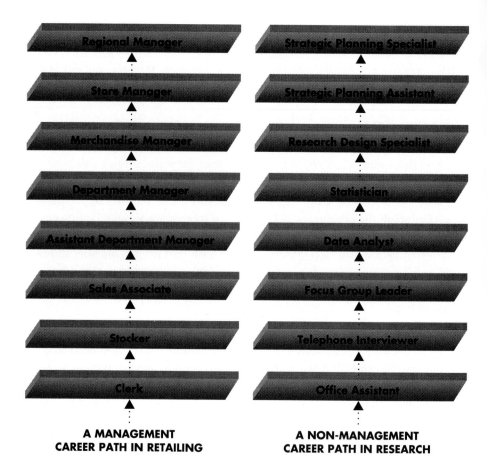

Fig. 23-1

Examples of career paths in business.

A MANAGEMENT CAREER PATH IN RETAILING	A NON-MANAGEMENT CAREER PATH IN RESEARCH
Regional Manager	Strategic Planning Specialist
Store Manager	Strategic Planning Assistant
Merchandise Manager	Research Design Specialist
Department Manager	Statistician
Assistant Department Manager	Data Analyst
Sales Associate	Focus Group Leader
Stocker	Telephone Interviewer
Clerk	Office Assistant

Career Counseling

For career development to be effective, employees must be aware of opportunities and plan their career paths. The human resources department offers career information and counseling services as a part of the career development program. Many companies have made career counseling a part of every employee's evaluation conference. Managers are often trained to provide career information to the employees they supervise.

Career counseling may result in an individual career plan. A **career plan** identifies the jobs that are a part of the employee's career path, the training and development needed to advance along the career path, and a tentative schedule for the plan's activities. The plan is jointly developed by the employee, a human resources specialist, and possibly the employee's manager.

Some companies have developed career centers. **Career centers** are facilities where career development activities are managed. Employees can visit the center to obtain career information (books, pamphlets, films, etc.), visit with career counselors, and schedule career planning workshops or testing as they begin to prepare for new jobs.

One tool companies have developed to help with career counseling is an assessment center. An **assessment center** provides structured testing in which employees are subjected to situations like those they will encounter in the new job to determine how they will perform. For example, assessments may be done in written and oral communications, decision making, and problem solving where employees are presented actual problems or situations. They must use the information to prepare and present solutions. As they present the solutions or solve the problem, they are evaluated by trained observers. At the end of the assessment process, a detailed individual report will be prepared and the results are used to develop a career plan for each employee.

Training and Development

The final part of a career development program is training so employees can develop the skill needed for changing job requirements and new jobs. If careful planning is done, training programs and other educational opportunities can be developed in adequate time to prepare employees for new job requirements. In that way, the business can be assured that it will have well-trained employees to fill job needs and employees will know they can get the training necessary for job changes.

IMPLEMENTING A CAREER DEVELOPMENT PROGRAM

Career planning does not just happen. It also cannot be considered the responsibility of employees alone. Businesses that want to match employees and jobs successfully must do several things to ensure that the career development program works well.

First, responsibility for organizing and managing the career development program must be assigned. Most companies assign the program to the human resources department. The human resources department will put together the people, materials, and procedures needed for the program.

Illus. 23-3
Education of managers and employees is needed before career development will work. What are some ways companies can provide information about the program to their personnel?

Jeff Greenberg, Photographer

Ethical Issues

MANAGING DIVERSITY

Questions:

1 What are some ways that businesses limit the chances of people who are not like the majority of employees from (a) being hired, (b) being satisfied and successful as an employee, and (c) being promoted?

2 What do you believe are the negative and positive points for each of the three common methods companies use to correct past employment problems from the viewpoint of (a) the people who are included in the program and (b) the people who are not included in the program?

3 How is the approach suggested by Dr. Thomas different from the other methods? Why does it have a better chance to solve the employment problem?

Source: R. Roosevelt Thomas, Jr., *Beyond Race and Gender*. New York: AMACOM, 1991.

Both nationally and internationally, the workforce is made up of more females, a larger percentage of employees from non-white ethnic and racial groups, a broader age range, and people with different family structures and career patterns (part-time employees, dual-career families, time out for family leave, etc.).

Government legislation and the social responsibility of individuals and organizations have resulted in businesses looking at past hiring and promotion practices. Many have found a long term pattern of discrimination where people have been denied the opportunity to work for a company or compete for certain jobs because of their gender, race, age, or a physical or mental disability. Even for those businesses that have not discriminated in employment practices, there is often an environment that is not open and supportive for people who were different from the majority of employees.

To correct those employment practices, several remedies have been attempted. They include:

1. An affirmative action program that seeks to identify applications for initial employment and promotions from groups that have been underrepresented in the company. Affirmative action is designed to increase the numbers of "minority" employees throughout the company.

2. Education and training programs that encourage people to recognize differences and value the backgrounds, cultures, and beliefs of others. Diversity training programs are designed to reduce conflicts and improve working relationships among people in the company.

3. Special mentoring and training programs for people from underrepresented groups to encourage those who have experienced employment discrimination to remain with the company and move up the career ladder.

There are advantages for each of the types of programs described but most have not been successful for a large number of companies. R. Roosevelt Thomas, Jr., founder of the American Institute for Managing Diversity, uses a fourth approach with the companies he assists. He calls the approach "managing diversity." He believes that a company has to analyze its entire structure to determine what helps employees succeed and what stands in their way of success. Then the organization needs to be redesigned to assure success for people who are hired in the business no matter what their race, gender, age, or other characteristics that make them unique. All employees must feel welcome and valuable in the organization and know they can succeed if they do the right things. The business must be organized to use and value the strengths and unique qualities of each employee hired.

Second, everyone in the business must be educated about the career development program and his/her role in career planning. Managers need to identify career opportunities in their departments and work with human resources personnel when changes are planned in their departments that will affect the career plans of employees. Managers also will have specific responsibilities in a career development program. They will evaluate employee performance and include career planning in evaluation conferences. They will help identify employees that are ready for career advancement. They will serve as coaches and mentors for their employees to help each employee make effective career choices.

Employees need to be aware of career development resources and how the career planning process works. They will be responsible for much of their individual career planning and development but need to know where to get help when needed. Employees will use performance evaluations and evaluation conferences to gather information to make career plans. They can then schedule assessments, counseling, and training to prepare for career advancement.

SPECIAL CAREER DEVELOPMENT PROGRAMS

Companies that offer career development programs should make the services available to all employees from the newest to the most experienced. However, there are situations where specific individuals or groups of employees participate in programs designed to meet specific needs in the company. Those programs may not be available to all employees.

Most large businesses have offered career planning, training, and counseling for employees selected to be managers. Not all employees have the opportunity to participate in management training. Those that are selected receive testing services, are moved through a specific set of jobs to receive experience in all parts of the business, and often are assigned to an experienced manager who serves as a role model and mentor.

Today, those same businesses are identifying groups of employees who have not had the opportunities to advance into specific careers. Employees from those groups are recruited into career development programs designed to increase the likelihood that they will successfully move up the career ladder. The special programs are most often directed at management positions and are provided to categories of employees (most often women and racial/ethnic minorities) who have not had adequate representation in management positions in the past. Companies want to ensure that those employees have opportunities to advance into positions that were closed to them in the past.

Non-management jobs can be targeted for specific career development programs as well. For example, many jobs are more frequently held by men than women or women than men. Companies may make extra efforts to encourage and prepare people from the underrepresented gender for those jobs. Companies may have difficulty finding qualified candidates for some jobs. Those jobs may be targeted for career development attention. Employees who are interested in or have the knowledge and skills that qualify them for those jobs that have been hard to fill will be encouraged to participate in the special programs. With these special efforts, companies are working to get the best possible use of human resources throughout the organization.

ORGANIZATIONAL DEVELOPMENT

Consider all of the ways that employees can contribute to the success or failure of a business. They can determine if product quality is going to be high or low, if customers are satisfied or dissatisfied, if equipment is maintained well or regularly breaks down, and if materials are wasted or conserved. You can probably think of many other ways that employees can help or hurt the business for which they work.

Studies of successful businesses reveal that the way employees are treated is one of the most important factors in how they feel about the business and the contributions they make to its success. Because of that, the way a company is structured, how work flows through an organization, and how employees work together and with their managers is now receiving a great deal of attention in business. It has led to a process called organizational development.

If you review the definition of organizational development presented earlier in the chapter, you will see that it attempts to improve the way work is accomplished in a business. An important emphasis of organizational development is to build effective work relationships. Managers work to make the employees feel that they are needed and involved in making the business a success. Two important elements of an effective organizational development program are effective management/employee relationships and making improvements in the work environment.

MANAGEMENT/EMPLOYEE RELATIONS

While managers and employees want their company to succeed, there are often differences in their goals. Managers are concerned about the profitability of the company and work hard to increase output and control costs. Those activities can conflict with the needs of employees, who want job security, good working conditions, and fair salaries and benefits.

Early in this century, as industry grew rapidly in the United States, very little was known about effective management procedures. Many business owners misused employees to help their businesses develop. Employees in those businesses had to work long hours with poor working conditions and low pay. While the government passed laws to improve some of the poor working conditions facing workers, individual workers still had little control over their wages, the hours they worked, and their job security. If employers wanted to treat them unfairly, there was little employees could do.

The Development of Labor Unions

One of the ways employees attempted to improve their working conditions was by forming labor unions. A **labor union** is an organization of employees

Lewis Hines/THE BETTMANN ARCHIVE

formed to negotiate with business owners. They hoped to benefit from their association by using their economic power as a large group of employees to improve their work situation.

The early history of labor relations was filled with conflicts and some violence as the unions tried to demonstrate their power and as owners tried to control the unions. Those conflicts often hurt businesses and resulted in union members losing their jobs. Sometimes people involved in the conflicts were injured or killed and property was damaged. The relationship between management and labor in the United States seemed to be getting worse rather than better.

Illus. 23-4
Children were commonly employed for long hours in unsafe working conditions in the early 1900s. What types of employment practices today might need government attention or would be the concern of labor unions?

Labor Laws

Because of the growing problems between labor and management, the federal government passed legislation concerning the rights and responsibilities of labor unions and management. The three most important laws were the Wagner Act, the Taft-Hartley Act, and the Landrum-Griffin Act. Those laws are summarized in Fig. 23-2 on page 576.

Union Membership

The extent of union membership varies according to the type of industry, occupation, and geographic area. Some industries such as mining, construction, and transportation have very high levels of union membership while others have practically none. Union membership increases and decreases based on levels of unemployment and the type of relationships between management and employees in particular industries, areas, or companies.

The most rapid union growth nationally occurred in the 1930s and 1940s. Total union membership actually declined in the 1980s and 1990s as a result of high levels of unemployment in industries that have typically had strong union membership, such as automobile manufacturing and steel production.

While union membership in white-collar and professional occupations has been relatively small, growth has occurred. In recent years, the number of bargaining units representing government employees, teachers, and clerical workers has increased. Workers in many service occupations are also increasing their participation in unions. Figure 23-3 on page 576 shows how union membership in the United States has changed since 1930.

Fig. 23-2
Federal labor legislation.

WAGNER ACT (1935)

- Also known as the National Labor Relations Act
- Guarantees the rights of workers to form unions and bargain collectively
- Prevents employers from using unfair labor practices, including discriminating against employees who attempt to form unions or refusing to bargain with unions
- Formed the National Labor Relations Board to oversee union/management activities

TAFT-HARTLEY ACT (1947)

- Provided balance in labor legislation to control the power of unions
- Made it illegal to require employers to hire only union members
- Unions cannot threaten employees to get them to join unions or charge excessive membership fees to control who joins a union
- Unions cannot negotiate unreasonable demands from employers, such as requiring the employer to hire a certain number of workers for a job when that number is not needed to complete the job
- The President of the United States is able to stop strikes for an 80-day "cooling off period" if the strike is not in the national interest

LANDRUM-GRIFFIN ACT (1959)

- Provides protection for individual union members from corrupt or irresponsible practices of union officials
- Union members are given the right to participate in union decisions, to receive reports on union activities and negotiated agreements with management, and to have fair hearings in any disciplinary actions

Fig. 23-3
Union membership in the United States from 1930 to 1990.

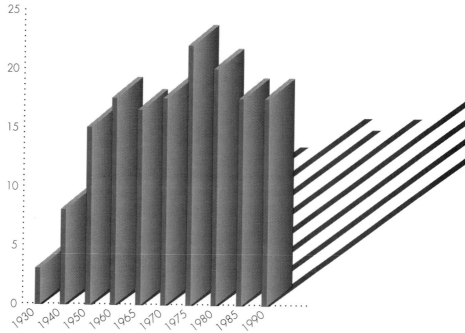

(in Millions)

Collective Bargaining

Unions and management attempt to reach agreements through collective bargaining. **Collective bargaining** involves representatives of management and labor meeting together to discuss and agree on conditions relating to employment. When they reach agreement, they develop a **labor contract**, a written document defining the rights and responsibilities of employees and management. The contract specifies such things as wages, hours, fringe benefits, working conditions, and disciplinary and grievance procedures. It is used to develop policies and rules and to settle disagreements between labor and management.

Union Objectives and Tactics

Labor unions have objectives that represent the needs of employees. The primary objectives are to obtain adequate wages, benefits, and working conditions for union members. In addition, unions work to protect job security and to ensure that members are treated fairly by management. Recently, some unions have attempted to influence major decisions made by management that can have an impact on company profitability, employees' jobs, and worker satisfaction.

To achieve those objectives, unions use several tactics. The primary tactic is to bargain with management for a favorable labor contract. They also represent union members in disagreements with management regarding employment conditions and practices.

When unions cannot reach satisfactory agreements with an employer, they sometimes boycott, picket, or strike. A **boycott** is a decision by union members not to buy the products of a company with which they have a dispute. **Picketing** is placing union members in front of a business to inform the public of their dispute and to encourage others not to enter the business. A **strike** occurs when union members refuse to go to work until the employer meets their demands.

Management Objectives and Tactics

The primary objectives of management when dealing with unions are to increase worker productivity and control the costs of labor. In addition, management wants to maintain control over important decisions on how work is done and on how the assignments are made to complete that work.

If management is unable to achieve its objectives through negotiations with a union, it has several other options. If union practices are violating the union contract or are causing damage to property or injury to other employees, management can go to court to obtain an injunction. An **injunction** directs the union to stop doing a specific act and is enforced by the court.

If a union strikes against a company, management may try to hire nonunion workers to replace the strikers so that the business can continue to operate. Just as a union can strike a business, management can also use a lockout to try and win a dispute with the union. A **lockout** is a temporary work stoppage where the employer does not allow employees to enter the business.

In the early 1980s, a new tactic in labor negotiations was attempted by some companies. Because the economy was in a long recession, many companies were unable to make a profit. Companies involved in labor negotiations asked unions to reduce wage scales and benefits that had been agreed to in earlier contracts. These requests were referred to as **give-backs**.

In the past, unions had always asked for increases in pay and benefits and were not willing to give up those gains. However, they were faced with high unemployment among union members and the likelihood that many more employees would lose their jobs if employers closed factories and businesses. Some unions agreed to the give-backs; but in return, they asked management for guarantees of job security and a greater voice in company operations.

Current Union-Management Relationships

While strikes, violence, and other conflicts between unions and management receive a great deal of publicity, there are many examples of good relationships between unions and employers. Many businesses have never had a union strike, and managers and union leaders work closely together to improve the company.

It has been found that continuing conflict between unions and management in some companies has been so expensive that everyone suffers. Employees lose their jobs and production decreases. Sometimes businesses have had to close. It takes a long time for a business to become profitable again and for employees to earn back the wages they lost as a result of a strike. Therefore, many companies and unions are now attempting to cooperate even more to meet the needs of the company and its employees.

Both unions and management are concerned about the jobs of employees and the changing skills needed for businesses to remain competitive. Many labor contracts now contain provisions for businesses to help employees find new jobs if the business reduces the size of the labor force. Also, labor and management are working together in some companies to provide opportunities for education and retraining. In that way, workers can transfer to newer, high-skilled jobs rather than just losing their old jobs.

IMPROVING THE WORK ENVIRONMENT

The needs and expectations of workers today are very different from those of workers in the past. Work is just one part of an employee's life. Of course, they want jobs that provide a reasonable wage or salary. But the amount of money earned is not always the most important thing. Today, employees are concerned about a variety of factors related to their work, including the work schedule and work conditions. Vacations, insurance, pensions, and other benefits are also important to most people. It is also clear that they want an interesting and challenging job as well as recognition for their work. Both personal and financial needs are important to employees, and managers must recognize those needs in order to maintain an effective workforce.

Employee Motivation

Managers must be concerned about worker motivation. **Motivation** can be defined as the reasons that cause people to act in a certain way. People attempt to satisfy their individual needs. For example, if a person is hungry, that need motivates that person to find a way to obtain food. If a person is bored or lonely, they will try to find entertainment or companionship.

The specific needs of individuals will be very different. However, all needs can be grouped into five broad categories: physical needs, safety needs, social needs, self-respect needs, and self-realization needs. The categories of needs are shown in Fig. 23-4 in the order of importance. The first concern of a person is for physical needs—food, shelter, clothing, and sleep. If a person is very tired or hungry, little else is important until those needs are met. In the same way, a person who is in a dangerous situation is more concerned about safety than about social or self-respect needs.

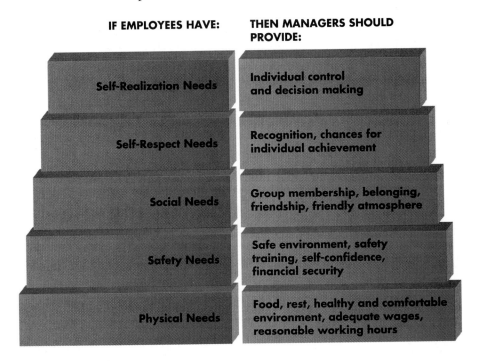

IF EMPLOYEES HAVE:

THEN MANAGERS SHOULD PROVIDE:

Self-Realization Needs	Individual control and decision making
Self-Respect Needs	Recognition, chances for individual achievement
Social Needs	Group membership, belonging, friendship, friendly atmosphere
Safety Needs	Safe environment, safety training, self-confidence, financial security
Physical Needs	Food, rest, healthy and comfortable environment, adequate wages, reasonable working hours

Fig. 23-4
Responding to the five levels of employee needs.

In the United States today, most employees' physical and safety needs are satisfied most of the time. Because these more basic needs are satisfied, social needs and personal needs such as self-respect and self-realization have grown in importance for many workers. Managers must find ways to satisfy those needs as a regular part of the employee's job. However, basic needs must continue to be satisfied as well. It is important for managers to realize that those needs cannot be ignored.

Job Design

To better understand how employees gain increased satisfaction from their jobs, studies have been completed to determine those factors that employees like most about their work. It was found that the greatest satisfaction occurs when a person (a) performs interesting work, (b) feels responsible for the work, (c) is recognized for good work, and (d) has a feeling of achievement.

These results show that employees are concerned with many things other than the amount of their paycheck or benefits like vacation days. It is surprising to many managers that while the amount of compensation is important, it is not necessarily more important than other factors related to the job. From those studies, efforts have been made to design jobs to better meet worker needs. **Job design** considers the kind of work and the way the work is organized.

One way companies try to gain efficiency and improve the quality of their products is to reduce the quantity and difficulty of the tasks performed by one worker. Formerly, it was believed that if one person did one thing over and over, the job could be completed quickly without errors. However, that job design resulted in boredom and a feeling of unimportance.

To overcome those problems, managers now try to get a variety of functions into a job. Making a job more interesting by adding variety to the tasks is called **job enlargement**. As an example, three workers on an assembly line might be responsible for three separate tasks, each one performing one task over and over. With job enlargement, however, each worker is trained to complete all three tasks. Thus, different tasks can periodically rotate among the employees. Moreover, the workers are given variety in their work, not more work to do. Another approach to job enlargement is cross training. With **cross training**, employees are trained to perform more than one job in the company even though they typically perform only one. Employees can be rotated to other jobs when an absence or illness occurs, while a replacement employee is being trained, when a significant increase or decrease in the amount of work occurs for a specific job, or simply to provide change and variety for employees. Employers have found that job enlargement and cross training have resulted in both greater productivity and greater job satisfaction if employees are involved in the decisions about the job changes.

Another method of job design to improve satisfaction is to get workers involved in decision making. Encouraging employee participation in decision making is known as **job enrichment**. For example, managers may allow workers to make choices about how a job should be done. They may ask for advice on how to improve performance or how to reduce errors.

Employee Participation

Some companies have developed work teams that are responsible for the entire assembly of a product, performance of a service, or operation of a small unit in the business. The team helps with goal setting, shares all of the tasks, and is responsible for the results. Companies using this system have found that team members develop a strong loyalty for the other members and take personal responsibility for the effective operation of the team and the quality of its work.

llus. 23-5
The use of employee work teams to make decisions often results in increased productivity and greater job satisfaction. What are some other methods of increasing employee participation in the work of a company?

A formal process of employee participation is known as quality circles or employee involvement teams. **Quality circles** are employee teams that meet regularly to solve problems and improve quality. The process begins with careful selection and training of team members. While the goal is to involve all employees in a quality circle in the long run, the first teams are made up of people who volunteer to work on the team. All team members participate in several training sessions designed to help them develop an effective team and improve communications, problem-solving skills, and decision-making skills.

The team then elects a leader and begins its work. It usually meets several times during the month with each meeting scheduled during work time. Meetings are long enough for the teams to identify problems and discuss possible solutions. The team brainstorms job-related problems, quality issues, or difficulties they are having with procedures. After they agree on the most important issues, they begin to identify possible solutions, changes that may be required, or additional information needed.

As soon as the team agrees on a solution, they work with managers to determine if the solution can be implemented and how to monitor progress and measure results. Because of the role of the quality circle in developing the solution, the employees usually take a great deal of responsibility for ensuring the solution works effectively.

Not all organizations have been satisfied with their employee involvement efforts. Some believe it gives too much authority to employees and takes away management responsibility. Other companies feel the team process takes employees away from their jobs too much. Companies who are using employee teams effectively believe they are successful because they have taken the time to prepare employees for their new roles and have carefully developed procedures and guidelines for the new employee/management relationships.

Companies continue to study the way they involve employees in the organization, and are finding that employees appreciate being involved when their contributions result in improvements in the organization and when their efforts are recognized by management. Organizational development has become an important function for many human resources departments. They continue to provide the normal range of employee services and help the organization recruit, train, and evaluate employees. However, they have found that assisting the organization to improve its structure, to organize work effectively, and to encourage effective relationships among employees and between management and employees is a way that the department can make an even greater contribution to the effectiveness of the business.

CHAPTER REVIEW 23

BUILDING VOCABULARY POWER

Define the following terms and concepts.

1. downsizing
2. restructuring
3. job security
4. career development
5. organizational development
6. career development program
7. career path
8. career plan
9. career centers
10. assessment center
11. labor union
12. collective bargaining
13. labor contract
14. boycott
15. picketing
16. strike
17. injunction
18. lockout
19. give-backs
20. motivation
21. job design
22. job enlargement
23. cross training
24. job enrichment
25. quality circles

REVIEWING FACTS

1. What types of pressures did businesses face in the 1980s and 1990s that affected employment?
2. When a large number of employees are terminated, what negative feelings might the remaining employees have toward the company?
3. What are two new responsibilities of human resources departments in today's organizations?
4. Why did companies believe it was appropriate to terminate employees without considering future employment needs?

5. What are the five requirements of a career development program?
6. What advantages do employees receive when career paths are available in a company?
7. How do employee evaluations aid employees and managers with career planning?
8. Who is involved in developing a career plan?
9. What department in a company is usually responsible for organizing and managing career development programs?
10. What are some examples of special career development programs that are not available to all employees?
11. What is one of the most important factors in how employees feel about an organization and the contributions they make to its success?
12. What are two important elements of an effective organizational development program?
13. How are managers' goals different from employees' goals?
14. Why were labor unions first organized?
15. How have businesses attempted to increase employee motivation and satisfaction with their jobs?

DISCUSSING IDEAS

1. In the scenario at the beginning of the chapter, why would a company terminate an employee like Jo Wu even though she was a very good employee and the company had paid some of the costs of her education?
2. Why are some companies having more difficulty finding the employees they need for effective operations?
3. What are the jobs that would make up a career path in an industry, company, or occupation with which you are familiar?
4. In what ways would an employee benefit from having a career plan developed?
5. How would the career center in a business be similar to or different from the career services offered by the counselors in a school?
6. Why have many companies had special career development programs for managers even though they did not provide similar career development programs for other employees?
7. What are some specific ways that employees contribute to the success or failure of a business?
8. Why have there often been conflicts between employees and management in companies and what can be done to improve management/employee relations?
9. What are some reasons that employees choose to join or not to join labor unions?
10. What are some advantages and disadvantages of cross training to the company and to employees?

A NALYZING INFORMATION

1. Identify the title of a management job that interests you. Using career information from your school counseling center or a library, prepare a description of the job and the education and experience requirements for the job. Now search the career information to identify an entry-level job and at least three other related jobs that have increasing requirements and responsibilities and could form a career path for you if you wanted to obtain the management job. Write a complete job description for each of the jobs.

2. Identify ways you believe companies could respond effectively to the challenge of increasing the diversity of employees throughout the organization and at all levels of employees from entry-level to management.

3. The Hendo Company has just experienced a four-week strike. During the strike, union members received 20 percent of their normal wages from the union strike fund. The average weekly wage of employees was $360. The company's average weekly sales before the strike were $120,000 with a profit of 4 percent of sales. During the strike, sales were 60 percent of normal and no profit was made on those sales.

    If employees received an 8 percent wage increase after the strike, how long will employees have to work to make up for the amount that was lost during the strike?

    If company sales increased 5 percent after the strike, (a) how much would be the weekly profit and (b) how long will it take the Hendo Company to replace the profits lost during the strike?

4. Conduct a survey of ten people who have been working full time for more than three years. Ask them to identify the two things they like most about their jobs. Combine your results with those of other class members. Make a chart that matches the responses with the appropriate categories of needs shown in Fig. 23-4.

5. With the rest of your classmates, identify one problem related to the operation of your school that you would like to study. Then divide the class into several "quality circles" of students (about 5-7 students per group). Discuss the problem to identify why the problem exists and how the school would be better if the problem were solved. Then propose several solutions and analyze each to determine the advantages and disadvantages of each. Select the one solution your group believes could be implemented and that would be acceptable to administrators, teachers, and students. Prepare a one-page written report from your group. Share your report with the other "quality circles."

REVIEW
23

S OLVING BUSINESS PROBLEMS

CASE 23-1

The MidSouth Textile company employs a large number of employees and has specific procedures for hiring and promotion. The company believes it is important that employees be able to work well together. Therefore, they do not advertise for new employees but ask current employees and managers to recommend people whenever there is an opening. No one will be hired that does not have a recommendation.

Once hired, each employee is assigned to an experienced employee for training. The experienced employee spends two weeks teaching the new person how to operate the equipment and perform other tasks. At the end of the two weeks, the new employee is moved into the vacant position. At the end of six weeks, the employee's performance is evaluated. New employees who cannot perform well enough to meet the company standards are terminated.

New assignments to more difficult jobs with higher pay are made at the end of six months. Supervisors identify the employees they believe are most qualified for the new assignments. Those not chosen must stay at the more routine jobs and do not get pay increases.

Every six months, employees can apply for transfers and promotions. They fill out a form on which they identify why they believe they should be considered for the job change. The company's top managers review the forms and each employee's performance evaluations. Those employees with the most outstanding performance are selected for job changes. The managers match the selected employees with the available jobs.

After five years with the company, an employee can be selected for the company's management training program. To be selected, the employee must have been promoted at least three times, must be recommended by his or her immediate supervisor, and must pass a management aptitude test. All new managers are selected from the management training program and promotions to management positions are made whenever openings occur.

Required:
1. What are the strengths and weaknesses of MidSouth's hiring and promotion procedures?
2. What changes would you recommend to improve the hiring and promotion procedures? Justify each of your recommendations and explain why it will improve employee motivation and organizational effectiveness.

CASE 23-2

The Orion Corporation recently implemented employee involvement teams as a part of an organizational development program. Seven-member employee teams were formed in each department. The teams received 20 hours of training and then were asked to survey the other employees in their department to identify an important problem that was affecting employee performance and motivation. The employee involvement team was asked to recommend a solution for the problem to the department manager.

The employees in the data entry department of the information management division were excited about the chance to participate in solving a problem they had been facing for some time. Eighteen of the twenty employees had school-aged children. Several times during the year, the employees needed to take time from work to attend parent-teacher conferences, help with projects in their child's school, or attend an important school activity involving their children. Orion had no policy that allowed employees time away from work for those activities. The employees either had to miss the school activities or call in sick. Most of the employees felt uncomfortable about taking a "sick-day" when they really were not sick. However, employees had no other way to get the time off.

The employee involvement team worked carefully to identify a solution to the problem that would meet the employees' needs and make sure that all of the work was done. They developed the following plan:

Each employee could have up to two half-day absences for school-related activities during the year. The absence would have to be scheduled at least one week in advance and only one employee could be absent at a time. The other employees agreed to complete the work of the absent employee before they left for the day without additional pay. The department manager could cancel the absence with one day's notice if the department had special assignments or extra work.

The employee involvement team recommended that the plan be implemented for six months. At the end of that time, if the manager and employees agreed that the department was operating effectively and the quality and quantity of work had not decreased, the plan would become permanent. All of the employees were excited about the new plan and were committed to making it work. The employee team submitted their plan to the department manager.

The manager rejected the employee recommendation. He identified two reasons for rejecting the plan: (1) The company could not have different policies concerning employee absences for each department. (2) Since all employees in the department did not have school-aged children, the policy would be unfair to those employees.

Required:

1. Do you believe most recommendations made by employee involvement teams should be accepted by managers? Why or why not?
2. How do you believe employees will feel about employee involvement based on the manager's response to their proposal? What should the manager do?
3. How could the Orion Corporation implement employee involvement teams to avoid the problem they now face in the data entry department?

REVIEW 23

Unit Summary

6-1 *Describe the role of human resources management in an organization and the major activities performed by human resources personnel.*

For many years, the human resources department (then known as personnel) was of little importance in the day-to-day operation of the business. Employees were hired, a compensation system was developed, and employee records were maintained. There was little regular contact between human resources personnel and either employees or managers.

Today, many companies have recognized that employees have changed and that management/employee relationships must change as well. The human resources department has the responsibility for leading those changes. They are called upon to ensure that an adequate number of employees is available, that they are well paid and trained, satisfied with their jobs, and productive. The major activities of human resources are recruitment and selection, training and development, compensation and benefits, performance evaluation, health and safety, and employee relations.

6-2 *Outline the procedures used in employee selection, promotion, and termination.*

Careful employee selection ensures that the best people with the skills needed for each job will be hired by a company. The procedures begin when a department identifies the need for an employee. The department manager works with the human resources department to identify the requirements for the position. Then the human resources department uses several sources to obtain applicants. A careful procedure of application, interviews, testing, and selection is followed.

When an employee has performed well and an opening at a higher or more specialized level occurs in the business, the employee should be considered for promotion. The company and the employee benefit from an internal promotion. The most difficult activity for human resources personnel and managers to perform is employee termination. An employee can be terminated because the position is no longer needed or because the employee's performance does not meet expectations.

UNIT SUMMARY

6-3 *Discuss the factors to be used in designing an effective compensation and benefits program for an organization.*

Employees are rewarded for their performance. The rewards include wages or salaries and a variety of employee benefits such as vacations, insurance, health and wellness programs, etc. If compensation and benefits programs are not carefully developed and managed, the company will not make enough money to continue to employ an adequate number of people. Or employees will be dissatisfied with the amount of compensation, the fairness of the system, or the type and amount of benefits they receive.

Human resources personnel evaluate jobs to determine their relative value. They study alternative compensation systems and choices of employee benefits. They must also be aware of legal requirements for compensation and benefits and administer government programs such as social security and workers compensation.

6-4 *Discuss the importance of employee training and development and the primary methods used for employee training.*

When faced with increasing competition, more companies are turning to training. Training increases the effectiveness of employees so they will complete their work faster, with higher quality, and with fewer mistakes. Much of the training in businesses, particularly small businesses, is done informally. Employees learn by watching experienced employees or by practicing on the job. However, formal training is being used more frequently.

The primary training methods are classroom, laboratory, apprenticeship, and on the job. In order to make sure that new employees get off to a good start and become an effective part of the company, companies are improving their employee orientation programs.

Determining the effectiveness of training requires that employee performance is evaluated. The human resources department works with company managers to design an evaluation program, prepare managers to evaluate employee performance objectively, and conduct effective evaluation conferences.

6-5 *Explain the purpose and characteristics of a career development program.*

Career development means that companies must determine their long-term employment needs, develop career paths for employees, and help those employees prepare career plans so their skills match the jobs that will be available in the company. The last part of a career development program is training so an employee can acquire the skills needed for changing job requirements or a new job.

Implementation of a career development program usually involves assigning the human resources department responsibility for organizing and managing the program. All employees and managers must be educated about the program and their roles in career planning. They need to be aware of career development resources and how the process of career planning works. Companies offering career development programs should make them available to all employees.

6-6 *Justify the need for organizational development to improve employee productivity and motivation.*

Companies can no longer operate in the way they have in the past and expect to be successful. New organizational patterns and different relationships between managers and employees must be considered. A traditional way that management/employee relationships have been defined is through labor unions and the labor contracts negotiated with companies. While labor union membership has declined in recent years, unions are still an important force in business. However, both unions and companies are exploring new relationships and new methods of cooperating.

Managers realize that employees must be motivated in order to perform effectively. There may be conflicts between the goals of managers and the needs of employees. However, employee needs should be identified and satisfied whenever possible.

One way of increasing employee satisfaction is through greater involvement in job-related decision making. Many companies are using job design, job enrichment, and employee participation teams to increase employee satisfaction.

Planning

Decision Making

anagement Responsibilities

OBJECTIVES

7-1 Define the role of managers in an organization and the functions that all managers perform.

7-2 Outline an effective procedure to be followed by managers when making decisions.

7-3 Identify important leadership skills needed by managers and how leadership is demonstrated in business.

7-4 Describe the important planning tools used by managers.

7-5 Explain the importance of organizing activities and the characteristics of an effective organization.

7-6 Present suggestions on ways for managers to implement the work of organizations effectively.

7-7 Illustrate the steps managers use in a controlling process to improve performance.

"Great leaders have three things going for them. First, they have strong personal values. Second, they have developed solid technical knowledge and skills in their field. Third, they have a vision of their future and the discipline to set goals and achieve that vision.

"Personal values show our commitment to be the best at what we do, to be honest with ourselves and others and to care about our families, friends, and communities. Learning is a life-long process that doesn't stop when you leave school. Finally, leaders know where they are going and have a plan to get there."

Jim Howard,
Chairman of the Board
and Chief Executive
Officer,
Northern States Power
Company

Professional Profile

A LEADER IN BUSINESS DEVELOPMENT

Heading a $3 billion manufacturing company that competes in markets worldwide presents daily challenges. But Glen Hiner faces the challenges by understanding the importance of relationships—relationships with customers, with employees, with stockholders, and with governments. As the chairman and CEO of Owens-Corning Fiberglas Corp., he emphasizes several priorities: customer satisfaction through high quality, low costs, and incomparable service; individual dignity for all employees so Owens-Corning is a preferred place of employment; and value to shareholders who have placed their trust in the company.

Owens-Corning Fiberglas Corp. is the world's top manufacturer of fiberglass materials. The materials are used as insulation in buildings, appliances, and other products. In addition, the company produces a variety of durable industrial materials that are used as substitutes for steel, wood, and aluminum. An example is a durable polyester resin that can be formed into underground petroleum storage tanks to prevent leakage.

Mr. Hiner earned a degree in electrical engineering from West Virginia University. He began work with General Electric and, during a 35-year career, advanced to the head of GE Plastics. In that position he developed his understanding of global business operations and expanded the annual sales of the GE division by 500 percent. Since coming to Owens-Corning in 1992, Mr. Hiner has focused on financial performance. Cash flow is improving while the company's debt has been reduced. Mr. Hiner recognizes that a successful company is built on the efforts of many managers. He knows that the executives who preceded him made important contributions to the company's success.

Glen Hiner,
Chairman and Chief
Executive Officer,
Owens-Corning
Fiberglas Corporation

INSPIRATIONAL IDEAS

"You need to recognize that you are not alone —you are a part of a team. Each member of the team has his or her own unique talents and insights that can be used to the benefit of the entire organization. Just as the best coaches are those who combine their athletes' individual talents with a strong sense of purpose, the best corporate leaders are those who encourage individual initiative while laying out a clear set of objectives and values."

Photo courtesy of Owens-Corning Fiberglas

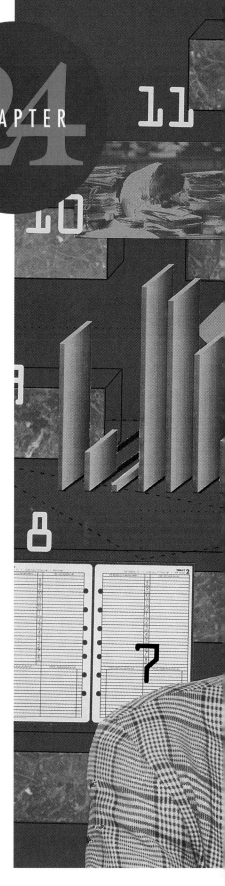

MANAGEMENT FUNCTIONS AND DECISION MAKING

CHAPTER 24

After studying this chapter you will be able to:

24-1 Define the four functions of management.

24-2 Differentiate between management and non-management employees and the various levels of management.

24-3 Describe the five major job responsibilities of supervisors.

24-4 Identify how managers use information and business research in their work.

24-5 Outline the steps in an effective decision-making process.

F or people who want to become managers, their first management position will probably be as a supervisor. Let's look at a typical situation in which an experienced employee considers the possibility of a promotion into management.

Anton Jacobs has worked for Freeden Computers for five years. It was his first job since graduating from Highmark Community College with a degree in Computer Science. He enjoys his work as a programming specialist, a position he has held for over two years now. The company recognized his ability, and he has moved up rapidly from his first job as programming assistant to his current position.

Anton is facing an important career decision. At the end of his last six-month performance evaluation conference, his manager told him that the programming supervisor would be promoted in three weeks. The manager wants Anton to consider applying for the supervisor's position.

The opportunity to move into a management position is exciting. The job would provide a higher salary and status as a manager. At the same time, Anton isn't sure he has the skills or the interest in being a supervisor. He has worked for several supervisors at Freeden and has seen that it isn't an easy job. All of the supervisors had been very good employees when they were promoted, but not all turned out to be effective supervisors. Some got along well with the people they supervised, while others did not. It seemed to Anton that supervisors were constantly dealing with employee complaints or with concerns from their managers. He has seen some supervisors work many extra hours each week to get all of their work done.

Anton really enjoys his work in programming, and he knows that he will not do as much of that work as a supervisor. Yet, he isn't sure if he wants to do programming for the rest of his career. He also knows that he enjoys working with and helping to train the new programming assistants. He really feels good when he sees them performing well and being promoted. His biggest concern, however, is that he really doesn't know very much about the supervisor's job, and he is concerned that he will not succeed. He already knows he is a good programmer. Freeden does not provide any training for prospective supervisors, and Anton's only preparation was a management course he completed while attending the community college.

MOVING INTO MANAGEMENT

Anton's experience is similar to that of many employees. They really do not know very much about the work of managers. If they have worked for effective managers, it may appear that the job is quite easy. On the other hand, employees may have had experiences with poor managers who make their own jobs difficult and cause problems for their employees.

Many employees believe they would like to be managers and often think they can do a better job than the managers for whom they work. However, when presented with the decision of whether to move into management, they may find the decision difficult to make. If an employee likes the work he/she does, moving into management will mean he/she can no longer do that work. Will an employee enjoy a management job as much? If the employee has been successful in his/her current job, a move into management can be very risky. What if the employee is not successful in the management position? It is not likely he/she will be able to move back into the previous job, and, indeed, may be fired if unsuccessful as a manager.

Understanding management and the work of management will make it easier for employees to choose a management career. If the company helps employees move into management with training programs, there will be less risk and a greater opportunity for employees to be successful. Some companies are now allowing employees an opportunity to work in a beginning management position for a short time before making a permanent decision. If the employee finds the job is not what was expected and if the company decides the new manager is not performing at the level required, an agreement can be reached for the employee to move back into the same type of job he/she held before.

Companies need good managers just as they need effective employees. Being able to identify managers from current employees allows a company to reward its employees with promotions and to have managers who understand company operations and policies. You can see why Anton would be a good candidate for a management position in Freeden Computers. If you were Anton, what decision would you make?

NATURE OF MANAGEMENT

Managers make things happen in business. From the original idea for a business, through the accumulation of the resources needed to operate the business, to the management of people, managers are responsible for the success or failure of the company. The decisions made by managers determine what a company will do and how well it will perform.

MANAGEMENT ACTIVITIES

Because there are so many types of managers, it is difficult to identify exactly what managers do. However, there are a number of activities that must be performed by all managers no matter what the type or size of the company. The president of a large international corporation made up of several companies and thousands of employees is a manager, but so is the owner of a small service business with one location and only a few employees. The people who are responsible for human resources departments and for purchasing departments, for a company's sales people, or for its information management activities are all managers. So are supervisors of people working on an assembly line, in a warehouse, or at data entry terminals. While each of these jobs involves many unique activities, each is also concerned with management.

Management is the process of accomplishing the goals of an organization through the effective use of people and other resources. As we learned earlier, those resources include money, buildings, equipment, and materials. The primary work of all managers can be grouped within four functions: (1) planning, (2) organizing, (3) implementing, and (4) controlling.

Illus. 24-2

The manager of a large manufacturing company and the manager of a small service business complete many of the same activities. How are their jobs similar and different?

Jeff Greenberg, Photographer   *Jeff Greenberg, Photographer*

Planning involves analyzing information and making decisions about what needs to be done. **Organizing** is concerned with determining how plans can most effectively be accomplished and arranging resources to complete work. A manager is **implementing** when carrying out the plans and helping employees to work effectively and is **controlling** when evaluating results to determine if the company's objectives have been accomplished as planned.

Operating a business is a very complex process. Even managers of small businesses must make product, marketing, personnel, and finance decisions every day. If the manager does not have an organized method for operating the business, problems will soon develop. The manager who knows how to plan, organize, implement, and control is prepared to make the decisions needed to operate a business successfully.

MANAGEMENT AND NON-MANAGEMENT EMPLOYEES

Many employees of a business complete activities that could be considered management activities. They might plan and organize their work or decide how to organize materials to complete work efficiently. An experienced employee may be given the responsibility to be the leader on a group project, and the group members may help the manager evaluate the project when it has been completed.

In each of these examples, the employee is getting valuable experience. That experience will help the employee to understand the work of managers and to prepare for possible promotion to a management position. If the company in

Miro Vintoniv/Stock, Boston

the earlier example had used these types of experiences to develop employees, Anton may have had a better idea of what it would be like to be a supervisor. Giving those types of responsibilities to employees can also be an effective motivating technique. However, just because employees perform some work that is similar to managers' responsibilities, the employees are not managers.

A **manager** completes all four management functions on a regular basis and has authority over other jobs and people. In each of the situations above, where employees were completing what seemed to be management functions, they either were doing those tasks infrequently, not completing all of the management functions, or were completing them for their job only.

There are typically several levels of management in most companies. A manager whose main job is to direct the work of employees is called a supervisor. **Supervisors** are typically the first (or beginning) level of management in a company and often have many non-managerial activities to perform as well. An **executive** is a top-level manager who spends almost all of his or her time on management functions. Executives have other managers reporting to them. Between executives and supervisors in larger organizations, there will be one or more levels of mid-managers.

A **mid-manager** completes all of the management functions, but spends most of the time on one management function such as planning or controlling, or is responsible for a specific part of the company's operations. Figure 24-1 on page 599 shows how the time spent on management functions changes for different levels of managers in a business.

Global Perspective

A MANAGEMENT CULTURE

Questions:

1 How might the concern for human relationships have contributed to the success of Japanese companies?

2 Why do practices that are developed from the culture of a company present difficult challenges to a company? What might be the effect of trying to change some of the Japanese management practices identified?

3 What are some management practices in the United States that relate to our culture?

Source: "Japan's White Collar Blues," *Fortune*, March 21, 1994, pp. 97-104.

Many companies have looked to the Japanese manufacturing systems as a model of quality and efficiency. Japanese companies have incorporated the latest technology, concentrated on employee training, and developed effective relationships between manufacturers, suppliers, and their customers so products move rapidly and at a low cost to the customer.

Surprisingly, the same systematic, efficient process is not always found in the offices of Japanese management. A culture that believes in job security, group decision making, and authority based on age and seniority has resulted in a system where the majority of personnel employed in manufacturing companies works in the offices rather than on the factory floor and human relationships are valued higher than reducing management costs.

During the rapid growth in Japanese companies of the 1970s and 1980s, a large number of young people were hired into beginning management positions. Now they find that it will take them 15 or 20 years to move into responsible positions because of the many layers of management.

Companies have such high salary costs they are not as able to spend money on the technology used to increase the efficiency of decision making and the quality of information managers need. Because there is not always enough work to do as the economy slows, some beginning jobs do not even have job titles or job descriptions. Young managers are finding that they are not always rewarded for hard work with promotions or increases in salary.

Until recently, Japanese companies were able to continue with the traditional management structures and philosophies. Companies were growing and profitable. The effectiveness of manufacturing hid the inefficiency of management. Now, companies are recognizing that continuing success depends on making changes in management.

Steps are being taken to increase performance incentives. Managers set goals and are held accountable for their achievements. Bonuses that used to be paid automatically are now withheld if goals are not achieved. Managers are being transferred to the production floor where there are sometime shortages of employees. Spending time in production not only helps with the staffing problem but gives managers a better idea about organizing work and effective operations.

Time-honored management patterns are hard to change. There is value in maintaining some of the cultural traditions as long as they don't lead to major problems in the company. But as Japanese companies have discovered, effective and efficient management is just as important to the success of companies as their world-renowned manufacturing processes.

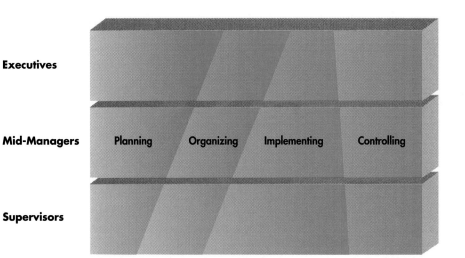

Executives

Mid-Managers   Planning   Organizing   Implementing   Controlling

Supervisors

You can see that as a manager moves up in the organization, responsibilities change. Supervisors work most directly with employees and are involved in the daily operations of the business. Therefore, they devote most of their management time to implementing. Executives work with other managers and are responsible for the long-term direction of the business. They spend most of their time on planning and organizing.

S UPERVISION

Supervisors are critical to the success of a business. They work directly with employees and are responsible for translating the company's plan into action. They must create an environment that motivates employees to do their best work. Let's examine the supervisor's job in detail to learn how supervisors can be effective managers.

THE SUPERVISOR'S JOB

Supervisors are often promoted from the area where they work. Usually, supervisors are selected from among the most experienced and most skilled workers. However, they may have little or no management training. As first-level managers, supervisors are responsible for the day-to-day activities of the company's employees. They need to understand and work with both employees and management. Supervisors must implement the decisions of management; at the same time, they must solve employee problems and present employee concerns to management.

The effectiveness of a supervisor's job is determined by two factors: the quality of the work of the employees and the satisfaction of the supervisor's employees. If work is not done well, management will not be pleased with the supervisor's job. And if employees are not happy with their work, they will not perform their jobs well for long.

Supervisors are sometimes called the most important managers in a business. Do you agree or disagree with that statement? Why?

Jeff Greenberg, Photographer

RESPONSIBILITIES OF SUPERVISORS

You learned earlier that supervisors often divide their time between management activities and other work. They are responsible for implementing the plans of executives by getting employees to perform effectively on a day-to-day basis. One supervisor's job may be very different from another's, especially from supervisors in other departments and companies. Employees have different levels of education, training, and experience. Some jobs are very technical while others require few specific technical skills or knowledge. Some supervisors manage experienced employees while others work with new employees. In spite of the differences in their jobs, however, supervisors still have a common set of responsibilities in all companies. Those responsibilities are summarized in Fig. 24-2.

Common responsibilities of supervisors.

Supervisor's Job Description

- **Communicating goals and directions**
- **Keeping management informed**
- **Evaluating and improving employee performance**
- **Motivating employees**
- **Using resources wisely**

Communicate the Goals and Directions of Management to Employees

In order for employees to complete work effectively, they must understand what needs to be done and why. Supervisors must be able to communicate effectively with employees. Employees must not only understand what is to be done; they must also know why and how they will benefit. Good supervisors are able to show employees the importance of the company's goals and help them see the importance of accomplishing the goals. Good supervisors help employees see how they can accomplish their own goals by helping the company to be successful.

Explain Employee Concerns and Ideas to Management

Employees want to feel that they are a part of the company and that their ideas and opinions are considered by management. Therefore, supervisors must take the time to talk with the people they supervise in order to find out their concerns, problems, and ideas. Then they must communicate those concerns to management and follow up to find out what action was taken. Employees like to work for a supervisor who is interested in them and their ideas. They will work hard for a company that is concerned about them and involves them in planning and decision making.

Evaluate and Improve Employee Performance

Supervisors get work done through individual employees. They need to be sure that each employee is performing as effectively as possible. Regular formal and informal evaluations can reveal the employee's strengths and weaknesses. Supervisors must be both positive and objective when they complete evaluations of employees. Good supervisors discuss these evaluations with their employees in ways that contribute to effective understanding, not conflict. They provide rewards and recognition for those employees who perform well. They also provide help for those employees who are not performing well so that their skills can be improved. This help might be in the form of advice and coaching, or it might be informal and formal training.

Encourage Employees to Do Their Best Work

All people have days when they enjoy working and other days when they do not. Employees' performance is affected by how they feel about their jobs. If they are unsure about what they are doing or fear they will be punished for poor work, employees are not able to perform very well. Supervisors need to create an atmosphere in which employees enjoy their work and do a good job. Employees want to feel accepted and comfortable. They want to know that they can get help if they have problems. They want others to realize that what they do is important and that they will be recognized for good work.

Use Resources Efficiently

Companies won't operate long if they are unable to make a profit. An important part of earning profits is controlling the costs of the business. Since supervisors are responsible for the day-to-day activities of a business, they have a great deal of control over whether a company makes a profit or a loss. Good supervisors continually look for ways to operate more efficiently and to use resources more effectively. They seek advice from employees and make suggestions to managers on how activities can be improved.

DAY-TO-DAY MANAGEMENT

Supervisors are essential to a business because they are responsible for the work of employees in the business. Each employee gets direction from a supervisor, and the supervisor is responsible for the work of each employee. It is important that supervisors are able to manage effectively their own work and the work of the employees for which they are responsible. Supervisors are responsible for planning, organizing, implementing, and controlling the daily work of their units.

Several management activities are important for day-to-day management. Those activities and the tools used to complete those activities are shown in Fig. 24-3.

Supervisors complete daily planning through the use of work schedules. Schedules are used to identify the work to be done and to plan the work of each employee. Supervisors decide what days of the week employees will work and which projects they will complete. If they schedule too few people, the work will not be completed. If too many employees are scheduled, costs will increase.

Time management is an important management skill for supervisors. A great deal of work must be done in a short time. Supervisors must be able to determine the work to be done, set priorities for the most important work, and ensure that it is completed. They must not only use their time effectively, but must help their employees determine how their time can be used most effectively each day.

Supervisors communicate every day with their employees. While much of the communication between supervisors and employees is oral, written communications are used as well. Whether oral or written, communications must be specific and clear. Supervisors need to plan their communications, determine the best method, and the best place and time to communicate the information. Supervisors should follow up on communications to ensure they are understood. Listening is an important communication skill for supervisors.

The final daily management skill for supervisors is quality control. A great deal of time is spent in some companies correcting errors and redoing work that was not done well the first time. Supervisors can reduce those problems by planning work carefully, developing quality standards, and checking the quality of the work being done regularly. In addition, supervisors can help employees

Work Schedules

Employee Weekly Time Sheet

NAME			DEPARTMENT		LOCATION
EMPLOYEE NUMBER		SOCIAL SECURITY NUMBER	PAYROLL CLASSIFICATION	SHIFT	FILE NUMBER

COMPLETE WEEKLY AND SUBMIT TO SUPERVISOR ON   EACH WEEK

DAY OF WEEK	MORNING		AFTERNOON		OVERTIME		FOR OFFICE USE	
	IN	OUT	IN	OUT	IN	OUT	REGULAR	OVERTIME
MONDAY								
TUESDAY								
WEDNESDAY								
THURSDAY								
FRIDAY								
SATURDAY								
SUNDAY								
TOTALS								

THIS FORM MUST BE RECEIVED IN PAYROLL BY _____ AM/PM ON _____ EACH WEEK.	SENT TO PAYROLL _____ AM/PM ON		RECEIVED IN PAYROLL _____ AM/PM ON	
	EMPLOYEE SIGNATURE	DATE	DEPARTMENT SUPERVISOR	DATE
	SUPERVISOR SIGNATURE	DATE	PAYROLL DEPARTMENT	DATE

Time Schedules

1 THURSDAY
DECEMBER, 19-- • 335th Day, 30 Days Left • 48th Week

APPOINTMENTS & SCHEDULED EVENTS   DAILY AND WORK RECORD

8
9
10
11
12
1
2
3
4
5
6
7
8

TO BE DONE TODAY (ACTION LIST)   EXPENSE & REIMBURSEMENT RECORD

Fig. 24-3

Common tools used by supervisors for day-to-day management.

Memos and Reports

ARBOR SHOES
MEMORANDUM

TO: Peter, Isabelle, Anita
CC: Philip, Marie
FROM: Adam
DATE: 10/25/--
SUBJECT: Holiday Promotions

Just a quick update on the plans for Holiday 19--. As you know, the marketing mix for fourth quarter will depend more heavily than ever on in-store promotions to gain that all-important impulse purchase.

Women's Dress and Evening Shoe Promotion

The tentative theme for the women's dress and evening shoe promotion is lights: *Styles to light up your holidays.* Components of the promotion include:
- Special lighted display
- 4-color flyer featuring sequined evening wear
- Sparkle-in-the-dark earrings with purchase

Evaluation Checklists

Personnel Evaluation

□ QUARTERLY   □ SEMI-ANNUAL   □ ANNUAL

EMPLOYEE		EMPLOYEE NUMBER	GRADE LEVEL	LAST EVALUATION DATE
TITLE		DEPARTMENT	LOCATION	PHONE

EVALUATION AREAS	POOR	FAIR	SATIS.	GOOD	EXCELLENT	BRIEF COMMENTS
KNOWLEDGE OF JOB						
ACHIEVES PLANNED RESULTS						
FELLOW EMPLOYEE RELATIONS						
CONSISTENCY						
QUALITY OF WORK						
ATTENDANCE RECORD						
ATTITUDE						

GENERAL COMMENTS

THIS EVALUATION □ WAS □ WAS NOT (SEE BELOW) DISCUSSED WITH EMPLOYEE ON

I HAVE READ THIS EVALUATION, MADE MY COMMENTS ON THE BACK OF THIS FORM, AND MY SIGNATURE DOES NOT NECESSARILY INDICATE THAT I AGREE WITH THIS EVALUATION.	SUPERVISOR'S SIGNATURE		DATE
	SUPERVISOR'S SIGNATURE		DATE
EMPLOYEE	DATE	PERSONNEL OFFICER'S SIGNATURE	DATE

recognize the importance of quality work so the employees will take responsibility for reducing errors and controlling costs.

IMPROVING SUPERVISORY SKILLS

One of the most difficult problems facing new supervisors is to spend less time on the non-managerial activities of the job and more time on management functions. Because supervisors are usually skilled employees, they often want to continue to do the work they were doing before being promoted. There are times when it doesn't appear their employees are doing the job as well as it can be done. Therefore, new supervisors are often tempted to do the job themselves. But supervisors need to rely on their employees to get the work done so they can concentrate on management activities.

Today, more companies are helping supervisors to develop and improve their management skills. Some companies provide formal training programs for new supervisors. They might, for instance, participate in management classes on a full-time basis for a few weeks, then continue training through a series of meetings and short training sessions. Or they might study training materials, such as books and audio or video tapes, for several months after they begin their supervisory duties. Other companies help supervisors develop their skills by paying for their attendance at management classes at a nearby college.

If companies do not provide training, the new supervisor needs to develop management skills individually by enrolling in classes, attending meetings, reading management books and magazines, participating in professional associations for managers, and other similar activities. Talking with and observing the work of experienced supervisors is another way to improve management skills.

USING MANAGEMENT INFORMATION

To do a good job of planning, organizing, implementing, and controlling, managers must have a great deal of information available. Records on production and sales, personnel, expenses, and profit or loss are needed before decisions can be made. Data must be collected, organized, and made available to managers so decisions can be made quickly and efficiently.

Even in very small businesses, the manager is unable to remember all of the information needed to make decisions. In large companies with many managers and hundreds of employees, it is impossible to operate without a systematic way to gather information for managers to use in decision making.

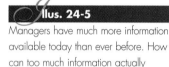

Illus. 24-5

Managers have much more information available today than ever before. How can too much information actually decrease a manager's effectiveness?

Bruce Ayres/Tony Stone Images

MANAGEMENT INFORMATION SYSTEMS

Management information systems were described in detail earlier in the textbook. Every company needs such a system as an important management tool. The management information systems of large companies use a mainframe or minicomputer to process all of the information needed by management. Because of the development of time-sharing systems and desktop computers with easy-to-use software, and the low cost of those systems, small companies are also using computer technology for information management. Managers find computers to be very helpful in controlling business operations.

Managers can use information systems to reduce the amount of time spent on controlling activities. If a manager reviewed all of the information collected on the operations in a business, there would be little time for other activities. Computers can be used to monitor the performance of activities in a company. If activities are performed as planned and standards are met, no management attention is needed. Differences between planned and actual performance are known as **variances**. When the computer identifies performance that is below standard, a variance report is printed for the manager. The **variance report** identifies standards that are not being met and the amount of difference between the standard and the actual performance. Through the use of the reports, managers can identify problems quickly and use their time to solve those problems.

BUSINESS RESEARCH

Management information systems are designed to provide needed data to managers so decisions can be made and problems can be solved. However, there are times when new problems arise or information is not available to answer questions or solve problems. When managers are unable to make decisions because of a lack of information, they may need to conduct research.

Business research is conducted in many areas to aid in decision making. Marketing research and product development research are two common areas. Personnel research studies are conducted on such topics as employee motivation and training techniques. Financial executives need the results of research that deal with decisions related to borrowing and investing. Research results are also needed regarding economic factors, such as those related to inflationary trends and forecasts of the level of economic activity for the country and for a particular type of business. The research described as well as other types of research help executives make important decisions relative to the growth and development of their companies.

Much of the needed business research is, of course, done by business itself. Most large companies have research departments or divisions that engage in research projects related to the specific problems of the company. Since research departments are expensive to maintain, small companies must depend to a considerable degree on professional research organizations.

Bureaus of business research and faculty members in universities conduct studies that are helpful to business. Extensive research is undertaken by various divisions of the federal government, and much of this research is available to and useful for business. Research studies that are useful to particular industries are made by trade associations. There are also many research organizations and individual consultants that may be used by a company to conduct a particular research study.

DECISION MAKING

In the process of planning, organizing, implementing, and controlling, managers are faced with problems that require making decisions. Some decisions are made at the top level of management, such as new products to be developed or markets that the business will enter. Other decisions are made by middle management, which may result in new ways of organizing work or different standards for evaluating performance. First-level managers such as department heads and supervisors make decisions about the daily operations of their units. It is important to the overall success of any business that the decisions be made as carefully as possible at every level of management.

PROBLEMS AND DECISION MAKING

Generally, a **problem** is a difficult situation requiring a solution. Problems usually do not have single solutions; instead, they have a series of possible solutions. There may be several good solutions, but there may also be several poor solutions. For example, the problem may be to find the most effective and efficient method to ship products from Texas to Illinois. Possible solutions are to ship by airplane, boat, train, or truck. Depending on the circumstances, any one of the shipping methods could be the best or the worst solution. To find the best solution, managers should follow a systematic approach to solving problems. That procedure is outlined in Fig. 24-4.

Fig. 24-4

Developing an effective solution to a problem.

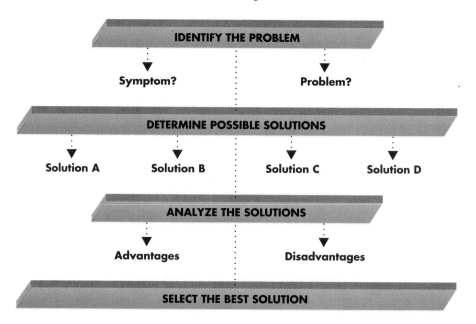

STEPS IN PROBLEM SOLVING

Every problem can be analyzed by following a series of steps. These steps include identifying the problem, listing possible solutions, analyzing the possible solutions, and selecting the best solution.

Identify the Problem

Before a manager can make a decision to solve a problem, the problem must first be located and identified. Often, a manager may not even be aware that a problem exists. For example, employees may be unhappy about another worker. The problem may not be known to a manager unless employees communicate this concern or it begins to affect their work.

A manager must also be careful not to identify a symptom as the problem. A **symptom** is a sign or indication of something that appears to be the problem. When a patient complains of a headache, the headache may be a symptom. The problem could be high blood pressure, a cold, or other illness. Falling sales in an appliance store is a symptom. The problem could be ineffective advertising, a bad store location, untrained sales people, low-quality products, poor service, and so on. Therefore, it will be difficult to change the symptom until the problem can be identified and corrected.

What are some reasons that sales are declining? Are fewer customers entering the appliance store? Are customers entering the store but not buying? Are customers buying but then returning the products because they are not performing as expected? Managers can often identify the problem by asking questions. The symptom can be used to identify questions that can isolate the problem.

Sometimes managers are unaware that problems exist until it is too late. They need regularly to review plans and performance to determine if operations are proceeding as planned. When any evidence appears that suggests a problem, it should be studied carefully rather than ignored. It is better to review symptoms and determine that there is no problem rather than to wait until problems are so big they are difficult to correct.

List Possible Solutions

Once a problem has been identified, a manager should begin to list all possible solutions. For example, if the problem is determining the best advertising medium to use, all possible ways to advertise should be listed. Every problem has at least two or more possible solutions, and no solution should be overlooked at this point in the problem-solving process.

There are many ways to identify possible solutions. Brainstorming, as discussed in an earlier chapter, is one method to develop a long list that can later be analyzed. Managers should review solutions that have been used in the past or that were considered for solving related problems. Discussing the problems with other managers helps to identify solutions. Reading and studying can keep managers aware of new types of solutions. Many managers recognize that employees and customers are sources of possible solutions.

Analyze the Solutions

The third step in problem solving is to analyze the solutions. This is done by studying each possible solution separately, comparing the solutions, and reducing the number of solutions to the best two or three. To study each solution thoroughly and objectively, information may be needed from business records, trade associations, libraries, consultants, and government sources. The use of management information and business research described earlier in this chapter is an important part of this step.

When all of the necessary information has been collected, the strengths and weaknesses of each solution are examined one by one. Then the solutions are compared. An attempt is made to classify the solutions in some way, such as extremely desirable, somewhat desirable, and least desirable. Some solutions may be too costly or impractical, while others may be inexpensive or be very practical. For example, in a list of solutions containing advertising media being considered by a small appliance store, it may be found that television is far too costly while newspaper advertising is quite inexpensive. After all the analyses have been completed, there may be two or three solutions that will effectively solve the problem.

For very important decisions, the managers may want to conduct an experiment to test one or more solutions. A likely solution is often tested in one part of the organization to see how it works. The results are then compared with other tests to determine which was more effective in solving the problem before using it throughout the business. The results of the experiment are analyzed to eliminate some solutions and to identify those that seem to be effective.

Select the Best Solution

The last step in problem solving is to make the final decision from among the remaining solutions. Some problems have to be solved quickly, but for very important decisions, managers take several days or more before selecting the solution. Only after much thought and deliberation is the final decision made and put into action. For certain problems, a manager may be able to make the decision and implement the solution. For others, the manager may need to seek the approval or cooperation of other managers first.

After a solution is selected, the manager will determine the best way to implement it and who will be a part of implementing the solution. As implementation occurs, the manager will gather information to determine if the solution is solving the problem or if additional efforts or even another solution is necessary.

BUILDING VOCABULARY POWER

Define the following terms and concepts.

1. management
2. planning
3. organizing
4. implementing
5. controlling
6. manager
7. supervisor
8. executive
9. mid-manager
10. variances
11. variance report
12. problem
13. symptom

REVIEWING FACTS

1. Do managers in both small and large companies perform similar types of activities?
2. Would a person who is responsible for planning and organizing the work for one job be considered a manager?
3. Which of the four management functions is performed most often by supervisors?
4. What employee qualifications are often used to select new supervisors?
5. What are the two factors that are used to determine the effectiveness of a supervisor's job?
6. Do supervisors have responsibility for employee evaluation? Why or why not?
7. What can new supervisors do to improve their management skills if the company does not have a training program?
8. Why is it important that data are collected, organized, and made available for managers?
9. What has made it possible for small companies to use computer technology for information management?
10. How do managers use variance reports?
11. What are some areas in which managers use business research?
12. How is a problem different from a symptom?
13. Why should managers identify more than one possible solution to a problem?
14. What are some ways to identify possible solutions to a problem?
15. What does a manager do after a solution is selected?

DISCUSSING IDEAS

1. How could a worker perform all four of the management functions and still not be a manager?
2. Why would large companies need middle-level managers who spend most of their time on one management function such as controlling?
3. List the advantages and disadvantages that Anton Jacobs should consider when deciding whether to apply for the supervisor's position at Freeden Computers.
4. What are some reasons that the best employee in a job may not make the best supervisor for other people in that job?
5. Why are most supervisors required to divide their time between supervisory responsibilities and other work?
6. Of the five areas of responsibility listed in Fig. 24-2, which do you believe is the most important to the success of the company and why?
7. What are some ways that supervisors can help employees manage their time better?
8. What skills do supervisors and other managers need to use to manage business information effectively?
9. Should all managers be involved in problem solving or should that be a responsibility of experienced managers and executives?
10. How can employees and customers assist with problem solving?

ANALYZING INFORMATION

1. Assume that your class has decided to hold an auction to raise funds for a charity. The auction will sell used, but useful, items that students and their families have in their homes but no longer need. Develop a chart with four headings: planning, organizing, implementing, controlling. Under each heading list the management activities that would have to be completed in order for a successful auction to be held.
2. During one month, three managers recorded the number of hours they spent on each of the four management functions. Mr. Groen spent 42 hours on planning activities, 26 hours on organizing activities, 83 hours on implementing activities, and 57 hours on controlling activities. Ms. Frink used 65 hours on planning, 24 hours on organizing, 36 hours on implementing, and 59 hours on controlling. Mr. Harrod spent 18 hours planning, 40 hours organizing, 60 hours implementing, and 74 hours controlling. For each manager, determine the total hours worked during the month and the percent of time devoted to each management function. Then determine the total percent of time spent by the three managers on each of the functions. Develop a chart to illustrate the results.

REVIEW 24

3. Keep a record of how you spend your time for two days. Record your activities for every half hour. After you have completed the list, review the use of your time. Identify the times when you believe you were using time effectively and the time when you believe you were not using time effectively. Then prepare a set of written recommendations on how you could more effectively manage your time in the future.

4. Identify an experienced supervisor who you can interview. Discuss information management with the supervisor. Prepare a chart with the following headings to focus your discussion on information available for decision making: Type of Information; Source of Information; Form of Information; Use of Information. Complete the chart with as many types of information as possible. Compare your chart with those prepared by your classmates.

5. A list of symptoms of business problems follows. For each symptom, write a question that could be used to help identify the actual problem.
   a. The rate of merchandise returns has increased greatly in the last six months in a department store.
   b. A new employee quits without giving notice.
   c. Advertising costs have increased by 10 percent this year.
   d. The number of customer accounts with debts over 60 days old is increasing.
   e. There have been a number of times that the assembly line has had to be stopped due to defective materials.

S OLVING BUSINESS PROBLEMS

CASE 24-1

Yvette and Eric are both considering careers as managers. One day they were discussing their views of a manager's work. The following conversation took place:

Eric: A manager's job is really very easy if the company hires good employees. All a manager has to do is make sure the work gets done.

Yvette: I think a manager has to be a good planner. If a manager can tell employees what to do, the employees will take it from there.

Eric: I wonder why companies have so many managers and spend time and money on management development.

Yvette: If you ask me, you are either a good manager or you are not. I do not think that taking classes in how to manage a company will do much good.

Eric: I agree. When you think about all of the different types of managers, there cannot be too many common things you could teach all managers.

Required:
1. Analyze the views of Yvette and Eric toward management. Do you agree or disagree?

2. Do you believe companies have too many managers and spend too much time and money on management training?
3. Can people be taught to be better managers?
4. What characteristics are common to all managers' jobs?

CASE 24-2

Jackson Blaine is the manager of the accounting department for the Overton Supply Company, an office supplies wholesaler. A standard was established that invoices would be keyed and mailed to customers within 24 hours after the order was received. Recently, Jackson learned that some invoices were not being mailed until three or four days after the order was received. Upon checking further, he discovered that his department did not always receive the necessary information from the shipping department on schedule.

Required:
1. What are some possible problems in this situation?
2. List the symptoms of the problems.
3. What are some alternative solutions?
4. How would you suggest that Jackson should proceed in this situation?

THE MANAGER AS LEADER CHAPTER

After studying this chapter you will be able to:

25-1 Define the concept of leadership and important characteristics of leaders.

25-2 Identify five important human relations skills needed by managers.

25-3 Discuss two viewpoints of managers about employees' attitudes toward work.

25-4 Compare three different leadership styles used by managers and when each is most effective.

25-5 Describe the importance of work rules in a business and procedures managers should follow in enforcing them.

Tomorrow is the date of the election for the president of the Student Council. Mark and Ellen are reviewing the four candidates before deciding on the one for whom each will vote.

Mark: *I'm not sure of the best qualifications for Student Council president. We want someone who is well known and has a good image because the president has to attend a lot of functions and represent our school.*

Ellen: *But our problem is that students don't seem to have a voice in the school. We need someone who is a good communicator to convince the administrators to listen to the students.*

Mark: *Maybe we need a Student Council that does more work rather than just talking about the problems. The president has to be able to motivate the other members to solve the problems of the school.*

Ellen: *When you think about it, it is hard to find anyone who can give us everything we need in a Student Council president. Do we have anyone running who has all of the characteristics that are important?*

Chapter 25 613

Anyone who is responsible for an organization must have a number of qualities and characteristics to meet their responsibilities successfully. Whether the president of a student group, the owner of a small business, or the supervisor of a department in a large company, each needs to be able to provide leadership in order for the organization to be effective. Understanding leadership and developing leadership skills is important for those who are planning for a career in business.

THE IMPORTANCE OF LEADERSHIP

Many years ago, it was assumed that managers had total authority over the employees in a business. The goal of management was to get the work of the business done. Therefore, it was expected that managers would tell employees what to do and the employees would complete the work as expected.

Today, we recognize that management is not that simple. To get work done effectively, employees must understand why the work is important and want to do the work. Managers who are able to earn the respect and cooperation of employees are known as leaders. They are much more effective than the managers who rely on the old approach to employee-manager relationships.

Leadership is the ability to influence individuals and groups to achieve organizational goals. Leadership includes the ability to apply effective human relations skills. **Human relations** refers to how well people get along together. Good human relations exist in a group of people who get along well together. In contrast, if poor human relations exist, a group then will have arguments, misunderstandings, hostility, and suspicion. Individuals, and often the entire group, will do things that interfere with the group's success rather than contributing to it.

Illus. 25-1

An effective manager must be concerned about the human relations within the work group. What should a manager do when it appears a conflict is developing between two employees?

Jeff Greenberg, Photographer

All managers must be concerned about their relationships with employees. Each has some responsibility for managing the work of others. Supervisors have a special reason to develop effective employee relationships. Because the supervisor has direct responsibility for the work of people, it is important that the supervisor has effective leadership and human relations skills. Those skills can be developed, and most management training programs today emphasize leadership and effective human relations.

LEADERSHIP CHARACTERISTICS

While managers are involved in many activities, one of the most important is creating an atmosphere that encourages employees to do their best work in order to make the business successful. Individual workers, however, have their own goals and needs. The closer the work done for the business meets the needs of individual workers, the greater the satisfaction is for both. Managers must work to satisfy the needs of each employee while also meeting the goals of the business. Success in this task requires leadership.

Because the quality of leadership is directly related to the success of an organization, it is important that managers possess certain leadership characteristics. Leaders help employees get work done correctly and willingly. A poor supervisor may be able to get workers to perform the necessary tasks, but the work may be done poorly and reluctantly. A good supervisor, on the other hand, is able to influence workers so that they enjoy their work and take pride in doing a good job.

To get others to perform well requires certain leadership characteristics. The common characteristics that effective leaders possess are shown in Fig. 25-1 on page 616. Having those characteristics does not ensure that a person will be a good leader. Leaders must also have an understanding of the work that must be done, and the business in which they work must be well organized. In addition to leadership skills, managers must be able to plan, organize, implement, and control work.

Leadership differs with each situation. It calls for more or less of a certain trait. Two managers who possess most of the leadership qualities will probably perform differently in any given leadership situation.

INFLUENCING PEOPLE

Leadership is used to influence people to accomplish the work of an organization. However, there are both negative and positive ways to influence others. Just because a manager is able to get others to do what he or she wants does not mean that the manager is an effective leader.

Managers are able to influence employees because of their power. **Power** is the ability to control behavior. There are several ways that managers obtain power. The type of power will determine how employees respond to managers. Four types of power available to managers are summarized in Fig. 25-2 on page 617.

Fig. 25-1

Effective leaders possess most of these traits.

Basic Leadership Traits

INTELLIGENCE

A certain amount of intelligence is needed to direct others. Leaders use their intelligence to study, learn, and improve their management skills. They also help the people they work with to learn and develop new skills. Leaders must use their intelligence effectively.

JUDGMENT

Leaders must make many decisions. They consider all facts carefully; apply knowledge, experience, and new information; and use good judgment.

OBJECTIVITY

Leaders must be able to look at all sides of a problem and not make biased judgements or statements. They gather information and do not rush into actions before considering the possible results. They value individual differences, not stereotypes or first impressions.

INITIATIVE

Leaders have ambition and persistence in reaching goals. They are self-starters who plan what they want to do and then do it. They have drive and are highly motivated. They encourage others to take actions and make decisions when appropriate.

DEPENDABILITY

Those who lead are consistent in their actions, and others can rely on them. They do not make promises that cannot be fulfilled. When they make a commitment, they follow through, and expect others to do the same. The people they work with can count on leaders to help them.

COOPERATION

Leaders understand the importance of other people and enjoy being with them. Thus, they work well with others. They understand that people working together can accomplish more than the same people working alone. They work to develop cooperative relations.

HONESTY

Leaders are honest and have high standards of personal integrity. They are ethical in decisions and their treatment of others.

COURAGE

Leaders possess the courage to make unpopular decisions and try new approaches in solving problems. They are willing to take risks to support others.

CONFIDENCE

Leaders have a great deal of self-confidence. They attempt to make the best decisions possible and trust their own judgment. They respect others and expect quality work.

STABILITY

Leaders are not highly emotional. You can depend on their reactions. They can help others to solve problems and reduce conflicts.

UNDERSTANDING

Leaders recognize that the feelings and ideas of others are important. They try to understand the people they work with. They encourage others to share their ideas, experiences, and opinions and show that each person is a valuable member of the organization.

TYPE OF POWER	RESULTS FROM
Position	The manager's position in the organization
Reward	The manager's control of rewards/punishments
Expert	The manager's knowledge and skill
Identity	The employee's perception of the manager

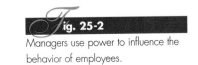

Fig. 25-2
Managers use power to influence the behavior of employees.

Position power comes from the position the manager holds in the organization. If a manager is an employee's boss, it is usually assumed that that manager can give directions and expect the employee to complete that work. If the manager does not supervise the employee, the employee would not expect to have to respond to that manager's request.

Reward power is based on the ability to control resources, rewards, and punishments. If a manager is able to determine who receives new equipment, needed supplies, and wage and salary increases, or to determine penalties for poor work or inappropriate performance, employees are likely to respond to the requests of that manager.

Expert power is given to people who are considered the most knowledgeable. When people are unsure of how to perform a task or what information is needed to solve a problem, they may turn to an expert. That person will be able to influence behavior because of the knowledge and skill he or she has.

Identity power is given to people because others identify with and want to be accepted by them. If an employee respects a manager and wants positive recognition from that person, the employee will likely do what the manager requests.

An analysis of the types of power shows that managers can influence their employees because of position or because of the rewards and punishments they control. However, those types of power are not related to the leadership characteristics discussed earlier. Employees do not determine those types of power; they are established because of the manager's position in the company.

Two types of power are given to the manager by employees. If employees consider the manager to be an expert, they will seek the manager's advice and help. If employees want the approval of the manager, they will respond to the requests of the manager. Both expert and identity power are related to effective leadership characteristics.

Sometimes people other than managers have power in an organization. Other employees can influence people's behavior because they can control rewards and punishments, are considered experts, or because other employees identify with them and want their approval. If those powerful employees support the work of the organization, they can have a positive influence on other employees. On the other hand, employees with power can be disruptive if they have different needs and goals than the organization. Employees may choose to be influenced by those people rather than by their managers.

DEVELOPING LEADERSHIP SKILLS

Leadership is important in the business world. Managers are often hired and evaluated on the basis of leadership characteristics. Through training and personal development, individuals can improve their leadership qualities. People can learn to be dependable, to have initiative, to cooperate with others, and so on. Training and experience can improve a manager's judgment in making business decisions. For the most part, people are not born to be leaders. Everyone can become an effective leader with preparation and practice.

Illus. 25-2

Selection procedures for managers often emphasize leadership characteristics. What are some ways a person's leadership ability could be evaluated in an employment interview?

Managers are not the only people in an organization who need leadership skills. Many businesses are using employee teams to plan work and make decisions. The team may include a manager, although many do not. Even when a manager is a part of the team, the leader of the group will not always be the manager. As the team completes various projects, individual team members may assume leadership for specific activities.

Companies evaluate the leadership abilities of employees when they are hired. Someone who has already developed many of the leadership characteristics and has had leadership experience will often be given preference in hiring. Training programs for employees emphasize team building and leadership development. Some companies allow employees to volunteer for leadership training while others expect everyone to be involved. Companies recognize that employees with leadership skills can make valuable contributions to their success.

HUMAN RELATIONS

Managers are continually in contact with employees, other managers, customers, and people from outside the business. Because of these contacts, the need for human relations skills is great. Earlier in the chapter, human relations was defined as how well people get along together. It is the manager's responsibility to work well with others and to help employees get along as well as possible with each other.

Several skills are involved in effective human relations. Those skills may be just as important to the success of a business as the skill to make decisions or the skill to operate a complicated piece of equipment. Human relations skills may be as difficult to develop as the other business skills listed. The important human relations skills needed by managers are (1) self-understanding, (2) understanding of others, (3) communication, (4) group building, and (5) developing job satisfaction.

SELF UNDERSTANDING

In order to work well with others, managers must have self understanding. Self understanding involves an awareness of your attitudes and opinions, your leadership style, your decision-making style, and your relationships with other people.

Employees look to managers for information and directions. They want managers to be able to make decisions, solve problems, and communicate expectations. If managers understand themselves and what other people expect of them, they can decide on the best way to work with people and the leadership style to use. They can use the understanding of their strengths, weaknesses, and how others perceive them to improve their skills as managers.

UNDERSTANDING OTHERS

Every individual is different. Each person has a different background as well as different attitudes, skills, and needs. A manager cannot treat everyone in the same way. Some people need a great deal of supervision; others do not. Some employees want to help make decisions, while others do not care to be involved in the decision-making process. Some people work harder when praised; others need to be criticized occasionally.

Managers need to know the best way to work with each employee. They need to be able to satisfy individual workers' needs and, at the same time, accomplish the goals of the company. The manager who understands the needs of employees will be a better manager.

COMMUNICATION

In an earlier chapter, you learned the importance of communication in business. Managers spend much of their time communicating. When breakdowns in communication occur, human relations problems are likely to develop.

Managers must understand what information needs to be communicated and what methods to use. They need to know when too much communication is occurring and when there is not enough. Managers must have skill in using official communications channels and in understanding informal channels.

Illus. 25-3

Many human relations problems occur when managers fail to recognize the unique qualities and differences among employees. Do you believe all employees should be treated the same by a manager? Why or why not?

Jeff Greenberg, Photographer

Managers do not just provide information, although they must be skilled in both written and oral communications. Listening is an important communication skill as well. By listening to employee concerns, managers can identify problems, determine needs, and respond to them more effectively.

GROUP BUILDING

When people in a company work well together, the company is able to produce more and be more profitable. When problems exist among people, it is difficult for a business to be successful.

People need to feel that they are a part of a group, that they are important, and that they can count on other group members for help. Managers that have group building skills are able to get people to work well together to accomplish the goals of the company. Groups that take responsibility for work and pride in the results reduce the amount of time managers must spend in monitoring the work of the group and ensuring that the work is completed.

DEVELOPING JOB SATISFACTION

Most people who work at a job for a reasonable length of time are not totally satisfied or dissatisfied with their jobs. However, some people enjoy their work much more than others. An employee's feelings about work may be very different from one day to the next. There are many reasons for these differences in job satisfaction. It can be influenced by factors such as the personal characteristics of employees and managers, the needs of the individuals, and the nature of the work itself.

Jeff Greenberg, Photographer

Managers must be aware of these factors if they want to deal effectively with employees and want to help employees maintain a high level of job satisfaction. For example, when two people with different backgrounds, values, and needs are asked to work together, there is a chance that human relations problems will arise. When individual needs are not satisfied or employees are not happy with their work, managers must be aware that problems are likely to occur.

People should be carefully matched with the kind of work they perform because personal characteristics can affect job performance. A shy person, or one who enjoys working alone, might perform better as a computer data entry operator rather than as a salesperson. A person who does not pay close attention to details may not be an effective quality inspector on a production line. Human resources departments often test new employees or those seeking a promotion in order to match people with appropriate jobs. Supervisors and other managers need to be careful when assigning tasks to employees. Whenever possible, they should match the job tasks with the needs and interests of the employees.

VIEWPOINTS ABOUT WORKERS

While management jobs include the same basic functions, the way individual managers deal with employees may be very different. Each manager has attitudes about people and work. Those attitudes help determine how the manager makes decisions, relates to other people, and treats employees. Studies have found that many managers have very different views of their employees. Some managers believe employees dislike work, while other managers have the opposite opinion.

DISLIKE FOR WORK

Some managers believe that employees dislike work and avoid it whenever possible. With this attitude, the manager is likely to assume that workers will not work any harder than necessary and will try to avoid responsibility. These managers expect that they will have to find ways to force employees to put forth the effort necessary for the organization to achieve its goals. They do not assume that employees will take individual initiative or be concerned about the quality of their work. As a result of these beliefs, this kind of manager closely supervises and controls workers and makes all important decisions.

ENJOYMENT OF WORK

A manager who believes employees generally enjoy their work will relate to people in a very different manner. These managers believe that employees obtain satisfaction from doing a job well. They assume that employees like responsibility and try to meet the goals of the organization as well as their own goals. Employees do not need close supervision and control if they like their work. The manager with this set of beliefs asks workers for their suggestions and ideas on how to complete the work. Employees are allowed a great deal of control over their own work and are not supervised closely.

A CHANGING VIEW OF EMPLOYEES

Studies have found that neither of the previous views is correct for all workers and all jobs. Although many managers tend to favor one viewpoint over the other, the manager who changes from one viewpoint to the other as circumstances change is likely to be the more effective manager. For example, a supervisor knows that for the jobs workers strongly dislike, closer supervision and control are needed. When employees are doing work they enjoy, less supervision and control are needed. Flexibility in a manager's viewpoint toward workers permits flexibility in their treatment.

Managers can influence whether employees like or dislike their work. When new employees are hired in a business, they are usually excited about the work and want to do a good job. Only when they find out the work is not something they enjoy or when they believe their manager does not trust them will they begin to require additional management attention.

If an employee or a group of workers does not seem to enjoy the work, things can be done to change attitudes. The manager can work with the employees to determine the reasons for their attitudes and to find out what they like and dislike about their work. The manager can find opportunities to involve employees, treat them with respect, and ensure that they have the opportunity to do work they enjoy. In that way, the manager may be able to begin to change employees' attitudes and gradually reduce the amount of supervision and control required.

LEADERSHIP STYLE

The general way a manager treats and directs employees is called **leadership style**. It includes the way a manager gives directions, handles problems, and makes decisions. Leadership style is influenced by many factors, including the manager's background, personality, and beliefs about whether employees like or dislike work. Because leadership style is influenced by numerous factors, each manager has a slightly different style from all other managers. However, leadership styles fall into three general categories. Those categories are autocratic, democratic, and open leadership.

AUTOCRATIC LEADERSHIP

The **autocratic leader** is one who gives direct, clear, and precise orders with detailed instructions as to what, when, and how work is to be done. Employees do not make decisions about the work being performed. When questions or problems arise, the leader handles them. Those who work for autocratic managers routinely perform tasks with little or no personal involvement in the work itself.

Efficiency is one of the reasons for using the autocratic style. The work is completed exactly the way the manager expects. Each worker generally has a clear idea of what is expected, and when there is doubt about how to perform, the manager is consulted. The autocratic leader believes that managers know what must be done and how it should be done to best achieve the goals of the organization. It is also assumed that workers do not have the knowledge or skills necessary to plan and carry out the work.

While some workers prefer leaders with autocratic styles, many others do not. A major disadvantage of the autocratic style is that it discourages employees from thinking about better ways of doing their work. As a result, some employees become bored and lose interest in their work. This type of leadership may lead to a decline in the quality and quantity of work. Human relations problems sometimes occur when supervisors use only an autocratic style. Certain employees are unsatisfied when they have limited opportunities to participate in decisions affecting their work. They begin to resent their supervisor and their company.

The autocratic style is effective in some situations. For example, it is often the best style to use in emergencies. Getting out a large rush order, for example, does not allow time for a supervisor to discuss the order with employees. It is much more efficient for a supervisor to give specific orders and to expect a rapid response. An autocratic style is often needed with temporary employees, such as part-time workers hired for short periods of time. The effective leader is one who knows when a situation calls for an autocratic style of leadership and uses it until that situation is over.

Ethical Issues

EMPLOYEE MANAGEMENT

Questions:

1. What are the advantages and disadvantages of the two solutions identified by the employee team?

2. What responsibility does the employee team have to management and to other employees in making a recommendation?

3. What recommendation do you believe the employee team should make? Why?

4. Do you believe that under the traditional autocratic management philosophy the same decision would be made? Why or why not?

The members of the third unit employee team of the EndCore Company were excited about their new responsibilities. EndCore is a packaging manufacturer. The third unit produces cardboard boxes. EndCore led the industry in total box sales for twenty years. However, during the past five years, they lost their market position and fell to fifth place in sales. The competition had improved quality and were able to undercut EndCore in product prices.

EndCore employees were trained for specific production jobs that had changed little over time. The management structure was very autocratic with managers responsible for all decisions. The company had a detailed list of work rules, which were strictly enforced. Employee-management relations were often strained.

Because of the declining performance, EndCore management decided to implement a new democratic management philosophy. Employee work teams would be formed to share in decision making with management. The company made a commitment to the new philosophy, the teams were formed, and training was provided to prepare the company for the new structure.

Now the unit three team had to find ways to reduce production costs so the company could price its boxes closer to the competition. The team reviewed all major manufacturing procedures in the unit to identify ways to cut costs. They developed several methods to change the way work was done and boxes were assembled for a cost savings of about 4 percent. This was an important savings, leaving the company's costs just slightly higher than those of competitors.

Just before making a final report to management, the team learned of a new automatic glue machine that was coming on the market. EndCore always hand-glued its boxes because the quality of the seals was much better. Gluing was a major part of the process, with over 15 percent of the employees used as box gluers. The new machine completely automated the gluing process and increased the speed with which boxes could be assembled. It had a 98 percent reliability rating—equal to the hand-gluing method. The cost of the machines was just under $1 million. However, the cost would be recovered in three years because production could be increased by 5 percent with a reduction in labor costs of 12 percent. Overall, using the gluing machines was estimated to cut the unit's production costs by almost 7 percent, which would put them below competitors' costs by more than 2 percent.

The employee team had found the solution needed by the company to make it competitive. However, implementing that solution would mean that at least 30 employees would lose their jobs.

DEMOCRATIC LEADERSHIP

The **democratic leader** is one who encourages workers to share in making decisions about work-related problems. When using the democratic style, managers discuss problems and solutions with employees, rather than merely announcing decisions. The manager may still make the final decision but only after discussing possible solutions with employees. Even when a decision is not involved, the democratic manager provides workers with assistance or encouragement and offers reasons about why certain work changes must occur. The principal characteristic of the democratic style, however, is that it gives workers an opportunity to become involved with the supervisor in the decision-making process.

Many workers prefer a manager who generally practices a democratic style of leadership. Employees who are permitted to influence decisions feel important and are more likely to carry out the decisions willingly. Workers who participate in the decision-making process are often highly motivated and, as a result, need not be as closely controlled and supervised.

As good as the democratic style may sound, however, it also has limitations. Not all people like to participate in decision making; some prefer to be told when and how to work. Also, the democratic style is time consuming because time must be taken from work to discuss problems. Furthermore, many jobs are fairly routine with little opportunity available for sharing in decision making. Workers sometimes become upset when they are asked to help make decisions on only unimportant matters.

The democratic leadership style is effective in many situations, especially when employees are interested in their work and are looking for more responsibility. It is also effective when workers have the knowledge to determine how best to perform their jobs. That is usually true for experienced or well-trained employees. When special problems arise and the manager wants to gather as many helpful ideas as possible, the democratic style is effective. Managers who assume that employees enjoy work are usually comfortable with this leadership style.

OPEN LEADERSHIP

The **open leader** is a manager who gives little or no direction to workers. Employees are given general instructions on the work to be done, but methods, details, and decisions are left to each individual. In the open style, any employee may become the leader when certain decisions must be made. Generally, each worker concentrates on specific tasks and is not often involved in the tasks of others.

The open style works best with experienced workers and in businesses where few major changes occur. If people have their own specialized jobs and are experts at them, the manager might use this style of leadership. If people work in many different locations, such as sales people or home-based employees, the open style may be required. Managers will not be able to control their work because of their location and it will not be feasible for groups of people to get together to make decisions.

Managers should be careful when using the open style of leadership with inexperienced employees or employees that have not been used to making their own decisions. When employees are not confident in their abilities or do not trust that managers will let them make their own decisions, they are likely to be ineffective with the open style. When effective teamwork is required, the open style can lead to confusion and lack of direction. Open leadership should be used very carefully and only after ensuring that employees are prepared for it and comfortable with the individual responsibility.

SITUATIONAL LEADERSHIP

The most effective manager is the one who selects a leadership style that best fits a particular situation. Whichever style is used, there are certain qualities that employees prefer in all managers. Those qualities are shown in Fig. 25-3.

Fig. 25-3

Employees prefer managers who possess these leadership qualities.

Employees prefer a manager who:

1. **Encourages employee participation and suggestions.**
2. **Keeps employees informed and shares employee ideas with upper management.**
3. **Works to build and maintain morale.**
4. **Is available to employees and easy to talk to.**
5. **Supports employee training and development.**
6. **Communicates effectively with employees.**
7. **Is considerate of the ideas and feelings of others.**
8. **Makes changes when needed rather than relying on past practices.**
9. **Supports employees who are doing their best even when mistakes are made.**
10. **Shows appreciation and provides recognition for good work.**

HANDLING EMPLOYEE PROBLEMS

Managers continually face the possibility of work-related problems. Conflicts between employees, disagreements with other managers, problems with customers, and other situations can make it difficult for the manager to accomplish the work of the business. Probably the most difficult situation faced by most managers is handling the personal problems of employees.

Sometimes employees face personal problems that affect their work. In most cases, the employee is able to resolve the problem, and it requires little or no action by the manager. At other times, a manager just needs to be sympathetic by listening to employees and showing an understanding of their situation. These situations occur infrequently, such as an employee who has an ill child or is late to work because of a transportation problem. Many businesses develop procedures that allow employees to deal with those types of problems.

In some situations, however, personal problems may be more serious and require more attention by managers. Problems such as drug or alcohol abuse, marital conflicts, or serious financial difficulties may result in employees being unable to perform their jobs well. Managers need to be aware of employees who are having difficulty on the job and try to determine the reasons for it. Then they need to work with the employee to get the necessary help to resolve the problem.

Illus. 25-5
Substance abuse is a serious problem in many communities. What are companies doing to reduce that problem in the workplace?

Jeff Greenberg, Photographer

Most managers are not trained to solve difficult personal problems, and they should not attempt it. But they should not ignore the problem either. Many business firms offer professional counseling and other services to help employees with personal problems. Managers need to make employees aware of those services and the importance of solving personal problems before they affect job performance. Managers should encourage employees to use the services available in the company when the problem first occurs. Then the manager should support the employee's decision to seek help.

Another potential human relations problem is disciplining workers who violate work rules. **Work rules** are regulations created to maintain an effective working environment in a business. There are certain expectations of employees that must be met if a business is to operate effectively. Those expectations might deal with hours of work, care of equipment, worker safety, and relationships among employees and between employees and management.

Many companies have developed work rules that apply to all employees. Other companies have unique sets of rules for workers in different divisions or for employees with different job classifications. For businesses with labor agreements, most important work rules are specified in the union contract.

Applicable procedures for handling violations and penalties are also specified. Procedures sometimes include an oral warning for the first violation, a written warning entered into the personnel file for the second violation, a short suspension, and finally termination if the problem continues. Penalties are usually more severe for serious violations of work rules. Also, there are normally protections for employees in the procedures that include hearings, appeals of penalties, and representation of the employee by the union.

If a business does not have a formal set of work rules, each manager needs to develop procedures and policies that tell employees what is expected of them and how the manager will resolve problems if they occur. If managers do not communicate expectations to employees and do not handle problems in a reasonable and equitable way, they soon lose the respect of the employees. Managers who involve employees in developing rules and procedures usually find greater support for those rules and fewer problems when penalties need to be applied for rules violations. Guidelines for managers to follow in enforcing work rules are listed in Fig. 25-4.

Management Guidelines for Enforcing Work Rules

Fig. 25-4

Employers must be objective, fair, and consistent when enforcing established work rules.

1. **Explain work rules and provide written copies of the rules to all employees.**
2. **Acquaint employees with penalties for work rule violations and make sure they understand the penalties as well as when and how they will be applied.**
3. **Investigate any violation thoroughly before taking action.**
4. **Consider any special circumstances before determining the violation and the penalty.**
5. **Act as soon as possible after investigating a violation and deciding on the action to be taken.**
6. **Inform the employee who violated a work rule of the rule that was violated, the penalty that will be applied, and the reason for the penalty.**
7. **Treat similar violations consistently.**
8. **Punish in private and praise in public.**
9. **Encourage employees to follow work rules by rewarding those who consistently follow the rules.**

Effective leaders are able to handle all types of work-related problems. The successful leader understands human behavior and applies good management and human relations principles in working with people. Conflicts certainly should not be created by the manager and usually are not. Even when conflicts and problems are created by others, they cannot be ignored. The effective manager tries at all times to help employees satisfy their own needs while also accomplishing the goals of the business.

BUILDING VOCABULARY POWER

Define the following terms and concepts.

1. leadership
2. human relations
3. power
4. position power
5. reward power
6. expert power
7. identity power
8. leadership style
9. autocratic leader
10. democratic leader
11. open leader
12. work rules

REVIEWING FACTS

1. If a manager has total authority over employees, how will work be assigned?
2. How do you know when good human relationships exist in a group?
3. What is required for managers to satisfy the needs of each employee while also meeting the goals of the business?
4. In addition to leadership characteristics, what is necessary for a person to be a good leader in business?
5. What are the characteristics of effective leaders?
6. What are examples of rewards managers can provide to employees?
7. What types of power are given to managers by employees?
8. Why do employees need leadership skills?
9. What are the important human relations skills needed by managers?
10. What are the two viewpoints managers have about workers?
11. What is involved in a manager's leadership style?
12. What type of leadership style is most effective for emergencies?
13. For what type of employees does the open leadership style typically work best?
14. What is the most difficult problem faced by most managers?
15. What should a manager do in a business that does not have a formal set of work rules?

DISCUSSING IDEAS

1. Why does the new approach to management work better than the old approach?
2. Is the leadership provided by the top executives of a company different than the leadership provided by supervisors?

3. Which are the most important leadership characteristics and why? Are there other characteristics of leaders not on the list that you believe are important?

4. What happens if managers use position and reward power but do not use the other two types?

5. What are some ways you can develop leadership skills while still in school?

6. It has been said that good leaders are born, not made. What evidence can you provide that the statement is not true?

7. Why do some managers continue to hold to the opinion that employees do not enjoy work even when it often leads to distrust and conflicts between employees and managers?

8. Why might a manager decide to use all three leadership styles at different times with the same group of employees?

9. Do you believe the characteristics that employees like to see in managers (Fig. 25-3) have changed from past years?

10. What types of procedures could companies develop to help employees deal with personal problems such as the illness of children, automobile trouble, dentist appointments, etc.? How would the procedures affect the profitability of the business?

A NALYZING INFORMATION

1. Identify ten people who are different in age, education, and work experience. In an interview with each, ask them to define the term "leadership." Then show them the list of characteristics shown in Fig. 25-1. Ask them to identify the top five from the list. Prepare a written report of the results of your interviews including one bar graph. Compare the results of your research with those of your classmates.

2. Select one of the five human relations skills discussed in the chapter or use the skill assigned to you by your teacher. Think of a situation that could occur in a business that demonstrates the effective or ineffective use of that skill. Then prepare a short script of dialogue between a manager and another person that illustrates the situation. Your scripts should contain at least four statements by each of the participants. After you have completed the script, review it with another classmate and then role play the situation for your classmates using the script. Your classmates should attempt to determine which human relations skill is being demonstrated and whether the role play demonstrates a positive or negative example of the skill.

3. Identify someone you believe is a good manager. Interview the person to determine their beliefs about (a) the use of power by a manager, (b) beliefs about whether people like or dislike work, and (c) leadership style. Prepare a chart that lists the major points on these topics from the textbook and compares these points with the viewpoints of the manager you interviewed. Share your findings in an oral report with your class.

REVIEW 25

4. With a group of your class members, brainstorm things supervisors can do to increase the job satisfaction of workers. Identify the things that would have a direct cost to the business and those that could be provided with no real cost to the business. Compare the list developed by your group with other groups in your class.

5. Compare the list of management guidelines for enforcing work rules in Fig. 25-4 with the procedures used by administrators and teachers to enforce the rules in your school. What are the similarities and differences?

S OLVING BUSINESS PROBLEMS

CASE 25-1

Sally Bensen had been a supervisor for five research specialists in the marketing department for nearly two years. The workers thought a great deal of Sally. In fact, many of them said she was the best supervisor they had ever had. Sally's manager, Juanita Sanchez, was most impressed with the good human relations among the employees and with the excellent work Sally's department did. The manager was so impressed that Sally was transferred to manage ten office assistants in the accounting department. Since Sally had prior accounting training and experience working as a bookkeeper, Juanita Sanchez thought she would be perfect in the new job.

After only two months, however, human relations in the accounting department had gone down and work output had declined. "What is happening, Sally?" Juanita asked. "Why isn't it working out?"

Sally responded, "I do not know. In the marketing department, I always discussed problems with the workers, and as a group we worked out solutions acceptable to everyone. In the accounting department, no one wants to discuss problems and solutions. They want me to solve all of the problems for them. That is just not my style."

Required:
1. Is it possible that a person might be an effective leader in one situation but not in another? Explain.
2. What type of leadership style does Sally practice?
3. Do you think that Sally would be more successful if she changed her leadership style to fit the situation in the accounting department? Explain.

CASE 25-2

Marge Faber was very upset because she had just suspended one of the employees she supervised, Josh Jordan. While he was a good worker, he had begun to develop a problem of coming to work late. Once, and sometimes twice, a week, he was five to ten minutes late.

The company had a policy on employee tardiness: a half hour of pay was deducted for any part of fifteen minutes the employee was late. If the employee was late more than thirty minutes, a verbal warning was given the first time, a written warning was given the second time, and the employee would be suspended for one week without pay for the third time.

Josh didn't seem to mind losing the money when he was late. Marge had talked to him recently about the problem, and he simply said he would try to do better. He had not been late for several weeks. Then two weeks ago, he was late thirty-five minutes on Tuesday. Last Thursday he was late by fifty minutes. Following company policy, Marge had given him both a verbal and written warning.

Yesterday, the city was hit by a heavy snowstorm. Because roads in the area were very slippery early in the morning, the company decided that employees who were late for work would not be penalized. Marge was surprised when Josh showed up on time. He said that he had used his new four wheel drive vehicle and had fun driving to work through the snow.

Today, Marge was furious when Josh walked in forty minutes late. She confronted him and told him he was suspended. Josh accused Marge of being unfair. He said the battery on his new vehicle had failed; otherwise, he would have been on time. Besides, the company hadn't penalized employees for tardiness yesterday, and then he had been on time. So, he shouldn't be penalized today.

Required:

1. What are the advantages and disadvantages of a policy such as the one described in the case?
2. Do you believe Josh Jordan was justified in his claim that Marge Faber was being unfair? Why or why not?
3. What do you think Marge should do after Josh returns from his suspension?

PLANNING AND ORGANIZING

After studying this chapter you will be able to:

26-1 Justify the use of a business plan for a new business.

26-2 Describe the five steps in strategic planning.

26-3 Provide examples of operational planning in a business.

26-4 List seven planning tools used by managers.

26-5 Identify four characteristics of a good organization.

26-6 Define two traditional types and one newer type of organization structure.

L isa O'Brien operates an antique furniture business called The Olde Tyme. It was established as a full-time business three years ago after operating for five years as a part-time business from Lisa's home. Lisa buys old furniture at auctions, flea markets, and yard sales. She then repairs and restores the furniture. The furniture is currently sold at a small store that she leases in a neighborhood shopping center.

When Lisa decided to change her business from part time to full time, she knew it would be expensive. She would need money for the store lease, for hiring several employees, for marketing expenses, and for increased operating expenses. When she approached her bank to borrow the money, the loan manager told her she would need to develop a business plan.

With the help of business faculty and students from the local college and materials provided by the Small Business Administration, Lisa studied the market, projected costs of operations, and wrote a business plan. Based on that plan, the bank loaned her the money to expand the business. Now, three years later, Lisa recognizes the importance of planning. She has followed a business plan and it has been a good guide for the development and operation of The Olde Tyme. She estimates that she spends over half of her time planning for the business. Some examples of those activities include determining the following:

- *The types and amounts of furniture to purchase.*
- *How much to spend on repairs and restoration.*
- *How to promote the business and its products.*
- *The number of employees needed, their compensation, and work schedules.*
- *What changes are occurring in customer wants and needs.*
- *What competing businesses are doing that could affect The Olde Tyme.*
- *How business expenses can be controlled.*

THE PLANNING FUNCTION

A **business plan** is a written description of the business and its operations with an analysis of the opportunities and risks it faces. It includes a detailed financial analysis showing the potential profitability. An outline of a business plan is shown in Fig. 26-1.

The business plan has given Lisa long-range goals and directions for the business as well as specific plans for operations, marketing, financial management, and human resource decisions. She uses the plan regularly and updates it each year.

Lisa O'Brien's analysis of the business shows that the market for antique furniture is growing faster than her sales. She is concerned that her neighborhood location is limiting her number of customers. Two possibilities exist for expansion. She can move to an antique mall that is opening in six months next to the largest shopping center in the area. Or, she can begin to sell her antiques by mail-order catalog, which would allow her business to reach customers beyond the local area.

As the owner of the business, Lisa knows that she has to plan carefully in order to make the best decision. The wrong plan could result in huge losses and the possible failure of her business. However, the correct decision could result in a much larger business, higher profits, and a great deal of personal satisfaction.

IMPORTANCE OF PLANNING

Not all managers spend as much time on planning as Lisa O'Brien. However, all managers are involved in planning in some way. Their decisions may be bigger or smaller than hers. Some managers make complex and expensive

Fig. 26-1
Outline of a business plan for a new business.

I. Introduction to the Business
   A. Description of Products and Services
   B. Owners and Ownership Structure
   C. Organization of the Business
   D. Long-term and Short-term Goals
   E. Current Strengths and Limitations

II. Description of the Industry
   A. Economic Characteristics
   B. Short- and Long-Term Potential of the Industry
   C. Analysis of Major Competitors

III. Market Analysis
   A. Description of Potential Customers
   B. Analysis of Purchase Behavior
   C. Identification of Target Markets
   D. Sales Forecasts

IV. Operations
   A. Organization of Operating Units
   B. Description of Operations Activities
   C. Analysis of Operating Strengths and Limitations
   D. Human Resource Plans

V. Marketing
   A. Description of Marketing Mix
   B. Analysis of Marketing Strengths and Limitations
   C. Procedures for Implementing Marketing Activities
   D. Evaluation Plans

VI. Financial Plan
   A. Startup Costs
   B. Semiannual Income and Expense Projections
   C. Monthly Cash Flow Budgets
   D. Annual Balance Sheets
   E. Financial Analysis
   F. Sources of Financing

decisions such as whether to build a new $20 million factory or to expand operations into another country. Other managers develop very short-term plans such as the employee work schedule for the next week.

Planning is probably the most important management activity. It sets the direction for the business and establishes specific goals. By planning, managers have guidance for making decisions. They use their plans to determine whether progress is being made. Planning also helps managers communicate with each other and coordinate activities.

LEVELS OF PLANNING

Two levels of planning are done in business—strategic planning and operational planning. **Strategic planning** is long term and provides broad goals and directions for the entire business. **Operational planning** is short term and identifies specific activities for each area of the business.

Howard Grey/Tony Stone Images

Strategic Planning

Changes in a business require planning over a long period of time. Developing and producing a new product can take five years or more. Building a new factory may require several years for planning and over a year for construction. A retail business that decides to take over the distribution function rather than use wholesalers needs more than a year to obtain the needed buildings and equipment, get appropriate approvals and licenses from state and local governments, and hire and train employees.

When Lisa O'Brien developed her business plan, she was involved in strategic planning. Faced with a decision to expand her business, she needs to do additional planning. These types of decisions cannot be made quickly. Managers need a great deal of information to determine if a particular decision will be profitable. Strategic planning provides the needed information and procedures for making effective decisions. Figure 26-2 describes the steps in strategic planning.

The top executives in a business are responsible for strategic planning. They use information collected from lower-level managers. In large companies, a special department may be organized to collect and analyze information and to develop proposals to be considered by the executives. Smaller companies may hire research firms or consultants to help with strategic planning. In the business described at the beginning of the chapter, Lisa O'Brien used people from a college and materials from a government agency for assistance.

Operational Planning

A good strategic plan tells managers where the business is going. They must then take actions in their areas to move the business toward those goals. Operational planning determines how work will be done, who will do it, and what resources will be needed to get the work done in a specific area of the business.

STEP 5: STRATEGIES
Managers identify the efforts expected from each area of the firm if goals are to be achieved.

STEP 4: GOALS
Managers develop outcomes for the business to achieve that fit within the mission.

STEP 3: MISSION
Managers agree on the most important purposes or directions for the firm based on the information collected.

STEP 2: INTERNAL ANALYSIS
Managers study factors inside the business that can affect success: operations, finances, personnel, other resources.

STEP 1: EXTERNAL ANALYSIS
Managers study factors outside the firm that can affect effective operations: customers, competitors, the economy, government.

Fig. 26-2
Strategic planning consists of a series of steps that set the direction for a business.

Operational plans in a factory could include developing department budgets, planning inventory levels and purchases of raw materials, setting production levels for each month, and preparing employee work schedules. Operational planning in a marketing department might include the development of promotional plans, identifying training for salespeople, deciding how to support retailers who will handle the product, and selecting pricing methods. A great deal of the operational planning in a business is the responsibility of middle-level managers and supervisors.

PLANNING TOOLS

All managers must develop skills in planning. There are a number of tools that can help in developing effective plans. Those tools are discussed next.

Goals

It has been said that you will never know when you have arrived if you don't know where you are going. Goals provide that direction for a business. Both large and small businesses need to develop goals. A small business owner may overreact to short-term problems or the actions of competitors if goals are not clearly stated.

Managers in large companies may take actions that conflict with those of other managers if they are not aware of goals. There are several characteristics of effective goals.

1. Goals must be specific and meaningful. The goal "to make a profit" is vague; however, the goal "to increase sales by $25,000 in the next six months" is much more specific. Managers must be careful in setting goals and must consider such factors as (1) the general economic conditions of the industry and local area, (2) past sales and profits, (3) the demand for products and services, (4) the reactions of current and prospective customers, (5) the resources of the

Goals provide direction for a business. Should the manager of a new business be as careful in setting goals as the manager of an established business?

business, (6) the actions of competitors, and other factors that influence the success of the business.

2. Goals must be achievable. While it is important that goals move the company forward, they must also be realistic. It is not useful to set a goal "to increase unit sales by 5 percent" if the company does not have the capability of manufacturing that many more units. If telemarketing salespeople are already completing many more calls each day than the industry average, it may not be realistic to set a higher goal for completing calls.

3. Goals should be clearly communicated and should be coordinated with each other. For a small business, goals may need to be communicated to all employees because they will be responsible for accomplishing those goals. Understanding the company's goals will make employees feel as if they are an important part of the business. Usually, they will work harder to achieve those goals.

A firm employing many managers requires a great deal of communication. Each department within a business has separate goals, but the goals must be coordinated. Assume, for example, that the sales manager of a firm decides to increase sales in a specific area of the country. The advertising manager, however, decides to reduce expenditures in the same area to use the money for a new product introduction. If advertising is needed to support the sales efforts, it is obvious that the managers have conflicting goals. Managers must work together so that goals can become consistent and complementary. If that happens, there is a much better chance for the goals to be accomplished with fewer conflicts among managers.

Budgets

The most widely used planning tool is the budget. As you learned previously, financial budgets assist managers in determining the best way to use available money to reach goals. When Lisa O'Brien applied for a loan, her banker required her to develop several long-term and short-term budgets for her new business. In that way, both Lisa and the banker could see how much money would be needed and how and if the new business could be profitable. When department managers complete operational planning, they complete one or more budgets for their departments.

Schedules

Just as budgets help in financial planning, schedules are valuable in planning for the most effective use of time. For most business purposes, a **schedule** is a time plan for reaching objectives. Schedules identify the tasks needed to be completed by a department or individual and the approximate time required to complete each task. A supervisor may develop a schedule to organize the work done by each employee for a day or a week (see Fig. 26-3). Schedules are usually used by production managers to plan the completion and shipment of orders. Schedules are also used by traveling salespeople to determine which customers to contact each day. Office supervisors need to schedule letters and reports to make sure they are completed on time.

Fig. 26-3

Schedules are used by managers as planning devices.

WORK SCHEDULE FOR JULY 23		SPECIAL ORDER DEPARTMENT	
Employee	Order 532	Order 533	Order 534
Shenker, M.	X		
Duffy, P.		X	
Gaston, S.			X
Robinson, J.			X
Kingston, C.		X	

Standards

Another planning tool for managers is the use of standards. A **standard** is a yardstick, or a measure, by which something is judged. In business, standards are set to ensure that the quality of work completed is always acceptable. Standards may set the number of defective products allowed on an assembly line or the number of calls a salesperson must make during a day. Because standards are used to control as well as to plan, the different types of standards are presented in Chapter 27. Managers are responsible for setting standards and for using those standards to judge performance. They also must know when to revise outdated standards.

Policies

As part of planning, managers frequently establish policies. **Policies** are guidelines used in making decisions regarding specific, recurring situations. A policy is often a general rule to be followed by the entire business or by specific departments.

A broad policy may state that the work of all employees must be evaluated by supervisors at least twice a year. Thus, even an employee who has been with the company for ten years must be evaluated. Policies help to reduce misunderstandings and encourage consistent decisions for similar conditions.

Procedures

A **procedure** is a list of steps to be followed for performing certain work. In order to implement the policy described in the previous paragraph, specific evaluation procedures must be developed. For routine tasks, procedures improve business efficiency and are of special help to employees who are learning a new job. The procedure shown in Fig. 26-4 would be a great help to a new employee in the catalog order department for the Johnson Company. Experienced employees can help managers design new procedures and improve old ones.

Research

In order to do a good job of planning, managers need to have a great deal of information available. To develop budgets, it helps to know how money was spent in past years, what certain tasks will cost, and how competitors are spending their money. Schedules will be improved if the manager knows how long it takes to complete certain jobs. Better standards and procedures can be established by carefully collecting information on the way jobs are performed. Research is used to collect data for managers and to provide the information needed to improve their planning decisions.

THE ORGANIZING FUNCTION

Planning is an extremely important function of management. However, before a plan can be put into operation, the company must be organized to best carry out the plan. We looked at a simple definition of organizing in Chapter 24. More specifically, *organizing* involves arranging resources and relationships between departments and employees and defining the responsibility each has for accomplishing the job. For example, when the plan is to start manufacturing a new product, it must be determined who is involved in accomplishing each part of the job. The following departments of the business probably need to be involved: research, manufacturing, human resources, sales, advertising, and finance. Each department then has specific responsibilities. To better understand the function of organization, it is necessary to become familiar with an organization chart and how it is used.

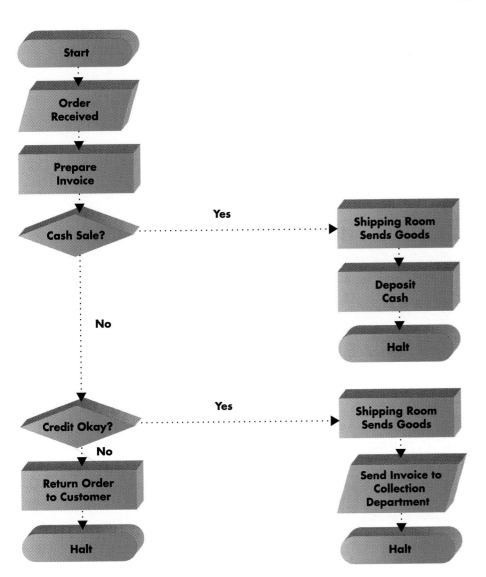

Fig. 26-4
Procedures may be placed in flowchart form.

ROLE OF ORGANIZATION CHARTS

A common device used in establishing a business is the organization chart; an example is shown in Fig. 26-5 on page 642. An **organization chart** is a visual device that shows the structure of an organization and the relationships among workers and divisions of work. The importance of the organization chart is to (1) indicate each employee's area of responsibility and to whom each reports, (2) coordinate the division of work and to make those divisions clear, (3) show the types of work done by the business, and (4) indicate lines of promotion.

Large organizations usually give new employees a booklet that explains the organization of the business and shows an organization chart. By understanding an organization chart, employees have some idea of where and how they fit into the company and what types of jobs are available. The organization chart can easily become outdated, however, as is often the case unless charts are revised when changes occur in the organizational structure.

Illus. 26-3

Work is done more efficiently if it is organized well. What are some ways that businesses can help employees to be more effective at organizing their work?

Jeff Greenberg, Photographer

Fig. 26-5

An organization chart depicts the structure of a business.

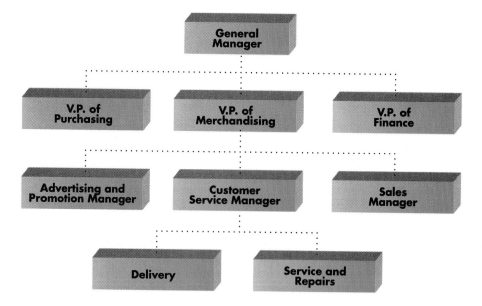

ELEMENTS OF ORGANIZATION

The manager of a new business has the complicated task of organizing the entire structure of the business. A manager for an ongoing business cannot risk ignoring the organization function either. Organization may need to change, for example, when goals are revised or when the business expands. Whether one is a manager of a new or existing department, division, or firm, the process of organizing involves three elements: the division of work, the facilities, and the employees.

Division of Work

In establishing an organization structure, the total work to be done must be divided into units, such as departments. The first consideration is the grouping of activities into broad, natural divisions, such as buying and selling. For small businesses, this may be all that is needed to divide the work into manageable units. For large businesses with many employees and activities, the major divisions may need to be further divided into units before departments of reasonable size can be formed. In a company with an effective division of work, departments are composed of related tasks, work flows smoothly within and among departments, and all responsibilities are assigned to employees.

Major divisions of work vary with the type of industry and business. Use of at least three divisions, however, is rather common. A retail store may be divided into purchasing, merchandising, and operations. A manufacturer's divisions may include production, marketing, and finance. Most businesses have an administrative unit and a human resources unit. An information management unit is also becoming quite common.

As a business grows, the number of major divisions must be increased or new units must be added to existing divisions. When a retail store expands, the basic divisions of buying and selling may be subdivided. Selling may be reclassified as marketing and subdivided into advertising, personal selling, and customer service. Buying, on the other hand, may include purchasing and receiving. Determining how to divide work into efficient units is based on (1) the type of work to be done in each business and (2) the amount of work to be done.

Organization is necessary in a small business as well as in a large business. For example, the owner of a retail store that sells electronic equipment has two employees—A and B. Employee A is placed in charge of sales by the owner, but is to call the owner if there is a problem. Employee A is also in charge of the store when the owner is absent. Employee B is in charge of servicing and repair, but is to bring any problem to the owner. Employee B is told that Employee A is in charge of the store when the owner is absent. This example illustrates how organizations assign responsibility and delegate authority.

Facilities

While divisions of work are being established, the physical aspects of organizing must also be considered. These aspects include providing necessary equipment and materials for employees to be able to complete their work, and arranging the layout of the facilities so that all work flows smoothly.

Work should move through the business as efficiently as possible. Employees should not have to waste time or motions, and work should not be delayed. A clerk, for example, who files and retrieves records frequently needs appropriate file storage located close to the work area in order to save steps.

Physical working conditions also have an effect on the morale of workers. Job satisfaction is influenced by lighting, temperature control, ventilation, color of walls, cleanliness of the building, quality of tools and equipment, and such added conveniences as parking facilities and break rooms.

Ilus. 26-4

The flow of work through a factory is an important consideration when designing a building. What examples can you identify from school, home, or a business in which the design of a building makes working there easier or more difficult?

Jeff Greenberg, Photographer

Employees

Dividing the work into manageable units and providing adequate equipment and facilities must be done with the workers in mind. In fact, organizing involves establishing good relationships among the employees, the work to be performed, and the facilities needed so that productivity will be high. In part, organization is a successful matching of the employee and the employee's materials and work.

CHARACTERISTICS OF GOOD ORGANIZATION

When a business is operated by one person, there is little need for an organization chart—all of the work is performed by one person. The need for organization increases when two or more persons work together. When people engage in any kind of cooperative activity, whether as members of an athletic team or as construction workers building a house, they can accomplish better results if the overall task is planned and organized so each person knows what is expected and how to perform the necessary work. There are several characteristics of good organization that apply to the management of work.

Responsibilities Are Assigned and Authority Is Delegated

Responsibility is the obligation to do an assigned task. In a good organization, the assigned tasks are clearly identified so that all employees know exactly the tasks for which they are responsible. **Authority** is the right to make decisions about work assignments and to require other employees to perform assigned tasks. Authority is delegated from the top of the organization down through the lowest levels.

One of the greatest mistakes in business is to assign responsibilities to employees without giving them sufficient authority to carry out those responsibilities. Each employee and each supervisor should know specifically (1) what each job is to accomplish, (2) what the duties are, (3) what authority accompanies the job, (4) who the manager in charge is, (5) who reports to the manager, and (6) what is considered satisfactory performance.

All sorts of problems arise if there is not a definite organization for a business. Unless employees specifically know their responsibilities, duties, and authority, they are not likely to do their best work. Furthermore, confusion is likely to exist most of the time. For instance, the person handling credit and the person handling sales may get into disputes through misunderstandings.

An organization chart that shows personnel and departments specifically places responsibility for major duties and shows authority. When responsibility and authority are understood, overlapping duties can be eliminated easily. By pointing out authority, such a chart can also be helpful in eliminating conflicts between individuals and between departments. The organization charts shown in Figs. 26-6, 26-7, and 26-8 point out how a business may grow from a one-person enterprise into a partnership with specialized duties, and then expand as additional employees assume certain responsibilities.

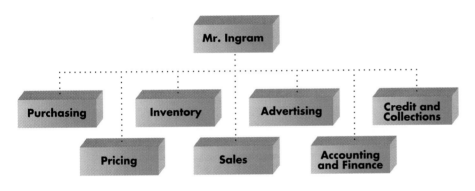

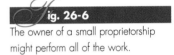

Fig. 26-6

The owner of a small proprietorship might perform all of the work.

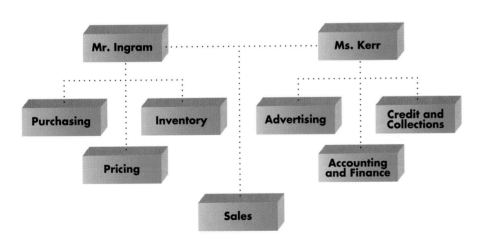

Fig. 26-7

There is a division of work in a partnership.

ig. 26-8

In an expanded partnership, there is a division of work and a delegation of authority.

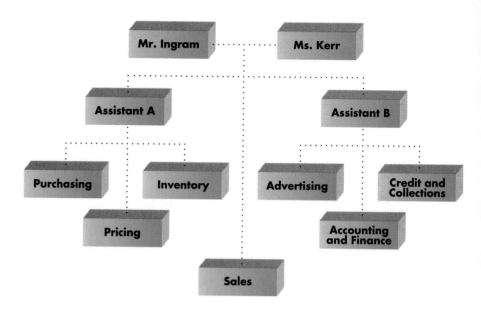

Quality of Work Is Evaluated

Accountability is the term used to relate each individual's responsibility to a superior in the organization for the amount and quality of work performed. When any manager assigns responsibility and delegates authority to an employee, the manager assumes the responsibility for ensuring that the work is completed and for evaluating the quality of that employee's performance. While the manager is ultimately responsible for the work, the employee is accountable to the executive for effectively performing the assigned work. Figure 26-9 shows in detail how the authority is delegated and the tasks are performed in a small rental business operated by an owner and two employees.

ig. 26-9

A manager can identify tasks and assign responsibilities to employees but is still accountable for their work.

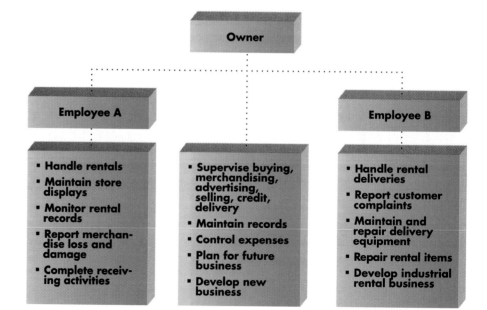

Unity of Command Is Practiced

A very important characteristic of good organization, **unity of command**, requires that no employee have more than one supervisor at a time. Confusion and disorganization result when a person has work assigned by and is accountable to more than one supervisor. The person may not know which assignment to perform first or may be given conflicting instructions regarding the same work assignment.

A Reasonable Span of Control Is Maintained

Span of control refers to the number of employees who are directly supervised by one person. The manager who supervises too many people is overworked and unable to perform all duties effectively. On the other hand, waste of valuable time results if management has too few people to supervise. In general, the span of control can be larger at the lower levels of an organization than at the higher levels. For example, the manager of a unit in a department store may supervise 15 or more sales people, while the president may find it difficult to supervise the work of four or five vice presidents.

Companies that have started to use work teams and that encourage employees to be more involved in planning and decision making have found that they can increase the span of control. Well-trained and motivated employees do not require as much direct supervision as those who must rely on managers for direction. These companies have been able to reduce the numbers of managers required or have been able to increase the size of their workforces without hiring additional managers.

Management Close-Up

PLANNING TO REORGANIZE HEALTH CARE

Questions:

1 Why is the cost of health care benefits increasing faster than the cost of most other products and services?

2 How do management decisions by health care providers in the areas of planning and organizing affect health care and insurance costs to other businesses?

3 What planning and organizing concepts and tools are demonstrated in the examples described above?

One of the biggest challenges facing managers today is the rising cost of keeping employees healthy. Most companies want to provide insurance or health care in order to keep employees healthy and on the job. For many companies, the cost of providing health care for employees is as much as 13-18 percent of the amount paid in salaries and wages. That amount has been increasing by 5-10 percent per year. For a number of reasons, costs are increasing so rapidly that many companies are cutting back on health care benefits or eliminating them totally.

Managers of hospitals, drug manufacturing companies, and other health care organizations are being forced to find new, more efficient ways of providing products and services. If they cannot, they will likely lose those customers who are unable to afford the rising costs. A significant amount of management time is devoted to careful planning so effective service can be provided at a reasonable cost. Some innovative ways to organize the delivery of health care are resulting from that planning.

- Costal Healthcare Group in Durham, North Carolina, helps hospitals by hiring and scheduling doctors. By taking over personnel responsibilities for over 300 hospitals, the company has reduced hospital costs by as much as 20 percent, which it can pass along to its customers.

- Mail order pharmacies sign contracts with large companies to provide prescription medications for employees at savings of 10-20 percent compared to using retail drug stores. Because all ordering, inventory, and operations are located in one area, the pharmacy costs can be controlled.

- Pyxis of San Diego has developed a system for dispensing prescription drugs in a hospital that works like an automated teller machine. The machines are used in hospitals to replace the typical drug storage cabinets. In the past, nurses had to locate the correct medication, measure the amount carefully, and record the information on the patient's record and in the hospital's billing system.

- InterPractice Systems of San Francisco has developed a complete computerized information system for HMOs. It maintains all patient records so health care providers can access the information instantly rather than searching through forms or questioning the patient. A summary of treatments and other information is entered into the computer rather than being written on paper. Patients with home computers review their bills, make appointments, and can even enter symptoms for an initial diagnosis of possible problems.

TYPES OF ORGANIZATIONAL STRUCTURES

The type of organizational structure identifies the relationships among departments and personnel and indicates the lines of communication and decision making. Two principal types of organizational structures have been used in business. They are (1) the line and (2) the line-and-staff organization. New ways of structuring organizations are now being tried by some companies.

Line Organization

In a **line organization**, all authority and responsibility can be traced in a direct line from the top executive down to the lowest employee level in the organization. A line organization is shown in Fig. 26-10 (sales is the only area for which the complete organization is shown). The lines joining the individual boxes indicate the lines of authority. The lines show, for example, that the president has authority over the sales manager; that the sales manager has authority over the assistant sales manager; that the assistant sales manager has authority over the branch manager; and that the branch managers have authority over the sales representatives. In addition, the lines describe how formal communications are expected to flow up and down the organization.

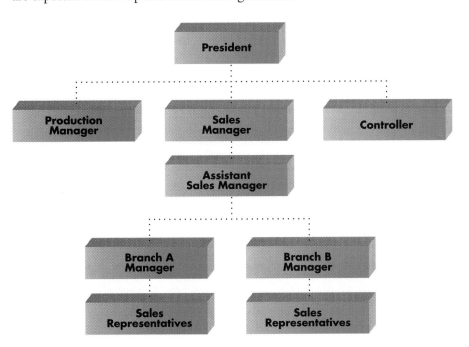

Fig. 26-10

Direct lines of authority and responsibility exist in a line organization.

In a line organization the president has direct control over all units of the business, but responsibilities and authority are passed along from one person to another, down to the lowest level of the organization. Under this form of organization, each person is responsible to only one manager who, in turn, is responsible to someone else. This type of organization can be very efficient, since new plans and ideas can be put into effect immediately in one area of the business without involvement from other areas. However, it often leads to many layers of management and isolation or lack of communication between departments and divisions.

Line-and-Staff Organization

As a business grows larger, the work increases in amount and often in complexity. The result is that line managers have greater difficulty in developing the skills they need in all of the areas of their responsibility. The **line-and-staff organization** adds staff specialists to a line organization. It is designed to solve the problem of complexity and still retain the advantages of direct and definite lines of authority. Staff specialists are added to the line organization to give advice and assistance to line personnel. Staff personnel have no authority over line personnel; that is, staff personnel cannot require anyone in the line organization to perform any task. They are there to help with specialized jobs. Thus, line personnel are still responsible to only one supervisor.

The line-and-staff organization in Fig. 26-11 is like the line organization in Fig. 26-10 except for the addition of the advertising specialist and the marketing research specialist. Their responsibility is to give specialized advice and assistance to the sales organization of the business and is indicated in the organization chart by the broken lines. The type of organization determines whether a manager must have expertise in a number of areas only generally related to the unit being managed or whether specialists will be available to help. Other examples of staff positions in some organizations are legal, information management, strategic planning, and human resources specialists.

Fig. 26-11

In a line-and-staff organization, staff specialists give advice and assistance to line personnel.

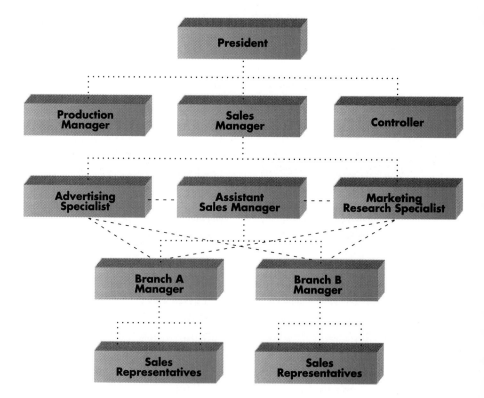

IMPROVING BUSINESS ORGANIZATION

Traditionally, businesses have used a **centralized organization** where all major planning and decision making is done by a group of top managers in the business. Recent studies of business organization have discovered that centralized organizations cause problems in some companies.

Large companies often develop very complex organizational structures. Those structures may result in communications problems and the need for a large number of policies and rules to control the organization. Individual managers and employees then begin to feel like unimportant parts of the business. They get frustrated when rules keep them from doing things they consider important or when it takes a long time to get decisions made.

To overcome these types of problems, some companies have developed a **decentralized organization**. In this structure, a very large business is divided into smaller operating units, and managers are given almost total responsibility and authority for the operation of those units. In many ways, the units operate as if they were independent companies. A large computer manufacturer provides an example of a decentralized organization. Rather than operating as one organization, it could be restructured by categories of products (mainframes, personal computers, accessory equipment) or by types of customers (industrial, government, international).

An even more flexible structure is the project organization. In a **project** or **matrix organization**, work teams are organized to complete a specific project, and a project manager with authority and responsibility for the project is identified. When a new project is developed, employees with the needed skills are asked to work on the project team. They work for that manager until the project is finished. Then they are assigned to a new project and another manager.

The project organization is used successfully in research firms, advertising agencies, and construction companies, but it is being considered by other types of businesses as well because it provides flexibility and allows for rapid change. The specific skills of managers and employees can be used as effectively as possible. Communications barriers are reduced and separate divisions of the business work well together. When employees are given new assignments using the project organization, care must be taken to define authority and responsibility. If these are not defined, problems with unity of command will result.

CHAPTER
REVIEW
26

BUILDING VOCABULARY POWER

Define the following terms and concepts.

1. business plan
2. strategic planning
3. operational planning
4. schedule
5. standard
6. policies
7. procedure
8. organization chart
9. responsibility
10. authority
11. accountability
12. unity of command
13. span of control
14. line organization
15. line-and-staff organization
16. centralized organization
17. decentralized organization
18. project (matrix) organization

REVIEWING FACTS

1. How does a business plan help the manager of a new business with planning?
2. What are the two levels of planning done in a business?
3. What level of management is responsible for strategic planning?
4. What are the three characteristics of an effective goal?
5. Explain how a schedule is used to help a manager plan.
6. Why are written procedures valuable for a new employee?
7. List four purposes of an organization chart.
8. What factors should be considered when establishing a division of work within a company?
9. How can you determine if authority and responsibility have been assigned properly?
10. Why should an employee report to only one supervisor?
11. How is span of control different at lower and upper levels of an organization?
12. What do broken lines in an organization chart mean?
13. Why can a manager be more of a specialist in a line-and-staff organization?
14. What types of problems often result within complex organizations?
15. How are employee assignments made in a project organization?

DISCUSSING IDEAS

1. What types of problems are likely to result if the owner of a small business does not develop a business plan?
2. Why do most executives spend much more time planning today than they did fifteen or twenty years ago?
3. Why is strategic planning done before operational planning?
4. How is your schedule of classes related to a business schedule?
5. Explain how the flowchart in Fig. 26-4 can help a new employee in the catalog order department.
6. Why should all employees in a company be familiar with the company's organization chart?
7. What problems are likely to result when responsibilities are assigned to an employee, but that employee is given no authority to carry out the assigned responsibilities?
8. Identify the result if a manager fails to assign duties and responsibilities to others.
9. If the sales manager of a nationwide organization and an office manager of a district office both have jurisdiction over salespeople working out of the district office, what can be done to avoid misunderstandings?
10. Why do most small business firms use a line organization rather than a line-and-staff organization?

ANALYZING INFORMATION

1. You and a friend plan to open a laundromat with twelve washing machines and four dryers. Write several policies that will help you plan the running of the business.
2. Draw an organization chart for an automobile dealer and service station based on the following facts:
   a. The owner of the business is J. M. Gray.
   b. The business consists of a service station, a used-car sales department, a repair department, and a parts department.
   c. Gray's daughter, Joan, acts as his assistant but also manages the parts department and supervises to a certain extent all of the other functions.
   d. B. L. O'Hara and three assistants have charge of the repair department.
   e. O. P. Thompson has charge of the used-car sales department, but a young woman by the name of Linda Williams spends most of her time selling the used cars.
   f. Gray's nephew, Jim Blake, takes care of the service station with the assistance of two part-time employees.

3. With the help of your teacher, identify five activities that must be completed by your class during the next three weeks. Then develop a schedule that shows how you plan to complete the activities.
4. Jane Sanchez has just developed a new game that she plans to sell by mail order for $20.50 during the next Christmas season. Write two long-term general goals and three short-term specific goals that would be appropriate as guides for Ms. Sanchez's new business.
5. Your class has been given three projects to complete: (a) To organize and write several sections of the school's student handbook. (b) To work with a local organization to collect food from the community for needy families. (c) To operate a Saturday morning recreation program for elementary students. Develop a project organization chart with a manager and at least five positions for each activity. Then assign specific class members to the positions in each project based on the activities to be completed and the person's interests and skills.

S OLVING BUSINESS PROBLEMS

CASE 26-1

Christine Jordan started a business 20 years ago as a one-person operation. It grew slowly for a while because Jordan did all of the work. As the business expanded, she hired more people. The business now employs 100 people. She is the president and manages the business personally. She has an open-door policy, and all employees are permitted and expected to come to her for answers to their problems. She has given responsibility to her sales manager, her production manager, and a purchasing agent, but she makes all of the decisions or approves the decisions before they are implemented. She thinks that an organization chart is unnecessary because everybody knows how the organization operates, and they understand that she is the boss.

Required:
1. What do you think about the efficiency of an organization of this type?
2. How do you think the department heads and the employees feel about the present type of organization and management?
3. Do you have any suggestions for the improvement of this business?

CASE 26-2

The Toyline Company makes and sells a line of children's toys. In six months, retail stores will begin buying the company's products in large quantities in preparation for the holiday shopping season. The marketing manager is confident that sales will be higher this year than last. Thus, several new salespeople have been hired and are being trained for the upcoming rush period. Increased advertising has also been planned.

The production manager, on the other hand, has been running into difficulties getting raw materials from the firm's only supplier. Production has been cut by 20 percent during the last two months, and the inventory of finished goods is less than planned. The production manager, not having received word to the contrary, has planned to keep the finished goods inventory at last year's level. There is no indication as to when the raw material problem will be solved. In addition, the labor contract with the union expires in three months and there has been discussion of a possible strike.

Required:

1. What management problems are apparent in the Toyline Company?
2. Why have these problems occurred?
3. Using the management tools discussed in the chapter, give examples of how each of the problems could be solved.

IMPLEMENTING AND CONTROLLING

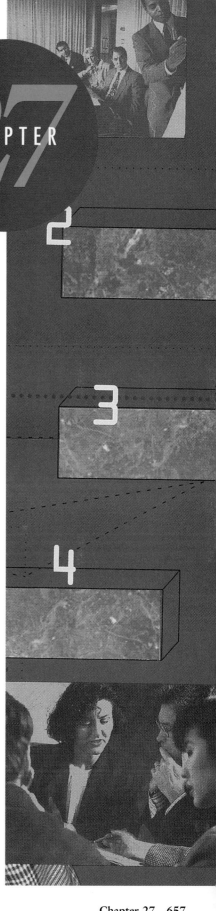

CHAPTER 27

After studying this chapter you will be able to:

27-1 Identify the major management tasks involved in implementing the work of an organization.

27-2 Explain the differences among three theories of employee motivation.

27-3 Discuss the steps in an effective change process.

27-4 Describe the controlling process and four types of business standards.

27-5 Recognize control methods businesses use for inventory, credit, theft, and health and safety.

*J*asmine had been hired as the manager of the new telemarketing department of an office supply company. The department was fully automated with computerized telephone and order processing systems. Jasmine was given a large budget to retrain current employees who had volunteered as well as to hire and train new employees for telephone sales. She had three months to organize the work and prepare the employees for their new tasks.

A strategy was developed to sell office supplies through catalogs. The promise to customers was that any order placed by 10 p.m. would be delivered by 9 a.m. the next day. A catalog was prepared and mailed to all businesses in the city. Follow-up telephone calls were made introducing the service and promoting the delivery guarantee.

Things got off to a good start. There was a real excitement among the employees when they made the sales calls to introduce the new service and the orders began to come in to the office. The employees seemed to enjoy using the new computer equipment and the training made them comfortable with their work. However, problems began to appear after the first month of operation.

The first problem occurred when Jasmine established sales quotas for each employee. With sales growing rapidly, it didn't seem difficult for most employees to make their quotas. However, some people had high sales volumes and others had few sales. Jasmine believed the quotas would encourage everyone to emphasize selling. Several employees complained that the quotas emphasized selling too much and resulted in pressure to perform.

The department began to experience some computer problems. When a high volume of calls came in, the computers would slow down. Employees would have to wait to get information on their screens and occasionally all of the information entered would be lost before the order could be processed. Also, it appeared that the company was not able to meet its goal of overnight delivery from time to time. The telemarketing employees were starting to receive customer complaints, which they were not prepared to handle.

The most serious problem was a rapid increase in employee dissatisfaction and turnover. The growing sales volume was putting pressure on Jasmine's department. While she was hiring and training new employees, it seemed there never were enough employees to handle the amount of business. New employees were receiving less training so they made more errors. Experienced employees were being asked to work overtime to meet the demand. Experienced employees, especially ones who had worked for the company before the change, were quitting or asking for transfers because of the pressure they were facing on the job.

Jasmine knew that her department was essential to the success of the company. If the department was not able to maintain and increase the level of sales and process orders efficiently, the new business strategy would fail. As the manager, she needed to figure out ways to solve the growing number of problems.

Jasmine is discovering what many experienced managers have learned. Plans are not effective unless they are implemented well. Changing conditions in a business create problems in the way work is accomplished.

As you learned in Chapter 24, implementing involves carrying out the plans and helping employees to work effectively. Controlling is used to evaluate results to determine if the company's objectives have been accomplished as planned. The majority of managers, especially supervisors and middle-level managers, spend a great deal of their time on implementing and controlling activities. In this chapter, we will finish our study of business management by examining these two important management activities.

THE IMPLEMENTING FUNCTION

Implementing is the management function of guiding employee actions toward achievement of a company's goals. The term *directing* is frequently used to refer to those implementing activities that managers use to guide the work of the people they supervise. Some of the common implementing activities are

Illus. 27-1
Supervisors must be able to implement the plans that have been developed. What types of information are available in business plans to help supervisors direct employees?

communicating, leading, and motivating. For example, a manager may communicate certain production goals to his or her subordinates, give the subordinates specific instructions about how to accomplish the goals, and provide rewards to those who successfully accomplish the goals.

IMPLEMENTING ACTIVITIES

To be successful at implementing, managers must be able to complete a number of activities effectively. The activities are designed to maintain the effectiveness of their employees. They include effective communications, motivating employees, developing effective work teams, and operations management.

Effective Communications

We studied the importance of communications in business and effective methods of communications in a previous chapter. Communications is an essential part of implementing work in a business. Managers need to be able to communicate plans and directions, gather feedback from employees, and identify and resolve communications problems. Both personal and organizational communications are important. Managing communications technology has become an important responsibility.

Employee Motivation

Motivation is the set of factors that cause a person to act in a certain way. An employee may be motivated to work hard and do the best job possible. On the other hand, an employee may choose to show up for work late, be unconcerned about errors, or interfere with the work of others. Motivation is both internal and external. Internal motivation is actions taken as a result of a person's beliefs, feelings, and attitudes. External motivation is the influences on a person's actions resulting from the actions of others and the environment.

To be able to motivate employees, managers must understand the employees' needs. People work to satisfy needs. Activities or results that provide high levels of needs satisfaction are likely to motivate employees. They will be chosen over the activities or results that are do not satisfy needs. Several theories of motivations will be reviewed in the next section.

Work Teams

Seldom do people work in total isolation. Most people work directly with others or rely on others in order to perform their work. It has been said that groups can accomplish more than the same number of people operating independently. Managers need to be able to develop effective work teams. A **work team** is a group of individuals who cooperate to achieve a common goal.

Effective work teams have several characteristics, as shown in Fig. 27-1. First, the members of the group understand and support its purpose. The activities that must be completed are clear, members know which of the activities they need to perform, and they have the knowledge and skills necessary to complete the activities. Group members are committed to making the group work and meet the expectations of others in the group. Finally, group members communicate well with each other and work to resolve problems within the group.

Fig. 27-1

Characteristics of effective work teams.

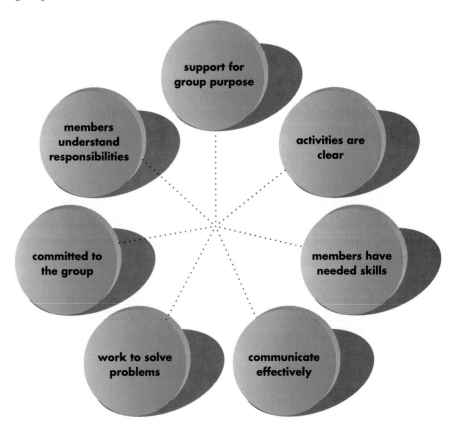

You can see that just because several people work together in a department does not ensure that they will be an effective work team. In fact, there are many reasons why they may not be an effective team. Managers can play an important role in developing the effectiveness of work teams. In order to develop effective teams, they must understand the characteristics described above and help to resolve problems in the group when they are observed.

Operations Management

Operations are the major activities of a business. Many types of activities occur in most businesses and often departments are organized to perform specialized operations. An important management responsibility is to ensure that the operations of a department are performed well.

Several activities are a part of operations management. Facilities, equipment, materials, and supplies must be available and organized in such a way that employees can perform their work. Employees need to be assigned to the appropriate tasks and scheduled to ensure that all work is completed on time. Activities are organized to ensure the greatest amount of work is accomplished on schedule.

Jeff Greenberg, Photographer

llus. 27-2
Ensuring effective operations is an important management responsibility. What are examples of operations that occur in a company with which you are familiar?

Operations management may be very simple in small departments with a limited number of employees and activities. However, it can be very complicated in other departments. Management of operations in the production areas of large manufacturing facilities requires skill in purchasing, production scheduling, inventory management, and quality control. Production managers must be familiar with concepts such as economic order quantity (the lowest-cost volume of inventory to reorder), just-in-time inventory control (keeping inventories at the lowest possible level to ensure continuous production), and statistical process control (careful measurement of the quality of production procedures).

MOTIVATION THEORIES

Think of the days you are excited to get up and go to school or work. You enjoy the day and work hard. Time seems to move faster than usual. Compare that to the days when it is impossible to get up and you dread going to work or school. The day seems to go on forever and you don't seem to be able to get anything done.

In the same way, you probably can identify teachers, coaches, or business people for whom you enjoy working and who seem to be able to encourage your best work. You also know others who you would prefer to avoid and for whom it is a struggle to perform well. What causes the differences?

We learned earlier that motivation causes people to act in certain ways. The examples above suggest that people have different levels of motivation depending on the day, the activities, and the people with whom they work. Managers attempt to understand motivation in order to get the best efforts from employees. Several theories attempt to describe employee motivation. Those theories are based on understanding and satisfying employee needs. The theories are summarized in Fig. 27-2.

Maslow's Hierarchy

Probably the best known theory of motivation is Maslow's Hierarchy of Needs. You will recall that Abraham Maslow described individual needs in five categories that form a hierarchy. The lowest level is physiological needs, followed by security, social, esteem, and self-actualization. According to the theory, people seek to satisfy the needs from lowest to highest. If needs cannot be satisfied on the job, employees will look elsewhere to receive satisfaction. Managers need to identify where each employee is on the hierarchy and help provide the necessary satisfaction with job assignments, compensation, and reinforcement.

McClelland's Achievement Motivation

While Maslow's theory was based on a common set of needs with which people are born, David McClelland believed that several important needs are developed and have strong influences on a person's behavior. He identified three major needs: the need for achievement, the need for affiliation, and the need for power.

McClelland suggested that people with a high **achievement need** take personal responsibility for their own work, set personal goals, and want immediate feedback on their work. People with a strong **affiliation need** are concerned about their relationships with others and work to get along well and fit in with a group. Finally, those with a **power need** want to influence and control others and to be responsible for a group's activities.

Managers who believe in McClelland's theory recognize that various jobs and activities provide better or worse opportunities for achievement, affiliation,

MASLOW'S HIERARCHY OF NEEDS

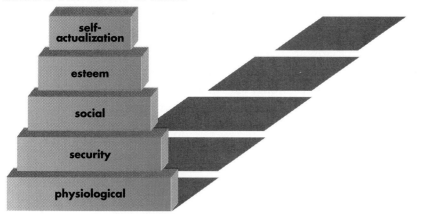

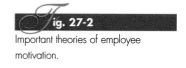

ig. 27-2

Important theories of employee motivation.

McCLELLAND'S ACHIEVEMENT THEORY

HERZBERG'S TWO FACTOR THEORY

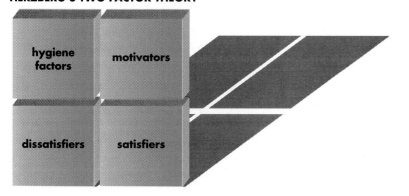

or power. The theory also suggests that the strength of the three needs can be changed over time with careful development.

Herzberg's Factors

Frederick Herzberg conducted studies of employees to identify what satisfied and dissatisfied them in their work. His research resulted in the identification of two distinct groups of factors that contributed to employee satisfaction or dissatisfaction.

He identified one group as hygiene factors. **Hygiene factors** provide dissatisfaction when they do not meet employee needs but do not contribute to satisfaction even when they are provided to employees. Examples of hygiene factors are the amount of pay and fringe benefits, working conditions, rules, the amount and type of supervision, and other things that are controlled by others.

Herzberg called the second group motivators. **Motivators** are factors that result in satisfaction. Motivators on a job include challenging work, recognition, achievement, accomplishment, increased responsibility, and personal development. Motivation factors are usually controlled by the individual.

The interesting part of Herzberg's theory is that the two types of factors and their results are separate from each other. In other words, hygiene factors can provide dissatisfaction but cannot improve satisfaction. For example, people will be dissatisfied by the level of their pay and fringe benefits but pay increases will not increase satisfaction. Pay increases and other extrinsic rewards will only prevent employees from being dissatisfied.

In the same way, Herzberg claimed that motivators provide satisfaction. In order to increase satisfaction, organizations should provide opportunities for interesting work, greater individual control and responsibility, and recognition for good work.

MANAGING CHANGE

The only thing that seems to be certain in business today is change. The size of companies is either increasing or shrinking. Technology is becoming an important part of all industries and most jobs. Businesses have moved into global competition. The workforce is increasingly diverse. Government agencies are increasing regulations in some areas while reducing them in others.

People are not always comfortable with change. Consider changes you have experienced. Examples could include moving, changing schools, relationships with family or friends, or an important decision. How did you react to that change? When it appears that things will be different, those affected by the change are likely to be very concerned.

When peoples' jobs or positions are threat-

Illus. 27-3

Change occurs regularly in businesses today. What are some examples of recent changes that have occurred in businesses in your community?

ened, when they are uncertain about how a change will affect them, or when they do not trust those responsible for planning the change, they will probably resist the change. It is important that managers work to overcome that resistance and to make change as comfortable as possible for the employees affected.

An effective change process involves several steps. They include planning, communicating, involving, educating, and supporting. The greatest resistance to change is experienced when it occurs suddenly, when people are not prepared, or when people don't understand the reasons for the change. When careful planning occurs, change can be accomplished successfully, and people affected will support the change.

Planning

Managers must be careful about moving too rapidly to make changes. They must be certain that change is needed and that the organization will be better off as a result of the change. Then a careful procedure should be undertaken to gather information, identify and study alternatives, and determine the consequences of change. Putting in place a careful planning procedure will help to assure that the best solutions will be developed and will give confidence to those involved in the final result.

Communicating

Sometimes managers believe it is best not to say anything to employees about possible changes until a final decision has been made and they are ready to take action. They believe that early information will create confusion and misunderstanding. People who study the change process recognize that it is almost impossible to conceal information about pending changes. Using informal communication and limited information, rumors and misinformation will spread. The result is usually more damaging to the organization than the result of early, direct communications from management.

Managers who have previously established effective communications with employees will be in a better position to communicate with them about possible changes than those who have not been effective. Since change occurs frequently in business, employees who are used to regular communications with their managers will not be shocked or surprised by information about potential changes. Open, two-way communications between managers and employees are a part of an effective work environment and should be used throughout the change process.

Involving

It is frequently said that people support what they create. Managers must recognize that employees can be the source of ideas on effective solutions and how to make change. Most effective change processes involve the people who will be affected in gathering information, considering alternatives, and testing solutions. It is usually not possible to involve everyone in all parts of the change process or to use a majority vote to decide on a change. However, employees will be more supportive when they know their voices will be heard and that they have input into plans that result in change.

Educating

Change in business does not just happen. If new products and services are developed, if new equipment and technology are introduced, or if the jobs of employees are redesigned, people will need to prepare. Usually, that means information and training. As plans for change are developed, managers must determine who will be affected and what new knowledge and skills will be required of employees. Then information meetings and training programs should be developed to prepare employees for the required changes.

Supporting

How willing are you to make a change if you are uncertain of the result? When people believe they will receive support from their organization, they are more willing to accept changes. All changes involve some amount of risk, and organizations cannot guarantee success. However, managers need to assure employees that there is support available to help them adjust to the change.

The support can take many forms. Part of the support is allowing time to adjust to change. Managers may provide more feedback on how employees are performing and be less critical of mistakes early in the process. Counseling, training, and additional information are other methods of support.

Sometimes changes have negative effects on employees that cannot be avoided. Employees may have to be terminated or undergo major job changes that can require reductions in pay, different working conditions, and so forth. Support is especially needed under those circumstances. Employees who lose their jobs need time to adjust. Companies may provide full or partial salary for several weeks or months while the people affected try to find new jobs. The companies may look for other positions in the organization and help employees retrain or relocate. They can also give preference to those employees when new positions open. Many companies now provide personal and career counseling, help with job-seeking skills, and even payment for employment services for employees who are terminated due to change.

THE CONTROLLING FUNCTION

"Employee absences have increased by 3 percent this year."

"Maintenance costs are down an average of $50 per vehicle."

"Salespeople in the southern district have increased new customer orders by 12.3 percent in a three-year period."

"An average of three employees per month are enrolling in the company's wellness program."

"The adjustments to the robot's computer program have reduced the variations in the seam to .0004 mm."

These statements provide very valuable information to managers. With the proper information, managers can tell how well activities are being performed. Reviewing performance is one part of the fourth management function—controlling. Managers must be able to determine if activities are performed well. If problems are occurring, managers need problem-solving skills to develop good solutions. In the last part of this chapter, we will study how managers complete the controlling function and how it improves the management process.

As we have learned, all managers complete the four management functions. Planning involves setting goals and directions for the business. Organizing deals with obtaining and arranging resources so the goals can be met. Implementing is responsible for carrying out the work of the organization. Controlling determines whether goals are being met and what actions must be taken if they are not being met.

While each of the functions includes a specific set of activities, they are all related. Planning improves if there is an effective organization to provide information to managers. Without effective planning, it is difficult to decide how to organize a business and what resources are needed. Implementation is impossible without plans and difficult with a poorly designed organization. Controlling cannot be completed unless the company has specific goals and plans. Figure 27-3 shows that management is a continuous process and that each function supports the others. Controlling is the final function and provides the information needed to improve the management process and business activities.

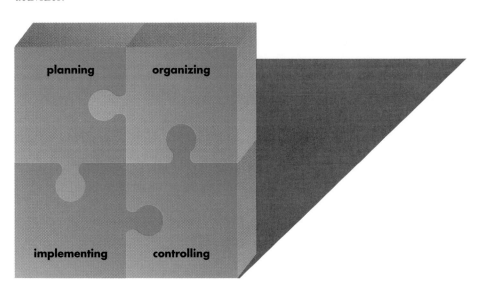

Fig. 27-3

The four functions of management are directly related.

THE BASIC STEPS

Controlling involves three basic steps:

1. Establishing standards for each of the company's goals and activities.

2. Measuring and comparing performance with the established standards to see if goals are met.

3. Taking corrective action when problems are identified.

The important activities in controlling are shown in the following example. A business has a goal to manufacture and deliver to a customer 1,000 made-to-order blankets by a specific date. The standard is to produce 25 items each day for 40 consecutive days. During the first ten days, only 200 blankets are produced. Because production is 50 blankets below the standard—250 blankets in ten days—the manager must take action to increase production during the remaining 30 days. The corrective action may include scheduling overtime work or assigning more workers to the task.

As another example, the manager of a shoe store wants to make sure that new styles of shoes sell rapidly. The standard is that 30 percent of all shoes in a new style are sold within one month. If only 20 percent of a certain style are sold after one month, corrective action must be taken. The manager may choose to increase the advertising for the shoes, give salespeople a higher commission for selling that style, or mark down the price to sell more. The manager will also want to use this information when planning purchases in the future.

Illus. 27-4
A manager of a shoe store follows the three-step controlling procedure. How might each of the steps described in the text apply to the shoe store?

In each example, the manager had to set a standard based on the work to be accomplished. Then the standard was used to see if the company's goals could be met. Finally, if the standard was not being met, the manager had to determine what could be done to correct the problem.

Notice that in both examples the manager did not wait very long to begin measuring performance. Controlling activities should be completed before the problem is too big or too expensive to correct.

TYPES OF STANDARDS

Standards are determined by managers in the planning stage. They are determined through study of the job, past experience, industry information, and input from experienced workers. The standards become the means for judging success and for applying controls.

Several types of standards are needed to control business operations. The standards used depend on the type of business, the size of the business, and the activities being controlled. The major types of standards used include quantity standards, quality standards, time standards, and cost standards.

Quantity Standards

Quantity standards are used frequently in business. Production managers specify the minimum number of units to be produced each hour, day, or month by individual workers or groups of workers. Sales managers establish the number of prospects that sales representatives must contact daily or weekly. Office supervisors may set an acceptable day's work for typists by the number of letters typed or indicate to data entry personnel the number of lines of information to be entered in one hour.

Quality Standards

Quantity standards alone are often not enough to judge an employee, a product, or a service. A fast worker, for example, can be very careless, or a slow worker can be extremely careful. Thus, the quality of the work performed is often just as important as the quantity produced.

Perfection—having no errors—may be the only acceptable standard for the products and services of a business. A battery that does not work will not sell. An invoice with pricing errors cannot be sent to a customer. An accountant cannot calculate the taxes of a client incorrectly. While perfection is the standard, it may not always be practical or cost effective to develop procedures to check every finished product. On an assembly line where thousands of products are produced every hour, sampling a few products each hour may be enough to identify when quality problems occur.

If quality standards are carefully set, they should not be lowered. Defective products that reach customers decrease sales or cause ill will. When customer confidence is lost because of poor product quality, the reputation of the business suffers. Management invites problems when quality standards are not given enough attention. A business in which all employees and managers are concerned about quality will be valued by its customers.

Time Standards

Time standards are closely related to quantity and quality standards. Most business activities can be measured by time. The amount of time it takes to complete an activity has an effect on costs, the quantity of work completed, and often on the quality of the work. Time standards are more important to some businesses than to others. Building contractors, bakeries, and newspaper publishers normally have very strict time schedules. If they do not meet the schedules, they suffer an immediate financial loss. Other businesses may not see the immediate financial loss, but failure to maintain time standards will result in fewer products being produced, poor coordination of activities between departments, or other problems.

Cost Standards

An important measure of the success or failure of a firm is financial profit or loss. While trying to increase profits, managers are constantly aware of two specific objectives: (1) to increase sales and (2) to decrease costs. Not all managers or employees are directly connected with work that increases sales. However, most employees and managers do influence costs. Wasting material or taking more time than necessary to perform a task adds to the cost of doing business. Increased costs, without a proportionate increase in sales, decreases profit. Business firms must be cost conscious at all times.

Generally, more attention is given to cost controls than to any other type of control. The control devices used, as a result, are numerous. One of the main purposes of the accounting department is to provide detailed cost information. This is why the head of an accounting department is often called a controller. Most managers, however, act as cost controllers in some way.

The most widely used controlling device is the budget. Budgets, like schedules and standards, are also planning devices. When a budget is prepared, it is a planning device; after that, it is a controlling device. Actual cost figures are collected and compared with estimated or planned figures. These comparisons permit judgments about the success of planning efforts and provide clues for making changes that will help assure that goals are reached.

MEASURING AND COMPARING PERFORMANCE

Standards become the basis for determining effective performance. Managers gather information on all parts of business operations. That information is compared with the standards to determine if the standards are being met. Whenever a variance is identified, a manager needs to identify the reasons for the difference.

It is possible that actual performance may exceed the standard. That may seem to be an ideal situation and the manager will not need to take any action. However, it is important to understand why the higher-than-expected performance occurred so that performance can be repeated. Also, the process for developing standards can be reviewed to determine why the standard was set lower than the possible performance.

The greatest concern of managers is when performance does not meet standards. It is important to identify as early as possible when lower-than-expected performance is occurring so corrective action can be taken. For that reason, performance must be monitored very frequently rather than waiting for several months. A delay in identifying performance problems may make it difficult to make changes before those problems have serious effects on the business.

Monitoring all of the activities for which managers are responsible can take a great deal of time. Managers can use information systems to reduce the amount of time spent on controlling activities. If a manager reviewed all of the information collected on the operations in a business, there would be little time for other activities. Computers can be used to monitor the performance of activities in a company. If activities are performed as planned and standards are met, no management attention is needed. When the computer identifies performance that is below standard, a variance report is printed for the manager. Through the use of the reports, managers can identify problems quickly and use their time to solve those problems.

TAKING CORRECTIVE ACTION

When a manager discovers that performance is not meeting standards, three possible actions can be taken:
1. Take steps to improve performance.
2. Change policies and procedures.
3. Revise the standard.

If careful planning has been done, managers should be reluctant to change standards. In the blanket manufacturing business, past experience should have been used to see if producing 25 items a day was reasonable. Only under unusual circumstances (major equipment breakdown, problems with suppliers, employee strikes, etc.) would the blanket managers reduce the standard. However, failure to meet the goal of 1,000 blankets by the specified date will not please the customer and may result in a loss of sales.

Most often, managers need to improve performance of activities when standards are not being met. This usually means making sure that the work is well organized, that supplies and materials are available when needed, that equipment is in good working order, and that employees are well trained and motivated.

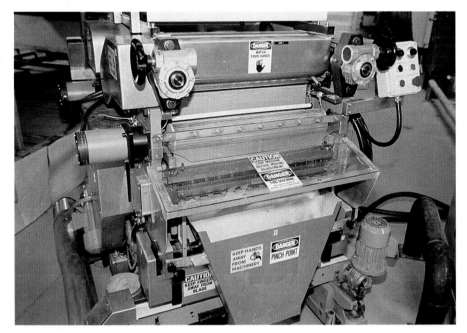

Jeff Greenberg, Photographer

Illus. 27-5
Standards need to be revised when procedures are changed or new equipment is added. How can managers develop effective standards for procedures or equipment with which they are unfamiliar?

Global Perspective

THE NEW GLOBAL MANAGEMENT

Questions:

1 What are some advantages and disadvantages of the original approach to international management compared to the new global management?

2 How can managers use the steps in managing effective change to implement the new global management?

3 Describe at least one way that each of the management functions (planning, organizing, implementing, and controlling) will be affected by global management.

Source: "Borderless Management," *Business Week,* May 23, 1994, pp. 24-26.

More and more businesses are moving into international markets. But many businesses have engaged in global competition for years. Companies such as Sony, Ford, IBM, Coca Cola, and Nestlés are experienced international businesses whose products are known worldwide. With years of experience, you would expect those companies to have perfected their management practices. But a major change is occurring. It is the new global management.

In the past, companies treated major international markets as if each were an independent business. They would develop a separate organization to serve each new area. A unique management structure with its own production, operations, marketing, and financing would be established with little interaction with the operations in the company's original country or in other parts of the world. There were important reasons for this management approach. Each market was viewed as separate and different.

European needs and competition were different from those in the United States, from Japan, or from South America. Differences in laws, language, and customs suggested that it would be more effective to develop a distinct operation in each area. Therefore, Ford had very different European and North American divisions. Each produced its own models of auto-

mobiles with independent research, production, and marketing divisions. Whirlpool discovered even more specific customer differences with Italians choosing front-loading washing machines and the French wanting top-loading models, so it was natural to keep operations separate.

However, the results proved to be less than perfect. Companies discovered a great deal of duplication as each market had its own demands for management, information, facilities, and finances. Often, companies found many of the international divisions were completing the same tasks and even making the same mistakes. With little or no communication among the units, managers were unable to learn from each other or to share resources and information. It was even difficult to move personnel from one international market to another because of the independence of each.

Today, these companies are recognizing two things. The needs of international markets are becoming more alike than different. Also, competition is becoming more intense with the same companies competing with each other in most international markets. Businesses are responding by consolidating their independent units into one global operation and coordinating their management and operations. One location provides services to a variety of international locations.

Occasionally, standards are not met because activities cannot be accomplished as planned, or policies and procedures are not appropriate. This is likely to happen when a business begins a new procedure, starts to use new equipment, or has other major changes. In this situation, managers may need to change the policies or procedures that are not working in order to meet the standards.

Finally, when the manager has explored all possibilities to improve performance and it still does not meet the standards, the standards themselves need to be evaluated. Planning is usually not exact. Conditions can change from the time plans and standards are developed and related activities are performed. Managers cannot expect that all standards will be appropriate.

When new planning procedures are used or new activities are implemented, planning is less likely to be accurate. Standards developed in those situations should be studied more carefully than the standards for ongoing activities or standards that have been developed in the same way for a long period of time.

Standards should be revised when it is clear they will not accurately reflect performance and attempts to improve performance have not been successful. When standards are changed, the new standards and the reasons for the changes should be clearly communicated to the employees affected. Also, the procedures for setting standards should be revised to increase the likelihood that standards developed in the future will be more accurate.

CONTROLLING COSTS

All managers constantly need to watch for areas where costs can be reduced. Excessive costs reduce the profit of a business. There are several areas in a business where managers can anticipate cost problems. They are inventory, credit, theft, and employee health and safety. Planning should be done in each area to prevent excessive costs from occurring.

Inventory

Manufacturers need to produce enough of each product to fill orders when they are received. They need enough raw materials to be able to produce those products. Wholesalers and retailers must maintain inventories to meet their customers' needs. In all types of businesses, if inventories are too low sales will be lost. If inventories are too high, costs of storage and handling will increase. There may be products in inventory that are never used or sold. In that situation, the company loses all of the money invested in those products.

Managers must keep accurate inventories to provide adequate product levels. Purchasing must be done carefully to select products that can be sold quickly at a profit. Products must be purchased at the right time and in the correct quantities to reduce the inventory cost of a company.

Newer methods of inventory management are being developed, such as just-in-time control. Inventories are kept at the lowest possible level to meet production and sales goals. Production time, sales activity, and purchasing requirements are studied carefully. Orders for materials are placed so they arrive just as they are needed. Production levels are set so the company has only enough products to fill orders as they are received. Effective inventory control methods can be very complicated. Both time and quantity controls are critical to reduce costs and meet customer needs.

Credit

Most businesses must be able to extend credit to customers. Businesses also use credit when buying products from suppliers. If credit is extended to customers and they do not pay their bills, the company loses money. Also, businesses that use credit too often when making purchases spend a great deal of money for interest payments.

As discussed earlier in the text, businesses must develop credit policies to reduce the amount of losses. Customers should be checked carefully before credit is given to them. Billing and collection procedures should be developed so that most accounts are collected on time. Managers need to watch the age of accounts because the longer an account is overdue, the greater the chance of loss to the company.

Managers responsible for purchasing must control the amount of money the company owes to other businesses. It is easy to make too many purchases on credit. When this happens, the interest charges are very high, and the company may not have enough money to pay all debts on time. Credit should be used when the company will lose money if the purchase is not made. Credit may also be needed for the purchase of expensive equipment or large orders of merchandise.

Managers must be sure bills are paid on time to protect the credit reputation of the business. If a cash discount is offered, it should be checked to see if the company will benefit from the use of the discount. Before credit is used, credit terms should be checked to see what it will cost. Credit can be a good business tool if used carefully.

Theft

By establishing theft controls, businesses usually are able to reduce losses. Specific steps can be taken to safeguard cash from loss. Protection against losses from forged, stolen, or worthless checks is another important controlling activity.

The theft of merchandise from warehouses and stores is a major concern of business. Retail stores are the hardest hit by such losses. Retailers lose billions of dollars annually due to crime, much of which is from theft of merchandise. Shoplifting by customers and employees equals six percent or more of total sales each year. Much of the loss occurs during the end-of-year holiday shopping season when stores are crowded and part-time persons are employed. Basic procedures followed by many retail businesses to reduce shoplifting are shown in Fig. 27-4.

Many stores, warehouses, and trucks are burglarized during the night or when merchandise is being transported. Security guards or special equipment

Common Methods for Controlling Shoplifting

1. Hire security guards (in uniform).
2. Hire store dectectives (not in uniform).
3. Install television cameras that scan entrances, exits, and checkout counters.
4. Place mirrors at key locations, which give views of various parts of the store.
5. Attach special inventory tags to products, which give a signal when products are taken from the store. (When an article is sold, the salesperson will remove the tag.)
6. Position station attendants at dressing rooms.
7. Keep unused checkout aisles closed.
8. Keep small, expensive items in locked display cases.
9. Post signs warning customers of the consequences of shoplifting.
10. Train employees on procedures to follow when they identify a shoplifter.

Fig. 27-4

Stores must protect themselves against loss from theft.

are frequently used to reduce the chances of such thefts. Many companies carry insurance against losses, but with high loss rates the cost of insurance is very high.

Health and Safety

Even when employees are absent from work because of sickness or injury, the company must continue to operate. Other employees must be available to fill in for the absent employee. Usually, the salary of both the absent employee and the substitute employee must be paid. Health insurance costs are often paid by the company as well. Studies estimate that the annual costs to many businesses for employee absence and health costs now exceed $10,000 for each employee.

Costs that result from health and safety problems can be reduced. Companies should provide safety training for all employees. Work areas and equipment should be inspected regularly to be sure they operate correctly and safely.

THE IMPORTANCE OF BUSINESS MANAGEMENT

Operating a business is a very complex process. Even managers of small businesses must make production, marketing, personnel, and finance decisions every day. If the manager does not have an organized method for operating the business, problems will soon develop.

A great deal of knowledge and skill is required for management. Even beginning supervisors need a great deal of education to be effective. No longer can business expect that any good employee can be an effective manager. The manager who knows how to plan, organize, implement, and control is prepared to make the decisions needed to operate a business. With effective leadership and communications and preparation in the use of technology, managers can contribute to the effectiveness of their organizations and the satisfaction of employees and customers.

CHAPTER REVIEW 27

BUILDING VOCABULARY POWER

Define the following terms and concepts.

1. motivation
2. work team
3. achievement need
4. affiliation need
5. power need
6. hygiene factors
7. motivators

REVIEWING FACTS

1. What is the importance of the implementing and controlling activities of management?
2. Which managers spend a great deal of their time on implementing and controlling activities?
3. Why do managers with effective business plans sometimes still have problems?
4. What are the major implementing activities managers can use to maintain the effectiveness of their employees?
5. What is the difference between internal and external motivation?
6. Why do managers need to develop effective work teams?
7. According to Abraham Maslow, how do people seek to satisfy their needs?
8. Does McClelland's theory of motivation suggest that people are born with the important needs that motivate them or that those needs are developed?
9. According to Herzberg, what types of factors provide employee satisfaction?
10. What are the steps in an effective change process?
11. What three activities do managers perform as a part of the controlling function?
12. What are the major types of standards used in business?
13. Why should managers be concerned if performance is higher than the standard?

14. What are the possible actions that can be taken if performance does not meet standards?
15. What areas of business operations should managers study in order to reduce costs?

D ISCUSSING IDEAS

1. Can managers be effective with implementing if they do not have good working relationships with the employees they supervise?
2. Which do you believe is most effective in increasing employee effectiveness—internal motivation or external motivation?
3. Why are businesses paying much more attention to developing effective work teams today than in the past?
4. What differences, if any, are there in the operations management of retail businesses, manufacturers, and service business?
5. Which of the three theories of motivation best describes the way you believe employees satisfy their needs and why?
6. What should a manager do if it is clear that employees do not want to make the changes that have been planned for an organization?
7. Provide an example of a business activity that demonstrates each of the four management functions.
8. What can happen if managers delay controlling activities for a long time after plans are implemented?
9. What are some examples of business activities where perfection is the only acceptable standard for performance?
10. Should managers delegate controlling activities to employees and employee teams? Why or why not?

A NALYZING INFORMATION

1. Many companies today are concerned about employee attitudes about their work environment. One company asks each employee to complete a survey every six months. The survey asks each employee to rate the effectiveness of his/her work group on seven characteristics. Each characteristic is rated on a five-point scale from 5 (very effective) to 1 (very ineffective). The average ratings of all employees are shown below for the January 30 and June 30 surveys.

Characteristic	*Jan. 30 rating*	*June 30 rating*
members support team purpose	3.5	3.8
activities are clear	2.0	2.2
members understand responsibilities	2.8	2.8

members have needed skills	4.8	4.6
members are committed to the group	3.5	4.0
members communicate effectively	4.1	4.8
team works to solve problems	4.0	3.6

    a. Calculate the amount of change (increase or decrease) for each item during the six-month period and the average rating for each item when the two ratings are combined.

    b. Prepare a rank-order listing of the characteristics based on the combined averages.

    c. Total the ratings for all characteristics for each of the ratings periods to determine an overall effectiveness rating for each period.

2. Develop a list of at least ten things you believe motivate employee performance. You can identify the items from your own ideas or by discussing the ideas with others. After the list is complete, prepare diagrams on separate sheets of paper that illustrate each of the three motivation theories discussed in the chapter. Then add the ten motivating items from your list in the appropriate locations on your three illustrations. Be prepared to discuss your diagrams and provide reasons for your decisions about the motivating items.

3. In the following chart, several items from a budget of a business are shown. The categories for which a budget amount has been determined are shown in Column 1. The budgeted amounts are shown in Column 2 and the actual amounts are shown in Column 3. Complete the chart by calculating the variance between the budgeted and actual amounts (Column 4) and the percentage increase or decrease (Column 5).

	Budget	Actual	Variance	% + or −
Sales	$680,000	$720,000		
Merchandise Returns	11,000	12,500		
Cost of Goods	229,400	240,000		
Operating Expenses	52,000	46,500		
Administrative Costs	34,000	31,500		
Marketing Expenses	306,000	350,500		
Net Profit	47,600	39,000		

4. Write a sample quantity standard, quality standard, and time standard for each of the following situations:

    a. A furniture factory building chairs.

    b. A salesperson calling on customers in a new territory.

    c. An assembly line manufacturing automobile tires.

    d. A cashier-checker at a supermarket.

5. Use library research to prepare a written report on one of the following topics dealing with control as a management activity:

    a. Methods of inventory management.

    b. The use of computers by managers.

REVIEW 27

c. Increasing product quality in American businesses.

d. How companies increase employee productivity.

SOLVING BUSINESS PROBLEMS

CASE 27-1

Ali's Buy-Rite Used Cars had experienced its third straight year of declining profits. While a few more cars were sold each year, the profit per sales was down. Ali had traditionally relied on a loyal group of customers who returned to buy a second and even third car, demonstrating their satisfaction with the company. Fewer customers were returning, however, and the company had to increase its promotional budget to attract new customers.

Ali believed two factors were contributing to the declining business. First, many new car dealers were now leasing many of their cars rather than selling them. This meant customers needed very low or no down payments and lower monthly payments. New car payments were now comparable to used car payments. Second, Ali's salespeople were getting more aggressive in order to sell cars. Because profits were down, more cars needed to be sold. Some customers were complaining they felt pressured by salespeople.

Ali decided the procedures used to sell automobiles had to change. He knew that several of the new auto dealers had gone to a one-price, no negotiation strategy where a low but fair price was put on each car. The car would be sold at that price so there would be no pressure from the salesperson regarding the price to be paid. Ali hoped the salespeople would help the customer select the best car rather than worrying about negotiating the best price.

Ali expected two problems in convincing the salespeople that the new sales strategy would be effective. First, it would require a different type of selling relationship with the customer, and some salespeople might have a hard time adjusting. Second, the salesperson would be paid a salary rather than a commission. Several of the top salespeople would not be able to make as much money as they could when sales were good, but all salespeople would make a decent salary.

Required:

1. How should Ali work with the salespeople to introduce the change?
2. How can Ali motivate the salespeople now that commissions will not be paid on sales?
3. What controlling activities could Ali undertake to be able to specifically determine why profits have been declining?

CASE 27-2

The business management class had just finished its study of management functions and the instructor wrote the following two paragraphs on the chalkboard:

"The work of managers has changed little in the past fifty years. The best way to learn to be an effective manager is with experience."

"Management in the 1990s is very different from management in the past. The best managers have spent years studying management and continue to participate in management education programs to learn the best management practices."

The instructor turned to the class and said, "There is still a great deal of debate about what makes an effective manager. The two sentences reflect very different views held by business people. Each of the viewpoints will determine who is hired as a manager in a business and how people prepare for management careers."

Required:

1. What is the meaning of the instructor's statement that each of the viewpoints will determine who is hired as a manager in a business and how people prepare for management careers?
2. How is the work of managers today similar to and different from the work of managers in the past?
3. Which of the sentences do you agree with and why?

Unit Summary

7-1 *Define the role of managers in an organization and the functions that all managers perform.*

Managers are responsible for the success of a business. Even though employees will do most of the work, if the company is not successful the fault will be placed on the manager. Managers exist in all businesses from the very small to extremely large. The first level of managers is the supervisor and the top level is the chief executive. Even though managers provide a vast number of activities, all managers complete the same four functions: planning, organizing, implementing, and controlling.

7-2 *Outline an effective procedure to be followed by managers when making decisions.*

Managers are confronted every day and nearly every hour of a day with questions and problems. They need to make decisions to answer the questions or solve the problems. Decisions need to be made well and quickly. Managers need skills in effective decision making in order to complete their work and lead the employees for whom they are responsible. Effective decision making requires a careful process of defining the problem, gathering information, determining and evaluating alternatives, and selecting the best option. Managers require information, must stay objective, and attempt to involve others in order to make the best decisions.

7-3 *Identify important leadership skills needed by managers and how leadership is demonstrated in business.*

Leadership is one of the most discussed topics in business management today. Business people have come to realize that a manager is not always an effective leader and that there are leaders in organizations who are not managers. It is also recognized that leaders are not born; leadership skills can be developed. Many companies are spending a great deal of time and money to identify important leadership skills and to develop training programs to improve the leadership skills of managers.

UNIT SUMMARY 7

7-4   *Describe the important planning tools used by managers.*

The management process begins with planning. One of the major differences between successful and unsuccessful companies is the use of a written business plan to guide the business. Both long-term and short-term planning is needed. Some managers spend most of their time setting the long-term direction and goals of a company. Even supervisors use planning skills, although their planning is directed at the day-to-day activities of their units. They do not typically spend as much time on planning as other managers. Managers must be skilled in the use of a number of planning tools including goals, budgets, standards, schedules, policies, procedures, and research.

7-5   *Explain the importance of organizing activities and the characteristics of an effective organization.*

Work is organized in order to perform it well and to use the resources of the company as effectively as possible. Once a company is large enough to employ more than one person, work is organized by dividing it among the employees. Traditional organization structures include a line organization, line-and staff, and matrix or project organizations. Many companies are redesigning their organizations to reduce the levels of management, to become more decentralized, and to involve work teams in planning and decision making.

7-6   *Present suggestions on ways for managers to implement the work of organizations effectively.*

Managers use the plans and organization of a business to implement work. Implementation involves the day-to-day work of the company. A number of activities are used by managers to ensure that work is completed successfully. They include communicating, motivating, using work teams, and operations management.

Employee motivation is necessary for effective operations. Managers use several motivation theories to determine how to meet employee needs with internal and external reinforcements. A particularly important challenge facing managers is to make needed changes in such a way that employees are comfortable and believe the organization will support them. Change must be implemented following a careful procedure of planning, communicating, involving, educating, and supporting.

7-7   *Illustrate the steps managers use in a controlling process to improve performance.*

The final step in management is controlling, or determining the effectiveness of activities. Controlling involves three steps. First, standards must be developed for all goals and activities. Next, performance must be measured and compared to the standards. Finally, corrective action must be taken if performance does not meet the standard.

Managers work with a number of standards including quantity, quality, time, and cost standards. With the increased competition being faced by managers, controlling costs has become especially important. Areas of cost control in most businesses include inventory, credit, theft, and health and safety.

Appendix

CAREER OPPORTUNITIES

Business careers are appealing because of the number of jobs available, opportunities for advancement, and variety of jobs. No matter what your interests, skills, or level of education and experience, there is a job that matches. Once you have obtained the first job, many opportunities open up. Advancement can occur with additional education or with continuing experience and training on the job.

You can identify career ladders in almost any business. If you begin work in a clerical position in a business, there is a progression to more specialized jobs in information management or office administration. You can progress from assistant manager to department manager or a highly specialized position in either area. Some people even progress to the very top of the company as executives. The same type of career path is available to people who begin as counter people in fast food restaurants, production workers in factories, or reservations clerks in hotels.

Because common areas of knowledge and skills are important to many types of businesses, you are not limited to one career ladder, one type of business, or one geographic area. People who begin in banking may change to an insurance career. Someone who is a salesperson for a computer-products company may decide to move to a building materials company for an increase in salary or more responsibilities. If job prospects are not particularly good in one part of the country, it is likely that a skilled business person can find employment in another region. Career paths in business are very flexible.

LEVELS OF EMPLOYMENT

In the business world, people work at all levels of a company. Beginning positions are obtained by people when they are still in high school with no experience and little understanding of business operations. The top positions in the world's largest corporations are held by people with many years of experience. Executives usually have worked in several areas of the business or often have experience in several businesses. Most business executives today have a college degree and, increasingly, they have graduate degrees.

There are several levels of employment in business. Those levels are based on the amount of education and experience required. Common levels are entry, career, specialist, management, and executive/entrepreneur.

Entry-level occupations usually involve routine activities and require little training. These jobs are open to people with little or no previous business education or experience. If you have not worked in business before, this is where you will begin. People hold entry-level jobs for only a short time until they have developed enough experience and skill for promotion. Examples of entry-level jobs are cashier, counter person, clerk, receptionist, and operator.

Career-level jobs require more complex duties. People in *career-level occupations* are able to control some of their work and will be responsible for some decisions. To be successful, they should have a basic understanding of business and skills in the areas in which they are working. They usually view their work as more than a job and have an interest in the area of business as a potential career. Career-level jobs include sales associate, reservations agent, word processor, teller, and customer service representative.

Specialists must be effective decision makers and have some leadership ability. *Specialist occupations* require a variety of skills in one or more business functions and extensive understanding of the operations of a specific company or industry. Specialists are the people considered the most skilled or expert in the activities they complete on the job. Specialists in businesses include buyers, researchers, analysts, professional salespeople, technicians, machine operators, and similar technical or skilled positions.

Supervisors/managers hold the first levels of management positions in companies. They must have a high level of knowledge in the parts of the organization that they supervise or manage. They also must be effective decision makers and have strong leadership ability. *Supervisor/management occupations* are responsible for specific units in a business and must make decisions about operations and personnel. The job titles associated with this level of employment are supervisor, assistant manager, and manager.

Executives/entrepreneurs perform all of the management tasks associated with owning a business or managing a major function, a large unit in a company, or the entire company. People who work in *executive/entrepreneur occupations* are fully responsible for the success or failure of the company. They must possess a comprehensive understanding of business and management. They will spend most of their time planning and evaluating the work of the organization. The positions held by executives/entrepreneurs are vice president, president, chief executive, and owner.

CAREERS IN INTERNATIONAL BUSINESS

The demise of the Soviet Union and the movement of many formerly Communist countries in Eastern Europe to adopt elements of a capitalistic economy are continuing evidence of the importance of international business. It has never been easier to travel to other countries, communicate with people around the world, buy goods produced in other places, and sell U.S. products and services abroad. We are members of a global community generally, and a global business community specifically. As businesses expand into international markets, so do the opportunities for international business careers.

International business careers have all of the advantages of working within the United States plus more. In addition to the excitement and challenge that accompanies work in any business career, international careers usually offer additional job choices and the chance to develop new skills, travel, and interact with a wide variety of people from different cultures.

If you want a career in international business, you will need to consider the skills required and develop plans for the necessary education and experience. In addition to the normal preparation for business, you will need knowledge and skills in other areas. The first area is the study of countries and cultures. It is not possible to know in which country you might be working as you prepare for an international career. However, there are specific types of information with which you should be familiar to be able to quickly learn about a particular country if you receive an international assignment. It is helpful to have a background in geography, world history, economics, political science, and current events.

The international business person needs to know something about the culture of the country in which the business will operate or to which the company's products and service are directed. Culture is the sum of the values, attitudes, beliefs, and habits of a specific group of people. While each culture is different, you can be prepared by learning about several of the major world cultures. A knowledgeable business person needs to know why cultures are different, what the important elements of each culture are, and how culture affects the way people think, make decisions, and act.

The economic environment of countries is an important part of international business as an area for study. A study of international economics includes an understanding of the monetary structure, banking system, natural and human resources, and economic traditions of countries. Business people need to be familiar with differences in political and legal structures, namely, the type of government, laws, and political methods of the country. An understanding of taxes, quotas, and trade agreements is also critical.

Currently, English is the international language of business. However, there is no substitute for understanding the language of your international contact. People are favorably impressed when you take the trouble to learn some of their language. It is difficult to predict which languages will be the most important in your future. Your commitment to study and learn a second language will impress employers as well as your international contacts. You will also find it easier to learn an additional language if needed later.

PREPARING FOR A BUSINESS CAREER

Preparing for a career in business may seem like trying to negotiate a maze. For people who are not familiar with business, it is difficult to understand what preparation is needed and how to obtain the job they want.

If you talk to people who have worked in business for many years, you will find that some did not plan or prepare for the job they currently hold. They often ended up there after starting in another part of the business in an entirely different occupation.

Today, a person is less likely to enter a business career without specific preparation. In your study of business, you have seen that it is quite complicated and requires a great deal of knowledge and skill in a number of areas. A successful business career is more likely for those people who understand the requirements and carefully plan to develop the necessary skills. In some ways, preparing for a business career is complicated, but in other ways it is really quite simple. It is often a matter of matching your personal qualities, education, and experience with a career path in business.

As you are well aware, good business education programs exist in high schools as well as in community and junior colleges and vocational/technical schools. Business is usually one of the largest degree programs in colleges and universities. You can complete a general business preparation or specialize in specific areas such as accounting, computer science, or marketing. Many businesses offer education and training programs for their employees or pay for some or all of the costs of college coursework. You can also attend conferences and seminars sponsored by businesses and professional associations.

Experience in business is always an advantage. Experience in working with people in any way can give you confidence and develop important communications and interpersonal skills. Even if you have not worked part time or full time in a business, other types of experiences are useful. Working on projects in an organization, writing for the yearbook or school newspaper, forming a Junior Achievement company, or helping in a parent's business are all examples of experiences that can develop skills important in business.

Most employers value experience when they hire employees. It is relatively easy to find an entry-level job if you are not particularly concerned about the type of work or working conditions. These entry-level jobs provide the work experience that will qualify you for the jobs you prefer. Even though the pay may not be as high as you would like and work schedules are sometimes difficult to manage with school and extracurricular activities, it important to have a good work record in your first jobs.

Beginning employees who stay with one employer for a length of time and receive favorable evaluations will find it easier to receive promotions or be hired by an employer offering a better job. Employees who take advantage of training, opportunities for leadership, or the chance to supervise other employees or work in other parts of the business will have an excellent employment record to use when applying for promotions or advanced jobs in other companies.

DEVELOPING A CAREER PLAN

Many people do little planning, even for the things that are most important to them. We know from our study of business that planning is an important skill. Businesses that use planning are much more successful than those that do not plan. While some people end up achieving what they want without plans, you are much more likely to be successful if you follow a plan. By developing a career plan, you will be able to practice an important business skill. In addition, your work can be shown to others to demonstrate your ability to plan.

The following steps provide an outline you might want to follow in developing a career plan:

1. Develop an understanding of business principles and concepts and the types of business careers. Study careers in depth to determine the industries, businesses, and jobs that are of most interest to you and the types of career paths related to those jobs.

2. Complete a self-assessment of your knowledge, skills, and attitudes that are related to those needed in business careers. Ask a counselor to assist you with appropriate interest and aptitude tests that can help you with your assessment. Get feedback from people who know you well (family, friends, teachers, employers) about their perceptions of the important skills, knowledge, and attitudes you have identified.

3. Identify the education and experience requirements for business careers that interest you. Compare those career requirements with your current preparation, and determine the additional education and experience you will need to qualify for those careers.

4. Discuss the education and experience you will need with people (counselors, business people) who are familiar with education programs and employment opportunities. Have them help you select those that fit your career plans and qualifications.

5. Develop a career plan that identifies the knowledge and skills needed for the career you have chosen and how each will be developed through a combination of education and experience. The plan can identify the jobs in a career ladder, the schools or education programs you plan to complete, how long you expect to take in moving through each step of the career ladder, and the ultimate career goal you would like to achieve.

PREPARING A CAREER PORTFOLIO

Portfolios have been used for many years by artists, models, and advertising people to demonstrate their abilities and present examples of their work. A *portfolio* is an organized collection of information and materials developed to represent yourself, your preparation, and your accomplishments. You might want to consider developing a career portfolio to help you with career planning and to represent yourself when you apply for jobs or for admission to an educational institution.

A portfolio should provide clear descriptions of your preparation, skills, and experience. Those descriptions can include examples of projects you have completed in school and on the job or for organizations to which you belong. They can even be work you have done as a hobby that demonstrates an important business skill. Evaluations of your skills and work evidenced through tests, checklists of competencies you have mastered, and performance reviews from employers can be included in your portfolio. In addition, you might ask people who know you well to write statements or recommendations that relate to your skills and abilities.

A portfolio can be developed over a long period of time. You might start it now and continue to add to it as you complete high school, go on for additional education, or move through jobs in your career ladder. You should prepare a portfolio that allows you to add and remove items. It should also protect the items so they remain in good condition. The portfolio should include your best and most recent materials.

A portfolio is a good way for you to identify important materials that will help you with your self-assessment. It also keeps materials organized so you can show them to others to demonstrate achievement, or as you apply for educational programs and jobs. Because it needs to communicate your preparation and skills effectively, it should be well organized, understandable, and easy for others to review.

Glossary

A **accountability:** the fact that each individual in an organization is responsible to a superior for the quality of work performed.

accounting records: financial records of the transactions of the business.

accounts payable: money owed for credit purchases.

accounts payable record: a record showing money owed and payments made by the business.

accounts receivable: the amount owed by customers.

accounts receivable record: a record showing what each customer owes and pays.

achievement need: take personal responsibility for work; set personal goals; want immediate feedback on work.

administered channel: a channel in which one organization takes a leadership position to benefit all channel members.

advertising: all forms of paid promotion that deliver a message to many people at the same time.

advertising budget: a plan of the amount of money a firm should spend for advertising based on estimated sales.

advertising media: the methods of delivering the promotional message to the intended audience.

advertising research: research done to test advertisements and the media that carry the advertisements.

affiliation need: concerned about relationships with others; work to get along well and fit in with a group.

aging the accounts: analyzing customers' account balances within categories based upon the number of days each customer's balance has remained unpaid.

applications software: consists of instructions for performing various types of tasks.

applied research: studies of existing product problems or design improvements for current products.

apprenticeship training: a specialized program for preparing skilled employees that is jointly organized and managed by labor unions and management and approved by the U.S. Department of Labor.

assessed valuation: the value of property determined by tax officials.

assessment center: provides structured testing in which employees are subjected to situations like those they will encounter in the new job to determine how they will perform.

asset book value: original cost less accumulated depreciation of an asset.

assets: things owned, such as cash and buildings.

authority: the right to make decisions about work assignments and to require other employees to perform assigned tasks.

autocratic leader: one who gives direct, clear, and precise orders with detailed instructions as to what, when, and how work is to be done.

automatic teller machine (ATM): enables bank customers to deposit, withdraw, or transfer funds by using a bank-provided plastic card.

automobile liability insurance: provides protection against damage caused by the insured's automobile to other people or to their property.

B **baby boom:** refers to the high birth rate period from 1945-1965.

baby bust: refers to the low birth rate period following the baby boom period.

balance of trade: the difference between money coming into and going out of a country.

balance of trade deficit: when more money leaves a country than comes in.

balance of trade surplus: when more money comes into a country than goes out.

balance sheet (statement of financial position): a financial statement that lists the assets, liabilities, and capital of a business.

bank: an institution that accepts demand deposits and makes commercial loans.

bank discount: interest deducted in advance from a loan.

bankruptcy: a legal process that allows selling assets to pay off debts.

bar codes: product identification labels containing a unique set of vertical bars that can be read using computer scanning equipment.

base plus incentive plan: a compensation plan that combines a minimum salary or wage with an incentive based on production or performance.

basic accounting formula: assets = liabilities + capital.

blind ad: an advertisement for a job opening that does not identify the company.

board of directors (directors or board): ruling body of a corporation.

bond: a long-term written promise to pay a definite sum of money at a specified time.

bonding: provides payment of damages to people who have losses resulting from the negligence or dishonesty of an employee or from the failure of the business to complete a contract.

bonus: money paid at the end of a specific period of time for performance that exceeds the expected standard.

book value: the value of a share of stock that is found by dividing the net worth (assets minus liabilities) of the corporation by the total number of shares outstanding.

borrowed capital (creditor capital): capital loaned to a business by others.

boycott: a decision by union members not to buy the products of a company with which they have a dispute.

brainstorming: a group discussion technique that is used to generate as many ideas as possible for solving a problem.

budget: a financial plan extending usually for one year.

budget plan: short-term credit usually covering a two- or three-month period.

building codes: codes that regulate physical features of structures.

burglary, robbery, and theft insurance: provides protection from loss due to robbery of money, goods, and various other business assets.

business: an organization that produces or distributes a good or service for profit.

business cycles: a pattern of irregular but repeated expansion and contraction of the GDP.

business ethics: a collection of principles and rules of conduct based on what is right and wrong for an organization.

business income insurance: insurance designed to compensate firms for loss of income during the time required to restore property damaged by an insured peril.

business plan: (1) a written description of the business and its operations with an analysis of the opportunities and risks it faces. (2) a written guide that helps the entrepreneur during the design and startup phases of the business.

buying: obtaining goods to be sold.

buying motives: the reasons people buy.

buying office: represents the products of many manufacturers and assists buyers in making purchases.

C **cafeteria plan:** a fringe benefit program in which employees can select the benefits that meet their personal needs.

capacity: earning power.

capital (net worth, owner's equity, shareholders' equity, stockholders' equity): what a business is worth after subtracting liabilities from assets.

capital budget: a financial plan for replacing fixed assets or acquiring new ones.

capital formation: the production of capital goods.

capital goods: buildings, tools, machines, and other equipment that are used to produce other goods but do not directly satisfy human wants.

capital stock: the general term applied to the shares of ownership of a corporation.

capitalism: an economic-political system in which private citizens are free to go into business for themselves, to produce whatever they choose to produce, and to distribute what they produce as they please.

career centers: facilities where career development activities are managed.

career development: a program that matches the long-term career planning of employees with the employment needs of the business.

career development program: provides a long-term focus on a company's employment needs combined with support for employees so they can prepare for future jobs in the company.

career path: a progression of related jobs with increasing skill requirements and responsibility.

career plan: identifies the jobs that are a part of the employee's career path, the training and development needed to advance along the career path, and a tentative schedule for the plan's activities.

cash-and-carry wholesaler: A wholesaler who operates much like a merchant wholesaler, except that the buyer must pay cash and transport the product from the wholesaler's business.

cash budget: an estimate of cash received and paid out.

cash discount: given if payment is received by a certain date.

cash flow: the movement of cash into and out of a business.

cashier's check: a check drawn on the bank that issues it, payable to the person designated by the purchaser of the check.

cease and desist: requires that a company stop using specific advertisements.

central processing unit (CPU): equipment that both stores and processes data in addition to controlling operating procedures.

centralized organization: all major planning and decision making is done by a group of top managers in the business.

certificate of deposit (CD): a time deposit savings account that requires an investor to deposit a specified sum for a fixed period at a fixed interest rate.

certified check: a check on which a bank certifies that a checking account customer's funds are being held specifically to pay the check when presented.

Certified Public Accountant (CPA): a person who has met a state's education, experience, and examination requirements.

channel integration: when one business owns the organizations at other levels of the channel.

channel members: businesses that participate in activities transferring goods and services from the producer to the user.

channels of distribution (marketing channels): the routes products and services follow, including the activities and participating organizations, while moving from the producer to the consumer.

character: an indication of one's moral obligation to pay debts.

charter (certificate of incorporation): an official document granted by a state giving power to run a corporation.

check: a written order on a bank to pay previously deposited money to a third party on demand.

chief information officer (CIO): the top computer executive.

chip (electronic chip, microprocessor, integrated circuit): a sliver of silicon containing circuits (transistors) through which electricity passes in order to process and store data.

classroom training: instruction accomplished in a room designed for a variety of training programs that emphasize knowledge and attitude development.

close corporation (closely held corporation): a corporation that does not offer its shares of stock for public sale.

coaching: regular observation of an employee by a supervisor or experienced employee with follow-up discussions on ways to improve performance.

code of ethics: a formal, published collection of values and rules used to guide the behavior of an organization toward its various stakeholders.

coinsurance: divides the risk between the insurer and the insured on a percentage basis.

collective bargaining: representatives of management and labor meeting together to discuss and agree on conditions relating to employment.

collision insurance: insurance that provides protection against damage to one's own car when it is in a collision with another car or object.

command economy: an economic system in which the method for determining what, how, and for whom goods and services are produced is decided by a central planning authority.

commercial bank: a financial institution that provides many services, such as handling time and demand deposits and commercial and consumer loans.

commercial businesses: firms engaged in marketing, in finance, and in furnishing services.

commercial credit: credit extended by one business to another business.

commercial loan: a loan made to a business.

commission plan: a compensation plan in which employees are paid a percentage of the volume of business for which they are responsible.

common stock: ownership that gives holders the right to participate in managing the business by having voting privileges and by sharing in the profits (dividends) if there are any.

communication: refers to the sharing of information, which results in a high degree of understanding between the message sender and receiver.

communication network: refers to how information flows through a business.

communism: forced socialism where all or almost all the productive resources of a nation are owned by the government.

comparable worth: paying workers equally for jobs with similar but not identical job requirements.

comparative advantage theory: to gain a trade advantage a country should specialize in products or services that it can provide more efficiently than other countries.

compensation: the money and other benefits people receive for work.

competition: rivalry among sellers for consumers' dollars.

comprehensive insurance: insurance that covers loss caused by flying objects, fire, theft, wind, hail, water, and vandalism.

computer integrated manufacturing: all of the manufacturing systems in a business are designed and managed using computers.

computer system: a combination of related elements (hardware and software) working together to achieve a common goal.

conditions: relate to economic and other matters such as the economic health of a community or nation and the extent of business competition that affects credit decisions.

conflict: a situation that develops when one person interferes with the achievement of another's goals.

consultant: an expert who is called upon to study a special problem and offer solutions.

consumer credit: credit extended by the retailer to the consumer.

consumer goods: products produced for sale to individuals and families for personal use.

consumer goods and services: goods and services that satisfy people's economic wants directly.

consumer loan: a loan made to an individual.

consumer panel: a group of people who offer opinions about a product or service.

Consumer Price Index (CPI): a measure of the average change in prices of consumer goods and services typically purchased by people living in urban areas.

containerization: products are packed in large shipping containers at the factory and then shipped using a number of transportation methods before being unpacked.

controlling: evaluating results to determine if the company's objectives have been accomplished as planned.

convenience goods: inexpensive items that consumers purchase regularly without a great deal of thought.

convenience stores: small stores located in neighborhoods or at convenient shopping locations that handle a variety of inexpensive, regularly purchased products such as foods, beverages, health care products, and household products.

convertible bonds: bonds that allow bondholders to exchange bonds for a prescribed number of shares of common stock.

cooperative: a business owned and operated by its user-members for the purpose of supplying themselves with goods and services.

copyright: similar to a patent in that the federal government gives an author the sole right to reproduce, publish, and sell literary or artistic work for the life of the author plus 50 years.

corporation: a business owned by a group of people and authorized by the state in which it is located to act as though it were a single person.

corrective advertising: a company must use a specific amount of its advertising budget to run new advertisements correcting misleading information.

cost of goods sold: the actual cost of the product to the selling company.

credit insurance: protection against losses on credit that is extended to customers.

credit life insurance: used by small loan companies, banks, and dealers who provide installment credit loans; the borrowers can buy sufficient life insurance to pay the balance of his or her debt in the event of death.

creditor capital: capital loaned to a business by others.

creditors: those to whom money is owed.

cross training: employees are trained to perform more than one job in the company even though they typically perform only one.

culture: (1) involves the shared values, beliefs, and behavior existing in an organization. (2) the customs, beliefs, values, and patterns of behavior of the people of a country or group.

customer oriented: businesses that direct company activities at satisfying customers.

cyberphobia: fear of computers.

cycle billing: billing that occurs when monthly statements are sent to certain customers on one day of the month and to other customers on other days of the month.

 data: original facts and figures that businesses generate.

data processing: electronically handling data that consist mostly of numbers and symbols but could also include a limited amount of text.

data processing service center: a business that processes data for other businesses for a fee.

database: a set of files maintained for decision making.

debentures: bonds that are not secured by assets but based upon the faith and credit of the corporation that issues them.

debit card: allows a person to make cash withdrawals from ATMs, pay bills by phone from bank accounts, and pay for on-site purchases such as foods and household items.

decentralized organization: a business is divided into smaller operating units and managers are given almost total responsibility and authority for the operation of those units.

decision support system (DSS): provides top-level executives with information needed to make decisions

affecting the future goals and direction of an organization.

decline stage: occurs when a product is introduced that is much better or easier to use, and customers begin to switch from the old product to the new product.

deductible: an arrangement that permits the insured to bear part of the loss in return for a lower premium.

demand: refers to the number of similar products that will be bought at a given time at a given price.

demand deposit: money put into a financial institution by depositors and which can be withdrawn at any time without penalty.

democratic leader: one who encourages workers to share in making decisions about work-related problems.

department stores: generally large full-service stores that carry many types of products for the home, such as furniture, appliances, clothing, and other household items.

depreciation: decrease in the value of an asset due to wear and age.

depression: a long and severe drop in the GDP.

direct advertising: promotions sent directly to a potential customer.

direct deposit: allows business to electronically transfer employees' paychecks directly from the employer's bank account to employees' bank accounts.

direct marketing: when producers sell directly to the ultimate consumer.

disability insurance: offers payments to employees who are no longer able to work because of accidents or illnesses.

discharge: the release of an employee from the company due to inappropriate work behavior.

discount stores: stores that offer a range of common items for a broad set of customers typically including apparel, household items, hardware, toys, and nonperishable food. (The products sell for less than the price at which they may be sold in other types of stores because of the volume of products sold and fewer services provided.)

discounts: reductions from the price of the product to encourage customers to buy.

disk drive: a device used to store and retrieve data on disks.

distortion: refers to how people consciously or unconsciously change messages.

distraction: anything that interferes with the sender's creating and delivering a message and the receiver's getting and interpreting a message.

distribution center: a large building designed to accumulate and redistribute products efficiently.

distribution planning: a method used by business to ensure that all important factors are considered when deciding on appropriate distribution methods and procedures.

dividends: profits distributed to stockholders on a per share basis.

domestic goods: products made by firms in the United States.

downsize: cutting back on the goods and services provided and thereby shrinking the size of a firm and the number of employees.

downsizing: a process where organizations are forced to cut the number of employees as well as reduce other costs.

drawer: the person who owns the account and signs the checks.

drive time: the most expensive advertising time on many commercial radio stations (the early morning and late afternoon hours when many people are in their cars and listening to the radio).

dumping: refers to the practice of selling goods in a foreign market at a price that is below cost or below what it charges in its own home country.

E **economic discrepancies:** differences between the offerings of a business and the requirements of a consumer.

economic growth: occurs when a country's output exceeds its population growth.

economic system: an organized way for a country to decide how to use its productive resources; that is, to decide what, how, and for whom goods and services will be produced.

economic wants: the desire for scarce material goods and services.

economics: the body of knowledge that relates to producing and using goods and services that satisfy human wants.

effectiveness: occurs when an organization makes the right decisions in deciding what products or services to offer customers or other users.

efficiency: occurs when an organization produces needed goods or services quickly at low cost.

electronic funds transfer (EFT): transferring money by computer rather than by check.

electronic mail (E-mail): transmits and stores documents through a data communication system without the printing of hard copy.

embargo: government bars companies from doing business with particular countries.

employee stock ownership: a bonus paid in the form of shares of company stock rather than in cash.

employee stock ownership plan (ESOP): permits employees to directly own the company in which they work by allowing them to buy shares in it.

employment requisition: a form requesting that a position in a department be filled by the human resources department.

employment turnover: the extent to which people enter and leave employment in a business during a year.

empowerment: lets workers decide how to perform their work tasks and offer ideas on how to improve the work process.

endorsement: the signature—usually on the back—that transfers a negotiable instrument.

entrepreneur: a person who starts, manages, and owns a business.

EOM: the time of payment is computed from the end of the month in which the merchandise is shipped.

ergonomics: the science of adapting equipment to the work and health needs of people.

ethics: the code of moral conduct that sets standards for what is valued as right or wrong behavior for a person or group.

evaluation conference: a scheduled meeting in which an employee and his or her immediate supervisor (or a human resources specialist) review the performance evaluation.

exchange rate: the value of one currency to another.

excise tax: a sales tax that applies only to selected goods and services, such as gasoline.

executive: a top-level manager who spends almost all of his or her time on management functions.

exit interview: a formal interview with an employee who is leaving a company to determine the person's attitudes and feelings about the company's policies and procedures, management, and operations.

expert power: given to people who are considered the most knowledgeable.

expert system: consists of software programs that help nonexperts make intelligent decisions.

export credit insurance: covers losses suffered if the purchasers of exports do not pay for their purchases.

exporting: when a company sells its goods and services to a foreign country.

exports: goods and services sold to other countries.

express service: a parcel service that guarantees the sender the shipment will arrive before a designated time.

extended coverage: additional insurance protection beyond the major peril.

F **facsimile (fax):** a machine that transmits a copy of a document from one location to another over telephone lines.

factoring companies (factors): specialize in lending money to businesses based on their accounts receivable.

factors of production: land, labor, capital goods, and management—the four basic resources that are combined to create useful goods and services.

factory outlets: a combination of a discount and specialty store that is owned by the manufacturer. (It is used to sell merchandise that cannot be sold through the normal marketing channels and offers only the brands of that manufacturer in a limited number of locations.)

false advertising: advertising that is misleading in a material respect or in any way that could influence the customer's purchase or use of the product.

feedback: a receiver's response to a sender's message.

fiber optic cable: a cable composed of hair-thin glass wires that simultaneously handle thousands of two-way voice, text/data, and TV transmissions at extremely fast speeds.

finance: deals with all money matters related to running a business.

financial statements: reports that summarize financial data over a period of time.

financing: providing money that is needed to perform various marketing activities, such as obtaining credit when buying and extending credit when selling.

fire insurance: insurance that provides funds to replace such items as buildings, furniture, machinery, raw materials, and finished products destroyed by fire.

fixed assets (plant assets): material assets that will last a long time.

flex-time: a plan for scheduling employee work in which some employees start early and leave early, while others start and finish late.

FOB destination: the seller pays the transportation charges to the destination.

FOB shipping point: the seller pays only the expense of delivering the goods to the transportation company.

foreign corporation: a corporation doing business in a state from which it did not receive its charter.

foreign goods: products made by firms in other countries.

forgery insurance: obtained by business people, banks, individuals, and other institutions to provide protection against loss caused by forged or altered checks and securities.

formal communication network: composed of different levels of management with information flowing upward, downward, and across an organization in a prescribed manner.

formal training: training that is carefully planned, managed, and evaluated.

franchise: a legal agreement between a company and a distributor to sell a product or service under special conditions.

franchisee: the distributor of a franchised product or service.

franchisor: the parent company of a franchise agreement that provides the product or service.

free trade: the elimination of most trade barriers.

fringe benefits: financial compensation in addition to salaries and wages.

Frost Belt: the colder northern half of the United States.

full disclosure: providing all information necessary for consumers to make an informed decision.

G **give-backs:** companies involved in labor negotiations ask unions to reduce wage scales and benefits that had been agreed to in earlier contracts.

glass ceiling: an invisible barrier to job advancement.

global competition: the ability of profit-making organizations to compete with other businesses in other countries.

grading and valuing: grouping goods according to size, quality, or other characteristics, and determining an appropriate price for products.

grapevine: an informal communication system that develops among workers.

graphical user interface (GUI): a software management package that uses symbols to select and shift among varied software application programs and provides common desktop tools, such as a notepad, calculator, clock, and calendar.

gross domestic product (GDP): the total market value of all goods produced and services provided in a country in a year.

group insurance: an insurance plan in which all employees can obtain insurance at a reasonable cost regardless of their health at a cost typically lower than if the coverage was purchased individually.

growth stage: when several brands of the new product are available.

H **hardware:** equipment that makes up a computer system.

health insurance: provides protection against the expenses of health care.

health maintenance organizations (HMOs): a cooperative agreement between a business and a group of physicians and other medical professionals to provide for the health care needs of the employees of the business.

home country: the country in which a multinational corporation has its headquarters.

host country: the foreign country where a multinational firm has production and service facilities.

human capital: the accumulated knowledge and skills of human beings —the total value of each person's education and acquired skills.

human relations: how well people get along together.

human resource planning: determines the types of jobs that are required for each part of the production procedure and the number of people needed for each job.

human resources management: a specific area of management that ensures that an adequate number of employees is available, that they are well-paid and trained, satisfied with their jobs, and productive.

hygiene factors: provide dissatisfaction when they do not meet employee needs but do not provide satisfaction when responding to employee needs.

Ⓘ **identity power:** given to people because others identify with and want to be accepted by them.

implementing: helping employees to work effectively.

importing: buying goods or services made in a foreign country.

imports: goods and services purchased from other countries.

income statement (statement of operations): a financial document that

reports total revenue and expenses for a specific period.

income statement budget: a plan showing projected sales, costs, and individual expense figures for a future period.

income tax: a tax levied against the profits of business firms and against earnings of individuals.

indirect marketing: when distribution takes place through channel members.

industrial businesses: firms that produce goods that are often used by other businesses or organizations to make things.

industrial goods: products that are to be used by another business.

industry: a word often used to refer to all businesses within a category.

inflation: a rapid rise in prices caused by an inadequate supply of goods and services.

infomercials: full-length television programs (30-60 minutes) produced to promote and sell a specific product.

informal communication network: consists of unofficial ways of sharing information in an organization.

informal training: training provided without careful planning, management, or evaluation.

information: data that have been processed in some way to make it useful.

information liability: responsibility for physical or economic injury arising from incorrect data or wrongful use of data.

information system: a computer system used to process data for the purpose of generating information from that data.

injunction: directs the union to stop doing a specific act and is enforced by the court.

input device: equipment that receives data and feeds it to the processor.

installment contract (conditional sales contract): an agreement under which the buyer promises to make regular payments until the goods are fully paid.

installment credit: credit used when a customer makes a sizable purchase and agrees to make payments over an extended but fixed period of time.

insurable interest: any interest in property that will suffer a possible financial loss if there is a loss of or damage to the property.

insurance agents: people who represent the insurance company and sell insurance to individuals and businesses.

insurance rate: the amount charged for a certain value of insurance.

insured: the persons or organization covered by the insurance policy.

insurer: a company that sells insurance.

integrated information system (IIS): an organized way to capture, process, store, retrieve, and distribute information for decision-making purposes for an organization.

international business: business activities that occur between two or more countries.

interstate commerce: business operations and transactions that cross over state lines.

intrapreneur: an employee who is given funds and freedom to create a special unit or department within a company in order to develop a new product, process, or service.

intrastate commerce: business transacted within a state.

introduction stage: when a brand-new product enters the market.

inventory management: determines the quantities of materials and supplies needed for production and the amount of finished products required to meet customer orders.

inventory turnover rate: the number of times during a year that a business is able to sell its average inventory.

investment banking firm: an organization that helps businesses raise capital.

investment company: an organization that specializes in the sale of a variety of stocks and bonds.

invoice: a form prepared by the vendor listing the goods shipped, the price, and the terms of sale.

job design: the kind of work and the way the work is organized.

job enlargement: making a job more interesting by adding variety to the tasks.

job enrichment: encouraging employee participation in decision making.

job evaluation: the process of ranking jobs in order according to their value based on specific characteristics of each job.

job security: the likelihood that employment will not be terminated.

job sharing: an employment plan that allows two people to share one full-time job.

job specification: information on the nature of the work done in a particular job, the necessary qualifications needed by the employee to do the work, and where the job fits in the organizational and wage structure of the company.

joint venture: two or more businesses that agree to make and/or sell a good or service.

knowledge workers: people who work with information.

labor: the human effort, either physical or mental, that goes into the production of goods and services.

labor contract: a written document defining the rights and responsibilities of employees and management.

labor force: most people aged 16 or over who are available for work, whether employed or unemployed.

labor participation rate: the percentage of the labor force either employed or actively seeking employment.

labor union: an organization of employees formed to negotiate with business owners.

laboratory training: training conducted in a special room designed to represent the equipment and procedures the employee will use on the job.

layaway plan: a purchase plan that permits a customer to make payments on an item until the item has been fully paid.

layoff: a temporary or permanent reduction in the number of employees resulting from a change in business conditions.

leadership: the ability to influence individuals and groups to achieve organizational goals.

leadership style: the general way a manager treats and directs employees.

lease: a contract that allows the use of an asset for a fee.

liabilities: claims against assets or things owed—the debts of a business.

liability insurance: provides protection for risks involved in operating a business.

licensing: a way to limit and control those who plan to enter certain types of businesses.

life insurance: provides money that is paid upon the death of the insured to a person or people identified in the insurance policy.

limited partnership: restricts the liability of a partner for the amount of the partner's investment.

line organization: all authority and responsibility may be traced in a direct line from the top executive down to the lowest employee level in the organization.

line-and-staff organization: the addition of staff specialists to a line organization.

list price: price quoted in price lists and catalogs of the vendor.

local area network (LAN): an electronic system that allows computer information to move over short distances between or among different computers.

lockout: a temporary work stoppage where the employer does not allow employees to enter the business.

long-term capital: capital that is borrowed for longer than a year.

long-term notes (term loans): loans written for periods of 1 to 15 years.

maker: the business or person who promises to pay the amount of the note.

management: the process of accomplishing the goals of an organization through the effective use of people and other resources.

management information system (MIS): provides upper-level managers with information needed to control the overall operations of an organization.

manager: a person who completes all four management functions on a regular basis and has authority over other jobs and people.

manufacturer brands: brand names established by a manufacturer of products for sale to a large market through a variety of businesses.

manufacturer's agent: an independent salesperson who is given the sole privilege of selling the products of a business in a given geographic area.

manufacturing: a special form of production in which raw and semifinished materials are processed and converted into finished products.

manufacturing firms: businesses that produce goods.

margin: term used to indicate the difference between the selling price and the cost of goods sold.

markdown: any amount by which the original selling price is reduced before an item is sold.

market: the types of buyers a business wishes to attract and where such buyers are located.

market economy: an economic system that determines what, how, and for whom goods and services are produced by coordinating individual choices through arrangements that aid buying and selling goods and services.

market research: the study of the people who buy a company's products or who may buy a new product.

market value: the value at which stock is bought and sold on any given day.

marketing: the process of planning and executing the conception, pricing, promotion, and distribution of ideas, goods, and services to create exchanges that satisfy individual and organizational objectives.

marketing concept: keeping the needs of the consumer uppermost in mind during the design, production, and distribution of a product.

marketing mix: the blending of all decisions that are related to the four elements of marketing.

marketing plan: a detailed written description of all marketing activities that a business must accomplish in order to sell a product.

marketing research: the study of all activities involved in the exchange of goods and services between businesses and consumers.

markup: the amount added to the cost of a product to determine its selling price.

mass production: (1) an assembly process in which a large number of products is produced, each of which is identical to the next. (2) occurs when up-to-date equipment and assembly line methods are used to produce large quantities of identical goods.

maturity date: date on which a loan must be repaid.

maturity stage: when there are many competing brands with very similar features.

medical payments insurance: a clause in an automobile insurance policy that will cover medical, surgical, hospital, and nursing expenses caused by accidental injuries to any occupant of the automobile, including the insured, regardless of the legal liability of the policyholder.

merchandise inventory: goods purchased to sell to customers at a profit.

merchandise market: a city where several major manufacturers are located or where those manufacturers have brought their new merchandise for display and sale.

merchandising budget: a budget that plans and controls the supply of merchandise to be sold to customers.

merchant wholesaler: a wholesaler who takes legal title to goods, offers credit to retailers, and provides other services, such as advertising and displaying merchandise.

mid-manager: a manager who completes all of the management functions but spends more time on one of the functions or is responsible for a specific part of the company's operations.

mixed economy: an economic system in which a combination of a market and a command economy are blended together to make decisions about what, how, and for whom goods and services are produced.

money market fund (money market account): an account where investments are made mostly in securities that pay interest.

monitor (video display screen): a television-like screen that immediately displays keyboarded data when it is entered in an information system.

monopoly: exists when competition is lacking for a product or service, or when producers are in a position to control the supply and price of goods or services.

mortgage bonds: bonds on which specific assets are pledged as a guarantee that the principal and interest will be paid according to the terms specified on the bonds.

motivation: the set of factors that cause a person to act in a certain way.

motivation research: the study of consumer buying behavior.

motivators: factors that result in satisfaction.

mouse (trackball): small hand-controlled device that guides a marker (pointer) to a list of commands that appears on the monitor.

multimedia: refers to the convergence of text, data, voice, and video through a microprocessor.

multinational firm: a business that owns or controls production or service facilities outside the country in which it is based.

multitasking: occurs when two or more software programs work simultaneously in the CPU.

mutual fund: pools the money of many small investors for the purchase of stocks and bonds.

mutual savings bank (savings bank): handles passbook savings accounts and loans, particularly mortgages.

N **natural resources:** anything provided by nature that affects the productive ability of a country.

negotiable instrument: written evidence of a contractual obligation, normally transferable from one person to another by endorsement.

net 30 days: payment is to be made within 30 days from the date on the invoice.

net profit: the difference between the selling price and all costs and expenses of the business.

no-fault insurance: each insurance company is required to pay the losses of its insured when an accident occurs, regardless of who might have been responsible for the loss.

nominal group technique (NGT): a process a leader uses to involve all group members to solve a difficult problem that may create conflicts among members.

non-tariff barriers: barriers other than tariffs that restrict imports.

nonbank bank (nonbank): an institution that offers only demand deposits or commercial loans, but not both.

noneconomic wants: desired wants that are not scarce.

nonprofit corporation: an organization that does not pay taxes and does not exist to make a profit.

nonverbal communications: delivering messages by means other than speaking or writing.

O **objections:** concerns or complaints expressed by the customer.

obsolescence: decrease in the value of an asset because it is out of date or inadequate.

officers: top executives who are hired to manage the business.

on-the-job training: formal or informal training done at the employee's workstation.

open ad: an advertisement announcing a job opening that identifies the company in which the job is located.

open corporation (public corporation): a corporation that offers its shares of stock for public sale.

open leader: a manager who gives little or no direction to workers.

open line of credit: permits borrowing up to a specified amount for a specified period of time.

open system: allows for the relatively free interchange of information among a variety of hardware and software systems.

operating expenses: the costs of operating a business.

operational information system (OIS): provides supervisors with information needed to make decisions about day-to-day business operations.

operational planning: short-term planning that identifies specific activities for each area of the business.

organization chart: a visual device that shows the structure of an organization and the relationships among workers and divisions of work.

organizational development: carefully planned changes in the structure and operation of a business so it can adjust successfully to the competitive environment.

organizing: determining how plans can most effectively be accomplished; arranging resources to complete work.

orientation program: a carefully designed introduction to the company, the work, and co-workers, and preparation for the job.

output: the quantity, or amount, produced within a given time.

output device: equipment that records, prints, or displays information in usable form.

Overseas Private Investment Corporation: a corporation that provides insurance coverage for businesses that suffer losses or damage to foreign investments.

owner capital (proprietary capital): money invested in the business by its owner or owners.

P **Pacific Rim:** countries located on the western edge of the Pacific Ocean.

packing list: a form that lists the packages or containers being shipped and their contents.

par value (stated value): a dollar value shown on a share of stock, which is an arbitrarily assigned amount that is used for bookkeeping purposes.

parcel shipment: the shipment of small packages.

parent firm: a company that controls another company.

partnership: a business owned by two or more persons.

patent: an agreement in which the federal government gives an inventor the sole right for 17 years to make, use, and sell an invention.

payee: the person to whom a note or check is payable.

pensions: regular payments made to an employee after retirement.

performance appraisal: the procedure used to determine how well employees perform their jobs.

peril: the cause of a loss for a person or organization.

personal property tax: a tax on such items as furniture, machinery, and equipment.

personal selling: promotion through direct, personal contact with a customer.

picketing: placing union members in front of a business to inform the public of their dispute and to encourage others not to enter the business.

piece-rate plan: a compensation plan that pays the employee a fixed rate for each unit of production.

piggyback service: a distribution method where truck trailers are loaded and placed on railroad cars to be shipped close to their final destination.

place (distribution): deals with the methods of transporting and storing goods, and making them available to customers.

planning: analyzing information and making decisions about what needs to be done.

point-of-sale terminal: cash registers that are connected to computers.

policies: guidelines used in making decisions regarding specific, recurring situations.

policy: the written agreement, or contract, between the insurer and the policyholder.

policyholder: the person or business purchasing insurance.

position power: comes from the position the manager holds in the organization.

power: the ability to control behavior.

power need: desire to influence and control others and to be responsible for a group's activities.

preferred provider organizations (PPOs): health care available from a selected set of physicians and health care facilities through negotiated contracts between the health care providers and the insurer.

preferred stock: ownership that gives holders preference over the common stockholders when distributing dividends or assets.

premium: a payment by the policyholder to the insurer for protection against a risk.

price: the monetary and the perceived value of the product or service.

price discrimination: setting different prices for different customers.

prime rate: the lowest rate of interest; the rate at which large banks loan large sums to the best-qualified borrowers.

prime time: the most expensive advertising time on television (between 6 p.m. and 11 p.m.).

private brands: brand names established by an individual business—usually a wholesaler or retailer—for sale to its customers.

private property: items of value that individuals can own, use, and sell.

privatization: when a state or country transfers its authority to provide a good or service to individuals or businesses.

problem: a difficult situation requiring a solution.

procedure: a list of steps to be followed for performing certain work.

producer: anyone who aids in creating a utility.

product: everything offered by a business to satisfy its customers.

product development: the process of developing or improving a product or service.

product life cycle: predicts the sales and profit performance of a given product.

product research: research done to develop new products or to discover improvements for existing products.

production: involves making a product or providing a service.

production oriented: businesses that emphasize decisions about what and how to produce and then how to sell the products.

production scheduling: identifies the steps required in a manufacturing process, the time required to complete each step, and the sequence of the steps.

productivity: refers to producing the largest quantity in the least time by using efficient methods and modern equipment.

professional liability insurance: provides protection from the types of financial losses resulting from providing professional services.

profit: the incentive, as well as the reward, for producing goods and services.

profit sharing: a bonus to each qualified employee based on a percentage of the profits earned by the company.

programmers: persons trained to prepare detailed instructions that direct computers to perform desired tasks in a specified manner.

progressive tax: tax based on the ability to pay.

project (matrix) organization: work teams are organized to complete a specific project and a project manager is identified with authority and responsibility for the project.

promissory note: an unconditional written promise to pay a certain sum of money, at a particular time or on demand, to the order of one who has obtained the note.

promotion: (1) providing information to consumers that will assist them in making a decision to purchase a product or service. (2) the advancement of an employee within a company to a position with more authority and responsibility.

property tax: a levy on material goods owned.

proportional tax (flat tax): tax rate remains the same regardless of the amount on which the tax is imposed.

proprietor: the owner-manager of a business.

prospectus: a version of registration statement for the Securities and Exchange Commission that contains extensive details about the company and its proposed sale of securities.

proxy: a written authorization for someone to vote in behalf of the person signing the proxy.

public franchise: a contract that permits a person or organization to use public property for private profit.

purchase order: a form that lists the merchandise being ordered from a supplier.

purchase requisitions: forms requesting the purchasing department to buy the items listed.

purchasing agent: the person in charge of the purchasing department.

pure research: research done without a specific product in mind.

quality circles: employee teams that meet regularly to solve problems and improve quality.

quality management: involves developing standards for all operations and products and measuring results using those standards.

quantity discount: used by sellers to encourage customers to buy in large quantities.

quasi-public corporation: a business that is important, but lacks the profit potential to attract private investors, and is often operated by local, state, or federal government.

quotas: limits placed on the quantity or value of units permitted to enter a country.

rack jobber: a wholesaler who takes legal title to goods and who usually works through large retail stores, especially food stores that carry nonfood items. (These wholesalers furnish racks or displays, stock shelves, price products, fix displays, and keep inventory records.)

real property tax: a tax levied on land and buildings.

real wages: the amount of goods and services that the money earned will buy.

recession: a decline in the GDP that continues for six months or more.

reconciliation statement: a summary that reveals the causes for the difference between the checkbook balance and the bank statement balance.

recycle: the reuse of products or product packaging whenever possible.

reengineering: occurs when traditional operating procedures are replaced by more efficient methods.

regressive tax: taxation wherein the actual tax rate decreases as the taxable amount increases.

regular charge credit: an account whereby a customer can charge a purchase at any time but must pay the amount owed in full by a specified date.

regular savings account (passbook savings account): allows customers to make deposits and withdrawals without financial penalties.

reinsurance: a method of reducing risk of a major loss by transferring part of the risk to another insurance company.

repossessed: taken back.

research: the systematic search for and interpretation of facts in an effort to solve problems.

researching and information gathering: studying buyer interests and needs, testing products, and gathering facts needed to make good marketing decisions.

responsibility: the obligation to do an assigned task.

restructuring: reorganizing work and resources to improve the effectiveness of the organization.

retailers: businesses that sell directly to final consumers.

retained earnings: profits that are put aside to run a business.

revolving credit: a credit plan that combines the features of regular charge credit and installment credit.

reward power: based on the ability to control resources, rewards, and punishments.

risk: the uncertainty that a loss may occur.

risk taking: assuming the risk of losses that may occur from fire, theft, damage, or other circumstances.

Rust Belt: the north central and northeastern states where major manufacturing centers were once dominant.

S-corporation: a special type of corporation that is taxed as if it were a partnership.

salary: compensation paid on other than an hourly basis, such as weekly or monthly.

sales budget: a forecast of the sales for a month, a few months, or a year.

sales finance company: specializes in purchasing installment sales contracts at a discount from businesses that need cash or that do not care to handle collections.

sales oriented: businesses that emphasize promotion in order to sell the products that have been produced.

sales tax: a tax levied on the retail price of goods and services at the time they are sold.

sanctions: a milder form of embargo where specific business ties with a foreign country are banned.

savings and loan association: specializes in savings accounts and home mortgage loans.

scanner: a computer input device used to read and store handwritten, typewritten, printed, or graphic material.

schedule: a time plan for reaching objectives.

seasonal discount: given to the buyer for ordering or taking delivery of goods in advance of the normal buying period.

secured loan (collateral loan): a loan that requires the borrower to pledge something of value as security.

securities: stocks and bonds.

self-directed work team: a group of skilled workers who are completely in charge of handling a significant component of a well-defined segment of work.

self-service merchandising: customers select the products they wish, take them to a cashier or checkout counter, and pay for them.

selling: providing personalized and persuasive information to customers to help them buy the goods they need.

selling price: the actual price paid for a company's products by the customer.

seniority: the length of time an employee has been with the company.

service firms: business that provide assistance to satisfy specialized needs through skilled workers.

services: (1) activities of value that do not result in the ownership of a physical product. (2) intangible products that result from a high degree of labor input and that satisfy consumer needs.

shares: equal parts of the division of ownership of a corporation.

shopping channels: television channels devoted exclusively to presenting merchandise for sale and accepting orders by telephone for direct shipment to customers.

shopping goods: goods that are bought less frequently than convenience goods, that usually have a higher price, and that require some buying thought.

short-term capital: borrowed capital that must be repaid within a year, and often in 30, 60, or 90 days.

small business: the term applied to any business that is operated by one or a few individuals.

smart card: a credit and debit card with a memory that stores financial, health, credit, and other kinds of data that can be read by computers.

social responsibility: the duty of a business to contribute to the well-being of society.

socialism: an economic-political system in which the government controls and regulates the means of production.

software: special instructions computers are provided to perform tasks.

sole proprietorship (proprietorship): a business owned and managed by one person.

span of control: the number of employees who are directly supervised by one person.

specialty goods: products that customers insist upon having and are willing to shop for until they find them.

specialty stores: stores that handle one category of products, such as shoes, jewelry, hardware, clothing, or furniture, but offer a wider choice of colors, sizes, and brands, and usually a high level of customer service.

specialty wholesaler: a wholesaler who specializes in one or only a very few types of merchandise.

stakeholders: the owners, customers, suppliers, employees, creditors, government, the general public, and other groups who are affected by a firm's action.

standard: a yardstick or measure by which something is judged.

stock rights: stockholders can buy one additional share of stock for each share owned at a price lower than the current market price.

stockholders (shareholders): owners of a corporation.

storing: holding goods until needed by consumers, such as on shelves, in storage rooms, or in warehouses.

straight salary: a specific amount of money for a long period of time worked (week, month).

strategic planning: long-term planning that provides broad goals and directions for the entire business.

strike: union members refuse to go to work until the employer meets their demands.

subsidiaries: the name for foreign operations that are branches or are separately registered as a legal entity.

substantiation: being able to prove all claims made about products and services in promotions.

suggestion selling: when the salesperson calls the attention of the customer to products that were not requested.

Sun Belt: the warmer southern half of the nation.

supermarkets: large stores that are well stocked with a variety of frequently purchased household products, with a primary emphasis on food items.

supervisor: a manager whose main job is to direct the work of employees.

supply: refers to the number of similar products that will be offered for sale at a particular time and at a particular price.

symptom: a sign or indication of something that appears to be the problem.

system software: composed of procedures and routines that serve the general purpose of operating the computer hardware, such as directing the CPU to calculate numbers, to store information, and to find information stored on disks.

systems analyst: reviews current and proposed changes and determines whether a new or modified computer system will be beneficial.

T **tape reels:** one-half inch wide magnetic tape used primarily by mainframe computers for processing information sequentially and/or as backup of data stored on disk.

target markets: groups of customers with very similar needs to whom the company can sell its product.

tariff: a tax on foreign goods.

telecommunications (data communications): a system involving the electronic movement of information from one location to another location.

telecommuting: allowing employees to work at home using computers rather than at the business.

telemarketing: a direct sales method that combines telephone sales with computer technology.

term insurance: life insurance that provides protection for a period of time specified in the policy.

terminal: consists of a keyboard and a monitor (with or without a CPU).

third world nations: countries that are underdeveloped, have few manufacturing firms, and have large numbers of poor people who possess few goods.

time deposit: money deposited for a fixed period.

time wage: a specific amount of money for each hour worked.

title: legal ownership.

title insurance: protection against losses that could occur if title to the property had not been legally transferred sometime in the past.

total quality management (TQM): a commitment to excellence that is accomplished by teamwork and continual improvement.

trade (functional) discount: a special deduction from the list price that is given to certain types of buyers, such as wholesalers or retailers, because the buyers perform certain functions for the seller.

trademark: a distinguishing name, symbol, or special mark placed on a good or service that is legally reserved for the sole use of the owner.

trading bloc: an arrangement between two or more countries to remove all restrictions on the sale of goods and services among them while imposing barriers to trade and investment from countries that are not part of the bloc.

transfer: the assignment of an employee to another job in the company that involves the same type of responsibility and authority.

transportation insurance: protection against damage, theft, or complete loss of goods while they are being shipped.

transporting: moving goods from where they were made to where consumers can buy them.

travelers' checks: checks purchased in fixed denominations by people who do not wish to carry large sums of cash.

treasury bill (T-bill): short-term security sold by the federal government to finance the cost of running the government.

treasury bonds: securities sold in $1,000 to $1 million amounts with maturities ranging from 10 to 30 years.

treasury notes: securities sold by the U.S. government in amounts of $1,000 up to $5,000 that generally mature in one to ten years.

trust company: manages property such as securities, real estate, and cash as directed by its customers.

U **underground economy:** income that escapes being recorded in the GDP.

underwriting: selling a new issue of a security, such as bonds, through an investment banking firm for a specified price.

unity of command: requires that no employee have more than one supervisor.

universal life insurance: combines term insurance with an investment fund.

unlimited financial liability: indicates that partners are responsible for their share of the business debts.

unsecured loans: credit extended by merely signing a promissory note and pledging nothing of value.

unsought goods: products that many customers will not shop for because they do not have a strong need for the product.

utility: the ability of a good or service to satisfy a want.

V **variance report:** identifies standards that are not being met and the amount of difference between the standard and the actual performance.

variances: differences between planned and actual performance.

vendor: the company from which goods are being ordered.

venture capitalists: usually a wealthy investor or investment group that lends large sums of money to promising new or expanding small companies.

voice messaging (voice mail): allows spoken messages to be received by special telephone equipment that records, stores, forwards, and plays back.

W **wages:** compensation paid on an hourly basis.

warehouses: buildings used to store large quantities of products until they can be sold.

whole life insurance: maintains insurance for the entire life of the insured as long as premiums are paid.

wholesalers: businesses that buy products from businesses and sell them to retailers or other businesses.

work rules: regulations created to maintain an effective working environment in a business.

work team: a group of individuals who cooperate to achieve a common goal.

working capital: the difference between current assets and current liabilities.

Z **zero population growth (ZPG):** the point at which births and deaths balance.

zoning: regulations that specify which land areas may be used for homes and which areas may be used for different types of businesses.

Index